D0074717

After the 'Death of Literature'

After the 'Death of Literature'

WEST GERMAN WRITING OF THE 1970s

Edited by
KEITH BULLIVANT

OSWALD WOLFF BOOKS
BERG PUBLISHERS
Oxford / New York / Munich
Distributed exclusively in the US and Canada by
St. Martin's Press, New York

First published in 1989 by
Berg Publishers Limited
– Editorial Offices –
77 Morrell Avenue, Oxford OX4 1NQ, UK
165 Taber Avenue, Providence, R.I. 02906, USA
Westermühlstraße 26, 8000 München 5, FRG

© Keith Bullivant 1989

All rights reserved.
No part of this publication may be reproduced in any form
or by any means without the written permission of
Berg Publishers Limited.

British Library Cataloguing in Publication Data
After the 'Death of Literature': West German Writing of the 1970s
1. German literature—20th century—
History and criticism
I. Bullivant, Keith
830.9′00914   PT401
ISBN 0–85496–037–6

Library of Congress Cataloging-in-Publication Data
After the 'Death of literature'.
Bibliography: p.
Includes index.
1. German literature—20th century—History and
criticism. I. Bullivant, Keith. II. Series.
PT403.A38 1989   830′.9′00914   87–26796
ISBN 0–85496–037–6

Printed in Great Britain by Short Run Press Ltd, Exeter

Contents

v

vi

Foreword

The sub-title of this volume, one of the first in English to address itself exclusively to the 1970s, immediately raises the question as to why it focuses on a single decade. It is, indeed, by no means always possible to talk meaningfully of a decade as a distinct cultural era and, as with any attempt at categorisation by period, to do so will inevitably mean a degree of oversimplification. The significance attached to the 1920s, for example, does, however, make the point that there are times when this approach is justified. As far as the Federal Republic of Germany is concerned, there is clear evidence from historians, literary critics and scholars that the pattern of the decades roughly corresponds to its significant phases. In the 1950s, the time of the 'Wirtschaftswunder', the 'return to business' as usual, in Konrad Adenauer's famous words, was reflected in the astonishing cultural continuity represented by the adherence to styles of writing established in the 1930s and by the individual careers of writers who had been writing at that time (indeed, Hans Dieter Schäfer and others have argued that the period 1930–60 should be viewed as a discrete epoch). The demands for a new literary beginning had come to very little. It was only at the very end of the 1950s that a new generation of writers came to the fore, most of whom were to play their part in the politicisation of West German cultural life in the stormy decade that reached its height in 1968.

With the election triumph in 1969 of Brandt's liberal coalition and the symbolic journey in 1970 of Grass and Siegfried Lenz with Chancellor Schmidt to pay tribute to the victims of the Warsaw Ghetto, there was generated a mood of great optimism that the 1970s would be a time of significant change. The intellectual life of that decade was dominated, however, by the major issues of the 'Radikalenerlaß', terrorism and state surveillance of the individual. Cultural commentators quickly claimed to detect a sense of disillusionment that the ideals of the Student Movement had not been fulfilled, a mood enhanced by the climate of political suspicion and distrust. By the middle of the decade it was widely asserted that 1973 had been a crucial 'Tendenzwende', when writers turned

away from activism to more private concerns, to a 'Neue Subjektivität' (examined on pp. 53–68 this volume by Moray McGowan).
Despite the importance for West German literature of the 1970s of
writers ascribed to this tendency, and despite the fact that the thesis
has much to recommend it, I feel that it is not accurate to see the
period entirely in this light. The 1970s, I would argue, were a highly
political decade, when writers, disturbed at what they sensed as
crucial threats to civil liberties, increasingly saw themselves as
'Radikale im öffentlichen Dienst' (in the phrase first used by Günter
Wallraff at the 'Schriftstellerkongreß' of 1974). It was only after the
relative normalisation of affairs that could be observed from around
1980 that the view of the Federal Republic as an 'Überwachungsstaat',
the writers' sense of alienation from the state that is charted by
Wilfried van der Will, ceased to dominate intellectual debates and
also faded as a literary theme.

My reading of the 1970s in the Federal Republic as a literary
period is, therefore, of a movement between the poles of 'Neue
Subjektivität' and politicisation. This is the key to the selection of
writers and themes examined in this volume. Collectively the essays
represent the coming together in the West German literary scene of
works written in German that are part of the space defined by the
two poles. The Austrians Bernhard and Handke are central, for
example, to 'Neue Subjektivität' (Bernhard is also a key figure in the
West German theatre of the period),[1] while Scharang is important
in the context of political realism and Wolfgruber and Innerhofer
take their place within the literature of the 'Arbeitswelt'. Austrian
and Swiss women writers are of great importance to the development of women's writing in West Germany, as can be seen in Juliet
Wigmore's essay (pp. 88–108 below), while Otto F. Walter's novel
Die Verwilderung (1977), though set in his native Switzerland, was
received in West Germany both as a political literary statement
relevant to the Federal Republic and as a work crucial to ongoing
debates about the nature of political realism.[2] Christa Wolf was not
only much discussed as another model for realist writing, but her
central theme of the tension between authority and the desire for
self-definition was essentially viewed as being highly relevant to the
West German situation, and she herself made this point. The
selective reception of literature from the GDR in the Federal Re-

1. See Helen Chambers' chapter on Bernhard (pp. 197–211 below) and Michael
Linstead's chapter on Handke (pp. 246–62 below).
2. See pp. 39f. below. Also in this connection see W. Martin Lüdke (ed.), *Nach dem
Protest*, Frankfurt on Main, 1979.

public had an important place in the profile of a decade that also saw the large-scale emigration of writers from the GDR to the West in the wake of Wolf Biermann's expulsion in 1976. The relationship of the literature of the German Democratic Republic to that of the Federal Republic provides the focus of Dennis Tate's essay (pp. 176–93).

The shaping of the volume in accordance with my reading of the 1970s has inevitably meant that writers and works of the period, important in themselves but falling outside the focal plane, have been omitted. Günter Grass is a particular case in point. While my favourite Grass novels *Aus dem Tagebuch einer Schnecke* (1972) and *Der Butt* (1977) are without doubt two of the major individual prose works written during the decade, Grass was not really central to the period, in the sense in which I have defined it and in the way that, for example, Böll, Walser and Handke, of the well-known writers, and Schneider and Kluge, of the names less familiar outside the Federal Republic, were. A different reading of the 1970s would, of course, produce a different selection of writers and themes, as collections of West German essays on the period show, but my view of Grass in the 1970s is supported by Peter Demetz in his excellent *After The Fires* (1986), who examines Grass's work and its centrality with regard to the 1960s and then proceeds to a defence of *Der Butt*, before examining Grass's work in the 1980s, when he sees the author as returning to the centre-stage of intellectual and political life. This is entirely in accord with my own reading of Grass; while he was a strangely marginal figure at times in the 1970s, no volume on the 1980s could possibly omit him. Grass played a prominent role within the Peace Movement in the first half of the decade and *Die Rättin* (1986) is the major literary expression of issues that dominated West German intellectual debates at the time. It must also be stressed that this book should not be viewed in isolation, but is part of a body of works, including my own *Realism Today* and *The Modern German Novel* and J.H. Reid's *The New East German Literature*, that are intended to complement and extend this volume.[3]

Though my views have been central to the shaping of this volume, a collection of essays by colleagues from the British Isles, the United States and Australia, with their own reading of the period and of the importance of individual writers, cannot have the structured coherence of a good monograph, unless an authoritarian editor were to

3. All titles by Berg Publishers (Oswald Wolff books): *Realism Today* and *The Modern German Novel* both Leamington Spa and New York, 1987; *The New East German Literature*, Oxford and New York, 1989.

Foreword

make it effectively a substitute for one. The inherent pluralism of the collection has its inevitable dangers and drawbacks, but internal contradictions are by no means undesirable when dealing with subject-matter that is far from cut and dried and represent the advantage that a volume of essays has over the monograph.

Whatever the shortcomings of the volume, it does serve to expose some recent myths: the 1960s in particular — and not just as far as German literature is concerned — have come to be seen as a legendary period of energy and creativity, the like of which, it is said, has not been seen since. Even for those older critics who are not children of the 1960s, such as Marcel Reich-Ranicki — for whom the Student Revolt meant, in effect, the destruction of German literature — , the 1970s in literature are seen as devoid of major themes and lacking in quality; Hans Magnus Enzensberger had, indeed, written them off by 1971 (in his poem 'Aufbruch in die siebziger Jahre'). Looking back from the late 1980s, however, the 1960s would seem to have been characterised by an awful lot of talking about literature, but many of the debates and much of the writing produced now appear ephemeral. On the evidence of the contributions to this volume, on the other hand, and in the light of the substantial body of writing available which it has not been possible to consider in detail here, the maligned 1970s now seem to have been very rich in literature and, as John Sandford's essay demonstrates, films of quality; the contributors to this volume very much hope that this examination will stimulate interest in a period so little known within German Studies in the English-speaking world.

Keith Bullivant
Gainesville, Florida, December 1988

DAVID ROBERTS

expansion a diversification of public sphere

it self element, authenticity, private values esp

— Introduction —

From the 1960s to the 1970s:
The Changing Contexts of German Literature

public space?
defining prob. = modernity a modernization for 68 gen. (not 3rd Reich = 1930 gen.)

? founded on romantic notion of lit as self-exp.

It is over forty years since the end of the Second World War and the contours of certain historical and literary periods are becoming discernible. For the Federal Republic classification by decade, e.g. the 'Restaurationszeit' in the 1950s, the political activism of the 1960s, the 'Tendenzwende' of the 1970s, serves as a kind of shorthand. At the beginning stands 'Stunde Null', the much questioned but apparently indispensible slogan for the radical caesura in German history brought about by the unconditional surrender of the Third Reich and the disappearance of national sovereignty. Although the absolute discontinuity suggested by the slogan has often been disputed, the myth of an absolute end and of an absolute beginning remains the founding fiction of the two German successors to the nation state created by Bismarck and destroyed by Hitler. The end of the nation state marked not only the conclusion to Germany's drive for European and world power, it opened the new stage of German and European history constituted by the division of Germany and Europe into two hostile power blocs. German history since 1945 is thus defined by the tension between a lost unity and the reality of the progressive consolidation — political, economic and military — of a divided Germany into its opposed camps. Here geopolitical position and economic potential have made the two Germanies the economic and military lynchpins of NATO and the Warsaw Pact respectively. Beyond that, the shattering of German sovereignty and identity, the massive physical destruction of German cities and the uprooting of its population all provided the preconditions for the Federal Republic and the German Democratic Republic to emerge as models for their respective capitalist or socialist systems. The pressures of division have thus resulted in the creation of two very different societies on German territory. The division was cemented by the building of the Berlin Wall in 1961 and recognised in the West by the new foreign policy of the Social Democrats after their electoral victory in 1969. Between 1961 and

1969 the post-war period, we may say, came to an end with the acceptance of the permanence of the provisional: *de facto* division in the place of an absent Peace Treaty.

The Berlin Wall and its consequences lent force to the thesis of two German literatures. In retrospect, however, the unity of the post-war generation, and by this I mean the writers born around 1930 — Günter Grass, Hans Magnus Enzensberger, Martin Walser, Alexander Kluge, Rolf Hochhuth, Siegfried Lenz in the West or Uwe Johnson and Christa Wolf in the East — must also be stressed. They shared the legacy of a personal experience of the Third Reich. Their task, precisely by virtue of being the post-war generation, was to overcome the shock, paralysis and resentment of their parents' generation and the cultural vacuum in the shadow of 'Stunde Null'. This is not to suggest that the burden of National Socialism and of Germany's fateful history this century has ceased to exercise the conscience of Germans of all ages or to determine the questions of individual and national identity, but rather that the understanding of literature for this generation is profoundly inter-connected with the duty of 'Bewältigung der Vergangenheit' in a way it could not be for the following generation born during or after the war. For Grass or Johnson or Hochhuth or Wolf the moral, political and didactic function of literature is the condition of their activity. It involves a view of the writer as critic, preceptor and conscience of the (divided) nation, for whom writing is, in Lenz's words, 'imaginary historiography'. That this expression of memory and identity is necessarily painful and self-critical only underlines the representative nature of the protest of the past against a forgetful present, for (national) identity presupposes not the alibi of 'Stunde Null' but the recall and reintegration of the repressed, the struggle against what the psychoanalysts Alexander and Margarete Mitscherlich called the inability to mourn (*Die Unfähigkeit zu trauern*, 1967). This moral task of post-war literature found international recognition in the award of the Nobel Prize to Heinrich Böll in 1972. Although the exploration of continuities between the Nazi past and the socialist present was long delayed in the GDR — Christa Wolf's *Kindheitsmuster* (1976) is a turning-point — the post-war generation in East and West must be seen as the mediator between past and present. They are above all historians of the age, for whom the present is defined by the past, for whom identity is not an individual but a collective question, a question of history, or in other words, the generation for whom the burden of collective guilt had to be accepted as an individual responsibility. Perhaps the most significant figure of this generation is Uwe Johnson. Through the search for

identity of the narrator-heroine of his 1,900 page novel *Jahrestage*
(1971–83) Johnson traces his journey from East to West Germany
and into emigration. The tragic history of Germany is carried
through to the post-national standpoint of exile and world history.
In this sense *Jahrestage* is *the* novel of the loss of German unity and ✗
identity, just as Peter Weiss's *Ästhetik des Widerstands* (1975–81) is *the*
epitaph on the resistance inside and outside Germany to Fascism
and on the defeat of socialism internally. *Jahrestage* in turn ends with
the crushing of the hopes of a socialist alternative to the disastrous
legacy of nationalism with the invasion of Czechoslovakia by forces
of the Warsaw Pact, including those of the German Democratic
Republic, in 1968.

The failure of the challenge to the status quo in both East and
West in 1968, for which Prague and Paris were the respective foci,
indicated the limits of possible political change in the two power
blocs. For East Germany Prague was one more reminder after Berlin
1953 and Hungary 1956 of the impossibility of reversing the consequences of German defeat. For Eastern Europe as a whole it meant
the end of the illusion of a reform of the Soviet system from within.
The nature of 'real existing socialism' (Rudolf Bahro's *Die Alternative*, 1977) could no longer be ignored. East German writers turned
increasingly in the 1970s to the inescapable realities of the antagonistic class structure of their society and the conflicts between the
individual and the state. Likewise the collapse of the high-flown
illusions of the Student Revolt in the West led to the abandonment
of the romantic dream of the revolutionary revitalisation of society.
The sobering process of revision demanded of the '68 generation led
to a painful but also liberating search for identity and self-definition
in the 1970s, whose driving force has frequently been described as
the appeal to personal experience, as the cult of authenticity. This
new subjectivity, as it was immediately labelled and just as immediately welcomed or deplored, was the most obvious symptom of a
more general shift in attitudes which both continued and apparently
negated the spirit of the Student Revolt of the late 1960s. Here it is
important to remember that the Student Movement in the Federal
Republic was part of a generational protest throughout the Western
world. The immediate target of the West German students was the
universities, the institutional symbol of the seemingly complete
restoration of the old social hierarchies after the caesura of 1945.
The protests of the young generation were the living evidence,
however, of the enormous transformations of West German society
since the end of the war. Just as this social transformation remained
long hidden by the continuities of Adenauer's restoration, so the

emergence of a student opposition as the vanguard of an increasingly information oriented society was disguised by the old rhetoric of class warfare and the illusions of an alliance between proletariat and intelligentsia. In retrospect 1968 appears increasingly as a watershed in the history of the Federal Republic, for it indicated how much West German society had become part of the Western world, how much its problems were now those of (post-) industrial capitalism. The Student Movement of the late 1960s stands as the explosive forerunner of the ongoing change from material to post-material values, identified and analysed by Ronald Inglehart in *The Silent Revolution* (1977) as characteristic of European society over the past two decades.

The Student Revolt of 1968 and the victory of the SPD in 1969 together marked the end of the post-war period in West Germany, and announced at the same time a change of literary generations, prefigured by the disintegration of the Gruppe 47. The claim to moral representation by the writers of the post-war generation was now directly challenged — the symbolic moment was Peter Handke's attack on the Gruppe 47 in Princeton in 1967. It was followed by the political attacks from the student left. The declarations of the death of literature sprang from the old revolutionary dream of translating words into deeds, which rejected the moral claims of literature as a tired substitute for direct action. And yet the decline of the Gruppe 47 in the 1960s was paralleled by the renewal of the theatre as a moral and political forum. Here, in the Schillerian pathos of Hochhuth or the documentary drama of Weiss or Heinar Kipphardt, the idea of engaged literature found powerful and persuasive expression. Moreover, the documentary drama and prose of the time derived much of its impact from the open break with the concept of a 'pure' literature. If *Waiting for Godot* expressed the stagnation and resignation of the 1950s, Weiss's *Marat/Sade* (1964), which renewed and fused in unique fashion the avantgarde impulses of Brecht and Artaud, dramatically incorporated revolutionary agitation of the 1960s. We can point to no such prominent role for the theatre in the 1970s, where the film, often in financial cooperation with television, has asserted its presence. The demise of the theatre as a moral-political forum seems to be closely related to the post-'68 change of attitudes. The turn away from the theatre towards prose and poetry as a vehicle of self-discovery and self-expression seems symptomatic of the often adduced contrast between the 'political' 1960s and the 'unpolitical' 1970s.

The critical weight accorded to subjectivity in West German literature in the 1970s and beyond is to a certain extent misleading,

since the recurrent theme of this literature is self and social alienation. The quest for the authentic self, for authentic experience,
which also provides the polemical impulse of much feminist writing,
has remained largely negative. Behind the opposition of the 'political' 1960s and the 'unpolitical' 1970s two contrasting responses to
the perennial question of the relationship between art and life can be
discerned. Where in the course of the 1960s more commitment and
literary realism increasingly came to be identified with political
engagement, the disappointments and reconsiderations in the wake
of the collapse of the Student Revolt led to a revised conception of
commitment and realism, which focused on the pressing issue of the
private sphere. The apparently private and the personal, as the
Women's Movement made clear, was now to be grasped as the
political. What had changed was the understanding of literary
experience and literary representation. For the post-'68 generation
the national past, the questions of national guilt, individual responsibility and identity no longer defined the symbolic-historical space of
their narratives. When they tackle these questions, it is in the form
of the autobiographical memoir. The exploration of the relation to
the (Nazi) past typically takes the form of the analysis of parent
and child relations, as for instance in Bernward Vesper's posthum-
ously published *Die Reise* (1971/7), Elisabeth Plessen's *Mitteilung an
den Adel* (1976), Peter Handke's *Wunschloses Unglück* (1972), or
Christoph Meckel's *Suchbild. Über meinen Vater* (1980). Such autobiographical studies document the roots of alienation, the silence
between the generations, the repressions of the past, the latent
energies which fuelled post-war reconstruction, but they are not
representative narratives in the wider sense.[1] Rather they are personal histories, sociological documents which contribute to the
mosaic of present and past. The backdrop to the new subjectivity of
the 1970s is not so much the national past as the world of consumer
capitalism and the global village of the omnipresent media. References to the 'Americanisation' of West German literature are indicative of this change of horizon, of the new context of what has been
called the 'culture of narcissism' (Christopher Lasch, 1980) in
Western society. And if we turn to the Women's Movement, the
Ecological or the Peace Movements, to take only the most striking
manifestations of the new politics after the Student Movement of the
1960s, they are social phenomena which cannot be described or
accounted for primarily in national terms.

Inglehart's cautiously optimistic analysis of the correlation be-

1. See Keith Bullivant, 'The Spectre of the Third Reich', pp. 139–54 below.

tween social and ideological change, based on a rising level of education, suggests perhaps too positive a view of the connection between industrial rationalisation and social rationality. Although Inglehart sees post-materialist values confined as yet to a minority of the population, above all the young and educated, his optimism seems sharply contradicted by the intellectual and literary atmosphere in the Federal Republic in the 1970s and 1980s. The pronounced pessimism of much writing of the 1970s appears to reflect no less than the protests against nuclear and ecological dangers a widespread existential Angst. If the symbolic space, the defining and determining task of the post-war generation, was the inescapable burden of the Third Reich, then the symbolic space of the '68 generation — and in *this* sense representative for the 1970s and beyond — is constituted by what we may call the problematic of modernity and modernisation (cf. here Jürgen Habermas's influential *Theorie des kommunikativen Handelns*, 1981). There is in Germany a long tradition of anti-capitalist critique which can be traced from the Romantics and Marx through to the teachings of the spiritual godfathers of the Student Revolt: the dialectic of enlightenment of Adorno and Horkheimer or the condemnation of one-dimensional man by Marcuse. This strain of romantic cultural pessimism and political utopianism enters of course into the Ecological Movement and explains to a large extent the differences between the traditional left, still committed in practise to endless growth, and the New Left. Inglehart points to the connections between the old critique and the new awareness of the limits and costs of growth, which is at the heart of the change of values he analyses. What can be observed in West Germany and in the Western world in general is the collapse of the uncritical belief in growth and progress which flowed from the long post-war boom and reached its inflationary end in the Vietnam War. This collapse, reinforced by the Oil Crisis of 1974, coincided with the collapse of the political hopes of '68 to form in West Germany a puzzling ideological amalgam, which defies the familiar political interpretative grid of left and right, progressive and reactionary.

The new ideological constellation of the 1970s and 1980s has provoked many attempts at explanation and interpretation, of which the most prominent have been the German arguments about 'Tendenzwende' in the mid-1970s and the currently thriving international debate on postmodernism. Applied to literature, 'Tendenzwende' suggested to the right the resurrection of literature after its supposed death and to the left a view of the new subjectivity as a betrayal of the concept of engaged writing. The ambiguities of the slogan indicated the greater success and even greater ambiguities of postmodernism, variously construed as a new stage of history or as the end of history altogether. The word started its career in the USA as the expression of a reaction to the modernist movement in the arts in the first third of the century but it has become more and more an umbrella term for ideological debates on cultural modernity. Increasingly central to this debate — and thus an important focus of the symbolic space of the 1970s and 1980s — is the critical question of the legacy of the Enlightenment (condemned for instance as patriarchal reason by the feminists) and the nature of the project of modernity. The return of Nietzsche, long banished because of his disturbing proximity to National Socialism's 'revaluation of values', is symptomatic of the ongoing revision of perspectives and the disintegration of the old (Marxist) certainties.

The literary reflections of the problematic of (post-)industrial society have been predominantly subjectivist. Here the search for orientation has typically taken the form of the suspicion of all systems and syntheses which ignore the individual subject. We find a similar reaction to the system as closed ideology and state apparatus of power among writers in the German Democratic Republic from the end of the 1960s on. (Ulrich Plenzdorf, Heiner Müller, Christa Wolf, Günter Kunert, Hans-Joachim Schädlich, Erich Loest are obvious examples.) In the German Democratic Republic, however, the 'subjective factor' remains an eminently political issue, which makes the individual confrontation or protest representative for East German society as a whole (here prototypically Volker Braun's *Unvollendete Geschichte*, 1975) in a way that the protocols, chronicles and confessions of the subject in the West cannot claim. If the new space of literature post-'68 is connected with the experience of alienation and the ambivalences of modernity, one consequence of this thematic is that this literature speaks largely to and for specific social and age groups or is gender based. The task of integrating the personal and the social becomes increasingly difficult for the writer and is itself a direct reflection of both alienation and differentiation. However, the one thing the literature of subjectivity does not call into question is the experiencing and suffering subject and the therapeutic act of writing itself. Indeed Handke now once again seeks to endow the writer with magical powers of recreation of (an ideal) reality, for writing is repetition, is restoration through mimesis (*Die Wiederholung*, 1986). This fetishisation of the romantic subject (which has quite a different function in the German Democratic Republic, as we can see in, for example Wolf's *Kein Ort Nirgends*, 1977) and the whole concept of literature as self-expression is all the more surprising as one of the most influential intellectual currents of the 1970s has been the attack on the subject in French poststructuralism. Between a view of the subject and of literature as the product of discourse which leaves no room for the fictions of author or authenticity and the directly historically, politically and socially defined subject in East German literature, the protocols of consciousness of much of the West German literature of the 1970s find themselves compelled to demonstrate the social reality of alienation underlying the dream of authentic experience. As commentators X have noted, it suggests all the signs of the exhaustion and approaching end of this thematic, which of course must also be seen against the larger historical perspectives of the writing of the older post-war generation in the 1970s and 1980s from Grass's *Tagebuch einer Schnecke* (1972) to Loest's *Völkerschlachtdenkmal* (1984).

Looking back over the literary and political scene since the watershed years of the Student Revolt and the first period of the SPD/FDP coalition under Brandt, which marked in retrospect a momentary high point of reconciliation between 'Geist' and 'Macht', we can discern two distinct developments, both of which have attracted the label 'Tendenzwende', and which might be seen as pointing backwards and forwards respectively.

The one, the overtly political, is characterised by the backlash against student radicalism (the notorious 'Radikalenerlaß' of 1972), the vicious press campaign against Böll and other suspect 'sympathisers' culminating in the anti-terrorist hysteria of 1977, when it seemed that a fragile democratic understanding would be swamped by a resurgence of old authoritarian attitudes. This reaction was reinforced by the attacks on the allegedly dangerous threat of a left cultural-political hegemony, directed at the post-war generation of writers and intellectuals, most prominently represented by Grass and Habermas. Grass's political engagement for the SPD placed him at the centre of controversy in the late 1960s. Habermas in turn was the catalyst and focal figure of the 'Historikerstreit' of 1986, which brought many of the polarising issues of the political 'Tendenzwende' to a head. In the debate the question of Germany's past and its meaning for the present was once again fought out. On one side the calls for a revived identification with national history and traditions, on the other the defence of the liberal democratic state as the product of defeat. The outcome of the debate makes it clear that the democratic self-understanding of the Federal Republic is not easily shaken.

As against these ongoing political tensions the other development can be read, as I have indicated, as involving a progressive redefinition of the political, carried out by the post-'68 generation. The search for alternatives to the existing system has found its most striking expression in the growth of the Greens, a hybrid coalition of groups which together form both a political party and a social movement. Not only have the Greens successfully contested the pragmatism of the established parties, more importantly, they have decisively altered public consciousness by setting the ecological agenda for the present and the future. If the political climate of the 1970s was largely determined by the reaction to the upheavals of the Student Movement, it was at the same time the evolution of the student generation which led to a new constellation of forces and issues placing the costs of industrial growth and the dangers of unlimited technological progress at the centre of attention in the 1980s.

Concomitant with this expansion of the political is a recognition of the complexity of modern, functionally differentiated society, which has changed the parameters and self-perception of the literary scene. The pluralism of differentiated society is reflected in the awareness, as Enzensberger argued in 1979, that its corollary is a decentering of the leading role of the writer as the critical voice of the public sphere. The contrast between the public role of the post-war generation, most notably in the 1960s, and the proliferation of counter-cultural movements and discourses in the 1970s and beyond is symptomatic of this paradigm and generation change.

The diffusion of the public sphere has been reinforced in turn by the multiplication of media. The book is but one form of information and entertainment among many in the age of the media, just as the theatre must compete with film, television and, more recently, video. For most authors income derives mainly from writing for news-papers, journals, radio, television or film. Only a small number of writers can live from their literary production, just as literature, in the sense it is usually understood by literary histories and depart-ments of literature, forms only a tiny percentage of total book production, not to speak of the media market as a whole. Even in the German Democratic Republic the high social and didactic import-ance attributed to literature has been modified and relativised by the SED's recognition since the 1960s that television is by far the most important and effective instrument of cultural policy and propaganda.

Literature, theatre and film were allotted an important role in the socialist transformation of society in East Germany after 1945. Cultural policy took (and takes) the form on the one hand of control — no book can appear without the imprimatur of the Ministry of

Culture, which is supervised in turn by the cultural sections attached to the Central Committee of the SED — and on the other hand of active encouragement of a literature of production, giving ideological support to the absolute priority of social and economic reconstruction. Censorship was exercised through the dogma of Socialist Realism, which demanded of the writer the correct (optimistic) historical perspective, while encouragement was concentrated in the campaigns to turn workers into writers and writers into workers ('Bitterfelder Weg'). This campaign was abandoned by the mid-1960s with the completion of reconstruction, the consolidation of state power and the switch of emphasis from heavy industry to the leading role of the 'scientific-technical revolution'. The New Economic Policy from the mid-1960s on, with its emphasis on planners, managers and technical specialists, openly ratified the class structure of real existing socialism and was accompanied by a sharpened censorship towards the literary intelligentsia, aimed at warding off the dangerous influence of the Czech reforms. A new *modus vivendi* between writers and the state appeared to establish itself after the end of the Ulbricht era and Honecker's accession to power in 1971. A greater tolerance towards writers became evident, whose limits, however, were clearly demonstrated by the exiling of Wolf Biermann in 1976 and the subsequent measures of repression against the protests of some 100 members of the Schriftstellerverband. As a consequence many writers left the German Democratic Republic, either voluntarily or involuntarily, either temporarily or permanently, so that one could now speak of a German–German literature based in West Berlin and the Federal Republic.

The SED has consistently sought to define from above the social scope and function of literature, actively so until the 1960s, thereafter more and more negatively in the form of repressive tolerance. The symbolic space of literature in the GDR is thus defined directly by the power of the cultural bureaucracy, and indirectly by the politicisation of all spheres; the subjection, that is, of civil society to the dictates of the state. Whether as critical support — as for instance in the production plays of Peter Hacks, Heiner Müller and Volker Braun in the 1950s and 1960s — or as critical dissent — as in the work of Erich Loest, Ulrich Plenzdorf, Christa Wolf, Stefan Heym and others in the 1970s and 1980s — literature in the German Democratic Republic cannot escape the oppressive realities of a closed society. One obvious aspect should be mentioned: the work of East German writers is read in a very different way inside the German Democratic Republic than it is outside. (Note for instance the reception of Wolf's *Kassandra*, 1983, in the West as a feminist anti-war text without reference to the parallels between German Democratic Republic and Troy.) Such basic differences of production and reception call into question Frank Trommler's argument in Thomas Koebner's collection *Tendenzen der deutschen Gegenwartsliteratur* (Vol. 2, 1984) that we can now once again speak of one German literature. Even if with Grass we see literature as the one forum left for German–German unity and identity, it would still seem more appropriate to speak of two separate, if increasingly interlocking, literary systems for Germany.

The elimination of the market in the German Democratic Republic has prevented the complete segmentation of art into the popular and the serious, the commercial and the subsidised, basic to capitalist societies. Communist Party denunciations of Western decadence have taken the double form of the rejection of serious modern art as distorted, negative and anarchistic and the exclusion as far as possible of the siren song of popular culture from jazz to rock. Behind this puritanism lies a normative concept of art drawn directly from the limited perspectives of the 'Bildungsbürgertum' of the nineteenth century, as the constant appeals in the German Democratic Republic to the national legacy of humanism, classicism and idealism make clear. The direct restriction of the population's cultural needs and interests only reinforces, however, the didactic dreariness of the official versions of the 'people's' culture. The ruling concept of literature in the German Democratic Republic is neither popular nor proletarian but emphatically 'positive'. The cultural-political impact of Plenzdorf's *Neue Leiden des jungen W.* (1973) lay in its ridiculing of official attitudes, the assertion of the need for alternative or counter cultures, and in the challenge to the standard model of the puritan, performance oriented social character. The hero's (ironically presented) anti-establishment cultural identity is of course close to the youth sub- and protest cultures of Western society. Neither the manipulations from above in the East nor the market manipulations of the culture industry in the West has produced the total conformity which Adorno or Marcuse predicted. On the contrary, the endless competitive pressure of the market and the corresponding differentiation of supply and demand contradict the pessimism and elitism of the theorists of the culture industry, who saw the work of art reduced to a mere commodity.[2]

Such radical 'purism' fuelled the iconoclastic impulses of the Student Revolt. The tendency to see all art as ideology was evident

2. See Dennis Tate, 'The 'Other' German Literature', pp. 176–93 below for further discussion of East German literature.

not only in the dismissal of literature as a system of false consciousness but also in the demand for a directly instrumentalised literature in the service of the revolution. However, given the present differentiation of the market and the plurality of tastes and interests, it is increasingly difficult to think of literature in representative terms, that is, as occupying the representative space of the classical bourgeois public sphere. Equally, the claim to represent the counter public sphere (cf. Negt/Kluge, *Öffentlichkeit und Erfahrung*, 1972), raised by the direct political challenges to 'representative' conceptions of literature, is itself relativised by the ever growing diversity of the market. The disintegration — but equally differentiation — of the public sphere simultaneously confirms and invalidates the pessimism of the critical theory of the fate of culture in capitalism, just as the idea of a counter public sphere confirms not so much the idea of a hegemonic culture as the plurality of (competing) subcultures. The writer in Western society, as opposed to state socialism, has to come to terms with the sense of the apparent irrelevance of his production in the face of an overwhelming media output. There is a clear parallel here with the pervasive sense of personal alienation which emerges from much of the writing of the new subjectivity in the 1970s, which can be seen as the image of the alienation of the writer and of literature in the world of consumer capitalism. Against such literary melancholy, however, we can also point to the wide currency of literary theories which dissolve the concept of literature itself into *écriture* or intertextuality, or to the success of writing directed to a specific public, for which of course the prime example for the 1970s is feminist literature.

To sum up — the Student Revolt of the late 1960s dramatised a significant shift of perspectives in West Germany, which can be described in terms of the end of the post-war period, the opening of the problems of post-industrial society, the critique of the Enlightenment and modernity, and the search for new values and orientations. For the German Democratic Republic the late 1960s and early 1970s also appear to represent a turning-point in that writers in the 1970s oriented themselves less and less to the idea of a socialist future and more and more to the really existing socialist present. This has brought with it a new emphasis on the 'subjective factor' and a more imaginative and sophisticated use of styles and forms, whilst simultaneously increasing tensions between writers and the state.

Select Bibliography

Rudolf Bahro, *Die Alternative*, Frankfurt on Main, 1977

Jan Berg, et al., *Sozialgeschichte der deutschen Literatur von 1918 bis zur Gegenwart*, Frankfurt on Main, 1981

Manfred Durzak (ed.), *Deutsche Gegenwartsliteratur. Ausgangspositionen und aktuelle Entwicklungen*, Stuttgart, 1981

Wolfgang Emmerich, *Kleine Literaturgeschichte der DDR*, Darmstadt and Neuwied, 1981

Helmut Fischbeck, *Literaturpolitik und Literaturkritik in der DDR*, Frankfurt on Main, 1976

Jürgen Habermas (ed.), *Stichworte zur 'Geistigen Situation der Zeit'*, 2 vols., Frankfurt on Main, 1979

Jürgen Habermas, *Theorie des kommunikativen Handelns*, 2 vols., Frankfurt on Main, 1981

Peter Uwe Hohendahl and Patricia Herminghouse (eds.), *Literatur der DDR in den siebziger Jahren*, Frankfurt on Main, 1983

Ronald Inglehart, *The Silent Revolution. Changing Values and Political Styles among Western Publics*, Princeton, NJ, 1977

Thomas Koebner (ed.), *Tendenzen der deutschen Gegenwartsliteratur*, vol. 2, *neuverfaßte Auflage*, Stuttgart, 1984

Helmut Kreuzer, *Veränderungen des Literaturbegriffs*, Göttingen, 1975

W. Martin Lüdke (ed.), *Nach dem Protest. Literatur im Umbruch*, Frankfurt on Main, 1979

Paul Michael Lützeler and Egon Schwarz (eds.), *Deutsche Literatur in der Bundesrepublik seit 1965*, Königstein, 1980

Oskar Negt and Alexander Kluge, *Öffentlichkeit und Erfahrung*, Frankfurt on Main, 1972

David Roberts, 'Tendenzwenden. Die sechziger und siebziger Jahre in literaturhistorischer Perspektive', *Deutsche Vierteljahresschrift* 56 (1982), pp. 290–313

——(ed.), *Tendenzwenden. Zum Kulturwandel der siebziger Jahre*, Berne, 1984

R. Hinton Thomas and Keith Bullivant, *Literature in Upheaval. West German Writers and the Challenge of the Sixties*, Manchester, 1974

PART I

Themes

WILFRIED VAN DER WILL

The Republic of Letters and the State

Permutations of 'Geist' and 'Macht' in the Federal Republic Since the Early 1970s

It is difficult to imagine the political life of the Federal Republic without the vociferous criticism of its intellectuals. But the incisively interventionist role of writers, artists, journalists and academics in matters concerning the fundamentals of democracy, the heinous heritage of National Socialism, and the defence of peace appeared finally to have come to a close in the mid-1980s. The most important of these 'old-guard' intellectuals, Heinrich Böll, died in July 1985. The obituaries referred to him as an 'institution'[1] of critical judgement in his own right. His death must be seen as a landmark ending the period when intellectuals saw it as their duty to act as extra-parliamentary custodians of democracy. They were able to achieve such public significance in a post-war situation where democracy had to be reconstructed and the influence of majority and minority opinions on the process of political decision-making had to be established. It was partly the desire of the Western Allied powers to build up democratic structures in the media of mass communication which ensured that so many critical intellectuals gained full-time or freelance positions in the liberal press and in the radio stations. Their privileged access to the media gave them a prominence in public affairs which could compete with that of politicians. This fact had motivated Chancellor Ludwig Erhard in the mid-1960s first to seek the intellectuals' support and, when this was not forthcoming, to denounce them as 'Banausen und Nichtskönner' and as 'ganz kleine Pinscher'.[2] It would however be erroneous to suggest, as the conservative sociologist Helmut Schelsky did in *Die Arbeit tun die*

---

1. Cf. Ulrich Greiwe, 'Die Instanz ist tot, ein großartiger Mensch wird vermißt', *Westermanns Monatshefte*, No. 7, 1986, p. 68.
2. In *Heute und die 30 Jahre davor. Erzählungen, Gedichte und Kommentare zu unserer Zeit*, 2nd edn, Munich, 1979, p. 125.

anderen (1975), that their influence was so exclusive as to amount to virtual domination of the press and television. These intellectuals were far from forming a kind of 'Priesterkaste' which supposedly had opened up for the masses seductive vistas of utopian socialism through the power of the word and the hold on public opinion exercised by this 'Reflexionselite'.[3] Such exaggerated estimation of the critical intellectuals' importance on the one hand was matched by their equally fallacious dismissal as inconsequential windbags on the other. In Helmut Heißenbüttel's novel *D'Alemberts Ende* (1970) they were depicted as unprincipled chameleons, exceptional only in the alacrity of their ideological adjustments and united as a class merely by the selfishness of their material desires. These were satisfied in a manner reminiscent of Brecht's 'Tuis' who as a service class earned money by 'leasing their intellect'.[4] Similarly, Karl Heinz Bohrer in a short, semi-fictional essay entitled *Die Ästhetik des Staates* (1984) could present a caricature of both political and literary life in West Germany as deeply provincial, conformist and opulent. Just as the politicians wallowed in flabbily imprecise language, so had the intellectuals spurned all aesthetic commitment in favour of a trendy and philistine communicativeness. They were gluttons for a culture of the 'juste milieu' which they consumed like so much 'crème fraîche'.[5]

Precisely which writers Bohrer had in mind with his short satirical sketch was not clear; but there was little doubt that he had developed an animus against any writing whose credentials were not clearly grounded in a solid commitment to aesthetic values, undiluted by confessions to political beliefs. To what extent the latter had influenced the creative work of authors in the immediate post-fascist decades need not concern us here. But it can hardly be gainsaid that what authority their political pronouncements may have had derived largely from the fame they enjoyed in the world of letters. The withdrawal of the intellectuals' voice from the arena of politics in the mid-1980s could not go unnoticed precisely because it had been so prominent before, indeed it had reached a crescendo in the early 1980s. It was not Böll's death alone that brought about this change. Günter Grass, having played a crucial role since 1965 through his

3. Helmut Schelsky, *Die Arbeit tun die anderen. Klassenkampf und Priesterherrschaft der Intellektuellen*, Munich, 1977, p. 131. See also J.H. Reid's chapter on Böll in this volume, p. 217.
4. 'Der TUI ist der Intellektuelle dieser Zeit der Märkte und Waren. Der Vermieter des Intellekts, Bertolt Brecht, *Der Tui-Roman, werkausgabe*, Frankfurt on Main, 1967, vol. 12, p. 611.
5. Cf. Karl Heinz Bohrer, 'Die Ästhetik des Staates', *Merkur*, No. 1, January 1984, pp. 1–15.

campaign speeches and involvement in several 'Wählerinitiativen' in support of the Social Democratic Party, absented himself from the Federal elections in January 1987 and went on sabbatical leave to Calcutta. Martin Walser, although still concerned in his fictional writings with political matters, notably the division of Germany, declined to take the vacant mantle of chief intellectual interventionist in politics by declaring that it was not for him to mount the politician's rostrum, which for the writer was a 'geliehenes Podest'.[6] Günter Wallraff, after the phenomenal controversy caused by his book *Ganz unten* (1985), a documentary account of the exploitation of the 'Gastarbeiter' which sold over 1.5 million copies in less than two years, decided to move to the Netherlands in the autumn of 1986 to escape what he called 'political persecution' and the tentacles of German bureaucracy. A less well-known figure, Wolfgang Hildesheimer, withdrew into 'das Pathos des Nicht-Mehr-Schreibens',[7] specifically because the world overshadowed by a final, scientifically engineered catastrophe could no longer be expressed in fiction. As for the younger writers, there are signs that in contradistinction to those influenced by the attitudes of the members of the Gruppe 47, which ceased its activities in 1968, they are looking for something more 'positive', more exclusively aesthetic, if not esoteric, than the moral and political commitment which informed the public stance of the older intellectuals. Perhaps now is the time to attempt a historical assessment of the critical intellectuals' public role in West Germany.

Such attempts have been made before and they have concentrated on the relationship between the Social Democratic Party and the literary intelligentsia.[8] True, the latter was unquestionably the most prominent group of extra-parliamentary political critics, but these also encompassed intellectuals from artistic, academic and journalistic backgrounds; and while the Social Democratic Party seemed for a substantial period to offer the only possibility for political commitment, this was at all times a precarious affair for intellec-

6. Walser originally used this term in a subtitle ('Wahlrede auf geliehenem Podest') in Martin Walser (ed.), *Die Alternative oder Brauchen wir eine neue Regierung?*, Reinbek nr. Hamburg (rororo), August 1961, p. 126. See also note 50 below.
7. Cf. 'Ich bin ein geständiger Täter', interview with Günter Wallraff in *Hamburger Rundschau*, 14.8.1986 and Ariane Thomalia, 'Die letzte Lesung des Wolfgang Hildesheimer?' *General-Anzeiger*, 23.10.1985, p. 11.
8. Cf. Merle Curtis Krueger, *Authors and the Opposition: West German Writers and the Social Democratic Party from 1945 to 1969*, Stuttgart, 1982; Helmut L. Müller, *Die literarische Republik. Westdeutsche Schriftsteller und die Politik*, Weinheim and Basel, 1982; K. Stuart Parkes, *Writers and Politics in West Germany*, London and Sydney, 1986.

tuals, even if one concedes that few of those with any prominence ever plumped for conservative positions. In some cases (Rolf Hochhuth has opted for the Free Democratic Party since the late 1960s) the preference for the SPD was short-lived, in others it was more definite and of longer duration. But from the late 1960s there had always been other political possibilities, for example the Aktion Demokratischer Fortschritt or the Deutsche Kommunistische Partei, and the arrival of the new social movements in the 1970s, the counter culture with its small co-operatives (playfully termed the 'culture of counters'), which led to the formation of the Green Party ('die Grünen') and its ultimate entry into the Federal Parliament in 1983, appears to have transformed the critical debate, originally opened up by the intellectuals and the Student Movement. It is therefore premature, if not wrong, to assess the intellectuals' political role exclusively in terms of their relationship with the SPD. This is not to deny that that relationship was crucial for the intellectuals, however, particularly at the time of the Social-Liberal Coalition. The outlines of a political and ideological history since the end of the 1960s of those polemically referred to by the media as 'intellectuals' might shed light not only on their unique position, but also on the development of the political agenda that, at a later stage, allowed them to retreat into the background.

Divisions in the Critical Intelligentsia and the Critique of the Consolidated Capitalist Society

In the same volume of *Kursbuch* (No. 15, 1968) which contained a vituperative critique of the literati by Hans Magnus Enzensberger and in which an influential reviewer and editor, Walter Boehlich, summarily declared the death of bourgeois literature, Karl Markus Michel published an epitaph on the Gruppe 47. While this group had been regarded by the Establishment as the centre of all dissatisfaction in and with the Federal Republic and was decried as the source of all subversion, Michel dismissed it as 'nicht einmal ein Papiertiger, sondern ein Schoßhund'.[9] Voices within the Gruppe 47 itself had begun to express similar misgivings. Heinrich Böll, in an article entitled 'Angst vor der Gruppe 47' had advanced trenchant self-criticism: 'Ein Schriftsteller, der funktioniert, ist keiner mehr', and he went on to ask: 'Ob eine Gruppe von Schriftstellern, wenn sie

9. Karl Markus Michel, 'Ein kranz für die Literatur. Fünf Variationen über eine These', *Kursbuch*, No. 15, 1986, p. 177

anfängt zu funktionieren, sich nicht auf eine absurde Weise mit der Gesellschaft konform erklärt?'[10] In a stinging diatribe in the literary journal *konkret* — subsequently broadcast by four radio stations — the well-known parodist Robert Neumann attacked the Gruppe 47 as a 'Literatur-Mafia' that, through the foundation of the 'Literarisches Colloquium', the money of the Ford Foundation and the cooperation of the city's Senate, had brought under its control, at least in West Berlin, a complete system of patronage in the form of prizes, grants and subsidies. In other words, the Gruppe 47 was not just part of the Establishment, it had committed 'Verrat an der Opposition gegen das [. . .] Establishment'.[11] Böll, along with Andersch, Enzensberger, Schnurre, Walser and Weiss, had already ceased attending its meetings which, because of internal dissensions, stopped in 1968 when Hans Werner Richter decided not to call the Group together again because the friendships within it had given way to irreconcilable ideological rifts. The Group had certainly failed to provide the rebellious students with critical or analytical concepts or, for that matter, with support and approval. Hence it could suddenly be classed as part of the very Establishment whose enemy it had prided itself on being. Yet some of its members did have considerable sympathies for the Extra-Parliamentary Opposition (Außerparlamentarische Opposition: APO) and the anti-authoritarian Student Movement, actively paving the way for the emergence of a younger, more professionally critical intelligentsia. Walter Jens, for example, had edited a volume of essays in time for the election campaign in 1965 in which the contradictions and shortcomings of the Erhard Government were analysed by young political scientists, sociologists and historians. This was a conscious attempt to replace the rather vague and wholesale condemnations contained in Walser's *Die Alternative* of 1961 with a more carefully researched analysis. At the same time it signalled a sociological shift in the locus of public criticism from a relatively small circle of freelance intellectuals to the broader stratum of the intelligentsia in the universities.

In 'Angst vor der Gruppe 47', Böll had clearly pointed to the reason for the dissensions within the Group: the willingness of a majority of its members to identify with the SPD and the consequent abandonment of their role as radical critics in society. He argued with considerable force that this role could not be claimed by those

---

10. Heinrich Böll, 'Angst vor der Gruppe 47' (originally in *Merkur*, 1965), in Reinhard Lettau (ed.), *Die Gruppe 47*, Neuwied and Berlin, 1967, p. 400.
11. Robert Neuman, 'Spezies. Gruppe 47 in Berlin', *konkret*, No. 5, May 1966, p. 37.

who were prepared 'einer Partei Sträußchen zu binden'[12] which was about to vote for the proposed 'Notstandsgesetze' (Emergency Laws), a party which, having betrayed 'die erste und einzige Anti-Atombegwegung in der Bundesrepublik',[13] was more fervently in favour of rearmament than the generals themselves, and a party aiming for a Grand Coalition. With the radicalisation of the students and the establishment of the Extra-Parliamentary Opposition, the intellectuals of the Gruppe 47 lost their unique position as ideologically non-conformist critics. They now found themselves in a political landscape in which they were outflanked by a movement of the young academic intelligentsia that captured public attention both by its protest in the streets and by the radicalism of its Marxist analysis. This produced a situation where some of the older intellectuals were drawn into tighter partisanship with the SPD, while others took camp closer to the 'revolutionary' and utopian positions of the anti-authoritarian students. Inevitably, severe disagreements arose amongst them. Grass attacked Böll and Andersch in his 'Büchner-Preis' speech (and elsewhere scolded Herbert Wehner, the chairman of the SPD's Parliamentary Party, for his duplicitous bargaining with the CDU); Walser attacked Grass and Hans Werner Richter in a radio broadcast; Richter attacked all those who did not actively defend the democratic state and instead allied themselves with the revolutionaries of the Third World. Ironically, at the very moment that democratic pluralism was taking root in Germany ('Die Gruppe 47 ist pluralistisch geblieben, die Gesellschaft ist es geworden',[14] Böll had observed), those who had stood for it most clearly fell out with each other and were denounced by the students as part of a subtle form of oppression by the 'ruling class'. 'Günter Grass probt die Anpassung',[15] was one critic's comment on his play *Davor* (1969). Other writers, like Enzensberger and Walser, were no longer prepared to credit the existing political system with any capacity to reform itself. In their view it had stagnated for too long and had ended up without any sizeable opposition in parliament. Democracy began to be seen as the rule of a clique elected by a majority that was thoroughly manipulated by the media industry:

Die parlamentarische Regierungsform ist vollends zur Fassade für ein Machtkartell geworden, das der verfassungsmäßige Souverain, das Volk, auf keine Weise mehr beseitigen kann [. . .]. In der Tat, was auf der

12. Böll, 'Angst vor der Gruppe 47', p. 397.
13. Ibid., p. 397.
14. Ibid., p. 391.
15. Peter Hamm in *konkret*, No. 2, Feb. 1969, p. 50.

Tagesordnung steht, ist nicht mehr der Kommunisnmus, sondern die Revolution. Das politische System der Bundesrepublik ist jenseits aller Reparatur. Mann kann ihm zustimmen, oder man muß es durch ein neues ersetzen. *Tertium non dabitur*[16]

Pointing an accusing finger at the all too reformist writers Enzensberger accorded not them but the students the honour of having created an historical situation of choice between the affirmation of the status quo and the possibility of opting for revolution. This was a gross overestimation of what the students had done, but it held true as far as the position of the intellectuals was concerned. They were indeed challenged to show where they stood. Inevitably, literature now had to become politicised, Enzensberger declared, irrespective of whether this would enhance the quality of the writing or, more likely, be to its detriment.

The dissensions, factions and frictions which were now becoming visible were not restricted, however, to the purely literary intelligentsia. The anti-authoritarian Student Movement, the protest against the 'Notstandsgesetze' and against the merely 'formal' democracy of the Grand Coalition brought to the fore warring armies of critical intellectuals from inside and outside the universities, on the left, in the centre and on the right of the political spectrum: the thinkers of the Frankfurt School of Social Research, Theodor W. Adorno, Max Horkheimer, Erich Fromm, Herbert Marcuse, Jürgen Habermas, amongst others, the psychoanalyst Alexander Mitscherlich, journalists such as Rudolf Augstein, Erich Kuby and Ulrike Meinhof, the theologians Martin Niemöller and Helmut Gollwitzer, all represented various shades of reformist criticism, tinged with reflections on the possibility of revolution; the philosopher Karl Jaspers held a position of liberal radicalism (cogently expounded in his long political essay of 1966 *Wohin treibt die Bundesrepublik?*), while conservative positions were intelligently defended by the sociologists Arnold Gehlen and Helmut Schelsky. The younger left-wing intelligentsia had created for itself a remarkable range of publication outlets: apart from established paperback series (Fischer, dtv, rororo) there were pirate editions (*Dialektik der Aufklärung*, by Horkheimer and Adorno was one of the first), a number of scholarly journals such as *Kursbuch, kürbiskern, Das Argument, Probleme des Klassenkampfs, Sozialistische Politik, Mehrwert*, political ones such as *konkret*, and a host of campus newspapers. Other important publica-

16. Hans Magnus Enzensberger, 'Klare Entscheidungen und trübe Aussichten', in Joachim Schickel (ed.), *Über Hans Magnus Enzensberger*, Frankfurt on Main, 1970, pp. 228f.

tions were specific paperback series, such as Rowohlt's *rororo aktuell* (started in 1961) and *edition suhrkamp* (which began in 1963 and was terminated in 1979, having run to one thousand volumes by then). These books and periodicals, which brought together contributions by a whole range of authors, illustrated in their own way that for all their distinction as creative writers, many literary intellectuals had by the second half of the 1960s merged with a larger critical intelligentsia in whose company they published their responses to the political and ideological challenges that this period posed. They were now no longer individual partisans fighting heroic battles on their own. Instead they became part of a larger constituency of protest that could exercise its fascination not just in the university towns, but beyond that in thousands of grammar schools in the smaller localities. In other words, almost an entire generation of young educated people, normally no more than a recruiting ground for a handful of future critical intellectuals, was advancing into the position of a socially critical intelligentsia. This was a public in its own right, which saw itself as an articulate agent for the whole society, whose main task was to free the mass of the population from the manipulative shackles of established politicians and the sensationalist media.

Within the broad mass of this intelligentsia, many of the older, well-known intellectuals retained a special status, not so much as leaders but because of the authority and publicity they lent to the arguments against the status quo. The campaign against the 'Notstandsgesetze' was unthinkable without the panoply of, as it were, VIP intellectuals who were at the forefront of the debate: Carl Amery, Ernst Bloch, Heinrich Böll, Hans Magnus Enzensberger, Erich Fried, Rolf Hochhuth, Walter Jens, Erich Kästner, Reinhard Lettau, Robert Neumann, Martin Walser and others. At major rallies, in Frankfurt in 1966 and elsewhere, they criticised the proposed laws — which were redrafted several times before finally being passed by the Bundestag in May 1968 — as legal tools that could easily be used by a dictator or an anti-democratic oligarchy to suspend the basic provisions for liberty in the Constitution, as had happened in the Weimar Republic. The conclusions that the various intellectuals drew from the defeat over the enactment of the emergency legislation showed a further deepening of the divisions amongst them: Hochhuth announced his resignation from the SPD and urged support for the Free Democrats as the only parliamentary guarantee for the survival of the democratic Constitution. In this he remained alone amongst writers, but was joined by the academic Peter Brückner. In the view of many other intellectuals an attempt had to be made to develop the broadly based alliance which had opposed the formation of the Grand Coalition into a permanent political force. As a result the so-called 'Gießener Kreis' published an appeal which pleaded not only for the strengthening of democracy in the Federal Republic, but also for a retrenchment of monopoly capitalist interests, a reduction of arms expenditure and a policy of reconciliation towards the East. This was signed by, amongst others, a number of prominent authors: Tankred Dorst, Max von der Grün, Wolfgang Hildesheimer, Christoph Meckel, Robert Neumann, Peter Rühmkorf, Dieter Süverkrüp, Günter Wallraff and Martin Walser. The appeal led to the formation of the Aktion Demokratischer Fortschritt in which, more than ten years before the foundation of the Green Party, the idea first surfaced of ensuring continuous reciprocal influence between the extra-parliamentary movement and its parliamentary representatives, with maximum accountability of the latter to its constituency. The ADF was to constitute an oppositional platform in parliament, which was to be used to promote discussion of policy concepts alternative to those of the established parties. The government was to be forced to engage in more transparent decision-making, and the new party, which would not have a centralist bureaucratic structure, was conceived above all as a watchdog of the democratic interest. The ADF was also similar to the later Greens in that it conceived of itself as a coalition of different extra-parliamentary groups and tendencies: 'Das Neue besteht darin, daß im Gegensatz zu unseren erstarrten und versteinerten Parteien die Kräfte des Bündnisses offen bleiben für immer neue Gruppen der Bewegung im Volke selbst. Sie wollen nicht an die Stelle dieser Bewegung eine Partei setzen, sondern die Bewegung selbst stärken und entwickeln'.[17] In truth, the ADF remained too exclusively orientated towards traditional notions of class consciousness, working-class solidarity and the Soviet model of socialism to make any real inroads into an electorate appalled by the Warsaw Pact invasion of Czechoslovakia in 1968. In the Federal Election of September 1969 the ADF fell well below the five per cent required to obtain representation in the Bundestag. The CDU/CSU received 46.1 per cent, the SPD 42.7 per cent and the FDP polled 5.8 per cent, enough to tip the balance and go into coalition with Brandt's Social Democrats, who had been supported wholeheartedly by such well-known writers as Günter Grass, Dieter Lattmann and Thaddäus Troll, with Heinrich Böll, Hans Werner Richter and

17. 'Aktions- und Wahlbündnis 1969. Neun Fragen und Antworten', *kürbiskern*, No. 4, Dec. 1968, p. 654.

Siegfried Lenz giving rather more guarded support.

There then followed a period when the Social-Liberal Coalition took the wind out of the intellectuals' critical sails. Many of them, grateful for the rational reforms in the universities and schools, for the policy towards the East ('Ostpolitik') and for progressive social legislation, saw this government as an executor of enlightened statesmanship. Significantly, when in December 1970 Brandt made his famous gesture of reconciliation with the Polish people by kneeling in front of the monument to the victims of National Socialism in the Warsaw Ghetto, he chose to be accompanied by two writers, Günter Grass and Siegfried Lenz. The national and foreign policies of the government appeared to be guided by the vision of a society promising a more equitable distribution of wealth, 'more democracy' at all levels and détente between East and West. The role of the writers as the 'Gewissen der Nation', critical of the authorities of the state, seemed to have become redundant. The Brandt Government had signalled that it understood democracy as a dynamic process which would gradually replace authoritarian attitudes at all levels of state power. To this extent the intellectuals, who were committed to the old Enlightenment ideal of emancipation from all blind obedience, could believe they had at last found an ally in a government ready, as it were, to share power with them. In a speech to the Verband deutscher Schriftsteller (Writers' Association) in 1970 Brandt indicated that he wished to bury the opposition which had existed between men of letters and State authority: 'Geist und Macht, das angeblich strenge Gegensatzpaar, üben oft und gerne Rollentausch. Denn so mächtig der Einfluß der Politik auf die Gesellschaft sein mag, längst hat sie ihre Macht teilen müssen: gerade Sie als Schriftsteller sollten Ihren Einfluß nicht unterschätzen'.[18] This was a flattering recognition of the writers' importance in the public discourse of politics. For a short time, the old opposition, if not antagonism, between the representatives of creative writing and art and those of power seemed to be suspended. The remaining enemies — as is evident from Böll's speeches and articles at the time — were the sensationalist Springer press, a target first identified by the students in 1968, and the rather conservative judiciary. When, after a failed vote of no confidence, proposed by the CDU/CSU in the Bundestag, Brandt decided to put the issue to the electorate in 1972, the SPD was vociferously supported by those intellectuals who had backed it in 1969, plus others from the

---

18. Willy Brandt, 'Braucht die Politik den Schriftsteller?', in Dieter Lattmann (ed.), *Einigkeit der Einzelgänger*, Munich, 1971, p. 12.

erstwhile ADF, like Max von der Grün. The SPD was returned with 45.8 per cent, its highest ever share of the vote. Since the FDP had also improved its standing (to 8.4 per cent), the foundation was laid for a continuation of the Social-Liberal Coalition. However, a number of issues, notably the nature of the democratic state in West Germany, now emerged which re-established the intellectuals in their accustomed role as defenders of fundamental democratic rights. In this process the rifts between the older intellectuals of the former Gruppe 47 gradually healed, while fresh divisions began to emerge between them and the younger intelligentsia.

The political environment had changed to such an extent that the intellectuals' extra-parliamentary criticism now had much greater resonance in society. Throughout the 1970s and the 1980s writers and artists did not simply revert to the role of isolated oppositionists, roaming over the political landscape like some unpredictable 'francs tireurs'. On the contrary, since their fame was now international and their function as cultural and social critics widely recognised, they found themselves surrounded by a politically alert audience much larger and more voluble than that of the 1950s and early 1960s. Sections of the governing parties, the students and senior school pupils had all been seized by the spirit of articulate anti-authoritarianism which for so long had appeared the prerogative of a tiny cultural elite. The aura of the creative genius which tradition-ally attached to that elite was dissipated by the writers themselves. By projecting themselves as critical citizens they were demonstrat-ing the value of the individual's public, political role which, at least in part, might be imitated by all, thus preparing the ground for that concept of participatory political citizenship which fired the 'new social movements' in the 1970s. Through their commitment in the political arena, the intellectuals sought to demonstrate in exemplary fashion how democracy in the Federal Republic might be extended if expanding critical spaces for debate could be secured within it. They further diminished their own aura by forming first a lobby and then a section within a trade union in order to advance their collective material interests. The foundation of the Verband deutscher Schrifts-teller (VS) in 1969 and its affiliation to the Print Union (the IG Druck und Papier) in 1973 concluded a process in which the extreme individualism that had torpedoed all such attempts since the 1840s[19] was finally overcome so that their collective interests could at least be represented by an effective bargaining organisation.

19. Cf. Friedhelm Kron, *Schriftsteller und Schriftstellerverbände. Schriftstellerberuf und Interessenpolitik 1842–1973*, Stuttgart, 1976.

The VS gave notice that writers no longer wished to be placed on a pedestal of rarefied admiration. Royalties, pension arrangements and benefits to authors from public libraries all had to be properly negotiated. With exaggerated pathos Böll demanded of the writers that they reject the posture of lowly supplicants to the publishers and state authorities: 'Wir verdanken diesem Staat nichts, er verdankt uns eine Menge; mag er also darauf gefaßt sein, daß er uns nicht länger auf dem Umweg über einen Pseudo-Geniekult oder auch nur auf dem Umweg über den Pseudo-Individualitätskult zerspalten und zersplittert halten und einzeln abfertigen kann'.[20] This sentence certainly resounded with a tone of solicitous pride *vis-à-vis* established authority. As such it was, of course, entirely in keeping with the spirit of anti-authoritarian republicanism with which writers had for a long time sought to inspire their fellow citizens. But in its plea *pro domo* and its organisational implications, Böll's remark also demonstrated that the writers had learnt from the corporatist anti-authoritarianism of the Student Movement.

The Intellectuals and the Problem of the State

Even in 1972 when the Social-Liberal Coalition, and the SPD in particular, had received an overwhelming vote of confidence from the electorate, the revolutionary illusions of the university were still by no means dead, finding expression in the foundation of a number of student communist parties, such as the KPD (Kommunistische Partei Deutschlands), the KPD (ML) (Marxistisch-Leninistisch) and the KBW (Kommunistischer Bund Westdeutschlands). Left-wing radicalism now became a joint target both of the writers who belonged to an older generation and of those who had emerged from the Student Movement. Grass had long warned the students about the futility of their radically anti-parliamentary politics, a warning now echoed by Böll and even Enzensberger. With his short novel *Lenz* (1973) Peter Schneider initiated a series of fictional accounts in which writers, who had been part of the anti-authoritarian movement, tried to come to terms with their experiences, describing the frustrations, illusions and disillusionments caused by the complete blockage of revolutionary change by established society. All these books were weighed down with a left-wing melancholia that had been induced by the disenchanted assessments of the immediate

20. Heinrich Böll, 'Ende der Bescheidenheit', in *Ende der Bescheidenheit. Schriften und Reden 1969–1972*, Munich, 1985, p. 65.

past now rife among the young intelligentsia. The whole complex of public struggles and intimate relationships was reviewed from the distance of escapist sojourns in sun-belt Europe. Here the sorrows about the political and emotional failures of the immediate past were soothed by the uninhibited warmth of southern proletariats and drowned in much grappa and red wine. These novels represented the disillusioned reflections of a lost intelligentsia which, uncertain of its own identity in terms of class, had sought to submerge itself in a supposedly revolutionary proletariat only to end up in political disorientation. In the later 1970s and early 1980s the intelligentsia portrayed in these novels went on to seek refuge in the hedonism of an alternative, neoromantic culture of small collectives.

Schneider's *Lenz*, modelled stylistically on Georg Büchner's story of the same name, concerns a student whose relationship with a young working-class woman has just ended. Following the typical pattern of penitently suppressing his middle-class identity, he looks for work on the conveyor belt of an electronics firm. Seen from the factory, the university appears as a milieu that is culturally and materially parasitic on the industrial proletariat. There is an intense yearning in Lenz to be able to see with the eyes of the under-privileged. If, as Karl Mannheim observed, identification with social positions and points of view that are not his own is a characteristic of the modern intellectual, then Schneider's Lenz is a typical example of such an attitude. Gradually he begins to understand that the desire for revolution is almost completely absent amongst the workers, that such longings are at best a pastime to alleviate the frustrations and impatience of students and at worst may be exploited as a mere salespitch for the syllogisms of the more established intellectuals. Having initially been swept along by the great avalanche of abstractions and theory which propelled the anti-authoritarian movement, Lenz now longs for the immediacy of concrete experience. He is the first literary figure embodying the 'Erfahrungshunger' (hunger for experience)[21] that inaugurated the 'new sensibility' of an entire generation of young intellectuals. Theory had become suspect not only because of the innate reductionism of abtractions and slogans, but also because it had patently failed to bring about an alliance between the intellectuals and the working class, leading instead to the disorientation of the former and to a serious misjudgement about the role of the latter in contemporary society. For all the analogies between Büchner's and Schneider's

21. Cf. Michael Rutschky, *Erfahrungshunger. Ein Essay über die siebziger Jahre*, Cologne, 1980. See also Peter Labanyi's essay on Schneider, pp. 321f. of this volume.

Lenz, important differences remain between the two texts. Whereas Büchner's Lenz had gone mad, roaming aimlessly in the no-man's land between the aristocracy and the bourgeoisie, Schneider's had to endure a similar, though by no means fatal, agony suspended between bourgeoisie and proletariat, from which he is only briefly relieved in the company of comrades in Italy. While Büchner's Lenz sinks into irreversible apathy, Schneider's proves to be a successful survivor, capable of re-adapting and re-integrating himself without resorting to terrorism or being absorbed by narcissistic resignation.

Returning to Germany, Lenz resolves at the end to 'stay put' ('dableiben'), thus leaving open the possibility of joining other forms of organised protest, for which the anti-authoritarian movement had paved the way, such as the citizens' initiatives ('Bürgerinitiativen') and the developing struggle over ecological issues. Lenz's disillusionment with the politics and student communism did not mean a disillusionment with politics as such. In contrast to this, other writers, amongst them Peter Handke and Botho Strauß, began to project intellectual life in their works as a paradox: totally alienated and forlorn amidst the huge dehumanised concrete structures of modernist architecture, the individual was at the same time deemed capable of reaching back to a kind of pre-dialectical, apolitical, childlike existence in harmony with fellow human beings and nature.[22] This utopian optimism and nostalgic yearning for a return to nature was not shared by Nicolas Born, for example, who marks a transitional position in the bifurcation rapidly developing between the political interventionism of the older intelligentsia and the narcissistic anarchism now fashionable with some of the younger writers. Born's novel *Die erdabgewandte Seite der Geschichte* (1976) deals with the decomposition of identity suffered by a petit-bourgeois intellectual. He writes radio essays about this problem and collects royalties for it. At one stage this first-person narrator reflects on his inability to develop a clear political persona with succinct political views and a capacity to act in an historically relevant manner. A typical member of what Karl Mannheim called the 'interstitial stratum of intellectuals',[23] he dissolves in ambiguity. The agenda of politics as circumscribed by the existing parties seems to him

---

22. Cf. Botho Strauß, *Die Hypochonder* (1971) and *Bekannte Gesichter, gemischte Gefühle (1974)*, Munich and Vienna, 1979; Peter Handke, *Als das Wünschen noch geholfen hat*, Frankfurt on Main, 1974; cf. also Michael Schneider, 'Botho Strauß, das bürgerliche Feuilleton und der Kultus des Verfalls: Zur Diagnose des neuen Lebensgefühls', in *Den Kopf verkehrt aufgesetzt oder Die melancholische Linke: Aspekte des Kulturverfalls in den siebziger Jahren*, Darmstadt and Neuwied, 1981.
23. Karl Mannheim, *Essays in the Sociology of Culture*, London, 1956, p. 104.

ludicrously irrelevant compared with the real issues of the time:

> Es gab kein öffentliches Bewußtsein, das die Industrie zurückentwickeln wollte in die Notwendigkeit, [. . .] und es gab kein öffentliches Bewußtsein, das sich selbst als den größten und letzten Wahnsinn begriff. Oder wie hätte es sonst zu diesen Staaten kommen sollen, zu diesen Regierungen? [. . .] Der Staat erließ ja unentwegt Gesetze zu seinem Schutz, so daß wir uns bald in seinem Schutz nicht mehr bewegen können.[24]

This neurosis of the state had developed in response to an anarchic attack on the status quo by a small group of terrorists who sought to force revolutionary change on society by violent means. It led them into a position of extreme social marginality but caused an over-reaction on the part of the state security forces which temporarily threatened the democratic consensus. The Baader-Meinhof group thought it legitimate to use violence in order to set an example to the rest of the Student Movement. The terrorist organisation assumed that such action by broad strata of the young intelligentsia might stir the mass of the population out of the political apathy into which it had been manipulated by Social Democratic reformism and the constant propaganda of the pro-capitalist mass media. In some notes made in prison, couched in the group's peculiar terminology, Ulrike Meinhof tried to explain the motivation and strategy of the self-designated Red Army Faction:

> Angeekelt von den Reproduktionsbedingungen, die sie im System vorfanden, der totalen Vermarktung und absoluten Verlogenheit in allen Bereichen des Überbaus, zutiefst entmutigt von den Aktionen der Studentenbewegung und der Apo hielten sie es für nötig, die Idee des bewaffneten Kampfes zu propagieren. Nicht weil sie so blind waren zu glauben, sie könnten diese Initiative bis zum Sieg der Revolution in Deutschland durchhalten, nicht weil sie sich einbildeten, sie könnten nicht erschossen und nicht verhaftet werden. Nicht weil sie die Situation so falsch einschätzten, die Massen würden sich auf ein solches Signal hin einfach erheben. Es ging darum, den ganzen Erkenntnisstand der Bewegung von 1967/68 historisch zu retten; es ging darum, den Kampf nicht mehr abreißen zu lassen.[25]

Precisely the opposite was achieved. The terrorism of the Red Army Faction and its successors checked the incipient public debate about the connections between authoritarianism, big business and National Socialism, and the question of German society's implication

24. Nicolas Born, *Die erdabgewandte Seite der Geschichte* (1976), Reinbek nr. Hamburg, 1979, pp. 187/8.
25. Quoted in Stefan Aust, *Der Baader Meinhof Komplex*, Hamburg, 1985, pp. 286/7.

in the murderous moral rigour of the terrorists[26] (Max Frisch) was stifled by the atmosphere of an ideological witchhunt. The terrorists considered the machinery of the 'late capitalist' state — which they termed Leviathan or Moby Dick — to be global in its hegemony and fascist in character. The declared targets were therefore the military and security forces of the United States and those of its prime ally, West Germany. The internal secret services (Verfassungsschutz — Office for the Protection of the Constitution) and the criminal investigation offices, far from withering under this attack, used it as an argument for further expansion. This could be justified all the more easily since in addition to the issue of terrorist violence, they had been assigned a very large target for close observation, that of the Student Movement, its graduates and any circles connected with such individuals and groups. From the late 1960s and early 1970s onwards the entire critical intelligentsia had been pinpointed for police surveillance. This was intensified by the 'Radikalenerlaß' (Decree on Extremists) of January 1972 which stipulated that all individuals who, because of real or alleged extremist activities, could be suspected of disloyalty to the Constitution were to be banned from employment in the civil service, including the teaching profession. The problems of armed struggle against the state and (allegedly) disloyal civil servants could together be used by the conservative press to create a climate of insecurity and hysteria which in the course of the 1970s reached such a remarkable degree of intensity that it began to threaten fundamental democratic rights. Once again it seemed that against the relatively recent traditions of democracy and the safeguarding of individual liberties the much older history of the authoritarian state ('Obrigkeitsstaat'), imposing the law from above, would reassert itself.

The exaggerated estimation of the terrorist threat, coupled with the eavesdropping practices ('Lauschangriffe') by the secret services and the muzzling of young intellectuals, ended the honeymoon between 'Macht' and 'Geist' shortly after the Brandt Government had been re-elected in 1972. The ruling politicians appeared to connive in and promote what was seen by many to be a dangerous strengthening of the repressive machinery of the state. The German PEN Club protested against the 'Radikalenerlaß', which, it deplored, affected freedom of speech in the radio and television stations and in the press. The state, eager to employ the most advanced

26. 'Was solche Menschen, Moralisten also, ihrerseits zu Gewalttätern hat werden lassen, die Frage ist unerwünscht . . ., Max Frisch: Rede vor den Delegierten des SPD-Parteitages. Hamburg, 1977', in Max Frisch, *Gesammelte Werke in zeitlicher Folge*, vol. VII, Frankfurt on Main, 1986, p. 36.

technological means in its defence, appeared ready to submit its citizens to comprehensive computer screening. It seemed increasingly that the state was undergoing a metamorphosis to emerge as a technocratic ogre. Specifically, the investigative practices of the Bundeskriminalamt in Wiesbaden (BKA — Federal Office of Criminal Investigation) were reconceived and reorganised in such a way as to make possible electronic scans of defined sections of the population ('Rasterfahndung') or computer-aided field searches ('Netzfahndung'). The BKA, which in 1971 had a budget of DM 54.8 million, was transformed into a modern computer centre and data bank whose budget a decade later had swelled to DM 290 million. These changes were masterminded by Dr Horst Herold who consequently became an object of much criticism by intellectuals. In a poem by Erich Fried, he was attacked for having suggested that all citizens should take part in the hunt for terrorists. In other words, the mass of the population was invited to act as police informers, while every student became a potential suspect. Herold himself, a highly articulate advocate of the 'gesellschaftssanitäre Aufgabe der Polizei'[27] liked to refer to his expensive new machine as 'Big Brother'. In a letter to the Federal Parliament in June 1972 the old-guard intellectuals 'warnen vor einer abermaligen Zerstörung der Keime einer freiheitlich demokratischen Grundordnung in Deutschland unter dem Vorwand ihrer Verteidigung'.[28] Herbert Wehner, the Deputy Chairman of the SPD, had used a similar argument even before the 'Radikalenerlaß' became official policy: 'Wenn man hier einmal anfängt, wo wird man enden? Wann wird die nächste Gruppe fällig sein und die übernächste? Ich sehe keinen Sinn darin, die freiheitliche Grundordnung durch den ersten Schritt zu ihrer Beseitigung schützen zu wollen'.[29] The witchhunt of the intelligentsia was on. (Brandt was later deeply to regret his Government's promulgation of this Decree.) Böll expressed his fear that the 'Radikalenerlaß' would breed rather than extinguish terrorism. Trying to inject a measure of democratic calm into the debate, he had warned in an article in *Der Spiegel* (January 1972), entitled 'Will Ulrike Meinhof Gnade oder freies Geleit?' that the measures taken by society against a few terrorists should be commensurate with the crime and that there should not be a hunt by 60 million people against six, as the mass tabloid *Bild* with its 10 million readers was urging. The

27. Horst Herold quoted in Aust, *Der Baader Meinhof Komplex*, p. 197.
28. In *Vaterland, Muttersprache. Deutsche Schriftsteller und ihr Staat seit 1945*, Berlin, 1979, p. 287.
29. Quoted in Peter Schneider, *. . . schon bist du ein Verfassungsfeind*, Berlin, 1975, pp. 91/2.

sustained campaign of vilification to which Böll was subsequently subjected on television and in newspaper articles reflected the extent to which the Federal Republic had already lost its democratic poise. If Böll had underestimated the violence of the terrorists, the reaction to his article showed that he had certainly not underestimated the power of the reactionary press and right-wing politicians to create an atmosphere of panic in which all critical citizens, particularly writers, artists, students, academics and journalists, might be browbeaten into silence by the preposterous suggestion that they were merely terrorism's fake front of decency. In his own novella, *Die verlorene Ehre der Katharina Blum* (1974), he showed how the mechanisms of collusion between the police, rich industrialists and the gutter press could operate to turn average citizens to violence. The climate in which an ordinary teacher could suddenly become suspected of being an 'enemy of the constitution' (a 'Verfassungsfeind') — a term quite alien to the original authors of the Constitution — was vividly portrayed in Peter Schneider's ... *schon bist du ein Verfassungsfeind* (1975). Böll's *Berichte zur Gesinnungslage der Nation* (1975) satirically pictured the crowded world of police informers engaged in spying upon each other. By the middle of the 1970s a gulf between the executive forces of the state and the intelligentsia had opened up that was now wider than ever. In this situation it was not surprising that the SPD received virtually no support from writers, artists and academics in its election campaign of 1976. Some had their houses and offices searched (Hans Magnus Enzensberger, Karl Markus Michel, Luise Rinser, Volker Schlöndorff, Günter Wallraff, Böll and his family five times), had had visits from the police, or had been targeted for police surveillance because they had allegedly sympathised either with terrorist groupings or with extreme left-wing organisations. The mood of suspicion, fuelled by the call for more drastic measures and ever greater surveillance, reached a high point in the autumn of 1977 (the so-called 'deutsche Herbst'). Terrorist offshoots of the RAF seeking to force the release of the Baader-Meinhof group from prison murdered first Siegfried Buback (April 1977), the top Federal Prosecutor at the Constitutional Court, then Jürgen Ponto (July 1977), the director of the Dresdner Bank, the second largest in Germany, and then Hanns Martin Schleyer (October 1977), the head of the powerful Industrialists' Federation (Bundesverband der Deutschen Industrie: BDI). During this 'deutsche Herbst' an atmosphere of intolerance arose in which critical intellectuals once again thought it paramount to defend the democratic basis of the country's political, administrative and legal institutions.

The extent to which the atmosphere had been poisoned, leading to dangerous misjudgements also on the part of some intellectuals, was highlighted at the beginning of 1976 by a poem on Article 3 (3) of the 'Grundgesetz' (Basic Law) in which Alfred Andersch likened the situation in the Federal Republic to that of Nazi Germany:

> ein volk von/ ex nazis/ und ihren mitläufern/ betreibt schon wieder/ seinen lieblingssport/ die hetzjagd auf/ kommunisten/ sozialisten/ human- isten/ dissidenten/ linke . . . ein geruch breitet sich aus/ der geruch einer maschine/ die gas erzeugt.[30]

This kind of imagery was based on the (false) assumption that democracy in the Federal Republic was too feeble to withstand contemporary tendencies towards intolerance, coercion and mental 'torture'. This assessment of the Federal Republic as, at least in some respects, a modern, more efficient version of a fascist state had the air of a self-fulfilling prophecy and as such was not dissimilar to the terrorists' own analysis. Other writers, however, began a debate on the legitimacy of the state or, more specifically, thought it necessary to inform their audience at large and the terrorists in particular that the latter's strategy played straight into the hands of the most reactionary and anti-democratic forces in the Federal Republic. At the same time the public was reminded of the degree to which police, administrative and judicial practices were falling short of true democratic standards and that the terrorist threat was actually a far lesser danger to the maintenance of freedom than the computer perfectionism of criminal and ideological investigation. These arguments were advanced in two volumes of the paperback series *rororo-aktuell*. The first, *Briefe zur Verteidigung der Republik*, appeared shortly after the murder of Hanns Martin Schleyer in November 1977 and had sold 135,000 copies by January 1978. Here some thirty authors, mainly in the form of open letters, pleaded both with the terrorists and with established politicians for a more realistic assessment of the situation. Amongst the contributors were writers such as Heinrich Böll, Nicolas Born, Günter Grass, Walter Jens, Siegfried Lenz and Martin Walser, well-known editors and journalists like Freimut Duve, Carl Amery and Axel Eggebrecht, and eminent university professors such as Iring Fetscher, Jürgen Habermas, Hartmut von Hentig and Oskar Negt. Bonn was by then beginning to look like a fortress in a civil war, as Marion Gräfin Dönhoff reminds us in her contribution: 'mitten in Bonn Sandsäcke, Stacheldraht, Panzerwagen. Ein zornerregendes Bild [. . .] In weni-

30. Alfred Andersch, 'Artikel 3(3)', in *Vaterland, Muttersprache*, pp. 297/8.

gen Jahren schon wird man sich dieser Episode nur noch als eines Alptraums erinnern'.[31] The main thrust of the many contributions was directed at the clamour for the re-introduction of the death penalty, at the notion that society as a whole was at war with an omnipresent urban guerilla — an *idée fixe* which Herold shared with his opponent Andreas Baader — and above all at the insidious criminalisation by the whole of the conservative press of the so-called 'Sympathisantenumfeld'. This was a vague term, but it served to suggest that beyond the relatively small circle of terrorists there was a vast terrain of sympathisers in which they could move under cover of anonymity. The *Frankfurter Allgemeine Zeitung* held that 'die Sympathisanten sind der bisher noch viel zu selten genannte harte Kern des Problems'.[32] *Welt am Sonntag* announced that the terrorist sympathisers were the 'hidden part of the iceberg'.[33] In this situation, one of the critical intellectuals rather aptly observed, 'der Begriff Sympathisant wird zum Geschoß'.[34] Such demagogic journalism was reinforced not by the politicians of the Social-Liberal Coalition, but by those of the conservative opposition, notably Strauss, Alfred Dregger and Hans Filbinger. However, the latter's fate showed that the intellectuals too were not without their sharpshooters. Filbinger was forced to resign as Minister President of Baden-Württemberg when Rolf Hochhuth, always on the look-out for supposedly lost archival material from the Third Reich, publicly accused him in February 1978 of having passed a death sentence against a rating in Hitler's navy just before the end of the war. It transpired that as a court-martial judge in occupied Norway, Filbinger had been involved in a number of such capital sentences and that his past was stained with Nazi ideology to a far greater extent than he had admitted in public. His resignation in August 1978 helped considerably to dispel the pessimism of all those who had feared that, if put to the test, the new democracy lacked the resources with which to defend itself effectively against the native traditions of authoritarianism on the conservative right. At the same time the documentarist, Günter Wallraff, began a one-man assault on the bastion of the tabloid press, *Bild-Zeitung*. Working under a false name, he had infiltrated the staff of the paper and in his book *Der Aufmacher* (1977), based on his experience there, he revealed the

31. Marion Gräfin Dönhoff, 'Die Proportionen nicht aus den Augen verlieren', in Freimut Duve, Heinrich Böll, Klaus Staeck (eds.), *Briefe zur Verteidigung der Republik*, Reinbek nr. Hamburg, Nov. 1977, p. 26.
32. Ibid., p. 173.
33. Ibid., p. 176.
34. Thaddäus Troll (ibid., p. 148).

murky practices of gutter-press journalism and the opprobrious thinking of its backroom strategists. Subsequent attempts by the paper to attach to him the odium of terrorist sympathiser and litigation brought against him by the Springer press only served to boost the sale of Wallraff's book and also gave him material for two sequels dedicated to the same target and exposing the many personal tragedies that *Bild* had inflicted by its ruthless sensationalism.

The second volume in the series *rororo aktuell* in which prominent intellectuals pleaded for more liberty appeared in October 1978, entitled *Briefe zur Verteidigung der bürgerlichen Freiheit*. Here the main burden of argumentation was pitted against the over-reaction by the legislative, administrative, judicial and security forces in the Federal Republic to the threat posed by a small gang of terrorist desperados who were in any case completely isolated both ideologically and politically. The authorities continually sought to legitimate their actions by involving the notion of the 'Rechtsstaat' (a state founded in law). The intellectual critics now raised the question to what extent this notion could serve as a sufficient guarantee for the continued existence of democracy. Filbinger had argued in his own defence that what was lawful under National Socialism could not suddenly be unlawful in the Federal Republic. There had indeed been no wholesale repeal of the law that applied between 1933 and 1945 since National Socialism had substantially left intact civic codes dating back as far as the previous century. But obviously, in any given state the way that the law is interpreted and administered is at least as important as the letter of the law itself. Oskar Negt pointed out: 'Der Faschismus hat für alles seine Gesetze gehabt, aber auch die beflissenen Vollzugsbeamten, die wichtiger für seine Bestandssicherung waren, als die marodierenden Horden'.[35] His argument reappeared in another contribution, significantly entitled 'Der Rechtsstaat allein ist nicht die Demokratie'. Here Freimut Duve, the editor of the whole series, insisted that while the law might prevent the arbitrary use of state power, its formal application could also be used to undermine democracy itself:

Es gibt auch autoritäre Staatssysteme, in denen die formalen Rechts-staatsprinzipien durchaus funktionieren, wo aber der Gesetzgeber selbst den Geist der Demokratie längst unterhöllt hat. Selbst in der brutalsten Verfolgung während der Naziherrschaft gab es Dutzende von Richtern, die sich formal auf sicherem Boden wähnten, die nur taten, was geltendes

35. Oskar Negt, 'Die Korrumpierung der politischen Moral', in Freimut Duve, Heinrich Böll, Klaus Staeck (eds.), *Briefe zur Verteidigung der bürgerlichen Freiheit*, Reinbek nr. Hamburg, Oct. 1978, p. 83.

Recht ihnen vorschrieb. Gewiß, es ist ein gewaltiger Sprung zwischen dem Rechtsstaat und der Willkürherrschaft, und wir müssen den Rechtsstaat mit Klauen und Zähnen verteidigen. Aber es ist ein ebenso gewaltiger Sprung zwischen den formalen Prinzipien des Rechtsstaates und der verfassungsmäßigen Verankerung der parlamentarischen Demokratie.[36]

The traditions which legitimated the authority of the state were, after all, largely derived from those of the Prussian state. They had not arisen out of a struggle for democracy and hence the law could regress to become a tool of arbitrary state power. If one were to locate precisely the critical space which the post-war West German intelligentsia inhabited it was to be found within the tensions and balances between the 'Rechtsstaat' and the constitution of democracy.

The emergence of the 'strong state' in the Federal Republic, notably since the introduction of the 'Radikalenerlaß', had by the middle of the decade brought about what was commonly referred to as a 'Tendenzwende' (i.e. a retrenchment of the democratic reform policies of the early 1970s). Enzensberger saw this development as a concerted attempt on the part of the authorities to beat back the challenge of the anti-authoritarian movement by means of a massively expanded security apparatus which deployed 'Polizei-Computer, Geheimdienste, Mobile Einsatzkommandos und die technisch avanciertesten Gefängnisse der Welt'.[37] It was this situation which inspired novels like the Kafkaesque *Die Herren des Morgengrauens* (1978) by Peter O. Chotjewitz and the ambitiously panoramic *Fürsorgliche Belagerung* (1979) by Heinrich Böll. The same situation had produced a student leaflet whose anonymous author (signing himself 'Mescalero') had confessed to a 'clandestine delight' ('klammheimliche Freude') at the murder of Siegfried Buback, followed by a frenetic outcry of indignation by a press[38] which overlooked the fact that the author of the leaflet had also declared his opposition to terrorism.

Towards the end of the decade, when there were distinct signs that the Federal and certain regional authorities were reducing the scope of their surveillance activities, Enzensberger, in a more relaxed mood, reflected on the legacy of the 1970s. The title of his essay — 'Der Sonnenstaat des Doktor Herold' (1979) — concealed

36. Freimut Duve, 'Der Rechtsstaat allein ist nicht die Demokratie', ibid., p. 174.
37. Hans Magnus Enzensberger, 'Traktat vom Trampeln', *Der Spiegel*, No. 25, 14.6.1976, p. 140.
38. Cf. Peter Brückner, *Die Mescalero-Affäre. Ein Lehrstück für Aufklärung und politische Kultur*, Gießen, pp. 40–4.

an acerbically ironic reference to Tomasso Campanella's utopia *City of the Sun* (ca. 1600). Enzensberger tried to explain historically the social and technological basis of the internal security systems which has been put in place and which amounted to a negative utopia. While the old Imperialist Germany relied on a type of police which, imbued with chauvinistic ideas, intervened in disturbances of law and order by sporting fearsome uniforms and wielding hefty truncheons, the new type of police was highly educated and typically worked behind computer terminals. Unlike its predecessor it did not act purely out of prejudice against 'Ausländer, Juden, Kommunisten, Langhaarige, Schwule, Künstler und Intellektuelle'[39] but obsessively pursued the ambitious goal of using its computers as an early warning system to prevent the malfunctioning of society. The professional preconditions for this new type of policeman included tertiary education, for 'seine Macht ist nicht aus dem Gewehrlauf, sondern aus der Software seines Computers gewachsen'.[40] Such policemen believe themselves to be social engineers:

> Ihr Ehrgeiz zielt weit über die bloße Repression hinaus auf die präventive Planung einer kybernetisch gesteuerten, störungsfreien Gesellschaft. Dabei fällt der Polizei aufgrund ihres 'Erkenntnisprivilegs' die Rolle eines zentralen Forschungs- und Entwicklungsapparates zu, der als Early Warning System fungiert. Der Polizist sieht sich als Grundlagenforscher und Sozialwissenschaftler, der anhand von empirisch gewonnenen Daten am mathematischen Simulationsmodell den gesellschaftlichen Gesamtprozeß antizipatorisch 'durchspielt'.[41]

Given the sophisticated networking of computer systems throughout the Federal Republic, data protection acts were, according to Enzensberger, merely a cosmetic exercise. He argued that, ironically, the technocratic designs of the security forces were the only utopian elements left in a society in which the utopias of traditional socialism had faded. The Federal Republic, investigative journalists now contended, was well on the way to becoming an 'Überwachungsstaat' ('surveillance state'). Enzensberger did not share this sombre vision. While his assessment in 1967 had been that the 'Grundgesetz' was merely the concession the ruling classes had had to make in order to continue with the capitalist system,[42] he now believed that democracy had grown firm enough to withstand these attempts to trans-

---

39. Hans Magnus Enzensberger, 'Der Sonnenstaat des Doktor Herold', *Der Spiegel*, No. 25, 18.6.1979, p. 73.
40. Ibid., p. 73.
41. Ibid., p. 73.
42. Cf. Enzensberger, 'Klare Entscheidungen', pp. 226/7.

form German society into a 'Neues Altantis der allgemeinen Inneren Sicherheit, eine Insel Felsenburg für Sozialautomaten.[43] This utopia had the tendency to self-destruct through its own grotesque mal-practices and hence could be looked at with some humour.

If, at the end of the 1970s, a more relaxed assessment of the nature of the West German state was possible, this was due in no small part to the same politicians of Social-Liberal Coalition who had inaug-urated a lacklustre politics of pragmatic crisis management. It was, above all, the Chancellor, Helmut Schmidt, who helped defuse the situation. By calling Max Frisch on to the platform of the Social Democratic Party Conference in 1977 and by pointedly seeking a dialogue with Böll, Frisch and Lenz about the state of the nation in that same autumn, when hysteria about terrorism was at its height, Schmidt signalled to a wider public that the critical intelligentsia was a legitimate part of democratic society. Such a gesture was necessary in order to save it from being associated ever more closely with the attitudes of the terrorists. In the following year the SPD-led regional governments began to restrict the practice of testing their civil servants' loyalty to the Constitution by means of special hear-ings. At the same time the intellectuals came under renewed attack from the conservative side with Franz Josef Strauss excoriating them as 'Ratten und Schmeißfliegen' who were too insignificant even to be taken to court.[44] Rhetoric of this kind was by now, of course, a not unfamiliar feature of the conservative politicians' relationship to the intelligentsia. Their wholly negative image had been given a certain academic respectability a little earlier in the aforementioned long polemical dissertation, *Die Arbeit tun die anderen. Klassenkampf und Priesterherrschaft der Intellektuellen* (1975), by the conservative sociologist Helmut Schelsky. He had declared that intellectuals constituted a latent social class in their own right, situated predominantly on the left, in command of the media and responsible for the wide currency of Marxist ideas. This kind of analysis built them up as bogey men with an influence so vast that it became difficult to explain why for most of the 1970s the majority of intellectuals had found themselves so very much on the defensive, notably against the very media they supposedly commanded.

---

43. Idem, 'Doktor Herold', p. 78.
44. Cf. Klaus Staeck (ed.), *Einschlägige Worte des Kandidaten Strauss*, Göttingen, 1979, p. 113 (also in *Der Spiegel*, No. 52, 25.12.1978).

The Reshaping of the Intelligentsia's Critical Role by the Politics of Protest in the 1980s

It became clear in the course of the 1970s that the critical intellectuals of the 'first hour', i.e. the Gruppe 47, the contributors to *Frankfurter Hefte* and a number of other journals, the members of the Frankfurt School of Social Research and a host of journalists, theologians and academics, would not be replaced by a new generation of intellectuals acting in the same capacity as critical opinion leaders with privileged accesss to the media. This role was an historical phenomenon specific to the period of post-fascist Germany. While political interventions by these intellectuals still retained their drama, quieter, more self-reflexive voices began to be heard on the literary scene. They too had been influenced by their experience of the extra-parliamentary upheavals of the 1960s and 1970s, but their conclusions were different from those of the older generation. The frustrations induced in the young intelligentsia by the foreclosure of revolutionary change had produced a situation in which some despaired of the possibility of reasoned action effecting anything other than more of the same disharmonising and alienating calamity that to them seemed to be the fate of modern society. Peter Handke and Botho Strauß, who typified this attitude, began to acquire large followings. Others were writing for journals that were founded towards the end of the 1970s, like *Freibeuter* and *Konkursbuch*. They subscribed in the main to the argument, first put forward by Horkheimer and Adorno in *Dialektik der Aufklärung* (1947), that technological rationality was tyrannical, reduced individuals to numbers and had as its most powerful executors the administrations of modern states which were a perversion of enlightened reason. The progress of technology was a regression of liberty. While Horkheimer and Adorno remained ultimately committed to the possibility of an enlightenment of 'enlightened reason' and hence to the liberating possibilities of rationality, their adherents in the late 1970s were sceptical, if not straightforwardly irrationalist. 'Modernism' was now the enemy. History and dialectics had to be abandoned in favour of withdrawal into the inner self, into nature, into an existence that both politically and socially was totally marginal. Such a stance, which was anarchic but non-violent, consigned its adherents to the very periphery of (extra-parliamentary) politics.

The battle-hardened political interventionists of the old-guard intelligentsia — who in 1980 recommended the electorate to vote SPD as the 'lesser evil' (just as they had done twenty years earlier)

— were drawn into their last fight in a new campaign for nuclear disarmament which at the same time spelt the swan song of their special role on the public stage. The majority had defined themselves politically in some relation to the SPD, with temporary interludes for some of them in other left-wing parties and organisations. The dramatist Franz Xaver Kroetz had belonged to the German Communist Party (DKP) all through the 1970s, but resigned from it in 1980. Between 1969 and 1974 Martin Walser, too, had sympathised with that party as the only one which was unambiguously anti-capitalist, but he withdrew his sympathies when in 1974 Willy Brandt had to resign because an East German spy had been allowed to penetrate the Chancellery. In his contribution to *Briefe zur Verteidigung der Republik*, Walser had thanked the Social Democrats for stemming the tide of anti-democratic demagogy:

> Die Sozialdemokraten haben der terroristischen Herausforderung gegenüber um eine öffentliche Fassung gerungen. Sie haben versucht, allen Verführungen zur Instinktentfesselung, zum Sichweiden, zum Sichtollfühlen, zum Auchdreinschlagenwollen zu widerstehen. Die Konservativen hatten — das bewies ein heißer Artikel Golo Manns ebenso wie die Forderung der Union nach Bundeswehr-Einsatz — genau das getan, was die Terroristen erreichen wollten: sie hätten Krieg gespielt.[45]

Another writer, Dieter Lattman, who had been instrumental in organising his peers within a trade union, had defied all caution and become a Member of Parliament for the SPD in 1972. But the strains between his role as an intellectual and his role as a member of a party caucus, between the ethics of independent public criticism and the tactics of party-political compromise, proved too much for him and he gave up in 1980. He summed up his experience in the following instructive sentences:

> Der Konflikt zwischen Geist und Macht — auch eine Gewaltenteilung — ist so alt wie notwendig. Im Gegensatz zur Politik, die ständig auf Kompromisse angewiesen ist und ihr Prinzip geradezu in der Relativierung vorgeblicher Eindeutigkeiten findet, müssen sich Literatur und Kunst die große Einseitigkeit leisten können, die moralische Energien zu einer übermenschlichen Anstrengung bündelt: zur Utopie einer gerechteren urdemokratischen Welt . . .[46]

45. Martin Walser, 'An die Sozialdemokratische Partei Deutschlands', in Duve, Böll, Staeck (eds.), *Briefe zur Verteidigung der Republik*, p. 159.
46. Dieter Lattmann, *Die Einsamkeit des Politikers*, Munich, 1977, p. 72.

Lattmann subsequently became committed to the cause of peace and was one of the speakers who addressed a large audience in the Dortmund Westfalenhalle on the occasion of the anniversary of the 'Krefelder Appell' that had been seminal in the rebirth of the Peace Movement in the 1980s.

The decision by the NATO Foreign and Defence Ministers in December 1979 to go ahead with a significant updating of weapons systems (the so-called 'dual track' decision) triggered a series of protests, in the course of which the structure of the political terrain and the position of the critical intellectuals within it changed significantly. Far from signalling a retreat from politics, the writers, foremost among them Böll, Grass and Jens, lent their fame, their oratory and the influence of their political reasoning to the Peace Movement. Between 1981 and 1985 they took a prominent part in the mass demonstrations. Böll dominated like an old patriarch, appealing repeatedly to the demonstrators to keep to non-violent means of protest and entreating the Governments first of Schmidt and then of Kohl to desist from inflicting on the nation the 'Waffenverseuchung', the 'Waffenpest',[47] that was threatening the very existence of life in the Federal Republic. By 1983 he had switched his political allegiance to the Greens. In February of that year, with a general election imminent, he announced that he was supporting the Greens because this party was unequivocally opposed to the presence of all nuclear weapons on German soil and because it had the most convincing economic programme on unemployment and environmentally beneficial technologies. He made it clear that his recommendation of the Greens was not a repudiation of the SPD and exhorted that party not to treat the Greens as lepers. In a major speech at a congress in Essen, entitled 'Keine Angst vor Systemveränderern', he argued that in view of the patent absurdities of an economic system which created an enormous destructive potential while at the same time throwing large numbers of people out of work, those who, like the Greens, pleaded for a fundamental rethink, should be welcomed with open arms and not given the cold shoulder.[48] In his last interview in 1985 he expressed the hope that after the General Election of 1987 a 'Red–Green Coalition' might be formed, substantially in order that the restoration of large-scale capitalism in post-war Germany might be redressed.[49] He had still

47. Heinrich Böll, 'Manuskript der Ansprache zur Friedensdemonstration vom 10.10.1981 in Bonn', in *Die 'Einfachheit' der 'kleinen' Leute. Schriften und Reden 1978–1981*, Munich, 1985, p. 203.
48. Idem, 'Keine Angst vor Systemveränderern', *die tageszeitung*, 4.3.1983, p. 10.
49. Cf. 'Ein Bundestag ohne Grüne wäre katastrophal', *Die Weltwoche*, 25.7.1985, p. 5.

not surrendered his long cherished hopes for a non-martial society and for a less Americanised, less commercialised culture.

As we remarked at the outset, Böll's death marks an incision in the history of post-war German intellectuals. Not least this is because he appeared by his political stance at the end to be passing on the torch of criticism to a younger intelligentsia, more exclusive in its political commitment, which would derive its legitimacy not from literary fame but from an electoral mandate. Walser, also of the 'old guard', indicated that he now wished to quit his 'borrowed rostrum',[50] particularly since the political microphones had been taken up by the Greens: 'Ich bin in der Hinsicht eigentlich ganz froh, daß die Grünen entstanden sind, daß also unser Herumempfinden einen politischen Ausdruck oder eine politische Form gefunden hat. Mich entlastet das. Ich bin sozusagen das Hinterfeld, das da seinen Stimmzettel abgibt'.[51] As for Grass, he had been at the forefront of protest against the NATO 'dual track' decision. In 1980 he and three other Berlin writers (Thomas Brasch, Sarah Kirsch and Peter Schneider) had sent a peace appeal to the Schmidt Government, admonishing the politicians not to engage in further preparations for war and not to invoke 'die Würde einer Nation', a concept which particularly in Germany had in the past justified the staging of large-scale bloodbaths.[52] In a widely televised discussion with writers in East Germany (December 1981, and again at a meeting in April 1983), Grass had expressed the view, generally shared by his fellow writers from both sides of the ideological divide, that Germans had a special duty not to allow a third world war to arise on their soil. In a manifesto of 1984, starkly entitled 'Verweigert Euch' (also signed by the Protestant pastor Heinrich Albertz, by the theologian Dorothee Sölle and by such writers as Hans Christoph Buch, Tankred Dorst, Jürgen Fuchs, Peter Härtling, Robert Jungk, Ursula Krechel, Dieter Lattmann, Guntram Vesper and Otto F. Walter), he had said that the stationing of Pershing IIs implicated the Bundeswehr in a first-strike strategy to 'decapitate' the enemy ('Enthauptungsstrategie').[53] This was at variance with the defensive nature of the German military as defined by the 'Grundgesetz'. In a subsequent speech, Grass explicitly incited young people to commit

50. Walser, 'Ich werde mich nicht an die deutsche Teilung gewöhnen', *Die Welt*, 29.9.1986, p. 9. See also note 6 above.
51. 'Der Lächerlichkeit die Würde zurückerobern', *die tageszeitung*, 30.9.1985.
52. Günter Grass, *Widerstand lernen. Politische Gegenreden 1980–1983*, Darmstadt und Neuwied, 1984, p. 14.
53. Ibid., p. 97.

an act that under the Nazi regime had been termed 'Wehrkraft-zersetzung' (subverting the morale of the armed forces).[54] All this received immense publicity, not least because there was a suggestion of criminal prosecution (which was later dropped). In a speech to Social Democrats in 1983 he had called for a revision of the Godesberg Programme in view of the ecologically counterproductive nature of industrial growth. Grass had expressed his wish for a coalition between the SPD and the Greens months before the latter were first elected into the Federal Parliament.[55] As we remarked earlier, however, having thus hinted at the future necessity for such an alliance he absented himself in the foothills of the election campaign 1986/7, taking sabbatical leave in Calcutta instead. It is unlikely that he did so merely because the reviews of his latest novel *Die Rättin* (1986) had not been all that glowing. Instead, it seems more likely that he found it difficult to locate a space for himself in the public political discourse, torn two ways as far as allegiance to a party was concerned. Grass's absence from the battleground of political persuasion is all the more surprising as he had accused other writers for withdrawing from the arena of politics. He had let it be known, for example that 'Peter Rühmkorf lebt schon seit vielen Jahren verschneckt'.[56] During the election campaign 1986/7 Rühm-korf hit back at such a majesterial assessment: 'Und wenn er in Kalkutta seine epischen Stoffballen weiterwälzt, dann singe ich gerade vor Björn Engholms erbauungsbedürftigen Truppen in der Kieler Fischräucherei'.[57]

The reasons for the intellectuals' shift towards the Greens, which at the same time explained their 'Wahlkampfenthaltung'[58] was analysed by Hans Magnus Enzensberger in a remarkable interview published by *Der Spiegel* shortly before the elections in January 1987. In it he continued a theme which he had first developed in an essay, also published in *Der Spiegel*, at the time of the Flick Affair. It had emerged that the CDU/CSU, the FDP and the SPD had all received large clandestine subventions from an industrialist, Friedrich Flick,

54. Ibid., p. 95.
55. Cf. 'Es gibt keinen Nährboden für reaktionäres Verhalten. Günter Grass über die mögliche Mehrheit links von der CDU/CSU', *Vorwärts*, 21.10.1982, p. 14 and 'Wir müßten uns wieder die alten Tugenden einüben. Günter Grass zum Thema 'Die Zukunft des Demokratischen Sozialismus', *Frankfurter Rundschau*, 22.6.1983, p. 14.
56. Peter Rühmkorf, 'Bleib erschütterbar, wähl SPD', in *Wählen — aber wen? Schriftsteller über Deutschland vor der Wahl*, Hamburg, 1986, p. 119.
57. Ibid., pp. 119/20.
58. Hans Magnus Enzensberger, 'Die Gesellschaft ist keine Hammelherde', *Der Spiegel*, No. 4, 19.1.1987, p. 67.

who held vast shareholdings, particularly in Daimler Benz. Given the position of moral, liberal-humanist or socialist reasoning which the intellectuals had adopted since the end of the Third Reich, it was not surprising that they gave vent to their disgust when the details of this scandal were exposed. Enzensberger argued that the affair was an index of the degree to which politics in the Federal Republic had become a cartelised game between politicians and big business, with the former receiving monetary donations and the latter special treatment in tax matters.[59] In the later interview he averred that 'die politische Klasse; der Bonner Zirkus', had become peripheral both to the social organisation of life and to the signal decisions affecting it: 'Die wirklichen Entscheidungen werden dezentral getroffen in einem weitverzweigten Nervensystem, das von keinem Punkt aus kontrollierbar ist [. . .] Dadurch verlieren die Zentralinstanzen an Autorität und an Gewicht. Ihr Spielraum schrumpft, aber auch ihre Gefährlichkeit nimmt ab. Die Regierung wird zum Papiertiger'.[60] It was because Social Democracy, in particular, had a long tradition of centralism and a firm belief in the institutions of central government as the levers of social reform that that party was now in irrevocable decline. Indeed, all the old established parties had become marginal to the real political experience of citizens today and when these parties fielded their star politicians in television discussions, all that could be heard was a 'reduziertes Murmeln',[61] a discourse in ready-made concepts and slogans that was completely divorced from reality. The decentralised politics of the present were determined by what he ironically called extra-parliamentary 'citizens' initiatives': on the one hand, those of big business like 'Siemens oder Nixdorf oder Hoechst' and those of the trades unions, the churches, the media, of parents, drivers, tax evaders and nature conservationists, on the other. The consequence was that the politicians had become the hostages of lobbyists and, incarcerated as a political class in Bonn, tended to think of the population as 'dumm und frech',[62] while this was precisely what society thought of the political class. Even if this part of the analysis bordered on caricature, it was nevertheless an indication of his and many other intellectuals' aversion to the staleness and corruption of the political discourse in the Federal Republic. Yet Enzensberger allowed for an exception. He made no secret of his sympathies for the Greens who, he thought,

59. Cf. Hans Magnus Enzensberger, 'Ein Bonner Memorandum', *Der Spiegel*, No. 48, 28.11.1983, pp. 35ff.
60. *Der Spiegel*, No. 4, 19.1.1987, p. 69.
61. Ibid., p. 67.
62. Ibid., p. 71.

displayed none of the careerism and remoteness from real life so typical of those who had come into politics through a party machine:

> Die meisten grünen Vertreter verfügen über irgendwelche praktischen Lebenserfahrungen außerhalb der Apparate. Manche kennen sogar den Zustand der Bargeldlosigkeit, der in Bonn unbekannt ist. Auffällig ist auch, daß sie sich für die Zukunft interessieren. Sogar ihre Defekte sind neuartig und jedenfalls interessanter als die selbstgefällige Dickhäuterei der Herren vom Kartell.[63]

In view of a number of manifest tendencies toward centralism, one of them being data collection by various ministries, Enzensberger, abandoning factual analysis, followed a modish preference for the regional and local rather than the national, continental or global. Despite such highly debatable aspects in his perception, it becomes clear that whatever the particular party-political allegiances of individual intellectuals, they saw in the emergence of the Green Party the possibility of passing on to a representative in parliament their public role as articulate tribunes of constitutional and democratic fundamentalism. It was for this role that the intellectuals had created a stage in the public life of post-fascist German society. Significantly, the extra-parliamentary interventionism in politics by famous intellectual figures (inside or outside the framework of 'Wählerinitiativen') was conspicuously absent in the run-up to the 1987 Federal Elections. This could not simply be understood as a default, nor had these figures consciously, as it were, handed over the baton of public criticism to the politicians. If the political role of the intellectuals had passed from them, then this was not only because they had vacated it, but also because it had disintegrated, tied as it was to the authority of the individual creative personality. This, at least, is the wider socio-historical context in which Enzensberger set his explanation of why there could be no successors to those who had acted as the 'ideologische Müllabfuhr'[64] of the post-fascist era and who were recognised as important counter-weights to the dominant figures of the Conservative Government ('Böll war die Gegenfigur zu Adenauer').[65] He summarily surmised that this was due to the disintegration of central authority and the attendant loss of charisma suffered by the outstanding cultural and political personality. In the interview referred to above, he constructed an analogy between the established politicians and the

63. Ibid., p. 74.
64. Ibid., p. 76.
65. Ibid., p. 76.

critics of power; both derived their importance for society from a concept of leadership whose authority was now no longer accorded universal recognition: 'in einer diffusen, dezentralisierten Gesellschaft (wird es) den Intellektuellen nicht anders ergehen als den Politikern: Auch ihre Autorität wird relativiert, ihre privilegierte Position ist im Schwinden'.[66] This was a far-reaching and not easily verifiable hypothesis. Although one would not wish to endorse it in all its ramifications, it could nevertheless be argued that the intellectuals' critical, extra-parliamentary role had been democratised, collectivised and given a parliamentary voice. The particular type of political commitment that was exhibited by a whole generation of intellectuals and so dramatically accompanied the development of democracy in West Germany appeared to have run its course. This came about not only because the representatives of the older generation of intellectuals had died or grown old, but also because a new critical intelligentsia, not predominantly located in the world of letters, but generated by the anti-authoritarian Student Movement, had taken over the substance of that commitment and made it an integral part of the political discourse in the Federal Republic. There was a continual necessity to table afresh questions that had centrally concerned the older intellectuals: vigilance against any revival of fascist or authoritarian attitudes; the distrust of power; the mistrust of large-scale capital, private or state-owned; the abhorrence of political corruption; the preservation of fundamental rights guaranteed in the Constitution; the opportunity for groups and individuals to gain public fora for their own political concerns; the relationship between East and West and, specifically, that between East and West Germany. To the extent that the Greens, in particular, have made all these concerns their own, they have, for the time being, narrowed the scope for extra-parliamentary criticism by individual intellectuals. It is in this sense that the Greens might be seen as the inheritors of a political agenda prepared by an older generation of intellectuals whose critical role they have largely taken over and redefined. Their 'fundamentalist' moral and political rigour is reminiscent of the purity of 'Geist' in comparison with the compromises of party-political pragmatism. For the time being, the republic of letters appears to be able to rely largely on the alertness of the general democratic public to keep at bay encroachments of civil liberties and the erosion of the Constitution by an authoritarian state. To this extent, it is not only the authority of the men of letters that has become diffused, but also their democratic spirit.

66. Ibid., p. 76.

Suggested Further Reading

P. Brandt and H. Ammon (eds.), *Die Linke und die nationale Frage*, Reinbek, 1981

K. Bullivant, 'Gewissen der Nation'? Schriftsteller und Politik in der Bundesrepublik', in G. Labroisse and F. van Ingen (eds.), *Literaturszene Bundesrepublik — ein Blick von draußen*, Amsterdam, 1988, pp. 59–78

R.A. Burns and W. van der Will, *Protest and Democracy in West Germany. Extra-Parliamentary Opposition and the Democratic Agenda*, London, 1988

J. Habermas, *Die Neue Unübersichtlichkeit*, Frankfurt on Main, 1985

G. Heidenreich, *Die ungeliebten Dichter. Dokumentation*, Frankfurt on Main, 1981

H.L. Müller, *Die literarische Republik. Westdeutsche Schriftsteller und die Politik*, Weinheim and Basel, 1982

K.S. Parkes, *Writers and Politics in West Germany*, London, 1986

K. Sontheimer, *Das Elend unserer Intellektuellen*, Hamburg, 1976

——, *Zeitenwende*, Hamburg, 1983

KEITH BULLIVANT

Political Realism of the 1970s

Despite the demands made by Hans Werner Richter for a new realist literature 'mit humanistisch-sozialistischem Einschlag', West German literature in the immediate post-war period was dominated not by 'political realism', but rather by a revival of the German idealist tradition, as represented initially by Jünger, Hesse, Benn, Kasack and then later by Gaiser amongst others. One contributory factor to this apoliticism was the suspicion of ideology amongst writers, engendered by the examples of both National Socialism and Stalinism, and by the general Cold War climate of the late 1940s and 1950s; another factor — not unrelated — was the contamination of the term 'realism' through the linguistic proximity to the Socialist Realism of the Eastern Bloc. In addition, the general pattern of rapidly growing affluence and social mobility in the new pluralist society of the new Federal Republic was such that, as Walter Jens put it, 'Begriffe wie "Klasse", "Arbeiter", "Bürger" und "parteiliche Ideologie" were 'nur noch Lehrbuch-Chiffren' for the majority of writers.[1] Until well into the 1960s, the most appropriate medium for writers who felt the need to take a stance on political issues was seen as lying outside imaginative literature — as the collections *Die Mauer oder Der 13. August* and *Die Alternative oder Brauchen wir eine neue Regierung?* (on the Federal elections of 1961) and the manifesto of the Gruppe 47 with regard to the *Spiegel* Affair of 1962 clearly show. The gradual politicisation of literature in the course of the 1960s found its initial literary expression in the documentary drama of the period, but — despite short-lived radical questioning of the social relevance of literature, especially in the famous *Kursbuch 15* — the debates in the Student Movement as to the nature of imaginative writing led to the rekindling of interest in the debates about political realism around 1930 within the Bund proletarisch-revolutionärer Schriftsteller and in the so-called 'Expressionismusdebatte' between Brecht and Lukács. This brought about the republishing of forgotten texts and lively debates within the Werkkreis Literatur der Arbeitswelt

1. Walter Jens, *Literatur und Politik*, Pfullingen, 1963, p. 5.

−36−

(which split away from the Gruppe 61 in 1970 to form a new literary grouping with avowedly political aims). The publications from the Werkkreis, the discussions by former student activists in *kürbiskern* and the *Literarische Hefte* and the subsequent founding of the Autoren-Edition in 1973 are testimony to the keen interest in political realism at this time and underline the dangerous oversimplification inherent in the notion that, by and large, writers in the 1970s were essentially concerned with personal, existential problems.

Despite the commonly held idea of the 'Tendenzwende' — as betokening a general turning away from politics — the 1970s were a thoroughly political decade, with intellectual life continuing to be dominated by a range of subjects originating within the Student Movement; particularly by that most radical product of '68, terrorism, as well as by the negative consequences of the security measures introduced in response to it, including the controversial 'Berufsverbot'. Treatment of these concerns is central to both non-fiction and imaginative literature of the period. The 1970s were also marked by the emergence of a feminist literature aiming, particularly in the initial phase, at a radical challenge to established patterns of sexual role ascription and at promoting group identity and social engagement; as such it is, in a very new sense, to be understood as political in nature. Moreover, the decade saw the appearance of a number of novels which constituted a new phase in the critical evaluation of the legacy of the Nazi past for the Federal Republic, some of which effectively put the West German Establishment on trial.[2] The notion of the literature of this period being essentially unpolitical also fails to take adequate account of the publication of a whole series of overtly political realist novels, such as Michael Scharang's *Charly Traktor* (1973) and *Sohn eines Landarbeiters* (1976), Max von der Grün's *Stellenweise Glatteis* (1973) and *Flächenbrand* (1978), August Kühn's chronicle of a Munich working-class family, *Zeit zum Aufstehn* (1975), Chotjewitz's *Der dreißigjährige Friede* (1977), the bulk of the production of the Autoren-Edition and lengthy sections of Peter Weiss's monumental three-part novel *Die Ästhetik des Widerstands* (1975–81).

A major starting-point of literary theories amongst those of the student generation still politically active was the rejection of established bourgeois literature as politically quietistic. Uwe Timm saw existing literary theory as constituting a defensive aesthetic code,

---

2. Cf. 'The Spectre of the Third Reich', pp. 139–54 below.

ensuring that literature did not address itself to burning social issues, but to 'das Überzeitliche, das Höhere, das Eigentliche, das Allgemeingültige, das nicht auf das Tagesgeschehen Gerichtete etc'.[3] Timm advanced the view that the politically committed author concerned with efficient communication with his audience should turn his back on aesthetic standards that equated quality with exclusivity and aim to produce literature with a wider appeal and which, at the same time, 'den Kapitalismus in Frage stellen könnte'. Timm advanced the view that this was most appropriately done in a popular negative 'Entwicklungsroman' — one which concentrated not on the development of extreme individualism, but described the path of an individual 'das aus seiner bornierten Vereinzelung zu einem kollektiven Bewußtsein gelangt, in einem Kollektiv lebt und arbeitet'.

Timm's *Heißer Sommer* (1974), Gerd Fuchs's *Beringer und die lange Wut* (1973), Ronald Lang's *Ein Hai in der Suppe oder Das Glück des Philipp Ronge* (1975) and Franz-Josef Degenhardt's *Brandstellen* (1975), all of which appeared in the imprint of the Autoren-Edition, showed the possibilities and, above all, the limitations inherent in the uncritical adoption of the popular novel form. All were heavily based on the experiences of the authors in the Student Movement and so, not surprisingly, were quite successful in portraying events of the time. All are marred, however, by the lack of adequate analysis of the inner workings of the minds of the central characters, making their political development very unconvincing. The questionable nature of the ending of these novels is compounded by the fact that we leave the heroes on the threshold of a new life which, we are given to understand, will be a more fulfilling one, but we have no clear idea as to what it will be or how it is to be brought about in political terms. We are left with an unconvincing happy end, as is the case with so many early Socialist Realist novels from the GDR, which these first novels from the Autoren-Edition, and a number of others from the 1970s, resemble in their basic form.

Such an unconvincing utopian ending is typical of a number of other realist novels of a more or less political nature from the 1970s, including Martin Walser's *Die Gallistl'sche Krankheit* (1972) and the best-known work on the experiences of the Student Movement, Peter Schneider's *Lenz* (1973). In the case of Schneider's 'Erzählung', however, it is precisely the skilful analysis of Lenz's turbulent state of mind, induced by intense dissatisfaction with the political debates of the later phase of the Student Movement and the distress at the

3. Cf. 'Zwischen Unterhaltung und Aufklärung', *kürbiskern*, 1972, No. 1, pp. 79–90.

end of his relationship with L., that makes us sceptical about the ultimate meaning of his experiences in Trento and what lies ahead for him after his return to Berlin. *Lenz*, like the other early novels dealing with this theme, is undoubtedly affected by the residue of the naive hope for radical social change that characterised aspects of the Student Movement and fails — or, it might be argued, comes too early to be able — to reflect the changed social reality. The optimism of all of these works is in marked contrast with Otto F. Walter's *Die Verwilderung* (1977), one of the later novels spawned by the Student Movement and which, in addition, reflects a very different notion of political realism.

Die Verwilderung rejects the faith in the persuasive powers of the popular novel form and corresponds instead to Alexander Kluge's interpretation of the nature of contémporary political realism.[4] Kluge starts from the assumption that present-day society is too complex to be reflected through an individual consciousness alone. Through 'aggressive Montage' subjective experience — the 'Realismus der Arbeitsweise des menschlichen Wahrnehmungsapparates'[5] — is to be contrasted with the objective 'Vermittlung der gegenständlichen Situation'. The aim is not the literary 'shaping' of social experience, but rather the liberation 'des auf die Wirklichkeit umformend reagierenden menschlichen Hirns' — the first step to social change. On the most straightforward level *Die Verwilderung*, a highly complex novel, concerns itself with the attempt to form a democratic cooperative that will turn its back on exploitation, the competition ethos and bourgeois notions of jealousy and property, even in the sexual sphere. The worthy citizens of the town of Jammers view this experiment in alternative life-style as an outrage and in the 'wahrscheinliches Ende' of the novel the commune is violently broken up and the leaders killed. The narrative is intercut with documentary material that, on the one hand, is designed to give support to the principles underlying the venture and, on the other, indicates the strength of conservative opinion in society opposed to such ideas. The author is clearly no neutral observer, but rather one who supports the utopian vision inherent in the novel — the 'auf demokratischem Weg herbeigeführte grundsätzliche Veränderung der Gesellschaft, mit dem Ziel [. . .], die Produktionsmittel in die Selbstverwaltung der Produzenten zu überführen'.[6] The novel moves

---

4. Cf. in this connection Peter Labanyi's essay on Kluge, pp. 263–95.
5. Cf. *Gelegenheitsarbeit einer Sklavin. Zur realistischen Methode*, Frankfurt on Main, 1975, pp. 216–18.
6. Walter and W. Martin Lüdke, 'Es hat sich etwas verändert', in W. Martin Lüdke (ed.), *Nach dem Protest*, Frankfurt on Main, 1979, p. 123.

between the poles of decent human values and the aggressive instincts seen as inherent in society. The author identifies himself with the hopes and dreams of the communards and explores the possibilities that he sees in their new life, but is incapable of ignoring the likely opposition. Instead of an unconvincing and glib happy end — or, for that matter, a crudely black-and-white picture of social attitudes — Walter, much in the manner advocated by Dieter Wellershoff, uses the novel as a simulator, exploring the possibility for social change and, in the process, compelling the reader to take up a stance on the issues raised — as is demanded by Kluge of such realism.

The persuasive 'likely ending' of *Die Verwilderung*, with its bleak picture of state oppression supported by radical social conservatism, struck a highly responsive chord in the Federal Republic, where this Swiss novel was essentially received as being applicable to the state of things in the so-called 'deutsche Herbst' of 1977.[7] The 1970s, far from having effected the changes that might have been expected from a liberal coalition government, had seen the introduction (initially by the ruling SPD in Hamburg) of the 'Radikalenerlaß' and the creation of an atmosphere of political distrust. The witch-hunt conducted by the Springer concern against the left and the intensification of surveillance necessitated by the wave of terrorism led to a suspicion of the state which is expressed vividly in the second half of the 1970s by the film *Deutschland im Herbst* (1978) and a series of political realist novels in which the negative utopia of the 'Überwachungsstaat' is in sharp contrast with the optimism of the novels of the Student Movement.

The best known of these novels — with Schlöndorff's film of it complementing the media furore caused by its initial appearance — is Böll's *Die verlorene Ehre der Katharina Blum* (1974). As in his contentious article 'Will Ulrike Meinhof Gnade oder freies Geleit?' (*Der Spiegel*, 1972), his attack on the overhasty condemnation of Ulrike Meinhof in the Springer press, Böll here endeavours, 'die Eskalation der terroristischen wie der polizeilichen Gewalt zu bremsen und einen gesellschaftlichen Denk- und Lernprozeß über die Frage einzuleiten, "wie Gewalt entstehen und wohin sie führen kann"'.[8] Although, as the narrator ('der Berichterstatter') tells us, the case of Katharina Blum is 'mehr oder weniger fiktiv', its authenticity — underlined by the quasi-documentary style — was immediately obvious to the public at the time, indeed, as Böll wrote

7. Ibid.
8. Jochen Vogt, 'Heinrich Böll', *Kritisches Lexikon zur deutschsprachigen Literatur der Gegenwart (KLG)*, p. 15.

somewhat ironically in the preface, 'Ähnlichkeiten mit den Prakti-
ken der "Bild"-Zeitung sind weder beabsichtigt noch zufällig, sondern unvermeidlich'.[9]

Central issues in *Die verlorene Ehre der Katharina Blum* are taken up
again and varied in his penultimate novel, *Fürsorgliche Belagerung*
(1979). The literary treatment of the tension between the individual
and social institutions proceeds from depiction of the terrorist threat
to Fritz Tolm, the president of the newspaper publishers' association, and members of his family. The novel is far more concerned,
however, with an examination of the effect on almost all spheres of
the family's life of the constant surveillance under which they are
forced to live and the introspection induced by this extreme situation
and the social isolation it brings with it — which in some cases
results in quite far-reaching personal re-evaluation. The actual
terrorist threat comes to nothing, but the drastic effect on individuals of the counter-measures that have to be taken is such that even
the previously most conformist members of the family (such as Fritz
and his daughter Sabine) are changed by the experience into 'Geg-
ner des Systems'. In a number of ways, the novel continues and
develops themes familiar not only from *Katharina Blum*, but also from
Böll's essays of the period, bringing out the way in which the distrust
of the state and of a substantial body of the populace is directed
against a generation critical of existing society. The whole tone of
the novel is in support of such criticism, with society being represented, on the one hand as decaying into decadence, on the other by
the concern of the Tolm family that, beneath the surface of a society
that seems, in any case, intolerant of fundamental criticism of it,
developments are taking place which represent an even more basic
threat to civilised values. By the end of the novel Fritz Tolm has
become fearful of a drift towards an authoritarian state, in which a
combination of tight security and close cooperation between powerful interest groups would put the individual at the mercy of the
system, whilst also ignoring vital environmental questions.

As in so many other of Böll's works, the corruption and the other
threats to the quality of human life are countered by a system of
authentic human values embodied by figures who are essentially
outsiders. Tolm, despite his professional achievements, has always
felt a certain schizophrenic attitude ('meine Zweibahnigkeit') to his
business activities: external success ultimately means nothing to
him. He has failed in the real task he set himself of using the
newspaper to counter the 'Nihilisierung durch den Nazismus' and

9. *Die verlorene Ehre der Katharina Blum*, Munich, 1976, p. 5

comes to admit: 'mir ist es nicht gelungen, das System zu täuschen, das System hat mich getäuscht'.[10] His sympathies lie increasingly with the youthful opposition, which, while not without its faults, is shown as offering real potential for social regeneration, unlike the terrorist scene, which represents idealism run amok and proceeds from concepts that are 'abstrakt und absurd' (as Böll put it in an interview).

Böll resisted any attempt to repeat here what he called the 'pamphletisch' quality of *Katharina Blum* or to aim for the panoramic picture of the time that some of his critics demanded of him; important figures are not given the chance to speak, so that we have to rely for information about them on those who do, and significant details of the various story lines are not explained. The book's open-endedness is an appropriate aesthetic reflection of our necessarily incomplete view of any modern complex issue, but, despite this, it adds up to a convincing and disturbing picture of this unhappy phase of the Federal Republic. Above all, it gives full expression to the sense of the gulf between the individual and the modern state that is nominally made up of such individuals, but which outwits and treats with suspicion those that challenge the given through their dreams of a better individual and collective existence.[11]

Böll was the first writer to deal with the personal consequences of public anxiety about terrorism, particularly as whipped up and turned against innocent individuals by unscrupulous sections of the press. By 1977/8 there was widespread apprehension amongst the German left which is vividly documented in Luise Rinser's account of the consequences for many innocent people of the hounding of those labelled 'Sympathisanten' or categorised as belonging to the 'geistigen Wegbreitern der roten Killer' (included in this list were Böll, Grass and Walter Jens) by the media and by right-wing politicians.[12] One of the many literary responses to the mood of the time, Peter O. Chotjewitz's 'Romanfragment' *Die Herren des Morgengrauens* (1978) was itself a spectacular victim of the intense suspicion amongst establishment circles of the left. This problematical novel, a fusion of a more or less autobiographical account of Chotjewitz's problems during his time as Andreas Baader's defence lawyer and a concern with the similarity between his experiences and those portrayed in Kafka's *Das Schloß*, had already been accepted by the

10. *Fürsorgliche Belagerung*, Cologne, 1979, p. 349
11. For further discussion of *Fürsorgliche Belagerung* see J.H. Reid's chapter on Böll in this volume, pp. 214ff.
12. Louise Rinser, *Kriegsspielzeug. Tagebuch 1972–8*, Frankfurt on Main, 1978, pp. 167–72.

editors of the Autoren-Edition but was rejected by the publishers (Bertelsmann) for very dubious reasons and without consultation with the editors; the protests of the Autoren-Edition (the authors of which imprint were accused of having 'eine bessere Ausbildung im Umgang mit Kalaschnikows [. . .] als in der Handhabung der deutschen Sprache')[13] led to its contract with Bertelsmann being cancelled and the novel having to be published by Rotbuch.

The response to the 'Überwachungsstaat' is at the heart of Franz-Josef Degenhardt's second novel, *Brandstellen* (1975), which traces the development of Bruno Kappel, a Hamburg lawyer, a man of the 1960s (whose contemporaries have either made their careers in the State Prosecutors' office or have become terrorists) from a dissatisfied but successful careerist into an activist in local politics in his home town, where, more or less by accident, he has become involved in a protest campaign. The evocation of the milieu is skilful and the linguistic accuracy of the fictional police records woven into the story excellent; the novel is however, like the earlier works about the Student Movement from the Autoren-Edition, flawed by the inappropriate choice of the more or less Socialist Realist 'Entwicklungsroman'. Kappel's development, presented at the end of the novel as culminating in an unambiguously socialist position, is far from convincing, with his decision to return to his home town seeming to rest more on the sexual appeal of his new lover and on a romantic dream of the simple life it can offer, than on a growth in true political awareness. Leaving aside the tricky question of the actual political impact of such extra-parliamentary opposition, his reaction might be felt to be understandable as an emotional response to the excesses of the state forces that are portrayed in the novel, but — bearing in mind the short-lived nature of his earlier activism and his apparently unstable character — hardly provides a pointer to a long-term politicisation.

Degenhardt's third novel, *Die Mißhandlung* (1979), adapts the form of the 'Entwicklungsroman', so that, instead of ending merely on the threshold of a new life, it shows us the process leading to change retrospectively and thereby presents us, at the same time, with some idea of the character's life after it. Moreover, while the conventional third-person narration in *Brandstellen* underlines the suggestion that Kappel is to be understood as an exemplary figure, the first-person account by Hans Dörner himself of his development from a conformist opportunist into a critic of society is clearly a

---

13. Cf. Gerd Fuchs, 'Die Maske fällt: Es wird der Putsch geprobt', *Literatur-Konkret*, 1977, pp. 8–10.

personal one, involving some sacrifice, and is thus all the more realistic for that. The suggestion at the beginning of the novel that he now engages in demonstrations on behalf of greater human rights again confronts us, however, with the problematical notion of the political persuasiveness of such activity outside the confines of the established political arena.

A different body of novels of political realism in the 1970s is constituted by the work of the Werkkreis Literatur der Arbeitswelt, which demonstrates during the decade a growing awareness of the problems of modern realism. The initial debates on this topic in the Werkkreis (reflected in the proceedings of its 1972 conference *Realistisch schreiben*) concentrated on the relevance of the 'Expressionismusdebatte' of the 1930s for contemporary political realist writing practice, on the examples of the BPRS (Bund proletarisch-revolutionärer Schriftsteller) and the novel of the GDR. By the mid 1970s, however, it became clear that writers were moving away from earlier models. Hermann Spix's *Elephteria oder die Reise ins Paradies* (1975) and Margot Schroeder's *Ich stehe meine Frau* (1975) represent two very different and remarkably successful socio-critical novels which, while tracing some development in their central characters, avoid the pitfalls of the simplistic 'Entwicklungsroman' used by others. In *Elephteria*, which also marks the most successful attempt at putting into practice the collective novel, i.e. one written with the collaboration of other members of the Werkkreis, the experiences of the eponymous central figure are placed in a wider context established by documentary material, with the montage construction sharply accentuating aspects of the situation that Elephteria, a Greek 'Gastarbeiterin', would not have been able to appreciate; in its use of technique it is very close to that adopted by Wallraff's 'Reportagen' of his middle period (for example the *Neue Reportagen* of 1972). *Ich stehe meine Frau*, on the other hand, is a highly subject-centric novel, focusing on the identity and other existential problems of Charlie Bieber, a woman torn between social expectations of her as wife and mother and her own 'authentic' needs. Charlie slowly comes to see that her problems are not merely personal, but part of the collective burden of women. There is no unconvincing development of her into a committed leader, however; she feels jealousy, for example, at the activities of others and is honest enough with herself to admit that she acts more out of emotional impulse than out of political conviction. Nevertheless, the novel — which, rightly, was received as an important text by the Women's Movement — succeeds precisely because of this openness, its accurate reflection of the experiences and mentality of a woman like Charlie and the effect that these have on personal development.

The modest success of this and other Werkkreis novels stems from the fact that no naive hope of immediate and radical change is put forward, attention is concentrated, instead, on the demonstration of how far aspects of contemporary society fall short of a humanitarian ideal. The limited perspective, the focus on individual experience of specific social problems — such as inadequate working conditions, redundancy threats, housing shortages and prejudice against minorities —, enables the didactic novelists from the Werkkreis to produce highly readable works that can inform both members of the same social group and sympathetic outsiders and thus help, to the extent that any literature can, in creating wider critical awareness.

The didactic novel, aiming to draw attention to problems of the working class through literature, is by no means peculiar to the Werkkreis in the 1970s. The increased literary exploration of the — in West German literature — neglected world of labour, particularly through the reworking in the novel of personal experiences or researched material by authors such as Chotjewitz (*Der dreißigjährige Friede*, 1977), Gerd Fuchs (*Ein Mann fürs Leben*, 1977) and others, such as Wilhelm Genazino, Franz Innerhofer and Gernot Wolfgruber, while owing, in stylistic terms, something to the influence of experimental and documentary literature, also demonstrates the wider impact of Werkkreis ideas. The fourth novel of Max von der Grün, co-founder of the Gruppe 61, seems to have benefited considerably from such influence: *Stellenweise Glatteis* (1973), based on careful research by the author, lacks the clichéd metaphorical portrayal of working conditions that marked and marred his earlier work (*Männer in zweifacher Nacht*, 1959; *Irrlicht und Feuer*, 1963; and *Zwei Briefe an Pospischiel*, 1968). The discovery of concealed listening devices in a firm's vehicles leads to tension and, finally, strike action, but also serves to reveal the compromised position of the union. Events are unwittingly set in motion by Karl Maiwald, through whose eyes the reader views events, and whose personal development runs parallel, to some extent, with the increasing tension in the firm. Previously he wanted nothing more than '[sich] um nichts kümmern [. . .] und in Ruhe gelassen werden', but is now alerted to practices in his place of work that affect him directly. He soon realises that he can achieve nothing as a loner and that collective action is more likely to have success, but is, even at the end of the novel, far from being a political activist, remaining uncertain and confused as to how to act.

The demonstration — as in *Stellenweise Glatteis* — of a far from complete process of growing awareness by an individual of the objective nature of his position, with the intent of persuading the reader along a parallel path of enlightenment and, thus, to political engagement, is one of the basic structuring principles of political realist writing. Such an exemplary process must, however, if it is to be realistic, not only take note of the inherent stability of modern industrial societies, but also due account of the considerable obstacles to such growth in political insight, and there is no doubt that, for the working class, the restricted linguistic horizon particularly bedevils self-orientation. Michael Scharang, whose earliest literary work (*Verfahren eines Verfahrens*, 1969) is an example of concrete or experimental literature, has made this problem the central theme of his later 'Hörspiele' and novels. The eponymous central figure of Scharang's novel *Charly Traktor* (1973), is as politically naive as von der Grün's Maiwald, but is considerably more disadvantaged in his efforts to maintain some degree of human dignity at his place of work by his inability to express himself adequately. He instinctively resents the authority of his employer, but, given that he cannot put his frustrations into words, this frequently comes out in the form of angry outbursts. Those parts of the novel narrated by Charly himself, so very reminiscent of Scharang's 'O-Ton' radio plays, through their sharp contrast with the tone of the authorial voice, are testimony to these difficulties. The real problem, in the view of the sympathetic narrator, lies in Charly's isolation from any political organisation that might help him. At the end of the novel there has been no dramatic change, but he has at last made contact with other, better informed fellow-workers and feels he has made a start at understanding something of his position and of acquiring the language necessary to this understanding.

Scharang's message of the need to educate the working class to a point where they can start to understand their social situation, and the need for group action if this situation is to be improved, is also that of August Kühn's family chronicle, *Zeit zum Aufstehn* (1975), which is also intended to be a sort of history book for workers. It provides a vivid survey of the political and social history of Germany over the last hundred years through the more or less chronological family history of the Kühn–Zwing family, based on oral accounts handed down through the generations and a whole range of documentary material from local Munich archives. This chronicle is then intercut with episodes from the life of the present family in the 1970s, which serve to emphasise the way in which, for this social group, there has been little improvement in living standards, but, rather, the perpetuation of social disadvantages. The authorial voice is also anxious to stress, however, that the consciousness of the working class is such that no helpful information is passed on from one generation to the next, with this process being compounded by the neglect of the social history of the working class in school history lessons. The novel is intended, therefore, as a graphic alternative history of Germany over the last hundred years, a crash course in political history designed to help promote an as yet absent critical awareness amongst a working-class readership, much in the manner of Hans-Dieter Baroth's novels *Aber es waren schöne Zeiten* (1978) and *Streuselkuchen in Ickern* (1980), which offer an alternative reading of the experiences of the working class in the immediate post-war period.

The politicisation of the 1960s led to a new critical awareness that questioned not only established literary forms — with the consequences that we have been examining —, but also the traditional portrayal of history. The young generation of literary and social historians began to turn its attention to the exploration of hitherto neglected subject areas: a particular concern was to supplement existing historical analyses in an attempt to understand more fully, through examination of the failure of democratic movements, the origins of the German state and, hence, the reasons for the lack of a strong German tradition of democracy. Other areas of interest were the development of a modern capitalist economy and of colonialism (where we note the continuation of interest in the Third World), and, a major focal-point of analysis, the rise and triumph of National Socialism in Germany and of fascism in general. A number of writers have spoken of the new insights gained through the confrontation with Marxist ideas in the late 1960s and the way in which this determined their writing in the 1970s.[14] Their new sense of the inadequacy of established historical perspectives led to these and other writers, in fiction and non-fiction, turning increasingly to historical topics and to a revival of the historical novel.

Uwe Timm's second novel *Morenga* (1978), perhaps the outstanding example of the form in the decade, amounts to an alternative account of the colonial era to that provided by the earlier 'Kolonialroman', with the personal interpretation of history of the authorial voice being supported, as in many a documentary work, by quotation from authentic source material. The author, essentially operating as compiler of information, concentrates our attention on the experiences of army veterinary surgeon Gottschalk in German South-West Africa (modern-day Namibia) by extensive and, to

14. Cf. the interviews with Degenhardt, Fuchs, Michael Schneider and others in Matthias Altenburg (ed.), *Fremde Mütter, fremde Väter, fremdes Land, Autoren im Gespräch*, Hamburg, 1986.

some extent, fictionalised extracts from his diaries. Gottschalk's otherwise unremarkable story is, however, then placed in a wider political and social context by the use of the montage technique: the individual experience is thus used, through its fusion with transindividual information of an historical kind, to facilitate a critical examination of the nature of the colonial system on both sides.

Timm's critical exposure of conditions in South-West Africa is not, however, to be understood as an attack on German colonialism in particular. Gottschalk's individual confrontation with colonialism, since it is so different from that of most settlers, and indeed, his or her own expectations, forces the reader to re-examine existing attitudes towards the colonial experience in general and the role of the colonists in particular. The suppression of the Hottentot uprising at the centre of the novel vividly accentuates the cultural and political role of the European nations as a collective force in Southern Africa; indeed, the collaboration of the British with the Germans in finally crushing Morenga, the Hottentot leader, is particularly significant, exemplifying the point that colonialism should be seen as the collective suppression and exploitation of underdeveloped people by the Europeans, rather than as an expression of the ambition of the individual nation. The location of the novel in Namibia, today effectively a part of South Africa, further links the events to the present, indeed, Morenga himself has great importance as the first rebel to use a new means of warfare (which we would now call guerrilla tactics). In Morenga, the 'Napoleon der Schwarzen', Uwe Timm rediscovered an historical figure who can be considered in many ways as the prefiguration of the great freedom fighters in the developing countries and the Third World, and who was, largely as a result of this novel — which was soon published in English in Southern Africa — swiftly adopted by SWAPO as a key symbolic figure of the struggle for freedom that they continue in Namibia. Timm thus confronts the modern reality of Southern Africa with its past through a figure who, in his day, fought for the category of human dignity that has still to be respected there and, through his example, still inspires a modern generation of those involved in the same struggle.

Morenga, while demonstrating the artistic potential of a revived form of the historical novel, is thematically unique in the 1970s. The major concern of the main body of historical novels published in the period was to demonstrate the relevance of the Nazi past for an understanding of the political present of the Federal Republic. While Bernt Engelmann was concerned to expose the Nazi past of leading West German industrialists and Manfred Franke

(*Mordverläufe*, 1973) and Peter O. Chotjewitz (*Saumlos*, 1979) set out
to show, in a more general way, the continuity between the racial
intolerance that burst out in the 'Kristallnacht' of November 1938
and that of the present day, Franz-Josef Degenhardt's *Zündschnüre*
(1973) and Gerd Fuchs's *Stunde Null* (1980) attempted to re-examine
the continuing implications of the situation at the end of the war.
Degenhardt demonstrates the unambiguous resistance of the young
communists at this time, implicitly arguing for a reappraisal of
conventional wisdoms as to the nature of opposition to National
Socialism and, more importantly, claiming that the potential for the
future inherent in that bravery was ignored and thus lost in the
post-war situation. Fuchs, on the other hand, shows in his picture of
life in the aftermath of the war in a small Hunsrück town the
dashing of hopes for change; in the founding of the Federal Republic
in 1949 he sees a lost opportunity, adding his voice to the swelling
chorus of those who, in the 1970s, came to call radically into
question the established notion of the state standing for a complete
break with the Nazi past. It is also noticeable how, during this time,
a younger generation turned to a related theme, the quizzical
examination of the early years of the Federal Republic — which has,
after all, lasted almost forty years — in the attempt to establish
shaping influences on the present of the 1970s. Outside literature
Fassbinder's film trilogy, *Die Ehe der Maria Braun* (1978), *Die Sehnsucht der Veronika Voß* (1982) and *Lola* (1981), portrays the first phases
of the life of the Republic as period pieces crucial to an understanding of the present, as is emphasised by the series of stills at the end of
the first film. Hans-Dieter Baroth's novel *Aber es waren schöne Zeiten*
(1978) offers an alternative account of a time that has, in the main,
passed into reassuring legend, and shows the origins of contemporary social and educational problems, while *Streuselkuchen in Ickern*
(1980), his examination of the 1950s, the time of the 'Wirtschaftswunder', examines the causes of the false values of the working class
of the present. One novel in particular, Peter O. Chotjewitz's *Der
dreißigjährige Friede* (1977) lays specific claim to offering a reinterpretation of the history of West Germany, with the intent of
exposing the impact of the early years on the present of the 1970s.

The novel, drawing on reports by, and conversations with, the
actors of the real-life drama on which it was based, traces the life of a
lower middle-class family, the Schütrumpfs, from the end of the
Second World War up to the 1970s, concentrating in particular on
the constraints imposed on the development of Jürgen, the son.
Despite his intelligence, he is unable to express his individual needs,
such that by the age of twenty, his 'Anpassung an die elterlichen

Lebensverhältnisse' is complete.[15] His major difficulty, the sympathetic authorial voice tells us, is that, like the vast majority of his generation, 'so gut wie keine politische Erziehung erhalten [hat]'. He comes into contact with activists in the factory where he works, discovering in the process the compromised past of its owners. His arson attack on the factory, seemingly a dramatic consequence of his political education is, in fact, an effort to avoid being abandoned by his girl-friend and, as such, yet another manifestation of the way in which his behaviour is determined by his petit-bourgeois background. The examination of Jürgen's life adds up to a body of criticism directed at the political immaturity of the middle classes, at the failure of the SPD and the trade union movement to act to counter this, at the activities of capitalist industry, shown both in the Third Reich and Federal Republic as being concerned only with its own interest, at the press and at the intolerance of a state that claims to be democratic. The novel demonstrates at times a certain heavy-handedness, but nevertheless adds up to a powerful appeal for a reappraisal of the social history of the Federal Republic.

The aim of any work of political realism has, ultimately, to be to influence opinion and to help to play a part in bringing about political action and, thereby, social change. It is not surprising, therefore, that one of the key concepts in the discussions about political realism in the 1970s — within the Autoren-Edition and the Werkkreis Literatur der Arbeitswelt in particular — was 'Brauchbarkeit'. While a proper examination of the political usefulness of literary works would necessitate a separate and very sophisticated analysis, the quite astounding sales figures of the Werkkreis novels in the Fischer Bücherei would certainly seem to suggest that they have had an informative and even unifying function amongst left-wing readers and, even, liberal sympathisers, which is a limited but perfectly legitimate role for political realism. The vastly different reception of the early novels of the Autoren-Edition and of Franz-Josef Degenhardt, reflecting very much the political position of the reviewers, would seem to point to their, on the other hand, having failed to reach beyond existing sympathisers. It is difficult to know how the reading public responded to Engelmann's deliberate use of the form of the thriller in *Großes Bundesverdienstkreuz* (1974), but there is no doubt as to the publicity generated by the court cases that ensued (and which he won). Böll's *Die verlorene Ehre der Katharina Blum* is a special case, given the publicity surrounding it and the impact of Schlöndorff's film, but *Fürsorgliche Belagerung* and other

15. *Der dreißigjährige Friede*, Düsseldorf, 1977, p. 76.

novels examined here, such as Walter's *Die Verwilderung* and Uwe Timm's *Morenga*, are anything but popular in concept, and their complex form would render any broadly based impact impossible.

As the 1980s draw to a close it becomes clear that the decade has been marked by an absence of political realism and it is naturally interesting to speculate as to the reasons for this. Have writers, for example, come to agree with one of the conclusions of Peter Weiss's *Die Ästhetik des Widerstands* — which is concerned with the attempt to develop a 'kämpferische Ästhetik' —, namely that high culture is not really capable of influencing political events? It is worth remembering at this point that one of the most frequently voiced ideas during the Student Movement, before the return of the faith in the didactic power of literature that, ultimately, lay at the heart of the political realism of the 1970s, was the necessity of their setting up 'Gegenmedien' under their own control and the experiences of recent years would seem to have reinforced the thinking behind that idea; certainly no work of political realism could attain the impact of *Holocaust* (1979), *Heimat* (1984) or *Väter und Söhne* (1986), the most prominent examples of critical realism in the television serial seen on West German screens in recent years. It is also clear that, whatever was claimed for political realism in the 1970s, no work of fiction has had the impact of Wallraff's latest reportages *Ganz unten* (1985), indeed, it is hard not to accept now the validity of the claims he made at the end of the 1960s for the impact of his sort of writing over 'literature'. Another important factor has undoubtedly been the creation of alternative forums for non-conformist political debate, particularly the Greens and the Peace Movement: it is striking that Heinrich Böll, so active in these spheres in his last years and who publicly embraced the Greens as 'his' party in his address to the Bonn peace demonstration of 1983, turned away from political realism in his last novel, *Frauen vor Flußlandschaft* (1985) and that Martin Walser has publicly expressed his relief that, with the establishment of the Greens in the political firmament of the Federal Republic, he has been able to retreat into 'das Hinterfeld', the true realm of literature.[16] The major political activity of writers in this decade, their involvement in the Peace Movement, has meant, in effect, a return to their extra-literary moral-political involvement that typified the engagement of committed writers until well into the 1960s; only one realist novel, Gerhard Zwerenz' *Der Bunker* (1982) has taken up the theme of the ultimate nuclear catastrophe, with Grass continuing in the style of *Der Butt* (1977) in his treatment of

16. In an interview in *die tageszeitung*, 30.9. 1985.

'die Vernichtung der Menschheit', in *Die Rättin* (1986). There are undoubtedly other factors that we can now clearly observe, including the depressing effect of the establishment of a right-of-centre government in Bonn (the second recent so-called 'Tendenzwende'), but we would also hazard the view that it is only in the 1980s that we can truly detect on a broad front the ebbing of optimistic energy generated by the Student Movement that some commentators wrongly claimed to detect in the early 1970s; this, perhaps more than anything else, would seem to explain the clear demise of political realism in the present decade.

Suggested Further Reading

Keith Bullivant, 'Politischer Realismus heute?', in A. Schöne (ed.), *Kontroversen, alte und neue* (proceedings of the 7th IVG Conference, Göttingen, 1985), vol. 10, Tübingen, 1986

——, *Realism Today*, Leamington Spa and New York, 1987, esp. pp. 43–64 and 106–49

Alexander Kluge, *Gelegenheitsarbeit einer Sklavin. Zur realistischen Methode*, Frankfurt on Main, 1975

Stephan Kohl, *Realismus. Theorie und Geschichte*, Munich, 1977

Peter Laemmle (ed.), *Realismus — welcher?*, Munich, 1976

Fredi Lerch (ed.), *Vorschlag zur Unversöhnlichkeit: Realismusdebatte Winter 1983/84*, Zurich, 1984

Uwe Timm and Gerd Fuchs (eds.), *Kontext 1. Literatur und Wirklichkeit*, Munich, 1976

MORAY McGOWAN

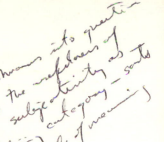

'Neue Subjektivität'

Most surveys of the West German literature of the 1970s[1] point out that outward-looking, socially critical and politically committed literature continued to be published beyond the supposed political and cultural 'Tendenzwende' of the mid-1970s,[2] beyond the revival of the capitalist consensus in mainstream politics and the retreat of the disillusioned rebels of the late 1960s 'von der Straße ins Kleingewerbe, in den Kräutergarten und in die Innerlichkeit'.[3] On the one hand, in 1973, two novels seen as prime examples of 'Neue Subjektivität' appeared, Karin Struck's *Klassenliebe* and Peter Schneider's *Lenz*; their success (75,000 copies by 1976 and 120,000 by 1980, respectively) certainly suggests they caught the spirit of the age. But on the other hand, the paperback edition of Günter Wallraff's first 'Industriereportagen' also sold over 300,000 copies in the 1970s. This was a highly politicised decade. Between 1975 and 1980 there were more strikes in West Germany than in the entire 1960s. The state's response to left-wing radicalism, in the form of the 'Radikalenerlaß' and the massive expansion of the surveillance state, provoked significant and often politically committed book-length responses, for example from Heinrich Böll, Peter Chotjewitz or Peter Schneider himself, as well as countless more easily overlooked shorter texts like the polemical epigrams of Arnfried Astel. The abuse and sometimes persecution critical intellectuals continued to suffer from the political right in the 1970s suggests that the latter were not aware of the former's withdrawal into a toothless privatism. It is also misleading to direct one's attention exclusively to the supposed politicisation and depoliticisation of one generation of one

1. This chapter largely focuses on *West German* literature without suggesting there are not specific Austrian, Swiss and GDR dimensions to the question of 'Neue Subjektivität'.
2. Clemens Graf Podewils (ed.), *Tendenzwende? Zur geistigen Situation in der Bundesrepublik*, Stuttgart, 1975; Klaus Bohnen, '"Tendenzwende": zu einer Kulturkontroverse der siebziger Jahre', in A. Schöne (ed.), *Kontroversen, alte und neue*, vol. 10, Tübingen, 1986; David Roberts (ed.), *Tendenzwenden. Aspekte des Kulturwandels der siebziger Jahre*, Frankfurt on Main, 1984.
3. Wolfgang Pohrt, *Endstation*, Berlin, 1982, p. 95

social group, that of the students, for this neglects other continuities both of political commitment and of apolitical inwardness in West German culture.

None the less there is widespread consensus that there was a revival of subjectivity in the literature of the 1970s after its relative neglect in the late 1960s. It is seen in the prevalence of autobiographical writing, whether purportedly factual — there was a revival of the diary form — or overtly fictionalised (Günter Grass, *Aus dem Tagebuch einer Schnecke*, 1972; Max Frisch, *Montauk*, 1975; Wolfgang Koeppen, *Jugend*, 1976; Peter Handke, *Das Gewicht der Welt*, 1977); in the biographies of parents, from Handke's *Wunschloses Unglück* (1972) via Karin Struck's *Die Mutter* (1975) to the wave of 'Vater-Bücher' at the end of the decade; in sensitive, inward-looking novels with telling titles (Hans Jürgen Fröhlich, *Im Garten der Gefühle*, 1975; Peter Handke, *Die Stunde der wahren Empfindung*, 1975; Nicolas Born, *Die erdabgewandte Seite der Geschichte*, 1976). Self-destructive subjectivity, expressed in madness, sickness, alcohol and drug abuse, was a common theme (Bernward Vesper, *Die Reise*; Maria Erlenberger, *Der Hunger nach Wahnsinn*; and Ernst Herhaus's *Kapitulation, Aufgang einer Krankheit*; all 1977) There was a comparable shift in drama from the political or historical plays of Weiss, Hochhuth or Kipphardt to the individual crises of identity and existence in the work of Botho Strauß or Thomas Bernhard, and indeed, though this aspect of his work was long overlooked, in the 'Kleinbürger' plays of Franz Xaver Kroetz. The poetry of the 1970s is also seen as marked by a broad shift from the public to the private, from the historically significant to the everyday, a trend represented in Jürgen Theobaldy's anthology *Und ich bewege mich doch . . . Gedichte vor und nach 1968* (1977) and characterised, almost caricatured, by Christoph Derschau's *Den Kopf voll Suff und Kino* (1976; in a fourth edition by 1979). The revived popularity of poetry, seen by many as the quintessentially subjective genre, was itself cited as evidence of the new subjectivity.

The disparateness of these examples of texts assigned at one time or another to 'Neue Subjektivität' — they could be continued almost indefinitely — suggests that the term is so wide and so inconsistently used as to tell us little. Certainly its use has been accompanied by lasting disagreement over its definition and especially its significance: a bourgeois irrelevance; a symptom of political escapism or resignation; literature returning to its real role after a self-destructive flirtation with politics; the product of heightened awareness of the dialectic of self and society; an act of resistance to those forces that threaten the human individual, etc. etc. There is evidence for all these views; their competing claims have generated sustained debate within and around literature in and since the 1970s which has itself become part of the object of investigation: 'Neue Subjektivität' may thus refer to qualities of texts, theories of literary effectiveness or ways of seeing. We will address some of these complexities by looking at the extent to which 'Neue Subjektivität' was 'new' and then at some prominent aspects of 'Subjektivität' in the literature of the 1970s.

Peter Rühmkorf's dating of 'die Geburtsstunde des neuen Ich-Gefühls mit Zerfall der Studentenbewegung'[4] is accurate only if one recognises that the gestation took place within the protest movement itself, where 'Neue Subjektivität' was anticipated in a number of ways.

The distrust of fictional modes of writing that produced the documentary literature of the 1960s established the literary merit of 'authenticity'. This survived the decline of documentary forms and helped legitimate texts of subjective experience in the climate of a new 'Ideologieverdacht' in the 1970s. For Jürgen Theobaldy the focus on personal experience was an attempt to state something 'Verläßliches' and 'Überprüfbares' in the face of the clichés of public discourse.[5]

Moreover, the attempted demystification of social processes in the 1960s had included the 'desublimation of literature':[6] Nicolas Born, on the cover of *Marktlage* (Cologne 1967), declares a move 'weg von der alten Poetik, die nur noch Anleitung zum Poetisieren ist; weg vom Symbol, Metapher, von allen Bedeutungsträgern'. His aim is a 'rohe, unartifizielle Formulierung' in which 'der Schreiber Dinge, Beziehungen, Umwelt direkt angeht, das heißt also Poesie nicht mit Worten erfindet': a rejection of poetic intensification in favour of naive reflection of experienced reality that continued in the 'Alltagslyrik' of the 1970s. Rolf Dieter Brinkmann, too, anticipated 'Alltagslyrik' — in a manner typical of the anti-elitist pop culture of the 1960s — by rejecting the aesthetic norms of bourgeois art in favour of quickly produced, accessible poetry of everyday experience.

4. Quoted in K. Bullivant and H.-J. Althof (eds.), *Subjektivität — Innerlichkeit — Abkehr vom Politischen? Tendenzen der deutschsprachigen Literatur der 70er Jahre*, Bonn, 1986, p. 367
5. *Und ich bewege mich doch . . . Gedichte vor und nach 1968*, Munich, 1977, p. 223. See also Julian Sierra-Ballester and Anthony Stephens' chapter on 'West German Poetry of the 1970s', p. 117.
6. R. Hinton Thomas and K. Bullivant, *Literature in Upheaval*, Manchester, 1974, pp. 78–81.

(*Keiner weiß mehr*, his autobiographical novel of marital breakdown and destructive self-immersion, would seem a central text of the new subjectivity, had it appeared in 1973 not 1968.)

Another continuity lies in the fact that the Student Movement, especially in its first, anti-authoritarian phase, was not only anti-capitalist, but also an existentialist revolt that stressed self-assertion. The term 'Neue Sensibilität', sometimes used interchangeably with 'Neue Subjektivität' or 'Neue Innerlichkeit' with reference to the 1970s, in fact originates with Herbert Marcuse. He argues (e.g. in *Essay on Liberation*, 1969) that the identification and mobilisation of the real subjective needs of the individual are inherently subversive of the false needs generated by capitalism. In *Eros and Civilisation* (1955; the German edition appeared in 1966 as the Student Movement was gathering momentum) Marcuse describes the pressure of social processes on individual psychology as such that 'psychological problems therefore turn into political problems: private disorder reflects [. . .] the disorder of the whole'.[7] This point — that the private is the political — was a key premise of the early Student Movement.

It was spontaneous and actionistic; the intrinsic sense of libera-tion engendered by the act of rebellion was as important as the extrinsic goal. It could be hedonistic: the subcultural celebration of sex, drugs and rock-'n'-roll as part of Marcuse's 'great refusal' could turn the rejection of consumer capitalism into parasitic dependence on its basic principle of wasteful abundance, as in Wolfgang Bauer's *Magic Afternoon* (1968),[8] another anticipation of inwardness like Brinkmann's *Keiner weiß mehr*. The political protest itself could be ambiguous: Christopher Lasch, surveying comparable develop-ments in America in *The Culture of Narcissism*, argues that 1960s radicalism was 'a form of therapy', quoting Susan Stern's memoir of the demonstrations at the 1968 Democratic Convention: 'I felt good [. . .] my body supple and strong and slim [. . .] I felt real'.[9] On the other hand, this very notion of subjective awakening was adopted as a criterion of political significance by such central figures of the protest movement as Rudi Dutschke, who declared in 1968: 'weil uns diese Aktionen innerlich verändern, sind sie politisch'.[10] Mar-

---

7. London, 1969, p. 21.
8. For a fuller discussion of *Magic Afternoon* see Anthony Waine's chapter on the influence of popular culture, pp. 69–73 of this present volume.
9. London, 1980, p. 7.
10. Quoted in Rolf Hosfeld and Helmut Peitsch, '"Weil uns diese Aktionen innerlich verändern, sind sie politisch". Bemerkungen zu vier Romanen über die Studen-tenbewegung', *Basis* 8, 1978, p. 102.

cuse himself was not descrying political action; the very next clause in *Eros and Civilisation* argues that the penetration of the private by the political means 'the cure of personal disorder depends more directly than before on the cure of the general disorder'.

It is in this context that in 1969, just when the 'rote Zellen' were achieving their greatest influence in the Student Movement, Dieter Wellershoff, in an essay called 'Zu privat: über eine Kategorie der Verdrängung', insisted on the critical potential of subjective literature: 'Indem sie die gesperrten und verstümmelten Kapazitäten des Menschen deutlich macht, zeigt sie den Preis der herrschenden Praxis und zugleich das Potential möglicher Veränderung'.[11] At the same time, Peter Schneider was paraphrasing Marcuse in calling on art to be 'die völlige Mobilisierung der Wünsche gegen die Wirklichkeit'.[12]

However, blind to or frightened of the subversive power of spontaneity and desire, the orthodox Marxists clung to their theoretical crutches and rejected the 'Neue Sensibilität' just as it was developing. As Nicolas Born's narrator says in *Die erdabgewandte Seite der Geschichte* (1976): 'Auf dem halben Weg zu uns hieß es umkehren, weg von uns; und wir ließen unsere Sachen in der allergrößten Unordnung zurück'.[13] This undialectic insensitivity, one could argue, and not the reassertion of subjectivity in the 1970s, was the real point at which the original impulses of the Student Movement were betrayed.

The success of Schneider's *Lenz*, or of Peter-Paul Zahl's *Von einem der auszog, Geld zu verdienen* (which flopped in 1970 at the height of left-wing orthodoxy but was a success on reissue in 1976), has much to do with the articulation of these contradictions. Lenz turns 'das weise Marxgesicht über seinem Bett' upside down: 'Um den Verstand abtropfen zu lassen [. . .] Er sah Marx in die Augen: "Was waren deine Träume, alter Besserwisser, nachts meine ich? Warst du eigentlich glücklich?"'.[14] Against the rigid certainties of Marxist rationalism, Lenz sets those aspects of human experience the arid socio-economic discourse neglects or denies. As Wolf Wondratschek says, 'An Marx, an die Wand geheftet, ist nur noch sein Bart politisch';[15] Lenz's questioning is not a rejection of politics, but an attempt to repoliticise an empty fetish by addressing its inadequacies.

Thus Lenz asks whether the members of his 'Betriebsgruppe'

11. *Literatur und Veränderung*, Cologne, 1969, p. 43.
12. *Ansprachen*, Berlin, 1970, p. 37.
13. Reinbek, 1979, p. 48.
14. Peter Schneider, *Lenz*, Berlin, 1973, p. 5.
15. Wondratschek, 'Zappa', in his *Omnibus*, Munich, 1972, p. 132.

really had no other interest in each other than 'diese sauberen Sätze von Mao Tse-tung [. . .] Wollten sie etwa nicht auch [. . .] ihre Genüsse und Schwierigkeiten miteinander austauschen? [. . .] Würden sich diese Bedürfnisse, die als Arbeitshindernisse galten, nicht hinter dem Rücken der Gruppe durchsetzen und durch ihre Unterdrückung die Arbeit behindern?'[16] Schneider's purpose is not to discredit Mao, but to criticise the group's denial of subjective reality which actually hinders the political work it is supposed to further and makes them, essentially, into other-determined consumers, even if of political ideology rather than material goods.

Lenz leaves Berlin to escape the instrumentalisation of the self; he soon leaves Rome too, rejecting the overvaluation by his friends there of psychology at the cost of the political. In Trento he finds a (romanticised) community whose synthesis of concrete political work and intact personal communication is mutually reinforcing. But it is not Lenz's community, and, deported back to Berlin, his resolve is 'dableiben': an open, dis-illusioned but not apathetic future based on a differentiated understanding of the interrelationship of the private and the political.

One variation of the 'Neue Subjektivität' of the 1970s is that which has learned this lesson that subjectivity may in fact render commitment more concrete by reflecting personal response to political or social experience ('sich einbringen' is more than simply a vogue expression of the 1970s). In this it continues the tradition of Marcuse's 'Neue Sensibilität' in the light of changed political and social conditions and helps lay the basis of the new alternative politics of the later 1970s and the 1980s, much wider in appeal and social base than that of the 1960s. In 1977 in the climate of the 'deutsche Herbst' Michael Buselmeier notes that pessimism and scepticism are now the dominant feelings amongst left-wing intellectuals — partly because the radical subjectivity of the Student Movement heightened awareness of the self's disintegration under social pressures. None the less the genuine left will 'auch unter den unfreundlichsten Bedingungen des Augenblicks ihre Utopie festhalten, sie nur vielleicht differenzierter vermitteln, indem sie z.B., nach einer Phase der Verdrängung und Ich-Ent-äußerung, die psychische Struktur und die Lebensgeschichte erforschen und diesen Prozeß als politisch begreifen'.[17]

There is another, opposite, sense in which 'Neue Subjektivität' is actually a product of, rather than a reaction to the late 1960s. The

16. Schneider, *Lenz*, p. 28.
17. 'Nach der Revolte', in W.M. Lüdke (ed.), *Literatur und Studentenbewegung*, Opladen, 1977, p. 160.

mistake of reading Enzensberger's essay 'Gemeinplätze, die neueste Literatur betreffend' in *Kursbuch* 15 (1968) as a declaration of the 'death of literature' is frequently pointed out; he in fact argues that literature is extremely tenacious. Misunderstanding his argument permits its easy refutation, for literature of course survived as, in fact, he said it would. However, it can still be shown that his essay subliminally prepares the ground for the rehabilitation of explicitly non-political literature. He himself describes his call to writers to direct their talent to political journalism as 'bescheidene, ja gerad-ezu bedürftige Vorschläge'. Much more forceful is his insistence that political reality is not 'ein literarisches Phänomen' and cannot therefore be effectively changed 'mit literarischen Mitteln'.[18] Neither when produced by a writer nor when consumed by a reader are *literary* statements of political criticism or commitment necessarily politically meaningful acts; indeed, they may function as catharsis or alibi.

However, he argues, precisely because literature is no substitute for political action, to attack it for its political impotence when your real target should be the political system it has proved powerless to change, is equally pointless. Demonstrating literature's political ineffectiveness, he preserves it by freeing it from the need to legit-imate itself politically. Enzensberger was of course calling for politi-cal commitment to be expressed in real action rather than literary shadow-boxing; but the essay's plea for the traditional separation of literature and politics is not so unlike Peter Handke's claim in 1966: 'Eine engagierte Literatur gibt es nicht. Der Begriff ist ein Wider-spruch in sich [. . .] der engagierte Schriftsteller kann sich als Schriftsteller nicht engagieren'.[19] As the 1970s progressed, litera-ture's renewed self-confidence revived aesthetic considerations and the bourgeois literary tradition, a development wholly in line with Enzensberger's diagnosis of its prospects.

'Subjectivity' is notoriously difficult to delineate, particularly literary subjectivity. With rare exceptions, all works of literature are products of an individual consciousness, and so are essentially 'subjective'. Even the 'Protokolls' seen as the epitome of the docu-mentary, objective phase of literature (e.g. Erika Runge's *Bottroper Protokolle*, 1968; Michael Scharang's 'O-Ton-Hörspiele' of the early 1970s) articulate the subjective experience of the interviewees, and the authorial subjectivity which influences the selection and order-ing of the material has affinities with the position of an omniscient

18. *Kursbuch 15 (1968)*, pp. 196 and 190 respectively.
19. Handke, *Ich bin ein Bewohner des Elfenbeinturms*, Frankfurt on Main, 1978, pp. 43 and 49.

narrator. The impact of Wallraff's 'Reportagen' results from the underpinning of his political commitment by the subjective authenticity of his reports: they are lived experience not second-hand analyses. Böll's political essays (like those of Peter Schneider or Ulrike Meinhof in the late 1960s), as well as his novels, have always been marked by a strong subjectivity in the sense of a willingness to commit himself in moral or socio-political debate.

But, as Böll remarked in 1977, 'es liegt mir wenig daran, mich mit mir selbst zu beschäftigen':[20] subjectivity as an authorial perspective must be distinguished from subjectivity as a theme of literature, a subject looking outward from a subject looking inward. The subjectivity of fictional characters (including apparently autobiographical narrators) should not be confused with that of the author. When Kroetz remarks of his characters in *Heimarbeit* 'Sie sind introvertiert',[21] or when Botho Strauß's *Trilogie des Wiedersehens* fills a whole art gallery with self-obsessed neurotics, neither author need necessarily share that condition.

Even 'subjectivity' restricted to the sense of narrators' view of themselves and their relation to the world covers a wide range of possibilities. The following analysis concentrates on two broad categories, in full awareness that they overlap, that there are others, that not every text by the cited authors follows the pattern shown here, and that even the cited texts may not be consistent within themselves.

The first group of examples essentially demonstrates the assumption of an intact subject. Grass's narrator in *Aus dem Tagebuch einer Schnecke* (1972) imposes his 'Ich' on the world with aggressive self-confidence: 'Ich schreibe auf regennasse Schieferdächer, in Bierpfützen, auf ein Förderband: Ich Ich Ich'.[22] Christa Wolf's narrator in *Nachdenken über Christa T.* is more tentative, declaring 'daß ich nur schreibend über die Dinge komme';[23] but she adds, in *Kein Ort. Nirgends*, 'daß ich in der Poesie wie in einem Spiegel mich zu sammeln, mich selber zu sehen, durch mich hindurch und über mich hinaus zu gehn versuche'.[24] Similarly, Karin Struck in *lieben* describes her literary self-examination as the attempt 'eine Person zu werden, die in die Welt gehen kann und ein Gesicht hat'.[25] In

20. Quoted in Theo Buck, 'Die Rückkehr des Individuums in der Literatur des letzten Jahrzehnts', in *Literatur und Gesellschaft in der BRD*, Bonn, 1979, p. 41.
21. *Spectaculum* 15, 1971, p. 323.
22. Reinbek, 1974, p. 158.
23. Halle, 1968, p. 44.
24. Berlin and Weimar, 1979, p. 51.
25. Frankfurt on Main, 1977, p. 449.

1976 Erika Runge declared her desire to write a novel, to do for
herself what she felt she had done for others in her documentary
texts, 'den Anspruch des Menschen auf Selbstverwirklichung, auf
Individualität, auch für meine Person zu vertreten'.[26] This brand of
subjectivity is sustained by forms of Enlightenment faith in the integrity of the subject, even if, as for Wolf, it must first be recovered.

Related to this position is the one which sees the subject as a
repository of resistance, and the new subjectivity therefore not as
'Reprivatisierung', but as a political act, 'nichts anderes denn der
Versuch, wider die Verfügungsgewalt einer Technokratie der au-
ßengesteuerten Sinne ein Widerstandspotential zu erhalten und zu
entwickeln, in dem wir unsere Identität finden und, wie schwierig
auch immer, autonome Selbstbestimmung verwirklichen'.[27] This,
clearly, combines an awareness of the threat of social pressures on
and even in the subject with Enlightenment optimism about its
preservation via Marcuse's 'great refusal'.

Two writers who combine a picture of a subject under profound
threat with a dogged insistence on the subject's capacity to resist it,
are Martin Walser and Franz Xaver Kroetz. Walser, whose novels,
such as *Die Gallistl'sche Krankheit* (1972), portray subjective crisis and
collapse, then, in *Seelenarbeit* (1979) (a title which encapsulates the
dialectic of the self and the social), posits human relationships as a
counterweight to self-disintegration.[28] Anton Kreuzberger, the hero
of Kroetz's novel *Der Mondscheinknecht* (1981), though handicapped
and socially marginalised like many characters in Kroetz's early
plays, fights free of his object existence. Like a Botho Strauß character, in trying to determine his identity through the act of writing he
heightens his sense of his self's fragility. However, this is balanced
by the conviction that struggle and self-assertion in the social
process — he is a skilled typesetter and trade-union activist —
create identity. 'Man muß sich wehren, wenn man ein Mensch sein
will', writes Kroetz on the cover. It may be this belief in active
processes of self-assertion that has led Walser and Kroetz, for
example, to be infrequently mentioned as proponents of 'Neue
Subjectivität' both by those who celebrate it as apolitical and by
those who damn it for the same reason.

But the important categories of 'Widerstand' and 'Weigerung'

26. Quoted in Helmut Kreuzer, 'Zur Literatur der siebziger Jahre in der Bundesrepublik', *Basis* 8, 1978, p. 12.
27. Wolfram Schütte (1975), quoted by Jost Hermand, 'Linke Sommergäste', *Basis*
8, 1978, p. 204.
28. Frankfurt on Main, 1979, p. 294. See also Anthony Waine's chapter on Walser,
esp. p. 352.

may become sophistic justifications for not writing committed literature, by claiming the political quality of the unpolitical. Thus H.-J. Heise wrote in 1975: 'So gesehen kann in einer Zeit, in der dem Lyriker das sogenannte engagierte Gedicht abverlangt wird, das Beharren auf seiner personalen Position sehr wohl ein politischer Akt sein — und zwar im Sinne der Weigerung'.[29] Jürgen Theobaldy's claim that 'Poesie ist eine Art Widerstand' is undermined by its location in the poem 'Harte Eier', a celebration of adolescent maleness. The unpolitical nature of unpolitical poetry is illustrated by a comparison of Theobaldy's 'Lob der Haut' with Volker von Törne's identically titled response.[30] Theobaldy's conversational celebration of everyday pleasures and his resigned observation of the frailty of the self encourages a comfortable consumer attitude to the textual experience (like Axel Springer's aim to give *Bild-Zeitung* readers the same pleasure they got from a cigarette). Von Törne, using equally everyday language, reverses expectations and deconstructs familiar metaphors to provoke a critical reflection on everyday reality absent from the self-satisfaction of the 'Alltagsdichter'.

Godehard Schramm in 'Ein Kleid aus Seide' (1975) looks back to the late 1960s: 'Wir rissen uns die Haut in Striemen ab/und nähten auf die nackten Knochen Lumpen,/nur weil die Menschen, die so radikal verneinten/[. . .] /die Häßlichkeit zu ihrem Gott erhoben'.[31] However the beauty he praises in rejection of this flagellatory severity is borrowed uncritically from advertising clichés: grapefruit from a desert greenhouse, roses from Palermo. These poets identify their texts as poems by their — fairly arbitrary — layout, and so lay claim to a poetic sensitivity to experience. But this is not 'Widerstand' or 'Weigerung', nor is it the radical passivity of Handke's poetic project in *Das Gewicht der Welt* (see below), but a capitulation before the world as its determinant structures present it to us.

Many of the 'Alltagslyriker' turn the 'Ich' into a self-legitimating fetish, much as the politicisation process of the late 1960s had done with 'Marxism' and 'the working class'. Thus they reverse and so repeat the contradictions of Lenz's 'Betriebsgruppe'. Both the middle-class intellectual aping a working-class perspective at odds with his subjective identity and the proponent of subjective authenticity blind to the depth to which social forces penetrate the apparently secure refuge of the self, perpetuate a false consciousness, for

---

29. 'Weigerung als Engagement', *Rheinische Merkur*, 12.9.1975, p. 17.
30. Printed side-by-side in Christoph Buchwald and Klaus Wagenbach (ed.), *Lesebuch. Deutsche Literatur der siebziger Jahre*, Berlin, 1984, pp. 94–5; 'Harte Eier' is on pp. 98–9.
31. *Meine Lust ist größer als mein Schmerz*, Munich, 1975, p. 82.

in post-industrial capitalism neither the working class nor the self possess the cohesive meaning which these two perspectives attribute to them.

An awareness of this is reflected in the opposite, very different ② category of 'Neue Subjektivität' to be considered here: that of writers who have abandoned, or wish actively to subvert, the belief in a self-determining subject. Nicolas Born's narrator in *Die erdabgewandte Seite der Geschichte* (1976) has lost faith in the constructs by which he has related to experience: 'Es ist so, dachte ich, daß ich alles nur noch durch mich selber erklären kann, außerhalb gibt es keine Erklärungen mehr'. But this is not the narcissism of an unbroken self-admiration; his disorientation extends to his own feelings and capacity for reason: 'ich verschwand aus mir, ich zerkrümelte'.[32]

Born's novel contains many anticipations of the neo-Romantic sensibility which has become progressively more pronounced in the work of Strauß and Handke, such as his narrator's articulation of the oppressiveness of reality and the need for the inexplicable, for 'eine Welt, die keinen Platz hatte in der Welt', if one is to escape spiritual death: a motif that anticipates a rehabilitation of imaginative literature: 'Die Geschichten, die wirklich passieren, kommen mir am lächerlichsten vor [. . .] Die Realität? O Mann [. . .] was haben wir da? [. . .] Vielleicht ist das krank. Aber sind wir nicht spätestens dann am Ende, wenn alles erklärt ist, wenn das letzte Geheimnis aus uns rausgewaschen ist wie ein Dreck?'[33]

Peter Handke's earliest texts indicated his scepticism towards the concept of a self-determining subject. *Selbstbezichtigung* (1966) assaults the assumption that saying 'I' is a criterion of selfhood. Almost every sentence in its twenty-two pages begins 'Ich', yet the 'Ich' produces only grammatical patterns void of identity. In *Kaspar* (1967) Handke shows how an 'individual' is created out of determinist building-blocks of language provided by social rule systems. These texts arguably address the problem of the loss of subjective identity more intensively than the first person statements in documentary texts which, concentrating on social existence, regard the subjective integrity of the statement-maker as unproblematic. In *Das Gewicht der Welt* (1977) Handke rejects all the 'Universal-Pictures', the social, political, psychological, ontological constructs that preform perception. He seeks to empty himself of this other-determined subjectivity by an 'unmittelbare, simultan festgehaltene

---

32. Reinbek, 1976, pp. 19 and 11 respectively.
33. Ibid., p. 26.

Reportage', a kind of automatic writing, in order to recover 'die vergessene, anonyme Sprache aller Menschen'.[34] Thus *Das Gewicht der Welt* aims in its self-imposed poetological severity to be neither an autobiography nor a fiction. But does this 'anonyme Sprache' exist outside the social and psychological determinants Handke has always loathed? Isn't this like the belief that children brought up in total isolation would, suddenly and perfectly, begin to speak the original language?

In Handke's *Die Stunde der wahren Empfindung* (1975) a random trio of objects — a leaf, a fragment of mirror, a hairslide — because it does not have 'meaning' (a construction which robs the individual of the immediacy of experience), floods Keuschnig, alienated by and from normality, with a sense of authentic existence: he feels 'eine hilflose Zuneigung zu allen [. . .] Ich habe eine Zukunft! dachte er triumphierend [. . .] ich kann mich ändern'.[35] Such passages remind us that Handke is not a relentless chronicler of negativity. But the experience of harmony and elation is not generated by Keuschnig's activity, but is passive, arbitrary, momentary: a religious revelation without a religion.

Botho Strauß's work up to and including *Rumor* (1980) shows the subject as profoundly vulnerable and in a state of dissolution. 'Ich, das Einzelwesen, vermehre mich, im Laufe meiner Auflösung, in grenzenloser Zellteilung', observes the narrator in 'Marlenes Schwester'.[36] In 'Theorie der Drohung' (1974) the narrator, instead of preserving his threatened identity by the act of writing, discovers that his every word is a plagiarism, and disintegrates into a 'Null-Person'. Schroubek writes in *Die Widmung* (1977): 'Das Leben hat, nach der Niederwerfung des Subjekts, damit begonnen, seinen Rest selber zu schreiben'.[37] Moreover, self-scrutiny destroys the sense of the self as an entity, and in *Die Widmung* Strauß rejects the suggestion that it is escapist: it is a gruesome process of mutilation that robs the self of its last refuge.[38] In *Rumor* biological as well as social determinisms reduce the 'teures Subjekt der Weltgeschichte, heiliges Ich' to a husk, 'überfüllt mit Mikrotexten, Codes und Alphabeten, Sprache überall und lauter Gesetzesherrschaft und fremde Ordnungen'.[39]

34. Salzburg, 1977, pp. 34 and 88.
35. Frankfurt on Main, 1975, pp. 81–3. See Michael Linstead's chapter on Handke, pp. 256–8 for further discussion of *Die Stunde der wahren Empfindung*.
36. Munich, 1974, p. 21.
37. Munich, 1979, p. 20.
38. Ibid., pp. 98–9.
39. Munich, 1980, pp. 144–5.

Yet recalling Enzensberger's assertion that literature is not politics, we should remember that literary portrayals of successful self-assertion are no substitute for self-assertion in society. Textual models for action may become reassurances that its necessity is not so urgent, whereas unbroken negativity in the text may generate a rage for change. This creates two unexpected affinities: on the one hand between documentary indictments of capitalistic exploitation and the fiction of radical negative subjectivity; on the other, between the texts of subjective self-assertion and the tradition — religious, bourgeois or socialist realist — of 'Erbauungsliteratur'. The political posture of a literary text is not a sufficient measure of its political quality. The distinction that suggests itself between 'Neue Subjektivität' as a politically progressive synthesis of self and social, therefore 'good', and 'Neue Innerlichkeit' as a reactionary inwardness, therefore 'bad', is misleading.

Strauß follows Adorno's argument that since the individual subject is an involuntary microcosm of social forces, then to insist, as the Enlightenment tradition does, on the integrity and capacity for self-determination of the individual is to cement the very conditions which block these aspirations. Strauß's icy negation can be a productive contrast to the self-satisfaction of many texts of 'Neue Subjektivität'. But he seems unwilling to accept that human identity is not static but dynamic; it is produced and preserved in interaction with other subjects and with social forces: the argument of the texts of Walser and Kroetz. Strauß's work *is* typical of much literature of 'Neue Subjektivität' in its negative image not only of political commitment but also of personal relationships.[40] This isolation hastens the decay of the subject threatened by outside pressures. Because Strauß, like Born or Handke, rejects the oppressive abstractions that make even subjective experience other-determined, he turns elsewhere for meaning. In this quest, 'Schrift' (*Die Widmung*) takes on quasi-mystical importance, displacing concrete action in the material world, a neo-Romantic position that becomes increasingly prominent in Strauß's work, as in that of Handke.

Women's writing in the 1970s developed out of 'Neue Subjektivität' in a double sense.[41] The Student Movement's own slogan

40. See: Volker Hage, 'Das Ende der Beziehungen. Über den Zustand der Liebe in neueren Roman und Erzählungen'; Hiltrud Gnüg, 'Schlechte Zeit für Liebe — Zeit für bessere Liebe? Das Thema Partnerbeziehungen in der gegenwärtigen Lyrik', in Michael Zeller (ed.), *Aufbrüche: Abschiede. Studien zur deutschen Literatur seit 1968*, Stuttgart, 1979, pp. 14–25 and 26–39 respectively.
41. For a fuller discussion of women's writing see Juliet Wigmore's chapter in this volume, pp. 88–107.

that the private is the political raised women's awareness of sexist structures in society that were ignored by orthodox left analysis. Women have played a key role in redefining, and widening the social base of, alternative politics (see e.g. Barbara Sichtermann, *Weiblichkeit. Zur Politik des Privaten*, 1983). But in the course of the 1970s much women's writing moved away from autobiography (Karin Struck, *Klassenliebe*, 1973), exemplary self-assertions (Verena Stefan, *Häutungen*, 1975) and emancipatory role models (Margot Schröder, *Der Schlachter empfiehlt immer noch Herz*, 1976). The Enlightenment goal of autonomous subjective identity was no longer sought but rejected as a patriarchal exclusion of the female.[42] The resulting, radically self-dissective subjectivity of some women's writing in the early 1980s (e.g. Anne Duden, *Übergang*, 1982) is close to that of Strauß. Both Strauß and the feminists have been significantly influenced by the post-Marxist amalgam of structuralism and psychoanalysis of French writers such as Foucault, Lacan and Derrida (and, in the case of the feminists, Cixous and Irigaray). In both cases, the intense concern with subjective identity in the 1970s has produced an awareness of this identity's dissolution and, as a result, variants of what one might call a critical narcissism: rather than into a limpid pool, Narcissus/a squints anxiously, distrustfully or playfully into a kaleidoscopic swirl of mirrors.

The many continuities (which does not mean identities) between 'Neue Subjektivität' and the 1960s may suggest that the real 'Tendenzwende' in 1970s literature was not the revival of subjectivity, but the relegitimation of invention, literary form and tradition which came later in the decade and in the 1980s. Wallraff's claim in 1968 that 'die genau beobachtete und registrierte Wirklichkeit ist immer phantastischer und spannender als die kühnste Phantasie eines Schriftstellers'[43] is in some ways nearer to the everyday authenticity of many 1970s texts than the latter are to the labyrinthine literary games of, say, Strauß's *Der junge Mann* (1984).

In 1981 Harald Hartung observed a 'Wiederkehr der Formen' as a result of dissatisfaction with the rootlessness, formlessness and listlessness of 1970s 'Parlandopoesie'. He quotes Michael Butor, who sees rhyme's value as forcing an idea 'eine Richtung zu suchen, die er niemals selbständig gewählt haben würde'.[44] The 'Alltagslyriker' of the 1970s distrusted form for precisely this reason; but as the

42. See Sigrid Weigel, *Die Stimme der Medusa*, Dülmen, 1987, Chapter 4: 'Von der "neuen Subjektivität" zur Subjektkritik'.
43. Quoted in Volker Hage, *Die Wiederkehr des Erzählers*, Frankfurt on Main, Berlin and Vienna, 1982, p. 8.
44. *Deutsche Lyrik seit 1965*, Munich, 1985, pp. 86–7.

1980s approached, they too rediscovered the constructive rather than constraining potential of form (e.g. Theobaldy, *Drinks*, 1979/1984; *Die Sommertour*, 1983). Literary traditions, which, as Enzensberger had predicted, were hard to kill off, were once more invoked. The crisis of authorial self-confidence in the ability to represent the world in literature, which both the reliance on documents and its apparent opposite, the retreat to an individual perspective, reflect (see Kurt Batt, *Die Exekution des Erzählers*, Frankfurt on Main, 1974), has provoked a reaction: the neo-Romantic return in the 1980s of attempts to transcend reality by aestheticising it, seen in the influence of Novalis on Strauß and Handke, and the return of the author (or the text) as a visionary force with the power to create counter-worlds. This 'resublimation' of the art 'desublimated' in the 1960s might seem to be a contribution to Schneider's 'Mobilisierung der Wünsche gegen die Wirklichkeit', which would be yet another hidden continuity with the 1960s. But the overall sense is rather one of immobilisation, of an anchoring of the desire within the hermetic world of the text.

The assertive self-confidence of the 1960s and its iconoclastic rejection — apparently subversive, always ambiguous — of traditional values manifested itself in several ways in the 1970s. Firstly, revived individualism and disillusion with collective paths to betterment led to the grasping hedonism of the 1980s yuppie. The right reoriented itself towards an unscrupulous post-industrial future, leaving the traditional left to the dogmas of its history or a conservative defence of hard-won social achievements. Secondly, partly from this same disillusion of 1960s hopes for a transformed world, partly from a more absolute sense of ineradicable antagonism between the self and the social, came the neo-Romantic pessimism of another failed Enlightenment. Thirdly, the political analysis of the contradictions of advanced capitalism in the 1960s, combined in the 1970s with the reassertion of the needs of the individual and the blunting of more extreme revolutionary hopes, also produced the more subtle grasp of the dialectics both of theory and practice and of subjective and objective needs and experiences, which characterises the alternative politics of the 1980s compared with the 1960s. The effects of literature are almost never quantifiable; but in the West German context the interrelated if often mutually antagonistic literary developments of the 1970s which bear the collective name 'Neue Subjektivität' could be seen as an important step in all three of these processes.

Suggested Further Reading

Peter Beicken, '"Neue Subjektivität". Zur Prosa der siebziger Jahre', in P.M. Lützeler and E. Schwarz, *Deutsche Literatur in der Bundesrepublik seit 1965*, Königstein, 1980, pp. 164–81

Hiltrud Gnüg, 'Was heißt "Neue Subjektivität"?', *Merkur* 356, 1978, pp. 60–75

Gerhard vom Hofe and Peter Pfaff, *Das Elend des Polyphem. Zum Thema der Subjektivität bei Thomas Berhnhard, Peter Handke, Wolfgang Koeppen und Botho Strauß*, Königstein, 1980

Ursula Reinhold and Grazyna Szarszewka-Kühl, 'Thesen zur Prosa-Entwicklung der siebziger Jahre in der BRD', *Weimarer Beiträge* 29, 1983, 4, pp. 625–37

Karen Ruoff, 'Rückblick auf die Wende zur "Neuen Subjektivität"', *Argument* 142, 1983, pp. 802–20

Michael Schneider, *Den Kopf verkehrt aufgesetzt, oder die melancholische Linke*, Darmstadt and Neuwied, 1981

Hinrich Seeba, 'Persönliches Engagement: Zur Autorenpoetik der siebziger Jahre', *Monatshefte* 73, 1981, 2, pp. 140–54

Hans-Gerhard Winter, 'Von der Dokumentarliteratur zur "neuen Subjektivität": Anmerkungen zur westdeutschen Literatur der siebziger Jahre', *seminar* 17, 1981, 2, pp. 99–113

ANTHONY WAINE

Recent German Writing and the Influence of Popular Culture

In a room littered with gin, wine and beer bottles, amongst which are also strewn records and discarded articles of clothing, a young writer and his girlfriend survey the blood-spattered furniture and carpets after their friends have just departed for hospital following a fight in which the girl has had her nose broken by her partner. We might expect the young writer and his girlfriend to be sobered by this spectacle. The reverse happens. They are 'turned on'. They begin fighting too, but fortunately they soon trade books rather than punches, as the following stage direction describes:

> BIRGIT: Geh jetzt hör auf . . . (Er boxt noch einmal fester, sie kratzt ihn, er schlägt sie, daß sie aufs Bett fällt, sie wirft ihm Bücher nach, er wirft Bücher zurück, es kommt zu einer regelrechten Bücherschlacht, bei der beide langsam immer *fröhlicher* werden. Bevor sie werfen, schreien sie die Autoren der Bücher. Also z.B.: Scheiß-Dürrenmatt, Scheiß-Pinter, Scheiß-Albee, Scheiß-Walser, Scheiß-Grass, dann fröhlicher werdend: Scheiß-Ionesco, Scheiß-Audiberti, Scheiß-Adamov, Scheiß-Genet, Scheiß-Anouilh, Scheiß-Beckett . . . (beide lachen schon) jetzt eine abschliessende Balgerei mit Klassikern: Scheiß-Goethe, Scheiß-Schiller . . . etc. -Regie).[1]

The scene is from the play *Magic Afternoon* by the Austrian Wolfgang Bauer (born 1941). The book fight serves to highlight comically yet realistically the sea-change occurring in German-speaking literature during the late 1960s. A new generation, whose dates of birth invariably fall between 1940 and 1948, surfaces declaring mock war not only against the long since departed symbols of high culture (Goethe, Schiller) but also on the still living, radical spirits of the European avant-garde. The modernist pantheon is well and truly desecrated.

What concerns us here is less why the desecration takes place — generational conflict and the climate of cultural revolt largely

---

1. Wolfgang Bauer, *Magic Afternoon. Change. Party for Six*, Cologne, 1972, pp. 28–9.

account for that — rather with what and with whom the pantheon is refurnished and repopulated. If Bauer is any guide, then it is being restocked with the paraphernalia and the ideology, or better still the anti-ideology of popular culture. But obviously it is not the popular culture associated for example with his fellow countrymen of the previous century, Raimund and Nestroy, whose plays fed on the local and national customs, rituals and myths of their Austrian homeland. As his choice of an English title intimates, Bauer is inspired by the lifestyle and the commercial, synthetic products imported from post-war urban British and American mass culture. Throughout this musical drama not a single record selected by the music-crazy characters is by a German-speaking artist or group. Wilson Pickett, The Rolling Stones and of course The Beatles provide the necessary ambience for a play whose setting and characters, as Wolfram Buddecke and Helmut Fuhrmann have rightly pointed out, echo the mood of The Kinks' evocative 'Sunny Afternoon'.[2]

Whilst it is indeed a sunny afternoon outside, Bauer's four young people, Charly, Birgit, Joe and Monika, typically choose to spend their leisure time indoors. Their quest is an internal one, as the ironic title cryptically suggests. The word 'magic' alludes to the state induced in the two men as they get high after smoking marijuana, whilst listening to the drug-inspired LP of The Beatles, *Sgt. Pepper's Lonely Hearts Club Band*. The drug culture of the late 1960s, especially because of its associations with rock music, is a ubiquitous theme of that growing corpus of serious German writing which has been steeped in modern international popular traditions. However, in this respect too Bauer's drama deserves our attention. Written against the backdrop of the 'swinging sixties', with the revolution in consciousness promulgated by academics, writers and rock-stars alike on both sides of the Atlantic, Bauer's message is decidedly cautionary. Whilst under the influence of the drug Charly and Joe sexually taunt and attempt to rape Birgit. She defends herself by fatally stabbing Joe. The play's title thus acquires a tragically ironic ring. The new culture, with which Bauer certainly identifies very closely, promises to magically transform the existence of a great many people but actually enslaves and deceives. It is illusory and escapist.

The fact is evident from his characters' discussions about what to do should they leave the flat. Characteristically it is the cinema which receives the most serious consideration:

2. Wolfram Buddecke and Helmut Fuhrmann, *Das deutschsprachige Drama seit 1945*, Munich, 1981, p. 429.

JOE: Im Kino is nix . . . außerdem mag i gar net ins Kino gehn heute . . .
BIRGIT: Im Kino ist überhaupt nichts.
CHARLY: Nein . . . ich hab alles durchgschaut . . . nichts, nicht einmal ein schlechter Film.
BIRGIT: Höchstens 'Der Perser und die Schwedin'. Aber das is ja auch nix.
JOE: Ich hab jetzt in Wien an herrlichen 'Herkules'-Film gsehn . . . 'Herkules und die Vampire' . . .
CHARLY: Kenn ich . . . den war ich vor zwei Jahren mit dem Pflegerl . . . der is gigantisch.[3]

Bauer is not satirically denigrating here or elsewhere in the play the cultural tastes *per se* of his bohemian clique, but rather he is critically demasking the clique's psychological dependency on the synthetic entertainment industry and the consumer society.

Paradoxically, whilst his fictional characters consume and are consumed by the products and trappings of mass culture, Bauer the playwright provides a model lesson in how to exploit this domain for positive artistic purposes. In particular his deployment of music, as his Graz friend and colleague, Peter Handke has noted,[4] is imaginative and utterly germane. It is used to underscore the highpoints and turning-points of the action as well as to create special mood effects. In addition, the records enable the characters to communicate deeply rooted emotions and attitudes, of which they are often only half aware. Early on in the play Birgit plays 'Penny Lane', whimsical, melodic with a soupcon of nostalgia for a lost childhood paradise. As the play progresses and the characters regress, their essential emotional emptiness becomes manifest and the music played, chosen this time by Charly, is 'Sgt. Pepper's Lonely Hearts Club Band'. In the latter half of the play, in order to evoke the male cynicism and chauvinism displayed towards both Monika (the girl with the broken nose) and Birgit, Bauer has Joe put on The Stones' 'Back Street Girl' whose refrain is the selfish and degrading 'Don't' want you part of my world/Just want you to be my back street girl'. After her killing of Joe the strangely becalmed Birgit chooses another record by The Stones, 'Play with Fire', with its coolly suppressed aggressiveness and muted sexuality.

Bauer not only used the music of the times to good dramatic effect and to appeal — if that was his intention — to the popular imagination. He also reproduced the hip, flippant conversational style of young people, which was to be repeated so skilfully in another play,

3. *Magic Afternoon*, pp. 19–20.
4. Quoted in Otto F. Riewoldt, 'Magic Wolfi oder "They never come back"', in H.L. Arnold (ed.), *Text und Kritik 59*, Munich, 1978, p. 40.

Die neuen Leiden des jungen W. by Ulrich Plenzdorf, a few years later in 1973. Like Plenzdorf's East German drop-out Edgar Wibeau, Bauer's slightly older clique of non-conformists are as concerned with style of living, fashions and physical appearances — three further by-products of contemporary mass culture — as he is. Edgar's fetish with genuine American jeans is the most overt expression of this. And just as Plenzdorf's play took the West German stage by storm, Bauer's created a furore and achieved popular notoriety.[5] In the 1969–70 theatre season *Magic Afternoon* became the second most performed play after Dürrenmatt's *Play Strindberg*, and in the period 1964–74 it shared fourth place with Handke's *Kaspar* (1967) in the table of the most frequently staged plays in the German-speaking world. Undoubtedly part of its success was also due to its avoidance of the political moralising — socially legitimate as this undoubtedly was — prevalent in the German theatre of the 1960s, which possibly had the effect of didactic overkill on the younger members of audiences. In contrast *Magic Afternoon* gave them their world, adroitly stylised, with its euphorias, its enticing superficialities and, crucially, its fatally dangerous moral vacuums.

Unfortunately, though perhaps not surprisingly in view of the background and tastes of much of the academic and cultural establishment, Bauer's style and his intentions have been sarcastically belittled and dismissed with remarks such as 'despite its naturalism, the action is pure melodrama'[6] and: 'What Bauer does offer the middle-aged, middle-class theatre-goer is the titillation of partaking vicariously in the obscene and callous world of dilettante drop-outs together with the reassurance of the evil effects of cannabis and social non-conformity. No wonder Bauer is so popular in the municipal theatres of Western Germany'.[7]

Bauer's play did indeed focus the public's and the critics' minds on the impact of the new, ephemeral values, habits and fashions on the mentality of the 1960s generation, albeit with the focus limited to the microcosm of a clique of bohemian young provincial Austrians imbibing the very latest offerings from the cornucopia of popular culture. His West German counterpart, Rolf Dieter Brinkmann (born in 1940), shares the same tastes but paints on a much broader canvas, so that the various historical layers of popular culture and its rapport with other social phenomena are apparent. The scope of Brinkmann's vision is well illustrated in a passage about London, which will be considered shortly. His major breakthrough as a

5. See Dieter Baacke, ibid., pp. 35–7.
6. Michael Patterson, *German Theatre Today*, London, 1976, p. 93.
7. Ibid., p. 94.

visionary and campaigner came with the publication provocatively entitled ACID at the turn of the decade, i.e. at almost the same time as *Magic Afternoon*'s appearance. Within the space of barely six years Brinkmann became a legendary and controversial figure who was successfully reconciling the worlds of so-called low and high culture to a degree which arguably only his fellow poet Wolf Wondratschek has so far achieved. A fatal accident involving a car in Westbourne Grove, London, in May 1975 tragically cut short Brinkmann's mission.[8]

ACID was the first major stage in this mission, tantamount to the westernising of German cultural life. It was originally conceived as a purely literary anthology, designed to introduce West German readers to that sphere of contemporary American literature which had grown both in size and import since the advent of the Beat writers in the early 1950s and now embraced 'sowohl den Trivialbereich wie den hochkulturellen [. . .] und für die Begriffe wie Pop oder Sub-Kultur nicht ausreichen'.[9] The resultant publication resembled more a magazine, containing poems, short stories, essays by the likes of Leslie Fiedler and William Burroughs, but also illustrations from underground periodicals and comics with sexually explicit photos and graphics particularly prominent, though many are intended more to amuse than to shock, a fact to which many of its critics seemed oblivious. Critics of both the Establishment and the anti-Establishment were quick to show their dissent and distaste. Martin Walser was stung into a political attack against the claims made by some of its contributors that drugs, in particular LSD, could change the world.[10] Others took exception more to the alleged pornographic contents and literary tastelessness. Hermand[11] and Kurz[12] are two such critics who can barely control their puritanical feelings of nausea at the kind of wares being plied by Rygulla and Brinkmann.

Perhaps Hermand and Kurz were really afraid of the subversiveness of the enterprise through which the hegemony of their bourgeois, elitist and essentially verbal culture would be eaten away by

8. See Wondratschek's tribute to his fellow poet 'Er war too much für Euch, Leute', *Chuck's Zimmer*, Munich, 1981, pp. 95–9.
9. R.D. Brinkmann and R.-R. Rygulla (eds.), ACID. *Neue amerikanische Szene*, Reinbek, 1983, p. 417.
10. Martin Walser, 'Über die neueste Stimmung im Westen', *Wie und wovon handelt Literatur*, Frankfurt on Main, 1973, pp. 7–41.
11. Jost Hermand, 'Pop oder die These vom Ende der Kunst', in M. Durzak (ed.), *Die deutsche Literatur der Gegenwart*, Stuttgart, 1971, pp. 285–99.
12. Paul Konrad Kurz, 'Beat-Pop-Underground', *Über moderne Literatur*, vol. 3, Frankfurt on Main, 1971, pp. 233–79.

the corrosive, acid-like power of the underground's art and artefacts. Brinkmann's opening remarks in his accompanying essay to ACID convey his belief that this is already happening:

> Bekannte literarische Vorstellungsmuster verwischen sich: der Raum dehnt sich aus, veränderte Dimensionen des Bewußtseins. Das Rück-koppelungssystem der Wörter, das in gewohnten grammatikalischen Ordnungen wirksam ist, entspricht längst nicht mehr tagtäglich zu machender sinnlicher Erfahrung, Jerry Lee Lewis über Klaviertasten gebeugt — ein altes Photo, überlagert von Vorstellungen heute mit Bildern von morgen vermischt mit dem schon entfernten Rock Bill Haleys and his Comets in den Echokammern des 'Grauen Raums' . . .[13]

How heretical of Brinkmann to mention the names of Jerry Lee Lewis and Bill Haley in the opening sentences of an essay — and a German one at that — on culture and aesthetics! But he is not doing so in order merely to provoke. He sincerely believes that the modern consciousness is so impregnated with 'Bilder' and 'Vorstellungen' (two of his favourite concepts) from the world of advertising, cartoons, magazines, postcards, posters, television, films, record sleeves and supermarket display signs that it is not merely impossible but unrealistic for any writer to try to maintain in his works a segregation between socio-cultural spheres or to filter out those elements that have not yet been intellectually sanctioned. He characterises the arbiters of such intellectual taste as being possessed of an 'akademisiertes Bewußtsein, das nur noch auf Wörter (Begriffe) zu reagieren versteht'.[14]

Brinkmann's hopes, nourished by the counter-culture's utopian tendencies, of displacing the 'akademisiertes Bewußtsein' proved short-lived. For both personal and political reasons the 1970s brought Brinkmann back down to reality. The sense of being part of a new class, transcending traditional divisions, based on age, life-style and a common democratised culture, gave way to a mood of dejection and rejection. This mood predominated in his last pub-lished collection of poems before his death entitled *Westwärts 1&2* (1975). His journeying westwards, which had been a principal feature of his mission to make himself and his fellow countrymen accept their westernised identity, continues but with a more critical and ironic detachment than hitherto. What is especially pronounced is his reassessment of some of the erstwhile symbols and arenas of popular culture, which are, however, refracted through a mind

13. ACID, p. 381.
14. Ibid., p. 385.

sensitised by a life-long exposure to that culture.

In his remarkable epic poem 'Einige sehr populäre Songs' one passage, describing an evening in London, vividly exemplifies this. It occurs quite suddenly in the course of an imagined recreation of Eva Braun's private life:

> ... Eva Braun, Milch

Glasfenster, Portale, Koma in einem schwedischen
Hotelzimmer, Spritzen ins Bein überm Socken
Halter. Nun werfen die Rechenmaschinen Knochen
in die Luft, Stanley Kubrik der Filmtrick ist

durchschaut trotz vier Kanalstereogeräuschen im
roten Plüschkino Sohos, wo ich eines regnerischen
Abends bin, allein durch London gehend, still,
zusammengefaßt in dem hellgrauen, windigen

Februarabend, zerfallenes London, elegische
Westendstraßen, elegische Reklamen, elegische
Theatergebäude und Stripteaseclubs, elegische
dreckige Buchläden im abgelagerten

trüben Staub ...

> ... Eva Braun, was sagtest du in dem
> Moment,

als das Foto gemacht wurde? Nach dem Film krieche
ich fröstelnd unter die dünne Decke eines billigen
Hotels in Bayswater, Haltestelle Odeon, das Monster
Viertel Londons, zerfallene Hinterhöfe, verscharrte

Körper, der gasbeheizte Kamin wärmt nicht, die
Zimmertapete ist fleckig, ich lese noch ein
Gedicht von Frank O'Hara und W.C. Williams, ich
trinke den Rest kalt gewordenen Kaffees aus dem

Pappbecher, der auf dem Marmor über dem Kamin
steht, ich bin allein in diesen amerikanischen
Gedichten und schaue mich darin um inmitten dieser
Londonnacht, gelbe Nebelbeleuchtung an den Straßen

Rändern, victorianische Monstersäulen und Portale
die ganze Straße entlang, Fenster mit Pappe davor,
Gardinenfetzen, und plötzlich, in der Stille, total
irrsinnig, erinnere ich mich an das Pausenzeichen

der BBC im Radio eines Morgens im Krieg. Ich
erinnere mich an die Nachkriegsschokolade der
englischen Soldaten, blaue Pflaumen an einem
Karren, der durch die Hinterhöfe geschoben wurde,

Straußwalzer, einen dunklen Kinoraum und Krieg.

Ein Knochen, in die Luft geworfen, ein Totschläger
Werkzeug auf der weißen Leinwand des Gedächtnisses,
ein flimmernder Schatten, hinter Zierblumen versteckt . . .[15]

In his introduction to *Westwärts 1&2* Brinkmann confessed: 'Ich
hätte gern viele Gedichte so einfach geschrieben wie Songs. Leider
kann ich nicht Gitarre spielen, ich kann nur Schreibmaschine
schreiben, dazu nur stotternd, mit zwei Fingern. Vielleicht ist mir
manchmal gelungen, die Gedichte einfach genug zu machen, wie
Songs, wie eine Tür aufmachen, aus der Sprache und den Festle-
gungen raus'.[16] The above extract from 'Einige sehr populäre Songs'
confirms that Brinkmann has indeed fused concrete, unpretentious
diction with the fluidity of a popular song. In fact just a few stanzas
later the narrator actually refers to 'dieses Rock 'n' Roll Lied über
euren/furchtbaren Wahnsinn, Eva Braun'. The apostrophising of
Hitler's mistress in this manner is indicative of that grotesque
collision of styles, subjects and cultures which lies at the heart of
Brinkmann's experience of contemporary European history. A modern American musical tradition is hijacked to convey a fantasy about
a German woman sexually involved with the leader of the Third
Reich. Moreover this popular medium, normally given to expressing
a younger generation's sense of joy, is turned to spotlight an older
generation's orgy of militarism and genocide. Historical reflections
are triggered off by the media's visual trivia such as a magazine
photograph. Western 'civilisation', not the perverted mind of a poet,
has brought about this schizophrenic mélange, part tragic, part
comical.

Tragedy and comedy are never very far apart either when the
narrator quoted in the extract moves through London's West End as
part of his cultural voyage westwards. Having just seen Stanley
Kubrick's science-fiction fantasy *2001: A Space Odyssey* he walks
along through the dark, wintry streets of Soho, which present a total
contrast to the summery images of London broadcast throughout
the western world in the seemingly dim and distant 'swinging
sixties'. That decade's magical aura is nowhere discernible in the
dozen stanzas describing his sojourn. On the contrary it is emphatically 'zerfallenes London', and as he scans the vista of urban
popular culture the obsessively repeated 'elegisch' reinforces the
sense of a bygone era. Such a feeling is strengthened by his explicit
reference to the 'victorianische' pillars and portals.

Indeed the whole atmosphere is reminiscent of some nineteenth-

15. Rolf Dieter Brinkmann, *Westwärts 1 & 2*, Reinbek, 1975, pp. 135–7.
16. Ibid., p. 7.

century melodrama or of a black and white horror movie set in fog-enshrouded, mid-winter London, as he talks of the hotel being in the 'Monster Viertel' and of the 'gelbe Nebelbeleuchtung' and 'Monstersäulen'. The choice of images is revealing. The combination of 'Nebel' and 'Beleuchtung' suggests associations with the lighting effects for the set of a popular movie, whilst the 'Monstersäulen und Portale' have connotations of grotesquely artificial stage scenery. It is quite appropriate therefore that he alludes to the 'weiße[n] Leinwand des Gedächtnisses' a little later, as if he were saying that the mind has been so conditioned by its exposure to the mass media, like the cinema, that it has actually become part of the machinery of that industry — echoes of Enzensberger's 'Bewußtseins-Industrie'! — and seemingly it registers reality with the aid of stockpiled images.

It is therefore totally in keeping with Brinkmann's imagination, filled with popular fantasies, that a large chunk of this section of 'Einige sehr populäre Songs' (entitled parodistically 'Historie') results from his obsessively curious response to the mass-produced photographic image of Eva Braun he comes across. Equally it is testimony to Brinkmann's realism that he should imply through this quasi-sensationalist investigation into German 'Historie' that for a member of his generation fascism is often no more than an association with some sepia photograph in a mass circulation magazine or newspaper. It does not matter how banal, trivial or superficial the objects are which captivate the imagination — 'kitschig und nachkoloriert' is how he describes the Eva Braun photo elsewhere — he is committed to acknowledging their impact on his audio-visually 'colonised' imagination.

The degree to which this colonisation has permeated his whole being is rendered visible by his choosing to read, alone in his hotel room, poems by two contemporary American writers, W.C. Williams and Frank O'Hara (a collection of whose poetry incidentally Brinkmann had introduced to German readers in the late 1960s). A West German alone in the heart of London finding solace in the works of two American poets! The message is ambivalent. It could be construed as one of deracination. Alternatively, however, it could also signify the narrator's effective westernisation. The lines following on from this particular image, and communicating the narrator's remarkable eureka-like flash of awareness may offer the key to the origins of this colonisation of consciousness: 'und plötzlich, in der Stille, total/irrsinnig, erinnere ich mich an das Pausenzeichen der BBC im Radio eines Morgens im Krieg. Ich/erinnere mich an die Nachkriegsschokolade der/englischen Soldaten'. These lines poignantly provide the historical perspective on Brinkmann's generation. Some of their most deeply rooted and decisive social influences were those transmitted at first intangibly and then physically by an alien culture seeking to penetrate the hearts and minds of a nation being prepared for a new identity.

If Brinkmann's contextualisation of this experience strikes the reader as almost incidental and fragmentary, the very same phenomenon is subjected to in-depth psychological and historical investigation in one of the bestselling novels of the 1970s, *Hubert oder Die Rückkehr nach Casablanca* (1978) by Peter Härtling. The author is something of an outsider in this chapter for his date of birth (1933) places him closer to the more established, so-called war generation of writers to which notably Grass, Lenz, Enzensberger and Walser belong. In fact the birthdate of the novel's anti-hero places him squarely within that generation. Hubert Windisch, we learn, first saw the light of day on 3 February 1923. Three experiences in particular determine Hubert's fate until the novel closes some forty years later in the mid-1960s. First is his early sense of alienation from and resentment towards his tyrannical, chauvinist father who, with the arrival of National Socialism, effectively leaves his family in order to pursue a career in the SS. The second decisive factor is his own experience, as a very young man, of military life and of the unheroic role he is assigned in the war as a small-time Nazi administrator in occupied Czechoslovakia. The third determinant, by no means unconnected to the first two, is his passion for the cinema.

From the outset the cinema provides escape from a reality that is unfulfilling, bewildering and often threatening: 'Hubert war sicher schon fünfzehn, als er, mehr aus Trotz gegen den Vater, sich an einem Nachmittag ein Billett kaufte und zum erstenmal in einer dieser schwachbeleuchteten Höhlen Unterschlupf suchte [. . .] Später wird das alles zu ihm gehören, eine zweite, bessere Heimat, Zuflucht, zahllose dämmrige Inseln, alle vertraut, keine der andern gleich.'[17] The cinema not only offers this womb-like atmosphere into which he can regress but also delivers roles to identify with and assume outside the cinema. The popular culture of the cinema comes to fulfil a compensatory function. Having been unable either to identify with the role model of the father, or to give free rein to his child's imagination through playing his own games, and having acquired a sense of male inadequacy in the virile world of Nazi ideology, he is given the welcome opportunity of assuming an ersatz

17. Peter Härtling, *Hubert oder Die Rückkehr nach Casablanca*, Frankfurt on Main, 1980, pp. 34–5.

identity via the stars of the German cinema such as Hans Albers.

With the ending of the war one might have expected the 21 – year-old Hubert's search for and indeed need for an ersatz identity to be extinguished. After all, the ideology which had so negatively influenced his childhood, adolescence, and early adulthood has disintegrated, whilst his father has committed suicide. Ironically, however, what his own society and culture had manifestly failed to do for Hubert's self-image, namely to instil in him a sense of belonging and a sense of being a real man, the American occupation of his country and in particular its film industry succeed in doing. Nor is it done against Hubert's better sense but with his full collaboration. He perceives in the Americans, for whom he works as a waiter in their officers' casino, an image of a more liberated mentality, reflected even in their physical deportment ('zuversichtlicher und leichter, als er es je gesehen hatte').[18] Speculatively he attributes this freer gait to their exposure to jazz, and in a passage of which Jack Kerouac would have been proud he muses:

> Gut, es könnte die Musik sein, die Schwarz wie Weiß so gehen machte, diese Musik, in der er sich badete, die in seinen Schlaf drang und selbst da noch an seinen Sehnen zupfte wie die Finger eines Gitarristen an den Saiten. Diese Musik, die frech war, die sich aus dem Abendland nichts machte, die zuschlug, pochte, patschte und umarmte, die einfach war und alle Schwierigkeiten aussprach, aussang, auskotzte.[19]

In the one throwaway remark 'die sich aus dem Abendland nichts machte' Härtling has provided a key insight (the antiquation of classical European culture) into his anti-hero's willing acceptance of his re-education. The next stage of Hubert's westernisation in this 'Bildungsroman' is his visit to an American cinema to see Humphrey Bogart in *The Maltese Falcon*, a film which marks an existential turning-point in Hubert's life: 'Verwirrt fühlte er, wie sein Gesicht auf das große, von Melancholie und Wissen erschöpfte Gesicht da oben antwortete, Falten spürbar wurden, Haut alterte. Auf Sam Spade hatte er gewartet'.[20] From then on begins a lifelong idolisation of Bogart which culminates in him seeing the actor in *Casablanca* in a small Parisian theatre-cinema.

The identification with Bogart proves to be a double-edged weapon for Hubert. It imbues him with that cool, manly confidence necessary to survive and succeed in the febrile climate of post-war

18. Ibid., p. 152.
19. Ibid., pp. 152–3.
20. Ibid., p. 158.

Germany. Yet imperceptibly it drives a wedge between Hubert and most of his fellow Germans as they eventually come to regard Hubert's Americanised image as eccentric and outmoded. When he does finally get to see *Casablanca* in the early 1960s it is a confrontation with his own identity crisis, which is the result of his early family circumstances but also the consequence of Germany's historical experiences in the first half of the century. Hubert's confusions and doubts are crystallised in Rick's lines from the film: 'Who are you, really? And what were you before? What did you do and what did you think?' These words, symptomatically left in their original English form, are chosen by Härtling to preface his novel. At the end of the film we learn: 'Sein Gesicht ist naß, er wischt die Tränen nicht ab'.[21]

The formidable power of popular culture, and in particular the cinema to mobilise our sentiments and manipulate our moods is also recognised by Wolf Wondratschek (born in 1943) in the poem 'Kino':

> Da sitz ich
> ganz hinten
> ganz allein
> im Kino
> und möcht gern
> tot sein
> mit Tränen
> in den Augen
> jahrelang
> mit beiden Armen
> auf der Lehne[22]

Despite its brevity and simplicity it is a deceptively complex and ambiguous poem.[23] Is he really alone (the only spectator) or does he simply feel alone in the cinema? Is the film still running or has the performance finished, and what kind of film is it anyway? Is the death wish real or is he being slightly self-mocking about the mood he is experiencing, that mood of self-indulgence in a sentimentality which records, films, so-called trivial literature can induce so freely? Has he entered into a fantasy world in which he has temporarily lost or suspended his own identity, like Härtling's cinema freak? Even the title is open-ended. The fact that he chooses to call his poem

21. Ibid., p. 211.
22. *Chuck's Zimmer*, p. 40.
23. Cf. Volker Hage's analysis of 'In den Autos' in W. Hinck (ed.), *Gedichte und Interpretationen 6*, Stuttgart, 1985, pp. 395–402.

'Kino' with no article, preposition or adjective may suggest that he wishes the experience to be viewed as more than an exceptional, unrepeatable moment in time, in contrast for example to Brink-mann's famous 'Einen jener klassischen', where we are given exact time, season, place and cause: 'Einen jener klassischen/schwarzen Tangos in Köln, Ende des/Monats August, da der Sommer schon/ganz verstaubt ist, kurz nach Laden/Schluß'.[24] By withholding all such realistic aids from the reader, Wondratschek may be saying that this experience is not only a familiar one for himself, but also for many cinema-goers.

If this is his intention, then the cinema gains a universal status similar to other institutions such as the Church. Indeed there is a temptation, prompted by the way in which the poet evokes the experience and the atmosphere, to view the cinema as the popular, modern surrogate for the Church. In both institutions the individual sits, passively and largely anonymously, confronted by icons, fables and myths. Death plays a central part in both the institutions' mythologies and consequently the individual is brought face to face not only with the fact of his own mortality but also with a sense of eternity. It is also true that the idea of worship is one common to both cinema and Church, though one of Wondratschek's most recent poems, 'Schluß mit dem Mist und den Mythen um Marylin Monroe' (1981), ends with a self-critical confession of the dangers of such idolatry: 'Sie war keine Göttin,/sie war Gift./ Und wir waren die Junkies,/die man im Kino/in der ersten Reihe trifft'.[25]

These lines do focus our attention on two further attributes of the cinema, which are also implicit in 'Kino', namely its power to spellbind and reduce us to near total dependency and its power to transform us into spectators or mere voyeurs. The final image 'mit beiden Armen auf der Lehne' reinforces the sense of inertia, as if the narrator has become an icon himself. Subconsciously it also comments on the individual in general in the age of technologically communicated mass culture. He is becoming increasingly sedentary, often with both arms resting on a chair or seat or table, whilst watching television, listening to the radio or listening to music through stereophonic headphones. Even live spectator sports are turning the comfort-seeking, affluent consumer into a static creature, whereas earlier in the period of more participatory, non-techno-logical culture he would be standing, moving, emotionally and physically involved in some mass spectacle or entertainment.

24. *Westwärts 1 & 2*, p. 25.
25. *Chuck's Zimmer*, p. 267.

Wondratschek's picture of this particular institution is the very opposite of a mass experience. The opening line 'Da sitz ich' not only emphasises the individual perspective but through the use of the detached 'da' (as opposed to 'hier') the individual appears to be almost placed outside himself, truly a spectator both of himself and of the film. The next two lines, containing the repetition of 'ganz', sharpen the focus on the individual who is detached ('hinten') but above all isolated ('allein'). We are reminded of the situation of the narrative 'I' in Brinkmann's poem, alone in the heart of London's entertainment quarter, and also of the self-ironising perspective on the individual and popular music in F.C. Delius's 'Einsamkeit eines alternden Stones-Fan' (1975) which describes the feelings of a Stones' fan purchasing their latest record in a 'Diskshop'(!), surrounded by the much younger clientele with 'Kopfhörer um die Ohren': 'Erinnerungen kommen hoch:/die Stones im Hyde-Park damals, da/war ich mittendrin, da hat sich was/bewegt mit uns. Jetzt/fühlt er sich beobachtet. Jetzt/fühlt er sich überlegen: die hängen hier rum,/ bei dieser immer schlechteren Musik,/leiden vielleicht an ihren Trips oder/an Langeweile, aber ich,/ . . . .'.[26]

All three poets are capturing an inescapable trait of modern popular culture, its ephemerality, which makes the individual acutely aware of his own transitoriness. Perhaps this explains Wondratschek's desire to indulge in and savour the mood evoked by the film for a short eternity and remain rooted to his seat for fear of losing the fleeting fantasy and returning to reality, a reality lonelier than that experienced in the cinema. Jörg Fauser (born in 1944) has critically identified the connection between metropolitan isolation and its antidote, metropolitan popular culture, when talking about his own experiences in essays or in novels such as *Alles wird gut* (1979). In one such essay he describes a visit to Berlin:

Ich wollte auch hinter Mauern nicht allein sein und ging wieder in die Bars, ins Getös, zu den Menschen. Die Menschen in Berlin konnten noch weniger als anderswo in der Stille leben, überall hämmerte der Rock, wimmerte der Jazz, seufzten die Orchester. Menschen meiner und der jüngeren Generation vermochten anscheinend nicht miteinander zu verkehren, ohne daß die Phone-Branche Kasse machte. Und dann die Kultur! Ohne Kultur ging es überhaupt nicht mehr ab. Irgendwann hatte ein Musikant gesungen: 'Everybody is in Show Biz', und ein anderer hatte, ebenso zynisch, sekundiert: 'Everybody is a Pop Star', und da hockten sie nun zusammen im Lärm und waren alle Stars und setzten

---

26. J. Theobaldy (ed.), *Und ich bewege mich doch. Gedichte vor und nach 1968*, Munich, 1977, p. 111. The poem is also discussed in Julian Sierra-Ballester and Anthony Stephens' chapter on 'West German Poetry of the 1970s', pp. 109f.

sich alle in Szene und wähnten sich als Künstler . . . Nirgendwo wurde
soviel kommuniziert wie in West-Berlin, nirgendwo soviel Stroh gedro-
schen und soviel heiße Luft erzeugt. Nirgendwo aber waren die Menschen einsamer, und jede Parole klang irgendwann wie ein Hilfeschrei aus
eisigster Verzweiflungskälte.[27]

Jörg Fauser and Wolf Wondratschek are in many ways archetypal
young writers of the 1970s. Having originally been politically active
in the late 1960s, both entered the 1970s suffering from the '68 Blues'
(Fauser), took drugs, savoured the twilight world of various German
cities, but also travelled abroad extensively. Both write knowl-
edgeably about sporting spectacles, in essays such as Fauser's
'Box-Abend' (1980) or in poems even, such as 'The Thrilla of
Manila' (1976), Wondratschek's tribute to Muhammad Ali. In
Hamburg's Reeperbahn district hangs an autographed photo of
Wondratschek in the bar of 'Die Ritze', one of Germany's most
famous training gymnasiums for boxers (echoes of Bertolt Brecht!).
Both writers have sought to reach wider audiences using popular
forms such as ballads, chansons, rock-'n'-roll songs, even to the
point of actually writing in the English language as Wondratschek
did or composing the texts for successful professional German rock
bands, which has been Fauser's metier for several years.

The response, especially in the case of Wondratschek, has been
extraordinary. Between 1974 and 1980 his four volumes of poetry,
now collected in one volume entitled *Chuck's Zimmer* (1981), sold
over 100,000 copies, making him easily Germany's best-selling poet
of the 1970s, and thereby gaining the grudging respect of Germany's
least swinging critics such as Marcel Reich-Ranicki. Many of Fauser's poems too, which invariably deal with aspects of popular culture
(e.g. 'Manchmal mit Lili Marlene' (1973), 'Amerika' (1979), 'Der
alte Mann und die See' (1977)) have appeared in anthologies of
German poetry of the 1970s, which have done much to establish the
genre of poetry as one which is read in circles far larger and more
heterogeneous than those traditionally associated with appreciating
what has often been, certainly in German culture, an esoteric
bastion of ART. Poets have become more reader-conscious and this
is undoubtedly attributable (as Brinkmann testifies) to the healthy
competition with and inspiration from the popular music industry,
the best of whose composers stand comparison with the leading
modern poets.[28]

27. Jörg Fauser, *Blues für Blondinen. Essays zur populären Kultur*, Frankfurt on Main,
   Berlin, Vienna, 1984, p. 15.
28. See V. Hage's introduction to *Lyrik für Leser. Deutsche Gedichte der siebziger Jahre*,
   Stuttgart, 1981, pp. 3–18.

Moving away from poetry to the field of semi-documentary fiction, another work betraying the imprint of popular culture, in particular the British variety, is *Der schöne Vogel Phönix*. It was written by a practically unknown man in his late twenties from Leer, East Friesland, called Jochen Schimmang. Appropriately and ironically subtitled *Erinnerungen eines Dreißigjährigen*, it was published in 1979 and promptly became a cult book, largely as a result of word of mouth. His first book, it achieved a circulation of 30,000 copies. In one sense it is a sequel to Härtling's *Hubert oder Die Rückkehr nach Casablanca*. If that novel explored the bedevilled search for identity of a member of the war generation and his poignant love affair with the products of the Hollywood dream factory, Schimmang's book traces the maturation process of one typical representative of the post-war generation and the key role played therein by various and at times unlikely heroes and idols of the British sporting and musical culture, which Schimmang has agreed (in a letter to the present writer, dated 23 November 1986) was tangibly close to the lives of his generation: 'Natürlich ist es zutreffend, daß mich — wie viele meiner Generation — die "populäre Kultur" aus dem anglo-amerikanischen Bereich stark beeinflußt hat. Mitte der 60er Jahre war dies beinahe unvermeidlich, denn die englische "Kulturrevolution" war uns doch näher als die chinesische. Es war also vor allem das Bild von "swinging London", das mich damals beeindruckte'.

Murnau, Schimmang's petit-bourgeois intellectual protagonist, therefore finds himself pulled in two directions by powerful forces at work in West German society in the second half of the 1960s. On the one hand he is fascinated by the glamour, the dynamism, the newness of mainly British youth culture with its appeal to that generation's healthy hedonism; on the other hand the social and political ferment at home and abroad attracts the young man's awakening moral conscience and political consciousness. In the story the categories are inseparable. The popular, the political and the private interweave and interact in the seismographic mind of Murnau, as the following memory recall shows: 'und im Mai, als ich wieder, diesmal mit frisch herausgenommenen Mandeln, im Lazarett lag, war Manchester United Europameister geworden, und in Frankreich gab es den größten Generalstreik der Geschichte'.[29] Nor is the reference to Manchester United purely arbitrary, for one of Murnau's earliest heroes was none other than the England midfield player, Nobby Stiles, who made his mark in England's World Cup triumph in 1966, when they beat West Germany in the Final. It is

29. Jochen Schimmang, *Der schöne Vogel Phönix*, Frankfurt on Main, 1979, p. 8.

ironic yet utterly credible that a young West German should identify
with and semi-idolise a member of England's football squad rather
than one of his own team's players (such as the redoubtable Uwe
Seeler). Just as Bogart's style instantly moved Härtling's Hubert, so
do the grit and the sense of purpose of a toothless, balding English
soccer player seep insidiously into Murnau's subconscious, so that
the latter is visited by Stiles in dreams at critical points in his
maturation. When Stiles' influence wanes, it is Mick Jagger's message at the 1969 Hyde Park concert to 'keep it cool' which Murnau
takes up as his new credo: 'Ich wechselte das Programm. Die
Kämpfe waren zu Ende. Nobby Stiles hatte abgedankt. Ab jetzt war
ich cool'.[30]

Still in search of the elusive identity which the semi-mythical
figures of 1960s mass culture had led him towards, Murnau's
journey takes him to Berlin, where he enrols as a student. His
conditioning there follows the well-trodden and well-documented
trail of reading and discussing Marx, Marcuse and Lenin, of exhaustive political involvement in left-wing groups and of the ensuing
disillusionment with the 'firm' as he cynically comes to regard his
'Kadergruppe' in the early 1970s. As his political ideals and his
private relationships both crumble, it is to the cinema that he
instinctively turns and where he finds his unhappy state of mind
mirrored in the anti-utopian images of films such as Visconti's *Death
in Venice*: 'Ich ging sehr viel ins Kino wie in meinen allerersten
Berliner Wochen. Sobald ich erst einmal das schützende Dunkel des
Kinosaals erreicht hatte und die Reklame vorüber war, fühlte ich
mich geborgen und bedauerte, daß diese Geborgenheit zeitlich
begrenzt war'.[31]

The words possess a déjà vu feel. They relate to the sentiments of
Wondratschek's poem and could have just as easily appeared in
Härtling's novel. They underline once again the central role which
institutions of popular culture have come to assume in the lives of all
members of modern society, whether intellectuals or not. This brief
survey of selected writers has served to refute any equation of
'popular' with 'unsophisticated', 'ordinary' or 'unimportant' cultural phenomena. We have seen rather that the term has acquired
the sense of 'widespread', 'universally respected' and 'democratic'
with regard to the status and power of those phenomena. To state
this fact in respect of the German-speaking intelligentsia's relationship to this area of culture is to identify a development of fairly

30. Ibid., p. 96.
31. Ibid., p. 265.

recent origin. Even a decade ago one would surely have judged it somewhat differently as Keith Bullivant did in his excellent account of 'Literature and Sub-culture'.[32] The chapter's title is symptomatic. At the time the prefix 'sub' seemed eminently apposite in as far as the new literature and the new culture were sub-terranean, sub-versive, yet also sub-ordinate, as if it were indeed a minority culture. His concluding remarks on ACID emphasise this: 'However, neither Brinkmann's own writings nor those of the American literature which he and his close associate, Ralf-Rainer Rygulla, have offered to the German public in translation (*Fuck you*, 1968, *Silver-screen*, 1969, and ACID, 1969) have done anything at all to make literature any less socially exclusive. They have themselves simply become fashionable in some trendy intellectual circles.'[33]

Modern German writing of the 1970s, of which this chapter provides a tiny yet hopefully representative sample, has come out of the ghetto of established, bourgeois, high culture and there is no likelihood of it returning. Equally it has also liberated itself from the ghetto of radical, avant-garde high culture, as the opening passage from Bauer's *Magic Afternoon* comically demonstrated, by admitting to and expressing those powerful forces which the products, the style and the ideology of late-twentieth-century popular culture have implanted and nurtured within us all. This culture is perceived as instinctual, dynamic, irrational, anti-intellectual. On the other hand, it can also be, as all these writers critically and self-critically remind us, escapist, ephemeral and anti-social. In this respect 'popular culture' is a misnomer. For, urbanised and synthetic as it is, it often appears as a privatising culture, i.e. one which both permits and compels the individual to experience it in a kind of isolation chamber. It is a retreat from social and cultural involvement, rather than a participation in it. Pre-industrial forms of this culture, and indeed earlier urban manifestations ('Biergarten', 'Kabarett', 'Laienspielgruppe', 'Gesangverein', Schalke 04 supporters' club et al) were participatory, communal cultural forms, sometimes institutionally formed and administered, but often organised in collaboration with the participant–spectators themselves. Even in the first half of this century the focal-point was as much local as national and expressed the cultural identity of a definable and structured community.

In a society such as Germany's, whose local and national cultural

32. R. Hinton Thomas and Keith Bullivant, *Literature in Upheaval. West German Writers and the Challenge of the 1960s*, Manchester, 1974, pp. 155–78.
33. Ibid., p. 157.

identity has been so fragmented, abused and manipulated from within and from outside, it is hardly surprising that its own indigenous traditions have been barely able to assert themselves against those imported from nations which not only happened to be the new military occupants but engaged in a policy of cultural imperialism using all the techniques and media of mass communication. The Americanisation of German-speaking Europe, towards which this Cool War was geared, was rejected or deliberately suppressed by writer after writer, intellectual after intellectual, up to the mid-1960s. But, despite Vietnam, it influenced a new generation that was much more responsive to its legacy. Furthermore, as this survey has illustrated, there was an equally vital Anglicisation process underway. Indeed, the much happier and productive co-existence of popular and highbrow culture in post-Osborne, post-Sillitoe, post-Lennon and -Jagger Britain undoubtedly served as a model for the likes of Brinkmann, Fauser and others who have spent long periods in this country, to emulate. Now, thanks to such developments, German-speaking literature is slowly forging an identity which is more westernised, more anti-intellectual, more anti-provincial, in short, more popular, than it may ever have been in its history.

Suggested Further Reading

Karl Heinz Bohrer, 'Die drei Kulturen', in J. Habermas (ed.), *Stichworte zur 'Geistigen Situation der Zeit'*, vol. 2, Frankfurt on Main, 1979, pp. 636–69

Iain Chambers, *Popular Culture. The Metropolitan Experience*, London and New York, 1986

Diedrich Diederichsen, Dick Hebdige, and Olaph-Dante Marx, *Schocker. Stile und Moden der Subkultur*, Reinbek, 1983

Diedrich Diederichsen, *Sexbeat. 1972 bix heute*, Cologne, 1985

Manfred Durzak, *Das Amerika-Bild in der deutschen Gegenwartsliteratur*, Stuttgart, 1979

Jost Hermand, *Pop International. Eine kritische Analyse*, Frankfurt on Main, 1971

Leo Lowenthal, *Literature, Popular Culture and Society*, Eaglewood Cliffs, N.J., 1961

D. Thompson (ed.), *Discrimination and Popular Culture*, London, 1964

Raymond Williams, *Communications*, London, 1962

JULIET WIGMORE

Feminist Writing in West Germany

The Women's Movement and Feminist Writing

Feminist writing needs to be considered against the background of the autonomous Women's Movement, of which it is an integral part. In West Germany, the movement itself emerged in the late 1960s, partly prompted by the student protests of 1968, and it came to the fore, as it did elsewhere in Europe, from about 1970. The early years saw the publication of many texts on feminist theory and politics, including translations of works by American and other European feminists. The interest in creative writing, on the other hand, developed more slowly, with most of the aesthetically more radical texts appearing only after about 1975. One consequence of the German Women's Movement has indeed been to stimulate much writing by women and so to initiate a change in the situation whereby women writing in German have long been far less visible than their counterparts in the English-speaking countries or in France.[1]

Feminist writing reflects many of the features and issues which have been central to the Women's Movement as a whole, including the fact that it comprises a diversity of standpoints which go under headings such as socialist feminist, radical feminist, separatist, and so on. Despite the variety of forms which feminist thinking takes, certain recurrent principles underlie it and will be mentioned here because they have in part motivated the selection of the writers to be discussed. At the same time, it should not be assumed that they define the parameters of feminist writing in any rigid way.

As a general principle, creative writing may be regarded as one means by which women seek to liberate themselves from the oppression which results from living in a male-defined social order in which women have been allocated the status of object. The feminist per-

---

1. Ways in which women writing in English have been misrepresented or unjustly overlooked are investigated in Johanna Russ, *How to Suppress Women's Writing*, London, 1983, and Dale Spender, *Mothers of the Novel*, London, 1986.

spective, in all contexts, presupposes an analysis of women's oppression, such as that formulated by Sigrid Weigel, with literature specifically in mind: 'Die Männer sind das erste, das eigentliche Geschlecht. Die Frauen werden in ihren Eigenschaften, Verhaltensweisen etc. stets in bezug auf die Männer definiert. In der männlichen Ordnung hat die Frau gelernt, sich selbst als untergeordnet, uneigentlich und unvollkommen zu betrachten'.[2] The process of liberation, therefore, means changing one's whole perception of the world, as a woman. The feminist writer thus specifically seeks a means by which she can become the subject through which the world is presented, instead of reiterating male-defined perspectives, which permit only inauthentic visions of women's lives. Indeed, the need to present an authentic account of women's perception of life accounts for the importance of the principle that 'the personal is political' ('das Private ist politisch') both in the Women's Movement as a whole and, not least, in feminist writing, as well as the emphasis on 'consciousness raising' ('Selbsterfahrung'). Because it marks a shift in perspective, feminist writing is, by definition, subversive of the status quo, and it can be regarded as an attempt to reclaim territory of which women have been deprived, including language itself.[3] The process of reclamation may also be seen in the wider context in which feminists endeavour to define 'themselves' (ourselves) and to make women visible, as has been achieved in part, notably in women's history and through investigations into the lives of contemporary women, be they housewives, mothers or paid workers in traditional or non-traditional spheres of activity. At the same time, the Women's Movement has created a platform for women to express themselves on issues such as sexuality, relations with men and with women, but also on more overtly political topics, such as abortion and the nuclear threat. Many of these aspects inform the literary works of feminist writers.

The first part of this survey of feminist writing will concentrate on the way feminist issues have become central in works by women writers, where they are presented largely in personal terms. Thereafter, I shall discuss some of the more innovative writers, who combine a feminist outlook with more radical modes of expression, with the result that the beginnings of a feminist aesthetic may be

2. Sigrid Weigel, 'Der schielende Blick. Thesen zur Geschichte weiblicher Schreibpraxis', in Inge Stephan and Sigrid Weigel (eds.), *Die verborgene Frau*, Berlin, 1983, pp. 83–137 (pp. 84–5).
3. For a discussion of this problem in linguistic terms, see Senta Trommel-Plötz, *Frauensprache: Sprache der Veränderung*, Frankfurt on Main, 1982, and Luise Pusch, *Das Deutsche als Männersprache*, Stuttgart, 1984.

said to be emerging.[4] Although the context is West German literature, Austrian and Swiss writers will be included, since the Women's Movement has an international flavour, in the West, and many of these writers have had an impact on feminist literary awareness in West Germany, where a number of feminist publishers are also established.[5] On the other hand, East German writers will only be mentioned when their work is directly relevant to the authors under discussion because, even though they may have had their work published in the West, it is not possible to do justice to them without taking into account the GDR context and the history of their reception, often belated, in West Germany. It must therefore suffice to note that many feminist writers have been profoundly influenced by the works of Christa Wolf in particular, especially by her novels *Nachdenken über Christa T.* (1968) and *Kindheitsmuster* (1976), apparently because of the attention they give to questions of identity, which, as will be shown, has been a central topic in works by certain Western feminist writers, such as Karin Struck.

Feminist Perspectives

(a) Karin Struck

An early novel in the history of recent feminist writing, Karin Struck's *Klassenliebe* (1973) is a personal account of the narrator's suffering, cast in diary form, and addressed to an absent lover, Z. . Historically, the diary form is a traditional means by which women have succeeded in writing creatively, especially before it was acceptable for women to become professional writers, for in Silvia Bovenschen's words: 'Der Brief, das Tagebuch haben keinen klar definierten Standort, hier durften Frauen sich tummeln'.[6] At the same time, this form is appropriate for the expression of personal perspectives, for it conveys a sense of authenticity by drawing the reader into the position of the first-person narrator. In *Klassenliebe*, the fact that the narrator's name is Karin, like that of the author herself, enhances the authentic quality. Nevertheless, her experi-

4. See Ricarda Schmidt, *Westdeutsche Frauenliteratur in den 70er Jahren*, Frankfurt on Main, 1982. I am grateful to Ricarda for greatly furthering my understanding of feminist writing through our many discussions.
5. For example, Frauenoffensive and Frauenbuchverlag in Munich.
6. Silvia Bovenschen, 'Über die Frage: Gibt es eine weibliche Ästhetik?', in Gabriele Dietze (ed.), *Die Überwindung der Sprachlosigkeit. Texte aus der neuen Frauenbewegung*, Darmstadt and Neuwied, 1979, pp. 82–115 (p. 109).

ences emerge as being not purely individual but, since they emanate from a sense of class conflict, as being of general significance.

Karin's immediate sense of suffering both inspires her writing and triggers memories of the past, in which she was oppressed by the conflict between her middle-class education at the Gymnasium, and later at university, and her working-class background. While she suffered at the hands of middle-class teachers and fellow pupils at school, she also notes the way she was oppressed specifically as a woman by the attitudes of men from her own class: 'Daß Kinder und Haushalt eine Arbeit ist, noch dazu, das begreifen sie nicht. Unbezahlte Arbeit. Und ich bin noch dazu ein Mensch weiblichen Geschlechts. Das kommt noch zu allem dazu'.[7] Thus, even when the basic cause of oppression is attributed to the class structure, women are shown to be the most downtrodden of all. This socialist feminist viewpoint, which gives primacy to class relations, is a strand which informs much feminist theory and creative writing, including that of Elfriede Jelinek, even into the 1980s, although generally speaking it was stronger in the early years of the women's liberation movement, before the shift to more radical positions, according to which women's oppression is attributed primarily to sex difference.

Karin experiences alienation, both as a result of class conflict in her own life and also in terms of sexual relationships. In this context, she finds that she has no adequate language in which to express her feelings, since all the terminology for sexual relations is male-defined, an issue which Verena Stefan tackles directly in *Häutungen* (1975). Karin's sense of alienation results in her being insecure about her own identity, which in turn exacerbates the sense of distance from her lover Z., who is also physically absent: 'Ich will Z. nicht stellvertretend lieben für etwas anderes. Z. ist Z. Z. als Z. lieben. Als Karin Z. als Z. lieben. Karin? Karin? Karin?' (p. 61). Both in this novel and in *Die Mutter*, Christa Wolf's novel *Nachdenken über Christa T.* is repeatedly invoked, suggesting that the author herself is concerned with searching for her own identity. The narrator in *Klassenliebe* contemplates suicide as the only apparent means of escape from her feelings of conflict and alienation, and she restrains herself from this step only by thinking of her unborn child. Her attitude suggests that for her motherhood is a means of justifying her existence, with the implication that giving life is itself of a value which is not open to question.

7. Karin Struck, *Klassenliebe*, 13th edn, Frankfurt on Main, 1978, p. 104. Page numbers in parentheses refer to this edition.

The issues of childbirth and motherhood form the central subject matter of Karin Struck's second novel, *Die Mutter* (1975). Through the eyes of the main protagonist, Nora, various aspects relating to motherhood are explored, initiated by the fact that Nora herself is expecting a child. Thus she reflects on her relationship with her own mother, and this is followed by a depiction of the attitudes and events in the maternity ward when she herself gives birth. She subsequently returns to the ward to visit a woman called Judith, to whom she has grown close, and with whom she shares not only the recent experience of childbirth but also her background in the working class. As a result of her encounter with Judith, which has sexual overtones, she declares that she will learn to write 'like Sappho' about the working class, which also means writing about motherhood: 'Die Mütter sind ja Arbeiterklasse. Wir sind ja Arbeiterklasse'.[8] The positive bond that she forges with Judith foreshadows the understanding that she reaches with her own mother in the final chapter, where it is associated with a sense of 'homecoming' in emotional terms, when she and her mother journey to her mothers's former home in Pommerania, now in the German Democratic Republic.

(b) Brigitte Schwaiger

Like Karin Struck's novels, those of Brigitte Schwaiger offer realistic accounts based on autobiographical material, although the social milieu depicted in Brigitte Schwaiger's fiction is solid middle class, 'gutbürgerlich', the main protagonist in a number of her works being the daughter of a doctor, as the author herself is. The novel *Wie kommt das Salz ins Meer* (1977) tells the story of the narrator's marriage to a man named Rolf, the pressure she experiences from her family, first to marry and then to stay married, especially because she has already disappointed her family through dropping out of the educational system, prompting her to reflect: 'Deine Heirat war für deine Familie die letzte Hoffnung'.[9] Through a satirical treatment of her own rigid, bourgeois family, the power of the nuclear family in the social structure is implicitly criticised: this can be seen, for example in the narrator's insight that her mother and grandmother welcome her marrying, even though they acknowledge to themselves that they did not find marriage a great source of happiness.

8. Idem, *Die Mutter*, 3rd edn, Frankfurt on Main, 1980, p. 272.
9. Brigitte Schwaiger, *Wie kommt das Salz ins Meer*, Reinbek nr. Hamburg 1979, p. 31. Further page numbers refer to this edition.

The narrator's own unhappy experience of marriage has general implications, as is evident when she first realises that she has lost something of her identity in losing her own name from her passport: 'Ich bin nicht ich. Ich bin Rolfs Frau' (p. 33). Rolf curtails her freedom in many conventional ways, yet she blames herself for destroying their marriage: 'Rolf ist erschöpft. Ich habe ihn ausgelaugt in dieser Ehe' (p. 112), and she asks herself: 'Ist es nicht Wahnsinn, dieses Paradies zu verlassen, nur weil der Mann hier mich langweilt?' (p. 112). The narrator's slightly naïve persona ironically understates the extent of the problems, as if they were purely personal issues, while her naivety actually allows a criticism of marriage as an institution to emerge.

In a later novel, *Lange Abwesenheit* (1980), Brigitte Schwaiger analyses her ambivalent feelings about her father, following his death. For, as a child, she sought his attention and approval, while resenting the fact that his commitments often kept him away from his family. Yet the narrator also objected to his prejudices and racist attitudes, directly primarily against the Jews, not least because his views have to some extent contaminated her own. Certain qualities represented by her father are distilled in the person of her lover, Birer, a man who is considerably older than herself, Jewish, and who in her mind both resembles her father and simultaneously offers a bastion against him: 'Er wird mein Geliebter, mit ihm werde ich mich behaupten gegen Vater'.[10] Yet she views Birer partly through her father's racist stereotype.

When her father eventually dies, she feels cheated, as if he has deliberately eluded her by dying in her absence: 'Hat sich einfach davongemacht, dieser Vater' (p. 80). It is the tension induced by his constant elusiveness, coupled with the bond which she had with him, that prompts her to examine their relationship in an attempt to comprehend certain aspects of her own personality, particularly the factors affecting her relationship with her lover. Thus, for the narrator, the exploration of her experience of her own father becomes a process of self-discovery, and the writing process is a therapeutic exercise, through which she increasingly gains consciousness of the forces which motivate her own behaviour.

(c) The Father as a Political Figure: Ruth Rehmann

Accounts of father figures have been frequent in recent years, and

10. Idem, *Lange Abwesenheit*, Reinbek nr. Hamburg, 1982, p. 28. Page numbers refer to this edition.

not only in novels by women writers. Yet the father–daughter relationship often seems to be particularly influential in moulding a woman's idea of herself, because individual fathers embody patriarchal attitudes inherent in society at large, and hence the presentation of a father figure may represent a politicised perspective. Thus, for example, in Ingeborg Bachmann's generally pre-feminist novel *Malina* (1971),[11] the narrator's father appears to her in a dream sequence as a Nazi doctor who murders her, which in essence parallels her suffering at the hands of her lover. Similarly, in Ruth Rehmann's autobiographical novel *Der Mann auf der Kanzel* (1979) a strong correlation emerges between facets of the father figure's character and certain oppressive elements of political history.

The narrator's father is a clergyman and a patriotic upholder of the imperial German spirit, for Ruth Rehmann, born in 1922, presents a longer historical perspective than most younger feminist writers. She pieces together her father's biography, which includes reflections on his role during the First World War and the Third Reich, aided by an elderly schoolmaster, who forms a link between the generations and who describes her father's loyalties in the words: 'Ihr Vater hatte drei Väter, den leiblichen, den Vater im Himmel und den Alten Kaiser und König von Preußen'.[12] As a consequence of his patriotic attitude, he was at first deceived by Hitler, until it was too late, whereupon he suffered strong conflicts because he was no longer able freely to express his moral scruples. Yet the story does not only tell the story of the father figure, for the narrator herself is also compelled to reflect on incidents from her own youth and to expose her own involvement in this period of German history. Thus, she tells how, as a young girl, she, like others of her generation, rushed to greet the Führer, despite her father's disapproval, and hence investigating her father's life also entails facing up to aspects of her own history. In this respect Ruth Rehmann's novel is 'political' in a wider sense than is Brigitte Schwaiger's account of her father, since it sheds light on her participation in historical events, in a way which is shared by many women of her generation, even though during the Third Reich women were largely excluded from political life.

(d) Autobiographical Perspectives

Autobiographical and biographical feminist writing covers a wide

---

11. Ingeborg Bachmann, *Werke*, vol. III, Munich and Zurich, 1978, pp. 174ff.
12. Ruth Rehmann, *Der Mann auf der Kanzel. Fragen an einen Vater*, 3rd edn, Munich,

range, some of it consciously political, while other works concentrate almost exclusively on personal experience. For example, the process by which a woman detaches herself from a man, already an aspect of *Wie kommt das Salz ins Meer*, is a frequent topic in feminist writing, and in Karin Petersen's novel *Das fette Jahr* (1978) it is even the sole focal-point. By contrast, similar subject-matter is presented in a wider context in Birgit Pausch's novel *Die Verweigerungen der Johanna Glauflügel* (1977), where Johanna's departure out of her marriage is but the first of her rebellions against social convention, followed by her leaving her alienating job as a nurse, leaving her country and her parents. These events, which suggest a gradual process of consciousness raising, enable her to liberate herself from the various oppressive mechanisms which are here shown to affect women particularly, though not exclusively.

In a different vein, Maria Erlenberger's novel *Der Hunger nach Wahnsinn* (1977), called a 'Bericht', presents a highly personal account of being treated for anorexia nervosa in a psychiatric hospital, where the narrator is diagnosed as schizophrenic. Many of the other patients, like her, suffer from complaints which are often thought to be induced by the pressure put on women specifically, for example through the notion of an ideal physical shape. Certain implicit criticisms of the hospital system too suggest that women are its passive victims: 'Die Ärzte stehen hier für die starke Welt des Mannes, und die Frauen sind klein und bittend. Die Frau ist der Patient des Mannes. Immer und überall'.[13] Eventually, the narrator is released from hospital into society, carrying a medical report that states that she is compliant ('angepaßt'), with its implication that this quality is a prerequisite for her liberation from direct male control.

(e) Female Friendship

Despite the political motivation for feminist writing, the relatively rare works which address themselves directly to the women's liberation movement sometimes have a didactic and stereotyped appearance, as is the case in Margot Schroeder's novel *Der Schlachter empfiehlt noch immer Herz* (1976), in which a housewife, Ola, joins a women's group campaigning against the threatened closure of a women's refuge in Hamburg ('Frauenhaus'). In the course of the

---

1986, p. 16.
13. Maria Erlenberger, *Der Hunger nach Wahnsinn*, Reinbek nr. Hamburg, 1977, p. 131.

campaign, there are discussions with men, within the framework of left-wing politics, in which standard positions are merely reiterated, without any real exploration of their significance for the campaign or for the characters. This narrative weakness becomes acute when Ola becomes involved in a lesbian relationship with a woman called Kathrin, which is alluded to only in terms of preformulated political views: 'irgendwie ärgert mich die Alternative der Lesben: Feminismus ist die Theorie, lesbisch sein die Praxis'.[14] Because Ola does not explore her own motives, the reader gains little insight into the link which might otherwise have emerged here between the personal and the political.

In marked contrast, Monika Sperr's novel *Die Freundin* (1980) tells in a third-person narrative the story of Anna, a kindergarten teacher and foster parent, who takes for granted her lifestyle as a socialist, feminist and lesbian, instead of theorising about these positions. Early in the novel, indeed, she attends a feminist conference, deriving from it not so much political insight as the support gained from being with other women, besides which political questions which may once have been of burning interest seem to her even a little irrelevant, such as the issues of 'political lesbians': 'Wie verläßlich ist die Sexualität von *Bewegungslesben*?'[15] In contrast to the recourse to slogans in Margot Schroeder's novel, Anna's thoughts on this issue are neither set down directly, nor are they predictable. Instead, her attitudes emerge through her lifestyle itself, which particularly involves her being supportive to others, mainly women. Foremost among them is her sometime lover, Edith, to whom she is still emotionally tied, while the constant demands which Edith places upon her present their relationship as realistic rather than politically sound. However, Anna, the giver, eventually meets an older woman, and there is a promise of a new attachment, in which she will receive support instead of constantly giving it. Thus, this novel reflects a more mature position, in which feminist lifestyles and principles are incorporated into a fictional narrative, which, despite its realistic style, avoids being either polemical or banal.

In a less overtly feminist novel entitled *Freundinnen* (1974) Caroline Muhr, born in 1925, explores the friendship between two older women, Ruth, a housewife, whose views are very conventional at the outset, and her childhood friend, Edda, a career woman, who chose not to marry, knowing that to do so would entail too many compromises. When they meet again after years of separation, Ruth's views

14. Margot Schroeder, *Der Schlachter empfiehlt noch immer Herz*, Munich, 1976, p. 86.
15. Monika Sperr, *Die Freundin*, Munich, 1983, p. 46.

gradually change under Edda's influence, and she begins to realise how limited her own experience is. While both women remain technically in heterosexual frameworks, Ruth becomes aware that she has fallen in love with Edda, a situation which is only resolved through Edda's untimely death. Some traditional ideas about women's emancipation are thus aired in this novel, while it is the intense friendship portrayed which places them in the modern feminist context.

In the works discussed so far, an authentic, personal narrative receives political significance because it reflects aspects of women's lives more generally. While one would not wish to make an absolute division, there are nevertheless some feminist initiatives which have a more radical appearance in aesthetic terms, and which, while still drawing on personal experience and autobiographical material in certain instances, open up new possibilities for expressing feminist perspectives.

The Emergence of Feminist Aesthetics

(a) Verena Stefan

Verena Stefan's novel *Häutungen* (1975) retains an autobiographical framework, within which the narrator describes how she detaches herself from men, starts to relate to women and emerges as an independent individual, yet it marks a considerable departure in aesthetic terms. In contrast to the realism of writers such as Margot Schroeder, *Häutungen* is structured partly by the use of imagery, particularly the title metaphor of the snake which sheds its skin, corresponding to the way the narrator dispenses with her old life, stage by stage, and 'grows' a new personality. As a mere shadow of the men to whom she relates initially, a 'Schattenhaut', she is dependent, saying with reference to a lover: 'ich brauchte ihn, weil ich mich nicht hatte'.[16] As she begins to understand the source of her oppression, in a chapter entitled 'Entzugserscheinungen' she starts to detach herself from sexual dependence on her lover, Samuel, while remaining dependent upon him for emotional support. The image of leaving behind an outer self recurs, as is expressed in a metaphor of removing shoes: 'ich war dabei umzusiedeln, wollte meine schuhe aus den gleisen neben ihm lösen, als ich merkte, dass sie festgewachsen waren, schlüpfte ich heraus und ging barfuss

---

16. Verena Stefan, *Häutungen*, 16th edn, Munich, 1981, p. 26. Further page numbers refer to this edition.

weiter. lange blieb Samuel neben den leeren schuhen stehen. er begriff nicht, wohin ich mein gesicht gewandt hatte, welche richtung ich eingeschlagen hatte, was ich so angestrengt suchte' (p. 65). The narrator goes to live with women and becomes sexually involved with Fenna, a situation described as 'Ausnahmezustand'. Finally, in a chapter entitled 'Kürbisfrau', the narrator can be seen to have metamorphosed completely into a new woman, Chloe, a writer, who is setting down her experiences. As if to suggest the extent of her detachment from her past, the narrative has here shifted from the first person to the third person.

In the introduction to the novel, Verena Stefan discusses the difficulty of writing about women's bodies and their sexuality, an obstacle which arises from the fact that all the available terminology is male-defined, and hence oppressive to women. Of the options open to her, she prefers clinical language, adopting terms such as 'Koitus' when writing about heterosexuality, where it is appropriate to convey the sense of detachment which the narrator has achieved. However, there remains the problem of how to describe new experiences, which call for a new language.

Häutungen has many innovatory features, including the integral part played by the various images from nature.[17] Beside these, however, the novel combines the genres of narrative, dialogue and poems, while also juxtaposing thoughts and ideas with theory and realistic details. This technique creates a sense of fluidity, which helps to convey a sense of gradual change by suggesting that various aspects of life are interconnected, and thereby depicting the narrator's search to become a whole person. Everything is related to the person of the narrating subject, who emerges as she narrates. Thus, for example, her insights are sometimes conveyed in poems, giving concrete form to her experiences.

Der eine küsste leidenschaftlich und wild, so daß ich zähne spürte,
    nichts als zähne —
Und ich küsste leidenschaftlich und wild.
Der andere küsste sanft und fand alles andere unreif und
    unerwachsen —
Und ich küsste sanft und erwachsen (p. 42).

17. The nature imagery has sometimes been criticised for suggesting an identification of women with nature and an implicit biological determinism. See Gabriele Goettle, 'Schleim oder Nichtschleim, das ist hier die Frage' and Brigitte Classen and Gabriele Goettle, '"Häutungen", eine Verwechslung von Anemone und Amazone', in Gabriele Dietze (ed.), as note 6, pp. 51–4 and pp. 55–9.

The echoing style graphically depicts the narrator's lack of self-determination, her 'Schattenhaut', while the many instances cited suggest that she is groping for general principles, which eventually give her insight into her situation.

Certain ritualised behaviour patterns, often embodied in language, are undermined in the novel. On the one hand, Verena Stefan creates neologisms, such as 'sexualitätsmüde' (p. 57), while on the other, she frequently breaks down conventional forms. Thus, for example, clichés of thought are called into question through mere syntactic variation: 'Ich bin verliebt / bin ich verliebt?' (p. 44). There is occasional use of zeugma, implying the incompatibility of matters which in reality often are assumed to go hand in hand: 'ich teilte meine wohnung und meine sexualität mit Samuel' (p. 52); and compound words are broken down into constituent morphemes, a technique which, at least in some cases, shows up a concealed ideology or significant ambiguity: 'herr schaft' (p. 35), 'unter leib' (p. 12).[18] Most of these formulations occur in her critique of living within a framework defined by men, and they recede after her lifestyle has changed.

Thus Verena Stefan attempts to chart the radical departure in the narrator's life through an appropriately original style, which renders *Häutungen*, still her only work of fiction, unconventional, with the result that it successfully avoids some of the many pitfalls of autobiographical writing, including banality and the sheer voyeurism which often arises from a purely realistic depiction.[19]

(b) Christa Reinig

Although it is not directly autobiographical in substance, Christa Reinig's novel *Entmannung* (1976) was inspired by the author's own reaction to the trial of a lesbian couple in Itzehoe, who were accused of conspiring to murder the husband of one of them. The trial, which figures in the novel, sparked off Christa Reinig's own interest in feminism, and in this respect the ambiguous title *Entmannung* in one sense implies a departure from a male-orientated style of writing and an attempt to find new ways of writing about women's liberation.

Nevertheless, in a second sense, 'Entmannung' applies to a man, Otto Kyra, who is the central figure in the novel, and whose

18. See Ricarda Schmidt, as note 4, pp. 60–8.
19. See Jutta Kolkenbrock-Netz and Marianne Schuller, 'Frau im Spiegel. Zum Verhältnis von autobiographischer Schreibweise und feministischer Praxis', in Irmela von der Lühe (ed.), *Entwürfe von Frauen in der Literatur des 20. Jahrhunderts*, Berlin, 1982, pp. 154–74.

research, as a doctor, into the nature of gender prompts him to seek to change sex. This he eventually achieves, after the death of Thea, his wife, when he leaves his flat dressed in her clothes, a symbolic gesture of departure, which is simultaneously subverted by the fact that he forgets his razor and decides not to return for it. Thus neither the transformation itself, nor his attitude towards it is unequivocal. Nevertheless, this event raises questions about the nature of gender, for when Otto Kyra finally metamorphoses into Valerie Solanas, dressed in a pair of unisex jeans, the androgynous image he projects does not imply a change in essence so much as mere elimination of the more excessive features of both masculinity and femininity, both of which have to be perceived as essential and static qualities in order for the idea of androgyny to be possible at all.

Otto Kyra is surrounded by four women who represent various female stereotypes, each of whom leaves him, and puts all men behind her, another aspect of the novel implicit in the title. The first woman, Doris, is a career woman who becomes a feminist and composes vicious attacks on men in two manifestos, eventually turning on Kyra in an act of violence, which results in her being committed to a mental hospital. By contrast, Klytemnestra, called Menni, is a housewife who becomes Kyra's mistress, subsequently attempting to throw off the domestic role and making a minor attack on her husband with a vegetable scraper — a far cry from the murder committed by her mythological namesake. Yet for this act of insubordination she receives a long prison sentence. Two other women also meet tragic ends, for Thea, a prostitute who becomes Otto's wife, dies of cervical cancer, while Xenia, the maid, commits suicide after being brutally assaulted and raped. Apart from them, there is Wölfi, a lesbian teenager from the GDR, who moves peripherally into Otto's circle, only to leave it again under inauspicious circumstances, having been accused of theft. Her departure from the household parallels the circumstances under which she left the GDR, for this action was not ideologically motivated but was purely a personal response to being taunted by her classmates because of her obsession with another young woman. Although she never becomes deeply involved with Kyra, or dependent upon him, she does not offer a truly positive alternative to the women who do because she has no principles but merely abdicates responsibility in the face of problems.

Entmannung contains many allusions to mythological and cultural traditions which have created or reinforced women's subjugation, an aspect which is wittily depicted, for instance, in an imaginary dialogue between Sigmund Freud and Alfred Hitchcock, both of whom have contributed to defining women as sex objects in their different fields. Freud's status, for example, is ironically subverted: 'Sigmund erzählt etwas von dem Zusammenhang der Wörter Wider-stand und Gegenstand. Er zitiert zum zehntausendsten Mal sein Glaubensbekenntnis "Anatomie ist Schicksal"'.[20] The familiar tone, together with the reduction of Freud's allegedly scientific account to a 'Glaubensbekenntnis' is liberating, for it helps to undermine his pervasive, male-orientated analysis. Similarly, Hitchcock's art is subverted, when at the end of the novel, Doris emerges to attack Kyra apparently from out of a life-sized photograph of Marilyn Monroe (a relic of Wölfi!), as if to suggest that the movie star herself were striking back on behalf of women from within the image created of her.

In a final metamorphosis which takes place under the direction of Gründgens, the characters appear as mythological figures, suggest-ing that the female stereotypes they represent have a perpetual validity, while only the names attached to their roles vary. Kyra himself is transformed into Valerie Solanas, the radical feminist author of the SCUM Manifesto (1968) ('Society for Cutting Up Men'), with whom he has previously had an exchange of views, during which she expressed a pessimistic attitude towards the possibility of women liberating themselves, a view which seems to be reflected by the novel as a whole.

Christa Reinig herself has stated that Otto Kyra is a mouthpiece for her own ideas and that she adopted a male persona because she was aware that her language and perceptions were shaped by male-defined viewpoints. Thus, Otto's attempt to renounce his 'masculinity' may be said to represent the author's own endeavour to transform her perceptions into truly feminine ones.[21] The fate of the two women in the Itzehoe trial, who were abused by the press and by the legal processes, as much for their aberrant sexuality as for their criminality, reverberates through the structure of the novel, in which the women around Kyra come to grief as soon as they attempt to stand up to men. The only possible solution, it is implied, is for men to change, as Otto himself attempts to do, yet this conclusion is not optimistic, for the final scenario suggests that any

---

20. Christa Reinig, *Entmannung*, 4th edn, Darmstadt, 1979, p. 28. Page numbers refer to this edition.
21. See Judith McAlister-Hermann, 'Literary Emasculation: Household Imagery in Christa Reinig's *Entmannung*', in Susan L. Cocalis and Kay Goodman (eds.), *Beyond the Eternal Feminine. Critical Essays on Women and German Literature*, Stuttgart, 1982, pp. 401–19 (pp. 403–4).

transformations are only partially effective.

(c) Barbara Frischmuth

Unlike Christa Reinig's *Entmannung*, a number of Barbara Frisch-muth's works are concerned with characters who succeed in chang-ing in the light of experience. Many of her novels, from the early work *Die Klosterschule* (1968) to *Bindungen* (1980) focus on women who are at a critical stage in their lives, sometimes caught in a conflict between what is expected of them and the possibilities which appear to be open to them, for instance. While autobiographical elements can be detected in her work, including for example, the frequent occurrence of women as single parents, as the author herself is, her novels are rarely confessional and, far from projecting an autobiographical style, they are narrated in a manner which suggests detachment.

These features are particularly apparent in the novel *Die Mystifi-kation der Sophie Silber* (1976), where the eponymous central figure is disorientated because she has reached a turning-point in her life. Having returned to Vienna after many years, she is about to take up residence in the apartment which she has inherited from her erst-while lover, Saul Silber, who died in her bedroom. At the same time, as a counterbalance to the sense of loss which prevails in this respect, she has recently been reconciled with the son she gave away for adoption, who is about to come to live with her as a lodger, an event which triggers memories of Sophie's rootless past.

This situation, as well as Sophie's state of mind, is elucidated through her contact with spirits of nature, who fulfil nature's tra-ditional function of healing, protecting and reconciling conflicts. At the same time, the remove from reality which this implies allows the usual boundaries placed on narrative fiction to be broken open. As a result, Sophie Silber's story is told in terms which transcend the restrictions of real time and space, despite the fact that it is based on her own memories. Much of her past is brought vividly alive through the perspective of the fairy Amaryllis Sternwieser, who has been the guardian spirit of generations of Sophie's family. As part of the broad perspective which this narrative technique allows, refer-ences are made to political events, including the mass emigration during the Third Reich, which was also undertaken by Saul Silber. The fairies and spirits of nature also emigrated at that time, a symbolic exodus which suggests that, through avoiding contamina-tion in this way, they may be regarded as the repository of all that is good and pure, available to be called upon in times of need.

In a central passage in the novel, Sophie and Amaryllis discuss the issue of changing one's personality, and Sophie asks: 'Genügt es, wenn wir die bleiben, die wir sind, oder dürfen wir nie damit aufhören, andere zu werden? Inwieweit aber können wir andere werden, ohne treulos gegen uns selbst zu sein? Und wenn wir uns selbst treu sind, inwieweit können wir andere werden?'[22] By the end, Sophie appears to have learnt that being faithful to oneself may actually demand change, since, in order to do justice to her own potential, she must throw off the constraints imposed by her past, a type of 'Fremdbestimmung' to which women are particularly susceptible. Sophie is then able to develop a positive new vision of the future: 'und sie sah dieses neue Leben vor sich, mit all seinen verborgenen Möglichkeiten' (p. 249). The encounter with the world of good spirits thus enables Sophie to begin a new life, something foreshadowed by the process of stepping outside contemporary reality.

Sophie Silber is the first novel of a trilogy, of which the following novel *Amy oder die Metamorphose* (1978) is set mainly in the real world. Amy herself, is nevertheless, a metamorphosis of the fairy Amaryllis Sternwieser, who here suffers and struggles as a human being, eventually accepting the responsibility of having a child, in the knowledge that she will have to bring it up on her own. The final novel of the trilogy *Kai oder die Liebe zu den Modellen* (1979) depicts Amy with her child, faced constantly with the various possibilities open to her with regard to his upbringing. Thus, in various ways Barbara Frischmuth, like Verena Stefan, does not merely reflect reality but steps outside the real world, to focus on change, potential and choices which have to be made.

(d) Jutta Heinrich

In a very different way from Barbara Frischmuth's world of spirits, Jutta Heinrich's novel *Das Geschlecht der Gedanken* (1977) also comprises a strong element of fantasy. The novel tells of the reaction of a young woman, Conni, to the psychological violence to which she has been subjected as part of her upbringing within the nuclear family,

---

22. Barbara Frischmuth, *Die Mystifikation der Sophie Silber*, 3rd edn, Munich, 1982, p. 121. Page numbers refer to this edition.
23. This novel was written in 1971, but not published until 1977. One publisher suggested that the subject-matter would have been more palatable, had the author agreed to have it published under a man's name. See Renate Möhrmann, 'Feministische Trends in der deutschen Gegenwartsliteratur', in Manfred Durzak (ed.), *Deutsche Gegenwartsliteratur. Ausgangspositionen und aktuelle Entwicklungen*, Stuttgart, 1981, pp. 336–58 (p. 354).

where the father is exaggeratedly patriarchal, while her mother is totally subservient, both socially and sexually. Conni is caught between the two role models, adopting a preference for the more powerful position occupied by her father, from which she is naturally excluded by virtue of her sex, while despising her mother's lack of assertiveness. As a result of being alienated from both the role models presented to her in such extreme form, she flees, as she says, into 'das Geschlecht der Gedanken',[24] that is, into fantasy and away from sex and gender roles. Because of this position, she forms no relationships but becomes isolated and, indeed, actively destructive of people around her, bringing humiliation and even death upon them as soon as she notices them falling into traditional gender roles.

A possibility of change occurs, however, for after the death of her father there are signs of a healing process. In a letter to her mother, Conni explains that she can only now, belatedly, begin to emerge as an adult, for hitherto she has been totally conditioned by her childhood experiences: 'Erwachsen werden heißt für mich, mitten im Leben mit gesteigerten Geburtsschmerzen auf die Welt zu kommen' (pp. 130–1). The nature of Conni's new start remains unspecified, for perhaps she, as the first-person narrator, is as yet unable to envisage what form it will take.

The achievement of *Das Geschlecht der Gedanken* resides in the power with which destructive aspects of an apparently normal family life are conveyed, and by the way they are integrated into Conni's fantasy world. Despite the extreme nature of the situation depicted, in a preface Jutta Heinrich suggests that the novel was intended to express a general truth about women's predicament: 'ich wollte die Ich-Erzählerin stellvertretend für mein Geschlecht so tief und hermetisch in eine undurchlässige Norm-alität, in die patriarchalische Ernst-haftigkeit einschließen, daß sie selbst zu einem verzerrten Spiegel der Macht-und-Ohnmacht-Strukturen werden muß' (p. 3). The very perversions which Conni's personality displays are thus to be seen as symptomatic of the prevailing power structures, which render some people, particularly women, completely 'power-less', a predicament which also emerges in Elfriede Jelinek's work.

(e) Elfriede Jelinek

Elfriede Jelinek's first overtly feminist work was *Die Liebhaberinnen*

24. Jutta Heinrich, *Das Geschlecht der Gedanken*, 4th edn, Munich, 1982, p. 27. Page

(1975), a novel which focuses on the plight of women in rural Austria. It centres on the story of two young women, Brigitte, a factory worker, and Paula, a countrywoman, who both have aspirations to improve their social standing, which is presented mainly in class terms. It is demonstrated that the most that women can hope for is to find a husband who offers them even marginally greater status and prosperity than they can achieve for themselves, for even in a society where both men and women have little scope for personal development, women come off worse. Despite the fact that Elfriede Jelinek attributes women's oppression mainly to the hierarchical social structure and not to men's behaviour, it emerges clearly that women are disadvantaged in relation to men specifically: 'wenn einer ein schicksal hat, dann ist es ein mann. wenn einer ein schicksal bekommt, dann ist es eine frau'.[25] According to this principle, through her marriage Brigitte becomes a caricature of a middle-class housewife and mother, while Paula, who initially had greater potential, gets pregnant and marries an alcoholic, resorts to prostitution and ends as a worker in the very factory which Brigitte left behind her. Thus, the novel presents in schematised form the idea that women at the bottom of the social scale inevitably become dependent upon men. None of the characters has any thought of attempting to change the situation as such, but instead they prefer to collaborate with the mechanisms of oppression in the hope of gaining from them.

As late as 1981, Elfriede Jelinek stated that she viewed the oppression of women as being only one aspect of a social struggle affecting men as well: '"Ich glaub" aber, daß der politische Kampf Vorrang hat, der Kampf aller Unterdrückten ob Männer oder Frauen'.[26] Despite this classic socialist feminist statement, Elfriede Jelinek's work has come to focus increasingly on the position of women specifically, as is evident, for instance, in the play entitled *Clara S.* (1981), which, alluding satirically to Clara Schumann, shows how she sacrifices her own musical career to that of her husband, Robert Schumann.

An earlier play, *Was geschah, nachdem Nora ihren Mann verlassen hatte* (1977/8), which was inspired by Ibsen's *A Doll's House* (1879), depicts a middle-class woman, Nora, attempting to lead an independent life after leaving her husband, Helmer, a wealthy industrialist,

numbers refer to this edition.
25. Elfriede Jelinek, *Die Liebhaberinnen*, Reinbek nr. Hamburg, 1975, p. 8.
26. Josef-Hermann Sauter, 'Interview mit Barbara Frischmuth, Elfriede Jelinek und Michael Scharang', *Wiemarer Beiträge* 27, 1981, 6, pp. 99–121 (p. 110).

the point at which Ibsen's play ends.[27] Nora seeks work in a factory, yet she is hampered in her attempts to become a working woman by her class and by constant sexual harrassment from men both in management and on the shop floor. The boss sees her as an asset which he can use in the cause of furthering his own ambitions, notably in a business deal designed to ruin Helmer. As part of this procedure, Nora is persuaded to perform 'sexual favours' for Helmer, which consists in her beating him, in disguise, while in exchange for this pleasure he reveals industrial secrets. This sado-masochistic role-playing ironically draws attention to the fact that, at the very moment when Nora appears to be in a position of power, she is actually controlled by all the men around her, including Helmer, who is only acting out the role of subordinate partner. Her own apparent power, on the other hand, is belied by her position at work and in her marriage, to which she is forced to return, both of them situations in which she is totally powerless.

Elfriede Jelinek's later novel *Die Klavierspielerin* (1983) focuses on the sadomasochistic inclinations of the main protagonist, Erika Kohut, which can be explained to a great extent as resulting from the imbalance of power in society at large, represented in Erika's life by her dominant mother. For her mother, with whom she lives, has kept her in isolation from other people and in bondage to the art of music, which she experiences as a form of oppression: 'In dieses Notationssystem ist Erika seit frühester Kindheit eingespannt[. . .] Dieses Rastersystem hat sie, im Verein mit ihrer Mutter, in ein un-zerreißbares Netz von Vorschriften, Verordnungen, von präzisen Geboten geschnürt'.[28] Her enslavement to music has been motivated by her mother's desire for status and prosperity, achievements which Erika has in part secured for them through becoming a music teacher. Yet the cost to her is great, for she has internalised the oppression which she has experienced directly at the hands of her mother and indirectly through society at large, which, in parallel to the relationship between Erika and her mother, is severely hierarchical. At the same time it is highly competitive, a characteristic which is reflected in the social function of music, which involves actual competitions, and in Erika's own life, in sexual competitiveness.

As a result of being oppressed and controlled, Erika relates to other people either aggressively, when she is in a superior position, such as in her capacity as teacher, or self-destructively, mainly in the

27. See Marlis Gerhardt, 'Wohin geht Nora? Auf der Suche nach der verlorenen Frau', *Kursbuch* 47, 1977, pp. 77–89.
28. Elfriede Jelinek, *Die Klavierspielerin*, Reinbek nr. Hamburg, 1983, p. 237.

context of sex, when she practises various forms of self-mutilation. As this behaviour occurs mainly in the way she relates to men, the type of oppression that she experiences appears to be particularly destructive of women in this society. The terms in which *Die Klavierspielerin* is couched are as brutal as those of *Das Geschlecht der Gedanken*, but the insights gained by the reader arise from the satirical treatment of Erika's behaviour, instead of through a direct, confessional style.

The literature which has arisen out of the Women's Movement of the 1970s thus reflects a wide range of issues affecting women, which are manifested in both personal and political terms. At the same time, the impetus to express ideas about women's oppression on the one hand and women's potential for liberation on the other has stimulated experiments with new narrative forms, in the attempt to express feminist perspectives. Some authors, whose work began to be known in the mid-1970s, only reached their full potential in the 1980s, among them Elfriede Jelinek, and many have continued to develop upon the foundations laid by feminist thinking. A significant effect of the feminist tendency is indeed that many women authors have emerged, of whom at least some have succeeded in establishing a reputation, a factor which in time may help to redress the balance in literature which has hitherto been so strongly loaded against women writers.

Select Bibliography

Primary Texts

Ingeborg Bachmann, *Malina* (Ingeborg Bachmann, *Werke* vol. III), Munich and Zurich, 1978
Maria Erlenberger, *Der Hunger nach Wahnsinn*, Reinbek nr. Hamburg, 1977
Barbara Frischmuth, *Die Mystifikation der Sophie Silber*, Salzburg, 1976
Jutta Heinrich, *Das Geschlecht der Gedanken*, Munich, 1977
Elfriede Jelinek, *Die Klavierspielerin*, Reinbek nr. Hamburg 1983
——, *Die Liebhaberinnen*, Reinbek nr. Hamburg 1975
——, *Was geschah, nachdem Nora ihren Mann verlassen hatte* (Elfriede Jelinek,

Theaterstücke), Cologne, 1984

Caroline Muhr, *Freundinnen*, Munich, 1974

Birgit Pausch, *Die Verweigerungen der Johanna Glauflügel*, Berlin, 1977

Karin Petersen, *Das fette Jahr*, Cologne, 1978

Ruth Rehmann, *Der Mann auf der Kanzel. Fragen an einen Vater*, Munich and Vienna, 1979

Christa Reinig, *Entmannung*, Düsseldorf, 1976

Margot Schroeder, *Der Schlachter empfiehlt noch immer Herz*, Munich, 1976

Brigitte Schwaiger, *Lange Abwesenheit*, Vienna and Hamburg, 1980

——, *Wie kommt das Salz ins Meer*, Vienna and Hamburg, 1977

Monika Sperr, *Die Freundin*, Munich, 1980

Verena Stefan, *Häutungen*, Munich, 1975

Karin Struck, *Klassenliebe*, Frankfurt on Main, 1973

——, *Die Mutter*, Frankfurt on Main, 1975

Background Reading

Silvia Bovenschen, 'Über die Frage: Gibt es eine weibliche Ästhetik?', in Gabriele Dietze (ed.), *Die Überwindung der Sprachlosigkeit. Texte aus der neuen Frauenbewegung*, Darmstadt and Neuwied, 1979, pp. 82–115

Susan L. Cocalis and Kay Goodman (eds.), *Beyond the Eternal Feminine. Critical Essays on Women and German Literature*, Stuttgart, 1982

Hiltrud Gnüg and Renate Möhrmann (eds.), *Frauen, Literatur, Geschichte. Schreibende Frauen vom Mittelalter bis zur Gegenwart*, Stuttgart, 1985

Jutta Kolkenbrock-Netz and Marianne Schuller, 'Frau im Spiegel. Zum Verhältnis von autobiographischer Schreibweise und feministischer Praxis', in Irmela von der Lühe (ed.), *Entwürfe von Frauen in der Literatur des 20. Jahrhunderts*, Berlin, 1982, pp. 154–74

Renate Möhrmann, 'Feministische Trends in der deutschen Gegenwartsliteratur', in Manfred Durzak (ed.), *Deutsche Gegenwartsliteratur*, Stuttgart, 1981, pp. 336–58

Heinz Puknus (ed.), *Neue Literatur der Frauen*, Munich, 1980

Ricarda Schmidt, *Westdeutsche Frauenliteratur in den 70er Jahren*, Frankfurt on Main, 1982

Hilde Schmölzer, *Frau sein und schreiben. Österreichische Schriftstellerinnen definieren sich selbst*, Vienna, 1982

Sigrid Weigel, 'Der schielende Blick. Thesen zur Geschichte weiblicher Schreibpraxis', in Inge Stephan and Sigrid Weigel, *Die verborgene Frau. Sechs Beiträge zu einer feministischen Literaturwissenschaft*, Berlin, 1983

JULIAN SIERRA-BALLESTER
AND ANTHONY STEPHENS

West German Poetry of the 1970s

To understand the main stream of West German poetry in the 1970s, it is necessary to recognise its conscious break with the 'high' manner of the Western European lyric which, in the German tradition, had reached its most recent culmination in the works of Paul Celan. Writing programmatically in 1976, Jürgen Theobaldy, a leading poet and polemicist of the new movement, is quite insistent that 'das, was die einzig mögliche Entwicklung der Lyrik von Baudelaire über Mallarmé bis hin zu Celan erschienen ist, mittlerweile als historisch abgeschlossene Phase genommen werden [muß]'.[1]

To form a first impression of the kind of poetic expression which accompanies such a programme, let us look at the opening stanzas of F.C. Delius's 'Einsamkeit eines alternden Stones-Fan' (1975), referred to earlier in this volume in a different context.[2] The poem, from Theobaldy's important anthology *Und ich bewege mich doch . . . Gedichte vor und nach 1968* (1977), is typical of the collection and of the new climate *per se*:

> Er latscht in den Diskshop und gleich
> auf die Platte los, die er will, die neuen Stones.
> Um ihn rum, Kopfhörer um die Ohren,
> die 10 oder 15 Jahre jüngeren Typen,
> die längst was andres hören.
>
> Die reglosen Gesichter
> regen ihn auf,
> diese Einsamkeit unter den Kopfhörern!
> Er nimmt die Platte und
> fühlt sich nicht sehr einsam.
> Er weiß nur, er überschaut
> den Plattenmarkt nicht mehr —
> Diplom-Physiker, da hab ich andre Sorgen —
> und weiß nicht, was ihn noch verbindet

1. Jürgen Theobaldy, 'Das Gedicht im Handgemenge', in Hans Bender and Michael Krüger (eds.), *Was alles hat Platz in einem Gedicht?*, Munich, 1977, p. 169.
2. See Anthony Waine's 'Recent German Writing and the Influence of Popular Culture', p. 82 in the present volume.

mit der, sagt er ironisch, nächsten Generation,
höchstens eine Demonstration, ein Joint,
etwas von dieser Mode.

Er sieht das Cover an:
gefällt mir eigentlich gar nicht, den Mick
solltest du wirklich langsam abschreiben,
aber sein Sound, den hat keiner mehr erreicht.
Und Mick sagts selber: Du wirst
irgendwann zu deiner eignen Parodie.
Dieser Satz geht ihm durch den Kopf
während der vier Schritte zur Kasse, irgendwann
wirst du zu deiner eignen Parodie.[3]

From these stanzas it is easy to see how the 'poetry of everyday experience' ('Alltagslyrik'), became the catchphrase of this decade. The conscious simplicity in word-choice and syntax, the deliberately prosaic quality of the language ensure that rhythms and feelings remain understated. The central figure of the poem is both 'he' and 'I', blending the autobiographical element with a casual, anecdotal presentation. Such a mixed perspective may suggest a certain nostalgia for the 'we' that marked the solidarity and enthusiasm of the late 1960s, and this is further borne out by the themes of ageing and loneliness. On the one hand, the poem makes no apology for being 'subjective'; the expression of personal experience constitutes a value in its own right. On the other, it is undeniable that what 'he' experiences is meant to stand for the complex historical position of a whole generation, one that began with the opposite of the passivity he sees about him but whose members now cannot escape the awareness that they are 'professional', settled and out of touch.

The everyday present which the poem evokes seems not very secure in itself. It is caught between the past of great moments, which justifies the anger at the blank faces of the next generation that never knew them, and the other, nearer past in which the old gods, like Mick Jagger, have grown old and become self-parodies. At the end of the poem the only future dimension is one of 'new disappointments'.[4] While the loss of confidence in most kinds of collective experience is entirely typical of West German poetry of the 1970s, the exploration of the purely personal sphere need not end as negatively as in this example. Certainly the past, in the sense of the years of the Student Revolution, is intractable, but there is a genuine

3. Jürgen Theobaldy (ed.), *Und ich bewege mich doch . . . Gedichte vor und nach 1968*, Munich, 1977, pp. 110ff.
4. P. 112: 'und abends die neue Platte mit/ neuen Enttäuschungen, die/ Vergangenheit ist Vergangenheit — / und nicht vorbei.'

sense of discovery in the new communicability of a genre which had, in the words of Jürgen Theobaldy, 'das Einverständnis mit dem Leser aufgekündigt'.[5]

In point of fact, West German poetry in the 1970s descended from its pedestal and became a vigorous and popular element of the Counter Culture of that decade. The use of everyday language as a poetic medium is in a sense similar to the vogue for dialect poetry in these years, since both mark the assertion of the writer's individuality against the multifarious pressures to conform.

Given the very large number of writers publishing their poems, reciting them at poetry festivals and/or having them preserved in anthologies, it would be pointless, within the scope of an essay such as this, to give long lists of names and titles. At best we can offer a sampling of representative poems and of statements with which authors justified their work. We cannot do justice to authors who remained creative throughout the 1970s but had made their impact before the decade began, such as Heißenbüttel, Fried or Jandl. Enzensberger, who merits a chapter of his own in the present volume, cannot be omitted here either because of the weight of his influence on the writers we are concerned with, although our treatment of him must remain summary. Considerations of space also prevent us from setting out to define phenomena, such as 'Neue Subjektivität', which are treated elsewhere in the volume,[6] and the same restriction applies to the poetry of East Germany and feminist writing in verse. Beginning in disillusionment, the poetry we are concerned with achieved a conscious integration with a relatively idyllic phase of West German Counter Culture. Not only did it find its legitimacy here, but the traditional domination of German poetry by 'great names' briefly gave way to a phase in which the tension between the social and existential claims imposed on this art form was minimised. The peculiar constellation of the Counter Culture in the later 1970s enabled not only a climate to arise in which anyone who wrote could and did feel themselves a poet in the fullest sense, but also it produced a free and easy association of individualism with an atmosphere of social protest, which it was not necessary to define or focus more precisely.

The immediate bases for understanding the poetry of the 1970s appear most evident in the middle 1960s. Walter Höllerer's *Thesen zum langen Gedicht* (1965) took a polemical stance against the cultivation of obscurity and esotericism and particularly against the mini-

5. Jürgen Theobaldy, 'Das Gedicht im Handgemenge', p. 170.
6. See Martin Kane's chapter on Enzensberger, pp. 227ff, and Moray McGowan on 'Neue Subjektivität', pp. 53ff.

mising of the poetic statement, the strong tendency of the modern poem 'zu Verstummen', in which Paul Celan had discerned one of its essential features.[7] Höllerer encourages German poets to be more discursive, to write as if they were speaking, not to condense their perceptions to the point where the reader is forced to decipher them, but rather to develop a 'bewegliche Schreibweise' in which one insight leads clearly and immediately to the next. Höllerer also pleads for a mixed poetic vocabulary in which 'subtile und triviale, literarische und alltägliche Ausdrücke' coexist.[8]

But more significant than any theoretical turning was the formation in 1966 of the 'Grand Coalition' in which the Social Democrats (SPD) joined the conservative parties in government, an event which convinced many West Germans of differing political persuasions that the role of a parliamentary opposition now had to be carried on outside parliament. So the APO ('außerparlamentarische Opposition') arose as a widespread, if somewhat haphazard, expression of political dissent. While it could not outlive Brandt's election victory of 1969 and never amounted to a political organisation, it did create the leftist consensus among students, younger intellectuals and writers which made the Student Revolution of the end of the 1960s possible. This extraordinarily short-lived movement, which already began to lose cohesion after the passing of the 'Notstandsgesetze' of May 1968 and whose rapid transformation of university life was equally rapidly reversed by the early 1970s, nevertheless was the formative experience of a whole generation and decisively influenced the course West German poetry was to take. Before the 'Radikalenerlaß' of 1972, which prohibited members of extremist organisations from entering public service, leftist political activism could be a fashion among the student generation or, indeed, be seriously pursued, without long-term negative consequences for the individual. From this time onwards, with membership of a Marxist student group an effective bar to future employment by all state institutions, leftist solidarity became a matter of full conviction and the readiness to pay for it; it could no longer be a matter of casual or spontaneous enthusiasm. Moreover, although the decade after 1970 was to see less than two hundred terrorists and their

---

7. Walter Höllerer, 'Thesen zum langen Gedicht', *Akzente*, 2/1965, p. 130, and *Theorie der modernen Lyrik. Dokumente zur Poetik I*, Hamburg, 1965, p. 436; c.f. Paul Celan, 'Rede anläßlich der Verleihung des Georg-Büchner-Preises' (1960), *Ausgewählte Gedichte. Zwei Reden*, Frankfurt on Main, 1967, p. 143: 'Gewiß, das Gedicht — das Gedicht heute . . . zeigt . . . eine starke Neigung zum Verstummen'.
8. Walter Höllerer, 'Thesen zum langen Gedicht', pp. 129f.

supporters sentenced in West Germany, the impact of terrorism on the West German consciousness was disproportionate. The risks entailed in being outspokenly leftist were an increasingly effective deterrent throughout the 1970s for those who still wanted a genuinely political Counter Culture.

The experiences that shape West German poetry of the early 1970s are, firstly, that of the collapse of the collective identity and its briefly enjoyed certainties and, secondly, the adventure or alienation that follows from being cast on one's own resources. The shock these events may produce is documented in Ursula Krechel's poem 'Jetzt ist es nicht mehr so' (1977):

> Jetzt ist es nicht mehr so
> daß wir müde, mit Blasen an den Füßen
> verdreckt und naß vom Wasserstrahl
> nach Hause kommen, essen, trinken
> und wieder weg ins Kino.
>
> Jetzt ist es nicht mehr so
> daß wir denken, wenigstens
> die Straße gehört uns.
> Und die Zukunft natürlich
> jetzt oder später, aber bald.
>
> [. . .]
>
> Jetzt ist es nicht mehr so
> daß wir jedem Arbeiter
> der aus der U-Bahn steigt mit Mütze
> gleich sagen können, was ihm fehlt
> und unserem Hausbesitzer auch.
>
> Jetzt haben wir plötzlich Zeit
> zu langen Diskussionen in den Betten.
> Verschwitzt, aber kalt bis in die Zehen
> sehen wir zum ersten Mal das Weiße
> in unseren Augen und erschrecken.[9]

Making poetry out of experience of a less dramatic and negative sort than Ursula Krechel evokes here, in other words: enhancing the value of the individual present by freeing it from the past, was surely a natural alternative for this generation. The therapeutic quality of 'Alltagslyrik' was not the least of its attractions. Thus far we have tended to emphasise the historical and emotional conditions from

---

9. From her collection of poems *Nach Mainz!*, Darmstadt and Neuwied, 1977, anthologised in Volker Hage (ed.), *Lyrik für Leser. Deutsche Gedichte der siebziger Jahre*, Stuttgart, 1980, pp. 139f.

which West German poetry of the 1970s arose. But we must also continue to pursue the line of theory which began with Höllerer's theses of 1965. Writing close to the end of the decade, Ludwig Völker quotes a series of statements by Nicolas Born, Günter Herburger and Rolf Dieter Brinkmann which seem to derive from Höllerer's position and make it more radical. As early as 1967, Nicolas Born demands that poetry abandon symbol, metaphor, profundity and ornamentation; in the same year, Günter Herburger says poetry must begin with 'dem Allernächsten [. . .] und nicht mit Sprüchen, die schon seit Jahrhunderten benutzt werden'. In the following year Rolf Dieter Brinkmann enunciated the imperative: 'man muß vergessen, daß es so etwas wie Kunst gibt! Und einfach anfangen'.[10]

If it seems somewhat paradoxical that the main principles of the poetry of the 1970s should have been stated before the Student Movement had even collapsed, whereas we have insisted previously that this event was decisive for the shape poetry actually assumed in this decade, then this merely points to the central paradox of the 1970s in West Germany: that they are, in a sense, over before they begin. Hans Magnus Enzensberger, always an acute observer of his own times, introduces the 1970s, with a wealth of ironies, as a decade of which very little can be expected, whose events have, as it were, already occurred. In his poem 'Aufbruch in die siebziger Jahre' (1971) he foresees a decade of stale emotions, repetitive experience, increasing bureaucratisation and, most percipiently, the younger generation's retreat from politics into passive self-centeredness: 'Die Gegenkultur/ baumelt an ihren Kopfhörern'.[11]

Enzensberger's own style in this poem is a sophisticated synthesis of the manners of Bertolt Brecht and Gottfried Benn, and certainly these two major figures stand, despite all their political differences, in a distinctly complementary relationship to one another as influences on the poets of Enzensberger's generation. For those poets who first emerge in the 1970s, however, sophistication can scarcely be a value in itself; rather, the significant shift of emphasis is towards the documentation of experience. As Michael Zeller points out, poetry of this kind flourished in the years 1968–71 in the service of political controversy. Later in the decade this was to be supplanted

---

10. Cf. Ludwig Völker, 'Benn/Brecht und die deutsche Lyrik der Gegenwart', in Lothar Jordan, Axel Marquardt and Winfried Woesler (eds.), *Lyrik — von allen Seiten. Gedichte und Aufsätze des ersten Lyrikertreffens in Münster*, Frankfurt on Main, 1981, p. 181.
11. Hans Magnus Enzensberger, *Gedichte 1955–1970*, Frankfurt on Main, 1971, p. 158.

by the documentation of private experience, but it is important to recognise that the techniques of 'Dokumentar-Lyrik' led to the opening up of thematic areas which had been previously closed to poetry, such as television, the press and oral history.[12]

Before approaching the vexed question of the 'simplicity' of West German poetry of the 1970s, it is worth considering the parallel drawn by Günter Blamberger between the situation of poetry in the immediate post-war years and the practice of 'Alltagslyrik' in the 1970s. He points out that 'Trümmerliteratur', the first literature to be written in Germany after the collapse of the Third Reich, shows many similarities of theory and practice to the poetry of everyday experience written in the 1970s: it is realistic, upholds basic human values, adheres closely to concrete experience and avoids complex abstractions. Blamberger sees both kinds of writing as dominated by a down-to-earth existentialism which proceeds from a loss of faith in the power of ideology and abstraction to represent and control reality.[13] If we accept this analogy, then we have in effect postulated a dual origin for the 'Alltagslyrik' of the 1970s. On the one hand we can see it as a consistent development by a number of different poets from Höllerer's theoretical statements of 1965; on the other, it appears as the most obvious, spontaneous reaction to the disillusionment stemming from the failure of the Student Movement.

These alternative origins point to a further paradox which West German poetry of the 1970s was fated to exercise repeatedly without achieving any clear resolution. It appears on the one hand as the desire to write directly, spontaneously and with an absolute minimum of theoretical preconceptions and, on the other, as the often futile struggle to divest oneself of theory in the strongly intellectual German poetic tradition. When it became apparent around 1975 that a new kind of poetry was being written, the portentous term 'Neue Subjektivität', together with related catchwords, was called into being and expounded in highly abstract language. Hiltrud Gnüg's essay on the subject in the issue of the periodical *Merkur* of January 1978 provides abundant examples of the irony attendant on propagating the dictum 'Nicht Dualismus, Eindimensionalität herrscht . . .'.[14] For trying to define this 'one-dimensionality' in positive terms gets her into difficulties with the concept of the poetic

12. Michael Zeller, *Gedichte haben Zeit. Aufriß einer zeitgenössischen Poetik*, Stuttgart, 1982, p. 250.
13. Günter Blamberger, 'Ein Gedicht, bitte — Zur Alltagslyrik der siebziger Jahre', in Harald Wentzlaff-Eggebert (ed.), *Die Legitimation der Alltagssprache in der modernen Lyrik. Antworten aus Europa und Lateinamerika*, Erlangen, 1984, pp. 187f.
14. Hiltrud Gnüg, 'Was heißt "Neue Subjektivität"?', *Merkur*, 1/1978, p. 74.

self or 'lyrisches Ich':

> Die private Erfahrung ist auch eine gesellschaftliche, doch sie erscheint nicht mehr in plakativen Losungen, sondern als Erfahrung eines höchst komplexen Subjekts. Neue Subjektivität — das heißt auch: An die Stelle des lyrischen Kunst-Ichs ist jetzt das authentische Ich getreten. Mit der Entzweiung von Kunstsprache und Alltagssprache fällt so auch die Unterscheidung von lyrischem Ich und Autor-Ich weitgehend weg.[15]

The problem with these statements is not merely that 'one-dimensionality' must at the same time be seen as 'highly complex', but that Hiltrud Gnüg confuses the issue of the fictionality of any literary work with the achievement of particular emotional effects. To create an impression of personal authenticity in a poem does not prevent the poem's fictional nature in a variety of senses. A number of similar incidents may be represented as a single experience without the atmosphere of authenticity being lost. An imaginary situation, evoked with skill, can notoriously appear more 'real' in literature than inept reportage. The 'authenticity' of a poem is not something that can ever be verified through the text alone, but is ultimately a function of the reader's response, in the sense of an ability or willingness to identify with it. The distinction between a poetic self and an 'authentic' self cannot be abolished within the text itself. The poetic self exists only as a function of a given text and remains so whether it presents itself to a reader as autobiographical, 'impersonal', or as a mixture of both. The attempt to get away from the connotations of the term 'lyrisches Ich' in discussions of German poetry is perfectly understandable. But it is confusing to see this as replacing one kind of 'self' with another, because a shift in authorial intention cannot alter the nature of the act of writing. It may, of course, influence the way the text is likely to be received by the reader whom it envisages.[16]

Another conundrum posed by Hiltrud Gnüg's description is the relation of individual experience to an involvement with social issues in the poetry of the late 1970s. The fundamental difficulty here is to make credible the claim that choosing to write on themes from the sphere of private, everyday existence does not mean turning one's back on the attitudes of political dissent so prominent in the first half of the decade. This problem is confronted by Jürgen Theobaldy in

15. Ibid., p. 67.
16. This point is argued in greater detail in: Anthony Stephens, 'Überlegungen zum lyrischen Ich', in Theo Elm and Gerd Hemmerich (eds.), *Zur Geschichtlichkeit der Moderne. Der Begriff der literarischen Moderne in Theorie und Deutung*, Munich, 1982, pp. 58ff.

the afterword to his anthology of 1977 *Und ich bewege mich doch. . .* in the form of a defence of Rolf Dieter Brinkmann's poetic techniques: 'Sie drücken nicht Protest aus, sie *sind* Protest, Einspruch, Gegen-bilder . . . ein Widerstand gegen die Massenmedien, Wirtschafts-verbände, Parteien und Ministerien mit ihren verstümmelnden, wirklichkeitsverzehrenden oder synthetischen Produkten. Der Bezug auf das Selbsterlebte ist der Versuch, Verläßliches, Überprüf-bares zu sagen angesichts der öffentlichen Parolen'.[17]

There is a tinge of absurdity about the claim that one is mounting an effective social protest by simply being oneself in verse. There is in fact very little in the theory of 'Alltagslyrik' to prevent its turning into narcissistic indulgence, except for the repeated assertion that it is meant to achieve the opposite by implication alone. Brinkmann had already, in the introduction to his book of poems *Die Piloten* of 1968, claimed to be writing more in the American than the German tradition and the cover, a montage of figures from American pop-culture, features a photograph of the author among them declaring in English: 'It is not enough to love art! One must be art!'.[18] If one then takes a sample of Brinkmann's poetic production from the early 1970s, entitled simply 'Ein Gedicht' (1975), it may well strike one primarily as sophisticated word-play:

> Hier steht ein Gedicht ohne einen Helden.
> In diesem Gedicht gibts keine Bäume. Kein Zimmer
> zum Hineingehen und Schlafen ist hier in dem
> Gedicht. Keine Farbe kannst du in diesem
>
> Gedicht hier sehen. Keine Gefühle sind
> in dem Gedicht. Nichts ist in diesem Gedicht
> hier zum Anfassen. Es gibt keine Gerüche hier in
> diesem Gedicht . . .
>
> [. . .]
>
> . . . In dem Gedicht erscheint auch kein
> Sommertag. Es ist niemals Dienstag in diesem Gedicht.
> Es gibt keinen Mittwoch in diesem Gedicht, es herrscht
> nicht Freitag in diesem Gedicht und kein Donnerstag
>
> fehlt in dem Gedicht hier. Es ist nicht Montag,
> Samstag und Sonntag in hier dem Gedicht. Das Gedicht
> hier ist nicht die Verneinung von Montag oder
> Donnerstag. Das Gedicht hört hier einfach auf.[19]

17. Theobaldy (ed.), *Und ich bewege mich doch . . .*, p. 223.
18. Rolf Dieter Brinkmann, *Die Piloten*, Cologne, 1968.
19. Hage (ed.), *Lyrik für Leser*, pp. 60–4.

This is the beginning and end of a text which has twenty-four stanzas, all in this vein. If it seems unfair to cite it against Theobaldy's claims for the social relevance of poetry such as Brinkmann's, then it must be remembered that the claims made are usually comprehensive. This applies equally to the passage we have quoted from Hiltrud Gnüg and to Theobaldy's various theoretical statements. The point is, surely, that effective social protest simply does not occur of itself, irrespective of what themes the text explores, but demands the realisation of a concrete and visible authorial intention. Programmatic statements about 'Neue Subjektivität', or whatever name is given to the trend, tended to become disingenuous on precisely this point by ignoring the effort and skill necessary to achieving any effect in poetry.

Commenting on Theobaldy's anthology, Harald Hartung observes that poems by Rühmkorf and Enzensberger stand out amid the 'new formlessness' like 'foreign bodies' or 'anachronisms' precisely because they exhibit so much formal discipline.[20] There is a clear analogy between the convictions that poetic form is something that can be dispensed with and that the social impact of a text can be left to look after itself. It is surprising that the work of Wolf Biermann, for example, which was so well known in the late 1970s because of the publicity attending his expulsion from East Germany in 1976, apparently did nothing to prevent such myths from being propagated. His case makes it spectacularly clear that there is nothing 'easy' about the poetry of social protest.

Perhaps the essential problem is that the claims are still made in the idiom of the beginning of the decade, when it was possible to believe that West German society as a whole could be swung towards the left, whereas in fact the 'Alltagslyrik' of the late 1970s is more reactive than aggressive. Its prime aim was to maintain an openness of communication at a time when this seemed threatened by the direction of West German society as a whole and its undoubted success lay in making poetry a genuinely popular means of expression within the Counter Culture. Günter Blamberger is right, at the conclusion of the essay we have previously quoted, to call attention to the following statement by F.C. Delius which gives a more realistic account of the motivation of West German poetry in the late 1970s than we find in the bulk of programmatic statements. Significantly, he first compares the restricted situation of the West German poet with that of a poet of genuinely popular appeal, Pablo Neruda:

20. Harald Hartung, 'Die eindimensionale Poesie', *Neue Rundschau*, 2/1978, p. 240.

'Unsere Leitsterne,' sagt Neruda, 'sind Kampf und Hoffnung. Doch es gibt keinen einsamen Kampf, keine einsamen Hoffnungen.' Neruda hatte leichter reden als wir. Wir (die bundesdeutsche Lyrikerzunft) schreiben in einer Gesellschaft, in der das Vergehen von Hören und Sehen, von Lesen, Schmecken, Fühlen, Lieben, Denken propagiert und durchgesetzt wird. (Selbst Lyriker, die gegen diese Entwicklung schreiben, merken manchmal schon nicht mehr, wie die kulturelle Perversion auf sie zurückschlägt: wenn *sie* sich schamhaft dafür verantwortlich fühlen, daß ihnen keiner oder kaum einer zuhört . . .)[21]

The reactive element in this statement is quite obvious. What deserves more careful consideration is the question of isolation and the missing audience. For the 1970s, after all, saw the inception of frequent and sometimes very large poetry festivals ('Lyrikertreffen') at which established writers and beginners were heard with equal enthusiasm. There was a mushrooming of small publishers, back-yard-presses and 'alternative' writing groups such as the 'Literatur-postamt Hamburg'. It was also the time in which the anthologies of major publishers were genuinely opened to little known poets. The *Lyrik-Katalog* of 1978, for example, contained poems by some eighty-one poets ranging from a few well-known writers, such as Rose Ausländer, Günter Grass and Helmut Heißenbüttel, whose work is quite atypical of the bulk of West German poetry in the 1970s, to many much younger poets in the tradition of 'Alltagslyrik'. These years also see a larger proportion of women poets getting into print.

It is more accurate, perhaps, to say that West German poetry in the 1970s was inclined to accept, consciously or unconsciously, the status and attitudes of a minority culture. It was in this decade that 'alternative' culture came heavily into vogue and 'Alltagslyrik' was one of its conspicuous manifestations. While it remains true that the attitude of this minority towards the culture of the mass media and the political establishment was as defensive or resigned as Delius's statement maintains, communication within the minority culture was much more open and effective, and this is where 'Alltagslyrik' came into its own. The alienation of the Counter Culture in its various forms and phases from the great majority of West Germans becomes evident if one looks at its sympathies and idols. Genuinely underprivileged minorities, such as 'Gastarbeiter', the young and long-term unemployed, drug users, and the targets of popular hostility, such as leftist radicals, homosexuals and feminists are

21. Jan Hans, Uwe Herms and Ralf Thenior (eds.), *Lyrik-Katalog Bundesrepublik. Gedichte: Biographien: Statements*, Munich, 1978, pp. 378f.; c.f. Blamberger, 'Ein Gedicht, bitte . . .', p. 205.

mentioned in the poetry with varying degrees of understanding or solidarity. The Counter Culture finds its idols, in the main, outside the Central European cultural sphere. Mikis Theodorakis, Pablo Neruda, the Argentinian 'tango' poets, Che Guevara (still!) and various figures from sub-cultures of the USA, such as Charles Bukowski, tend to be invoked, rather than Rosa Luxemburg, Marx or Hölderlin.

Despite all these qualifications, F.C. Delius's pessimistic statement preserves a core of realism, since the examples of 'Alltagslyrik' that have most impact a decade later are not long, self-indulgent meanderings, but rather those terser statements in which the grievances of individuals are expressed who genuinely feel disadvantaged or oppressed by the majority. This form is perhaps most convincing when it is a plea to be heard that doubts its own success, as in the following lines by Ute Erb:

Liebesmarkt

Wo man mit menschlichen Gefühlen handelt,
steh ich am Pranger,
ständig abgewandelt
von Frau zu Mutter,
Dienerin und Hur,
Abtreiberin,
und jeden Monat banger,
werd älter ich,
und ich verschenk mich nur.[22]

Ute Erb's poem owes its strength to its directness, concreteness and lack of ornamentation. It is an effective condensation of what feminist literature has often expressed at greater length, but less memorably. The limits of 'Alltagslyrik' appear in its lack of formal sophistication, which may be deliberate, but has its own risks. The urgency and terseness of 'Liebesmarkt' avoids these, but a great deal of 'Alltagslyrik' has not aged well because its lack of formal discipline goes hand in hand with a kind of complacency.

It is important to remember that the tradition of more sophisticated lyric writing in German did not die out in the 1970s, despite the many programmatic announcements of its end and the quantitative dominance of 'Alltagslyrik'. The poetry of Sarah Kirsch, to take only one example, made no concessions to the fashion of 'Alltagslyrik' after her voluntary exile to West Germany in 1977. Her style re-

22. *Lyrik-Katalog Bundesrepublik*, p. 92.

mained disciplined, complex and imaginative, as in the following poem from *Katzenleben*, published in 1984:

Die Dämmerung

Es ist dunkelgrün unter dem Regen
Den alten Gewölben der Eichen
Halshoch das ungeschnitten Gras
Die tiefen schleifenden Wolken
Treffen Menschen die auf dem Grund
Des Meeres in versunkenen Dörfern
Träumerisch umgehn und Hunde schweben
Durch ein widersinniges Dasein
Die schwarzen Algen der treibende Tang
Schwimmenden Vögel fliegenden Fische
Bringen viel Unruhe mit sich
Über den Dächern sehn wir die Kiele
Englischer Kriegsschiffe ziehn.[23]

That this is no less possible in poetry of the late 1970s is shown by Hans Magnus Enzensberger's *Der Untergang der Titanic*, first published in 1978. This is a major poetic achievement of the 1970s which stands quite outside the trends which predominate, a long, moving and successful poem in thirty-three 'cantos', the same number as in Dante's 'Purgatorio'. Dante is only one of the many literary and cultural points of reference in the text, which skilfully counterpoints various different time-levels and lines of thematic association in order to confront the West German present with various real or imaginary alternatives. Enzensberger also uses documentary style to great advantage, blending it with the other elements with a much greater freedom and verve than is usually found in the documentary techniques of 'Alltagslyrik'. In short, Enzensberger's poem demonstrates all that literary sophistication which the advocates of 'Neue Subjektivität' had declared obsolete and deliberately set out to exclude from their writing.[24]

The early 1980s do not mark a turning in the direction of West German poetry. While 1980 sees the violent confrontations between police and squatters ('Hausbesetzer'), which have been termed 'an entirely new oppositional movement', and while the inauguration of President Reagan and the immediate increase in tensions between East and West may have produced from 1981 onwards the 'wave of

23. Sarah Kirsch, *Katzenleben*, Stuttgart 1984, p. 56.
24. For a fuller discussion of this poem see Martin Kane's chapter on Enzensberger, pp. 237–42.

fear' ('Angstwelle') and, simultaneously, the sharp increase in the size and number of peace demonstrations, one cannot say that these factors caused the great majority of West German poets to write differently.[25] 'Alltagslyrik' continued to flourish, after all, throughout the West German obsession with terrorism in 1977–8, and it would be inaccurate to see the abandoning of the style as a direct response to political events.

Hans Dieter Schäfer predicted in 1981 the demise of the prevailing poetic style of the 1970s and this was fulfilled by about the end of 1983. But the decisive change was towards the greater formal discipline and sophistication which most older and established poets had, in any event, maintained throughout the decade.[26] The disavowal of poetic craftsmanship seems to have encountered its own natural limits, as the often straggling or amorphous 'slice of life' manner became uninteresting to its own practitioners. It is important to note that the forms of disseminating poetry which became popular in the 1970s — 'Lyrikertreffen' with public readings, a wealth of small publishing firms and 'do-it-yourself' editions — have continued to flourish up to the present, but those who write and publish poetry more as a hobby have tended to follow the example of the professional writers, such as Wondratschek and Theobaldy, in giving up the cult of 'lässiges Daherreden' and its concomitant themes and authorial positions.[27] From this perspective, we can conclude that the characteristic poetry of the 1970s may be seen as an initially vigorous, experimental divergence from the strong German tradition of form-conscious and intellectual poetry, which certainly achieved its aims, but, in doing so, lost impetus and ended quietly in the early 1980s.

25. Ingrid Müller-Münsch et al., *Besetzung — weil das Wünschen nicht geholfen hat*, Hamburg, 1981, p. 6; see also 'Es gibt eine Explosion von Ängsten', *Der Spiegel*, 16/1981, pp. 17–22; and Freimut Duve, Heinrich Böll and Klaus Staeck (eds.), *Zuviel Pazifismus?*, Hamburg, 1981, passim.
26. Hans Dieter Schäfer, 'Zusammenhänge der deutschen Gegenwartslyrik', *Lyrik — von allen Seiten*, p. 65; for further useful information on the end of 'Alltagslyrik' c.f. Blamberger, *Ein Gedicht, bitte . . .*, pp. 203f.
27. Schäfer, 'Zusammenhänge der deutschen Gegenwartslyrik', p. 65.

Suggested Further Reading

Heinz Ludwig Arnold (ed.), *Literaturbetrieb in der Bundesrepublik Deutschland: Ein kritisches Handbuch,* 2nd edn, Munich, 1981

——, *Die Gruppe 47: Ein kritischer Grundriß,* Munich, 1980

——, *Politische Lyrik,* 3rd edn, Munich, 1984

Peter Bekes et al., *Deutsche Gegenwartslyrik von Biermann bis Zahl. Interpretationen,* Munich, 1982

Wolfgang Bentin (ed.) *Deutsche Literatur Geschichte. Von den Anfängen bis zur Gegenwart,* Stuttgart, 1979

Otto F. Best and Hans-Jürgen Schmitt (eds.), *Die deutsche Literatur: Ein Abriß in Text und Darstellung,* vol. 16, chapter II: 'Lyrik', Stuttgart, 1977

Peter Brückner, *Versuch, uns und anderen die Bundesrepublik zu erklären: Politik 81,* Berlin, 1979(1978)

Hans Magnus Enzensberger, *Museum der modernen Poesie: eingerichtet von Hans Magnus Enzensberger,* Frankfurt on Main, 1980

Hugo Friedrich, *Die Struktur der modernen Lyrik: Von der Mitte des 19. bis zur Mitte des 20. Jahrhunderts,* Hamburg, 1973(1956)

Ulrich Fulleborn, *Deutsche Prosagedichte des 20. Jahrhunderts: Ein Textsammlung in Zusammenarbeit mit Klaus Dieter Dencker,* Munich, 1976

Hiltrud Gnüg, *Entstehung und Krise lyrischer Subjektivität: Vom klassischen lyrischen Ich zur modernen Erfahrungswirklichkeit,* Stuttgart, 1983

Reinhold Grimm (ed.), *Zur Lyrik-Diskussion: Wissenschaftliche Buchgesellschaft, 'Wege der Forschung',* vol. CXI, Darmstadt, 1974

Michael Hamburger, *Die Dialektik der modernen Lyrik: Von Baudelaire bis zur Konkreten Poesie* original title: *The Truth of Poetry* (1969), Munich, 1972

——, *German Poetry 1910–1975: An Anthology* translated and edited by Michael Hamburger, Manchester, 1977

Harald Hartung, 'Pop als "postmoderne" Literatur: Die deutsche Szene, Brinkmann und andere', *Die Neue Rundschau,* 1971/4, pp. 723–42

Walter Hinck (ed.), *Gedichte und Interpretationen,* vol. 6, *Gegenwart,* Stuttgart, 1982

Walther Killy, *Elemente der Lyrik,* Munich, 1972

Otto Knörrisch, *Die Deutsche Lyrik der Gegenwart 1945–1970,* Stuttgart, 1971

Dieter Lattmann (ed.), *Kindlers Literaturgeschichte der Gegenwart, Autoren — Werke — Themen — Tendenzen seit 1945: Die Literatur der Bundesrepublik Deutschland II, Lyrik: Karl Krolow, Dramatik: Hellmuth Karasek,* Frankfurt on Main, 1980(1973)

Peter Mosler, *Was wir wollten, was wir wurden: 'Studentenrevolte zehn Jahre danach'. Mit einer Chronologie von Wolfgang Kraushaar,* Hamburg, 1982(1977)

Malcolm Pasley (ed.), *Germany: A Companion to German Studies,* London and New York, 1982(1972)

William H. Rey, *Poesie der Antipoesie: Moderne deutsche Lyrik — Genesis — Theorie — Struktur,* Heidelberg, 1978

Peter Rühmkorf, *Strömungslehre I: Poesie,* Hamburg, 1978

Peter M. Stephan, '"Theorie des offenen Gedichts?"': Deutsche Gedichte der Gegenwart im Spiegel der Anthologien', *Literaturmagazin 14*

——, 'Die Literatur blüht im Tal', *Gespräche — Essays — Neue Prosa und Lyrik*, Hamburg, 1981, pp. 133–49

Jürgen Theobaldy, '"Begrenzte Weiten": Amerika-Bilder in der westdeutschen Lyrik', *Akzente*, 1976/5, pp. 402–17

—— and Gustav Zürcher, '"Veränderung der Lyrik: Über westdeutsche Gedichte seit 1965'', Munich, 1976

Hans Peter Thurn, 'Literatur und Alltag im 20. Jahrhundert', K. Hammerich and Michael Klein (eds.), *Materialien zur Soziologie des Alltags*, Opladen, 1978

Karl H. Van D'Elden, *West German Poets on Society and Politics: Interviews with an Introduction by Karl H. Van Đ'Elden*, Hamline University, Detroit, 1979

Peter Wapnewski, *Zumutungen: Essays zur Literatur des 20. Jahrhunderts*, Düsseldorf, 1979

X Frank Wolff/Eberhard Windaus (eds.), *Studentenbewegung 1967–1969: Protokolle und Materialien*, Frankfurt on Main, 1977

DONNA L. HOFFMEISTER

The Novel of the Everyday

The social and ideological definitions of self are a basic preoccupation of contemporary German, Austrian, and Swiss literature and
the deconstruction of self, as expounded by Michel Foucault and
Jacques Derrida, are at the centre of literary theory. The well-
established devices: non-linear, discontinuous narration, varying
pronouns and tenses for the protagonists, and conscious stylisation
have been the means for expressing radical disruptions of self in
contemporary fiction, in the fictionalised biographies of Christa
Wolf, Max Frisch or Wolfgang Koeppen, for instance, or in Uwe
Johnson's *Jahrestage* (1970–83). The decentring process on the stage
has similar components. Language is continually varied without any
binding perspective, whether satirical or serious, being communicated in the plays of Peter Handke, Botho Strauß or Thomas
Bernhard. The language is too disjunctive, the oscillation of perspectives too extreme to give the characters even the vaguest of contours.
Fragmented identity stems from the lack of comfortable, confident,
agreed-upon vantage-points or what Habermas calls the 'Neue
Unübersichtlichkeit'.[1] The holistic versions of self that were the
mainstay of the literature of the past, in the 'Bildungsroman' of the
nineteenth and earlier twentieth centuries, for instance, now seem
suspect and manipulated. Contemporary writers thus explore the
self not so much as *terra incognita* (with the implicit possibility of
revelations from the unconscious) but rather as a familiar site
crisscrossed by mental traffic often bizarrely out of synchrony.

What are the access routes between these literary images of
human identity and current history? How do we define the macro-
historical situation, which Fredric Jameson argues is the absent
cause of any given text.[2] I work from two premises: first of all,
literature is not an autonomous construct but rather an expression of

1. Jürgen Habermas, 'Die Neue Unübersichtlichkeit: Die Krise des Wohlfahrtstaates
   und die Erschöpfung utopischer Energien', in Habermas, *Die Neue Unübersichtlichkeit*, Frankfurt on Main, 1985
2. Fredric Jameson, *The Political Unconscious: Narrative as a Socially Symbolic Act*, Ithaca,
   NY, 1981, p. 82

the social world. The perspective of modernism and its critical counter-part, 'New Criticism', postulated aesthetically absolute fiction-making. But modernism is loosening its hold on our interpretation of litera-ture and a sociological reading of literature is gaining credence. However, the relationship between the literary world and exter-nality is not easy to define, for literature clearly does not transcribe reality. If accuracy were a literary criteria, sociological treatises and factory manuals might be bestsellers, which is not the case. The world in literature is organised and selected in accordance with the requirements of the reading process, which is both a limiting and a liberating experience. Oscar Wilde's comment that nature imitates art expresses both the opportunity and the predicament of literary credibility. A novel, for instance, may select certain aspects of reality so cleverly that readers fail to notice all that is omitted. The world of the reader appears to coalesce with the world of fiction. The willing suspension of disbelief is essential to the literary experience. That is the opportunity. But there is also a risk for the writer, in that the freedom implicit in this act of organisation is also a significant burden. Organising a world of fiction is never value-free. My second thesis is that literary language is unavoidably referential in that it crystallises the writers' double responsibility to their concrete hu-man condition and to their dreams of change. The alchemy, whereby the writer's world is internalised by a reader, is inseparable from the writer's self-aware involvement in his or her historical situation. There is a double complexity between the everyday world and the finished novel: the complexity of the novel's derivation from the everyday and the conscious referentiality of the writer to his every-day.

What is common to a group of writers with which I am concerned here is their ability to place the whole discussion of the self within the realm of everyday life, indeed they include banality within the compass of their literary works, in order to connect the blankness of existence, the abandonment of human uniqueness with this one fundamental aspect of daily living, namely the workplace, which has hardly ever been conceded entry to the life of literature. Dozens of novels written in the last decade describe how protagonists attempt to forge a sense of personal identity by means of everyday experi-ences, specifically their experiences of the workplace. These two concerns: the self and everyday life, have become symptomatic for much of present-day literature. There is a central historical signifi-cance which is not yet understood. What has broken down is precisely the modernist distinction between aesthetically absolute fiction-making and aesthetically uninteresting everyday reality. Contemporary fiction of the everyday forges special links between externality and the worlds of fiction and I am not here merely repeating the old Chekovian distinction between event and atmosphere. Traditionally the unexceptional event commanded literary space and the public's interest. Such is still the case with American soap operas, which relate how Americans become ill, have accidents, go to hospitals, fall in and out of love and flirt with adultery. What is not true is that these events occur with such frequency and such drama or that they constitute the basic fabric of American life, which is much more concerned with doing a routine job routinely, shopping for groceries, going to bed at night, waking up in the morning, showering and brushing one's teeth. If fiction is to articulate such mundaneness, it must dig beneath soap opera melodrama, resist the temptation simply to manipulate expectations of drama by relocating them; in effect it must suppress the exceptional events which also occur in life. Precisely the fiction of the everyday points to a different understanding of experience. In fact, fiction of the everyday may be a deliberate reaction against the current marketability of high drama and synthetic intensity. Inadequacy, falling short, is the leitmotif for literature of the everyday: work is inadequate for people, people feel inadequate for work and yet the emancipation from the performance principle, the emergence of a non-alienated conception of work, as already urged by Marcuse in *Eros and Civilization* in 1955, seems as remote as ever. Although these authors explore the work world without any utopian dreams, they explore it with great urgency, for it is precisely here, in this uncharted Amazon of contemporary man's daily experience, that the historical rifts may be opening in the apparently impregnable blandness of the administered society. How the self is defined, how it depends on work reality and how that reality might be transformed are the fundamental obsessions to which the novelists under discussion here give verbal shape.

The depiction of everyday work reality in fiction since 1970 is not a bright one: the portrayal, for instance, of unskilled labour by Ludwig Fels in *Ein Unding der Liebe* (1981) or of skilled labour in Martin Walser's *Seelenarbeit* (1979), of physical labour in Franz Innerhofer's novel about farmwork, *Schöne Tage* (1974), or in Hans-Dieter Baroth's story about coal-mining in *Streuselkuchen in Ickern* (1980).[3] The discontinuity of personal experience and estrangement

3. I should state at this point that, in this essay, I in no way attempt to cover the body of theoretical debates about, or the range of novels of the everyday, as represented by the work of the Werkkreis Literatur der Arbeitswelt. Analyses of these aspects are provided by Bullivant and Hahn/Naumann (see Suggested Further Reading).

of factory work is depicted by the Swiss writers Silvio Blatter in *Genormte Tage, verschüttete Zeit* (1976) and Franz Böni in *Die Wanderarbeiter* (1981). Nicolas Born deals with the radical breaks and shocks of a journalist in *Die Fälschung* (1979) and Hermann Lenz with the tranquil despair of a writer in *Ein Fremdling* (1983), while Peter Rosei in *Das schnelle Glück* (1980) and Wilhelm Genazino in *Fremde Kämpfe* (1984) deal with unemployment and its psychic dislocations. These writers are all concerned with what happens to the self in a de-centered work world. The personal identity of their protagonists influences the kind of work they do. At the same time the protagonists in these novels are modified by the identity they acquire through their work. To varying degrees they become what they do. In other words, work is a human product and man is a product of work. This mutuality between identity and work does not lead, however to behaviourism, on the one hand, or to psychologism, on the other, but forces itself outward toward history. It is a wheel with spikes on it. Formerly Naturalism's goal aimed also toward an historical perspective. The newer Naturalists are more self-consciously history oriented.

This literature of the everyday is one response to the heated debate about human identity and the function of literature being carried on both in literature itself and by the theorists, primarily the deconstructionists and their opponents. A concern with identity is the starting-point for modernists and post-modernists alike. Literature of the everyday comes to terms with the fictive articulation of dispersed, decentred identity by inverting the identity obsessions of the modernists. For in literature of the everyday identity does not decompose but rather the perspective about oneself and the world which seems natural and appropriate is, in fact, shown to be relative to one particular socio-historical environment. The social location of identity is the preoccupation of these texts. All perspectives are demonstrated to be dependent on the ideologising influence of their social contexts.

The best way to understand this renewal of realism is to look closely at two seminal texts. Part of the power of Kafka's *Der Prozeß* lies in the reader's sense that it is portraying the landscape, more precisely the workscape, of the twentieth century for the first time. The principle of office work: its hierarchies, anonymities, repressed dramas and pervasive depersonalisation constitute a claustrophobic world which is only gradually being mapped out in concrete literary

---

My concern here is to present the work of two important writers whose work is little known outside West Germany and Austria

terms fifty years after Kakfa. Two writers, Gernot Wolfgruber and Wilhelm Genazino, have produced rather intriguing articulations of this twentieth-century workspace, Wolfgruber in a novel entitled *Niemandsland* (1978)[4] and Genazino in a trilogy of three short prose works about an office worker called Abschaffel (1977–9).[5]

In his portrayal of the character Georg Klein, Wolfgruber traces the painful, confusing, anxiety-ridden experiences of upward mobility; for when Georg Klein moves from blue- to white-collar work, he no longer wants to identify himself with factory workers, but he finds no firm confirmation of his newly acquired status either. Wolfgruber portrays in a relentless, absorbing fashion the disorientation and reorientation of a person who switches work worlds. By the end of the novel the no-man's-land which lay between the factory in which Klein once worked and the dying works, the last free space, is covered over by a large low building. In no-man's-land the spectre of freedom disappears into a pervasive, anonymous work reality, which is unable to impart to Klein a sense of personal well-being.

The novel focuses on Klein's analyses of his own situation. Through the process of interpretation and reinterpretation on his part we see how his understanding of his world is formed implicitly by his social background: his upbringing, family traditions, norms and expectations, his education and the social factors which bear on his sense of values. His working-class background has both a restrictive as well as a liberating influence on him in so far as Klein continues to struggle against it when he upgrades his work status. His father worked for the railroad and he sees no reason why his own son should not be content with such work also. But Klein's inability to adapt causes him to quit his apprenticeship for work of lesser status at the factory and then to quit one factory job after another in his insistent search for alternatives. He deems his father's advice to be thoughtless, automatic sentences with which he tries to stifle his children's hopes of a life different from his own. Getting an office job means a changed relationship with his family, first indifference and then genuine shame for them. When he finds himself sitting with his mother in a restaurant, he feels his annoyance choking him and he utters one disdainful remark after another in order to show how different he is from her. But the crisis of adjusting to new class norms affords Klein an even greater rupture with his background. He

4. Gernot Wolfgruber, *Niemandsland*, Salzburg, 1978. Subsequent page references to this novel are inserted into the text
5. Wilhelm Genazino, *Abschaffel* (I), Reinbek, 1977; *Die Vernichtung der Sorgen* (II), Reinbek, 1978; *Falsche Jahre* (III), Reinbek, 1979. Page references are inserted into the text

changes his circle of acquaintances, his reading habits, the manner in which he spends his leisure time, his dress, etiquette, and eating habits and his relations with women and experiences this new life as prefabricated. The novel depicts how the kind of work one is involved in determines the content and form of large segments of everyday life. The title *Niemandsland* articulates the brittle, artificial, subsuming nature of Klein's new everyday reality. Upward mobility is predicated on this cleavage between a past and a present identity. In the life systems of our century the only way forward for Klein is by constructing a different identity but he is fully aware in the end of the enormous costs of freeing himself from the expectations and commitments of his upbringing. Advancement is bought at the cost of anxiety.

Klein attempts to understand the principles underlying the behaviour of white-collar workers so that he might fit in better, but his interpretations of this new social constellation and his calculations of how he should bear himself in new situations prove faulty. He is revealing the limitations of his working-class horizon. He feels so self-conscious about buying a book on good manners that he has it wrapped as a gift. Even after he has memorised the book, he decides that such socially sanctioned class behaviour would never become second nature to him. He cannot imagine why anyone would want to know how to eat oysters, for instance. He thinks that office workers have more learning than blue-collar workers. The polite, clean-nosed and well-combed graduates of the Gymnasium obviously have advantages on the job market which the loud, rough, lackadaisical apprentices do not have, but he learns that such class-oriented conduct has little to do with how much one knows. But then he thinks that he has perhaps only read the wrong books; his evaluations of his situation always contain a tentative recasting of any and all conclusions. He justifies changing his voting behaviour when his new acquaintances from work make fun of the working-class party. He has to buy a new car, wear a clean shirt to work everyday and learn about cheese, wine, Persian carpets, dog pedigrees and genuine furniture and to pretend as if this strange knowledge were all self-evident. The manner in which he passes his leisure time is a kind of conspicuous consumption. He goes to coffee houses instead of working-class bars and is occasionally aware how senseless such behaviour is. In order to protect himself from threats to his new identity he avoids his former co-workers from the factory and makes sure he does not throw away his cigarette in the manner in which workers do. He watches over his behaviour in almost phobic fashion. He has to be particularly careful of language-use. At work he has to learn to say 'Bürobeginn' instead of 'Arbeitsbeginn' (p. 99) and cumbersome sentences such as 'Entschuldigung, darf ich Sie einen Augenblick stören?' (p. 99). He is never sure how middle-class office workers swear. This newly acquired stock of knowledge about the bureaucratic world help him to meet the threats of unfamiliar situations but he gradually becomes aware in the novel how cliché-ridden and reductive his perceptions are. Again and again he is disappointed to learn in what a mediocre fashion his middle-class acquaintances furnish their apartments and how limited their reading habits are. He admits to himself how stupid it was to think putting on a white shirt might wipe out his previous identity. But like the white shirt, he exchanges his working-class girlfriend for a middle-class wife. And the status anxiety which is not solved by the work organisation continues to fester in the private sphere, leading to attempted suicide and eventually divorce. Significant biographical shocks are necessary steps for the upwardly mobile and, of course, it is through such shocks that the author forces us to question class behaviour as such. Klein is not being satirised, simply because there is no archimedean point, no 'correct' perspective, from which to launch a satire.

Wolfgruber's novel traces how Klein's perspectives are drastically shaped by his work experiences. His view is modified also by his own awareness of the disparity between his expectations and his concrete experiences. But awareness of office hierarchies, dependencies, constraints and monotony are pushed aside. His consciousness admits only those perspectives with which he can cope at that point. By means of distortion and forgetting he survives one crisis after another. Klein did not form any relationships with assembly-line workers but later fondly remembers having done so. As a manual worker he said he would never identify workers with their mechanical movements but does so when his white-collar job requires this of him. As a manual worker he was often explosive in expressing his dissatisfaction but cannot understand such behaviour on the part of manual workers when he is no longer one of them. In order to legitimise his present work situation, Klein has to repudiate earlier realities and memories. The necessity for Klein to maintain a false consciousness and false values in order for him to survive is one central issue of the novel. All the more significant for his construction of meaning is the stabilised perception he reaches toward the end of the novel. Klein can no longer understand how he could have had such utopian views of office work. He no longer gets extra pleasure in not having to punch the time clock as manual workers do. Office work resembles factory work in its monotony, in the discontent it causes and in the indignity of power relations. Above all he realises that the management of the firm has interests opposed to his, whether he is a manual labourer or an office worker. He wanted to believe that he was destined for upward mobility and that such a change in status was an enviable social good. In the end he questions whether his promotion into the white-collar ranks truly matters. Relativising the mobility ethos is a major issue of the novel as a whole. Klein's false consciousness gradually gives way to sobriety and resignation. For him the future no longer assumes superiority over the past. The prospect of not being able to imagine a work alternative better than the one he presently has, a view he found abhorrent at the beginning, has now become his own. His realisation that white-collar work is not necessarily better than his work in the factory is the determinate judgement with which the novel ends. Klein's sheer survival in the work world with all his anxiety, disillusions and compromises places in question the traditional process of 'Bildung' which the novel both enacts and subverts. The reader's journey with Klein's consciousness through the bureaucratic work world ends in a cancellation of all the elements which have seemed to define that consciousness: struggle, development, critical awareness, memory. Klein's story tells us that the era of the unique consciousness may be at an end. But consciousness persists as such. The reader is virtually forced to make the transition from psychology to history.

Abschaffel, the protagonist of Genazino's novels, is not searching for an identity based on work but is fleeing from it. The first sentence of the first novel makes clear that he works only because he must. But the role he must play as a well-adjusted white-collar worker requires that he at least maintain appearances. Since bureaucratic work is repulsive to him, he develops strategies of role distance to deal with it. But they are a questionable remedy. For to escape from himself requires that he project his self-disdain onto others, which is an energy consuming activity Abschaffel calls work. In this behaviour he is both following an established linguistic transference in German of the concept of work into emotional life ('Trauerarbeit', 'Seelenarbeit') and effectively draining the workplace itself of its claim to the psychic energy of work. Abschaffel's sense of panic keeps him in perpetual motion, pacing his apartment, loitering through bordellos, chasing around town. But the insight he would most like to repress forces its way into his consciousness: 'Ich kann nicht mehr arbeiten[. . .]. Ich kann mein Leben nicht anerkennen, weil es würdelos und blöd ist' (pp. 178–9, II). The issue which this trilogy raises is whether people with a sense of personal deficiency choose boring work or whether particularly boring work leads to psychic deformities. Both Klein and Abschaffel survive their work traumas with an identity barely intact, with a world view which is more cynical than wise and with a relationship to work which is more submissive than sovereign. In the third novel about Abschaffel a psychotherapist diagnoses Abschaffel's problem as 'Starrheit des Berufslebens' (p. 150, III). He claims Abschaffel chose an occupation which makes no demands on him because he needs his energies for working through his emotions toward his parents. This diagnosis is convincing in the context of the novels: Abschaffel's dislike for his parents' norms, values, behaviour and lifestyle and his emotional attachment to them are indeed related to his inability to accommodate to his work reality. But a certain banality clings to these diagnoses which draws the reader's attention towards the whole questions of transforming social issues into therapeutic ones. At the same time Abschaffel's quest for a privatistic overview leads him to a judgement of his father's working life. The reader both accompanies Abschaffel on his quest and becomes critical of his criticism.

He defines his father as a 'hoffnungsloses kleines Arbeitstier, das an seine Verhältnisse ausgeliefert war' (p. 26, III). His stinginess, his concern with cleanliness, his gluttony and his tyranny all derive, in Abschaffel's opinion, from his disappointment with his work. His situation is made wretched by his keeping his disappointment to himself and by boasting about his job to his son. His stinginess derives from the frustration that his earnings are inadequate. He permits himself only one pleasure, a pack of cigarettes a day, he has only three coats his entire life and he never lets a crust of bread go to waste. 'Diese Art von Mangelleben hielt der Vater für DAS LEBEN überhaupt' (p. 48, I). He does not go to his mother's funeral, in order to save the tram fare, does not allow a neighbour to give his son a pair of much wanted ice skates because he will not pay the entrance fee at the ice station and refuses to go on Sunday walks with his family because not being able to eat in a restaurant along the way humiliates him. The perverse family relationships, deriving from his father's frustrations with his work have a determining influence on Abschaffel's life. Abschaffel's everyday routine is dictated by his overwhelming rejection of his father's lifestyle and by his conviction that despite all his efforts he will always be like his father: 'billig geizig, schäbig' (p. 169, III). Because of his fear of identifying with his father he avoids buying cheap shaving brushes, gets pleasure from throwing away expensive items and puts an extra slice of meat on his bread as compensation. His scorn and sympathy for his father, his hatred and partiality for his mother and his confused involvement with their lives weave a constraining web which keep Abschaffel from changing his life. He is timid and indecisive. Only in his mind does he contrive a kind of imaginary independence. With both Klein and Abschaffel a radical rejection of a perspective results only in its equally sterile inversion.

Much of Genazino's trilogy is devoted to Abschaffel's perceptions about office work. Unlike Klein, Abschaffel is too cynical and worldly wise to expect to find meaning in work. There is nothing about his work experience which does not meet with his scorn. It is a deception, for instance, to attach status to jobs with titles such as 'Exportkaufmann, Importkaufmann oder Speditionskaufmann' (p. 7, I), when all these workers do is to telephone a little and kill time by filling out forms or dictating letters. Abschaffel spends time at work, for instance, twisting the hair of his eyebrows. His desk partner will never do much more than arrange his scissors, glue, and paper clips in an orderly fashion before he leaves work for home. When Abschaffel has sat motionless at his desk for two hours he is afraid that a viscous fluid is collecting in his eyes like that of crocodiles. The only consolation is to observe the even more vacuous life of fish in an aquarium. Office workers attribute their jobs to failure in school; without school dropouts no bureaucracy would exist. The boredom of office work can be broken by tossing paper clips down secretaries' blouses and by walking to the toilet frequently to wash one's hands. Cleanliness, over-correctness and unimaginativeness typify, in Abschaffel's view, the people he works with. Only one of Abschaffel's colleagues has a truly unique way of breaking the routine by displaying sentiments and attitudes not appropriate for office decorum: he keeps a bottle of wine hidden in his waste basket, wishes everyone a good weekend on Monday and calls himself Marquis de pommes frites (p. 44, II). He succeeds in having bizarre regulations enforced, such as the installation of five wheels on every office chair, and criticises stipulations governing the use of the office photocopying machines in such a way that both the boss and his co-workers think he is on their side. Other office employees can be easily recognised outside the office; they are the ones who wash down their food in fast-serve restaurants. The question whether the bureaucratic structure which demands conformity and an overconcern with regulations brings about such deformity, or whether disciplined, submissive people choose to become bureaucrats is one Abschaffel asks but leaves unanswered. For in literary terms this circularity is embodied in Abschaffel's perspective. His ironies and criticisms draw attention to the continuity between his co-workers' petty escapisms and those of his own devising.

Abschaffel develops strategies for dealing with his everyday work life, but criticism, rejection and role distance are a kind of work which consume his energies and leave him exhausted. Every firm, in his opinion, seems like a pseudo family because people see one another on a day-to-day basis. He tries to keep relations impersonal by taking off his glasses so that his co-workers seem only like moving spots in the background. The man sitting opposite him never dares to begin a conversation with him. His working life distorts all time into an alternation between rush and emptiness. He has trouble therefore making decisions in his spare time. He tries to coordinate taking a bath and preparing a meal but finds it all too hectic. He never takes sick leave and spends his vacations anxiously at home, not knowing what to do with himself. The mediocrity of his work world continually asserts itself. For this mediocrity signifies his own mediocrity. Again and again he says to himself that he can no longer endure his work until he is finally led to admit this to another person: 'Ich kann nicht mehr arbeiten, verstehen Sie' (p. 178, II). The perfect inner balance of alienation is always liable to collapse into its opposite, radical incapacity for work. And the reader's response is necessarily double; Abschaffel's failure cannot be construed as a criticism of him as a person, for he has already thought of every possible criticism; such failure can only be read as the atrophy of the entire Western institution of work and puritanical achievement.

Throughout most of the three novels, Abschaffel diverts his attention from this painful insight by means of time-killing diversions or critical observations of his surroundings. He wants to kill time without being aware of doing so. He imagines messing up his hair, blowing smoke through his nose while greeting someone at the door. He feels proud that he is able to put matches into a matchbox with the fingers of one hand. Sometimes he just gazes at his eyelashes. He annotates as everyday insanity the joy he feels fetching his clean underwear from the laundry. Abschaffel repeats sentences obsessively to himself, changing words here and there: 'aber selbstverständlich' becomes 'aber selbsterklärlich' (pp. 20–1, I). 'Eine Portion Eis mit Früchten' becomes 'eine Portion Eis zum Furchten' (p. 39, I). He designates these caprices as 'die Arbeit des Beobachtens und Bemerkens' (p. 44, I). Although there is the sense of a quest echoing throughout Abschaffel's formulations, the text is as trapped as he is, circling around the empty centre of the workplace.

As a timid person, Abschaffel's means of distancing himself from his work identity seem rather feeble. He refuses to take vacations like other office workers do. Utopian or positive solutions are not imaginable to this astute pessimist and cynical office worker. In all this the reader gradually becomes aware that the large scale on which these petty events are laid out is necessary. Genazino's books are crowded with events, both actual and imaginary; yet nothing happens and nothing can happen. The three novels are a continuously narrated monologue of free indirect thoughts. Abschaffel is constantly catching onto his own psychological tricks. His confusion is the reader's and his insights into his own confusion are the reader's also. Such a double awareness lends a macabre humour to the novels: reading the new regulations of his apartment building, Abschaffel asks himself if standing in front of the new regulations might be against the regulations. It is part of his behaviour to abstract himself from situations and to ask general questions about the significance of his behaviour. When he catches himself throwing away a carton, he says he would rather not appear as if he were able to accommodate to everyday life by throwing away cartons. He signals to the reader that he knows he is distracted, that he knows he tells lies, and that he has difficulty coming to terms with his own contradictions. His own name Abschaffel relates to a life in neutral gear, a state similar to death. He has rid himself of the dreams, desires, and the ability to be sad. Genazino's theme is similar to Handke's, whose figures often register their irritation and disgust with events and things of everyday life and stand outside themselves in self-observation. But unlike Handke's protagonists, Abschaffel's neurosis put this self in question. The reader is drawn into Abschaffel's comprehensively portrayed society of bureaucracy but is aware of the other world of unstated historical, critical issues, which for all his restless detachment Abschaffel can never confront.

These two character novels of social-psychological realism, which relate successively the everyday events of its protagonists, Georg Klein and Abschaffel, and the long-term crises which develop out of work existence, have little external action. We are more attached to the events of their minds, than to the non-events of their worlds in which they are exchangeable cogs in the machine. As in Alain Robbe-Grillet's *nouveau roman* insignificant details of everyday life, the quasi-automatic behaviour which we learn to forget, are caught with precision. Many of Abschaffel's observations lead nowhere. The expectation that details in literature have greater significance than in everyday life, that readers should pay attention to every single incident is deliberately subverted. The style, which is ascetic, brittle and without poetic flourish, communicates the threat of a Beckettian void but without Beckett's metaphysical stylisation. Genazino even denies us an ending. Genazino's trilogy of the white-collar worker Abschaffel gives penetrating glimpses of disappointment, consumer terror, human want and indifference. Abschaffel, whose neuroses are fostered by his everyday work life, is capable neither of vigorous resistance nor of total capitulation. The only solution within the frame of the novel and within Abschaffel's consciousness seems to be dogged accommodation to a work situation which will not humanise him. Genazino's novels lay bare the brutal reality of office work and his refusal to suggest remedies underpins his diagnosis. The more thoroughly Abschaffel pursues his question for personal answers, the more that quest dissolves into the perpetuum mobile of the work place. In Genazino's literary moment, the 1970s, the author himself seems to expose the inadequacy of the analytical, psychologically driven literary explanations through a repeated short-circuiting of all explanations.

How can literature which deals with the hassle, boredom, and noise of daily living inspire reader interest? The very choice of words, the referential language and circumscribed form would not meet the criteria of modernist literature. For here trivialities and nihilisms jostle one another. The answer has to lie in the intersection of postmodernism with the structural emptiness of ever more rationalised work experience in the smoothly functioning technologies of late capitalism. The modernist assault on the autonomous self has deposited its fragments in a wholly controlled work environment, where endless lip service is paid to the needs of the self, while the self which must actually live atrophies inexorably. At the opposite extreme from Gothic romances, these texts invite the reader to join an anxious and disoriented hero on a quest for clarity about the opaque repetitions of the everyday. This literature does not reroot its readers however or give them the catharsis of despair. It is uncomfortable literature and not easily consumed. For there seems to be no constancy in human identity as articulated in contemporary German literature and no reality principle against which the private vision of it is to be measured.

Suggested Further Reading

Keith Bullivant, 'Bürgerliche Literatur und Arbeitswelt', in Götz Groß-klaus and Eberhard Lämmert (eds.), *Literatur in einer industriellen Kultur*, special number of the *Jahrbuch der Deutschen Schillergesellschaft*, Marbach,

1988, pp. 303–21

——, *Realism Today*, Leamington Spa and New York, 1987, esp. pp. 46–51 and 136–47

Ulla Hahn and Uwe Naumann, 'Romane mit Gebrauchswert', *Basis 8*, Frankfurt on Main, 1978, pp. 155–73

R. Hinton Thomas and Keith Bullivant, *Literature in Upheaval. West German Writers and the Challenge of the 1960s*, Manchester, 1974 (see Chapter 5 for a general review of Gruppe 61 and the Werkkreis up to ca. 1972)

Werkkreis Literatur der Arbeitswelt, *Realistisch schreiben*, Erkenswick, 1972

There are no lengthy analyses of the work of Wolfgruber and Genazino, apart from the excellent essay by Martin Lüdke and Sigrid Lüdke-Haertel (on Wolfgruber) and that by Thomas Reschke (on Genazino) in Heinz Ludwig Arnold's *Kritisches Lexikon zur deutschsprachigen Gegenwartsliteratur* (KLG); both of these contain such bibliographical references as exist. My own essay on Baroth is due to appear in KLG during 1989.

KEITH BULLIVANT

The Spectre of the Third Reich
The West German Novel of the 1970s and National Socialism

Although time does not stand still, it was something of a surprise to hear, in a report in the autumn of 1985 by the German correspondent of the BBC, of the apparent lack of public interest in the trial of alleged war-criminals, then taking place in Berlin and since abandoned. While this does not necessarily betoken a longer-lasting tendency, it is in marked contrast to the great attention paid to the problem of the Nazi past within and without literature in the 1970s, which reached its high point with the prolonged public debate over the TV series *Holocaust* in 1979. By the 1970s the Second World War had been over for a quarter of a century and yet this, the third phase of the West German response to the legacy of the recent past, was in many ways more intense and painful than those that went before. Before considering the way in which the novel of the period deals with National Socialism, it is important to examine briefly the earlier phases of the response to the Third Reich and to attempt to throw into relief thereby what is special about the 1970s.

By the 1960s it had become an established part of the classification of West German literature that the 1940s and 1950s had reflected a general 'Bewältigung der Vergangenheit', an overcoming of the past, as a prelude to normalisation. It has long been clear, however, that this was far from being the case: the rapid development of the Cold War situation led to the Western allies rushing through and reducing to a farce the process of so-called de-Nazification, so that key positions of responsibility in the legislature and in commerce could be assumed by the only people with appropriate experience — in many cases former Nazis. Despite the long-lived myth of 1945 marking a 'Stunde Null' for Germany, the Currency Reform of 1948 and the Marshall Plan marked the restoration to power and influence of a compromised generation. This was to be one of the themes of the novel of the 1970s. In literature there was, despite attempts to establish a socio-critical realism, also a considerable degree of continuity. Not only did the Cold War climate rapidly lead to any critical realism being equated with Socialist Realism and thus viewed as near-treasonable, the post-war intellectual and literary scene was dominated by an older generation steeped in the tradition of German idealism. Just as the dangers of fascism in the 1930s had been seen primarily as endangering the German spirit ('Geist') so, in the aftermath of the war, was the German tragedy conceived of in essentially aesthetic categories. Thus Thomas Mann, while in no way trying to excuse what had happened, in 1945 describes National Socialism as resulting from a secret alliance of the German soul with the demonic, as reflecting the German rejection of the rational thought of the Enlightenment and an inherent 'Altertümlichkeit der Seele, welche sich den chtonischen, irrationalen und dämonischen Kräften des Lebens [. . .] nahe fühlt'.[1] After all the horrors of National Socialism, Mann was still explaining it in the same terms that he had used in the 1920s and 1930s, terms that in no way addressed themselves to it as a political force. Not for the first time, Mann, whose stance against the Nazis was one of the most unambiguous amongst conservative German writers and intellectuals, reveals himself to be the most prominent example of the peculiar German middle-class inability to think in political categories that contributed to the lack of real opposition to Hitler and which was to re-emerge with surprising vigour in intellectual circles after the war.

Given this, it is not surprising to find that, at this time, the German literary scene was essentially dominated by writers such as Hermann Hesse, Ernst Jünger and Gottfried Benn, whose concern was with the magical inner world of the spirit, rather than with the 'platten Realitäten der bürgerlichen Welt', as Jünger put it.[2] Literature, pronounced Frank Thieß, in the 1950s president of one of the representative cultural academies, had nothing at all to do with what '[man] im gemeinen Verstande für Realität hält'.[3] Hermann Kasack's *Die Stadt hinter dem Strom* (1947), a novel which offers an allegorical portrayal of life after the collapse of Germany as a life beyond the river of death, was widely held to be *the* representative novel of its time, and was praised by a contemporary critic for offering 'das Spiegelbild unserer "verlorenen" Epoche, [. . .] eine großartige dichterische Vision alles Werdens, Daseins und Vergehens'.[4] Hans Egon Holthusen, the outstanding literary critic of the late 1940s and the 1950s, held it to be the concern of literature at this time 'die aus allen Fugen geratene Welt wieder in Ordnung zu

1. 'Deutschland und die Deutschen', *Werke*, XI, Frankfurt on Main, 1960, p. 1143.
2. Jünger, *Das Abenteuerliche Herz, Gesammelte Werke*, vol. 9, Stuttgart, 1979, p. 173.
3. Thieß, *Dichtung und Wirklichkeit*, Wiesbaden, 1962, p. 9.
4. Gerhard Pohl in *Aufbau*, 1948, No. 8, p. 653.

denken [. . .], das alte Wahre in neuer Sprache wiederherzustellen'.[5]
To these long-established and now revived non-political modes of
thinking was added another, one which had its origins in Germany,
but which now returned via France — Existentialism. Despite the
stimulus provided here by Sartre, the movement in Germany lacked
the political engagement it had in French intellectual circles, and in
literature it led to nothing more than a variant on the apocalyptic
view of the end of the war and its aftermath, or, as with Alfred
Andersch, to a concern with individual freedom, rather than social
issues and, in stylistic terms — despite his public claim to be an
'Anti-Symbolist' —, to a propensity for more or less timeless symbols that, again, was not that far removed from the writing of more
avowedly conservative writers.

In all these various ways, the political, intellectual and literary
climate of the 1940s and 1950s militated against a deep examination
of the legacy of the Nazi past. At the time, however, it was widely
believed that it *had* been dealt with and that normalisation was now
the order of the day. There did emerge, towards the end of the
decade, a new generation of writers desirous of looking quizzically
at the Nazi era, and Günter Grass's *Die Blechtrommel* (1959)[6] inspired a number of clones in the following years, but the second
phase was really ushered in by external events. Adolf Eichmann was
captured in South America and put on trial by the Israelis in
Jerusalem in 1960; the man in the glass booth confronted Germany
with unanswered questions and helped to bring about the Frankfurt
Auschwitz trials, which lasted from 1962–4. The literary response
was a series of documentary dramas, most notably Hochhuth's *Der
Stellvertreter* (1962), Kipphardt's *Der Hund des Generals* (1962) and *Joel
Brand* (1965) and, above all, Peter Weiss's *Die Ermittlung* (1965),
which was based on the press reports of the Frankfurt trials. Kipphardt and Weiss, in particular, broke through the comfortable
myth of National Socialism having been the work of a small group of
madmen, to ask telling and highly differentiated questions about
personal guilt and also about the involvement of German business in
National Socialism. The wider debate about the Nazi past, fuelled
further by the controversy surrounding the President of the Federal
Republic, Heinrich Lübke, and the Chancellor of the late 1960s,
Kurt Georg Kiesinger, both of whom had been members of the Nazi
Party, played its part in the politicisation of intellectual and cultural

---

5. Holthusen, *Der unbehauste Mensch*, Munich, 1951, p. 33.
6. The style of this novel was, interestingly enough in this context, chosen in part as a
   conscious response to the symbolism of Andersch's *Sansibar oder Der Letzte Grund*,
   1957.

life during the decade, which reached its high point in the Student Revolt of the 1967–9. It was during this time that to the moral anger at the role of ex-Nazis in public life and the atrocities of the concentration camps, with which a young generation was confronted for the first time, was added a concern with the nature of fascism of such. Particularly Marxian thinking seems to have had the effect of enabling a number of writers born during the Third Reich to view the period for the first time with some sense of clarity: 'Der Marxismus', says Gerd Fuchs, looking back,

> bot mir eine völlig neue, stringente Faschismusanalyse, die nach all den Verquältheiten der Jahre vorher geradezu befreiende Wirkung hatte. Erst der Marxismus ermöglichte mir eine wirklich analytische Bearbeitung des Phänomens Faschismus, und das heißt nicht nur Distanzierung von dieser historischen Epoche, sondern auch Distanz zu mir selber als Produkt dieser Epoche.[7]

If we compare the academic programmes of social scientific and historical institutes before and after the Student Revolt, or look at the dissertation titles of the time, the intensity of the theoretical preoccupation with National Socialism becomes clear.

This study of German fascism also served to bring out into the open for the first time just how many important positions in the Federal Republic were filled by former Nazis. As a result a whole generation, and with it the state, was condemned. In non-fiction, documentary literature and the novel the compromised past of a number of former Nazis was revealed. Bernt Engelmann, in his novels *Großes Bundesverdienstkreuz* (1974) and *Die Laufmasche* (1979), draws on the 'faction' thriller, as established by Frederick Forsyth with *The Odessa File* and *The Day of the Jackal*, to draw attention through the medium of a popular form of fiction to the penetration of state organisations by ex-Nazis, their collaboration with right-wing politicians like Franz Josef Strauss and to the Nazi past of some of West Germany's leading industrialists, notably Hanns Martin Schleyer, the Chairman of Mercedes Benz and of the Bundesverband der Deutschen Industrie, who was to be kidnapped and murdered in 1977 by the Red Army Faction. In his second novel Engelmann uses the thriller form to show the way in which, in Munich, the American occupation forces had, in their fear of Communism, been responsible for the over-hasty re-habilitation of leading former Nazis and their restoration to power and influence.

---

7. In Matthias Altenburg, *Fremde Mütter, fremde Väter, fremdes Land*, Hamburg, 1986. Quoted in Helmut Peitsch, 'Die rätselhafte Vergangenheit', *die tat*, 3.10.1986.

Engelmann's obsession with the guilt of members of the West German Establishment did, through the ensuing court cases, have some success in drawing public attention to the issue, but, in concentrating on individual guilt, his 'faction' novels have the effect of confirming National Socialism as the product of the machinations of evil opportunists. Others, with a less simplistic view of the phenomenon, succeed in highlighting the more important point: to show that the notion of 1945 as a caesura was a myth. Gerd Fuchs's novel of 1980, called *Stunde Null* and set in the same region as Edgar Reitz's film *Heimat* (1984), focuses on the time immediately after the war, bringing out vividly the mood of the period, above all the determination on all sides to start afresh. Even the CDU had in its 'Ahlener Programm' of 1947 a clear anti-capitalist platform designed to keep those who had helped Hitler to power away from a regenerated industry based on public ownership. *Stunde Null* charts the bitter disappointment of those who had to witness the restoration to power and influence of businessmen who had been heavily involved in the Third Reich. It is typical of a number of historical novels of the late 1970s — historical novels in the sense of Georg Lukács, i.e. which narrate past events as the pre-history of the present. In this sense aspects of Uwe Johnson's *Jahrestage* (1970–83) and, in particular, a vital dimension of Günter Grass's *Aus dem Tagebuch einer Schnecke* (1972) should be placed in this category. Grass, in his role within the latter novel of responsible father, is anxious to stress to his children that the intolerance of National Socialism towards the Jews, which he had experienced as a child, is still alive today, but directed at other social victims. At another point in the novel the fanaticism of an SS soldier is portrayed as being parallelled in his son's activities within the SDS (Sozialistischer Deutscher Studentenbund).

One of the various methods used by Grass to place his material in a modern context is to complement the story of the sufferings and ultimate emigration of the majority of Danzig Jews with interviews he had conducted with survivors in Israel. The publication of Peter O. Chotjewitz's *Saumlos* (1979), which also takes up the fate of a Jewish community (this time in a small town in Hessen) and attempts, at the same time, to show the continuance of intolerance in the present, was accompanied by a companion volume of interviews with survivors in Israel (*Wer mit Tränen sät*, 1979). The narrator of this novel returns more or less by accident to the village in which he had been brought up after the war and stumbles across an expert in local history who excites his curiosity as to the fate of the Jewish community, which had at one time outnumbered the Christian one.

Using the form of the thriller — with a nod, indeed, in the direction of Hitchcock — Chotjewitz unravels through his narrator a sordid story of exploitation and murder. There have, it transpires, been other, earlier attempts to solve this mystery, but then, as now, a solid wall of silence and non-cooperation by the villagers, together with the disappearance of official records, made it difficult to prove individual guilt. No one has done, seen or heard anything and, anyway, the suggestion of persecution of the Jews is communist propaganda. The narrator does succeed, to his own satisfaction, in getting to the likely truth of the matter, but the sense of village unity holds out against him to the end and renders conclusive proof impossible. *Saumlos* — the fictional name of the village, and one chosen to suggest unfinished business — is an historical novel in that it makes clear just how much the repressed past is part of the present: not only is the wealth of leading villagers based on cheaply acquired Jewish property, but the same village unity that manifested itself in intolerance of the Jews in the 1930s is now used against other outsider groups.

A final novel belongs in this context: Manfred Franke's *Mordverläufe* (1973), the attempt to recreate the events of the Kristallnacht in a small Rhineland town. This, artistically one of the major works of the decade, gives a multi-perspectival impression of the events of 10 November 1938 and those that led up to them. It is a sort of documentary work, in that it draws on a vast array of 'ready mades' — including interviews with eye-witnesses, court records, newspaper reports, police transcripts of interviews with suspects — that are assembled in a vast collage. Franke did actually set out to produce a conventional novel from the material he assembled, but he rapidly realised that he would be over-simplifying a complex issue, rendered even more difficult by the time gap, if he did so. The result not only succeeds in recreating the mood in the town, it also alerts us to the degree of central pressure exerted on local party branches in the wake of the Grynszpan attack on Ernst von Rath in Paris on 7 November 1938. Above all, however, it sounds a cautionary word to those, like Engelmann, with black-and-white notions of guilt. Even more than in *Saumlos*, the unravelling of evidence at this distance in time is fraught with difficulties — contradictory statements, the incompleteness of official records, the unreliability of memory and outright lying being the main ones. Like Chotjewitz, Franke does succeed in putting together a likely pattern of guilt, from which it becomes clear that, where action has been taken, it is the small fry, those unable to engage expert counsel, that have been offered up for symbolic punishment. Those at the heart of the horrors of that night escaped — indeed, as in *Saumlos*, their post-war affluence is based on their having used their positions in the Nazi Party to buy up Jewish property cheaply.

In the overall context of the West German examination of the Nazi past, perhaps the most striking thing about *Saumlos* and *Mordverläufe* is the shift of focus away from *causes célèbres* to the more humdrum reality of life in the Third Reich, which, through its concentration on the penetration of German society by the Nazis, in turn asks far more uncomfortable questions about national and individual guilt than had hitherto been the case. This examination of 'everyday Fascism', as Reinhard Lettau has termed it, constitutes in quantitative terms the major concern with National Socialism in the 1970s, and receives a final impetus at the end of the decade with the screening of *Holocaust* (1979). Throughout this period a large number of non-fictional accounts of all sorts of aspects of life in the Third Reich appear, which collectively serve to show how extensively the life of the nation was affected by the Nazis. Mention should be made in this connection of one particularly admirable autobiographical novel, Hannsferdinand Döbler's *Kein Alibi* (1980), subtitled *Ein deutscher Roman 1915–45*. Döbler tells us that the writing of the novel was precipitated by his attendance in the 1960s of a war crimes trial, when he was forced to ask himself: 'bin ich ein besserer Mensch? Oder nur ohne eigenes Verdienst ohne Schuld?'. Döbler came from a conservative academic family, one that had, like so many others, an ambivalent attitude to the Nazis, in that they were repelled by certain plebeian features of the movement, yet saw in Hitler the chance to realise certain nationalist aims. Döbler himself remained somewhat aloof until conscripted and commissioned. He rapidly came to accept, as a professional soldier, the obligations of his oath of allegiance, which enabled him to justify deportation of Jews from Holland and ill-treatment of Russian prisoners of war. By the end of the war he even formed a suicide squad to defend to the last, if necessary. A fusion of diary entries and memories of the time with the comments of the Döbler of today highlights with great honesty his acceptance of the thought-processes of the regime. Above all, he presents his former self as the embodiment of what he now regards as typically middle-class ruthless opportunism and also of patterns of military behaviour which, with their emphasis on loyalty to orders and on the need to distinguish themselves through heroism, enabled them to go along with the horrors of the Second World War.

Döbler's novel is typical of a body of often highly autobiographical novels dealing with the experience of the Third Reich which, far from being literary *mea culpas*, use the portrayal of individual experience to draw attention to the wider implications of the experience of National Socialism. Perhaps the best known of these is Walter Kempowski's *Tadellöser und Wolff* (1971). This novel, the first in a 'German chronicle', in which Kempowski sets himself the task of explaining the rise of Nazism, is a rich evocation of the author's childhood in Rostock. Its popularity undoubtedly has something to do with nostalgia, since it evokes powerful memories of territories now lost to West Germany, in the manner of Siegfried Lenz's East Prussian novels and Horst Bienek's Gleiwitz trilogy. The real achievement of this novel, however, is the way in which autobiographical material is used to go beyond the loving evocation of the past and to probe into the relationship of the middle-class world to National Socialism. Within the family we range over a variety of political opinions, from the convinced Nazi, Uncle Richard, to Kempowski's unpolitical mother, whose concern is with decent human values. The picture of the bourgeois adult world in the 1930s and during the war is conveyed through the eyes of the young Walter, as he then was, and it is precisely the naive voice of the child that exposes the inconsistencies in family attitudes. He brings together material gleaned from talking to his family and other records to recreate simultaneously the world as experienced then by the adults and, at the same time, by the younger generation. Childish innocence at points throws the opportunism of the adults into particular relief, but it serves at the same time to warn us against making facile judgements: Walter himself collects pictures of war heroes, much in the way that the youth of today collects pictures of sports or pop stars and his rebellion against the Hitler Youth is born of a determination to keep his long hair, rather that of political resistance.

Kempowski probes his father's involvement with the Nazis and is not afraid to present the reader with information that points to political conformism. But there is no attempt to pillory the father, indeed, the reader is left to read between the lines to deduce the father's position. In this respect Kempowski's affectionate treatment of a misguided father differs from a whole series of others, which, in effect, wage war on the parental generation. For the student of German literature it is tempting to view this as yet another manifestation of a struggle between the generations that occasionally surfaces as a catalyst to writing, but the anguish in the treatment of the relationship with the individual — rather than a stylised — parent would seem to point to a particularly traumatised relationship between son and father. To try and help us understand this, and thus to shed some light on developments in literature during the 1970s, reference can usefully be made at this point to certain ideas put forward by the writer and critic, Michael Schneider, and the well-known German-Jewish sociologist Norbert Elias.[8]

Common to both of these writers is the idea that the parental generation, those who were already adults during the Third Reich, far from coming to terms with their own relationship to National Socialism, had simply repressed their past; the motto of the first Adenauer regime, 'business as usual', and the emphasis on the reacquistion of material prosperity were, in such an analysis, the particular expressions of this process. There was, it is conceded, a small group of prominent West German politicians — Adenauer, Heuss and Willy Brandt, for example — which, while adult during the Third Reich, was not tarred with its brush but rather had a self-evident sense of belonging to a tradition merely interrupted by the Nazis. The public claim to the continuance of this tradition, together with the heady excitement engendered by the various phases of West Germany's international rehabilitation in the early 1950s, provided the motor of national endeavour during the time of the so-called 'Wirtschaftswunder'. For a younger generation, Elias claims, those who had not experienced the Germany which their parents were trying frenetically to re-establish in the 1950s, — the whole crusade was meaningless and, more importantly, begged the question as to the significance of the Nazi past. This would seem to be the underlying message of Fassbinder's film *Die Ehe der Maria Braun* (1978). While the Cold War situation and growing national pride in the achievements of the West German economy dominated the political scene these potential problems remained in abeyance. In the 1960s, however, this was to change. The first hiccups in the upward surge of German expansion occurred and, perhaps more importantly, the relationship to the United States began to be questioned, while a young generation, not held in thrall by the rebuilding of the country, reached adulthood; *then* fundamental questions *were* asked, particularly under the stimulus of the war trials referred to above. The real turning-point came at the time of the Student Revolt of the late 1960s, when the concern with fascism led to the wholesale breakdown of relations within families, as the parental generation was tried and found guilty of complicity in the crimes of the National Socialists. For Michael Schneider it was

8. Cf. Elias, 'Gedanken über die Bundesrepublik', *Merkur*, 1985, pp. 733–55 and Schneider, 'Nicht alle sind tot, die begraben sind. Versuch über meine Nachkriegs-Kindheit', *Nur tote Fische schwimmen mit dem Strom*, Cologne, 1984. Page references in the text are from these sources.

Marxist thinking that gave him the tools to break through 'die Mauer des Schweigens, die die Kriegsgeneration hinter ihrer monströsen Vergangenheit aufgerichtet hatte', by confronting the 'dämonologischen Faschismusbegriff unserer Erzieher, Lehrer und Professoren' with a materialist analysis of the phenomenon of fascism.[9] If further proof was needed of the complicity of the parental generation, it was provided by a series of revelations about the Nazi past of a number of prominent persons and, to compound this, the whole surveillance apparatus of the state, unleashed in the anti-terrorist hysteria of the early 1970s, was seen to confirm for many — and this effect was, indeed, the avowed aim of the Baader-Meinhof Group — that the Federal Republic was nothing but the continuation of the Third Reich. In this situation questions of national and personal identity became inextricably intermingled: 'Für das Identitätsbewußtsein dieser jüngeren Generationen als Deutsche wurde die offene Auseinandersetzung mit der Vergangenheit dringlicher', recognised Elias (p. 51). To the general concern with the relationship between the Establishments of both the Federal Republic and the National Socialist state was added an examination of individual childhood experience. Those born from, roughly speaking, 1930 onwards, noted in retrospect (much as Michael Schneider had done) not only an exclusion from history lessons of a thorough-going analysis of the causes and nature of National Socialism, but also an avoidance by parents of questions from their inquisitive children; at best, the fathers emerged as those who had done their duty at the Front, who were but victims of the system: 'Die Auskünfte der Väter blieben in der Regel anekdotisch und beschränkten sich auf bestimmte Kriegs- und Fronterlebnisse, in denen sie als wehrlose Befehlsempfänger, als Opfer eines 'totalitären Systems', dem sie hilflos ausgesetzt waren' (p. 11). The suppression of the trauma induced by the collapse of the Third Reich and the death of Hitler led to the real past being buried. Schneider says of his own childhood: 'Unsere Lust zu fragen, unsere kindliche Frage- und Widerspruchsbereitschaft wurde von Anfang an gebremst, weil, ließ man unserer Wißbegierde erst einmal freien Lauf, sie sich wie ein Lauffeuer ausbreiten und früher oder später an den Hauptnerv ihrer [. . .] Verdrängung ihrer Nazi-Vergangenheit rühren konnte';[10] his own father avoided all questions by making 'eine höhere Fügung' responsible for Hitler and National Socialism (p. 16). In this 'Glashaus-

---

9. In Altenburg; quoted in Peitsch, 'Die rätselhafte Vergangenheit'.
10. Schneider, 'Väter und Söhne, posthum. Das beschädigte Verhältnis zweier Generationen', in *Den Kopf verkehrt aufgesetzt oder Die melancholische Linke. Aspekte des Kulturzerfalls in den siebziger Jahren*, Darmstadt and Neuwied, 1981, p. 11.

atmosphäre', as it has been widely described, children, inevitably, did not get to know their parents properly, indeed, the social psychologist Alexander Mitscherlich has labelled them 'die vater-lose Generation'. The generation concerned had previously viewed themselves as the unfortunate victims of an authoritarian concept of parenthood, but, with the insights gained in the late 1960s, child-hood experience was now viewed in a different and even more painful light.

The need to exorcise the trauma of the past and to confront oneself with parental involvement in the Nazi past, as a necessary first step to authentic self-definition, is a common theme in the autobiographical novel of the 1970s, with a particular sub-group, the so-called 'Väter-romane', representing the particularly anguished attempt to come to terms with the criminal past of their parents. The first, and most striking of these is Bernward Vesper's *Die Reise* (1971/7). Vesper, son of the Nazi writer Will Vesper and lover of the terrorist Gudrun Ensslin, documents his desperate attempt to pour out his 'Rebellion gegen die zwanzig Jahre im Elternhaus, gegen den Vater, die Manipulation, die Verführung, die Vergeudung der Jugend'. His need is to find some way of coping with the existential burden produced by his childhood experiences and some indication of the weight of these is given by the fact that he committed suicide in 1971, before the book was finished. Another harrowing example of this type of novel is provided by Günter Seuren's *Abschied von einem Mörder* (1978), which deals with the author's discovery of the reality of his father's wartime activities: he is the murderer of the title. These novels are clear indications of the way in which, and, as Elias and Schneider claimed, the *extent* to which the past was suppressed by the parental generation, creating unidentifiable tensions and problems during childhood, which finally surfaced in the 1970s. Perhaps because of the pain, they ultimately tell us less than other novels written at about the same time, in which the fictionalised biographies of others form the basis of novels narrated by a sym-pathetic author with the degree of distance that enables him to bring out more fully the nature of the existential problems engen-dered by the parental Nazi past.

Hermann Peter Piwitt's *Die Gärten im März* (1979)[11] is concerned with Ponto, a helpless drinker, at least as far as the outside world can tell. His friend, the narrator, knows another Ponto, however, who drinks in order 'sich von innen [zu] begucken', and who cannot forget that, 'wenn es den Rausch nicht gäbe, man die Nüchternheit

---

11. Reinbek, 1979; all quotations from this edition.

erträglich machen müßte'. Drink is his escape from the torments caused by the memories of childhood. His father had been a high-ranking SA officer who terrorised his family, forced Ponto's older brother to volunteer for military service and even nominated neighbours for the Nazi sterilisation programme. Ponto recreates his past by sorting through the memorabilia in the attic of his parents' house and, thereby, comes to recognise that he has, from the beginning, been robbed of a proper childhood and later life. He now has no authentic existence on to which he can cling and, as a result, is condemned to an anxiety-ridden existence. His drinking represents not only the attempt to make this reduced life more bearable, but also the attempt to suppress the anger that has built up within him: 'die Katatonie', he says, 'ist der letzte Versuch, Gewalt zu vermeiden'. One day Ponto disappears; the narrator clings to the belief that he is continuing with his search for his true self, but one character suggests that he has joined the terrorists, and the reader cannot exclude the possibility of suicide.

Perhaps the fullest, certainly the most readable treatment of the burden of the Nazi past on the generation raised, or born, during the 1930s is provided by Peter Härtling's *Hubert oder Die Rückkehr nach Casablanca* (1978), referred to earlier in this volume in a different context.[12] The body of Härtling's work consists of what he calls 'Geschichten gegen die Geschichte [. . .] erzählen'; the rejection, in other words, of what he regards as a falsely harmonising and homogenising tendency in historical accounts of Germany's recent past, which, he feels, fail to take full account of individual experience. The other motif of his work, which in turn informs his counter-interpretation of history, is the story of his own family. His father, he has said in *Nachgetragene Liebe* (1980), his own 'Vaterroman', 'hinterließ mich mit einer Geschichte, die ich seit dreißig Jahren nicht zu Ende schreiben kann', and, indeed, the bulk of his novels consist in the reworking of that story. *Hubert* represents another variation on this theme, but it is striking, in the 1970s, how much more anguished the lives of his protagonists are. Hubert's father is a radical German nationalist who spends the 1920s working to counter the 'Schmach von Versailles' and the 1930s preparing for war. The family house is dominated by the image of man as warrior, but the somewhat sickly and dreamy Hubert disappoints his father, who constantly reminds him: 'Aus dir wird nie ein richtiger Mann' (p. 12). One side of Hubert longs to escape from his father's world,

12. Darmstadt and Neuwied, 1978; all quotations from this edition. See also Anthony Waine's chapter on the influence of popular culture, pp. 78–80 above.

but another side of him wants desperately to be part of the machismo embodied in the military world. He volunteers for war service, but is only given a desk job. He retreats behind a mask that enables him to stand apart from the war, such that, even when confronted with information about the horrors of Auschwitz and Theresienstadt, it does not touch him: 'Was sie sagt, will er nicht sehen. Es ist Vaters entsetzliche, von Planern und Tätern aufgewühlte kriegerische Welt' (p. 111). This statement proves to be truer than he realised, since it emerges that Hubert's father, who committed suicide in 1944, was a mass murderer. At the end of the war Hubert deludes himself that, although he 'zwanzig Jahre nicht er selbst gewesen [ist]' (p. 151), he will now be his own man. Very quickly, however, both in the de-Nazification procedures and in a chance acquaintance he makes, he is brought up against the ghost of his father, forced to 'sich rechtfertigen für etwas, das er nicht gewesen war' (p. 223). He begins to fear that he will 'Vater nie verlieren'. He takes refuge in role-playing and also by burying himself in work. But while all around him respond adroitly to 'normalisation' and increasing affluence, Hubert, apparently part of all this, is ill at ease. He lacks 'ein Stück meines Lebens, die Zeit hat mir meine Vergangenheit verdorben und ich leide darunter. Meine Phantasie reicht nicht aus, mich anders und neu zu erinnern'. With the death of his mother, the only person who knew his true life story, he is confronted once more, and far more intensely, with his father: he sees that, since the end of the war, he has 'auf einer Insel gelebt und angenommen, daß seine Zeit auch die Zeit der anderen sei' (p. 271). He can now see how others have suppressed the past, whereas it evokes for him sense of a 'Trauer, die er allein nicht aushalten konnte' (ibid). To escape, he now immerses himself in the persona of Rick Blane (= Bogart) from Michael Curtiz's film *Casablanca* (hence the sub-title of the novel) and is increasingly unable to distinguish between dream and reality. In an attempt to explain something of his problems to his wife, he tells her a version of his life based on the plot of *Casablanca*, allotting himself, significantly enough, the role of someone who shoots 'einen namenlosen Mörder' (freely based on Blane's shooting of Strasser, the Gestapo major). But his desperate attempt to shape his existence by, in effect, killing his father and acquiring a sense of personal past, is a disaster: his professional and personal lives fall apart completely and he exists only in a world of imagination run riot, in the pose of 'männlicher Einsamkeit' he has assumed from Bogart, but which, as Laszlo tells Rick in the film, is a role he has adopted to try and escape from himself. Then one day he picks up a girl hitch-hiker and finds that, since she is not traumatised by the Nazi past, he can tell her everything. The narratorial tone and the fact that, in the final scene of the novel, he is still wearing his Bogart-style fedora, make us wonder whether he isn't deluding himself that he has now laid the ghost of his father, but, in the figure of Effi, the hitch-hiker, Härtling identifies something which ties in with the lack of interest in the war crimes trials of 1985: she takes the line that what Hubert tells her all happened a long time ago and need not concern him any longer.

The same difference in attitude between the generations comes out in Grass's 'erzählender Essay' *Kopfgeburten oder Die Deutschen sterben aus* (1980), a work in the style of the earlier *Aus dem Tagebuch einer Schnecke*. In this fusion of autobiography and fiction Grass dwells at length on his sense of the particular guilt of the Germans for the Third Reich and all it stood for; this, it is clear from a number of Grass's speeches within the context of the 'Friedensbewegung', gives the Germans a particular responsibility in attempts to secure world peace. He is also aware that there was no 'Stunde Null', that, in the case of so many of the generation above his, including writers, there were merely 'trübe Übergänge'. But he refuses to blame such people, convinced that, had he been just a few years older, his path would have been similar to that of Wolfgang Weyrauch; he has been spared true personal guilt by an accident of birth (but he has gone out of his way elsewhere to indicate the extent of his youthful enthusiasm during the Third Reich). Harm, a fictional school-teacher in *Kopfgeburten* who is markedly younger than Grass, has no understanding at all for Grass's preoccupation with such questions, however:

> "Was haben wir denn damit zu tun?" schreit Harm seine Dörte an. "Wir sind nach der Scheiße geboren. Wir haben ganz anderen Mist zu verantworten. Doch überall fragt man uns, ob es bei uns wieder Nazis gibt. Als würde sich alle Welt das wünschen. Nein! Wir haben andere Sorgen. Nicht diese ewige Dazumalkacke. Sondern was morgen ist. Wie wir das hinkriegen, die achtziger Jahre. Und zwar ohne Strauß. Da, der ist auch nur von vorgestern. Der will noch immer Stalingrad halten.[13]

There is a certain irony here, in that not only were there clear signs in the attitudes of present-day West German youth revealed by analyses in *Der Spiegel* prior to the Federal Elections of 1987 which brought out its concern only with individual problems of the present and the future, much in the manner of Grass's Harm, but also Franz Josef Strauss and others on the right wing of the ruling coalition argued very strongly that Germans should now re-assert their sense

13. *Kopfgeburten oder Die Deutschen sterben aus*, Darmstadt and Neuwied, 1980, p. 67.

of national pride and bury the Hitler era 'in der Versenkung oder
Versunkenheit besser gesagt'.[14] The result of this sort of attitude,
together with the consequences of some clumsy remarks by Dr Kohl,
argued Hans Magnus Enzensberger — normally a reliable seismo-
graph of intellectual trends — was that 'wir haben seit 1945 kaum
Jahre erlebt, in denen so viel über die Verbrechen des Dritten
Reiches nachgedacht, geschrieben, gestritten wurde wie jetzt. Auschwitz ist gegenwärtiger denn je. Die Leute, die unsere Geschichte
zuschaufeln wollten, haben sich als Ausgräber erwiesen'.[15] Here he
perhaps goes too far, but there seems little doubt that a wide range
of issues raised about National Socialism continue to surface —
in, for example, discussions over Kipphardt's *Bruder Eichmann* in
1982, the republication of Michael Schneider's *Die Wiedergutmachung*
(1977/86), the projected performance of Fassbinder's allegedly anti-
Semitic play *Der Müll, die Stadt und der Tod* at the end of 1985, the
controversy over the Nazi past of the Austrian President, Kurt
Waldheim, the trial in Jerusalem of an alleged Auschwitz guard
deported from the USA and in France of Klaus Barbie, the 'Schläch-
ter von Lyon', not to mention Peter Schneider's treatment of Josef
Mengele in his contentious short novel *Vati* (1987). While it no
longer has the prominent place in the novel that it occupied in the
1970s, the spectre of the Nazi past continues to haunt the cultural
and intellectual life of the West German present, no matter how
pressing the concerns of those generations born after 1945.

Suggested Further Reading

Although there are a number of works dealing with the legacy of the Nazi
past in recent GDR literature, there are very few studies of the treatment of
this theme in the West German novel of the 1970's. Examinations of various
aspects of it are contained in

Keith Bullivant, *Realism Today*, Leamington Spa and New York, 1987,
esp. pp. 157–70 and 199–207
Norbert Mecklenburg, 'Faschismus und Alltag in der deutschen Genwarts-
prosa. Kempowski und andere', in Hans Wagener (ed.), *Gegenwartslitera-*

14. Quoted in *Der Spiegel*, 2, 1987, p. 25.
15. '"Die Gesellschaft ist keine Hammelherde", *Spiegel*-Gespräch mit Hans Magnus
Enzensberger', 19.1.1987, p. 77.

tur und Drittes Reich, Stuttgart, 1977

Alexander and Margarete Mitscherlich, *Die Unfähigkeit zu trauern*, Munich, 1967

Helmut Peitsch, 'Realistische Vergangenheitsbewältigung? Probleme literarischer Faschismusdarstellungen in Romanen der Autoren Edition', in Gerd Mattenklott and Gerhart Pickerodt (eds.), *Literatur der siebziger Jahre*, Berlin 1985 (Sonderband of *Das Argument*, no. AS 108)

——,'Die Väter-Welle und die Literaturkritik', in K. Bullivant and Hans-Joachim Althof (eds.), *Subjektivität — Innerlichkeit — Abkehr vom Politischen? Tendenzen der deutschsprachigen Literatur der 70er Jahre*, Bonn, 1986 (DAAD)

Michael Schneider, 'Deutschland Traum und Trauma', in Schneider, *Den Kopf verkehrt aufgesetzt oder Die melancholische Linke*, Darmstadt and Neuwied, 1981, pp. 7–80

——, 'Nicht alle sind tot, die begraben sind. Versuch über meine Nachkriegs-Kindheit', in Schneider, *Nur tote Fische schwimmen mit dem Strom*, Cologne, 1984, pp. 9–33

[handwritten annotations in top margin: "not very original - much relabel? or not relevant to ...ground or ... only you ...", "— see fn #32", and below title "(not ... plans)"]

JOHN SANDFORD

The 'Literaturverfilmungswelle'

It can hardly have escaped the attention of observers of the German cultural scene that the 1970s were a decade in which the West German cinema produced an extraordinarily large number of 'Literaturverfilmungen'.[1] There was nothing new in the phenomenon itself: after all, film-makers have, more or less since the beginnings of the cinema, regularly adapted literary texts for the screen, and this has been especially the case in Germany. But what seemed to be distinctive about the 'Literaturverfilmungswelle' of the 1970s was both the quantity of film adaptations and the exalted status in the literary canon of the texts used as a basis for some of the most successful films.

It is almost certainly the case that these factors were instrumental in helping to ensure the widespread familiarity that the New German Cinema had come to enjoy abroad by the early 1980s. There can be few German departments — in schools, let alone in higher education — that have not had their showings of *Effi Briest*, of *Die verlorene Ehre der Katharina Blum*, or of *Die Blechtrommel*, presented and perceived not so much as 'films', but as cinematic renderings of specific, much-read and much-studied literary texts. Indeed, the advent of video has meant that there are probably few educational establishments that do not now possess their own cassettes — often of doubtful legality — of at least some of the 'classic' 'Literaturverfilmungen' of the 1970s. And this 'classic' status is closely tied to the status of the original literary text: enquiries among first-year university students of German as to their familiarity with modern German cinema invariably indicate that a majority of them have been shown films that are predominantly 'Literaturverfilmungen' during their sixth-form years. Indeed, the impression is inescapable that *Die verlorene Ehre der Katharina Blum* has, in its Schlöndorff / von Trotta film version, become *the* 'German department film' of all time. The

1. Eric Rentschler's book *German Film and Literature. Adaptations and Transformations*, New York and London,1986, contains a very full list of 'Adaptations in German film history' (pp. 336–65); according to this no fewer than 129 'Literaturverfilmungen' were made in West Germany in the 1970s.

high demand for these 'Literaturverfilmungen' is also attested by the experiences of distributors of 16mm versions of German films — in particular the German Film Libraries and Goethe Institutes, 'semi-official' institutions whose distribution and exhibition policies did so much in the 1970s to introduce foreign audiences — and not just educational establishments — to German films and thereby promote the much wider familiarity that the New German Cinema was enjoying abroad by the latter part of the decade.

'Literaturverfilmungen' in this 'classic' form can be identified as those that have been generally perceived as films of high quality in their own right based on literary works that are equally of high quality: in other words, 'good films of good books'. The general critical acclaim at their release and their current status in retrospective assessments of post-war German film suggest that in addition to those already mentioned — Fassbinder's *Fontane Effi Briest* (1973), Schlöndorff / von Trotta's *Die verlorene Ehre der Katharina Blum* (1975), and Schlöndorff's *Die Blechtrommel* (1979) — other films of the 1970s that have attained this status of 'classic Literaturverfilmungen' would have to include at least Wim Wenders' *Falsche Bewegung* (1974) (based on *Wilhelm Meisters Lehrjahre*), Eric Rohmer's *Die Marquise von O.* (1976), and Werner Herzog's *Woyzeck* (1979). If one steps slightly beyond the strict confines of the 1970s the list could be joined by, for instance, Schlöndorff's *Der junge Törleß* (1966) and *Eine Liebe von Swann* (1984), and Fassbinder's 13-part *Berlin Alexanderplatz* of 1980.[2]

2. These films have been the subject of a number of detailed analyses, including in particular: (on *Effi Briest*) William R. Magretta, 'Reading the Writerly Film', in Andrew Horton and Joan Magretta (eds.), *Modern European Filmmakers and the Art of Adaptation*, New York, 1981, pp. 248–62; Jürgen Wolff, 'Verfahren der Literaturrezeption im Film, dargestellt am Beispiel der Effi-Briest-Verfilmungen von Luderer und Fassbinder', *Der Deutschunterricht*, 33, 1981, 4, pp. 47–75; (on *Katharina Blum*) Jack Zipes, 'The Political Dimensions of *The Lost Honor of Katharina Blum*, *New German Critique*, 12, 1977, pp. 75–84; David Head, '"Der Autor muß respektiert werden" — Schlöndorff/Trotta's *Die verlorene Ehre der Katharina Blum* and Brecht's Critique of Film Adaptation', *German Life and Letters*, 32, 1979, pp. 248–64; William R. Magretta and Joan Magretta, 'Story and Discourse', in Horton and Magretta (eds.), *Modern European Filmmakers*, pp. 278–94; (on *Die Blechtrommel*) David Head, 'Volker Schlöndorff's *Die Blechtrommel* and the "Literaturverfilmung" Debate', *German Life and Letters*, 36, 1983, pp. 347–67; (on *Falsche Bewegung*) Peter Harcourt, 'Adaptation through Inversion', Horton and Magretta (eds.), *Modern European Filmmakers*, pp. 263–77; (on *Die Marquise von O.*) Alan Spiegel, 'The Cinematic Text', in Horton and Magretta (eds.), *Modern European Filmmakers*, pp. 313–28; Thomas Bauermeister, 'Erzählte und dargestellte Konversation. Der Heiratsantrag des Grafen in Kleists und Eric Rohmers *Die Marquise von O.*, in Klaus Kanzog (ed.), *Erzählstrukturen — Filmstrukturen. Erzählungen Heinrich von Kleists und ihre filmische Realisation*, W. Berlin, 1981, pp. 90–141; (on *Der*

If the 'good book / good film' category epitomises the best remembered 'Literaturverfilmungen' that were widely received and perceived *as* adaptations, there were also films in the 1970s that failed to achieve in the cinema acclaim and status on a par with their literary 'Vorlagen' ('good book / bad film'): this was certainly the case with Alexander Petrović's star-studded but wooden adaptation of *Gruppenbild mit Dame* (1977), and with Wolf Gremm's *Tod oder Freiheit* (1978), which 'updated' *Die Räuber* into the era of Baader and Meinhof. On the other hand there were films that did just the opposite, 'rehabilitating' largely forgotten or neglected authors by (re-)introducing their works to a wider public: Fassbinder was particularly adept at bringing Bavarian writers to a national and international audience in such films as *Pioniere in Ingolstadt* (1971) and *Wildwechsel* (1972), based on plays by Marieluise Fleisser and Franz Xaver Kroetz respectively, and *Bolwieser* (1977), which led to a distinct Oskar Maria Graf renaissance. A similar service for one of the more neglected of the Mann family (Klaus) was performed in 1981 by István Szábo's *Mephisto*.

Some directors also undoubtedly helped sales of their *own* less well-known books by turning them into films: here too Fassbinder was exemplary, with his *Katzelmacher* of 1969 and *Die bitteren Tränen der Petra von Kant* of 1972. Alexander Kluge also made films of writings of his own that in themselves were, and remain, relatively little read: thus one of the most important early films of the New German Cinema, *Abschied von gestern* (1966), was adapted by Kluge from his own short story 'Anita G.', and later he turned his story 'Ein Bolschewist des Kapitals' into the much better-known 1976 film *Der starke Ferdinand*.[3] Other writers who became directors of their own works included Horst Bienek (*Die Zelle*, 1971), Peter Handke (*Die linkshändige Frau*, 1977), and, at the beginning of the eighties, Reiner Kunze (*Die wunderbaren Jahre*, 1980).[4]

---

junge Törleß) Eric Rentschler, 'Specularity and Spectacle in Schlöndorff's *Young Törless*', in Rentschler (ed.), *German Film*, pp. 176–92; (on *Berlin Alexanderplatz*) Eric Rentschler, 'Terms of Dismemberment: the Body in/and/of Fassbinder's *Berlin Alexanderplatz*', ibid., pp. 305–21.

3. On *Abschied von gestern* see Miriam Hansen, 'Space of History, Language of Time: Kluge's *Yesterday Girl*', in Rentschler (ed.), *German Film*, pp. 193–216; on *Der starke Ferdinand* see Timothy Corrigan, *New German Film. The Displaced Image*, Austin, Tex., 1983, pp. 95–119. For an examination of Kluge's corpus see Peter Labanyi's chapter, pp. 263–95 of this volume.

4. On *Die Zelle* see J.J. White, 'Horst Bienek's *Die Zelle* — Novel and Film', *German Life and Letters*, 32, 1979, pp. 229–47; on *Die linkshändige Frau* see Timothy Corrigan, 'The Tension of Translation: Handke's *The Left-Handed Woman*', in Rentschler (ed.), *German Film*, pp. 260–75.

Not all the best-received 'Literaturverfilmungen' of the 1970s were based on German works, though this was the case with a strikingly large majority. Thus Wim Wenders made a version (*Der scharlachrote Buchstabe*, 1973) of Hawthorne's *Scarlet Letter*, and Hans Wilhelm Geißendörfer of Ibsen's *The Wild Duck* (1976), whilst Schlöndorff's *Der Fangschuß* (1976) was based on Marguerite Yourcenar's novel *Coup de Grâce*.[5] Two of the most successful — in terms of international exhibition — of West German films in the 1970s were also based on non-German novels, though both had German settings: Wim Wenders' *Der amerikanische Freund* (1977), based on novels by Patricia Highsmith, and Fassbinder's *Eine Reise ins Licht* (1978), based on Nabokov's novel *Despair*. Nor were the directors of cinema versions of German texts necessarily all German — though here again the exceptions were few in number, including the already-mentioned István Szábo and Eric Rohmer, whilst at the beginning of the decade perhaps the best-known of all films based on a German text was made by Luchino Visconti (*Death in Venice*, 1970).

One particularly distinctive group of 'Literaturverfilmungen' have been the transformations that have been so radical as to fail to make the breakthrough to anything approaching a mass audience — films that are however well-known to, and often highly valued by, small numbers of cinéastes. The most consistent creators of radical transformations of this type have been Jean-Marie Straub and Danièle Huillet, who began in the 1960s with *Machorka Muff* (1963), based on Böll's story 'Hauptstädtisches Journal', and *Nicht versöhnt* (1965), based on the same author's *Billard um halbzehn*. In the 1970s the Straubs made a version (1970) of Corneille's play *Othon*, of Brecht's *Die Geschäfte des Herrn Julius Caesar* (*Geschichtsunterricht*, 1972), and of Schönberg's opera *Moses und Aron* (1975). Their 1984 film *Klassenverhältnisse*, based on Kafka's *Amerika*, though still a distinctively Straubian rendering, seems to have been found more 'accessible' by critics and — larger — audiences.[6]

When one looks back over the history of the German cinema, the preponderance of 'Literaturverfilmungen' among the major films of the 1970s becomes striking, though it can also be seen as part of a pattern of successive waves of literary adaptations that have charac-

5. On *Der Fangschuß* see Corrigan, *New German Film*, pp. 71–93.
6. An indication of the popularity of Straub/Huillet among film specialists lies in the large number of studies of their work that have appeared in Britain and America in particular — in contrast to their almost total lack of impact with the film-going public as a whole. On *Geschichtsunterricht* see Maureen Turim, 'Textuality and Theatricality in Brecht and Straub/Huillet', in Rentschler (ed.), *German Film*, pp. 231–45.

terised German film-making since its early beginnings. Certainly there are precedents for classic adaptations of major literary texts in the Weimar years: one has only to think of Lang's *Die Nibelungen* (1924), of Pabst's *Die Büchse der Pandora* (1929) and *Die Dreigroschenoper* (1931), or of Sternberg's *Der blaue Engel* (1930). Yet such films are, by comparison with the 1970s, relatively few and far between. The 'classics', not just of Weimar, but of the pre-1960s German cinema in general, are on the whole *not* versions of major literary texts. Thus, of the three films that probably more than any others epitomise for the film-club public at large the 'expressionist' German cinema — *Das Cabinet des Dr Caligari*, *Nosferatu*, and *Metropolis* — only *Nosferatu* is a reworking of a novel: Bram Stoker's *Dracula* is in any case neither German nor a 'classic' of the traditional literary canon, and has long been eclipsed by the numerous Dracula films to such an extent that Herzog's 1979 'remake' of *Nosferatu* pays homage to this *cinematic* tradition — and in particular to Murnau — rather than to Stoker.

One could similarly look at the early sound cinema in Germany: again there *are* 'Literaturverfilmungen' of major German works, but again many of the now most familiar film genres from the pre-war period— such as the proletarian films like *Kuhle Wampe*, the documentaries of Berlin life (*Berlin, Sinfonie einer Großstadt*), the 'Bergfilme' (*Das blaue Licht*), the documentaries of the Third Reich (*Triumph des Willens*), and the more notorious Nazi propaganda pieces (*Hitlerjunge Quex*) — show little tendency to engage in 'classic Literaturverfilmung'. And in the fifteen or so years immediately following the war there is arguably only one 'Literaturverfilmung' that merits this epithet: the Gorski / Gründgens *Faust* of 1960.

In fact, the penchant for 'Literaturverfilmung' in the 1970s becomes even more distinctive if one looks at the lengthy list of lesser-known reworkings of major texts produced during the decade.[7] Why, then, do film-makers make 'Literaturverfilmungen', and why

---

7. Such a list would include: Heinrich Böll, *Ende einer Dienstfahrt* (Hans-Dieter Schwarze, 1971) — *Ansichten eines Clowns* (Vojtech Jasny, 1976); Bertolt Brecht, *Baal* (Volker Schlöndorff, 1970); Theodor Fontane, *Der Stechlin* (Rolf Hädrich,1975) — *Cécile* (Dagmar Damek, 1977) — *Grete Minde* (Heidi Genée, 1975) — *Kriegsgefangen* (Theodor Mezger, 1979); Goethe, *Die Wahlverwandtschaften* (Rudolf Thome, 1975) — *Götz von Berlichingen* (Wolfgang Liebeneiner, 1979); E.T.A. Hoffmann, *Die Elixiere des Teufels* (Manfred Purzer, 1976); Ödon von Horváth, *Geschichten aus dem Wienerwald* (Maximilian Schell, 1979); Heinrich von Kleist, *Die Verlobung in San Domingo* (Hans Jürgen Syberberg, 1970) — *Das Erdbeben in Chili* (Helmer Sanders-Brahms, 1975); Siegfried Lenz, *Die Deutschstunde* (Peter Beauvais, 1971); Thomas Mann, *Unordnung und frühes Leid* (Franz Seitz, 1977) — *Buddenbrooks* (Franz Peter Wirth, 1979); C.F. Meyer, *Die Richterin* (Daniel Schmid,

in particular were so many produced in West Germany in the 1970s? One answer to the first question is given at a very practical level by Volker Schlöndorff, one of the most assiduous and most prominent of the Federal Republic's 'Literaturverfilmer'. It is, according to Schlöndorff, simply *easier* and less time-consuming for a film director to film a book than to sit down and create a detailed original film-script first:

> Die höchste Form eines Drehbuchs ist natürlich ein Literaturwerk. [. . .] Ein Autor arbeitet ja doch meist an einem Buch jahrelang [. . .] Beim Drehbuchschreiben nimmt man an, 8 Wochen, gut, sagen wir drei Monate, dabei kann nicht dasselbe rauskommen. Ich will damit nicht das Drehbuch disqualifizieren, ich sage nur, daß ich deshalb eher Literatur verfilme, weil ich niemanden kenne, der sich mit vergleichbarem Ernst hier an ein Drehbuch setzen könnte, und ich schon gar nicht.[8]

The image that Schlöndorff projects here of the hard-pressed director who turns, *faute de mieux*, to ready-made literary 'Vorlagen' is expressive of the position that West German directors found themselves in in the 1970s. The New German Cinema was, by international standards, a decidedly low-budget affair. Its films tended to be made by relatively small teams, and its directors had to do much more than simply direct: in a context far removed from the clear division of labour of the factory production system of Hollywood they were obliged to attend to all aspects of the production of their films, from the initial conception even through to the final distribution. The Federal Republic's cinema simply did not produce native script-writers: that was something that by and large the directors were expected to do, and it was something that, as Schlöndorff indicates, many of them found easier to do if they worked from already extant texts.

Yet Schlöndorff's mundane explanation for the 'Literaturverfilmungswelle' is hardly an adequate one. There have, after all, been plenty of other examples of 'new' national cinemas whose directors have experienced constraints of time and money similar to those adduced by Schlöndorff, but who have not resorted to the expedient of literary adaptation to overcome them. The 'neo-realist' cinema of post-war Italy, the French 'Nouvelle Vague', and the more recent

---

1977); Friedrich Schiller, *Don Carlos* (Hans Wilhelm Geissendörfer, 1971); Adalbert Stifter, *Der Hochwald* (Hajo Baumgärtner, 1978); Theodor Storm, *Der Schimmelreiter* (Alfred Weidenmann, 1978); Martin Walser, *Das Einhorn* (Peter Patzak, 1978). The film titles are not always the same as the book titles given here; for details of the former see Rentschler (ed.), *German Film*, pp. 351–6.

8. Hans Günther Pflaum (ed.), *Jahrbuch Film 78/79*, Munich, 1978, p. 115.

cinematic revivals in Australia and Great Britain have not been characterised by a plethora of literary adaptations. Indeed, on the contrary, they seem to be distinguished by a decided *avoidance* of involvement with the literary heritage — an avoidance that makes precisely this apparent infatuation on the part of the West German cinema one of its most distinct characteristics.

Historically, one of the functions of 'Literaturverfilmung' has been a legitimatory one. The cinema has from the outset suffered from a 'Legitimationsdefizit' as compared with the other arts, not least because of its appeal to a mass audience, and the fact that that appeal has been seen to stem from the absence of any prerequisite 'literacy' on the part of that audience in order for its products to be enjoyed by them. This in its turn is reflected in the cinema's alleged tendency towards 'trivial' subject-matter and treatments. Not surprisingly, such an elitist dismissal of the cinema has been particularly characteristic of its reception in Germany, with its singularly stratified conceptions of 'Bildung' and 'Kultur'. Thus Paul Heyse, writing in 1913, saw in the cinema an instrument of debasement that would merely encourage 'die Neigung des Volkes zum Bilderbesehen',[9] a sentiment widely shared by the self-appointed guardians of cultural values during the cinema's early years.

It was only natural that the cinema's response to its proclaimed inferiority would consist in part in attempting to climb aboard the 'Bildungskanon' from which its detractors were resolutely excluding it 'Literaturverfilmung' provided a natural means of asserting the cinema's right to respectability. And that no more so than in German: as Anton Kaes suggests, the comparison with America, whose less class-bound society lacked an equivalent of the German 'Bildungsbürgertum', is instructive, for there a need to film the literary classics was not so urgently felt: 'In Deutschland dagegen mußte sich das Kino von der Literatur als dem klassischen Medium des sich darin selbst darstellenden Bürgertums rechtfertigen. Daß sich das Kino zur kulturellen Legitimation dabei der hohen Literatur als Stoff bediente, zeigt den idealistischen Einschlag der deutschen Kultur'.[10] In the Third Reich a new pressure for legitimation came into operation, again pushing film-makers in the direction of

---

9. Quoted in Anton Kaes (ed.), *Kino-Debatte. Texte zum Verhältnis von Literatur und Film 1909–1929*, Munich and Tübingen, 1978, p. 89. Kaes's book is an invaluable anthology of source material on the early stages of the 'Literaturverfilmung' debate in Germany. See also Siegbert Prawer, 'A New Muse Climbs Parnassus: German Debates about Literature and the Cinema 1909–1929', *German Life and Letters*, 32, 1979, pp. 196–205.
10. Kaes (ed.), *Kino-Debatte*, p. 11.

'Literaturverfilmung': now it was not the cinema that was seeking to valorise itself, but the state, and it did this by encouraging film-makers to appropriate the national classical heritage in the service of Nazi ideology — at a time when, ironically, some directors were in any case seeking to escape official prescriptions precisely by a recourse to literary adaptation on *their* own terms. After the war, literary adaptation was again a marked characteristic not so much of the cinema but of television in its early years. Once more the sense of a 'Legitimationsdefizit' seemed to be at work, with the result that in 1954 every one of the 'Fernsehspiele' broadcast by the Bayerischer Rundfunk and the Süddeutscher Rundfunk was an adaptation of a pre-existing literary text; the same was true in the following year of the output of the Sender Freies Berlin, the Hessischer Rundfunk, and, again, of the Süddeutscher Rundfunk.[11]

Was it then once again a desire to legitimate the cinema in the face of an elitist cultural Establishment that led so many film-makers in the 1970s to make films of books? In a sense, the answer is yes, but the Establishment was not quite that 'Bildungsbürgertum' which confronted the early film-makers, and nor was its power wielded through the mechanisms of a totalitarian state. Yet in an odd kind of way, echoes of both of these previous experiences of German film-makers were at work: the directors of the New German Cinema found themselves by the mid 1970s very much beholden to a new 'Mäzenatentum', a network of semi-state institutions that seemed to be conspiring towards the exclusive sponsorship of one particular type of cinema — the 'Literaturverfilmung'.

The public subsidy system of the West German cinema has been much admired and much envied abroad. The West German film-makers themselves have viewed it less sanguinely, not infrequently voicing complaints about the pressure and constraints that it implied for them. Yet few of them could have done without it, as commercial profitability was decidedly not a characteristic of the New German Cinema in its first decade or so: indeed, it was not until 1975 that it produced a film — *Die verlorene Ehre der Katharina Blum* — that even actually recouped its expenses.

Most West German films in the 1970s were made with public money from a variety of sources: the 'Länder', in the shape of their Kuratorium Junger Deutscher Film; the Bundesministerium des Innern, with its various film prizes; local authorities, with their

---

11. Knut Hickethier, *Das Fernsehspiel in der Bundesrepublik. Themen, Form, Struktur, Theorie und Geschichte 1951–1977*, Stuttgart, 1980, pp. 81–3. Hickethier's book looks in detail at the nature and implications of 'Literaturadaption und -rezeption im Fernsehspiel' (pp. 77–214).

financial incentives for local productions; and — most importantly — the Filmförderungsanstalt and the broadcasting corporations. The Filmförderungsanstalt was originally set up on the basis of the 1968 'Filmförderungsgesetz' (FFG), a most unfortunate instrument as far as most young film-makers were concerned, as it was designed to reward and encourage *commercial* success by established *producers*, as opposed to *artistic* excellence by new *directors*. Its much-criticised 'Förderungsmechanik' resulted in the production of interminable mediocre but money-spinning *series* — most notably of the films of the 'Sexwelle'. With an SPD government now in power, the FFG was revised in 1974 in a direction that was more favourable to newcomers — in particular by the inclusion of provisions for 'Projektförderung', the allocation of loans for the realisation of promising film-scripts, rather than the provision of rewards for the commercial success of films already made.[12] But 'Projektförderung' was to turn out to be one of the most important instruments pushing the New German Cinema in the direction of an over-production of 'Literaturverfilmungen'. The other was television.

The relation between the cinema and television has been a fraught one in all those countries where the new medium has been perceived as a threat to the old. In West Germany, a decade later than in Britain, the possession of a television set became the norm for most families in the course of the 1960s. Thus in 1957 there were around one million sets in the Federal Republic; by the early 1970s a virtual saturation level of close on nineteen million was reached. This growth in television ownership was strikingly paralleled by a steep fall in cinema attendance: whereas in 1957 West Germans made 801 million visits to the cinema, by 1970 this figure had dropped to 160 million, with a further fall to around 115 million by the mid-1970s.[13]

One response of the cinema to the competition of television lay in a specialisation of its product — searching out and concentrating on those things that television could not do. But what those things were depended very much on local conditions: in America in particular a better-funded film industry turned to technical and generic specialisation wide-screen formats and big-budget 'epics' and 'blockbusters'.

12. In 1979 the 'Filmförderungsgesetz' ('Gesetz über Maßnahmen zur Förderung des deutschen Films') was revised yet again, this time to provide grants on the basis of more subtle criteria than the simple presentation of a promising 'Drehbuch'. For the text of the 'FFG' see *Media Perspektiven*, 1979, 7, pp. 486–502; also Willi Bär and Hans Jürgen Weber (eds)., *Fischer Film Almanach 1980*, Frankfurt on Main 1980, pp. 167–200.
13. Figures taken from Georg Roeber and Gerhard Jacoby, *Handbuch der filmwirtschaftlichen Medienbereiche*, Pullach, 1973, p. 932, and Burkhard Dreher, *Zur Lage und Entwicklung der deutschen Filmwirtschaft*, W. Berlin, 1978, p. 69.

The underfinanced West German cinema resorted to changes in thematic emphasis, seeking out in particular those areas that television, the 'family medium', could not explore. Here too was a factor that — along with the 'Filmförderungsgesetz', the advent of the 'permissive society', and the growing influx of non-German-speaking 'Gastarbeiter' — conspired towards the wave of soft-core pornography that brought the salvation of several commercial film producers in the early 1970s.

Initially, the broadcasting corporations resolutely resisted demands that they should in some way compensate the film industry for the damage that television seemed to be doing. Then, in 1974, they came up with the 'Film/Fernseh-Abkommen', an agreement that was to turn television into a major *sponsor* of the New German Cinema. Their motives were not entirely disinterested, as there was a distinct possibility that a levy on the transmission of films would be written into the new 'Filmförderungsgesetz', but there were also influential figures in broadcasting who regarded the struggling New German Cinema with much sympathy and admiration.

The 'Film/Fernseh-Abkommen' — an agreement between, on the one side, the ARD and the ZDF (West Germany's first and second TV channels), and, on the other, the Filmförderungsanstalt — introduced three main areas of support for film-makers by the broadcasting corporations: co-production — in quantitative terms by far the most important rubric —, 'Vorabkäufe', and *ex gratia* contributions to the 'Projektförderung' budget of the 'Filmförderungsanstalt'.[14] The film sponsorship covered by this agreement was not without precedent in German television: as in other countries, the broadcasting corporations had their own film and drama departments engaged in in-house productions, and working alongside a long-established tradition of subcontracting programme production to outside companies and the purchase of transmission rights for independently produced cinema films.

These arrangements, together with the New German Cinema's dependence on such public bodies as the Filmförderungsanstalt, the Kuratorium Junger Deutscher Film, the Bundesministerium des Innern, and the various Land and city authorities, meant that by the mid 1970s a cinema had been created in West Germany that was peculiarly subject to the specific constraints that shape *public* rather than private bodies. The cinema, traditionally a commercial opera-

14. For the text of the 'Film/Fernseh-Abkommen' see *Media Perspektiven*, 1980, 7, pp. 515–21. Apart from increases in the budget, the 1980 version is otherwise substantially identical with that of 1974.

tion, found itself in the Federal Republic increasingly beholden to taxpayers, electors, and politicians, rather than to shareholders and financiers. It was an enthralment mediated via 'Kommissionen', and one that seemed to push relentlessly in the direction of 'Literaturverfilmung'.

'Die Kommissionen', wrote Hans Blumenberg, the film critic of *Die Zeit*, in 1977 'fördern eine erstickende Mittelmäßigkeit, in spätestens drei Jahren werden sie es geschafft haben, daß die gesamte bürgerliche Literatur des neunzehnten Jahrhunderts, am liebsten Fontane und Storm, in schönen, langweiligen Bebilderungen für den Deutschunterricht der gymnasialen Mittelstufen zur Verfügung steht'.[15] For all its ironic hyperbole, Blumenberg's lament touched on a sore point, and was widely echoed in statements by the film-makers themselves, who coined the term 'Gremienkino' to describe the new genre that public subsidy seemed to be creating. Volker Schlöndorff wryly summed up the situation with the remark: 'heute [werden] die Filme für elf Leute gemacht, [. . .] acht davon sitzen in der Projektkommission'.[16] Equally apodictic was Blumenberg's observation, in another 1977 article, 'der deutsche Film wird zu Tode subventioniert' — the reason being that 'sich zu viele Filmemacher bei ihren Projekten weniger an ihren eigenen Ideen und möglichen Zuschauerbedürfnissen orientieren als an den Chancen, durch thematisch wie stilistisch abgesicherte Projekte bei den diversen Förderungsgremien Gelder zu bekommen'.[17]

Two factors repeatedly stressed by critics of the system are of especial significance here: firstly the stress on *scripts* — on 'Drehbücher' — as the prerequisite evidence demanded for the award of a subsidy, and secondly the fact that, given the nature of the system that had been created, scripts of a particular kind — namely *literary* scripts — stood a demonstrably better chance of success. As Alexander Kluge, the most prominent and perceptive spokesman of the New German Cinema, put it in 1978: 'Weg mit dem schematischen Drehbuch, das die Förderungsgremien verlangen [. . .]. Das ist die Quelle der Literaturverfilmung und der Einengung. Der Film ist

---

15. *Die Zeit*, 2 September 1977. Cf. in similar vein Hubert Haslberger's remark 'Verwerflich ist keineswegs der durchaus angebrachte Respekt vor Fontane, Storm und Eichendorff — verwerflich ist die Meinung, diesem Respekt müsse man unbedingt dadurch Ausdruck verleihen, daß man keines der großen Werke des 19. Jahrhunderts unverfilmt läßt'. ('Trotz allem keine Polemik: Literaturverfilmung, das ungeliebte Schoßkind', in Hans Günther Pflaum (ed.), *Jahrbuch Film 79/80*, Munich, 1979, pp. 90–9 [94].)

16. Quoted in *Süddeutsche Zeitung*, 20/21 August 1977.

17. *Die Zeit*, 26 August 1977. Similarly Haslberger 'Trotz allem keine Polemik', talks of 'Literaturverfilmung' as the 'Weg des geringsten Widerstands'.

durch das Buch in seinem Horizont schon eingegrenzt, bevor er überhaupt anfängt.[18]

In fact the actual wording of the relevant sections of both the 'Filmförderungsgesetz' and the 'Film/Fernseh-Abkommen' is — inevitably — vague and relatively unprescriptive. The former contains a general statement of intent — 'die Qualität des deutschen Films auf breiter Grundlage zu steigern und die Struktur der Filmwirtschaft zu verbessern' (§2[1]1), and a catalogue of criteria for 'nicht förderungswürdige Filme' (§19) — criteria that include the depiction of 'sexuelle Vorgänge oder Brutalitäten in aufdringlich vergröbernder spekulativer Form', projects that 'gegen die Verfassung oder gegen die Gesetze verstoßen oder das sittliche oder religiöse Gefühl verletzen', or quite simply films that 'nach dem Gesamteindruck von geringer Qualität sind'. The 'Film/Fernseh-Abkommen' added further provisions, embracing in its first paragraph both these conditions already laid down in the 'Filmförderungsgesetz' *and* the various 'Rundfunkgesetze', and, in an important further elaboration, describing its aims as 'durch Gemeinschaftsproduktionen und Projektförderungsmaßnahmen die Herstellung von Filmen zu ermöglichen, die den Voraussetzungen des Filmförderungsgesetzes [. . .] und der Rundfunkgesetze entsprechen, und dadurch das Programmangebot sowohl der Filmtheater als auch des Fernsehens zu bereichern' (§1).

The anchoring of film production to the requirements of the 'Rundfunkgesetze' and the object of enriching 'das Programmangebot [. . .] des Fernsehens' represented a major and largely unprecedented constraint on the stylistic and thematic parameters of the German cinema, creating what was in effect an 'öffentlich-rechtliches Kino'. Admittedly, although films funded within the framework of the 'Film/Fernseh-Abkommen' were destined ultimately — usually after a two-year run in the cinemas — for television transmission, the agreement did specify that this did not mean that the object was to produce 'television films': 'Vorrangig den Fernsehinteressen dienende Filme sollen nicht Gegenstand der Gemeinschaftsproduktion sein' (§4). Yet it is noteworthy that the agreement's provisions for an annual 'Projektförderung' grant to the Filmförderungsanstalt did make such a requirement of that ostensibly *cinema* aid body: 'Die Rundfunkanstalten gehen davon aus, daß unter den von der Vergabekommission geförderten Filmen sich in angemessenem Umfang Projekte befinden, die [. . .] erwarten lassen, daß sie auch für eine Verwertung im Fernsehen geeignet sind' (§10,2). And certainly the

18. Hans Günther Pflaum (ed.), *Jahrbuch Film 78/79*, Munich, 1978, p. 117.

film-makers themselves were in no doubt about the constraints on their work that television implied, observing in their 1979 'Hamburger Erklärung': 'Die Fernsehanstalten produzieren mit ihren Programmrastern Strukturen von Filmen, die der Filmsprache nicht entsprechen'.[19]

The 'Rundfunkgesetze' of the West German 'Länder', which provide the legal basis for the functioning of both the ARD and the ZDF, typically enjoin upon the broadcasting corporations the threefold task — familiar from the BBC — of 'educating', 'entertaining', and 'informing' their listeners and viewers. Thus, for example, the Bavarian 'Rundfunkgesetz' states that 'Sendungen [. . .] dienen der Bildung, Unterrichtung und Unterhaltung', whilst in Hessen the function of broadcasting is designated as 'die Verbreitung von Nachrichten und Darbietungen bildender, unterrichtender und unterhaltender Art'. They further elaborate requirements of 'objectivity', 'neutrality', 'balance', 'decency', and 'constitutionality'.[20] These were then the criteria to which film-makers too — precisely at the same time, one should not forget, of the 'Tendenzwende' in West German public life — were to be beholden if they wished to obtain subvention money from the two most important public sources.

Clearly, the requirements of the 'Rundfunkgesetze' could be most simply met by that familiar legitimatory device of resorting to the 'cultural heritage'. There was already an inherent generic tendency in television to work — in contradistinction to much of the best cinema — from ideas to images rather than the other way round. This was compounded by the feeling that films of books, and above all films of 'great books', would ideally meet at least two of the three legally prescribed functions of broadcasting: 'Unterhaltung' and 'Bildung', whilst ensuring that its other principles were not transgressed either.

But above and beyond these legalistic considerations another factor was at work too — a rather more mundane one that harks back to Schlöndorff's lament about the pressure of finding time to write a decent script. The members of the grant-awarding 'Gremien' — appointees of political groups, the broadcasting corporations, the Churches, unions, and various film-industry organisations — were also people for whom time was precious, who — at least this was how film-makers tended to perceive them — did not have time to cope with unfamiliar and detailed original 'Drehbücher'. And so

19. 'Hamburger Erklärung', in Willi Bär and Hans Jürgen Weber (eds.), *Fischer Film Almanach 1980*, Frankfurt on Main, 1980, pp. 205–9
20. Texts of the 'Landesrundfunkgesetze' can be found in Günter Herrmann, *Rundfunkgesetze: Fernsehen und Hörfunk, Textsammlung*, Cologne, 1977.

they were fed the familiar classics of German literature: these, aspiring film-makers quickly learnt, stood a much better chance of attracting a positive response from those who controlled the purse-strings of public subsidy.

It was, then, not just 'Literaturverfilmungen', but adaptations of a specific sort that became the norm in the West German 'Subventionskino' of the 1970s: adaptations, that is, predominantly of German texts, of German texts that, as often as not, had acquired an aura of 'respectability' through their status in the literary canon, and moreover, adaptations that had as much to do with the aesthetics of television as with those of the cinema. It is striking that it was not until the late 1970s, and even then only in small numbers, that West German films began to break out of the constraints of the standard TV-screen format. West German 'Literaturverfilmungen' are notably lacking in long- and tracking shots, resorting instead to the more specifically 'televisual' techniques of close-ups and head-shots and the manipulation of images by zoom lenses. The spacious landscapes that come across so effectively in wide-screen cinema are replaced by more intimate settings, frequently indoors, that give to many of these films a spatial feel akin to that of the 1920s 'Kammerspielfilme.' A lot are, at best, 'Fernsehfilme'; many hover uneasily close to the genre of the 'television play'.[21]

At least one — hardly disinterested — observer of the film scene in the 1970s saw nothing wrong in the effects that the dependence on television was having on the West German cinema. This was Günter Rohrbach, head of television entertainment at the Westdeutscher Rundfunk, who even went so far as to hail — approvingly — the birth of a new genre, the 'amphibischer Film', suited equally for presentation on television and in the cinema.[22] Most film-makers were much less happy with the situation, however, and when they met in Hamburg at the end of the decade they issued a declaration that looked back to that earlier statement of intent by young German film-makers, the 'Oberhausener Manifest' of 1962. 'Phantasie läßt sich nicht verwalten', proclaimed the 'Hamburger Erklärung': 'Gremienköpfe können nicht bestimmen, was der produktive Film tun soll. Der deutsche Film der achtziger Jahre kann nicht mehr von Gremien, Anstalten und Interessengruppen so wie bisher fremdbestimmt werden'.[23]

---

21. For a discussion of the arguments over the generic specificity of the two media see Hickethier, *Das Fernsehspiel*, pp. 38–65.
22. 'Das Subventions-TV. Plädoyer für den amphibischen Film', in Hans Günther Pflaum (ed.), *Jahrbuch Film 77/78*, Munich, 1977, pp. 95–100.
23. See note 19 above.

It would be wrong to elevate the gloomy assessments of the 'Hamburger Erklärung' to the status of the last word on the mood and activities of the West German cinema in the 1970s. The view from outside was, of course, much more positive. But then the outside world was both privileged and more restricted in its perceptions of the New German Cinema. Privileged in that it was presented with what were by and large some of the best (though by no means *all* of the best) West German films of the decade. Restricted in that that very filtering process meant that film-goers not living in West Germany could not assess the full range of the country's production. The extent to which, in numerical terms, 'Literaturverfilmungen' dominated the domestic film market, and the sheer mediocrity of some of these products, was masked to the outside world by the selective export of films that were either not 'Literaturverfilmungen' at all, or if they were, of films that were *good* 'Literaturverfilmungen'. Unequal delays in foreign releases and distribution also meant that the outside world could not appreciate so readily the stages through which the West German cinema evolved in the 1970s. In fact, many of the earlier 'Literaturverfilmungen' had been imaginative, creative readings and transformations of the texts they were inspired by. It was not until the mid 1970s that the more stultifying effects of the public sponsorship arrangements began to manifest themselves, and by the late 1970s a number of directors had already begun to achieve a degree of financial independence that freed them of the need to pay obeisance to the 'Gremien' of the 'Film/Fernseh-Abkommen'.[24]

It would be equally wrong to insist mechanistically that West German directors were somehow 'pushed' into making 'Literaturverfilmungen' by force of circumstances. Clearly, as in any other country, many were in any case attracted by particular texts, authors, and themes that made 'Literaturverfilmung' a natural ambition for them. Not surprisingly, such cases seemed to correlate closely with some of the most admired and most successful 'Literaturverfilmungen' of the decade, as did some of the other films in which directors used a 'respectable' literary 'Vorlage' as a vehicle for the mediation of radical, and sometimes hotly contemporary, political analyses.

Such a 'subversive' use of literary texts was inevitable in a situation where predominantly radical directors were engaging with

---

24. Eric Rentschler even discusses the peak of the 'Literaturverfilmungswelle', which he dates as occurring in 1977, as a 'Literaturverfilmungs*krise*'. ('Germany Before Autumn: The Literature Adaptation Crisis', *West German Film in the Course of Time. Reflections on the Twenty Years since Oberhausen*, Bedford Hills, N.Y., 1984, pp. 129–57.)

the constraints of an increasingly cautious and conservative sponsor-ship system.[25] It was a state of affairs that Schlöndorff and Böll were to parody in their acerbic contribution to one of the most radical — and genuinely independent — films of the decade, *Deutschland im Herbst* (1977): their sketch shows the agonised contortions via which a broadcasting corporation's programme commissioners come to turn down a showing of *Antigone* because of its inherent violence and portrayal of rebellious women. Schlöndorff was in any case not only one of the most persistent, but also, in financial terms, increasingly one of the most successful of the 1970s 'Literaturverfilmer'. His brashly commercial approach brought him a degree of indepen-dence from the 'Gremien' that was reflected in the thematic radical-ism of such films as *Die verlorene Ehre der Katharina Blum*. But it was a radicalism of content mediated — and, in the eyes of many critics, *compromised* — by a formal adherence to the 'production values' of the classic thriller and the sentimental romance. The film's shrill tones were far removed from the understated whimsical self-re-flexivity of Böll's novel.

Yet this was clearly a kind of 'Literaturverfilmung' that paid off in terms of audience appeal: *Die verlorene Ehre der Katharina Blum* played for months to packed houses throughout West Germany, and be-came the first of the New German Cinema's films to actually show a profit. (Though sales of the *Bild-Zeitung* and the national hysteria over terrorism seemed unaffected by the film's popularity: both continued to grow.) Schlöndorff / von Trotta's was a kind of 'Litera-turverfilmung' that, in formal terms, operated at an opposite ex-treme from the work of Jean-Marie Straub and Danièle Huillet. Equally determined to tease out the radical implications of the texts they adapted, Straub / Huillet remained uncompromisingly radical too in the formal techniques with which they achieved this. Their film versions of works by Böll, Brecht, Corneille, Schönberg, and now Kafka are landmarks of a determinedly purist cinema that eschews the commercial compromises — and success — of Volker Schlöndorff and Margarethe von Trotta.

The polar extremes of the literary adaptations of Schlöndorff / von Trotta and Straub / Huillet, which recall the Lukács / Brecht paradigm of earlier debates over form and content in radical litera-ture, are both products of a strand in West German film-making that has been less constrained by the dictates of public sponsorship than the majority of New German directors. Apart from the fact that

25. See Miriam Hansen, 'Cooperative Auteur Cinema and Oppositional Public Sphere: Alexander Kluge's Contribution to *Germany in Autumn*', *New German Critique*, 24–5, 1981–2, pp.36–56.

both pairs of directors have regularly sought financial backing outside Germany, Schlöndorff / von Trotta — and even more so in recent years Schlöndorff on his own — have become, through commercial success, increasingly independent, whilst Straub and Huillet were making films on low budgets that simply did not need major financial backing.

In a sense, Rainer Werner Fassbinder stood between these two poles.[26] His 'Literaturverfilmungen' of the 1970s were — with the singular exception of the 'international film' *Despair* (1977) — not overtly laden with 'production values' à la Schlöndorff / von Trotta, nor were they radical experiments in the manner of Straub / Huillet. Nor — and this was the hallmark of Fassbinder's adaptation technique — were they as immediately political: for all the patently political implications of the end product, Fassbinder's primary interest in the literary texts that he filmed was clearly a personal one. Whether it was Kroetz's *Wildwechsel* (film version 1972), Ibsen's *Doll's House* (filmed as *Nora Helmer*, 1973), Fontane's *Effi Briest* (1974), Graf's *Bolwieser* (1977), Nabokov's *Despair* (1977), or Döblin's *Berlin Alexanderplatz* (1980), Fassbinder's adaptations latched on to protagonists and circumstances that embodied his own recurrent obsessions of personal loneliness, alienation, and emotional blackmail as the apparently inescapable base-line of human relationships.

These characteristics of the Fassbinder 'Literaturverfilmung' are epitomised in his 1974 version of *Effi Briest*, which remains one of the most distinctive and accomplished adaptations of the decade — indeed, of German cinema as a whole. Although the subject-matter was of a deeply personal significance for Fassbinder, he managed to make tangible its broader political implications — explicitly in the film's lengthy subtitle — whilst at the same time rendering homage to his original source. The title *Fontane Effi Briest* is a manifesto of this intent: this is very much a 'film of the book' that makes no secret of its literary origins. With its episodic structure, its intertitles, its voice-over excerpts (read by Fassbinder himself), and its deliberate use of a monochrome film-stock, it carefully draws attention through its own textuality to that of Fontane's book.[27]

The extent to which a given 'Literaturverfilmung' was an 'accurate'

---

26. On Fassbinder and the 'Gremien' see Sheila Johnston, 'A Star is Born: Fassbinder and the New German Cinema', *New German Critique*, 24–5, 1981–2, pp. 57–72.
27. William R. Magretta quotes Fassbinder as saying of *Fontane Effi Briest*: 'it is completely clear that it is a film about the relationship between the author and the story he tells, and not a film based on that story'. (Horton and Magretta (eds.), *Modern European Filmmakers*, p. 248.)

or 'adequate' rendering of the literary work in question was a question that was inevitably much asked by German critics in the 1970s when confronted with films like *Effi Briest*. It was an old debate in Germany, and one that all too often perpetuated some questionable unspoken premises about the comparative artistic 'worth' of the two media and the nature of inter-medial adaptation in general. Hostility towards the filmic adaptation of literary texts has been a given of writing on the cinema from the very beginning in a way that has not been characteristic of analyses of the other arts: whereas poets can with relative impunity allow themselves to be inspired by painters, painters by dramatists, or dramatists by historians, film-makers who have had the temerity to try their hand at 'Literaturverfilmung' have regularly been castigated for 'betraying' their sources.[28]

The simplistic 'adaptation-as-betrayal' approach was not without its exponents in the 1970s. Indeed, the marked paucity of theoretical writings on the cinema in West Germany — itself a sorry comment on the general level of film culture there — is paralleled by a corresponding dearth of analytical engagement with the 'Literaturverfilmungswelle'. Certainly a number of *articles* were stimulated by the unwonted abundance of current adaptations, many of them looking in detail at particular films.[29] But only one full-length book — Irmela Schneider's *Der verwandelte Text. Wege zu einer Theorie der Literaturverfilmung* (1981) — made any serious attempt to look in depth at the nature of filmic adaptation in general using the insights of semiotic analysis.[30]

Schneider's central thesis was derived from Umberto Eco's suggestion that for any given object there is a 'Wahrnehmungsmodell' that is identical irrespective of the medium employed at any given time. Film adaptations were thus recreations in cinematic form of the 'Wahrnehmungsmodelle' that had originally been expressed in words: 'Wenn das ikonische Zeichen mit irgendetwas Eigenschaften gemeinsam hat, dann nicht mit dem Gegenstand, sondern mit dem Wahrnehmungsmodell des Gegenstandes. Es ist konstruierbar und erkennbar auf Grund derselben geistigen Operationen, die wir

28. See Kaes, *Kino-Debatte, passim,* for numerous examples of these attitudes.
29. See, for instance, the special number of *Der Deutschunterricht* (33, 1981, 4) devoted to 'Literatur und Film'.
30. Tübingen 1981. Page references are indicated in my text. Schneider's ideas are presented in more compact form in her article 'Überlegungen zu einer Semiotik der Literaturverfilmung', *Zeitschrift für Literaturwissenschaft und Linguistik (LiLi)*, 36, 1979, pp. 31–49. See also in this same number Wolfram Buddecke and Jörg Hienger, 'Verfilmte Literatur. Probleme der Transformation und der Popularisierung', pp. 12–30.

vollziehen, um das Perzept zu konstruieren, unabhängig von der Materie, in der sich diese Beziehungen verwirklichen' (p. 42). There is, Schneider proposed, for any given text a 'deep structure' behind the manifest 'surface structure', and the root of much mischief in facile 'comparisons' between film and book lay in an ignorance of these different levels: the successful cinematic adaptation of a literary text was not the one that slavishly sought to reenact the 'story', 'characters', and 'settings' of its original, but rather the one that got to work on the underlying 'deep structure' that ultimately informed it (p. 47).

Schneider's observations represented a more rigorous theoretisation of what perceptive critics have been practising for some time: establishing *how* and *why* 'Literaturverfilmungen' had effected particular transformations, and assessing them in the last analysis on their merits *as films* rather than on the basis of some 'comparison' with the 'original' — a 'comparison' in which the odds were invariably stacked in favour of the book. But by the end of the 1970s it became obvious that at least one group of people in West Germany were increasingly anxious to reassert the links between book and film, and that was the publishers. If the effect of literature on the cinema is an area of study where much work still remains to be done, the effect of cinema on literature — and more precisely, on the *reception* of literature — has been scarcely explored at all.

As more and more of German classic and modern literature is 'processed' by the 'Literaturverfilmer' it becomes correspondingly difficult to read German literature without a preconceived notion of what particular characters and settings 'look like'. The sixth-formers and Abiturienten who study *Die verlorene Ehre der Katharina Blum* as a 'set text' after having seen the film first are not alone in coming to the book as something 'secondary', in feeling that Heinrich Böll has perhaps left some things out, and added others. It is difficult not to picture Katharina as the actress Angela Winkler, just as a reading of *Der Tod in Venedig*, *Effi Briest*, or *Berlin Alexanderplatz* cannot now be disentangled from images of Dirk Bogarde, Hanna Schygulla, or Günter Lamprecht. Publishers, anxious to cash in on 'tie-ins' and 'spin-offs', have assiduously promoted these associations, reminding us — in case we have forgotten — of what these protagonists 'look like' by placing their photographs on the front covers of the paperback editions of the books.[31]

---

31. At least one writer is also clearly unable to resist the temptation to refer back in his latest novel to the 'Verfilmung' of an earlier work: Günter Grass in *Die Rättin* (Darmstadt and Neuwied, 1986) not only resurrects Oskar Matzerath, but also has an unnamed Volker Schlöndorff attend Oskar's birthday party: 'Einer der

The 'Literaturverfilmungswelle' of the 1970s demonstrably helped to boost sales of classic works of literature, to unearth ignored and forgotten masterpieces, and to bring extra prominence to contemporary works. In the 1980s video cassettes of films are already available — for hire or purchase — at prices comparable with those of books. 'Literaturverfilmung' has been traditionally perceived as the phenomenon of 'the film of the book': given the German filmmakers' proneness to film major works of literature, it seems unavoidable that German literature will now increasingly be marketed, perceived, and read as 'the book of the film'.[32]

Suggested Further Reading

Willi Bär and Hans Jürgen Weber, *Fischer Film Almanach*, Frankfurt on Main (annually since 1980)

Wolfram Buddecke and Jörg Hienger, 'Verfilmte Literatur. Probleme der Transformation und der Popularisierung', *Zeitschrift für Literaturwissenschaft und Linguistik (LiLi)*, 36, 1979, pp. 31–49

Timothy Corrigan, *New German Film. The Displaced Image*, Austin, Tex., 1983

Der Deutschunterricht, 33, 1981, 4 (special number on 'Literatur und Film')

Robert Fischer and Joe Hembus, *Der Neue Deutsche Film 1960–1980*, Munich, 1981

James Franklin, *New German Cinema*, Boston, Mass., 1983 and Bromley, Kent, 1986

German Life and Letters, 32, 1979, 3 (special film number)

David Head, 'Volker Schlöndorff's *Die Blechtrommel* and the "Literaturverfilmung" Debate', *German Life and Letters*, 36, 1983, pp. 347–67

Knut Hickethier, *Das Fernsehspiel in der Bundesrepublik. Themen, Form, Struktur, Theorie und Geschichte 1951–1977*, Stuttgart, 1980

Andrew Horton and Joan Magretta (eds.), *Modern European Filmmakers and the Art of Adaptation*, New York, 1981

Filmemacher, dem es vor nicht allzu langer Zeit gelungen war, mit eigener Produktion den Jugendjahren des Geburtstagskindes nahezukommen, bestätigte: Genau das, Oskars exemplarisches Außenseitertum habe er zeigen wollen' (p.489).

32. Parts of this article elaborate topics I have already examined in detail elsewhere in '"Literaturverfilmung" and the New German Cinema', *Publications of the English Goethe Society*, 52, 1982, pp. 67–89, and 'The Paid Pipers of Oberhausen: Public Sponsorship and the West German Cinema', *Journal of the Association for the Study of German Politics*, 6, 1983, pp. 3–23. I am grateful to the editors of these journals for permission to make further use of this material.

Anton Kaes (ed.), *Kino-Debatte. Texte zum Verhältnis von Literatur und Film 1909–1929*, Munich and Tübingen, 1978

Klaus Kanzog (ed.), *Erzählstrukturen — Filmstrukturen. Erzählungen Heinrich von Kleists und ihre filmische Realisation*, W. Berlin, 1981

New German Critique, 24–5, 1981/82 (special double number on New German Cinema)

Hans Günther Pflaum, *Jahrbuch Film*, Munich (annually since 1977)

—— and Hans Helmut Prinzler, *Film in der Bundesrepublik Deutschland. Der neue deutsche Film*, Munich, 1979

Klaus Phillips, *New German Filmmakers. From Oberhausen through the 1970s*, New York, 1984

Eric Rentschler, *West German Film in the Course of Time. Reflections on the Twenty Years since Oberhausen*, Bedford Hills, NY, 1984

——, *German Film and Literature. Adaptations and Transformations*, New York and London, 1986

John Sandford, *The New German Cinema*, London and Tatowa, NJ, 1980, and New York, 1982

——, ' "Literaturverfilmung" and the New German Cinema', *Publications of the English Goethe Society*, 52, 1982, pp. 67–89

——, 'The Paid Pipers of Oberhausen: Public Sponsorship and the West German Cinema', *Journal of the Association for the Study of German Politics*, 6, 1983, pp. 3–23

Irmela Schneider, *Der verwandelte Text. Wege zu einer Theorie der Literaturverfilmung*, Tübingen, 1981

DENNIS TATE

The 'Other' German Literature
Convergence and Cross-Fertilisation

In the 1970s the literature of the German Democratic Republic became a force to be reckoned with in the cultural life of the Federal Republic. The pronounced change in West German attitudes to East German authors which largely coincided with the beginning of the decade is well illustrated by Heinrich Böll's review of Stefan Heym's novel *Der König David Bericht* in the autumn of 1972.[1] The very fact that a preeminent author such as Böll was prepared to devote his critical attentions, in *Der Spiegel*, to the latest work of an East German counterpart is in itself significant, for, despite the apparent dominance of professional literary commentators such as Fritz Raddatz and Marcel Reich-Ranicki in the efforts of the early 1970s to publicise the emergence of a new quality of writing in the GDR, it is the evident respect with which Böll, as a creative writer, regards Heym and many of his East German colleagues which tells us more about the way literary relations between the two German states were developing. Böll's opening sentence — 'Daß Autoren immer Ärger machen (und haben), ist hinlänglich bekannt' — which he develops into the leitmotiv of his review, underlines his sense of identity with Heym and his fictional mouthpiece, the scribe Ethan, at the court of the ruthlessly authoritarian King Solomon. Certain moral qualities and painful experiences provide, for Böll, not only the essential continuity between the author in the Old Testament era of Heym's imagination and the present day, but also the similarity in the situation of authors in the two German states. Only a minority amongst writers have the talent to produce work which has 'Weltniveau' and speaks to a wide readership; and when this talent is combined with the incorruptibility of an Ethan in the pursuit of the truth about his own age, the inevitable result is conflict with authorities whose hegemony is threatened and who endeavour to silence this dissenting voice with whatever means they have available.

---

1. Reprinted in *Essayistische Schriften und Reden*, vol. 2, Cologne, 1979, pp. 595–8.

Böll's striking unwillingness to differentiate between the situation of the two German literatures in their respective states is also, of course, a consequence of the exceptional circumstances in which both he and Heym found themselves in the autumn of 1972. In the Federal Republic it was the year of the 'Radikalenerlaß', a period of what Böll had just described as 'Intellektuellenhetze', organised by right-wing politicians and the Springer press, most notably against himself, after his appeal, in his previous *Spiegel* article, for a less hysterical response to the threat posed by the Red Army Faction. In the GDR, in contrast, quite radical changes in cultural policy, away from the repressiveness of the last years of Ulbricht's leadership, had been signalled by the 'no taboos' speech of December 1971 by the newly installed Erich Honecker. But although the publication of Ulrich Plenzdorf's *Die neuen Leiden des jungen W.* in the first issue of *Sinn und Form* in 1972 indicated the potential for critical cultural debate under Honecker, Heym was still suffering from the virtual ban on publication of his work in the GDR imposed in 1965. The fact that *Der König David Bericht* had appeared only in the Federal Republic emphasised a continuing difference between Western pluralism and the SED's limited ideological tolerance, a difference Böll clearly acknowledged in his comments on the impossibility of Ethan fulfilling official hagiographical expectations in his biography of King David, but without wishing to restrict the relevance of Heym's novel to the GDR or Eastern Europe, as Reich-Ranicki had done in a review for *Die Zeit* entitled 'König David alias Stalin'. For Böll the problems recently faced by Daniel Ellsberg in the USA in publishing his *Pentagon Papers* represented just as valid a point of reference as that of the Stalin era in the GDR.

Towards the end of this revealing review Böll broadened his focus to remind his readers that Heym was by no means alone in enjoying his respect as a literary equal. Coupling Heym's name with those of several other East German authors — Wolf Biermann, Franz Fühmann, Reiner Kunze, Christa Wolf, Rolf Schneider, Günter Kunert and Stephan Hermlin — he declared that GDR literature was now 'längst international anerkannt'. His list demonstrated that his sympathies and knowledge were by no means restricted to the 'dissidents' highlighted in the West German media since the middle 1960s following the publication there of works banned in the GDR (such as Biermann's *Die Drahtharfe*, 1965, and Kunze's *Sensible Wege*, 1969). They also encompassed authors who had enjoyed considerable official recognition in the GDR in the previous decade, both as instigators of cultural debate (notably Hermlin) and as creators of influential works (Wolf's *Der geteilte Himmel*, 1963, or Fühmann's *Das*

−177−

Judenauto, 1962, for example) subsequently published in the Federal Republic. Whether this yet amounted to *international* recognition is open to question: Böll's choice of adverb may have involved some deliberate exaggeration as a means of exposing the absurdity of the GDR's refusal to publish one of its best-known authors, at the time when it was seeking international recognition itself by bodies such as the United Nations. In the face of this contradiction Böll made his boldest assertion, setting relations between authors in the two German states above the complexities of the formal political relations developing slowly in the context of Willy Brandt's 'Ostpolitik': not only was East German literature internationally recognised, but 'die literarische Wiedervereinigung' had 'längst stattgefunden'.

The nature of the reunification Böll evidently had in mind here, based on equality of status of authors in the two states and their critical independence from political authority, had nothing in common with the national aspirations of the West German right, which had had a bearing on the patronising titles of earlier anthologies of GDR literature, such as Reich-Ranicki's *Auch dort erzählt Deutschland* (1960) and Balluseck's *Gedichte von Drüben: Lyrik und Propagandaverse aus Mitteldeutschland* (1963), and on the assumption that the best literature from the GDR was of a non-political kind: when Johannes Bobrowski was awarded the Gruppe 47 Prize in 1961, it was claimed to be for 'tief unpolitische, ziemlich traditionalistische, schöne Lyrik'![2] Böll's reference to reunification did implicitly acknowledge that there had been a period (from the late 1940s until the middle 1960s) of rigid separation of the two German cultures, when the terms 'socialist' and 'critical' realism might have been legitimately used as a shorthand to differentiate between literatures pursuing quite different objectives and between the work of authors who had little direct contact with one another. But there had been decisive changes, marked in the GDR by the political disenchantment of Ulbricht's final years and in the Federal Republic by the restoration of creative confidence following the 'death of literature' debate of the late 1960s, which had transformed not only Böll's understanding of how much common ground now existed (even though others would have avoided the emotive reference to 'Wiedervereinigung').

The wider West German awareness of this process of convergence was not greatly facilitated before the 1970s by the activities of its publishers, whose presentation of the small number of East German authors they printed tended to disguise the very fact that they came from the GDR.[3] A notable exception was Klaus Wagenbach in West

2. R. Lettau (ed.), *Die Gruppe 47: Bericht, Kritik, Polemik*, Neuwied, 1967, p. 178.
3. See H.-J. Schmitt, 'Zur Wirkungsgeschichte der DDR-Literatur' in H.-J. Schmitt

Berlin, whose *Lesebuch: Deutsche Literatur der sechziger Jahre* of 1968 sought to demonstrate how authors in all the German-speaking states (including some ten GDR authors in a total of around fifty) had come to see the primary function of their writing as that of questioning their respective status quo. By organising his collection of short prose texts and poems according to theme, Wagenbach underlined the extent to which his cross-section of authors complemented each other in their treatment of such major issues as the legacy of the Hitler years, social stagnation, the 'non-bucolic' modern experience of nature, industrial alienation, and the threat of nuclear war.[4]

If Wagenbach's *Lesebuch* proved a modest revelation of an unacknowledged degree of literary convergence, it was Christa Wolf's novel *Nachdenken über Christa T.*, published in the spring of 1969 in the Federal Republic, which first created an awareness of the possibilities of cross-fertilisation between the two German literatures as a genuine two-way process. The pivotal position of Wolf's novel in the literary development of the GDR is now undisputed, despite the controversy it originally provoked in the GDR itself; its reception in the Federal Republic has proven a fascinating case-study in the rapid change of attitude around 1970 of West German critics to East German literature.[5] Its first Western reviewers, viewing it purely in a GDR context, largely failed to recognise the breakthrough it represented there, regarding its polemic against cultural-political norms as a sign of political resignation. Only later was *Christa T.* understood as a sensitive reappraisal of the idea of personal wholeness central to German classicism and the early Marx, as a work marking the liberation of Wolf's generation from its misunderstanding of the basic message of the *Communist Manifesto*, that 'die freie Entwicklung eines jeden' has to precede 'die freie Entwicklung aller' rather than vice-versa. (Stephan Hermlin's autobiographical *Abendlicht* of 1979 dates his bewildered realisation of what this passage actually means as having occurred in the middle 1960s; the fact that many West German intellectuals associated with the Student Movement, in their preoccupation with political activism, had similarly failed to grasp this basic point also emerged in the 1970s, notably in the work of Peter Schneider.)[6] Where the quality of *Christa T.* was

(ed.), *Die Literatur der DDR* (Hansers Sozialgeschichte der deutschen Literatur, vol. 11), Munich, 1983, pp. 20–5.

4. See his afterword to the *Lesebuch*, Berlin, 1968, pp. 175–84.

5. M. Behn (ed.), *Wirkungsgeschichte von Christa Wolfs 'Nachdenken über Christa T.'*, Königstein, 1978.

6. *Abendlicht*, Berlin, 1979, pp. 20–2; P. Schneider, 'Über den Unterschied von

acknowledged, it was often in terms of her having 'learnt' from her Western counterparts: as Reich-Ranicki put it, 'über die Techniken und Ausdrucksmittel, die Christa Wolf offenbar von westlichen Autoren übernommen hat, verfügt sie [. . .] sehr sicher und ganz natürlich'.[7] There is not a little irony in the fact that Uwe Johnson's *Mutmaßungen über Jakob* — a work conceived in the GDR to expose the clichés of Socialist Realism — is the most quoted 'Western' influence in reviews of *Christa T.*: a revealing distortion being per-petuated by Eberhard Mannack in his *Zwei deutsche Literaturen?* as late as 1977. It took Hans Mayer, uniquely placed as the key figure in literary criticism in the GDR in the 1950s before his emigration to the Federal Republic and more aware than most professional re-viewers of the potential of East German literature, to underline the wider significance of *Christa T.*. What Wolf describes as 'die Schwierigkeit, *ich* zu sagen' is not only rooted in the literary develop-ment of the GDR. It is equally applicable to the permanent threat to individuality in Western societies: '[Die Schwierigkeit, *ich* zu sagen] bedeutet in einer Gesellschaft der Selbstentfremdung, sei sie nach kapitalistischen oder sozialistischen Produktionsverhältnissen angelegt, den schmerzhaften Vorgang für jeden einzelnen, die An-passungsklischees zu durchbrechen und sich [. . .] in seiner Beson-derheit zu erkennen'.[8] Mayer's point about the accessibility of the central issue of *Christa T.* to a West German readership, made in the first issue of *Die Neue Rundschau* to appear in 1970, set the pattern for the decade. Quickly followed by sensitive detailed analyses of Wolf's novel by Heinrich Mohr and Manfred Jäger as well as by the author's own lucid elaboration of her aesthetic of 'subjective authen-ticity' in essays and interviews published in the early 1970s, Mayer's article was the starting-point for the reception of Christa Wolf in the West as a literary model, which, from today's perspective, is now also being described as a 'Publikumserfolg, der in der Nachkriegs-zeit seinesgleichen sucht'.[9]

The other important point of contact between the two German literatures on the threshold of the 1970s was one established less obtrusively, although it raised political issues scarcely less sensitive than Wolf's portrayal of the inadequacies of the socialist present-day had done. It arose from the elaboration of the radical strain in the

---

Literatur und Politik', in *Atempause: Versuch, meine Gedanken über Literatur und Kunst zu ordnen*, Darmstadt, 1977, pp. 162–74.

7. Behn (ed.), *Wirkungsgeschichte*, p. 64.
8. Ibid, p. 94.
9. W. Mauser (ed.), *Erinnerte Zukunft: Elf Studien zum Werk Christa Wolfs*, Würzburg, 1985, p. 7.

cultural heritage to which both German states laid official claim, in conscious opposition to the legitimation both sought to derive from the classical humanism of Goethe and Schiller. The Hölderlin bicentenary in 1970 placed fresh focus on the great patriotic poet, who could be shown to have been more genuinely inspired by the spirit of the French Revolution than the classicists who scorned his moral integrity and his creative independence from convention — a figure symbolising the utopian aspirations of authors in both states. The ostensibly historical task of commemorating Hölderlin, the poet who, in his *Hyperion*, had lamented the 'Zerrissenheit der Deutschen', allowed East German authors — virtually for the first time since the 1950s, when Ulbricht officially promulgated the doctrine of the 'zwei deutsche Literaturen' — to express a sense of shared purpose with their Western counterparts. Stephan Hermlin was able to express his wish to have Martin Walser's essay 'Hölderlin auf dem Dachboden' published in the GDR, while indicating his frustration at the cultural stagnation in the GDR which made such an aspiration, for the moment, unfulfillable: '"Warum Dichter sein in dürftiger Zeit", hatte Hölderlin geschrieben. Zeiten bleiben nicht immer dürftig'.[10] The bicentenary spawned an impressive variety of literary texts by East and West German authors in the early 1970s, ranging from Walser's speech at the Tübingen festivities and Hermlin's radio play *Scardanelli* to major poems by Wolf Biermann and Volker Braun, and culminating in substantial biographical portraits both in prose — Gerhard Wolf's *Der arme Hölderlin* (1972) — and in drama — Peter Weiss's *Hölderlin* (1971) — which use 'epic' methods to underline the contemporary significance of the conflicts they recreate. Both of these portraits evoke the sense of political radicalism thwarted in a period of restoration of the old order, with distinct echoes of the GDR of Ulbricht's final years and the aftermath of the Student Movement in the Federal Republic. Gerhard Wolf's is, if anything, more bitter, offering little assurance that cultural history is not about to repeat itself; it is left to Peter Weiss to preserve, through his imagined meeting between the aged Hölderlin and the young Marx in the final scene, the utopian hope of a productive synthesis between the transformation of the economic order and 'die visionäre Formung tiefster persönlicher Erfahrung'.[11]

10. *Lektüre 1960–71*, Berlin, 1979, p. 117.
11. B. Greiner's essay — 'Zersprungene Identität: Bildnisse des Schriftstellers in zeitgenössischen Dichtungen über Hölderlin', in K. Lamers (ed.), *Die deutsche Teilung im Spiegel der Literatur*, Stuttgart, 1978, pp. 85–120 — seriously underestimates the critical force of some of the East German views of Hölderlin, especially Gerhard Wolf's. I have offered a rather different reading of *Der arme Hölderlin* in

The changes in cultural policy in the GDR following the conception of *Der arme Hölderlin* suggested that Wolf's 'epic' perspective on Hölderlin had underestimated the scope for progress and that Weiss's defiant utopianism might have been more appropriate to the GDR of Erich Honecker. This is not to suggest, however, that Honecker's 'no taboos' speech of December 1971 led to the rapid appearance of major literary works held back from publication during the preceding years: Heym's *König David Bericht* was not released for publication there until 1973, while Hermann Kant's *Das Impressum*, the first East German text of 1972 to be published simultaneously in both states after raising expectations that it would be a worthy successor to *Nachdenken über Christa T.*, proved a great disappointment. The author of the much-admired *Die Aula* had produced an 'Entwicklungsroman' centred on the life of a respected newspaper editor, which revealed virtually nothing of the awareness of the widespread individual alienation from state authority that had given Christa Wolf's novel its wider German significance. Initially, it was the new quality of public debate on literary issues which attracted the attention, and sometimes the envy, of West German intellectuals: creative writers in the GDR were defending notions of subjectivity and originality which took them completely outside any conventional definition of Socialist Realism. Adolf Endler and Günter Kunert dominated a debate on lyric poetry, linking quality with 'Grenzüberschreitung' and rejecting the parochiality of, in Kunert's phrase, 'eine Literatur für streng presbyterianische Handwerksgesellen von Orten unter 30,000 Einwohnern über das presbyterianische Handwerksgesellenproblem'.[12] The authenticity of Plenzdorf's portrayal, in *Die neuen Leiden des jungen W.*, of working-class experience and the rebelliousness of the younger generation was praised by Hermlin at the outset of a controversy thoroughly documented in leading periodicals like *Sinn und Form* and *Neue Deutsche Literatur*. The Seventh Writers' Congress in December 1973 underlined the extent to which the authors themselves were collectively undertaking this radical redefinition of literary priorities, within which, as Franz Fühmann polemically put it, the pursuit of truth rather than wishful thinking was now recognised as being the motivating force of a socialist literature.

The prestigious annual anthology of new writing, *Tintenfisch*, published in West Berlin, devoted a section of its 1974 edition to the

---

The East German Novel: Identity, Community, Continuity, Bath and New York, 1984, pp. 189–97.
12. *Tintenfisch*, no. 7, Berlin, 1974, pp. 60–8.

documentation of this debate. Its editor, Michael Krüger, prefaced his selection of material with the hope that it might prove 'vorbildlich [. . .] für die Belebung der westdeutschen Auseinandersetzung, die vornehmlich entweder an ihrem Ekel über Literatur herumwürgt oder ihr alleiniges Heil in der Literatur der Arbeitswelt sucht, wenn nicht findet'.[13] Equally without precedent, an East German study of contemporary West German prose, Kurt Batt's *Die Exekution des Erzählers*, first published in the GDR in 1972, was being taken seriously in the Federal Republic as an analysis of the roots of this literary crisis.[14] Batt's survey of the fiction of the late 1960s and early 1970s — however much it was open to criticism as an attempt to judge a plurality of prose styles according to old-fashioned criteria of realism — anticipated the revival of confidence in established narrative techniques in the later 1970s, in the way he devoted special praise to Böll's harmonisation of documentary and fictional elements in *Gruppenbild mit Dame* (1971) and insisted on historical perspective as the key to the recovery of a literature which had confused the 'Ende des bürgerlichen Individualismus' with the 'Ende des Menschen als Subjekt überhaupt'. Batt's relative openness to the work of authors actively pursuing the task of 'Vergangenheitsbewältigung' despite their personal unacceptability in the GDR — he highlights a North German strain of realism exemplified by Johnson, Kempowski and Lenz — also served to encourage the production of the autobiographical fiction which became such a vital element in the East German literature of the decade.

The rapid growth in the prestige of East German writing in the Federal Republic led some authors, understandably, to distrust the motives of the Western media which were suddenly giving them such prominence. Jurek Becker's speech to the Seventh Writers' Congress warned against the dangers of their work being exploited for political attacks on the authority of the SED and to promote reactionary 'gesamtdeutsche Hoffnungen'.[15] He took care, however, to exclude fellow-authors in the West from his strictures, since the greatly extended opportunities for West German citizens to travel into the GDR following the signing of the 'Grundlagenvertrag' in 1972 had encouraged much closer personal contacts between authors, especially those living in East and West Berlin. As Günter Grass reported in his *Kopfgeburten* (1980), there were regular, unpublicised,

13. Ibid.
14. Republished in *Revolte intern: Betrachtungen zur Literatur in der BRD*, Leipzig, 1974, pp. 191–273; the West German edition appeared in Munich in 1975.
15. *Neue Deutsche Literatur* (Feb. 1974), pp. 55–60.

meetings after 1973 which brought him, together with Western colleagues such as Nicolas Born, Peter Schneider and Christoph Meckel, into productive literary discussions with Becker, Sarah Kirsch, Kunert and hitherto unknown younger authors like Thomas Brasch and Hans-Joachim Schädlich. Even though such close personal contacts might still have been exceptional, there was an evident increase in intellectual cross-fertilisation from this period onwards.

The most striking case of the impact of East German writing in the West over the 1970s was in the area of feminist aesthetics, in which Christa Wolf, Irmtraud Morgner, Sarah Kirsch and, later, Maxie Wander all had a significant role to play. They countered the hostility of Western feminist writing to the formalisation of experience in literature by demonstrating the effectiveness of integrating historical perspective, fantasy and socialist commitment within an aesthetic of 'subjective authenticity'. Wolf's stories *Unter den Linden* (1973), Kirsch's poems *Zaubersprüche* (1973), Morgner's montage-novel *Trobadora Beatriz* (1974) and the tongue-in-cheek accounts of changes in sexual identity from the anthology *Blitz aus heiterm Himmel* (1974) were all published rapidly in the West and have since contributed widely to the feminist debate.[16] In 1976 one of the Federal Republic's best-known female authors in the field of documentary literature, Erika Runge, announced her conversion to a style of writing based on Christa Wolf's, which would encompass 'das Subjekt in der komplexen Vielseitigkeit seiner Individualität'.[17] Ironically, just afterwards, Maxie Wander showed that there is no necessary contradiction between this goal and the documentary method: her collection of interviews with women, *Guten Morgen, du Schöne* (1977), has since become a model in the West for the uninhibited discussion of the relationship between private and working experience in the pursuit of self-realisation. This East German women's literature has faced few problems of accessibility in the West. In his *Spiegel* review of *Guten Morgen, du Schöne*, the recently exiled Thomas Brasch doubted whether the explicit promotion of sexual equality in the GDR Constitution had led to significant differences in women's lives there: for him, both states have remained essentially 'Industriegesellschaften' and the frustrations articulated by Maxie Wander's interviewees result from a German obsession with 'Leistung' which predates the post-war division.[18]

16. See J. Serke, *Frauen schreiben: Ein neues Kapitel deutschsprachiger Literatur*, Frankfurt on Main, 1982 esp. pp. 19–22.
17. 'Überlegungen beim Abschied von der Dokumentarliteratur', in U. Timm and G. Fuchs (eds.), *Kontext 1: Literatur und Wirklichkeit*, Munich, 1976, pp. 97–119.

Brasch's comments help to indicate why the new feminist dimension in East German writing in the 1970s also led its authors into a direct confrontation with the psychological legacy of the Third Reich which they had previously believed to be less their concern than that of their West German colleagues. As it had been an article of faith in the GDR that the socialist German state had made a clean break with the fascist past, there was — apart from modest exceptions like Fühmann's *Das Judenauto* — nothing published there to compare with the West German tradition begun with works like Grass's *Die Blechtrommel*. It was therefore a clear acknowledgment that there was a lot of ground to be made up in seeking to match the achievements of West German authors in the area of 'Vergangenheitsbewältigung' when Christa Wolf began work on her autobiographical novel *Kindheitsmuster* (1976), indicating in her narrative framework the tortuous process by which she overcame her fear of confronting her own past. The fact that this is part of a generational process is evident in the many thematic similarities between Wolf's novel and Franz Fühmann's *22 Tage oder die Hälfte des Lebens* (1973) or Hermann Kant's *Der Aufenthalt* (1977), while drama of the quality of Heiner Müller's *Germania Tod in Berlin* (1977) or Volker Braun's *Simplex Deutsch* (1980) seeks to objectivise the essential personal issues by locating them within a broader historical canvas.[19] Looking at this group of works in relation to their major Western counterparts of the 1970s — Böll's *Gruppenbild mit Dame*, Weiss' *Ästhetik des Widerstands* (1975–83) or Siegfried Lenz's *Heimatmuseum* (1978), for example — it is difficult to isolate distinguishing 'East German' features: the brutal force of Müller's portrayal results in just as idiosyncratic a manner from his self-liberation from cultural-political norms as Fühmann's fragmentary, self-questioning diary or Kant's rigorously restricted focus on the immediate post-war months. The secondary significance of the direct comments on the contemporary GDR in these major works caused some bewilderment in the Federal Republic as to how they should be assessed. In an article of 1978 on *Kindheitsmuster*, Böll castigated reviewers for their condescending appraisal of Wolf's novel, for their evident expectation that a work with such critical power should culminate in some demonstrative rejection of the GDR. He argued that it should be viewed first and foremost not as a work of East German literature

---

18. *Der Spiegel* (no. 31, 1978), pp. 137–8.
19. See Patricia Herminghouse, 'Vergangenheit als Problem der Gegenwart: Zur Darstellung des Faschismus in der neueren DDR-Literatur', in P.U. Hohendahl and P. Herminghouse (eds.), *Literatur der DDR in den siebziger Jahren*, Frankfurt on Main, 1983, pp. 259–94.

but as a significant variation on the central theme of recent German writing in general: 'Die verfluchte, immer wieder und immer wieder mit Recht gestellte Frage: Wie war das denn nun eigentlich? ist nur zu beantworten in der Literatur als ganzem, als über Jahrzehnte sich ausbreitendem Versuch, der viele Variationen, viele Intonationen, unzählig viele Ausdrucksformen hat'.[20]

The appearance of *Kindheitsmuster*, a work conceived and written in the first half of the 1970s and published late in 1976, marks an important turning-point within the process of convergence taking place gradually over these years, as a result of similarities in authors' experience in their respective political environment and from their common historical identity as Germans. This process accelerated markedly after the expatriation of Wolf Biermann from the GDR, the public protest of most established East German authors (couched in the Marxist terms of the importance of self-critical public debate) against the Politbüro's decision, and the ensuing turmoil which led figures like Becker, Sarah Kirsch and Kunert to leave the GDR. Even the major authors who remained in the GDR (Hermlin, Heym, Wolf and Fühmann, for example) now began to discuss not only the historical responsibilities their German identity imposed on them, but also their longer-term vision of the 'Kulturnation', with a new openness. They clearly felt less constrained by loyalty to Honecker and had lost their confidence of the earlier 1970s that the GDR alone might provide the basis for real progress towards this ideal. In the Federal Republic, the political violence of the autumn of 1977 (the assassinations of Buback and Schleyer, the recapture of the hijacked aircraft at Mogadischu, and the simultaneous deaths of Baader, Ensslin and Raspe in Stammheim prison) created a widespread sense of despair amongst intellectuals which gave the term 'der deutsche Herbst' almost permanent connotations. These unconnected, but largely overlapping, events in the two German states triggered a succession of publications in the Federal Republic, in which East German authors were substantially involved and which sought to define elements of common German identity more explicitly than before. The eighth number of Rowohlt's *Literaturmagazin* (1977), edited by Nicolas Born, was entitled 'Die Sprache des großen Bruders: Gibt es ein ost-westliches Kartell der Unterdrückung?'; *Tintenfisch* No. 15 (1978), 'Deutschland: Das Kind mit zwei Köpfen', was described by its editor, H.C. Buch, as an attempt to revive the patriotic ideals of Hölderlin and to demonstrate that there was at least a literary basis for German unity in the

20. K. Sauer (ed.), *Christa Wolf: Materialienbuch*, Darmstadt, 1979, p. 11.

longer term; and, in the face of the official celebrations of 1979 in both states of three decades of independent achievements, Jochen Jung's anthology *Deutschland, Deutschland* and Klaus Wagenbach's stocktaking *Vaterland, Muttersprache* reasserted the alternative view of a continuity of post-war literary endeavour to bring about a German ideal which neither state looked like achieving alone.[21]

For the same reason that publications of this kind could only appear outside the GDR, West German authors were less constrained about commenting directly on the provisionality of the two German states than their colleagues in the GDR. Martin Walser was particularly outspoken in his speech of October 1977 in suggesting that the time had now come to refuse any further recognition of the Federal Republic and the GDR, in the interests of keeping open 'die Wunde namens Deutschland'. East German authors, in contrast, remained unwilling to engage in any discussion about the political future of the GDR, even where their work of the later 1970s reveals an almost total preoccupation with their identity as German intellectuals. Rainer Kirsch's essay of 1978, 'Wertschätzung der Umfelder: Zum Begriff des Nationalen', differentiates carefully between the state as an organisational necessity ('ein Dienstleistungsbetrieb') and national aspirations which form part of the longing for mankind's progress towards the Marxist dream of a 'Weltgemeinschaft freier Individuen'. It is futile, in his view, given the present confrontational state of East–West relationships, to try to envisage possible changes to the division of Germany, yet he remains, as a citizen of the GDR, firmly committed to the idea of the German nation 'für mögliche bessere Zeiten'.[22] This carefully weighed formulation of utopian aspirations amidst the deteriorating intra-German and international relationships of the late 1970s is echoed by a wide range of Kirsch's East German colleagues around the same time. The most remarkable of these statements, because it was made publicly in the GDR, at an otherwise featureless Eighth Writers' Congress in May 1978, was Stephan Hermlin's. His forthright assertion that the three basic elements in his identity as a writer — his Germanness, his communist commitment, and the sense of historical continuity which made him a 'spätbürgerlicher Schriftsteller' — were inextricably linked, led him to insist on the absolute

21. See H. Mohr, 'Entwicklungslinien der Literatur im geteilten Deutschland', in P.G. Klussmann and H. Mohr (eds.), *Literatur im geteilten Deutschland*, Bonn, 1980, pp. 47–58; H.L. Müller, 'Vaterland versus Muttersprache: Deutsche Schriftsteller und deutsche Nation', *Aus Politik und Zeitgeschichte* (20.3.1982), pp. 31–7.
22. Walser, *Wer ist ein Schriftsteller?*, Frankfurt on Main, 1979, pp. 94–101; J. Jung (ed.), *Deutschland, Deutschland: 47 Schriftsteller aus der BRD und der DDR schreiben über ihr Land*, Salzburg, 1979, pp. 141–6.

distinction between the rationality of politicians and 'das Vorrecht des Dichters, vernunftlos zu träumen'. For this reason, literature could not be 'deckungsgleich mit der Existenz von Staaten'.[23]

Statements like these do, of course, imply a continuing endorsement of the conservative view of literary quality indicated by Kurt Batt's attack on the 'Exekution des Erzählers' earlier in the decade, and tend to assume that this view was by now reestablished in the Federal Republic. Günter Kunert was able to argue soon afterwards, in his essay 'Deutsche Literatur in Ost und West', that the factor unifying the best recent writing in both states was its triumph over concerted efforts to water down established criteria: the ravages of SED cultural policy had been no more destructive than 'das Moment geistigen Terrorismus' behind the West German cultural radicalism of the late 1960s, which had regarded 'jedes ästhetische Gebilde' as 'bürgerlicher Scheißdreck' — in both cases the result had been 'Sinnverlust'.[24] This literary conservatism behind the utopian German perspectives of the late 1970s is exemplified by the two major works of East German authors published in both states in 1979, Hermlin's *Abendlicht* and Christa Wolf's *Kein Ort. Nirgends.* *Abendlicht* stands apart among the autobiographical novels of the 1970s as a sustained achievement in poetic prose, illuminating, in a succession of fragmentary recollections, the sources of Hermlin's creative inspiration in German literature, music and landscape as well as the strength of a political commitment forged in opposition to fascism. It was received in the Federal Republic as a masterpiece of German prose — 'eines der großen Beispiele unserer Literatur', as Reinhard Lettau put it[25] — and, perhaps because of its undisputed aesthetic qualities, as being somehow above the ideological conflict between the two states. *Kein Ort. Nirgends*, refining the 'epic' techniques Wolf's husband Gerhard had employed in *Der arme Hölderlin*, is another evocation of the 'deutsche Misere' which depends on the long-established idea of the poet as the incarnation of the human aspiration to self-fulfilment. (Wolf does, of course, add her own distinctive perspective, in presenting the moral integrity of her dual protagonists, Kleist and Karoline von Günderrode, as a 'feminine' alternative to the destructive masculinity of the machine age whose birth they witness.) On its specifically German plane it is strikingly similar to Grass's *Das Treffen in Telgte*, another work of 1979 which endorses the 'timeless' notion of the poet — now in the historical

23. 'In den Kämpfen dieser Zeit', *Aufsätze, Reportagen, Reden, Interviews*, Munich, 1980, pp. 123–8.
24. *Diesseits des Erinnerns: Aufsätze*, Munich, 1982, pp. 185–8.
25. *Der Spiegel* (no. 49, 1979), pp. 240–5.

context of the aftermath of the Thirty Years War — as the guardian of the values which constitute 'das andere, das wahrhaftige Deutschland'.

While stressing the extent to which the two German literatures grew closer together in this traditionalistic, patriotic vein in the later 1970s, it should not be forgotten that there was also at this time a succession of works exclusively critical of Honecker's GDR and published only in the West, to which sections of its media devoted their predominant attention. Even though the first years of Honecker's administration had been characterised by an unusually small number of banned works — Heym's *Fünf Tage im Juni* (1974) being one of the few to be rejected, despite his rehabilitation the previous year — the Biermann crisis was also in this respect a significant turning-point. Prose works such as Reiner Kunze's *Die wunderbaren Jahre* (1976), H.-J. Schädlich's *Versuchte Nähe* (1977), Jurek Becker's *Schlaflose Tage* (1978), Stefan Heym's *Collin* and Rolf Schneider's *November* (both 1979) all portrayed the contemporary GDR in terms unacceptably bleak to the SED. They were subsequently marketed vigorously in the Federal Republic in exaggeratedly anti-communist terms and further publicised, wherever possible, in film versions.[26] While the fact of the authors concerned being harassed, in some cases to the extent of forcing them to leave the GDR, produced many public expressions of solidarity both inside and outside the GDR — Grass's energetic efforts on behalf of Schädlich, Biermann's admission, in a review of *Collin*, of how he had previously underestimated Heym's integrity, the general protest to Honecker in 1979 by eight members of the GDR Schriftstellerverband — these were often accompanied by attempts to counter the exploitation of their work for narrow political purposes. Böll again provides a good example of this in his support for Kunze. After praising, in a review of 1976 in *Die Zeit*, the uniqueness of *Die wunderbaren Jahre* as a source of vivid images of young people's harsh experience in the GDR, he adopted a more generalised German perspective a year later in his eulogy for Kunze, when the latter was being awarded the 'Büchner-Preis'. Now underlining the common international task of all German authors to improve, through the quality of their writing, the deservedly poor reputation of Germans in general, Böll described the exile of a figure like Kunze from the GDR as an occasion for sadness rather than parochial triumph in the Federal Republic: 'Ein Land wird ärmer ohne seine Autoren, und an dieser Verarmung kann uns nicht gelegen sein, seien wir froh

26. See G. Davis, '"Bloß kein Berufs-Dissident werden!"': Zum Phänomen der DDR-Literatur in der Bundesrepublik', in P.M. Lützeler and E. Schwarz (eds.), *Deutsche Literatur in der Bundesrepublik seit 1965*, Königstein, 1980, pp. 233–9.

um jeden, der dort bleiben will und bleiben kann'. What *Die wunderbaren Jahre* was now seen as offering was 'mehr Auskunft über Deutschland [. . .] als ganze Fluten von Propagandaliteratur' (my emphasis).[27]

With the passage of time it has also become evident that the impact of these highly publicised works has generally been of a transitory or a non-literary kind. Schneider's *November* was quickly recognised as being an unconvincing artefact, in its attempt to contain the experience of such totally different individuals as Kunze and Biermann within the personality of his female protagonist; Becker's *Schlaflose Tage* is a rather colourless transfer of an identity-crisis to a fictional schoolmaster, and was rightly criticised by Raddatz in *Die Zeit* as 'sein schwächstes, unkünstlerischstes Buch'; *Collin* has survived mainly as a substantial piece of political journalism, while *Die wunderbaren Jahre*, following the polemical film-version of 1980, lost what remained of its original literary significance as a variant on the presentation of adolescent conflict in Plenzdorf's *Die neuen Leiden des jungen W.* or Braun's *Unvollendete Geschichte* (1975). For the understanding of life in the GDR in a decade surprisingly deficient in works with specific East German locations, fiction like this will continue to serve a limited function as political information, alongside prose of the quality of Plenzdorf's or Braun's which *was* published in the GDR: but as a body of literature it appears to confirm the belief articulated by Günter Kunert just previously, that major novels rarely emerge directly from a period of political upheaval.[28]

As the 1970s came to an end, the bitter internal conflicts provoked within the East German cultural world by the Biermann affair were no longer sufficiently acute to divert the attention of the West German media from the urgent international issues which were intensifying the sense of common purpose built up over the decade by leading authors in both German states. The apprehension expressed by Grass in *Kopfgeburten* during his ruminations on the dawning of 'Orwells Jahrzehnt' — over the onset of a new arms race between the superpowers, the ecological threats to the planet's survival, and the grotesque contrast between European affluence and Third World starvation — was to be closely echoed in the two major East German novels of the early 1980s, Irmtraud Morgner's *Amanda* (1983) and Christa Wolf's *Kassandra* (1983), which both provide a personalised documentary framework to the fantastic and

27. *Essayistische Schriften und Reden*, vol. 3, Cologne, 1980, pp. 394–7, 477–82.
28. J. Walther, *Meinetwegen Schmetterlinge: Gespräche mit Schriftstellern*, Berlin, 1973, p. 97.

mythical events they describe. This intense common awareness of
unprecedented dangers led, in turn, to the formal meetings of
authors from the two German states (the first organised by Hermlin
in East Berlin in December 1981, the second by Grass in West Berlin
in April 1983), which were a public acknowledgement of their joint
responsibility as Germans, the children of Hitler's Reich, to ensure
that war should never again break out on German soil.

These meetings not only represented the culmination of a decade
of literary *rapprochement*: they also drew attention to the immense
difficulties involved in the longer term in keeping cultural aspirations separate from inter-governmental relationships. The fact that
the East Berlin 'Begegnung zur Friedensförderung' was immediately preceded by a joint declaration of Erich Honecker and Helmut
Schmidt also to the effect that Germans must never again be responsible for the outbreak of war, while giving an encouraging
indication that official inner-German detente might help to defuse
superpower tensions, actually threatened the fragile sense of community Hermlin had helped to achieve in bringing together in a
public forum leading authors from both states, including recent
exiles from the GDR. The ambiguous position that Hermann Kant,
who had become President of the GDR Schriftstellerverband in the
aftermath of the Biermann affair, and Hermlin himself, as a con-
fidant of Honecker, were felt to occupy between authorial independence and party loyalty created a significant hurdle to further progress in this direction. In the early 1980s a succession of former East
German authors now living in the West, including Kunze, Schädlich, Sarah Kirsch and Jürgen Fuchs, protested vigorously against
any hint of collaboration with what they saw as agents of repressive
East German authority. They also responded indignantly to the
view expressed by Bernt Engelmann, Chairman of the West German
Schritstellerverband at the time, that a clear distinction needed to be
maintained between any political consideration of reunification —
'Wiederherstellung eines deutschen Nationalstaates' — and the
utopian literary projections of a humanistic longing for German
brotherhood. These bitter public exchanges about the precise nature
of the German dimension which had developed such emotional force
during the later 1970s may be one reason why there has recently
been much less direct reference to the idea of the 'Kulturnation' and
little sign of a continuing preoccupation with the suffering poet
amidst the 'deutsche Misere' of past centuries.

What has not changed, however, is the conviction built up over
the 1970s that the critical functions of writers in the two German
states are not essentially different, and that the technological

imperatives to which both German states respond in an often ruthless manner are a major cause of the individual disorientation which has become the central theme of both literatures. It may even be that a literature once ridiculed in the West for its naive optimism now retains just enough sober determination not to abandon hope of human progress to appeal to a West German readership more profoundly than the work of its own authors often does. As Michael Schneider, a trenchant critic of the 'Katastrophismus der westdeutschen Kulturszene' in the 1980s, has argued, a work like *Kassandra* can provide an example of the 'Vermenschlichung [. . .] im Vorfeld der Katastrophe'[29] which he finds dangerously lacking in the recent literature of the Federal Republic.

Suggested Further Reading

It is not my intention here to offer an exhaustive bibliography of good analyses of the literature of the GDR in this period; this can be obtained from, amongst other sources, Hohendahl and Herminghouse, Wallace, Reid or my own contribution to *The Modern German Novel* (see below). The works listed here relate rather to the focus of my essay.

Manfred Behn, *DDR-Literatur in der Bundesrepublik*, Meisenheim, 1977

Geoffrey V. Davis, 'Bloß kein Berufs-Dissident werden!', in Paul Michael Lützeler and Egon Schwarz (eds.), *Deutsche Literatur in der Bundesrepublik seit 1965*, Königstein, 1980, pp. 230–45

Wolfgang Emmerich, 'Jenseits der Tabus?', in idem., *Kleine Literaturgeschichte der DDR*, Darmstadt and Neuwied, 1981, pp. 179–228

Peter Uwe Hohendahl and Patricia Herminghouse (eds.), *Literatur der DDR in den siebziger Jahren*, Frankfurt on Main, 1983

Paul Gerhard Klussmann and Heinrich Mohr (eds.), *Literatur im geteilten Deutschland*, Bonn, 1980

Eberhard Mannack, *Zwei deutsche Literaturen*, Kronberg, 1977

Hans Mayer, 'Literatur heute im geteilten Deutschland', in Werner Link (ed.), *Schriftsteller und Politik in Deutschland*, Düsseldorf, 1979, pp. 115–29

J.H. Reid, *The New East German Literature*, Oxford and New York, 1989, (Berg/Oswald Wolff)

Dennis Tate, 'The Novel in the German Democratic Republic', in Keith Bullivant (ed.), *The Modern German Novel*, Leamington Spa and New York,

29. *Nur tote Fische schwimmen mit dem Strom: Aufsätze*, Cologne, 1984, p. 161.

1987 (Berg/Oswald Wolff), pp. 3–18

——, '"Breadth and Diversity": Socialist Realism in the GDR', in Michael Scriven and Dennis Tate (eds.), *European Socialist Realism*, Oxford and New York, 1988 (Berg), pp. 60–78

Ian Wallace (ed.), *The GDR under Honecker 1971–1981*, Dundee, 1981

—— , *The Writer and Society in the GDR*, Tayport, 1984

PART II

Writers

HELEN CHAMBERS

Thomas Bernhard

Thomas Bernhard, the poet of paradox, the connoisseur of contradictions, is highly regarded by professional 'Germanisten' in his
native Austria. The response of non-academic critics and the general
readership tends to be more emotional. Personal reactions to his
savage attacks on Austrian life and culture show that his works
repeatedly strike a nerve, and the reviewer, feeling pain, rejects its
source for reasons that are often unconvincing in aesthetic terms.
Outside Austria there is less to interfere with the direct appreciation
of his artistic achievement and with the appearance of translations
his fame is spreading. George Steiner in 1976 saw him as 'the most
original, concentrated novelist writing in German'.[1] Peter Demetz,
referring to *Alte Meister* (1984), asserted: 'Er schreibt sich eben
energisch und unbeirrt in die Weltliteratur ein',[2] a judgement reiterated in Franz Josef Görtz's assessment of Bernhard's novel,
Auslöschung (1986): 'So rätselhaft einleuchtend pflegt Weltliteratur
zu sein ... und Thomas Bernhard zählt nun dazu'.[3] His fellow
Austrian Ingeborg Bachmann figures as the positively drawn poet-
ess in *Auslöschung* and, writing in the early 1970s, she put her finger
both on Bernhard's literary worth and on the problems he poses: 'In
diesen Büchern ist alles genau, von der schlimmsten Genauigkeit,
wir kennen nur die Sache noch nicht, die hier so genau beschrieben
wird, also uns selber nicht'. Our problem is one of being too close to
subject-matter, that is, existence in our own time: 'Wie sehr diese
Bücher die Zeit zeigen, was sie gar nicht beabsichtigen, wird eine
spätre erkennen, wie eine spätre Zeit Kafka begriffen hat'.[4]

   Despite the fact that his works share a whole range of features
with those of other contemporary writers: pessimism, provocative-
ness, existential uncertainty, scepticism about language, and autobiographical tendencies, to name a few, they present interpretative
difficulties of a peculiar kind. For this reason it may be instructive to

1. *TLS*, 13 February 1976.
2. *FAZ* 1985.
3. *FAZ*, 30 September 1986.
4. Ingeborg Bachmann, *Werke*, vol. 4, Munich, 1978, pp. 361–4.

base a study of Bernhard on salient aspects of the critical reception of his works. Since the appearance of his first novel, *Frost*, in 1963, apart from a three-year gap between *Amras* (1964) and *Verstörung* (1967), Bernhard has produced at least one new publication a year, totalling about forty to date. The secondary literature is acquiring corresponding proportions. Bernhard, with a characteristically double thrust, sums up the would-be literary critic's position in a formulation which is at once an inward-looking *cri de coeur* and a sardonic observation of painfully general validity: 'Schon gleich, wenn wir etwas angehen, ersticken wir in dem ungeheueren Material, das uns zur Verfügung steht auf allen Gebieten, das ist die Wahrheit, sagte er, dachte ich. Und obwohl wir das wissen, gehen wir unsere sogenannten Geistesprobleme immer wieder an, lassen uns auf das Unmögliche ein: ein *Geistesprodukt zu erzeugen. Das ist Wahnsinn!* so er, dachte ich'.[5]

A recurrent critical strategy employed to abstract the essence of Bernhard's works is the listing of themes. Manfred Mixner writes of the poetic objectivisation of his experience of 'Angst, Qual, Schuld und Einsamkeit';[6] G. Schloz itemises the ingredients of *Vor dem Ruhestand* (1979) as 'Tristesse, Inzest, Infamie, Verlogenheit, Wahn'.[7] Other common factors from such lists are disease, darkness, death and despair. Using a more sophisticated but related tactic Wendelin Schmidt-Dengler has formulated Eleven Theses on Thomas Bernhard's Works.[8] The present study too has had recourse to this approach. The lists formulated are often shocking or at least disturbing and by this means the critic's own response to an accumulation of negative themes finds expression. They also reflect Bernhard's habit of naming abstractions repeatedly and his chronic underuse of pronouns. His obsessive attacks on and attempted exorcism of his disturbing subject-matter involves relentless naming of the source of torment. It is part of the pervasive ambiguity of the work that it is often hard to decide whether such insistent nominal repetition is effective, deadening or irritating.

A further aspect of Bernhard's style pointed up by the critics' lists is his repeated use of keywords, or groups of related words which emerge again and again in his works, suggesting that we are being confronted with a code or pattern. One such recurrent motif is

5. *Der Untergeher*, Frankfurt on Main, 1983, p. 96.
6. Manfred Mixner, 'Vom Leben zum Tode', in M. Jurgensen (ed.), *Bernhard Annäherungen*, Berne, 1981, p. 76.
7. *Christ und Welt*, 6 July 1979.
8. Wendelin Schmidt-Dengler, *Der Übertreibungskünstler. Zu Thomas Bernhard*, Vienna, 1986, pp. 107–11.

'rücksichtslos / Rücksichtslosigkeit'. This has a relatively straight-forward and constant function, expressing the conviction that in order to survive, egotism is of the essence, but as survival is a heroic achievement against the odds, the ostensibly negative term is often, but not inevitably, used positively. A recurrent word complex such as 'Kunst / künstlich / Kunststück' with its virtually inexhaustible family of elaborate compounds — the comic and sinister variants 'Kunstpudelnummer' and 'Kunstzertrümmerer' from *Die Macht der Gewohnheit* (1974) are typical — forms the basis of a more intricate thematic pattern in the works. It is as if the literary text conforms to an underlying formula whose elements are amenable to extensive permutation and combination, without fundamentally altering the meaning.

The structure and style of Bernhard's works has, by author and commentators alike, frequently been termed both mathematical and musical. Repetition of keywords and motifs is fundamental to both these views of his works. Their function is comparable to that of themes in music and symbols in mathematics. Both create their own framework of reference, established by repetition and by a technique of question and answer. Similarly, Bernhard in his works creates his own frame of reference by techniques of repetition and variation, and his language, like music and mathematics, can be seen as a coded formulation, in this case of the artist's statement about reality. It is possible to decode Bernhard's works in variety of ways, indeed their highly formalised nature provokes such an approach. Schopen-hauerian, Nietzschean, Freudian and Wittgensteinian interpreta-tions are all plausible, although the multiplicity of the possibilities underlines the injudiciousness of embracing any single philosophical or psychological interpretation. In *Frost*, Strauch, in the struggle to order the fluctuating chaos of his perception of inner and outer reality, claims: 'Ich habe eine Notenschrift meiner Angst erfunden' (F, p. 113).[9] The same is true of Bernhard. He has invented a means of notation, a set of verbal equivalents for his perception of existence, of which fear is a vital aspect. In *Der Kulterer*, first written in 1962 and reworked as a film script in 1973, the artist figure expresses a comparable idea of the coding, or in other words, aesthetic ordering of reality, this time in more positive terms. The prisoner Kulterer undergoes a sublime spiritual experience, the overwhelming intima-tion of an underlying order in creation through art: 'Wirkungen beruhten plötzlich tatsächlich auf Ursachen. Auf einmal hatte es das, was auch er "Hierarchie" nannte, gegeben. Anarchie schaltete

9. See Author's Note at the end of this essay for key.

sich, wie er dachte, von selbst, links und rechts seines Weges aus. Und er entdeckte auf den Stützpfeilern der Mathematik die Poesie, die Musik, die alles zusammenhält' (K, p. 101). Poetry, equated with music, the force which provides an ultimate coherence to existence, is seen to be founded on mathematics, that is on an abstract, logical system. As systems all three — music, language and mathematics — are capable of infinite variation, and although self-sufficient, they none the less reflect the play of relationships between things in the real world. It is revealing in this early work to see such an unequivocally positive interpretation of the power of art, even though its relationship to the real world remains problematic. The works which followed *Der Kulterer* in the early to mid-1970s with their predominantly dark perspectives have been succeeded by works in which the relatively more positive orientation of *Der Kulterer* becomes increasingly discernible.

Another striking feature of Bernhard's reception is the critics' tendency to imitate his style. The explanation for this lies in fundamental formal qualitites of Bernhard's writing. The ease of parody points both to its closeness to mannerism[10] and to its strong acoustic appeal. Imitation occurs with both positive and negative intent. The apotheosis of parodistic Bernhard criticism is Eberhard Falcke's review of *Auslöschung*, entitled 'Abschreiben. Eine Auflehnung',[11] in which, blinkered by his own expectations and his identification of recurrent themes and techniques, he fails to recognise Bernhard's achievement. It is a work in which familiar problems of alienation from family and home, of self-doubt and the search for an individual identity in spite of himself, the world and death are pursued with dynamic linguistic force, and there are significant innovations in both content and form. Falcke's formulation, 'daß es sich bei dieser Bernhardschen sogenannten Neuerscheinungung um gar nichts anderes handeln kann als um eine ungeheuerliche Wiederholungsinfamie', may serve as an indication of the seductive nature of Bernhard's prose. From the original Falcke has taken the device of provocative exaggeration with comic effect, the use of a proper noun to express a mode of existence, 'sogenannt' to denote the writer's scepticism *vis-à-vis* the ontological status of certain man-made concepts, and the combined acoustic and intellectual appeal of the compound noun, all of which are typical of the model. Ironically the very phenom-

---

10. C.f. Martin Esslin, 'Ein neuer Manierismus? Randbemerkungen zu einigen Werken von Gert Jonke und Thomas Bernhard', *Modern Austrian Literature*, 13, 1980, 1, pp. 111f.
11. *Der Spiegel*, 45, 1986.

enon of writing (and thus thinking) along lines prescribed by another irresistible consciousness is one of Bernhard's central themes. Falcke is hoist with his own petard. In earlier novels particularly, such as *Frost* (1972) and *Verstörung* (1979) the narrator is progressively sucked into the world he is observing and the expression of his observations becomes infected by the style of the dominant figure in the narrative. In later works, instead of showing this phenomenon from the perspective of the involuntary victim we see it from the viewpoint of the intellectually dominant character. Reger, the music critic, in *Alte Meister* has turned the museum attendant, Irrsigler, into a mouthpiece for his thoughts; Murau in *Auslöschung* sees himself as feeding ideas into his pupil Gambetti's mind. Human relationships in Bernhard's works are predominantly power struggles where monomaniac self-assertion is countered by techniques of evasion and protest. The theme of verbal domination, a feat often accomplished by Bernhard the writer over his readers, may well in turn derive from his exposure as a child to the intellectual dominance of his much admired writer grandfather.

A feature of his style which insinuates itself effortlessly into the critical diction is his habit of making sweeping generalisations. His writing over long stretches is abstract and polemical. He tells you how catastrophic existence is rather than showing you by means of description or narrative. This deliberate strategy whereby words, not things or people, are the reality of the text, looks more like philosophy, or indeed literary criticism, than fiction and for this reason the reviewer is tempted to reflect the mode. One finds a surprising number of absolute statements in the secondary literature, a preserve where an objective critical approach more commonly precludes sweeping generalisations about writers whose work is still in progress. Benjamin Heinrichs's statement for example: 'Wie alle Bernhard Figuren scheitert auch Bruscon',[12] is an oversimplification which fails to take account of the roles of narrator figures in his prose — particularly in *Holzfällen* (1984) where the evening described has been a confrontation of the narrator with his past and results in his achieving a degree of self-knowledge — or of such figures in the plays as the rebellious Queen of the Night in *Der Ignorant und der Wahnsinnige* (1972) who refuses to function further as a coloratura machine, and Voss in *Ritter, Dene, Voss* who triumphantly manipulates his sisters by means of his madness. Such positive achievements are never unambiguous, but should not be dismissed as capitulations to life. Similarly Gudrun Mauch's observation:

12. *Die Zeit*, 23 August 1985, on *Der Theatermacher.*

'Auch im Roman *Korrektur* ist wie in allen Werken Thomas Bernhards ständig die Rede von der finstersten Verzweiflung',[13] is an overstatement which does less than justice to the differentiated texture of Bernhard's works. There is much that is comic in the recognisably human eccentricities of his figures, and although, for example, one might argue that the plight of Caribaldi and his circus artistes (*Die Macht der Gewohnheit*) in their doomed interdependence is an expression of despair at the futility of existence, the fact that Caribaldi does not give up and will manifestly live to fight another day can equally be seen as an affirmation of the self.

Bernhard's own use of absolute statements is rather different. It is a symptom of his unwillingness to compromise at any level. In *Auslöschung*, ironically the work to date in which, relatively speaking, there is the greatest evidence of balance, harmony and a willingness not to lay the blame for the ills of existence elsewhere, he explicitly discusses the function of exaggeration, announcing the theme early on: 'Um etwas begreiflich zu machen, müssen wir übertreiben [. . .] nur die Übertreibung macht anschaulich' (A, p. 128). The question is, what does the exaggeration make clear? This statement seems to suggest that exaggeration draws attention to objective truth, and is necessary because of the reader's deadened responses; that it is pointing outwards towards aspects of external reality, and Bernhard's many tirades, though unacceptable at face value because of their extremity, undeniably contain a measure of objective truth. Although one may not agree that all doctors are charlatans, all artists are cheats, sexual reproduction serves exclusively to add to the sum of misery in the world, the Catholic Church cripples development and Goethe is the grave-digger of the German 'Geist', the notions convey a nagging sensation of truth. The narrator in *Frost* generalises thus: 'Denn das Aufgeschriebene stimmt nicht. Kein Aufgeschriebenes stimmt' (F, p. 129). This statement can be viewed from various angles. It can be seen as an expression of artistic despair, of extreme scepticism about the power of language. It can also be seen both as a truism and as a self-invalidating thesis. Bernhard's use of language is such that even when he abandons his tortuous syntactical *tours de force* the meaning is fraught with ambiguity. The style is turned in on itself while ostensibly, at times aphoristically, pointing away from itself. The same is generally true of his uncompromising tirades. On the one hand they express the intensity of the subjective aggression, rage and disgust of the writer, but at the same time, in their extremity,

13. Gudrun Mauch, 'Thomas Bernhards Roman *Korrektur*. Zum autobiographisch fundierten Pessimismus Thomas Bernhards', in H. Zeman (ed.), *Studien zur österreichischen Erzählliteratur der Gegenwart*, Amsterdam, 1982, p. 89.

they demand a response from the reader; they involve him often to the extent of extracting a grudging recognition of the truth underlying the distortion. Towards the end of *Auslöschung* the narrator expatiates on the theme of exaggeration explaining that for him the art of exaggeration is at the same time his signal distinction and a survival technique. It is typical of Bernhard that such a fundamental aspect of his style is viewed both positively and negatively. Exaggeration is a means of escape from reality, both outer in the form of 'die eigentliche Tatsache' and inner in the form of 'Geistesüberdruß' (A, p. 611), but it is also consummate artistry. However this apparently key statement on the art of exaggeration, which cannot but be seen as a comment on Bernhard's own literary practice, is destabilised by Gambetti's reaction: 'das laute ungehinderte Gambettilachen' (A, p. 611). This is not the cruel and desperate laughter of the earlier works, of die Gute in *Ein Fest für Boris* (1980), for example, confronted in Boris's death by corroboration of the absurdity of existence, but genuinely free and spontaneous laughter which questions the pontificating of the self-absorbed narrator, and shows that Bernhard speaks with more than one voice. For all the accusations of 'Größenwahn' that come his way, his own more flippant, self-deprecatory remarks deserve to be taken more seriously; or to put it another way, paradoxically Bernhard deserves to be taken less seriously.

One final aspect of Bernhard's use of uncompromising generalisation can be observed in Murau's comments in *Auslöschung* on the German language:

Schon die deutsche Sprache ist genau genommen eine häßliche, eine, wie gesagt, nicht nur alles Gedachte zu Boden drückende, sondern durch ihre Schwerfälligkeit auch alles gemein verfälschende, sie ist gar nicht imstande, einen Wahrheitsgehalt tatsächlich als solchen tatsächlichen Wahrheitsgehalt wiederzugeben, sie verfälscht alles von Natur aus, sie ist eine rohe Sprache ohne jede Musikalität, und wäre sie nicht meine Muttersprache, ich würde sie nicht sprechen . . . Die deutschen Dichter haben immer nur ein ganz primitives Instrumentarium zur Verfügung gehabt, sagte ich zu Gambetti, dadurch haben sie es hundertmal schwerer als alle anderen. (A, p. 239)

Here, as with his violent attacks on his hated, beloved homeland, one has the sense that he is not only expressing disgust and frustration, but is attacking his quarry in the hope that it will resist. Die Gute expresses such a hope in *Ein Fest für Boris* (EF, p. 33). Such violent acts of aggression are the product of a radical desire to provoke the object to defend itself, to prove itself other than that which the unmistakable thrust of the polemic suggests. In a world of numbing routine and unreflecting acceptance of mediocrity at all levels the tirade is the poet's challenge: simultaneously an expression of despair and an act of faith, of hope that the victim may at last be provoked to demonstrate its viability. That the German language is allegedly so inherently awkward provides an additional challenge to the poet and the acceptance of challenge is the life-blood of Bernhard's works.

A further critical tactic is to compare him with other writers, particularly, but not exclusively, Austrians. This, too, reflects Bernhard's practice but has its origins more significantly in other factors. Bernhard invites comparison by frequently prefacing his works with quotations, most often from the French *philosophes*, Montaigne, Voltaire, Pascal, or from Novalis. Equally, within the texts and to an ever-increasing degree he refers to, cites and delivers devastating discourses on great artists and philosophers of the past. Reger, the unpleasantly patronising central character in *Alte Meister* for example, indulges in an elaborate double hatchet job on Stifter and Heidegger, which is also directed at the Germans for being taken in by pseudo-art and pseudo-philosophy. Reading such a rampant piece of exaggeration is a perplexing experience. Is this a gratuitous act of provocation on Bernhard's part aimed at his predominantly well-heeled, well-read public? Is it one of his intellectual experiments to test how far he can go? Some might say that with the mention of Heidegger's underpants he has sunk to the level of cheap jokes and that the whole thing is too exasperating to be taken seriously, including the final twist when Reger reveals that he is related to both his distinguished targets, 'mit Stifter von der Mutterseite her, mit Heidegger von der Vaterseite her' (AM, p. 95). However seriously or otherwise one is prepared to take such outbursts two things are clear: the introduction of the names of great artists and philosophers forces a comparison between them and the living writer, Bernhard, although it is possible to appreciate his works without prior knowledge of the figures to whom he refers, simply through the texture of associations. Secondly, the great artist figures, both performing and creative, are frequently examined from the angle of their reception and the reception of art is often the focus of critical attention. The inherent irony and self-referential dimension to this preoccupation is obvious and it, like so much in Bernhard's works, can cause the reader to shift uncomfortably in his seat, uncertain whether Bernhard includes himself in or out of the target area. At this point as elsewhere the line between literature and reality, personal and fictional utterance becomes hard to distinguish. Generally speaking Bernhard is critical of the public's obtuse responses to art rather than of works of art themselves.

Apart from the explicitly provoked comparisons with other writers the critics have not been slow to try to pin down Bernhard's qualities by means of reference to fellow artists, living and dead. He has Novalis's death and darkness-related utopianism, Nestroy's tragi-comic vein, Hofmannsthal's *Sprachskepsis*. Kraus's polemics, Kafka's nightmarish precision and, for all his disclaimers, Stifter, the god-father of modern Austrian literature, cannot be excluded from comparative approaches to the works of a man who spent hours in the Stifterian pursuit of formative walks with a grandfather and who evokes a natural world which impinges mysteriously and relentlessly on man's existence. There is not scope here to pursue all of these tempting avenues of approach, and the list can certainly be extended far beyond the key areas of early Romanticism and Austrian litera-ture to Thomas Mann, Chekhov and Beckett among numerous others. It is important, however, to consider why such a compara-tive mode has been so consistently adopted. This can be attributed to a significant degree to the initially disturbing, alienating and exaggeratedly negative impact of Bernhard's work. Setting him side by side with other writers is part of an attempt to render familiar something outlandish and at times repellent. It is reassuring by a legitimate process of comparison to establish that he is none the less familiar, for that in turn helps to explain the attraction of something that is superficially so alien. Most of the comparative assaults on Bernhard's works have resulted in analogies that remain partial and thus illuminate his originality.

If one considers for example his relationship to early Romanticism and in particular to Novalis — as evidenced in the Fürst's utterances in *Verstörung*: 'Wir haben die Welt in unserem Denken noch nicht überwunden' (V, p. 168), and: 'In die Wissenschaft lasse sich wie in eine Landschaft schauen [. . .] in welcher alle Jahreszeiten immer gleichzeitig sind' (V, p. 172) — we find the expression of aspirations akin to the Romantic desire for a synthesis of nature and 'Geist', of outer and inner reality. The motif of the simultaneity of the seasons, an echo of Strauch's dream in *Frost*, recalls Klingsohr's fairy tale in *Heinrich von Ofterdingen*, where the existing laws of nature epitomised by the revolution of the seasons have to be destroyed in order to usher in a new golden age founded on the power of poetry. Strauch's dream of an unknown but familiar iridescent landscape where the wind plays ageless music on the hard grass, the human beings are in ever-changing chromatic harmony with their surroundings, dis-tinguishable only by their wonderfully differentiated voices, and the trees reach up into the infinite, is a utopian vision closely akin to the products of the early Romantic imagination. But the dream becomes a nightmare as Strauch's head swells up, obscuring the light and rolling down the hill annihilating all life. The dream is prefaced by Strauch's comment: 'Die Phantasie ist der Tod des Menschen' (F, p. 36). His imagination, that is the power of his head, for poetry and reason are virtually equivalent concepts in Bernhard's works, has not permitted him to accept the vision. The painful consciousness of the truth about life, entailing the knowledge of death, has prevailed. The motif of darkness and death is crucial to Novalis's thinking about the achievement of ideal harmony through the supremacy of the imagination, but Bernhard differs from him in that, despite sharing his ardent longing for an ideal universe and the resolution of all contradictions, he cannot make the leap of faith required to achieve this, even imaginatively, for more than a brief moment. Novalis's magical idealism is echoed but the abyss of scepticism inevitably swallows it. For all the potent resonances of Novalis in Bernhard's work there is a further fundamental difference which illuminates the first. In Bernhard's poetic universe the power of love, on which Novalis founds his hopes, is absent. Nevertheless Bernhard's repeated creation of utopian visions, even if they must be denied by the logic of existence, forms a strong positive undercurrent in works where despair and destruction of self and world prevail.

T.S. Eliot, with whom Bernhard was preoccupied in the late 1950s and early 1960s, furnishes an explanation of the relationship between the artist and his predecessors which is particularly apt in Bernhard's case and further vindicates the critics' approach to him. Relevant to the point of view of the writer, in this instance a writer whose acquaintance with and vital interest in the European literary and philosophical tradition is beyond doubt, is Eliot's definition of tradition:

> It cannot be inherited, and if you want it you must obtain it by great labour. It involves in the first place a historical sense, which [. . .] involves a perception, not only of the pastness of the past, but of its presence; the historical sense compels a man to write not merely with his own generation in his bones, but with a feeling that the whole literature of Europe from Homer and within it the whole literature of his own country has a simultaneous existence and composes a simultaneous order.[14]

This is true of Bernhard in a narrowly historical sense, particularly with regard to the recent Nazi period which is integrated into such diverse works as *Frost*, *Die Ursache. Eine Andeutung* (1975), *Vor dem*

14. T.S. Eliot, *The Sacred Wood*, London, 1960, p. 49.

Ruhestand and *Auslöschung* as vital to an understanding of the present. It is also true in a more general way of the many hierarchical, feudal and conservative configurations that he evokes, with their attendant servant–master relationships, which clearly derive from the historical structures of Austrian society. On the side of reception Eliot adequately accounts for the need to evaluate the artist, in our case Bernhard, with reference to his peers: 'You cannot value him alone; you must set him, for contrast and comparison, among the dead. I mean this as a principle of aesthetic not merely historical criticism', and goes on to argue that the 'existing monuments form an ideal order among themselves which is modified by the introduction of the new (the really new) work of art among them'.[15] Although one might share Terry Eagleton's misgivings about the 'ideal' order, his sneering paraphrase to the effect that 'the existing classics within the cramped space of Tradition politely reshuffle their positions to make room for a newcomer'[16] does less than justice to Eliot. Subsequent literary criticism will certainly have to include Bernhard in its evaluative order while his highly personal style has added a new dimension to German literature. Eliot's own works form part of the tradition in which Bernhard writes. Of *The Waste Land*, which greatly interested Bernhard, Eliot said that it could be seen not so much as 'an important bit of social criticism' but as 'the relief of a personal and wholly insignificant grouse against life; it is just a piece of rhythmical grumbling'.[17] This remark, complete with self-irony, can be transferred with ease to Bernhard's works, without in either case restricting their wide appeal.

A final common critical response, less fruitful than the comparative impulse, involves the assertion that Bernhard is writing the same book over and over again. This stance is given some slight credence by his own comments to the effect that he abhors autobiography and that he does not write novels, only shorter or longer prose pieces, suggesting that his opus is one long artistic statement about existence, published piecemeal. The charge seems no more appropriate in the case of Bernhard than of many writers. One could equally argue that Kleist, for instance, or Stifter or Fontane wrote and rewrote the same book, if by that one means that there are easily identifiable thematic and stylistic constants, keywords and key preconceptions underpinned by a coherent, though not necessarily unambiguous view of existence. If one means, however, that there is

15. Ibid.
16. Terry Eagelton, *Literary Theory*, Oxford, 1983, p. 39.
17. M. Drabble (ed.), *The Oxford Companion to English Literature*, Oxford, 1985, p. 1047.

no perceptible artistic development and variation then that is true neither of Bernhard nor of the others.

Bernhard Sorg's rough division of Bernhard's work by decades up to 1981 sees the 1950s as devoted primarily to lyric poetry, the 1960s to prose writing and the 1970s to plays and autobiographical pieces.[18] In the 1980s, having abandoned poetry, he has been moving more or less alternately between longer prose pieces and shorter narratives, autobiographical works and plays. To consider Bernhard simply as a writer of the 1970s thus produces a distorted emphasis on the author as dramatist and autobiographer, although the decade does include the nicely contrasting trio of stories, *Midland in Stilfs*, *Der Wetterfleck* and *Am Ortler* (1971), the small masterpiece *Gehen* (1971), and *Korrektur* (1975) which can be seen as the conclusion to a stage in his development as a novelist.

The autobiographical works with their more conventional narrative mode are for many readers the most accessible part of Bernhard's opus. Despite the obligatory misgivings about the relevance of an artist's life to an evaluation of his works, what we learn from them is welcome illumination on a psychological level, and they represent an important part of Bernhard's literary output. They can be viewed as a symptom of the new subjectivity in the literature of the period and, with their stylised literary form, they can stand on their own quasi as works of fiction, which on one level, owing to Bernhard's customary techniques of exaggeration and distortion, they indubitably are. Apart from the final work, *Ein Kind* (1982), dealing with his painful early relationship with his mother, each short volume has a subtitle underlining the personal significance both of the period treated and of the act of narration for the writer. *Die Ursache. Eine Andeutung* (1975) is Bernhard's evocative but selective account of the restrictions on his development as a youngster in a Salzburg boarding-school, first under Nazi then Catholic control. *Der Keller. Eine Entziehung* (1976) describes how he wrenches himself free from the deadening influence of the Gymnasium to work in a dingy grocer's shop and study music. *Der Atem. Eine Entscheidung* (1978) evokes in excruciating detail the lung disease which brought him face to face with death, and his effort of will to escape. *Die Kälte. Eine Isolation* (1981) tells of his stay in a sanatorium, conveying, as in the others, the mental and emotional environment which is more important than, though indivisible from, the physical one. It is here that his decision to write crystallises and, out of near despair,

---

18. Bernhard Sorg, 'Thomas Bernhard', in H.L. Arnold (ed.), *Kritisches Lexikon zur deutschsprachigen Gegenwartsliteratur*, Munich, 1978.

commitment to life and art asserts itself. Each of these works is remarkable not only as a piece of carefully focused, selective self-analysis and as an act of self-assertion, but also for its simultaneous evocation of social institutions and their smothering effect. The boarding-school, the Gymnasium, the hospital and the sanatorium are all made both real and almost mythological, as one witnesses not only Bernhard's struggle for emotional, intellectual and physical survival, but also the universal conflict between the individual and the institutions that enmesh him.

The best of Bernhard's plays that emerged in the 1970s, *Der Ignorant und der Wahnsinnige* (1972), *Die Macht der Gewohnheit* (1974) and *Immanuel Kant* (1978), can all be seen to derive from his experience of life, and are another way of coping with it. Often reminiscent of the cabaret in style, they are generally viewed as caprices, lighter pieces tossed off as relaxation from the more serious business of prose writing. Bernhard's theatre is characterised by a preponderance of demanding virtuoso monologue roles. His skeletal, repetitive and unpunctuated texts provide wide scope for skilled performers such as Bernhard Minetti and Bruno Ganz for whom he has written specifically on many occasions. There can be no doubt that these plays work on the stage, although conventional plot, characterisation and dialogue are discarded. Like the other works they treat of man's struggle against existence, and despite what can be seen as a large number of own goals by the characters the situation is desperate but not always serious. Again personal polemic is intimately bound up with criticism of national and international institutions. Man's relationship to his cultural, intellectual, political and historical context is under scrutiny. Charges by the critics of gratuitous banality, brutality or tedium are not uncommon, but conservative responses to modern theatre are one of Bernhard's targets and he has a large following of satisfied customers.

A final consideration of why Bernhard's works, despite repellent subject-matter and perplexing or irritating technique, find such widespread acclaim suggests that at the core of his art is an ability to combine the subjective and the objective, the inner and outer world. A simultaneous closeness to and remoteness from recognisable reality is the hallmark of his works. This operates on all levels. On a linguistic plane not only does he produce formulations of spiralling artificial complexity, he also recreates the rhythms of natural speech. Corroboration of this lies in the fact that he is eminently quotable, and in Minetti's observation that Bernhard's lines are easy to learn.[19] He has captured the quintessence of human speech. Comments such as Manfred Jurgensen's, 'es gibt sehr wenig äußerliche Wirklichkeit im literarischen Schaffen Thomas Bernhards',[20] stem from a partial view and are wide of the mark. One can certainly find pages on end where the flow of a character's thoughts circles incessantly round abstractions, but there are other passages where the evocation of external reality is oppressive in its immediacy. For example, the description of die Ebenhöh's sickroom in *Verstörung* (V, pp. 28f.) with its unpleasant smells, the absent companion's abandoned book and the invalid's laundered but unclean garments strewn around is an image of telling sensual as well as emotional impact. In a review of *Vor dem Ruhestand* Benjamin Heinrichs, approaching the phenomenon from another angle, comments: 'Da beschreibt einer die Faschisten nicht aus aufgeklärtem sicherem Abstand sondern aus höhnischer Ferne und verzweifelter Nähe zugleich',[21] and it is precisely this combination of remoteness and proximity to the subject-matter which is the pivotal factor in Bernhard's works. In his artistic struggle with the problems of existence he tries to stand back, to give a distanced, even metaphysical account of the reality he despises, but he is unable, in all honesty, to abstract himself in this way and is sucked back into the inescapable aspects of actual existence which clamour to be formulated. It is from this constant tension that the dynamic force of his prose derives. It is reflected in the central image — or reality — of characters constantly on the move, walking, going physically and mentally between diametrically opposed goals. And although the acuteness of this conflict between mental mastery of the world and the world's mastery over us is often expressed in unrealistically exaggerated terms, the exaggeration does not destroy or replace the reality, it simply recreates certain facets of it. As Walter Weiss astutely comments, the mixture that Thomas Bernhard produces is 'zugleich Verzerrung und Erhellung der Wirklichkeit'[22] and therein lies its charm.

Editorial postscript: Just as this volume was going to press we sadly learned of the death of Thomas Bernhard.

Thomas Bernhard, 10 February 1931 – 12 February 1989

19. Thomas Bernhard, *Der Weltverbesserer*, Bochum, 1980, p. 222.
20. Manfred Jurgensen, *Erzählformen des fiktionalen Ich: Beiträge zum deutschen Gegenwartsroman*, Berne and Munich, 1980, p. 36.
21. *Die Zeit*, 6 July 1979.
22. Walter Weiss, 'Thomas Bernhard — Peter Handke: Parallelen und Gegensätze', in A. Pittertschatscher (ed.), *Literarisches Kolloquium Linz 1984. Thomas Bernhard. Materialien*, Linz, 1985, p. 14.

Thomas Bernhard

Author's Note

The following editions and abbreviations are used for Bernhard's works (all editions are published in Frankfurt on Main unless otherwise indicated):

A = *Auslöschung*, 1986
AM = *Alte Meister*, 1984
EF = *Eine Fest für Boris*, 1980
F = *Frost*, 1972
K = *Der Kulterer*, 1976
V = *Verstörung*, 1979

Also note:

Der Weltverbesserer, Bochum, 1980
Der Untergeher, 1983

Select Bibliography

K. Bartsch, D. Goltschnigg and G. Melzer (eds.), *In Sachen Thomas Bernhard*, Königstein/Ts., 1983

Ulrich Greiner, *Der Tod des Nachsommers. Aufsätze, Porträts, Kritiken zur österreichischen Gegenwartsliteratur*, Munich, 1979

M. Jurgensen (ed.), *Bernhard Annäherungen*, Berne, 1981

Barbara Saunders, *Contemporary German Autobiography. Literary Approaches to the Problem of Identity*, London, 1985

Wendelin Schmidt-Dengler, *Der Übertreibungskünstler. Zu Thomas Bernhard*, Vienna, 1986

W.G. Sebald, *Die Beschreibung des Unglücks. Zur österreichischen Literatur von Stifter bis Handke*, Salzburg, 1985

Bernhard Sorg, 'Thomas Bernhard', in H.L. Arnold (ed.), *Kritisches Lexikon zur deutschen Gegenwartsliteratur*, Munich, 1978

Hans Wolfschütz, 'Thomas Bernhard: The Mask of Death', in A. Best and H. Wolfschütz (eds.), *Modern Austrian Writing*, London, 1980

J.H. REID

The End of Urbanity
Heinrich Böll in the 1970s*

The 1970s were turbulent years for Böll personally. When in 1970 he was elected president of the West German branch of PEN and in the following year became president of PEN International, the first German ever to take up this office, few can have expected that within months he was to become in his own country the target of an unparalleled campaign of vilification from sections of the media and the right-wing political parties. In spite of some provocative speeches, notably 'Die Freiheit der Kunst' (1966), Böll's reputation was still largely that of a popular author, whose works were re-spected for their moral impetus but whose admonitions were sufficiently consoling not to offend conservative readers too deeply. Now he was thrust into the political limelight as the commentator on the Federal Republic's problems and sins. He developed a public persona, an image which he did not especially welcome, which placed him in the centre of controversy. In 1972 he was awarded the Nobel Prize for Literature, the first German to be so honoured since 1929; but the normally nationalistic press was not pleased and Franz Josef Strauss went so far as to accuse the Swedish Academy of meddling in the Federal elections, which were taking place at the same time. By the end of the decade relations with officialdom in his own country had deteriorated to such an extent that in 1979 he turned down the offer of a 'Bundesverdienstkreuz', one of the Federal Republic's highest honours.

Hitherto he had consistently been described as a 'Catholic writer', a term he always repudiated: as far as the public was concerned, he said, his Catholicism was a question of which Church he paid tax to, anything else being his private affair (I, pp. 56f.).[1] In 1970, however, he stopped paying his church tax in protest against what he saw as the Church's materialism, and in 1976 he officially left the Church

---

* Some of the material in this essay is based on my *Heinrich Böll: A German for his time*, Leamington Spa and New York, 1987.

1. See Author's Note at the end of this essay for key.

-212-

altogether. Nevertheless, he continued to practise his religion and was buried according to Catholic rites in 1985. His works remained immensely popular. The relative optimism of *Gruppenbild mit Dame* (1971), however, had given way at the end of the decade to the defiant gloom of *Fürsorgliche Belagerung* (1979).[2] The very titles of the two novels which begin and end the decade indicate a shift in perceptions: the former implies community, it contains a visual image of harmony with each participant in his or her right place; the latter is ominously martial, suggesting the situation of the beleaguered intellectual.

In 1970 Böll moved from the outskirts of Cologne into a flat near the city centre. He described the area in the television feature 'Hülchrather Straße Nr 7', which was broadcast in March 1972. The law courts lay not far off, the bell of a neighbouring school served as an alarm-clock, the Rhine was only a short distance away, and from his window he could observe the children playing and the foreign refuse-collectors dealing with the 'Wohlstandsmüll'. He had, he said, moved 'aus der Schein-Individualität, der in Wirklichkeit total genormten Weekend-Gartenaktivität des Vororts im Grünen, zurück in die Anonymität, oder sollte man sagen: Urbanität?' (E 2, p. 585). This 'urbanity' consisted in the first place of having all the shops and services he needed within a few minutes walk; but, more importantly, cities had a greater continuity of tradition than villages, even if this was only to be found in isolated spots, and they could be more tolerant: 'Urbanität besteht in der Duldung von Erscheinungen, die statistisch längst abgeschrieben sind — Urbanität kann es auf dem Land nicht geben' (p. 594). Traffic congestion was already a problem — perhaps one could transform the roofs of the cars parked bumper to bumper into children's playgrounds (p. 592). The supermarket was threatening to replace the corner shop — but he believed that the city was resilient enough to repel this alien (p. 593). Already, however, rows of perfectly habitable houses were being rased in the service of the 'god of profit' — and 'Profit und Urbanität schließen einander aus' (p. 594). By 1977 he was an infrequent visitor to Cologne — although he still had a flat there, it was only his secondary residence, as he preferred to work in his house in the Eifel (Vormweg, p. 84) — and in 1982 he gave up his flat in Cologne altogether. Cologne had become 'alien' to him, he said; the neighbourliness and community of street life had

---

2. See Keith Bullivant's chapter on 'Political Realism', pp. 41f, for further discussion of *Fürsorgliche Belagerung* in addition to my examination in this chapter.

been destroyed by traffic; civilisation was dominated by the motor-car, and the motor-car was an 'Isolationsinstrument, kein Kommunikationsinstrument' — pedestrian precincts were no solution, but merely the attempt to create artificial life (E 2, p. 585). This is one way in which Böll saw the 1970s as regressive. The democratic cities, that great achievement of the Renaissance, the Enlightenment and technological advance in the nineteenth century, had become, by the end of the decade, the scene of intolerance, profiteering and the technological nightmare.

This shift in Böll's allegiance to a physical milieu is reflected in his novels. *Gruppenbild mit Dame* appeared a few months before the television feature, with which it shares a number of characteristics. It is a novel about 'Urbanität', in the sense outlined above, and the threat to it posed by 'Profit' and intolerance. Leni Gruyten has managed to retain the spacious flat she inherited from her parents in a part of the city which was 'only' 35 per cent destroyed in the war; she does not patronise supermarkets, preferring the individual services of the small shopkeeper; the continuity of urban traditions is indicated by her orgiastic encounter with a bump in the road surface which she remembers from forty years previously. She personally practises urbane tolerance; her tenants are frequently foreign workers, with one of whom she eventually forms an attachment. This 'Urbanität', however, is under threat. The small retail business is about to disappear in the wake of the area's 'Strukturwandel' (R 5, p. 12); because of Leni's refusal to sleep with one of her tenants he has been spreading rumours of her immorality and she is subject to catcalls and insults when she passes along the street; she is in debt and about to be evicted from her flat by her nephews the Hoysers, who regard the low rents she charges her tenants as 'Marktzersetzung' (R 5, p. 332), and in any case wish to develop what has become a prime site. In keeping with Böll's confidence in these years, the novel ends with Leni's at least temporary success in the battle to keep her flat; an unlikely coalition of forces — a music critic, a florist, a civil servant, a rich capitalist, Turkish and Portuguese refuse-collectors, a Russian ex-prisoner of war and a retired graveyard worker — combines to thwart the bailiffs; community and solidarity are still possible and effective in an urban environment.

By the time of *Fürsorgliche Belagerung* this is no longer the case. Most of the later novel is set in the countryside, in the nineteenth-century villa 'Tolmshoven', the village of Hubreichen, or the hamlet of Blorr with its thirty-four electors, seven of whom, unaccountably, voted SPD in the recent elections. The city is the place to which Erna Breuer is forced to flee when her village privacy is

invaded by the security precautions taken on behalf of her prominent neighbour Sabine Tolm; but the city is a nightmare of noise,
the din of the motorway and its feeder roads robs the inhabitants of
their sleep and destroys any vestiges of community there might have
been. Villages are little better. When Rolf and Veronica came to live
in Hubreichen they encountered open hostility, stone-throwing and
threats to burn their house down; Hubreichen's order and peace is
from time to time broken by inexplicable acts of violence, when
people can bear the stillness no longer. The tolerance of urbanity is
not to be found here either. And in any case these villages are
threatened by advancing industrialisation — Iffenhoven, where
Käte was born, was rased to make way for a coal-mine and Tolmshoven is due to suffer a similar fate.

Initially Böll greeted the new decade with an enthusiasm reminiscent of the words of Brecht's Galileo on the dawning of the New
Age. A speech he delivered in 1970 contained the words:

> Ich deute mir diese internationale gegenwärtige Bewegtheit von den
> Fabriken bis in die heiligsten Offizien, von den Akademien bis in Lehr-
> lingsheime hinein, in Armeen und Strafanstalten, in Kirchen, Schulen,
> Familien, in der Kunst und in der Antikunst — ich deute mir diese
> Bewegtheit als den großen Versuch, die alten Rahmen aufzugeben oder
> zu zerstören, als eine Vorstufe oder Vorbedingung zur Brüderlichkeit. (E
> 2, p. 466).

Böll's anti-authoritarianism allowed him to sympathise with the
Student Movement of the late 1960s: he had made common cause with
the student leaders in opposing the 'Notstandsgesetze' (Emergency
Legislation) passed by the Grand Coalition, and had defended the
students on numerous occasions against the demagoguery of *Bild*
and *Welt*. In 1969 he had been one of the founders of the West
German Schriftstellerveband. The titles of two major addresses to
the organisation, 'Ende der Bescheidenheit' and 'Einigkeit der
Einzelgänger', implied a new and aggressive self-confidence; Böll,
hitherto best known for the individuality of his 'little men', the
victims of an all-embracing bureaucracy, was now preaching the
virtues of solidarity. The election of the first post-war Social Democratic government in the Federal Republic in 1969 was 'sensational'
— other countries were more accustomed to a regular pendulum
swing of power between opposing parties; Willy Brandt's success
was a 'Gegengewicht gegen die Entwicklung, die 1949 begonnen
hat' (I, p. 510). In 1969 Böll's mistrust of the SPD, which had
formed a coalition with the CDU under a former Nazi and had
helped to push through the 'Notstandsgesetze' had prevented him

from giving Brandt public support. But in the election campaign of 1972 he even made speeches on behalf of the party as a member of Günter Grass's 'Sozialdemokratische Wählerinitiative': 'Die Bundesrepublik hat sich seit Beginn der sozial-liberalen Koalition gewandelt, mit ihr die Welt um sie herum', he declared in Cleves (E 2, p. 599). Brandt's 'Ostpolitik' represented the 'Bereinigung der Reste von 45 in Europa' (I, p. 587). Böll admired Brandt personally; his commitment to the SPD was based largely on this admiration (I, p. 162), and when Brandt was forced to resign over the Guillaume affair in 1974 his sympathies with the party rapidly cooled. In any case he had been deeply disappointed by the 'Radikalenerlaß' of 1972, against which he spoke out on numerous occasions and whose undemocratic and illogical nature is the subject of the satires *Berichte zur Gesinnungslage der Nation* (1975) and 'Du fährst zu oft nach Heidelberg' (1977). Although in the elections of 1976 he wrote a number of pieces against the CDU for *Konkret*, he was also suggesting ironically that there was no need for a change of party since the SPD was as friendly towards industry and capital as any CDU government could be (E 3, p. 360). In 1963 he had written sceptically on the contemporary political scene: 'Wir nähern uns dem Einparteienstaat, der ein paar linke Flügelchen rauschen lassen wird. Im übrigen: lauter Mitten' (E 1, p. 534). In October 1976 he had reverted to this position: the FRG was a 'Land, wo links und Rechts sich um die Besetzung der Mitte streiten, die Mitte immer mehr nach rechts hin radikalisieren' (E 3, p. 403). The dynamism he had diagnosed in 1970 had by 1977 given way to the 'Gelähmtheit unserer Gesellschaft'; the lack of any official encouragement to citizens to make use of their freedom had a paralysing effect (Kesting, p. 74). The 'Feigheit der SPD' was largely to blame for this paralysis, the ruling party's failure to stand up for the intellectuals who had supported it and now found themselves denounced by the right-wing media and politicians (Riese, p. 27).

Böll's personal bitterness was understandable. As president of PEN he had spared no effort on behalf of persecuted writers the world over, but with decidedly mixed results. When he engaged in negotiations which had necessarily to remain secret, he was accused of inactivity, of not wishing to offend his readers in the Soviet Union; when he was successful, as in the case of Peter Huchel and Andrej Amalrik, he received no credit. His intervention on behalf of Ulrike Meinhof in January 1972 created the most spectacular controversy. Wishing primarily to calm the waters in order to give Frau Meinhof the opportunity to surrender in the hope of a fair trial, Böll succeeded only in reaping a whirlwind of accusations and calumny; he was a 'Salon-Anarchist', a 'Sympathisant des Linksfaschismus'; within a month the material for a whole book documenting the affair could be collected.[3] After the murder of Günter von Drenkmann, President of the West Berlin Supreme Court, in December 1974 he was publicly blamed for having 'manured the soil' on which such violence flourished. The lawsuit Böll embarked on to clear his name dragged on until 1981, when he finally received satisfaction. But the same accusations were to reappear in 1977 when Hanns Martin Schleyer was kidnapped and his bodyguards murdered: *Quick*, for example, published his photograph alongside one of the murder scene, and the *Neue Ruhr-Zeitung* accused him of paving the way for terrorism.

The reasons for Böll's problems with the press and the politicians were complex ones. They had largely to do with the long-standing hostility between conservative politicians and intellectuals in Germany which has been documented by Dietz Bering.[4] To the vilification of intellectuals by the National Socialists and their predecessors there came the specific problem of the post-war division of Germany and the Cold War, which created a situation in which intellectuals on both sides of the Iron Curtain were expected to make public statements on current affairs but only supportive ones, anything less being regarded as, according to context, a betrayal of 'freedom' or a betrayal of 'socialism'. The most comprehensive attack on West German intellectuals came in 1975 from the conservative sociologist Helmut Schelsky in his book *Die Arbeit tun die anderen*, and Böll was one of the main targets of his polemic. The new 'Priesterkaste', said Schelsky, was the intelligentsia, concerned not for the welfare of those they claimed to represent, but rather for their own power, decrying all that West German society had achieved in the thirty years since the end of the war, devaluing the very virtues that their own wealth depended on, namely industriousness and 'Leistung', and claiming that traditional exploitation still existed in order to disguise their own striving to subject society to their will.[5] Böll replied that intellectuals had had the role of 'Gewissen der Nation' forced upon them by others, the real conscience of the nation ought to be parliament, but since West Germany lacked the political culture that countries such as France possessed, others were being thrust into the gap (I, pp. 417ff.). Nevertheless, it has to be said that

3. Frank Grützbach (ed.), *Heinrich Böll: Freies Geleit für Ulrike Meinhof. Ein Artikel und seine Folgen*, Cologne, 1972.
4. Dietz Bering, *Die Intellektuellen. Geschichte eines Schimpfwortes*, Stuttgart, 1978.
5. Helmut Schelsky, *Die Arbeit tun die anderen. Klassenkampf und Priesterherrschaft der Intellektuellen*, Munich, 1977.

Böll's intervention on behalf of Ulrike Meinhof was unwise in the manner in which it was made. In spite of his belated recognition of the values of solidarity Böll remained too much the 'Einzelgänger', there was perhaps not enough 'Einigkeit' in his intervention, and when over a hundred writers signed a declaration of support in July 1972 it was already too late.

In view of these developments it would not have been surprising if Böll became a pessimist, and this was suggested to him in 1977 by Hanjo Kesting. He denied being pessimistic — Kesting was confusing pessimism and melancholy; the latter was a 'Grundstimmung' and contained a strong ingredient of humour (Kesting, p. 74). Böll wrote a number of humorous satires in the late 1970s, and there is indeed a certain bitter melancholy about, for example, his 'Deutsche Utopien', in which Grass and Dutschke are invited to afternoon coffee with the family Strauss or Alfred Dregger wishes to change the name of the University of Frankfurt into 'Rosa-Luxemburg-Universität', accusing the SPD of 'Verrat am Marxismus' when they resist the change (GE, pp. 440, 444). In fact Böll continued to be directly involved in current affairs throughout the 1970s and right up to his death in 1985. In this respect he did not change direction. Together with Günter Grass and Carola Stern he founded the periodical *L'76 Demokratie und Sozialismus* in 1976. He was co-editor of various pamphlets in the series *rororo aktuell*: *Briefe zur Verteidigung der Republik* (1977), *Briefe zur Verteidigung der bürgerlichen Freiheit* (1978), *Kämpfen für die sanfte Republik* (1980) and other later volumes. At least since 1969, when he commented on the Sakharov memorandum (E 2, pp. 347ff.), he had been concerned at the threat to the earth's ecology posed by technological progress, and his concern led him in 1977 to urge the formation of a new party to take up this issue which the traditional parties were ignoring (Riese, pp. 23f.) — the Greens were founded two years later. His support for the Peace Movement during the early 1980s falls outside the scope of this essay, but it hardly implied the attitude of one who had turned away from social and political affairs.

Nevertheless, as we have seen, a distinct change can be detected in Böll's literary output between the novels *Gruppenbild mit Dame* and *Fürsorgliche Belagerung*. He himself was never dogmatic on literary styles and methods — indeed he reserved much of his scorn for the dogmatists, whether they were advocating the *nouveau roman* or documentary literature (E 1, p. 356; E 3, p. 49). He took up the term 'Tendenzwende' on a number of occasions, describing, for example, Peter Weiss's *Die Ästhetik des Widerstands*, the first volume of which appeared in 1975, as a potential model for a worthwhile change of direction, whereas the 'Tendenzwende' propagated by the media was one only for opportunists (E 3, p. 429). What is no doubt significant about Weiss's novel in this context is its combination of political commitment and subjective, personal experience — a 'Neue Subjektivität' rather than a 'Neue Innerlichkeit'. Earlier, however, Böll had praised Peter Handke's 1972 novel, *Wunschloses Unglück* (E 3, p. 32), admittedly Handke's most socially 'relevant' text, but in 1977 he denied that 'die sogenannte neue Innerlichkeit' was necessarily a retreat; it was perhaps a correction of the too superficial involvement in politics which had characterised the late 1960s and early 1970s: 'das, was Handke etwa schreibt und andere auch, ist ein sozusagen ewiger Strom in der Literatur, der auch nicht abgebrochen werden darf' (Riese, p. 21). Handke had been quite right to declare that there was no such thing as 'engagierte Literatur', only 'engagierte Literaten'. Alessandro Manzoni's *I promessi sposi* (1827) which Böll was reading at the time, was not a directly political novel, but its depiction of people's irrational fear of the plague could be read as an allegory of the current West German fear of intellectuals (Riese, p. 20). Böll's reading of Manzoni may well have influenced the writing of *Fürsorgliche Belagerung*. The existential themes which many critics have diagnosed as characteristic of 1970s literature[6] are very strong in this novel. It describes the irrational and hopeless search for security in a world dominated by 'Angst', and does so not in political but in existential terms. In a discussion in Paris in 1978 Böll characterised the heavy security precautions taken on behalf of politicians in the wake of the Schleyer kidnapping as a sign of the general human condition: 'Wir sind ja bedroht von Berührungsängsten und von der Tatsache, daß wir alle in Festungen leben' (I, p. 707). His words anticipate the novel which appeared a year later.

There are, of course, existentialist motifs in *Gruppenbild mit Dame*. These are to be found especially in the scenes during the last few months of the war, when the fear of the Nazis and the fear of destruction by bombing-raids combine to drive everyone into each other's arms, and when Leni and Boris set up their private love-nest in the graveyard vaults. The parallel which this implies between 1978, the setting of *Fürsorgliche Belagerung*, and 1945 is in itself startling. *Gruppenbild mit Dame*, however, is to a greater extent than

6. Helmut Kreuzer, 'Neue Subjektivität. Zur Literatur der siebziger Jahre in der Bundesrepublik Deutschland', in Manfred Durzak (ed.), *Deutsche Gegenwartsliteratur. Ausgangspunkte und aktuelle Entwicklungen*, Stuttgart, 1981, pp. 77–106; David Roberts, 'Tendenzwenden. Die sechziger und siebziger Jahre in literaturgeschichtlicher Perspektive', *DVLG* 56, 1982, pp. 290–313.

any other of Böll's works a social novel in the eighteenth- and nineteenth-century tradition. This has to do with the sense of community and urbanity it creates, as I have already suggested. It is also conveyed by Böll's portrayal of twentieth-century German history. In *Billard um halbzehn* (1959) Böll had already attempted to survey German history from Wilhelm II to Adenauer, but in an extraordinarily circumscribed manner, refracting it through the minds of a limited number of persons within a few hours of a single day and within a highly restricted geographical area. What gives *Gruppenbild mit Dame* its spaciousness is Böll's use of multiple personal narrators, all of whom freely roam in space and time and have their own individual biography. In true 'epic' style digressions are numerous, whether these are the story of the 'Verf.''s jacket, Margret's blushing fits or Lev's rejection of 'Leistung'. It fruitfully develops the documentary manner of the time. The 'Verf.' himself is drawn into the action, and the story which he set out to document runs away from him in the end as he discovers that it is impossible to remain the neutral, objective observer he set out to be. If he is indeed a kind of Günter Wallraff,[7] then he is one who is forced to confront the dilemma of the committed documentarist, namely that documentation is never neutral — here again subjectivity is programmatic. Böll's early novels, as I have attempted to show elsewhere,[8] contained some of the hallmarks of modernism, the most notable of which was a tendency towards aesthetic autonomy. It was a position, however, from which he increasingly diverged. *Gruppenbild mit Dame* is 'post-modernist' at least in the sense that it never sets up an aesthetic sphere separate from the reader's own reality. This, too, is an aspect of its 'urbanity'. Altogether it conveys the optimistic mood of dynamism which Böll felt to characterise the beginning of the decade.

In 1972, to the surprise of most of his readers, Böll published a slim volume of poems, a manifestation of subjectivity of another kind. Two had previously appeared under a pseudonym, others had been published elsewhere. In 1975 an expanded edition included political collages by Böll's friend Klaus Staeck, and a further expanded edition appeared in 1981. These are occasional poems, poems which on the whole confront reality directly and in a personal, subjective manner. In Volker Hage's phrase it is 'Lyrik für

7. Jochen Vogt, *Heinrich Böll*, Munich, 1978, p. 105
8. J.H. Reid, 'Heinrich Böll: From modernism to post-modernism and beyond', in K. Bullivant (ed.), *The Modern German Novel*, Leamington Spa and New York, 1987, pp. 109–25.

Leser',[9] far removed from the hermetic modernist poetry fashionable in the 1950s after the model of Gottfried Benn. They are partly 'Zeitgedichte', commenting on issues of the day — 'Aufforderung zum "Oho"-Sagen' (1971) looks forward to the day in 1978 when the Bundeswehr will have lost half its Starfighters and people may at last begin to prick up their ears; 'sieben jahre und zwanzig später' (1972), a gloss on Ingeborg Bachmann's 'Früher Mittag', protests against the 'Radikalenerlaß' which had just been passed — the Nazi 'Henker' of the original have become *Bild* and *Welt*. Some celebrate friendship and conviviality, either being dedicated to individuals, or as in 'Für Hans Werner Richter (und Toni natürlich)' (1979) in the tradition of Klopstock's *Der Zürchersee*, remembering past meetings and excursions. The longest poem of the collection, 'Köln III Spaziergang am Nachmittag des Pfingstsonntags 30. Mai 1971', belongs to the context of *Gruppenbild mit Dame* and 'Hülchrather Straße Nr 7': the city is being destroyed in a 'Thirty Years War' waged in the name of 'Profit'; 'St. Gereon' (the church) is juxtaposed with 'St. Gerling' (the insurance company which Böll's friend Wallraff was later to investigate); not far off, completing the unholy trinity, is 'St. WDR'. On his walk through Cologne the poet is constantly aware of the letter in his pocket containing the ultimatum he has received from his church: pay up (your church taxes) or get out. His sister Grete, who died ten years previously of leukaemia, is an important personal motif — blood cancer is related metaphorically to the life-destroying activities of Church and industry.

The narrative technique of *Die verlorene Ehre der Katharina Blum* (1974) follows on less from that of *Gruppenbild mit Dame*, as some have suggested, than from that of *Ende einer Dienstfahrt* (1966). In both *Dienstfahrt* and *Katharina Blum* the narrators are shadowy figures who are never allowed to develop the personality and biography of the 'Verf.' in *Gruppenbild*. To that extent *Die verlorene Ehre der Katharina Blum* is a less 'urbane' novel. As in *Dienstfahrt* the real figures of power are never seen, whether it is the 'Präsident' manipulating the organs of justice to suppress publicity in the case of the Gruhls, or, in the case of Katharina, Lüding, a word from whom is sufficient to turn the bloodhounds of the press off the trail of Sträubleder and on to that of Blorna. Similarly a word from Beizmenne is sufficient to have the telephones of suspects tapped — a motif which anticipates the total surveillance of *Fürsorgliche Belagerung*. The 'Verstecke' which Böll could still find in cities in 1971 (E 2,

---

9. Volker Hage (ed.), *Lyrik für Leser. Deutsche Gedichte der siebziger Jahre*, Stuttgart, 1980.

p. 593), places of tolerance, eccentricity and traditions, have become few and far between. Katharina can preserve some of her privacy — the police never do find out who the 'Herrenbesuch' was — and like Leni Gruyten she does not lack friends, she has her community of helpers. By *Fürsorgliche Belagerung* (1979) the Tolms can keep nothing secret from the authorities — unless, as they once did in Moscow, they write messages to one another and subsequently flush them down the toilet. Furthermore there is little evidence of solidarity or community spirit in this novel, where merely reading a book about Castro in a bus is enough to provoke violent hostility. Again the development of Böll's narrative technique is revealing. Manfred Durzak suggested that *Katharina Blum* was a more subjective work than *Das Brot der frühen Jahre* (1955) because in contrast to the earlier work the reader never sees the two lovers together (I, pp. 321ff.). Since in *Das Brot der frühen Jahre* we only see Hedwig through the eyes of Fendrich, the first-person narrator, this seems a dubious assertion. However, inasmuch as *Die verlorene Ehre der Katharina Blum* has an anonymous narrator mediating between reader and story it may be regarded as an example of subjective narration, while its open polemical commitment to attacking the Springer press makes it highly subjective in another sense. *Berichte zur Gesinnungslage der Nation*, while sharing the polemical impetus of its predecessor, is undoubtedly 'objective' in technique, since it lacks any overt narrator at all. These modern-day 'Dunkelmännerbriefe' (I, pp. 658f.) reproduce 'reports' from rival anti-terrorist organisations which turn out to be spying on each other's members. What is significant about *Fürsorgliche Belagerung* in this context is that Böll has reverted to a narrative technique he employed extensively in the 1950s, notably in *Haus ohne Hüter* (1954) and *Billard um halbzehn* (1959): indirect interior monologue, whereby each chapter has its separate personal focaliser and the extradiegetic narrator has all but disappeared. This is 'objective' narrative, as *Gruppenbild mit Dame* was not. At the beginning of the 1970s Böll employed overt, personal narrators; by the end of the decade the sense of community which they conveyed has been lost and the individual characters are living in narrative isolation, each fearful in his or her own armoured cell. The Federal Republic of 1979 had become a much less 'urbane' place to live in than it had appeared in 1971.

It is therefore perhaps not surprising that Böll took a renewed interest in the short-story form. The vast majority of his short stories were written before 1960. Between 1975 and 1980, however, he published ten short pieces. Some are decidedly nostalgic. 'Bis daß der Tod euch scheidet' (1976), 'Rendezvous mit Margret' (1978) and, almost programmatic through its title, 'Nostalgie oder Fett-flecken' (1980), could have appeared twenty years previously. Like so many of Böll's famous contributions to the genre, they conform to the short-story pattern of the brief encounter which illuminates past and present, and they plunge the reader *in medias res* right from the opening sentence. The others are satires, again a genre in which Böll had excelled twenty years previously: 'Erwünschte Reportage' (1975), 'Höflichkeit bei verschiedenen unvermeidlichen Gesetzesübertretungen', 'Du fährst zu oft nach Heidelberg' and 'Geständnis eines Flugzeugentführers' (1977), 'Deutsche Uto-pien I' (1978) and 'Deutsche Utopien II' (1979). Unlike Böll's earlier satires, with the possible exception of 'Hauptstädtisches Journal', they are almost entirely topical and seem unlikely to last longer than the issues which inspired them. 'Geständnis eines Flugzeugentführers' is unique in Böll's works, the only example of a satire wholly at the expense of a country other than the Federal Republic, in this case the Soviet Union. In 1960 Böll had declared that a West German satire on Walter Ulbricht was just as misguided as an East German satire on Konrad Adenauer would be — both were 'ein Ausweichen vor der eigenen Wirklichkeit' (E 1, p. 390), and accordingly the Clown, Hans Schnier, refuses to perform his West German satires when he visits Erfurt. Was Böll in 1977 trying to demonstrate that in spite of his adversaries' accusations he was just as aware of Soviet shortcomings as he was of those of his fellow-countrymen? In fact from 1973 onwards his books were no longer available in the Soviet Union, partly because in that year its government signed the Universal Copyright Convention and would for the first time have had to pay to publish them, partly because of Böll's criticism of its policies over dissidents.[10]

Böll's optimism about the artist's ability to influence events was severely shaken in the course of the decade. It is reflected in his attitude to the avant-garde. His television feature had already pointed out how easy it was to block the narrow streets of Cologne with a refuse lorry (E 2, p. 590). In *Gruppenbild mit Dame* the tables are turned on the oppressors in a carnivalistic 'Happening' when the streets are closed off by several refuse lorries and the bailiffs are prevented from reaching Leni's flat. As a citizen of Cologne Böll was fascinated by the carnival which dominated street life once a year and referred to it on numerous occasions. 'Fasching ist eine Erfin-dung der Boheme, der Karneval stammt aus dem Volk, er ist klassenlos' (E 1, p. 362). The masks of carnival enabled people to be

10. Martin Hüttel, 'Böll in der Sowjetunion', *L'80*, 1981, no. 18, pp. 98–107.

their true selves, to remove the masks of their daily lives (E 1, pp. 180ff.); masked as a clown Hans Schnier hopes to confront Marie on her return from Rome and persuade her to return. But in *Die verlorene Ehre der Katharina Blum*, carnival — one is reminded here of Bakhtin's chronotope[11] — that great democratic festival in which the world's values and hierarchies are momentarily reversed, has been taken over by the profiteers (R 5, p. 388), and it is the police who use its cover to help them to arrest those who refuse to conform to the Federal Republic's militarism. In *Fürsorgliche Belagerung* this, too, has become the fate of the 'Helft-Leni-Komitee''s 'Happening': now it is the police who use the fictitious traffic-jam in order to apprehend the terrorists. One reason for this change in Böll's outlook is the development of urban terrorism in the Federal Republic. 'Happenings' were associated with student protest in the early days of the movement. Initially Böll, and many others like him, regarded Fritz Teufel, for example, as 'ein liebenswürdiger Anarchist' (I, p. 698). But when the antics turned into bank robberies, kidnappings and murder they were no longer amusing. Helmut Heißenbüttel even found associations of Joseph Beuys's famous multi-pocketed waistcoat in the 'Händehochselbstschußmaschine' with which Bewerloh, the terrorist of *Fürsorgliche Belagerung*, commits suicide (FB, p. 375).[12] In 1974 Böll was still willing to see the police and the media as a greater potential threat to civil liberties than the terrorists — hence his choice of a harmless army deserter as the object of the police search in *Die verlorene Ehre der Katharina Blum*; by 1979 he was portraying terrorists and security men as two sides of the same coin.[13] Moreover the avant-garde, viewed optimistically by Böll in *Ende einer Dienstfahrt* and *Gruppenbild mit Dame* as capable of transforming society into something more humane, has now been completely assimilated. Both Frederick Le Boche's 'One minute piece of art' in *Die verlorene Ehre der Katharina Blum* and Rotgimpel's 'Ignition Art' in *Berichte zur Gesinnungslage der Nation* belong to the Establishment.

Böll's development in the 1970s is thus not unambiguous. His direct political involvement as *citizen* continued; it is reflected in a

11. M.M. Bakhtin, 'Forms of Time and of the Chronotope in the Novel. Notes towards a Historical Poetics', in Michael Holquist (ed.), *M.M. Bakhtin, The Dialogic Imagination. Four Essays*, Austin and London, 1981, pp. 84–258
12. Helmut Heißenbüttel, 'Erzählung von einem sentimentalen Wirrkopf und Trottel? Heinrich Bölls "Fürsorgliche Belagerung" und die Kritik', *Freibeuter*, 1980, No. 4, p. 158
13. See my 'Back to the Billiards Table? — Heinrich Böll's *Fürsorgliche Belagerung*', *FMLS* 19, 1983, pp. 126–41.

number of the satires he published. The novel, *Fürsorgliche Belagerung*, and some of the short stories written at the end of the decade, however, imply a reversion to positions which were more characteristic of the Böll of the 1950s. One other feature of *Fürsorgliche Belagerung* may briefly be mentioned by way of conclusion, its portrayal of women. The one area in which the 1970s may indubitably be regarded as progressive is that of the development of a feminist consciousness. *Gruppenbild mit Dame* is centred on a woman; but although Karin Struck was fascinated by the figure of Leni Gruyten (I, pp. 251ff.), Böll's heroine is characterised less by consciousness than by unconsciousness, naïve spontaneity. Katharina Blum similarly lacks feminist awareness, but she combines Leni's sexual emancipation — divorcing her husband and repulsing Sträubleder's advances — with a career as a successful professional woman, a unique development in Böll's major works. With *Fürsorgliche Belagerung*, however, Böll reverts to the female stereotypes of his earlier fiction: Käte Tolm is a warm-hearted mother-figure; her daughter Sabine is wealthy enough to live a life of unemancipated domestic idleness. Here, too, finally, in Böll's depiction of women's role as not social but familial, we may detect a regression to a kind of 'inwardness'.

Author's Note

The following editions and abbreviations are used for Böll's works:

E 1–3 = *Werke. Essayistische Schriften und Reden*, edited by Bernd Balzer, 3 vols., Cologne, n.d. [1978]
FB = *Fürsorgliche Belagerung. Roman*, Cologne, 1979
GE = *Gesammelte Erzählungen*, vol. 2, Cologne and Bornheim-Merten, 1981
I = *Werke. Interviews I*, edited by Bernd Balzer, Cologne, n.d. [1978]
R 5 = *Werke. Romane und Erzählungen*, vol. 5, edited by Bernd Balzer, Cologne, n.d. [1977]

Conversations and interviews not included in the collected works:

Kesting = '"Ich bin kein Repräsentant!" Heinrich Böll im Gespräch mit Hanjo Kesting', *die horen* 25, 1980, No. 120, pp. 67–85
Riese = Heinrich Böll and Hans-Peter Riese, 'Schriftsteller in dieser

Republik. Gespräch über Selbstverständlichkeiten', *L'76*, No. 6, 1977, pp. 5–37

Vormweg = Heinrich Böll and Heinrich Vormweg, *Weil die Stadt so fremd geworden ist . . . Gespräche*, Bornheim-Merten, 1985

Select Bibliography

Peter Bekes et al., *Deutsche Gegenwartslyrik von Biermann bis Zahl. Interpretationen*, Munich, 1982

Hans Joachim Bernhard, 'Positionen und Tendenzen in der Literatur der BRD Mitte der siebziger Jahre', *Weimarer Beiträge* 23, 1977, No. 12, pp. 53–84

Martin Durzak (ed.), *Deutsche Gegenwartsliteratur. Ausgangspositionen und aktuelle Entwicklungen*, Stuttgart, 1981

W. Martin Lüdke (ed.), *Nach dem Protest. Literatur im Umbruch*, Frankfurt on Main, 1979

Paul Michael Lützeler and Egon Schwarz (eds.), *Deutsche Literatur in der Bundesrepublik seit 1965*, Königstein, 1980

Marcel Reich-Ranicki, *Entgegnung. Zur deutschen Literatur der siebziger Jahre*, Stuttgart, 1979

Ursula Reinhold, *Tendenzen und Autoren. Zur Literatur der siebziger Jahre in der BRD*, E. Berlin, 1982

—— and Grazyna Szarszawska-Kühl, 'Thesen zur Prosaentwicklung der siebziger Jahre in der BRD', *Weimarer Beiträge* 29, 1983, pp. 625–37

David Roberts, 'Tendenzwenden. Die sechziger und siebziger Jahre in literaturgeschichtlicher Perspektive', *DVLG* 56, 1982, pp. 290–313

——(ed.), *Tendenzwenden. Aspekte des Kulturwandels der siebziger Jahre*, Frankfurt on Main, 1984

Michael Schneider, *Den Kopf verkehrt aufgesetzt oder Die melancholische Linke. Aspekte des Kulturzerfalls in den siebziger Jahren*, Darmstadt, 1981

Klaus Schuhmann, *Weltbild und Poetik. Zur Wirklichkeitsdarstellung in der Lyrik der BRD bis zur Mitte der siebziger Jahre*, E. Berlin, 1979

Michael Zeller (ed.), *Aufbrüche. Abschiede. Studien zur deutschen Literatur seit 1968*, Stuttgart, 1980

MARTIN KANE

Chasing the Chameleon
With Hans Magnus Enzensberger
Into the 1970s and Beyond

Man muß [. . .] ein Thema finden, das einerseits jeden
interessiert, wirklich jeden interessiert, und das andererseits
einen politischen Aspekt hat [. . . man] muß Sachen
machen, die man noch nicht kann. Die Sachen werden
immer dann interessanter, wenn man etwas macht, was
man noch nicht vollständig beherrscht. Natürlich könnte
ich alle zwei Jahre einen Gedichtband publizieren. Ich
weiß, wie das geht, sozusagen. Ich kann das. Aber das ist
schon schlecht, sondern man muß sich dann Sachen
heraussuchen, die man noch nicht kann, und die muß man
lernen [. . .].[1]

Andenken

Also was die siebziger Jahre betrifft,
kann ich mich kurz fassen.
Die Auskunft war immer besetzt.
Die wundersame Brotvermehrung
beschränkte sich auf Düsseldorf und Umgebung.
Die furchtbare Nachricht lief über den Ticker,
wurde zur Kenntnis genommen und archiviert.

Widerstandslos, im großen und ganzen,
haben sie sich selber verschluckt,
die siebziger Jahre,
ohne Gewähr für Nachgeborene,
Türken und Arbeitslose.
Daß irgendwer ihrer mit Nachsicht gedächte,
wäre zuviel verlangt.[2]

What, in attempting to assess Hans Magnus Enzensberger's contribution to German literature in the 1970s, are we to make of these

1. 'Interview mit Hans Magnus Enzensberger', *Weimarer Beiträge*, 1971, vol. 5,
p. 90.
2. Enzensberger, *Die Furie des Verschwindens. Gedichte*, Frankfurt on Main, 1980, p. 9.

two statements? On the one hand the words of a man not taking the easy way out, but consumed by intellectual energy and curiosity; on the other the weary despair of a lyrical persona defeated by the ways of a world he has been unable to fathom. Are we to assume that in the period which separates their publication — some nine years — Enzensberger has undergone a sea-change of sorts, that he has been overwhelmed by the same wave of political resignation which had swept so many of his contemporaries — 'prominente[r] linke[r] Galionsfiguren des letzten Jahrzehnts'[3] — into the arms of 'Neue Innerlichkeit'?

Certainly this is what many commentators on the two major volumes of poetry which he produced in the 1970s — *Mausoleum. Siebenunddreißig Balladen aus der Geschichte des Fortschritts* (1975), and *Der Untergang der Titanic* (1978) — concluded. Curt Hohoff entitled his remarks on *Mausoleum*: 'Enzensbergers Balladen. Ein trauriges, oft zynisches Par lando',[4] while Aurel Schmidt detected in the work, 'eine tiefe Skepsis: der Zustand der Linken heute'.[5] Dagmar Ploetz in her discussion of *Der Untergang der Titanic* suggested that the poem might represent 'eine neue Art von Existentialismus angesichts der alltäglichen Apokalypse',[6] while Uwe Schultz noted a dramatic turnabout in Enzensberger's development: 'Am Anfang tobte der Zorn, und jetzt wird der Zynismus zelebriert'.[7] But perhaps the most acerbic in his appraisal of thé road along which the poet had gone was Karl Heinz Bohrer. In *Merkur* he wrote in scathing comparison of the old and new Enzensberger: 'Der Dichter, der wie kein anderer identisch war mit der politischen Hohnrede, kein Ironiker bloß, ein Aggressor vielmehr, der seine Triumphe zwar kühl, aber lange genoß, schwört der gefährlichen Kategorie Zukunft unverhohlen ab, vorerst mal', and, casting in passing a large question-mark over his intellectual integrity, feigned breathless astonishment at Enzensberger's apparent *volte face*: 'Ein tolles Stück aber ist es nun doch, plötzlich mit dem glatten Gegenteil von allem herauszukommen, was gestern noch galt'.[8]

What is missing in all these comments is an awareness that

3. Herbert Claas and Karl-Heinz Götze, 'Ästhetik und Politik bei Hans Magnus Enzensberger und Peter Weiss', *Das Argument*, 115, 1979, p. 369.
4. Curt Hohoff, 'Enzensbergers Balladen. Ein trauriges, oft zynisches Parlando', *Rheinischer Merkur*, 10.10.1975.
5. Aurel Schmidt, 'Der Fortschritt, der keiner war', *Basler Nationalzeitung*, 8.11.1975.
6. Dagmar Ploetz, 'Jemand, der die Zeitgenossenschaft aufkündigt', *Deutsche Volkszeitung*, 30.11.1978.
7. Uwe Schultz, 'Kunststücke des nie versinkenden Korkens', *Stuttgarter Zeitung*, 17.10.1978.
8. Karl Heinz Bohrer, 'Getarnte Anarchie', *Merkur*, 12, 1978, pp. 1275 ff.

pessimism, cynicism and elements of existential hopelessness are nothing new in Enzensberger's writing; that they have always coexisted with those more positive and critical tendencies which one expected from a poet once seen as the heir apparent to the legacy of Brecht and who has intermittently understood himself as a Marxist writer. The strong element of the clown in him, of the wilful anarchist who led Peter Weiss to declare that 'man weiß nie, wo man ihn hat',[9] have always permitted Enzensberger to hold together in close, if sometimes precarious, balance seemingly quite contradictory elements. If we look back to his first two volumes of poetry, *verteidigung der wölfe* (1957) and *landessprache* (1960), which secured him an early reputation as the angry young man of post-war German literature, we may readily ascertain that much more than sharp political observation in combination with irate and virtuoso poetic formulation of the contemporary realities of 'Wirtschaftswunder' Germany are at the heart of the startling ferocity of this early work. In scrutinising for instance poems such as *drift I* and *drift II*, the claims made for Enzensberger as the 'Erbe Brechts'[10] in particular seem very wide of the mark. As may be confirmed by his subsequent confrontations with Brecht — the poem 'weiterung', for instance (bl, p. 50)[11] — Enzensberger would never be able to subscribe to that unrelenting faith in humanity which characterises all of Brecht's work (even in the darkest times) and which — to take a single, especially striking example — is crystallised in a poem such as 'Die Maske des Bösen'. Enzensberger is, as Hans Egon Holthusen was the first to point out, too much in thrall to a 'widrigen Geschmack von Welt, der als eine Abart der Sartreschen nausée gelten darf'[12] ever to be a genuine Brechtian. One might add furthermore that it is also difficult to reconcile the intellectual animal who would shortly produce the sharp political essays of *Einzelheiten* (1962) with the poet who, in these *drift* poems is able to evoke, in images of acrid pungency, a sense of all-pervasive existentialist despair:

> . . . du treibst
> ohne rückkehr, hirt der lügen,
> mörder schuldlos im heißen wind:
> schlag die augen auf und sieh

9. Peter Weiss, *Notizbücher 1971–1980*, Frankfurt on Main, 1981, vol. 2, p. 741.
10. Walter Jens, 'Paukenschlag und Kantilene', *Die Zeit*, 5.8.1960.
11. See Author's Note at the end of this essay for key.
12. Hans Egon Holthusen, 'Die Zornigen, die Gesellschaft und das Glück, *Kritisches Verstehen. Neue Aufsätze zur Literatur*, Munich, 1961, p. 146.

> diesen himmel aus kalk, trink
> den tränenwein: das ist das harz der welt,
> trink ihn dein lebtag, er ist alt,
> er schmeckt nach vielen mündern,
> nach vieler nacht, nach langer drift,
> bitter, dunkel, nach asche. (vw, p. 42)

This is not an isolated example. The images in *drift I* of ashen corrosiveness and the sense of embitterment and drifting aimlessness they convey abound in Enzensberger's early poetry. In 'bitte einsteigen türen schließen' we read: 'ein galliger abschied / trieft aufs geleis./ ich hab ein herz aus koks' (vw, p. 46), while in 'geburtstagsbrief' we find the lines: 'wie asche langsam / zieht der pilz die fäden im gehirn' (vw, p. 51). It is one of the paradoxes of both *verteidigung der wölfe* and *landessprache* that lines such as these are found alongside poetic statements which are much more aggressively and explicitly political in provenance. That the 'Ingrimm seiner Lyrik'[13] as Karl Krolow has called it, which is a vigorous expression of hostility to the institutions and forces which make up the Establishment of the Federal Republic and is directed (in a poem such as 'landessprache' for instance) at the political machinery of the state, the military and industrial capitalism in all its ramifications, should rub shoulders with profound disenchantment of an existentialist nature gives us the vital clue as to what has always most seriously troubled Enzensberger's readers and critics: his ability to change voice and switch mask with bewildering ease. In a country which has frequently wished to impose on its more distinguished writers the burden of high moral purpose, slippery elusiveness is an unwelcome, deeply suspect commodity.

This elusiveness has its roots, in part, in the recognition, as Auden once put it, that 'poetry makes nothing happen'[14] and in the realisation that the implicit claims which a vociferous political poetry makes for its effectiveness may find little echo in reality. This would undoubtedly have been a hard nut to swallow for a poet who had professed such unambivalently polemical ambitions for his poems and who had wished them to be understood as 'Inschriften, Plakate, Flugblätter, in eine Mauer geritzt, auf eine Mauer geklebt, vor einer Mauer verteilt'[15] or as 'gebrauchsgegenstände, nicht geschenkartikel im engeren sinne'.[16]

13. Karl Krolow, *Aspekte zeitgenössischer Lyrik*, Gutersloh, 1961, p. 115.
14. W.H. Auden, 'In Memory of W.B. Yeats', in Edward Mendelson (ed.), *The English Auden. Poems, Essays and Dramatic Writings 1927–1939*, London,. 1977, p. 241.
15. In 'beiblatt' issued with *verteidigung der wölfe*.
16. In 'gebrauchsanweisungen' issued with *landessprache*.

One of Enzensberger's answers to this dilemma — another of his masks or escape routes — is to venture into the realm of the grotesque, to respond to the intractabilities of the political sphere by creating absurd and fantastical counter-worlds.

Of key importance here is 'utopia', chosen significantly to open both the selections of his poetry — *Gedichte 1955–1970* (1971) and *Dreiunddreißig Gedichte* (1981) — which Enzensberger himself compiled.

utopia

der tag steigt auf mit großer kraft
schlägt durch die wolken seine klauen
der milchmann trommelt auf seinen kannen
sonaten: himmelan steigen die bräutigame
auf rolltreppen: wild mit großer kraft
werden schwarze und weiße hüte geschwenkt.
die bienen streiken. durch die wolken
radschlagen die prokuristen,
aus den dachluken zwitschern päpste.
ergriffenheit herrscht und spott
und jubel. segelschiffe
werden aus bilanzen gefaltet.
der kanzler schussert mit einem strolch
um den geheimfonds. die liebe
wird polizeilich gestattet,
ausgerufen wird eine amnestie
für die sager der wahrheit.
die bäcker schenken semmeln
den musikanten. die schmiede
beschlagen mit eisernen kreuzen
die esel. wie eine meuterei
bricht das glück, wie ein löwe aus.
die wucherer, mit apfelblüten
und mit radieschen beworfen,
versteinern. zu kies geschlagen,
zieren sie wasserspiele und gärten.
überall steigen ballone auf,
die lustflotte steht unter dampf:
steigt ein, ihr milchmänner,
bräutigame und strolche!
macht los! mit großer kraft
steigt auf

der tag. (vw, p. 26)

This poem is — to borrow Enzensberger's comment on another of his poems, 'bildzeitung', which had sprung from a feeling that organised political activity in the 1950s seemed out of the question — the product of an 'Erfahrung der Ohnmacht'.[17] But the release from feelings of political impotence which 'utopia' sketches is also simultaneously a release from the burdens of intellect. The utopia depicted here is one where poetical, not political, solutions are operative. The poem's bizarre images in which Popes are reduced to twittering innocuous birds, finance and economics are transformed into trivial, fun pursuits, and the heroes of the day are the milkman who plays sonatas on his churns and the 'bräutigame' and 'strolche' who can love and lust for life, suggest that utopia is only possible in terms of the absurd; it is conceivable only as an exhilarating Erewhon created from the full blast of the poet's anarchic and fanciful imagination freed from the constraints of logic and reason.

It is hard to recognise in this and other of his poems in the absurdist mode the painstaking political essayist who in analyses of the language of *Spiegel* and the *Frankfurter Allgemeine Zeitung* for instance, built a devastating case on the basis of closely compiled fact and detail. He has moved instead into the company of Christian Morgenstern who regarded the deliberate vagaries of his own brand of humour as a welcome liberation from the oppressive strictures of a rational and materialistic approach to the world. In his notes on the *Galgenlieder* Morgenstern wrote: 'Im Übrigen ist Humor eben Humor und hat jederzeit seinen eigenen Sinn und -Ernst für sich. Ja, es ist seine Mission, zumindest heutzutage, im Menschen den dumpfen trübseligen Ernst, in den ihn eine materialistische Gegenwart verstrickt hält, ein wenig aufzulockern, anzubröckeln'.[18]

As with Morgenstern's poems, the topsyturvy, but essentially benevolent never-never lands which Enzensberger creates may be seen as an explosive reaction against the labyrinthine intellectual difficulties of a rational approach to the social and political environment and the sense of frustrated helplessness this inevitably engenders. They may also however be seen as a kind of lifeline, exemplifying what Wallace Stevens seemed to be saying when he observed that: 'We never survive intellectually. But emotionally we arrive constantly (as in poetry, happiness, high mountains, vistas)'.[19]

This sanguine view of the solace which poetry might offer was, by the late 1960s, one to which Enzensberger could no longer subscribe. In his third volume of poetry, *blindenschrift* (1964), the desire

---

17. Hilde Domin (ed.), *Nachkrieg und Unfrieden. Gedichte als Index 1945–1970*, Neuwied and Berlin, 1970, p. 36.
18. Christian Morgenstern, *Über die Galgenlieder*, Berlin, 1921, p. 14.
19. Wallace Stevens, 'Adagia', *Opus Posthumous*, New York, 1957, p. 173.

to set in motion political shock waves — as well as the faith in the power of poetry to do this — which had been implicit in the predominant tone of *verteidigung der wölfe* and *landessprache* are replaced by serious reservations and questions about the effectiveness of poetry and the voice of the individual poet. Poems in the volume such as 'mund', 'windgriff' and 'ufer' may be read not only as metaphors of non-communication, but also as indications of Enzensberger's nagging doubts about the range and influence of his voice as a political poet. In his now celebrated and much-discussed essay 'Gemeinplätze, die Neueste Literatur betreffend', first published in 1968 in *Kursbuch* 15, these doubts were expanded into a powerful onslaught on the relevance of literature as a pursuit worthy of creative writers anxious to demonstrate their commitment to political affairs. In a complex, but always good-humoured argument, Enzensberger urged his fellow writers to abandon their novels, poems and plays and to apply their way with words to more factual and polemical work which would make a much needed contribution to what he called the 'politische Alphabetisierung Deutschlands'.[20]

It seemed, in his involvement from 1965 on with *Kursbuch*, that Enzensberger was following his own prescription. By 1972, a journal which had aimed at an initial circulation of 5,000 and had a strong literary orientation was selling something in the region of 50,000 copies and had almost totally abandoned any preoccupation with *belles lettres*. Scarcely a single poem or prose fragment found its way into issues which were now given over to lengthy explorations of specific areas of social and political concern: 'Kritik der Zukunft' (No. 14), 'Dialektik der Befreiung' (No. 16), or 'Die Klassenkämpfe in Italien' (No. 26) for instance.

Not surprisingly, however, considering Enzensberger's propensity for delivering the unexpected, it emerged that he had not burned quite all of his literary bridges. Peter Hamm's caustic comment that Enzensberger had 'jedenfalls bis auf weiteres — die Produktion von Rauschmitteln eingestellt'[21] proved, like the death of Mark Twain, to have been somewhat exaggerated. The volume *Gedichte 1955 — 1970* contained some thirty new poems which Enzensberger had written and been storing in his desk drawer since publishing *blindenschrift* in 1964. It was clear, however, that, having ceremonially incinerated once and for all his mantle as the heir-apparent to

20. Also in Enzensberger, *Palaver. Politische Überlegungen (1967–1973)*, Frankfurt on Main, 1974.
21. Peter Hamm, 'Opposition — am Beispiel H.M. Enzensberger', in Joachim Schickel (ed.), *Über Hans Magnus Enzensberger*, Frankfurt on Main, 1970, p. 254.

Bertolt Brecht in the 'Gemeinplätze' article, if he were ever to return to poetry it would not be to the sparsely wrought and personal poems — expressions of self-doubt and nagging conscience — of *blindenschrift*. The plea he had made in the *Kursbuch* article for a much more productive engagement of the writer's energies could never be met by the poetry of private reflection. This is confirmed by the majority of these new poems. Private lyricism has not been totally abandoned, as 'Das leere Haus', reflections on the memories evoked by the imminent demolition of a house in Berlin, indicates, (G, p. 120) but much more striking is the use of the impersonal poetic techniques of montage, as for instance in 'Vorschlag zur Strafrechtsreform', (G, p. 143) a parodistic text constructed from excerpts from the 'Strafgesetzbuch', or 'Berliner Modell 1967' (G, p. 146) which invents a mock solution to the student disturbances of the late 1960s out of the description of an industrial computer system. There are also poems here which are used to expand some of the arguments raised by 'Gemeinplätze, die Neueste Literatur betreffend'. 'Der Papier-Truthahn', for instance, gives a cryptic, perhaps self-ironic picture of the bourgeois revolutionary-cum-media performer, developing a strand of Enzensberger's much earlier essay 'Die Bewußtseins-Industrie'[22] to show the way in which radical political ideas may effectively be defused by making them a marketable commodity. A career may be made when the professional dissident becomes society's favourite clown:

> Den ganz echten Revolutionär
> finden Sie heute auf Seite 30
> der Unterhaltungsbeilage
>
> Der ganz echte Revolutionär
> kann über den Kommunismüs
> nur noch mitleidig lächeln
>
> Der ganz echte Revolutionär
> steht irgendwo ganz weit links von Mao
> vor der Fernsehkamera
>
> Der ganz echte Revolutionär
> bekämpft das System
> mit knallharten Interviews
>
> Der ganz echte Revolutionär
> ist volltransistorisiert
> selbstklebend und pflegeleicht

22. Enzensberger, *Einzelheiten 1. Bewußtseins-Industrie*, Frankfurt on Main, 1962, p. 7–17.

Der ganz echte Revolutionär
kriegt das Maul nicht zu
Er ist ungeheuer gefährlich
Er ist unser Lieblingsclown. (G, p. 153)

Similarly, in 'Ein letzter Beitrag zu der Frage ob Literatur?' he directs ironic reassurance to those fellow writers and intellectuals who persist in fretting about the social usefulness of their role:

Fürchtet euch nicht!
Krümmt euch vor Anstrengung
oder schiebt eine ruhige Kugel,
aber habt keine Angst.
Es kommt nicht auf uns an.
Dafür werden wir doch bezahlt. (G, p. 160)

What also filters through in many of these new poems is that sense of humorous, mildly distanced scepticism which was to colour so much of what Enzensberger would produce in the 1970s. If they represent a shift in poetic emphasis, it was soon to transpire that they were not the only surprises which Enzensberger had up his sleeve.

Mausoleum, published in 1975 was Enzensberger's first entirely new volume of poems in over a decade and represented yet another fresh departure in the development of his poetry. Consisting of portraits of thirty-seven figures crucial to the intellectual and social development of the Western world, the volume begins with Giovanni de' Dondi the fourteenth-century Italian clockmaker, and concludes with the Argentinian revolutionary Ernesto Guevara de la Serna. *En route* it takes in astronomers, philosophers, surgeons, biologists, explorers, anthropologists and inventors; it embraces figures as celebrated as Gutenberg, Machiavelli or Leibnitz, and as relatively obscure as Charles Messier, Ignaz Semmelweiss or the English mathematician Alan Turing. This is not, however, the solemn compilation of a 'Hall of Fame' erected in honour of the inventive and wise. The full title of the volume — *Mausoleum: Siebenunddreißig Balladen aus der Geschichte des Fortschritts* — prepares us for the question-mark which Enzensberger sets against conventional notions of progress and the personalities of those who forge it. In the poem on the Marquis de Condorcet (1743–94), for instance, we are asked how the French philosopher's professed confidence in the progress of the human mind can be squared with the phial of poison which he perpetually bore about his person and which he was eventually to use in his prison cell as a way of cheating the guillotine.

Or, juxtaposed with his statement, 'Die Barbarei ist für immer besiegt', we find the question, 'was es mit dieser Philosophie für eine Bewandtnis hat: / ist sie Beschwörung, wohlriechender Hohn, Stoßgebet, idée fixe, oder Bluff?' (M, p. 50)

In form these poems are very diverse, but are unified by a vision that removes the makers of intellectual history from their pedestals, confronts them with an unblinking, demythologising gaze, and exposes the sombre side of their personalities and the less savoury implications of their discoveries, observations or achievements. The brand of iconoclasm they reveal is not entirely new ground for Enzensberger. In a much earlier poem 'ratschlag auf höchster ebene' the so-called 'makers of history' are reviled as 'schüttere wölfe, geschminkte keiler, kastraten/mit herzklaps' (vw, p. 72) while in the poem 'zweifel' he had noted that 'die spuren des fortschritts sind blutig' (bl, p. 37). What is different here in *Mausoleum*, however is that crime, as Brecht once remarked, is given a name, an address and a contour. What is always revealed is the frailty of the man at the heart of the reputation; we are invariably presented not with the titan of legend, but with the severely truncated personality, the psychological or emotional cripple or the bearer — witting or unwitting — of cruelty or inhumanity. Alexander von Humboldt, for instance, is not only a botanist and explorer, he is the outrider of the exploitation and destruction of the primitive societies he set out to observe. In a somewhat different vein, the grim remorselessness of Thomas Malthus's economic and demographic conclusions are contrasted with his cosy domestic circumstances; there is something inexplicably chilling here about the image Enzensberger gives us of the prophet of catastrophe being served buttered muffins by a rosy-cheeked wife. Or Isambard Kingdom Brunel, maniacally single-minded and afflicted with a congenital melancholia for which the only anodyne was a series of grandiose engineering projects: the Thames tunnel, the vast, neo-Gothic extravaganza of Paddington Station and, finally, a flotilla of iron ships, each more monstrous than its predecessor. Surveying the famous photograph of Brunel heroically posed before a massive anchor chain, Enzensberger gives us a fresh perspective, compounded of compassion and debunk, on this atrabilious genius: 'Halb Chaplin und halb Galeerensklave: ein Pessimist im Zylinder' (M, p. 76).

The poems of *Mausoleum* introduce themselves as ballads, but in fact considerably stretch accepted definitions of the genre. Many of them incorporate large slabs of prose — in which the portrait of Oliver Evans, the American inventor, for instance, is entirely writ-ten. Elsewhere however, Enzensberger exploits the variety permitted by his elastic interpretation of the ballad form to accommodate terse characterisation, dramatic narrative and extensive use of quotation, either from the writings of the subject of the poem or from those of his contemporaries. These italicised quotations have an important and varied function in the poems. They support Enzensberger's mainly sceptical presentation of his subject, either by their ironic contrast to the standard image of the man, or by supplying information about him which the myth has neglected. Overall they reinforce Enzensberger's main purpose in this collection — to challenge the reader to a reassessment of the received ideas about the nature of genius, the roots of the inventiveness of the civilised mind and the progress which has supposedly flowed from it.

In conclusion it must be noted that *Mausoleum*, in the vast intellectual sweep it attempts to encompass, fulfills Enzensberger's own aggressive demand made in the 1968 *Kursbuch* article that literature, if it is to have any purpose and justification, must set its sights on the goal of 'politische Alphabetisierung'. He can scarcely have envisaged, however, that this, his own next wholly new volume of poetry, would fulfill it on such an elevated level.

In this discussion of *Mausoleum* we have, chronologically speaking leap-frogged over one of Enzensberger's crucial experiences of the late 1960s — his stay in Cuba 1968-9 — which was to culminate, ultimately, in one of the literary events of the late 1970s, his long, free-verse narrative poem *Der Untergang der Titanic*. This work has a complicated genesis which begins with Enzensberger abandoning his Visiting Fellowship at the Center of Advanced Studies at the Wesleyan University in the USA in January 1968. His open letter of resignation finds Enzensberger in militantly unambiguous mood: nothing here of the despairing cynic or the elusive clown who will not permit himself to be pinned down. He writes, in explanation of his decision:

> Ich halte die Klasse, welche in den Vereinigten Staaten von Amerika an der Herrschaft ist, und die Regierung, welche die Geschäfte dieser Klasse führt, für gemeingefährlich. Es bedroht jene Klasse, auf verschiedene Weise und in verschiedenem Grad, jeden einzelnen von uns. Sie liegt mit über einer Milliarde von Menschen in einem unerklärten Krieg; sie führt diesen Krieg mit allen Mitteln, vom Ausrottungs-Bombardement bis zu den ausgefeiltesten Techniken der Bewußtseins-Manipulation. Ihr Ziel ist die politische, ökonomische und militärische Weltherrschaft. Ihr Todfeind ist die Revolution.

He concludes by declaring his intention to decamp to Cuba in the belief that 'ich den Cubanern von größerem Nutzen sein kann als den Studenten der Wesleyan University, und daß ich noch von ihnen zu lernen habe'.[23]

This 'Offener Brief' was a flamboyant act: simultaneously a rejection of US imperialism and a gesture of solidarity with the Cubans and their revolution. The documentary drama *Das Verhör von Habana* — product of some 1,000 sides of transcribed tape-recordings of the public hearings held in the wake of the abortive Bay of Pigs invasion of April 1961 — was a further gesture in this direction, as was a first version of the *Titanic* poem. Whether the poem was as partisan in its support of the Cuban revolution as is *Das Verhör von Habana* we shall never know, since it was posted off to Paris, never reached its destination and, as Enzensberger had not been able to make a copy of it ('Es war ein Gedicht ohne Durch-schlag'; T, p. 21) was lost forever.

If Wolfram Schütte can speculate, however, that in the original version *Titanic* and iceberg were conceived as images for an immi-nent clash between American capitalism and a socialist Cuba,[24] it is clear that by the time that Enzensberger came to rewrite the poem eight years later the metaphor had been substantially redrawn. The enthusiasm for a new socialist society created out of a dictatorship overthrown by Marxist revolution which — one may reasonably speculate — inspired the original conception of the work, has clearly faded in the later version. Instead, as Class, Götze and other commentators have argued, the poem seems to have caught the tide of a general mood of 'Untergang' prevalent among the left in the late 1970s.[25]

Although the recreated version has undergone substantial ideo-logical refurbishing, it is still unable to provide an answer to our question why, after having been drawn to Cuba along with so many of his intellectual contemporaries to see the fruits of the revolution at first hand, Enzensberger should choose this moment — at a point when the problem of the sugar harvest might have seemed of more pressing interest — to preoccupy himself with a maritime tragedy which had taken place some fifty years previously.

Its thirty-three cantos interspersed with sundry poems as well as 'Bildbeschreibungen, polemische Gedichte, erkenntnistheoretische Modelle und Vergleiche'[26] remind us throughout how readily the

23. Enzensberger, 'Offener Brief an den Präsidenten der Wesleyan University', repr. in Schickel (ed.) (cf. note 21), pp. 233ff.
24. Wolfram Schütte, 'Den roten Faden verloren', *Frankfurter Rundschau*, 17.10.1978.
25. See, for instance, Ulrich Greiner, 'Der Untergang der Titanic. Das Desaster der Linken ist nicht nur ein Desaster der Linken. Anmerkungen zur Situation', *Frankfurter Allgemeine Zeitung*, 19.10.1978.

sinking of the *Titanic* offers itself, not only as exemplification of man's eternal hubris, but also as a prophetic political metaphor. Enzensberger fully exploits the symbolism enshrined in the ship and her first and last voyage to create the image of a capitalist class society on the brink of disaster. This opulently appointed, but fatally ill-prepared vessel, transporting the wealthy and impoverished in rigidly separated stratification, and sailing blindly towards hazards arrogantly ignored by those in charge of her, provides both a vision of the state of pre-1914 capitalism and may also be stretched to cover the political and social circumstances of the present day. In the second canto, for instance, we are told what no one needs to explain to the mass of emigrants travelling steerage, huddled meekly below decks, too timid to lay claim to their right to survive; namely that 'die Erste Klasse zuerst drankommt, / daß es nie genug Milch und nie genug Schuhe / und nie genug Rettungsboote für alle gibt' (T, p. 11).

It is reasonable to imagine that this is where Enzensberger had put the principal emphasis in the first, and subsequently lost, version of the poem, since he would have written it with the events of 1968 — which had, however briefly and fragmentarily, threatened sections of the established order in Western Europe — still reverberating in his consciousness. But he, as well as history itself, have moved on meanwhile; or at least, to judge from the faintly scathing view he gives in this later version of his own earlier self, his intellectual perspectives, as well as his temperamental disposition towards the prospect of revolutionary change have distinctly shifted.

For what is immediately obvious about Enzensberger's bravura performance in the new version is that he does not permit himself to be seduced and restricted by the political and social clichés which may be harvested so easily from the fate of the *Titanic*. One is surprised indeed, on recalling his role in the late 1960s as the hard-nosed *anti-littérateur* who had urged that all creative writers should abandon *belles lettres* and redirect their talents to the dispelling of political illiteracy, to see the kinds of literary interests and values he has rediscovered in this poem: the speculative play with personae; the notion that art, in its treatment of the monumental issues, may be a source of entertainment and diversion; and that it may be more concerned with the formal conundrums set by the representation of metaphysical questions than with their possible baleful consequences.

Unexpected interruptions to the main thread of the poem such as 'Apokalypse. Umbrisch, etwa 1490' are not, for instance, to be

---

26. Publisher's notice issued with *Der Untergang der Titanic*.

regarded as Enzensberger's attempt to situate his *Titanic* poem in the context of an apocalyptical awareness which has teased the imagination of writers and artists universally throughout history. The admiring, if mildly ironical account here of the tribulations of a Carmelite monk working through the rigours of an Abruzzi winter, and the stifling, dusty summer which follows it, to complete on time a commissioned painting of the Apocalypse, is too lacking in the solemnity required by such an endeavour. Firmly anchored in the question, 'Wie fängt man es an, / den Weltuntergang zu malen?', it is instead a pursuit of the personal and artistic pitfalls which surround an enterprise of this kind. Metaphysical dread becomes a matter of solving problems of form to a deadline: 'technische Fragen, Kompositionsprobleme. / Die ganze Welt zu zerstören macht viel Arbeit' (T, p. 12). On the successful completion of his painting we see the monk sitting down contentedly with family and friends to a table of fresh truffles, wine and snipe. 'Angst' has been banished in aesthetic resolution.

Entertaining excursions of this kind cannot obscure the note of resignation which provides the linking factor for the startling diversity of form, voice and language in this poem. The sheer delight and virtuosity which Enzensberger displays in the dramatisation of event and setting (to experience what it is to drown, read canto 14), or in finding his way into the skin of the multifarious individuals (stoker, Russian exile, engineer, textile manufacturer, wild-eyed poet) caught up in the real and mythical incidents which make up the *Titanic* legend, do little to disguise the poem's restrained pessimism, leavened though it is, as the subtitle suggests, by an undercurrent of humour.

Enzensberger's 'Zwei Randbemerkungen zum Weltuntergang' published in *Kursbuch* 52 of May 1978, prepare us for this vein of lightly ironised melancholy. In a self-acknowledged mocking undertone, he postpones here the prospect of utopia, castigating 'die Arroganz dieser akademischen Exorzisten' and 'Theoretiker, gefesselt an die philosophischen Traditionen des deutschen Idealismus' for their refusal to see that the laws of history are beyond rational comprehension. The treatment of the *Titanic* catastrophe in tandem with his evaluation of his Cuba experiences sets the same question-mark against the future. The sinking of this extravagant emblem of capitalism did not signal the end of what it symbolised, while from the cosy fug of his Berlin room 'die sonderbar leichten Tage der Euphorie' in Cuba are but a dim memory, the promise and example they seemed to offer never having borne fruit.

In the climax of his poem — in its final, mysterious and ominous cantos — Enzensberger attempts a macabre merging of these strands. We see his room filled with those who have escaped to tell the tale; not only the figures we know from the *Titanic*, but those who have lived through other traumatic events of our century which have failed to deliver promised new beginnings out of cataclysm. 'Wir glaubten noch an ein Ende, damals / (Wann: "damals"? 1912? 18? 45? 68?), / und das heißt: an einen Anfang. / Aber inzwischen wissen wir: / Das Dinner geht weiter / . . .' (T, p. 97). The *Titanic*, and all she represents, lives on, while these bedraggled survivors (concentration camp victims? War deserters? Disillusioned revolutionaries of the late 1960s and 1970s?) mingle together, water lapping round their ankles, awaiting the ultimate catastrophe.

In a *Zeit* interview in September 1980 about his new publishing venture — the intellectual glossy, *Trans-Atlantik* — Enzensberger stated that his main interest was 'die Untersuchung der Wirklichkeit mit literarischen Mitteln'.[27] *Der Untergang der Titanic*, along with *Mausoleum* and other miscellaneous poems written in the 1970s, demonstrates that Enzensberger was not, in reaffirming the value of literature, restricting himself to the blend of literary reportage and political essay with which — in getting *Trans-Atlantik* off the ground — he and his collaborator, Gaston Salvatore, were seeking to 'aus der Zielgruppe der Einverstandenen auszubrechen' in order to reach a much wider audience. That poems also had their place in this scheme of things is confirmed by the 'Zehn Lieder für Ingrid Caven'[28] and the volume *Die Furie des Verschwindens* (1980). The 'Zehn Lieder' were first issued in recorded form as *Der Abendstern*: the dissonant effects of Peer Caven's music in combination with Ingrid Caven's *chansonnière* delivery providing the perfect counterpoint to the amiable irony of Enzensberger's raw, at times brutal texts which trace, at one end of the scale, the twilight lives of drug-dealers and -addicts and ageing prostitutes and, at the other, speculate about the final unsuspecting moments before the Bomb shatters the cosy orderliness of Federal Republican complacency.

Enzensberger's collaboration with Ingrid and Peer Caven takes us back in tone, and sometimes in theme, to the decadent cabaret world of a bygone Germany. Echoes of Tucholsky and Brecht abound, and while the peremptory 'Hereinspaziert!' which opens the poem 'Bundeswalzer' is inviting us to view not the world of Lulu and her admirers but that of the contemporary Bundesrepublik one thinks inevitably of Wedekind's 'Menagerie':

27. 'Die Wahrheit ist immer riskant'. ZEIT-Gespräch mit Hans Magnus Enzensberger über die neue Zeitschrift "Transatlantik", *Die Zeit*, 19.9.1980.
28. Enzensberger, *Die Gedichte*, Frankfurt on Main, 1983, pp. 327–41.

Hereinspaziert! Hier, wo das Geld ist,
hier spielt auch die Blasmusik.
Nur herein, nur keine Bange
vor der Bundesrepublik!

Ist sie nicht in Wirklichkeit
fast so schön wie im Prospekt,
wie von einer großen Zunge
strahlend sauber abgeleckt?[29]

In its disaffected, but not ill-tempered contemplation of the social
and psychological wreckage of West Germany today, *Die Furie des
Verschwindens* may be said to be from the same mould as the 'Zehn
Lieder für Ingrid Caven': it has little which can offer us much cheer.
We are confronted not just with the most obvious victims — the
'Türken und Arbeitslose' of 'Andenken' — but a whole range of
casualties, be they the stranded, failed academic in 'Die Drei-
unddreißigjährige' who had 'sich das alles ganz anders vorgestellt'
(F, p. 13), the divorcing couple in 'Die Scheidung' destroying each
other with 'Rache' and 'stumme Kampf' (F, p. 171), or the desolate,
self-deluding or embittered erstwhile revolutionaries of 'Die müde
Sache':

Aus dem Nebenzimmer ruft jemand: Nicht um uns
geht es hier, es geht um die Sache! — Allerhand
(sage ich), solche Töne, lange nicht mehr gehört.
Das muß der Schulfunk sein. Du natürlich, angeödet
wie immer, schweigst! — Finsteres Schweigen. — (F, 18)

In contrast, however, to the tone of his early poetry the fate of the
damaged, exploited, or merely apathetic is not registered here in
terms of rebellious outrage; the moralistic rant occasionally to be
found in a poem such as 'landessprache' has been replaced by a still
sharp, but now somewhat wry irony. The sneer of the revolutionary
at the complaisant petit bourgeois in the final line — 'ihr / ändert
die welt nicht' — of 'verteidigung der wölfe gegen die lämmer', has
been ousted by a certain reserve at the prospect of reordering the
world into a more attractive and humane place. Indeed, strange
things seem to have happened in this continuation, in another mode,
of the scepticism and pessimistic resignation of *Mausoleum* and *Der
Untergang der Titanic*: even the much-reviled Spießbürger of 'verteidigung der wölfe gegen die lämmer' and 'an einen mann in der
trambahn' (vw, p. 77) seems to have been reappraised and under-

29. Ibid., p. 338.

gone a certain rehabilitation. As we consider, in the poem 'Der Angestellte', the unsparing, but sympathetic picture — 'seinen Jammer hat niemand bemerkt' — of what for the younger Enzensberger would have been a hate figure, or, when in the essay 'Zur Verteidigung der Normalität',[30] we see him springing to the defence of what he would once have found abhorrent, we can only murmur in agreement with one of the voices in 'Die Frösche von Bikini' — the long, central poem ('Gedicht, Streitgespräch, Halluzination und Seelendrama')[31] in *Die Furie des Verschwinden* — who remarks, 'Merkwürdig, / was einem alles sympathisch wird mit der Zeit' (F, p. 46).

What, finally, is one to make of Hans Magnus Enzensberger? Where does one locate the Enzensberger who, in *Gespräche mit Marx und Engels* (1973) — a collection of miscellaneous notes, letters, recollections, documents and reports by individuals who had known or had contact with Marx and Engels — can reconstruct in a very positive and affirmative way the legacy of Marxist thought, but is also the author of the essay 'Das höchste Stadium der Unterentwicklung. Eine Hypothese über den Real Existierenden Sozialismus', published first in *Trans-Atlantik* and subsequently in *Politische Brosamen* (1982). This essay, with its catalogue — illustrated with anecdote and personal experiences — of the mismanagement, waste, paranoia and corruption which seem to be an inescapable feature of all socialist societies reminds us of what David Caute once called the 'hard pillow' for Western European socialists — the total failure to find their beliefs and ideals borne out by the experience of those societies where socialism is supposedly already an established fact. The juxtaposition of these two works may in fact help us to come closer to an understanding of the real Enzensberger (if such an animal exists), bringing together as they do the utopian lured by the attractions of the Marxist 'Gedankengut', and the unremitting realist who cannot turn a blind eye to the way it has been implemented in practice. This solution, ultimately, may be more useful than seeing him as an irreducibly complex bundle of contradictory intellectual and lyrical personae, or than pinning on him the readily available labels of slippery, doubt-ridden anarchist or elusive, creative clown.

But perhaps the most satisfactory escape from a definitive explanation for Enzensberger's multifarious talents may be to grasp at the excuse he himself has used in a brilliant but tantalising essay

30. Enzensberger, *Politische Brosamen*, Frankfurt on Main, 1982, p. 207 ff.
31. Peter Demetz, "Kunerts Abgründe, Enzensbergers Träume', *Frankfurter Allgemeine Zeitung*, 1982, 18.11.1980.

which raises more questions than it answers. In bringing 'Das Ende der Konsequenz' to a conclusion he notes: 'Ich möchte diese Frage, wie die meisten, die mich interessieren, offenlassen'.[32]

Author's Note

The following editions and abbreviations are used for Enzensberger's works (all editions published in Frankfurt on Main unless otherwise indicated):

bl = *blindenschrift*, 1964
G = *Gedichte 1965–1970*, 1971
M = *Mausoleum. Siebenunddreißig Balladen aus der Geschichte des Fortschritts*, 1975
T = *Der Untergang der Titanic*, 1978
vw = *verteidigung der wölfe*, 1957

Other works by Enzensberger referred to in the text were published as follows:

landessprache, 1960
Einzelheiten 1. Bewußtseins-Industrie, 1962
Das Verhör von Habana, 1970
(as editor) *Gespräche mit Marx und Engels*, 1973
Palaver. Politische Überlegungen (1967–1973), 1974
Die Furie des Verschwindens. Gedichte, 1980
Dreiunddreßig Gedichte, Stuttgart, 1981
Politische Brosamen, 1982
Die Gedichte, 1983

Suggested Further Reading

Heinz Ludwig Arnold, *Hans Magnus Enzensberger*, Munich, 1985 (*Text und Kritik* no. 49, 2nd edn). (This contains an excellent bibliography)
Frank Dietschreit, and Barbara Heinze-Dietschreit, *Hans Magnus Enzensberger*, Stuttgart, 1986
Reinhold Grimm, *Hans Magnus Enzensberger*, Frankfurt on Main, 1984
——, *Texturen. Essays und anderes zu Hans Magnus Enzensberger*, New York, 1984

32. Enzensberger, *Politische Brosamen*, p. 30.

Hans Magnus Enzensberger

Bärbel Gutzat, *Bewußtseinsinhalte kritischer Lyrik*, Wiesbaden, 1977 (on
  Enzensberger's first three volumes of poetry)
Joachim Schickel (ed.), *Über Hans Magnus Enzensberger*, Frankfurt on Main,
  1970
Arrigo Subiotto (ed.), *Hans Magnus Enzensberger*, Leicester, 1985

On Enzensberger in his capacity as a leading West German intellectual
readers are recommended to consult

Keith S. Parkes, *Writers and Politics in West Germany*, London, 1986, pp.
  182–204

*Handke
reception
disc. of works (1/2) (1/2)*

MICHAEL LINSTEAD

Peter Handke

The 1970s were a prolific decade for Peter Handke. During those years he published six novels, three plays, two volumes of essays and poems, one journal, and two film scripts, as well as directing the film of his own novel *Die linkshändige Frau* (1976). What is more, his last novel of the 1970s, *Langsame Heimkehr* (1979), was the first part of a tetralogy which was to stretch into the 1980s. The 1970s were also a very successful decade for Handke in terms of sales and critical appreciation. During the 1960s, after he had moved from Graz to West Germany, Handke was very much the *enfant terrible* of the literary establishment, especially after the première of *Publikumsbe-schimpfung* in 1966. By the first few years of the 1970s it seemed, to judge from the critics, that Handke had become part of the main-stream as the emphasis turned away from politics and the public sphere towards the investigation and exploration in literature of the inner self, the whole spectrum of its desires, feelings and anxieties: 'Das Subjekt als Erfahrungssubjekt wird zum einzigen Garanten der wahren Empfindung, so wie die Empfindungen (Authentizität) zum einzigen Maßstab des wahren bzw. falschen Bewußtseins werden'.[1] A contextualisation of Handke within West German literature of the 1970s — the era of the 'Tendenzwende', 'Neue Subjektivität' and 'Neue Innerlichkeit', to use the common slogans — must be approached, however, only with a certain amount of caution. Although he seems on the surface to be a prime figure, if not *the* prime figure, within such categories, it must be borne in mind that Handke has always maintained a distance from West Germany and its cultural life, particularly in the 1970s when he lived for the most part in Paris (from 1973) before moving back to Austria at the end of the decade.

There have clearly been numerous critical attempts to come to terms with the 1970s and the literature it produced, and on many issues these essays are in agreement. Helmut Kreuzer notes in 1976

---

1. David Roberts, 'Tendenzwenden. Die sechziger und siebziger Jahre in literatur-historischer Perspektive', *DVjs*, 56, 1982, 2, p. 300.

a new 'Rückzug auf das eigene Ich', which means for him that the themes of the literature are now existential rather than political or social: he names 'das Gebären, das Kindsein, das Lieben, die Krankheit, der Selbstmord und der Tod'.[2] This is a conclusion which is supported by David Roberts some six years later, who writes of 'diese Wende zum Existentiellen' as a reaction to the 'Verdrängung des Persönlichen und Privaten während der Studentenrevolte'.[3] For Kreuzer, as for others, this involves an incorporation into writing of autobiographical elements on a scale unknown in the 1960s. These can be quite explicit, as in Karin Struck's *Klassenliebe* (1973) or Verena Stefan's *Häutungen* (1975), (part of whose subtitle is *Autobiografische Aufzeichnungen*), or they can be integrated into a seemingly fictional text, as in Handke's *Die Stunde der wahren Empfindung* (1975) or Peter Schneider's *Lenz* (1973). Kreuzer discusses both the Handke novel and the Schneider story, as indeed do most commentators when attempting to characterise the 1970s, and sees many similarities, notably 'Motive der Vereinzelung, Langeweile, der Angst und der Schuld, der Bewegung ohne Ziel'.[4] But there is, as Roberts points out, an ambivalence within this 'return to the self'. The subject may be the only guarantor of true feeling but at the same time there is the problem 'daß das Subjekt immer wieder die eigene Schemenhaftigkeit empfindet, daß es "eigentlich" eine Rolle, eine Maske, ein Teil der anonymen Masse ist'.[5] This situation is reproduced in many of Handke's works of the 1970s: the retreat into the self involves first of all the rejection or destruction of the false self, the mask or masks which the whole range of activity involved in living as a social being has forced one to adopt. This is by no means an easy task for Handke's characters, especially as the demands of this social, public existence keep reasserting themselves. Kreuzer makes a further point in his comparison of Handke and Schneider: that both authors strive to emancipate their main figures, to release them 'in ein sinnhaftes Leben'.[6] The nature however of this 'sinnhaftes Leben' into which Gregor Keuschnig and Lenz enter differs radically, a point Kreuzer does not take up. Kreuzer's early essay highlights a problem then with definitions of the literature of the 1970s. It is too easy to just band together all such subjective literature under the headings

2. Helmut Kreuzer, 'Zur Literatur der siebziger Jahre in der Bundesrepublik', *Basis*, 8, 1978, p. 12.
3. Roberts, 'Tendenzwenden', p. 299.
4. Kreuzer, 'Zur Literatur', p. 24.
5. Roberts, 'Tendenzwenden', p. 300.
6. Kreuzer, 'Zur Literatur', p. 24.

'Neue Subjektivität' or 'Neue Innerlichkeit' and to present these terms as interchangeable: some more accurate differentiation is called for.

In his 1977 essay, 'Die Rückkehr des Individuums in der Literatur des letzten Jahrzehnts', Theo Buck offers steps towards such a differentiation. He lists a number of familiar themes of the contemporary literature and interprets the concentration on the self as betokening some form of resistance to the state of society in the Federal Republic at the time. Thus the drift towards existential themes is a result of 'Verdrossenheit gegenüber Staat und Partei [. . .] das erschütterte Vertrauen in die wirtschaftliche Stabilität [. . .] Bewußtsein von der "Abschaffung des Einzelnen" in der materiellen Produktion [. . .] Zweifel an der wissenschaftlichen Rationalität, die generelle Skepsis hinsichtlich des Fortschritts der Menschheit'.[7] Buck feels able to distinguish three groups within the 'Neue Subjektivität': 'Erstens die neue Variante des Elfenbeinturms, zweitens eine Marcuse-Linie, drittens die Identifikation mit dem neuen Werther-Syndrom'.[8] The authors he connects with these groups are Handke, in the first case, Schneider and Struck in the second, and Botho Strauß and Rolf Dieter Brinkmann in the third. Handke is clearly significant enough to be included in Buck's discussion, but the basis of his inclusion is largely the essay 'Ich bin ein Bewohner des Elfenbeinturms' of 1967 as well as his accusation of 'Beschreibungsimpotenz' at the meeting of the Gruppe 47 at Princeton in 1966. This immediately relativises the validity of Buck's thesis for Handke: that the concentration on the self expressed resistance to West German society in the 1970s. But Buck has touched, perhaps accidentally, upon a more important point, namely that the origins and practice of Handke's subjective writing lie much further back, in the 1960s in fact, and that any convergence with other writers in the 1970s is attributable rather to a movement or development on their part than on his.

The 1967 essay 'Ich bin ein Bewohner des Elfenbeinturms', whose title immediately distances it from the contemporary politicisation of literature, opens with a definitive statement: 'Literatur ist für mich lange Zeit das Mittel gewesen, über mich selber, wenn nicht klar, so doch klarer zu werden' (BE, p. 19).[9] This statement is valid for Handke the writer as well as Handke the reader. The content of the

7. Theo Buck, 'Die Rückkehr des Individuums in der Literatur des letzten Jahrzehnts', in *Literatur und Gesellschaft in der Bundesrepublik Deutschland. Neue Tendenzen der Gegenwartsliteratur* (DAAD), Bonn-Bad Godesberg, 1979, pp. 43–4.
8. Ibid., p. 49.
9. See Author's Note at the end of this essay for key.

literature he reads, and of his own writing, is derived from real personal experience: 'Überhaupt scheint mir der Fortschritt der Literatur in einem allmählichen Entfernen von unnötigen Fiktionen zu bestehen. Immer mehr Vehikel fallen weg, die Geschichte wird unnötig, das Erfinden wird unnötig, es geht mehr um die Mitteilung von Erfahrungen, sprachlichen und nicht sprachlichen' (BE, p. 24). The representation of political reality in literature only leads, for Handke, to abstraction rather than concretism. The only kind of reality he can depict is personal and subjective: 'Es interessiert mich als Autor übrigens gar nicht, die Wirklichkeit zu zeigen oder zu bewältigen, sondern es geht mir darum, *meine* Wirklichkeit zu zeigen. . . . Das Erforschen und Bewältigen der Wirklichkeit (ich weiß gar nicht, was das ist) überlasse ich den Wissenschaften' (BE p. 25). Hence his writing, even at this pre-'Tendenzwende' stage in West German literature as a whole, is firmly directed towards self-knowledge and self-growth: 'Ich habe keine Themen, über die ich schreiben möchte, ich habe nur ein Thema: über mich selbst klar, klarer zu werden, mich kennenzulernen oder nicht kennenzulernen [. . .] aufmerksam zu werden und aufmerksam zu machen: sensibler, empfindlicher, genauer zu machen und zu werden' (BE p. 26). This exploration and constant undermining and redefining of the self serves Handke's main expectation of all literature, 'ein Zerbrechen aller endgültig scheinenden Weltbilder' (BE, p. 20).

'Ich bin überzeugt von der begriffsauflösenden und damit zukunftsmächtigen Kraft des poetischen Denkens [. . .] Das hoffnungsbestimmte poetische Denken, das die Welt immer wieder neu anfangen läßt, wenn ich sie in meiner Verstocktheit schon für versiegelt hielt':[10] this is the central statement of Handke's 'Büchner-Preis' speech of 1973 'Die Geborgenheit unter der Schädeldecke'. It is often quoted by critics as a central statement within the definition of the 'Neue Subjektivität' as well, but we see now that it is firmly linked to Handke's earlier desire from the 1960s for a literature which breaks open our ossified perception of the world: this intention within Handke's writing predates the slogans and the buzzwords by some six years. In Handke's case then we must speak rather of a happy coincidence between his writing and that of many other authors in the 1970s, but this coincidence is not sameness: there is still the need for more precise determination of the differences as well as the similarities.

The difficulties involved in a contextualisation of Handke begin to

10. Peter Handke, *Als das Wünschen noch geholfen hat*, Frankfurt on Main, 1974, pp. 76 and 80.

lie uneasily with the urgent need to construct one in Hans-Gerhard Winter's essay 'Von der Dokumentarliteratur zur "neuen Subjektivität": Anmerkungen zur westdeutschen Literatur der siebziger Jahre' of 1981. Winter runs through the familiar themes of the 'Neue Subjektivität' and discusses Schneider's *Lenz*, Handke's *Die Stunde der wahren Empfindung* and Brigitte Schwaiger's *Wie kommt das Salz ins Meer* (1977). He then provides three groups of writers 'auf deren Werke der Begriff "neue Subjektivität" angewendet werden kann'.[11] The first group is the generation of the Student Movement: Peter Schneider, Nicolas Born, Bernward Vesper. The second contains authors connected with the Women's Movement: Brigitte Schwaiger, Karin Struck, Verena Stefan. The third group consists of one author: Peter Handke. Winter does not go any further into this group other than to recognise that Handke is clearly different from the other two groups and that he is also too important to be left out, but a more precise determination of his writing is lacking.

The beginnings of a more differentiated analysis of Handke's position can be seen in Peter Beicken's essay '"Neue Subjektivität": Zur Prosa der siebziger Jahre' of 1980. Beicken 'isolates' 'verschiedene Aspekte [. . .], die in der Literatur nicht in dieser Reinform auftreten, wohl aber doch als Bestimmungsfaktoren im komplexen Beobachtungsfeld nachzuweisen sind'.[12] The first is the 'Rückgriff auf die Subjektivität als Sensibilisierung der instrumentellen Vernunft': Beicken lists Walser's later works *Jenseits der Liebe* (1976), *Ein fliehendes Pferd* (1978) and *Seelenarbeit* (1979). The second is the 'Prinzip der Selbsterfahrung auf der Basis autobiographischer Authentizität und fiktionaler Komposition': here Beicken lists Roland Lang's *Die Mansarde* (1979) and Claudia Storz's *Jessica mit Konstruktionsfehlern* (1977). The third aspect is 'die rigorose Ausweitung der Gefühle in der Reflexion, der Nachweis der Empfindungen in Raum des Denkens', for which Botho Strauß stands. The final aspect is represented by Handke, 'der aus der intellektuellen Ichforschung eines Botho Strauß die konsequente Selbstdurchdringung des Subjekts macht mit dem Ziel der Konvergenz von Bewußtsein und Erleben in der poetisierten Empfindung'. This 'convergence' is the state in, for example, Handke's novel, *Der kurze Brief zum langen Abschied* (1972), 'in dem einem das Sehen schon ein Erkennen war',[13] it is a magical directness of experience outside the constrictions of any systems of mediation between the self and the world

11. *Seminar*, 17, 1981, 2, pp. 110–11.
12. Paul Michael Lützeler and Egon Schwarz (eds.), *Deutsche Literatur in der Bundesrepublik seit 1965*, Königstein, 1980, p. 170.
13. Peter Handke, *Der kurze Brief zum langen Abschied*, Frankfurt on Main, 1974, p. 36.

such as language, perception patterns or the responsibilities and expectations of a social role.

This is clearly not the same kind of 'Neue Subjektivität' we see in authors such as Schneider. In *Lenz* the concentration on and awareness of the self achieved by the main figure during his stay in Italy leads to a new balance between the personal and the political. Lenz does not flee into the self but seeks to restore a deficit so that his political existence can continue, only now alongside and involved in his personal existence. This restoration of a deficit may take place within another country, but Lenz does return to West Berlin, albeit at the insistence of the Italian police, and does intend to remain there. The problems and their solutions are sited within an historical framework — experience of West Berlin 'K'-Gruppen, disappointment with the direction of the Student Movement, personal guilt about his mother's death, experience of Eurocommunism in Italy. Lenz achieves what he does achieve as a result of living and experiencing as an historical being. Handke has his protagonists 'restore the deficit' or 'connection' through a magical moment when inner world and outer world converge and thereby transcend the mediating forces which have kept them apart. This is an element completely lacking in Schneider's writing.

One could then place Handke perhaps not so much under the heading 'new subjectivity' as under that of the 'new irrationalism'. Stephan Reinhardt, in his 1979 essay 'Nach innen führt der geheimnisvolle Weg, aber er führt auch wieder heraus', notes that 'diese Skepsis gegenüber der Ratio und die Bereitschaft zum Irrationalen [. . .] in den letzten Jahren sprunghaft gewachsen [sind]'. The result has been 'das Ende der neuen Aufklärung und die "Wende zum Mystischen"'. Any confidence 'durch sinnvollen Gebrauch von Verstand und Vernunft die Weltverhältnisse [. . .] erklären zu können' has disappeared: now the aim is 'den etablierten Sinn aufzubrechen durch Wahnhaftes, durch das ganz Andere, Spontane, die abgelebten Muster durch eine neue Sehweise, und sei es die des Wahnsinns, in neuem Licht erscheinen zu lassen'.[14] This direction is much nearer to Handke's writing in the 1970s than many of the other formulations. Within the framework of the 'Tendenzwende' it has become necessary for some critics to distinguish therefore between the two main terms, 'Neue Subjektivität' and 'Neue Innerlichkeit'.

14. W. Martin Lüdke (ed.), *Nach dem Protest. Literatur im Umbruch*, Frankfurt on Main, 1979, pp. 159–60. See also Klaus Peter, 'The "New Irrationalism" in West Germany', *The Germanic Review*, 61, 1986, 1, pp. 19–28.

In fact Roman Ritter makes such a distinction as early as 1976 in his essay 'Die "Neue Innerlichkeit" — von innen und aussen betrachtet', in which he deals with Struck, Handke and Brinkmann. He specifies two groups of writers and plays them off against each other:

> Die einen wollen Subjektivität einbringen in die literarische Aneignung der Realität, um ein Mehr an Wirklichkeit erfassen zu können. Für die anderen ist das Subjektive am Verhältnis zur Wirklichkeit das entscheidende Kriterium ihres Realitäts- und Literaturverständnisses. Die einen nehmen das Subjekt — und damit auch sich selbst — ernst, weil sie den Einzelnen als gesellschaftliches Wesen begreifen; sie wollen Individuum und Gesellschaft nicht zerreißen, sondern konkretisieren und anschaulicher machen.[...] Die andere Gruppe sieht einen letztlich unversöhnlichen Gegensatz zwischen Individuum und Gesellschaft, der verabsolutiert wird. Die Entwicklung von Gesellschaft und Individuum wird enthistorisiert.[15]

For Ritter, Handke clearly belongs to this second group. This petrification of the relationship between the individual and society, as opposed to one of dialectical interplay between the two as in Schneider's *Lenz*, leads Keith Bullivant and others to distinguish between 'Neue Innerlichkeit' and 'Neue Subjektivität'. In the 1982 essay 'Subjektivität — Innerlichkeit — Abkehr vom Politischen?' Bullivant argues that 'Neue Innerlichkeit' is characterised by an 'Abkehr von oder Absage an Politik' and a withdrawal into 'wesentlich als autonom präsentierte Innenräume'.[16] This is the position of Handke, Thomas Bernhard and others. The term 'Neue Subjektivität' — examples are Uwe Timm, Franz Xaver Kroetz, Wolfgang Koeppen, Peter Schneider, Karin Struck — is 'die Aufarbeitung von durch Kollision des Selbst mit der Umwelt produzierten Erlebnisstoffen, "die Darstellung des Einzelschicksals im Wechselspiel mit der politischen, sozialen und historischen Umwelt"'.[17] In Handke's work there is no such interplay but rather an ossified antagonism between the individual and society. The latter is presented as a place where genuine individual identity has been lost and replaced by a false role or mask. The rejection and discarding of this mask marks the beginning of a drive for emancipation and self-growth in many of Handke's characters, but this lack of contact with the 'political, social and historical environment' means that this only takes place

---

15. U. Timm and G. Fuchs (eds.), *kontext 1. Literatur und Wirklichkeit*, Munich, 1976, p. 239
16. Cf. K. Bullivant and H. J. Althof (eds.), *Subjektivität — Innerlichkeit — Abkehr vom Politischen?*, Bonn, 1986, p. 369
17. Ibid., p. 369

within the inner world of each character, and as such it seems elevated and unreal. Individual change and development are only ever asserted, they are never truly tested within a recognisable social reality.

The narrator in *Der kurze Brief zum langen Abschied* (1972) is 'on the run' from his childhood and anxieties associated with it, and from his estranged wife Judith. He has come to America in the hope that he can change, that he can free himself from the legacy of the narrowness of his upbringing in rural Austria, and that he can overcome the destructive relationship with Judith. Various elements — the American landscape, conversations, reading-material — contribute to a new acceptance of his own identity and the opening up of possibilities within him, possibilities which had been restricted until then. Hence, the false self of the narrator before his journey is reassessed and revised. The relationship with Judith is also ended peacefully and harmoniously. The disappointment with Handke's novel is that these achievements and the possibilities of a different future only remain stated or asserted, they are never portrayed in any fulfilment: the novel remains, in Handke's words, 'die Fiktion eines Entwicklungsromans'.[18] This is a pattern which Handke is to reproduce to a greater or lesser extent in four books which dominate his production in the 1970s and which can be linked together under a thematic heading of an investigation of the power of social roles and possible emancipation from them. In the biography of his mother *Wunschloses Unglück* (1972), the play *Die Unvernünftigen sterben aus* (1973), and the novels *Die Stunde der wahren Empfindung* (1975) and *Die linkshändige Frau* (1976) Handke presents on the one hand an historically sited analysis of the pressures, for example on his mother, to live a socialised, normative existence, but on the other hand he portrays any liberation from such forces outside such an historical framework within the terms of an irrational, almost mystical 'moment of true feeling' when social existence is magically transcended.

In *Wunschloses Unglück* any notion of emancipation can only be extremely tentative. The book charts the life of Handke's mother who committed suicide in 1971 at the age of fifty-one. It is not only about her life however; it is also about the problems her son has in writing of that life. The danger is that such a life, whose course was determined from birth according to a pre-set pattern or 'model' of how women should live their lives in male-dominated rural Austria, can only be represented via a pre-set model of a woman's biography.

18. Michael Scharang (ed.), *Über Peter Handke*, Frankfurt on Main, 1973, p. 88

This is something Handke wishes to avoid. In order to express what is private in public sentences, Handke finds himself having to reflect constantly upon the already available models of the literary representation of his subject-matter: 'Aus den Übereinstimmungen und Widersprüchlichkeiten ergibt sich dann die eigentliche Schreibtätigkeit' (WU, pp. 45–6).

The construction of the false self of women's social existence in the Austrian environment of the 1920s and 1930s is achieved through the exclusion of a private life. Existence for women is public, and therefore always visible, always able to be controlled. This means no room of your own, no secrets, no individual futures, no desires: 'Selten wunschlos und irgendwie glücklich, meistens wunschlos und ein bißchen unglücklich' (WU, p. 19). Under such conditions women's lives are transparent, reduced to the deadening progression of a local children's game: 'Müde/Matt/Krank/Schwerkrank/Tot' (WU, p. 17). This strait-jacket of expectation and propriety so permeates the mind that the oppression becomes internalised and self-reproducing, thus rendering any notions of spontaneity or 'differentness' fearsome and unwanted: 'Spontan zu leben [. . .] das hieß schon, eine Art Unwesen treiben' (WU, p. 52). The subversive potential of education and genuine self-growth is stifled and controlled by the patriarchy as well: 'Es fing damit an, daß meine Mutter plötzlich Lust zu etwas bekam: sie wollte lernen; denn beim Lernen damals als Kind hatte sie etwas von sich selber gefühlt. [. . .] Zum ersten Mal ein Wunsch, und er wurde auch ausgesprochen [. . .] Meine Mutter erzählte, sie habe den Großvater 'gebettelt', etwas lernen zu dürfen. Aber das kam nicht in Frage: Handbewegungen genügten, um das abzutun; man winkte ab, es war undenkbar' (WU, p. 20). Mental confinement is complemented by a physical confinement to the house: 'outside' was the yard and 'inside' was 'ausnahmslos das eigene Haus ohne eigenes Zimmer' (WU, p. 19). Her sexuality too is regulated and defined by her internalisation of social demands. Her feelings of this lack of control over her own body cause her to avoid affairs, and later she only goes out with 'KAVALIERE' where there is no question of sexual involvement. Her sexuality is only allowed to assert itself in its totally public function: motherhood. To all other intents and purposes she becomes *sexless*: 'Sie wurde ein neutrales Wesen, veräußerte sich in den täglichen Kram' (WU, p. 38). Estranged from her feelings and hopes, with her body and inner world requisitioned by others, she becomes a concretism of a process with which Handke first concerned himself in his play *Kaspar* (1968), namely 'die lebenszerstörende Wirkung einer entfremdeten Existenzform, in der es keine Möglichkeit der Selbstentfaltung gibt'.[19]

There is no escape for Handke's mother. Her tentative efforts to do so, to live a different life once the children have moved away, come to nought. She lives a life in which interpersonal contact is entangled in such a system of prescriptions and rules that any freedom of movement within these relationships is seen as a deviation from the strict norm. Each person, trapped within this institutionalisation of human relations, becomes isolated within the alienated forms of human intercourse, and any notion of personal development is abandoned: 'Sie war; sie wurde; sie wurde nichts' (WU, p. 44). The false self remains rigidly in place as Handke's mother drifts into 'die fleischgewordene animalische Verlassenheit' (WU, p. 77) with no feelings, no recognition of her environment, loss of care for her children. She is stranded between hatred of this public, managed existence and a fear of death: 'Das bloße Existieren wurde zu einer Tortur. Aber ebenso grauste sie sich vor dem Sterben' (WU, p. 90). Her suicide represents an escape but it is also a capitulation under the pressure of normative forces which provided her with a ready-made social identity, at the centre of which was a void.

In his next published work, *Die Unvernünftigen sterben aus* (1973), Handke constructs a tension and conflict similar to that of *Wunschloses Unglück*. The poles of this tension could be stated in terms of 'rational' and 'irrational'. The 'rational' pole is that of the public sphere, the outer world, the sphere of order, of a clinical technology, of an hierarchical class system, into which the characters fit at various levels. On the other hand there is the 'irrational' pole, the private sphere, inner world, the sphere of disorder, of spontaneity of action. The main figure, Quitt, is situated within this tension, pulled at one time towards his responsibilities as a public figure, towards his role as an entrepreneur within a consumerist society, which demands 'rational' behaviour from him if he is to protect his interests effectively. At other times Quitt leans towards 'irrational' self-assertion, towards commitment to his own wishes and needs outside the constraints placed upon the role-bearer by his social responsibilities. The conflict is then between playing a role and living out one's 'true' identity. It becomes clear during the play, however, that Quitt's 'irrationality' — he breaks a price cartel agreement with other entrepreneurs — only serves to support his 'rational' self's need for commercial gain and advantage: 'Ich werde mich nicht an die Absprache halten. Ich werde ihre Preise ruinieren und sie selber

19. Manfred Mixner, *Peter Handke*, Kronberg, 1977, p. 185

dazu' (U, p. 55). The entrepreneur in Quitt is such an internalised position that he cannot resist the coercion to exploit material — in this case the 'irrational' material of his inner world — for profit. Quitt cannot escape from his public identity, and indeed the pretence of such an escape is employed to further consolidate and advance that identity: the false self remains supreme throughout. This is why, at the end of the play, Quitt commits suicide. He realises the inescapability of his situation — 'ich stecke immer noch tief in meiner Rolle' (U, p. 98) — and also its numbing emptiness: 'Mein Selbstbewußtsein ist das Bewußtsein von einem Haufen Unrat in einem unendlichen leeren Raum' (U, p. 96). The role and the self merge as one: 'Außen hielten die Muskeln eine tote Haut fest [. . .] diese tote Haut, das war schon mein wahres Gesicht' (U, p. 98).

In *Wunschloses Unglück* and *Die Unvernünftigen sterben aus* Handke shows, in two different ways, how the discarding of the false self, which living as a social being has produced, cannot be accomplished on the basis of a simple decision. Handke's mother was never able to make such a decision anyway, and Quitt is so much a product of his role that the 'mask' of the false identity is in fact the only identity he possesses. Such is the all-pervading nature of this role that any resistance to it takes on the ambiguous value of also being an extension of it. The problem then of how such public existences can be discarded in order for a process of emancipation to be initiated is overcome in *Die Stunde der wahren Empfindung* and *Die linkshändige Frau* by the introduction of uncontrollable, subconscious elements from within the main characters which *force* them to reassess radically their previous existences and to embark upon a period of painful self-growth. Hence, for Gregor Keuschnig it is a dream of a 'Lustmord' (SWE, p. 45), for Marianne an 'Erleuchtung' (LF, p. 23).

Die Stunde der wahren Empfindung would seem to be a fictional exposition of the aesthetic programme of the 'Büchner-Preis' speech. Gregor Keuschnig is subjected to an experience — he dreams of having murdered an old woman — which throws him out of the normal run of things and which allows the world eventually to begin anew. This irrational encroachment on his otherwise public, rational life — Keuschnig is a bureaucrat, a press attaché at the Austrian Embassy in Paris — deprives him of the feeling that his life is in any way genuine or that it contains 'sense'. The dream — described as a 'jolt' — destroys the false public edifice of confidence and coherence around Keuschnig and allows his inner world to break out of the constraints the outer world had placed upon it. The public life is revealed then to be merely a game or pretence, 'eine Vortäuschung' to be lived 'der Form nach' (SWE, p. 7). Its 'sense' is illusory. Keuschnig is now thrown into 'non-sense' ('Sinnlosigkeit') and Handke is interested in whether this can be used to help him realise a genuine identity. Without the secure crutches of convention and habit Keuschnig spends most of the novel exploring the change the dream has caused within him. This change is likened to a 'Wachzustand' whereas his former life was upheld by 'die schlaf-wandlerischen Sicherheiten' (SWE, p. 35). The dream enables him to discard the artificial ordering of the world, its fabricated coher-ence, and to head towards emancipation by increasing his con-fidence in his own ability to form his own world. This is a notion of self-definition which was completely unavailable to Handke's mother or Quitt; it is also a notion which is to have a central position in *Die linkshändige Frau.*

This drive to forge a true identity manifests itself in various ways in various scenes throughout the novel; only one of them can be dealt with briefly here. From his office window Keuschnig sees a girl watering plants in another office; he rushes to her room and they have sex on the floor. Afterwards, in spite of the impersonal nature of this encounter, he feels very close to her: 'Er konnte sie selbstverständlich anschauen, ohne Anstrengung; ohne die Angst, sich zu verraten. [. . .] Er hatte vor ihr kein Versteckspiel nötig, nie mehr [. . .]. Sie hatten voreinander keine Geheimnisse, aber ein gemeinsames Geheimnis vor den anderen' (SWE, p. 55). Unlike the rest of the world he no longer needs to concentrate on the outer form, the appearance of his life. With the girl his inner world is trans-formed into action and his actions are the result of the externalisa-tion of the momentary rush of sexual urge without the checks and hindrances of social constraint or morality. Keuschnig's conscious-ness becomes his world, private becomes public. The encounter with her is in the totally direct present as if the world were new with no system or order.

The world becomes new in another central episode of the book. Keuschnig sees before him three objects, 'ein Kastanienblatt: ein Stück von einem Taschenspiegel: eine Kinderzopfspange' (SWE, p. 81). These objects suddenly become 'Wunderdinge'. Keuschnig reacts with '"Wer sagt denn, daß die Welt schon entdeckt ist?"' (ibid.). There are still things to be discovered in the world, it is not completely parcelled up or, in the words of the 'Büchner-Preis' speech, 'versiegelt'. The three objects at his feet are defunctional-ised, they lose their meaning within anthropocentric systems of value and coherence and are 'set free' via what Handke calls 'dieses mystische Erlebnis'.[20] This applies also to the experiencing conscious-ness, so that Keuschnig can maintain: '"Ich habe eine Zukunft! [. . .].

"Ich kann mich ändern"' (SWE, pp. 82–3).

This future under the sign of a true identity is only touched upon at the end of the novel: for most of the time Handke depicts the difficulty Keuschnig has in reconciling the new-found aspects of his inner world with his former existence. Only once his wife has left him, his child has run away, and he has contemplated suicide does he break through to the beginning of this new future. He is aided in this by observing his child and admiring her independence: 'Sie saß da, für sich allein' (SWE, p. 131). The child is neither determined from without nor does she attempt to judge or determine others: she is only true to herself. The change in Keuschnig can only be documented from without at the end of the novel. The narrative perspective turns from his inner world to an objective third-person stance and Gregor Keuschnig becomes 'der Mann'. Keuschnig as an experienced character thus dissipates somewhat and we do not see the self-growth he has attained integrated through action into a public existence. Rather, the novel charts a beginning exemplified by its open end of six dots. The false self may have been discarded but the true identity has still to be revealed.

The fourth text in this thematic grouping, *Die linkshändige Frau*, attempts this revelation. Having broken up her marriage with Bruno as a result of an 'Erleuchtung', Marianne attempts to live on her own with her child and to develop her self outside the boundaries of a relationship which had been characterised by the dominance and brutality of the male partner. This self-growth also takes place almost completely outside social involvement: society is a place where true identity is lost and replaced by a pre-determined role, what Handke terms 'die vorausbestimmte Biographie'.[21] Marianne withdraws into her inner spaces but the narrative does not follow her there. Rather, Handke employs a cold, sober, detached stance, reminiscent of a screenplay, where actions are described without any psychological intention or interpretation. This distance serves of course to support Marianne's isolation, so that from the start the various stages of this self-growth are largely withheld from us. We can only observe from without, as we had to do with Keuschnig on the last page of his novel, and attempt to draw our own conclusions.

The final long scene shows a partial reintegration into society when Marianne throws a party and all the various characters in the story turn up. It is a party, however, which has an unreal, arid

---

20. H.L. Arnold, 'Gespräch mit Peter Handke', in *Peter Handke*, ed. H.L. Arnold, *Text und Kritik*, vol. 24/24a, Munich, 1978, p. 36
21. 'Und plötzlich wird das Paar wieder denkbar', *Der Spiegel*, 32, 1978, 28, p. 140.

quality about it, which is not alleviated by the narrative tone. Social hierarchies, previous arguments and misunderstandings between people are 'magically' overcome. Complete strangers embrace each other and a publisher kneels in front of a salesgirl and kisses the ends of her fingers. Marianne's self-growth is untested by this event and the very final scene has her isolated again on her terrace, drawing. However, as W. Martin Lüdke points out in connection with the story, isolation is a means within a process of development and not that process's goal: 'Das Alleinsein wird [. . .] als gelungene Individuierung gesetzt, und nicht als ein notwendiges Moment im Prozeß der Identitätsfindung verstanden. Was im Versuch der Emanzipation ein Mittel sein kann, erscheint hier weithin als Zweck'.[22] With isolation enjoying this position it is also no wonder that a collective attempt to change women's subordinate role in society should be given such short shrift, as in the parody and ridiculing of the figure of Franziska and her women's group.

Marianne's self is presented then as not being able to stabilise itself within a social context, 'in der — immer problematischen — Auseinandersetzung mit anderen'.[23] Any emancipation must necessitate withdrawing from society altogether, rather than attempting to change one's position within that society. Marianne's problems are existentialised and thereby lose much of their historical specificity: 'Es stellt sich bald heraus, daß es hier weniger um die gesellschaftlichen Strukturen und Bedingungen der Unterdrückung und Ausbeutung geht, als um das alte Handke-Thema der vergewaltigten Individualität überhaupt. Gesellschaft erscheint hier fast nur als Negation'.[24] The 'exotic' nature of this emancipation is presented, perhaps unconsciously, in the song text from which the book derives its title. The longed-for state of the individual in the collective, where true identity is still maintained, is placed outside recognisable society:

Ich möchte dich IN EINEM FREMDEN ERDTEIL sehen
Denn da werde ich dich unter den anderen endlich allein sehen
Und du wirst unter tausend anderen MICH sehen
Und wir werden endlich aufeinander zugehen (LF, p. 102)

The problem of the representation of this emancipation or self-growth remains in Handke's writing because of his view of the

22. W. Martin Lüdke, 'Peter Handke und seine Dichtung', *Universitas*, 36, 1981, 6, p. 573
23. Ibid., p. 574
24. R. Nägele and R. Voris, *Peter Handke*, Munich, 1978, p. 68

relationship between the individual and society as one of petrified antagonism. The way out of this impasse is either to show the individual in the isolation of his or her 'free' inner spaces, or for that antagonism to be momentarily bridged in an almost mystical instant of 'connection' between the two apparently irreconcilable elements. The latter is what happens in Handke's last book of the 1970s, *Langsame Heimkehr* (1979).

The critic Peter Pütz characterises the novel as an attempt to find 'Zusammenhang, Form und "Heil" verheißende Harmonie'.[25] This 'connection' and the need for it is mentioned in the very first sentence of the book where Handke writes of the geologist Valentin Sorger: 'Sorger hatte schon einige ihm nah gekommene Menschen überlebt und empfand keine Sehnsucht mehr, doch oft eine selbstlose Daseinslust und zuzeiten ein animalisch gewordenes, auf die Augenlider drückendes Bedürfnis nach Heil' (LH, p. 1). This need for healing does not involve the agency of other people — Sorger has after all 'survived' the intrusion of anyone else into his life — and in this he is a descendant of Marianne. At the end of her story she is alone, drawing pictures, 'jeden Gegenstand in allen Einzelheiten' (LF, p. 131). Sorger's work as a geologist has a similar function of registering, recording and giving form to the world — in this case the landscape of Alaska — but with links to giving him thereby a sense of the form of his own inner world as well.

This is achieved on almost the last page of the novel, where, in a direct reference back to that first sentence, the narrator addresses Sorger: 'Das phantasielose, blutsaugerische Elend ließ von dir ab, und du spürtest deine Lider wie gesalbt von dem ewigen wilden Bedürfnis nach Erlösung' (LH, p. 199). Between these two passages the novel sets out the beginnings of Sorger's 'slow homecoming', his search for and experience of a 'gesetzgebender Augenblick' (LH, p. 168). This 'law', 'connection' or 'form' is not however already present in phenomena, ready to be found, but must be searched for and invented, 'nicht *ge*funden, sondern *er*funden'.[26] This involves the agency of the individual imagination as the inner world asserts itself and its own sense of order against the 'final images' of the outer world.

The 'gesetzgebender Augenblick', the moment when Sorger's inner world connects with and changes the outer world, happens in a coffee-shop in New York. Sorger experiences an overwhelming consciousness of being in the process of time, of being an historical

25. Peter Pütz, *Peter Handke*, Frankfurt on Main, 1982, p. 109
26. Ibid., p. 111

subject. With this connection established between himself and history and the isolation of Alaska broken through, a potential for action towards another individual is set free: ' "Es ist [. . .] mein geschichtlicher Augenblick: ich lerne (ja, ich kann noch lernen), daß die Geschichte nicht bloß eine Aufeinanderfolge von Übeln ist, die einer wie ich nur ohnmächtig schmähen kann — sondern auch, seit jeher, eine von jedermann (auch von mir) fortsetzbare, friedensstiftende *Form*" ' (LH, p. 168). Sorger meets an old friend Esch who is plagued with job, family and money problems. They sit together in the coffee-shop and, in a scene which has strong mystical overtones, Sorger 'heals' Esch in an instant of 'connection' between himself and the world:

> Sorger wünschte sich seine Macht herbei und verwandelte sich (es war schwer) in die Nische, in der sie beide sassen, wölbte sich über den Zufallsbekannten und nahm ihn, der über seinen Zustand schon erstaunt den Kopf zu schütteln begann und sich zwischendurch wieder höflich das Taschentuch borgte, in sich auf, bis sich der starre Torso des anderen allmählich neu belebte und einen zunächst grotesken, dann liebenswürdigen Kinderkopf bekam und sich schließlich die Arme rieb, aus denen, wie er sagte, eben "die Angst wegschwirrte". (LH, pp. 173–4)

Sorger becomes the comforting father in this scene and Esch his child, and this relationship is then transferred into the religious realm as Sorger becomes his priest: 'Sorger wurde sein Vorsprecher: befahl und verbot ihm (der in seiner Nach-Angst gerne gehorsam war); sprach ihn frei von Schmerz; weissagte ihm Gutes und gab ihm schließlich den Segen' (LH, pp. 177–8).

Sorger overcomes at this moment the 'Ekel und Trennungsschmerz zwischen ihm und der Welt' (LH, p. 190) and 'returns home' equipped with his true identity. The terms in which Handke presents this reestablished 'connection' however denote merely a transcendence of the normative, socialising forces so effectively portrayed in *Wunschloses Unglück*. Handke's total faith in the individual's ability to retreat into the safety of supposedly autonomous inner spaces — the elements of 'Neue Innerlichkeit' in his writing — contrasts with the depiction of his mother's life in its social and historical context or with that of Quitt the entrepreneur: neither of them had such an inner world at their disposal. Rather, their public identities, their false selves, were all-encompassing, such was the power and penetration of social demands into the private sphere. What is more, these pressures will still exist to force people into false identities as long as emancipation is perceived as an individual act of flight rather than a collective action for change.

Author's Note

The following editions and abbreviations are used for Handke's works (all editions are published in Frankfurt on Main):

BE = *Ich bin ein Bewohner des Elfbeinturms*, 1972
LF = *Die linkshändige Frau*, 1976
LH = *Langsame Heimkehr*, 1979
SWE = *Die Stunde der wahren Empfindung*, 1978
U = *Die Unvernünftigen sterben aus*, 1974
WU = *Wunschloses Unglück*, 1975

Also note:

Als das Wünschen noch geholfen hat, 1974
Der kurze Brief zum langen Abschied, 1974

Suggested Further Reading

Peter Pütz's excellent essay on Handke in *Kritisches Lexikon zur deutschsprachigen Gegenwartsliteratur* contains a comprehensive listing of secondary literature on the author. Of the various book publications, the following are recommended:

Manfred Durzak, *Peter Handke und die Gegenwartsliteratur*, Stuttgart, 1982
Raimund Fellinger, *Peter Handke*, Frankfurt on Main, 1984
Norbert Gabriel, *Peter Handke und Österreich*, Bonn, 1983
Norbert Honsza, *Zu Peter Handke. Zwischen Experiment und Tradition*, Stuttgart, 1982
Manfred Jurgensen (ed.), *Handke, Ansätze, Analysen, Anmerkungen*, Berne and Munich, 1979
June Schlueter, *The Plays and Novels of Peter Handke*, Pittsburgh, NJ, 1981

PETER LABANYI

Surrendering to the Logic of Flow
Reading Alexander Kluge

Every story, all history, is exemplary; it contains an opportunity —
often refused — for learning. History and literature (and film) are,
for Alexander Kluge, modes of understanding yoked together by the
myriad ways they respond to our existential hunger for meaning. In
the present age, no innocent answers are possible. Towards the end
of his film interrogation of Germany's relationship to its history, *Die
Patriotin* (1979), the following comment is made by the storyteller, a
knee, which is all that remains of a German soldier who died at
Stalingrad: '*Die Geschichte sind wir*, die Toten und Totenteile. [. . .]
Jede Zelle eines Körpers, die nicht umkommen wollte, weiß den
Anfang des Abendlandes, bis zu den Sternen hin und wie es einmal
endet. Nur das zänkische Gehirn weiß es nicht' (DP, p. 166).[1]
Within each cell is inscribed the past and the destiny of the human
species. Kluge's breathtaking phylogenetic simultaneity, his com-
passionate vision of history as 'Trauerarbeit', are allied with a belief
that we should trust the wisdom of the body, of our needs, wishes
and senses, rather than that of the 'quarrelsome' mind.

This is not to advocate irrationalism, for reason, when uncoupled
from human interests as in technocracy, lends itself to instrumentalisation for inhuman ends, which it achieves with a perfectionistic
barbarity of which 'brute' instinct is incapable. This 'dialectic of
enlightenment' underlies the reclaiming of the body in cultural
discussion in the Federal Republic during the 1970s — the logical
extension of the attempt to ground the 'subjective factor' on a
materialist basis: in keywords, from 'Phantasie' in the late 1960s, via
'Erfahrung' and 'Sinnlichkeit' to, simply, 'Körper'. This project was
given added impetus by sexual-political debates initiated within the
New Women's Movement and, more recently, by the therapy boom.
Its wider context is an ecological ethic, which urges the replacement
of abstraction, linearity and the mechanistic by concreteness, process

1. See Author's Note at the end of this essay for key.

and the holistic.

Conventional medicine often makes us feel 'better' only temporarily because it suppresses the symptoms without getting at the causes of an illness. Alternative medicine, by contrast, respects the body as a totality; it not only accepts the symptoms but may even reproduce or exacerbate them in order to activate the body's own self-regulatory healing processes, from which, even though we may initially have to feel 'worse', the organism emerges more resistant. Consider the following passage from 'Die ganze Weihnacht soll es sein' according to this therapeutic perspective:

> Ihr Schematismus, ihre Rigidität. Aber die existiert nicht ohne das ganze Weihnachtsgefühl — Lämmer in Island werden von ihren Hirten gerade noch vor dem Schneesturm in eine warme Scheune gebracht. Eine Hebamme im zwölften Jahrhundert hat sich im Schneesturm bei Schwanebeck verirrt. Plötzlich sieht sie das Licht des Türmers im Domturm der nahen Stadt, der hinaufsteigt, um Heilig Abend einzublasen. Sie folgt diesem Licht und findet zum Öfchen. In der gesamten DDR Weihnachten, bis nach Polen hinein, den Balkan hinunter usf. "Meine Gerty ist genau Heilig Abend 1952, 20 Uhr, geboren." Kriegsweihnacht. 24.12.42 in Stalingrad; die eingekesselte Armee improvisiert Behelfschristbäume. Weihnachten 1974, die Massenbewegung in überfüllten Zügen nach Süden. Diesmal keine "weiße Weihnacht", in früheren Zeiten weiße Weihnacht. "Ich erinnere mich aus meiner Kindheit, daß Weihnachten immer Schnee gelegen hat. Der Schnee hat geknirscht. Allerdings war da auch mehr Landklima, wo ich her bin." Ein Meteorologe sagt: Die Wetterverhältnisse zum 24. Dezember haben sich in den letzten 50 Jahren nicht absolut geändert. Lichter, die Kinderperspektive. Die öffentliche Stadt stirbt ab 14 Uhr allmählich aus. In der Landschaft draußen Unterfahren von Rundfunkprogrammen (Autoradio), ein Sender wandert ein, ein anderer Sender wandert aus. Sechs Konkurrenzversionen des Weihnachtsoratoriums. Im Kanon dazu (verschiedene Anfangszeiten) *Hänsel und Gretel*; Weihnachtstrost der Politiker. Für Nachrichten über Tatsachen ist ab 16 Uhr kein Platz. (GeS, pp. 192–3).

Accelerating social and cultural change, the drastic transformation of the physical environment, disasters public and private, professional and domestic, wars and threats of war all disrupt the time-scales of our everyday lives and provoke compensatory yearnings for security and, above all, meaningfulness. This need for reassurance (closure) is met by conventional stories and plots, which narrate from an identifiable perspective and satisfyingly culminate in a conclusion that confers meaning on what has gone before. The above passage, the first half of a four-paragraph text, does not work in this way. Not even the 'ending' offers any resolution, rather it merely adds another micro-narrative: 'In einer westfälischen Familie wurde am Heiligabend in einer Dachkammer die Großmutter gefunden, die sich erhängt hatte. Um die Stimmung während der Feiertage nicht zu beschädigen, beschloß die Familie, den Fund geheimzuhalten und die Tote erst am 3. Feiertag zu entdecken. Zu diesem Zeitpunkt war auch der Abtransport zu bewerkstelligen' (GeS, p. 194).

Here at least the focus is, relatively, sustained. By contrast, in the opening two paragraphs of 'Die ganze Weihnacht soll es sein', both the perspective and the subject-matter change almost from sentence to sentence, while the style is even more elliptical. The effect depends on the montage of different levels and perspectives. The reader has to negotiate breaks in space and time: from lambs in modern Iceland to a midwife in twelfth-century Germany; from Christmas on a national scale (the GDR, Poland, the Balkans) to the most intimate experience of the birth of a child; from Stalingrad in 1942 to Germany 1974; from a subjective but concrete recollection of childhood to the abstracted voice of the 'expert'. The meaning of Christmas ('die *ganze* Weihnacht') lies not in any one of these particles but in all of them and their interactions simultaneously. The passage assembles several of Kluge's recurrent preoccupations: Christmas (as the opposite of the everyday), Stalingrad, wishes, a dialectical grasp of ideology, memory, technocracy, childhood and its relics in adult life (*Hänsel und Gretel*), the consciousness industry, along with the allusion to Germany's problematic national identity in the title. But the real content of the passage is to be found in its *form*. For Kluge, a totality can only be made up of fragments. The unmediated confrontations here serve, dialectically, both to register and to sublate the artificial, ideologically motivated divisions between past and present, subjective and objective, imagination and fact. It is to overcome these that simultaneity is for Kluge, as we shall see, both a quintessential technique and an epistemological imperative. In his work as both film-maker and writer, authenticity is less a matter of verifiability than of proportion. It is irrelevant whether the elements in the above passage are 'documentary' or invention. When the second paragraph of 'Die ganze Weihnacht soll es sein' was reproduced in *Filmkritik*, it was indeed misattributed to Kluge's fictional collection, *Lernprozesse mit tödlichem Ausgang* (1973). The text is in fact taken from the 'theoretical' section of *Gelegenheitsarbeit einer Sklavin: Zur realistischen Methode* (1975), though Kluge's fictions, as well as his film outlines, are full of such compressed, asyndetic miniatures.

The assembly of relatively autonomous particles by means of montage leaves breaks, to negotiate which we must activate our associative faculties; these gaps provide space for our own experience. Meaning is not contained within the text, as a kernel waiting to be extracted; it must be constituted amid each reading process. Whereas a conventional narrative rewards us with a prepackaged meaning that temporarily pacifies our yearning for meaning in our lives, Kluge's texts radicalise our sense of discontinuity and contingency by embodying it in their forms. Like holistic therapies, such texts exacerbate the very symptoms that make us turn to narratives in the first place. But the ultimate, utopian goal is that, having been through such taxing literary simulations, the reader should be able to apply the synthesising skills exercised, the ability to cope with contradiction and complexity, in everyday life itself.

It is this refusal to harmonise contradictions, to subsume complexity under a monolithic perspective and a linear narrative thread, that has gained Kluge the reputation of being a 'difficult' writer. We may manage to synthesise two paragraphs, but suppose we are dealing with text-constellations of a hundred pages and more? Kluge has generally been regarded as a peripheral figure in the literary scene of the Federal Republic, not least because of his simultaneous activities as a film-maker and theoretician. Two premises underlie this essay: firstly that all of Kluge's work in each medium is a totality (although the emphasis here will be on his writing, which has received less attention than his films); secondly that Kluge is one of the most 'difficult' writers in the Federal Republic because, as his elliptical, unelaborated, even 'un-literary' style along with the substance and organisation of his writing suggest, he has called into question the very fundaments of literature. Kluge exemplifies Benjamin's model of the writer as producer, who radically thinks through his own work and its technique, its relationship to the literary means of production: 'Ein Autor, der die Schriftsteller nichts lehrt, lehrt niemanden'.[2]

Kluge is, though under very different circumstances and using different modes, following trails opened up by Benjamin: with his utopian view of (especially silent) cinema; his centring of montage as structural principle; his idiosyncratic bricolage of Marx and Freud, Jewish philosophy, 'Märchen' and childhood; his love of quotations, allied with a passion for collecting; his eclecticism, curiosity and obsessiveness as an intellectual *flâneur*; his preference for fragments and for essayistic and paradigmatic forms; his use of allegory,

---

2. Walter Benjamin, 'Der Autor als Produzent', in *Versuche über Brecht*, Frankfurt on Main, 1966, p. 110.

nourished by a mimetic sense for correspondences inspired by the hologrammatic world-view of Romanticism; his fascination with the explosive force ('shock') of images of all kinds, and his allied affinities with Surrealism; his advocation of a 'distracted' interest on the part of reader and viewer; his commitment to the ethical, exemplary purpose of narrative; his attempt to fuse subjectivity and materialism into a redemptive vision of history as simultaneity; his personal as well as intellectual relationship with Theodor Adorno; and above all, with his reliance on immediate concrete experience as cognitive touchstone. Kluge's first film, the short *Brutalität in Stein* (1961), was a thoroughly Benjaminesque reflection on the 'ruins' left behind by the Third Reich in the shape of the arena at Nuremberg and the memories of the Nazi past embodied in it. Kluge has indeed acknowledged his debt to Benjamin, whose ideas — on how the historical ripeness of the cinema was both grounded in and summoned forth new structures of human perception and reception of works of art — stimulated some of Kluge's first attempts to define the distinct potential of film as a medium. The contrasts with literature which Kluge brought out in his early essays on the cinema were decisively to the latter's advantage.[3] Whereas literary language is schematic, neither concrete nor abstract, the material of film is, Kluge points out, always concrete — images — while montage enables it to form concepts in the viewer's mind. This associative quality, which is analogous to the workings of the human brain, also entails that film has the capacity to organise complex aggregates of material. Yet, paradoxically, it seems to have been precisely the 'sceptical' approach from the vantage-point of film that revealed the potential of *writing* for Kluge. The 'cinematic' qualities of 'Die ganze Weihnacht soll es sein' — montage, perspectivism, simultaneity — are only the most immediately obvious results. As we shall see, the cinema underlies not simply all of Kluge's production at the level of form and organisation but the direction taken by his thought too.

Michael Rutschky has argued that the cult of the cinema among the left in the Federal Republic during the 1970s was in part motivated by that very hunger for experience which was prepared to settle for sensuality if sense could not be constituted. Rutschky maintains that this sector of the audience went to the cinema partly to escape from the depression and disorientation of the years between the demise of the Student Movement and the 'deutsche Herbst'. Notwithstanding strong intellectual and political sympathies — symbolised, among other things, by Kluge's association

3. Cf. 'Die Utopie Film', *Merkur* 201 (December 1964), pp. 1, 135–46.

with the umbrella organisation of the non-dogmatic left, the Sozialistische Büro, with the political-cultural quarterly *Ästhetik und Kom-
munikation*, as well as, of course, his roots in and connections with the
Frankfurt School — this could explain the problematic position of
Kluge. For what his texts and films register in their fragmentary
forms and themes (especially in the shape of his characters' 'hunger
for meaning') and evoke in the reader and viewer through their
unsynthesised complexity is, precisely, disorientation.

It is understandable that, before the 1970s, Kluge was regarded
primarily as a film-maker, for whom writing was either second-best
— when he was unable to make films — or merely the literary
(albeit seminal) stage of the film-making process. Indeed, Kluge
himself contributed to such a view by maintaining that the stories in
his first collection, *Lebensläufe* (1962), were conceived as films; while
his second book, *Schlachtbeschreibung* (1964), was based on research
for a proposed film on Stalingrad. In one sense the 'filmic' dimension in *Lebensläufe* is reflected in the montage technique whereby its
fragmentary and perspectivist textures are orchestrated. The more
documentary origins of *Schlachtbeschreibung* are mirrored in its non-
narrative and classificatory organisation: we are offered a sequence
of antagonistic diachronic accounts along with synchronic materials.
Schlachtbeschreibung can also, reflecting Kluge's legal training, be read
as a 'trial' — with evidence, witnesses, background material and
summing-up — in which the 'verdict' is left to the reader. Both
books were intended to be, and indeed were, read as radical disruptions of conventional fictional narratives — an outcome of their
uncompromising, defamiliarising perspectivism. In *Schlachtbeschreibung* in particular, and to a lesser extent in some of the stories in
Lebensläufe, this perspectivism resulted from the juxtaposition of
different language-sources and registers. It is not enough to see
perspectivism simply as a 'cinematic' technique provocatively transposed to literature. Such an approach does not adequately account
for Kluge's intense *linguistic* awareness in both books, as revealed by
his use of mimicry, quotations and documents — a sensibility
already manifest in the way he handled textual materials in *Brutalität
in Stein*.

Consistent with this filmic precedent, documents are deployed in
Lebensläufe and *Schlachtbeschreibung* not for authenticity but as raw
material for ideology criticism by the reader, for whose 'judgement'
the practical consciousness of a whole spectrum of bureaucratic,
hierarchical and authoritarian modes of thought — ranging from
Kant to the Prussian officer corps, from Nazi scientists to the law —
is displayed at first hand. This refusal to absorb and harmonise

material into a homogeneous style and monolithic narrative is one of Kluge's trademarks. It entails that the texts do not so much read like film outlines as offer materials out of which 'conventional' linear narratives could be fashioned. In the resulting 'writerly' texts, the completion and connection is to be carried out by the reader, though generally Kluge's selection and presentation has been so skilful that the outcome is anything but playfully open (nor could it be, given his historically determinate cognitive thrust and subject-matter). At the same time, the fragmentation is not only strategic but realistic: the anti-organic forms correspond to the synthetic nature of the individual in the modern world. The 'Lebensläufe' in the title also connote the discontinuous 'lives' each character leads. Its combination of language-consciousness and defamiliarising forms resulted in the identification of *Lebensläufe* with the strain of experimental prose fashionable during the early 1960s — misleadingly, as comparison with the subsequent development of, say, Heißenbüttel and Jürgen Becker shows. The consignment of *Schlachtbeschreibung* to the subsequent mode of documentary writing proved scarcely less helpful. Kluge himself was to warn against such a categorisation in an afterword to the book on its reissue in 1968 — the height of the documentary wave.

The occasional story in journals apart, Kluge published no new fiction for almost ten years after *Schlachtbeschreibung*, during which time he helped instead to lay the foundations of the New German Cinema by both his campaigning and practical example. The problem of how to classify his writing was suspended. In tune with the 'death of literature' proclaimed during the late 1960s, it seemed as though Kluge's scepticism towards literature, the counterpart of his utopian enthusiasm for film, had now become dominant, and that he could henceforth reassuringly be regarded first and foremost as a film-maker.

Between the early 1970s and the early 1980s, however, Kluge published not only some 2,000 pages of theoretical writing but no less than 1,200 pages of new fiction, while managing to sustain his output of individual, and increasingly also collective, feature films. It is paradoxical that Kluge's 'rediscovery' of literary production, whether in fiction or theory, can be traced back precisely to the political and intellectual upheavals of the Student Movement, whose impact on his work was already reflected in the title of his second feature film, *Die Artisten in der Zirkuskuppel: ratlos* (1968). Having just established himself as a film-maker with *Abschied von gestern* (1966), based on one of the stories in *Lebensläufe*, Kluge now was driven to interrogate the premises of his production and withdrew at the end of the decade to Ulm to investigate the grammar of the medium by making experimental 'science-fiction' films. These were by no means without political and intellectual content, for from this period onwards Kluge also began to immerse himself in Marxist theory. The first precipitate was the appearance in 1972 of a major work in the tradition of the Frankfurt School, *Öffentlichkeit und Erfahrung*, written with the sociologist Oskar Negt. Inspired by the disintegration of the Student Movement and the subsequent disorientation of the left, the book set out initially to provide a corrective continuation of Habermas's *Strukturwandel der Öffentlichkeit* (1962) in the light of the electronic-media explosion and the debates on press and public opinion during the 1960s. In part thanks to Kluge's untameable curiosity, the project mushroomed until *Öffentlichkeit und Erfahrung* became an encyclopaedia of the interests of the non-dogmatic left in the early 1970s. Its subject-matter included political-economic analysis of late capitalism, the state and legitimation; working-class culture and socialisation; labour history; Marxist theoretical traditions, relating in particular to the question of class consciousness; a conceptualisation of the 'subjective factor', along with its determinants (family, work, and their different time-scales) and constituents (sensuality, experience and phantasy); the structures of the mass media, especially television, and the mechanisms of their reception; fascism; language; architecture and ideology; education; children, etc., etc. Even more remarkable than the eclectic scope is, however, the book's form. Ostensibly divided into six chapters, together with excursuses and twenty historical appendices, *Öffentlichkeit und Erfahrung* is, in reality, a patchwork of relatively autonomous sections. The text is further broken up by the meandering footnote microessays, the use of bold type for emphasis and italics for often lengthy quotations ('documents'), as well as by illustrations. Such a fracturing notation demands a more active and 'distracted' form of reading. The intention is, precisely, that the very form of the book will enact its central argument — namely the need to devise subdominant ('proletarisch' — used, in part, as a utopian metaphor) oppositional counter-strategies to the colonisation of the human senses and imagination by a late capitalist consciousness industry geared to closure. By negotiating the 'breaks' between different areas of experience — public/private, objective/subjective, work/family — the reader is both made aware of and momentarily, during the reading process, overcomes the compartmentalisations and exclusion-mechanisms on which capitalism depends to sustain and reproduce itself. Thus, in a sense that is crucial to all of Kluge's work, the book's deeper content is to be found in its *form*. Despite certain affinities with Kluge's earliest writings, on university self-government and on cultural policy,[4] at the level of content and strategic interest *Öffentlichkeit und Erfahrung* grows more logically out of Negt's involvement in worker education. However, the book marks a new departure for Kluge in a more important sense: from now on, not only will film, fiction and theory be the components of a single interlocking production, but Kluge's fictions will also incorporate analytical perspectives and conceptual categories from his own theoretical work. The results are twofold. Firstly, together with Kluge's preference for paradigmatic forms and his tendency to transplant material between books and media, this blurs the boundaries between theory and fiction, and even between individual 'works'. Kluge can be seen to be engaged in one vast, cumulative 'work in progress', a kaleidoscopic montage of all his writings — and, even, his films — whose possible interconnections, and hence meanings, are multiplied as each new component is added to the constellation. Sometimes the connections between texts in different volumes are stronger than those between texts in the same volume. This partly accounts for the fact that Kluge has so far produced no less than three different versions of *Schlachtbeschreibung*: a paradigm of the work not as organic product but as process, as Brechtian 'Versuch'.

The second result of the cooperation between theory and fiction is that, after *Öffentlichkeit und Erfahrung*, Kluge's fictions are now characterised by an intellectual saturation at two levels: not only that of the ideologies he is attacking, as in *Lebensläufe*, but also that of his own evolving thought (though Kluge sometimes teasingly elides the two). Thus Kluge's second collection of fictions, *Lernprozesse mit tödlichem Ausgang* (1973), on the one hand thematically and, so far as a few of the stories are concerned, formally relates back to *Lebensläufe* but, more significantly, it shares a common genesis with the theoretical *Öffentlichkeit und Erfahrung* project. This is the case too with the film *Gelegenheitsarbeit einer Sklavin*, which also appeared in 1973 and which Kluge explicitly describes as complementary to the theoretical book. This parallelism of film, fiction and theory was to be sublated into cooperative synthesis with *Die Patriotin* (1979) and, to a lesser degree, *Die Macht der Gefühle* (1984), where all three dimensions — film-script and notes; fictions; theoretical fragments — are assembled in a single multi-media volume: the quintessential

---

4. Cf. *Die Universitäts-Selbstverwaltung: Ihre Geschichte und gegenwärtige Rechtsform*, Frankfurt on Main, 1958, and *Kulturpolitik und Ausgabenkontrolle: Zur Theorie und Praxis der Rechnungsprüfung* (with Hellmut Becker), Frankfurt on Main, 1961.

Kluge work.

From the early 1970s onwards, dipping into a Kluge text at random it is often difficult to tell whether one is dealing with 'fiction' or 'theory', as our opening example demonstrated. There is a playful element here, as the footnotes, formulae, diagrams and other pseudo-academic trappings scattered throughout Kluge's *fictions* from the 1970s suggest. Meanwhile the use of illustrations in the fictions simultaneously connotes 'the filmic' — or rather its absence — and thus, dialectically, exposes the limits of literature when it comes, for instance, to capturing a person's physical appearance. At a more serious level, the blurring of the boundaries between fiction and theory — as in the incorporation of essayistic passages in fiction and micro-narratives in theory — embodies Kluge's conviction that subjective and objective, imaginative and cognitive, feelings and concepts, can be compartmentalised only at the cost of distortions. One motive of all Kluge's work is to combat such division at all levels in society; not simply with his ideas but at a formal level — by montage.

This applies, for instance, to the exclusion-mechanisms of the bourgeois public sphere, which determine what is considered 'public' and what 'private', but more fundamentally to the division of labour and resultant uneven development of human faculties legitimated by the former and shown, in its 'lethal consequences', in operation in *Lernprozesse*. In this respect, the book is no less a collection of exemplary case-histories than was *Lebensläufe*. This time, however, the focus is not on the question of the continuities between the Third Reich and the Federal Republic but on 'tradition' in the broader sense as, literally, a process of carrying over values and ideas from one epoch to the next: 'Eine Armada erstklassiger Individualisten in einer Zeit kollektiver Kämpfe' (LP, p. 9).

However, this is too generalised to do justice to the richness and diversity of material that *Lernprozesse* contains, much of which cannot be subsumed under such a heading. The book's themes could also be conceptualised, more precisely though more abstractly, as an exploration of how the epochal phenomenon of 'Sinnentzug' (LP, p. 5), which corresponds to what Habermas terms 'motivation crisis', provokes 'unreasonable' reactions among people, because their 'hunger for meaning' only becomes intensified by the latter's increasing scarcity, as they 'learn' to their cost. The withdrawal symptoms that result are explored in a number of different sites, such as, once again, the Third Reich; modern Frankfurt; organised crime and the police; women; Easter; nuclear war. As always with Kluge, the texts contain paradigmatic resonances too, such as the incorporation of material on Stalingrad as a flashback in the title story. That 'Lernprozesse mit tödlichem Ausgang' marshals a dazzling arsenal of narrative strategies and anti-auratic devices is appropriate, given that the text sets itself the ultimate task: to describe the destruction of the world. But this also serves as a pretext for presenting ideology-criticism in the guise of science-fiction: the hubristic reconstruction of capitalism, this time on a galactic scale, is set against the utopian efforts of the surviving Chinese to rebuild the landscape of the planet. Those who refuse to learn from history are condemned to repeat it, like the four 'survivors' from Stalingrad: the text culminates in the year 2103 with another crisis. *Lernprozesse* also explores motifs, such as time, revenge, labour power, which will be seminal in Kluge's subsequent writing, both fictional and theoretical. Yet, as a corrective to refining Kluge's literary work down to the ideology-criticism of intellectual traditions and the elaboration and testing of his own conceptual categories in various sites, we need to remind ourselves that his narrative *and cognitive* motive in writing stories is to grasp individual experience, however attenuated it may be by the circumstances.

To take an example, instead of, like Habermas, updating Nietzsche's insight into how human reason's critical liquidation of dogmas and illusions culminates not in freedom but in nihilism, what Kluge does is to anthropomorphise this notion in an analogous individual: H., 'der letzte Vertreter der Kritischen Theorie' (LP, p. 199). A conference on 'Science in Change' has been overtaken by events; a crisis has brought the world to the brink of nuclear war. H. has hidden himself away in a basement room in the conference hotel, in order hastily to register his reactions: 'Falls es noch zur Veröffentlichung eines Bändchens kommen wird, wird es folgende Notiz erhalten' (ibid.) — whereupon the text continues with an unacknowledged borrowing from Habermas's own slim volume about crises, *Legitimationsprobleme im Spätkapitalismus* (1973), complete with an appropriate quotation from Nietzsche (maxims from whom are scattered throughout *Lernprozesse*). By contrast, a nuclear physicist, having found a piano in one of the rooms in the hotel, is playing Schubert 'Lieder' to a waitress: 'Die *vielleicht letzten Stunden vor einem Weltende* will Philipps mit einem menschlichen, d.h. musikalischen Interesse verbringen' (LP, p. 195). Unlike Philipps, who seeks out human, sensual contact, H. is imprisoned within abstraction and regards an interruption of his conceptual flow by another human being 'als unerträglichen Zusatz äusserer Realität zur überflutenden inneren' (LP, p. 199, n. 9). Despite Kluge's extreme perspectivism and disrupted chronology, despite his mastery of theoretical and technocratic discourses, what ultimately interests him in 'Projekt: Groß-Weißafrika' is the spectrum of individual responses to the crisis. Even though an individual standpoint and subject is necessarily relativised in a text such as this, it is always there as an implicit criterion. This is true even of the overwhelmingly objectivist first version of *Schlachtbeschreibung*, which interpolates occasional fictional micro-narratives amid the official language-sources: '"In die Erde gekrallt"/G. krallte sich in die Erde, steinhart gefroren, ein Nagel brach. Der Panzer sah zu, überrollte dann den G.' (SB, p. 91). As laconic as a children's rhyme, such a text unflinchingly reproduces the microscopic significance of an individual fate in a catastrophe of the scale of Stalingrad. Yet that it is ultimately individual experience, the life, suffering and death of human beings, that concerns Kluge is symbolised by the fact that, even though this is the only mention of G. in the entire book, he is accorded a place in the 'Personenliste' along with Hitler, von Manstein, Paulus and the other principal actors. At the same time, however, even this micro-narrative embodies the idea underlying *Schlachtbeschreibung* and many of Kluge's other fictions: the 'fatal consequences' of wilfully trying to apply instinctive or obsolete behaviour ('krallte') in an inappropriate environment ('steinhart gefroren') or amid new circumstances ('der Panzer'), instead of surrendering to the logic of the situation and improvising.[5]

By now it should be clear that the difficulties facing the reader of Kluge's texts — which can be rationalised as therapeutic side-effects — are but minor compared to those confronting somebody attempting an overview of his work. Such an enterprise is not merely academic but artificial: the attempt by what Kluge calls 'conceptual imperialists' to elevate themselves, like judges, over a situation and to reduce dynamic process to a static result. Given the scope and complexity of his work and its myriad and mobile interconnections, such an enterprise is almost bound to fail, for, to an even greater extent than with other writers, all readings are provisional — not simply because Kluge's *oeuvre* is work in progress but because it is also organised like a circuit-diagram, which permits an almost

---

5. It is not merely a metaphor that is 'punished' in 'In die Erde gekrallt' but, by implication, an entire literary and ideological tradition (documented elsewhere in *Schlachtbeschreibung*) erected on a pathetic and anthropocentric attitude towards Nature: 'Dieser Dunst der kurländischen Erde ließ mich dumpf spüren, was uns dies Land zu bieten hatte. Ich krallte die Finger in die satte Erde, die mich anzusaugen schien. Diesen Boden hatten wir erobert. Nun forderte er von uns; auf einmal war er uns verpflichtendes Symbol' (Ernst von Salomon, *Die Geächteten* (1930), Hamburg 1962, p. 50).

unlimited number of paths and connections to be pursued. This quality, the way in which elements can be recombined, is not the outcome of using montage as a structuring principle. On the contrary, the latter is demanded by the nature of Kluge's writing process, which corresponds to his description of film-making: 'Es werden enge Realitätsausschnitte, Momentaufnahmen, gebildet und miteinander zu einem Zusammenhang montiert' (GeS, p. 202).

An idea of this process can be gained if we grasp that, even though Kluge rearranges his texts and endlessly transplants passages from one context to another, he does little reworking of the verbal surface of his writing. Indeed he treats his own transplanted texts no differently from the quotations that permeate his books. Such self-borrowings appear to function for Kluge as personal 'documents', in that they register the particular nexus of ideas and experiences that existed at the moment of their composition. Stressing in the foreword to *Neue Geschichten. Hefte 1–18: 'Unheimlichkeit der Zeit'* (1977) that it is not one of his theoretical books (notwithstanding the thematic and formal affinities), Kluge notes that he does not 'correct' errors and misunderstandings that have come into being during the writing process. For the form in which the stories are narrated is 'ein *Gefühl*, das nur einmal mißt, und war es theoretisch [. . .] falsch, dann ist es falsch und mißt so auch' (italics added, NG, p. 9). Retrospectively to rework his stories to emphasise their connections and fit them into an overall scheme would be to succumb to precisely the kind of hierarchical and deductive thinking that Kluge opposes. Despite the above distinction made by Kluge, this applies to his non-fictional writing too. Thus the theoretical 'extracts' included in the volume *Die Patriotin* are taken over almost verbatim into *Geschichte und Eigensinn*, suggesting that the genesis of the latter project too corresponds to the inductive, combinatory technique of film-making, whereby relatively autonomous passages are generated and subsequently assembled into a 'Zusammenhang'.

Thus the stories in *Neue Geschichten* are offered as 'Geschichten ohne Oberbegriff' (ibid.) and arranged in the 'Heften' that correspond to their composition. This entails that clusters of stories that have evident thematic connections with one another are scattered over more than one 'Heft'. As the latter term suggests, the heterogeneous quality of *Neue Geschichten* resembles a collected volume of a periodical — in which some topics take up a whole number, others are followed up over several issues, complete with interviews, pictures, 'captions', and even photo-features — recalling Tretyakov's vision of the newspaper as a modern 'epic'. Once again, the book's content is to be found in its *form*. Consistent with this, if the overall concern of all Kluge's work can be seen as the question of 'Zusammenhang', its literary 'use-value' is to challenge the reader to exercise his or her synthesising skills to establish connections and create an overall context that is subjectively satisfying. This is exactly what Negt and Kluge set out to do in the almost 1,300 pages of *Geschichte und Eigensinn* (1981), which originated as a continuation of *Öffentlichkeit und Erfahrung* but grew to become a fitting theoretical counterpart to the encyclopaedic *Neue Geschichten*. The increased scale of both books is matched by the increased fragmentation and abbreviation of their constituent texts, whose relative autonomy symbolises their narrative and conceptual productivity, which offers innumerable strands for the reader to follow up, associate and connect.

Merely to echo Kluge, however, and collapse the contents of his texts into their forms is to capitulate before the richness of his work, in which sustained arguments and patterns can be seen to evolve over a quarter of a century. The range of subject-matter is immense: war, the Nazi era, Stalingrad, the circus, pre-history, science-fiction, the law, crime, the police, industrial security, prostitution, child-rearing, relationships, nature, the Student Movement, the Frankfurt School, technocracy, as well as Kluge's birthplace, Halberstadt, and the history of his family. This material is explored in a bewildering variety of textual modes: curriculum vitae, dialogue, interview, transcript, letters, verse, quotations (from real and invented sources), diary entries, formulae, footnotes and appendices. Unity is not provided at the level of 'style', for Kluge's writing is not just perspectivist in narrative form but polyphonic in texture. It absorbs a plurality of discourses: from colloquialism to scientific and academic language; from the lapidary sentences of 'In die Erde gekrallt' to intricate conceptualising periods of twenty lines or more. A further element of discontinuity is provided by the quotations from a huge variety of sources that punctuate Kluge's writing: ranging from philosophical texts to songs, official documents to children's verse, scientific works to poetry. Like the documents, and like the illustrations (photographs, paintings, drawings, maps, diagrams, tables, collages and sketches by the author himself), the function of such 'found' elements is, as with Kluge's films, all of which contain unstaged sequences and borrowed visual material, to keep the texts porous, open to reality, instead of trying to create the illusion of an organic and autonomous textual whole. Once again this synthetic quality corresponds to the discontinuities of individual experience in the contemporary world.

It is the aggregate of all these anti-auratic elements that gives

Kluge's texts, in whatever mode, their unmistakable appearance. The eye is assaulted by the breaks in the page layout: sections, subsections, subheadings, interpolated quotations and verses, dialogue, passages in bold type or white on black, passages in boxes, parallel columns of type, as well as ubiquitous footnotes and illustrations. This carefully contrived *visual* quality, which works against the harmonising tendency of prose as a medium, lays bare the mainspring of Kluge's output: 'Der Ausgangspunkt ist nicht eine Idee, sondern ein *Bild*'.[6] This motivates the discontinuous forms of all Kluge's work, for rather than beginning with an abstract notion and deducing a plot or an argument from it, Kluge starts with the concrete — whether a visual image, a quotation or a document — and explores its associations and connections *inductively*, in the writing process, the results of which exploration are subsequently assembled into a text; or, of course, into a film, the cardinal principle of which medium is montage.

Brecht was among those who recognised the inductive lesson that film could teach literature. Like Kluge, he too grasped that 'naive realism' was helpless before the complexity of reality and had to be replaced by 'construction':[7] by montage. The raw material of film is always concrete rather than abstract, and thus the film-making process is not the execution of a preconceived plan but exploratory. Because of what Clausewitz calls 'Reibung',[8] the 'friction' of reality, some element of improvisation is always necessary, in military strategy and film-making alike. This requires a 'passive' attitude on the part of the director: to allow the logic of the content to emerge, rather than trying to impose a linear pattern on it: 'Die Substanz konzentrieren ja, Substanz wegen eines "roten Fadens" wegschieben: nein'.[9] Such a content-centred aesthetic must avoid what the Soviet film-maker Vertov called 'premature synthesis' and rely on 'foreground' devices such as montage, so that the relatively 'passive' film or text can be completed via the resultant gaps by an active viewer or reader, in his or her own head on the basis of his or her own experience. In this respect, what Adorno refers to as the 'emancipation of the material' in a work of art is identical with the emancipation of the person receiving it and, irrespective of the material's ideological tendency, is of evident political significance.

6. Interview with Ulrich Gregor, in *Herzog/Kluge/Straub*, Munich, 1976, p. 154.
7. Cf. Bertolt Brecht, 'Dreigroschenprozeß', in *Gesammelte Werke*, Frankfurt on Main, 1967, vol. xviii, esp. pp. 157, 161–2.
8. Cf. the interviews and other film-theoretical materials in Kluge's *Ulmer Dramaturgien. Reibungsverluste* (with Klaus Eder), Munich, 1980.
9. Alexander Kluge, *Die Artisten in der Zirkuskuppel: ratlos*, Munich, 1968 p. 146.

Kluge explicitly relates his view of realism to the methodology of Marx as outlined in the 1857 Introduction to the *Grundrisse*, where the dialectical movement, beginning with the concrete, moving to the abstract and returning to a now conceptually and relationally saturated concrete, is described. The parallel with Kluge's own working methods in his films and fictions, where the stories are saturated by both 'documented' ideological and his own analytical subtexts, is evident. Indeed the humanistic-utopian Marx of the *Paris Manuscripts* in particular has, especially from the early 1970s onwards, been an endless inspiration for Kluge's work in fiction and also film, not simply for his theory. The affinity is crystallised in the 'filmic' premise, which Kluge quotes repeatedly: 'Die Sinnlichkeit [. . .] muß die Basis aller Wissenschaft sein' (GeS, p. 212). In that both employ radical dialectical techniques of analysis, perspectivism and confrontation to grasp reality in its authentic, complex and antagonistic proportions, the 'film sense' and the 'sociological imagination' of Marxism are one.

However, as Marx says elsewhere, to be sensual is to suffer, which reminds us that for Kluge realism, indeed his work as a whole, is motivated not by an affirmation of reality but by protest (GeS, pp. 187–222): against the various terroristic reality-principles that cause human suffering. It is the collisions between human wishes and reality (history) that are the central concern of his work. While the experimental materials, the case-histories, are yielded by Kluge's fictions, the conceptualisation of this is carried out in his theoretical writings, supremely in *Geschichte und Eigensinn* (1981), which in 'unfinished' texture, form and even format pays homage to the inexhaustible conceptual laboratory of the *Grundrisse*. Yet the relationship between fiction and theory is, like that between experiment and hypothesis, dialectical — to the extent that Kluge toys with ideas, which will later be developed in the latter book with Negt, in fictionalised form in *Neue Geschichten* and in some of the new texts in the 1978 edition of *Schlachtbeschreibung*. This applies not just to the concretisation in narratives of generalised themes such as 'revenge' and its time-scales, but to the elaboration of specific theoretical concepts.

One example is 'Rachegefühl als Freizeitthema', in which three members of the Frankfurt School of Social Research are having a break in a nearby café. The bonus of such an environment is that, not only can they determine their object of study, they can now also work collectively, rather than subject to the academic division of labour. The three colleagues focus on one of the central questions of Marxist debate, but with an emphasis appropriate to *Neue Geschich-*

ten. If the working class is the collective *subject* of societal transformation, in that case, so runs the argument, it is also the carrier of a
'verdichteten Form des Protestgefühls, der Rache' (NG, p. 198).
They launch into a dizzying elaboration of this idea, which culminates in the following passage, which has to be quoted in full:

> Hinrichs, der sich derweil ausgeruht hat, sagt: Nochmal ganz *einfach.*
> Ableitung! Sinnlichkeit ist ein Arbeitsmittel, nicht wahr? Nein, ruft
> Grabbe, ein Rohstoff. Ein Produktionsverhältnis, sagt Putermann. Ich
> meine, sagt Putermann: die Sinne, ich meine die 5 Sinne, Augen, Ohren,
> Nase — Grabbe ruft dazwischen: Zunge! — , Hinrichs: Und dann die
> Hirnsinne, ich zähle davon 15, und die kulturellen Programmsinne . . .
> Grabbe: Oder Kultursinne (gekocht, roh, naturschön, "von Bedeutung"
> usf.). Jetzt ist es wieder kompliziert. Hinrichs sagt: Nochmals ganz
> *einfach.* Putermanns 5 Sinne und meinetwegen noch die Hirnsinne dazu
> als Produkt der Weltgeschichte (etwa 1 Million Jahre). Darauf setzt sich,
> ihr kennt alle die Stellen, die *Sinnlichkeit des Habens* (etwa 800 Jahre).
> Davon koppelt sich ab, und zwar zwingend, die *Sinnlichkeit des Nichthabens*
> (also die Reststücke der Sinne, die nicht ins Haben passen, das
> Quälerische im Haben: der Protest). — Und diese Nichthaben-Sinne
> (ebenfalls ca. 800 Jahre alt, aber in der Masse zehnjährig), also nochmal
> ruhig, fängt Hinrichs neu an, dies zusammengezählt zu Sinnlichkeit
> des Nichthabens bedeutet Rohstoff (Wurzel = Radikalität, die Dinge an
> der Wurzel fassen), Werkzeuge (= Bewegung), daraus entsteht eine
> imaginäre gesellschaftliche Fabrik (Raum, Öffentlichkeit), daraus ge-
> macht: Produktionsverhältnis — und das ist doch "Zeit" (denn das geht
> nicht, daß wir in Nichtzeiten Gefühle produzieren, die brauchen Zeit,
> nehme ich die Zeit weg, nehme ich auch das Gefühl weg). (NG,
> pp. 199–200)

Dialogue has been collapsed into prose to create a labyrinthine
montage. The effect of such a polyphonic passage, which combines
characteristically meticulous punctuation and an equally characteristic refusal to differentiate direct speech from the narrative voice,
depends on the uniformity of the medium of print. As in a musical
score the raw material is provided, with careful notation, to be
activated and articulated by the reader. At an immediate level, the
associative intoxication of the passage shows how intensity of conceptualisation — here embodied in its primary form, as speech —
and intelligibility do not necessarily go hand in hand. Kluge has,
following Adorno, expressed his suspicion of a spurious and atomis-
ing clarity because it wilfully reduces the real antagonistic complexity of reality. Instead he has endorsed the subversive, anti-
systematic cognitive strategies of 'essayism' advocated by his
mentor.[10] At the same time, the fundamentalist Marxism — the
footnote reference is to the *Paris Manuscripts* — and the presence of

categories such as 'Sinnlichkeit', 'Protest', 'Öffentlichkeit', 'Zeit' and 'Gefühle', all of which are central in Kluge's theoretical work, makes such a passage self-reflexive too. Yet in its elliptical over-complexity, which Hinrichs repeatedly tries to bring under some control, it is also grotesque. For here this quality derives as much from the fact that the three colleagues are failing to cooperate. As a result, form overrides even content as 'progressive' as that here — a recurrent theme in the texts on the Student Movement elsewhere in *Neue Geschichten*. To underline this, also present in the café, though not a full member of this 'Politbüro' (NG, p. 200), is Putermann's girlfriend, to whom he allots time '"wie auf Lebensmittelkarte"' (NG, p. 197). The irony is that while the three 'experts' are discussing protest, revenge and how lack of time destroys human feeling, Billie Dahmert is *experiencing* precisely these sensations towards Putermann, whose conceptual authoritarianism is mirrored in his conduct of personal relationships. Revenge is taken in the paragraph that follows, which dismantles several of the key concepts from Billie's point of view: '*Gefühle* hatte sie immer, insbesondere das des Nichthabens im Hinblick auf Putermann' (NG, p. 200). If a concept is to be alive, it must be tested against lived experience. As Kluge's films in particular repeatedly affirm, it is no accident that reified, technocratic thinking is identified with the male and concrete ex-perience and sensuality with the female. However, the story as a whole endorses the categories that it is satirising in the mouths of Putermann and his colleagues because it depicts why his relation-ship with Billie is doomed to failure: 'Unheimlichkeit der Zeit'. Putermann's reaction to a speculative comment by Grabbe signals the end of the coffee break: 'Das ist eine Hypothese, sagte Puter-mann übergangslos' (NG, p. 202). The time for associative phantasy is over; the reality-principle of compartmentalised positivistic social science has been reasserted. But Kluge does not state this in the text, preferring to use association himself. Immediately beneath, there is a wartime photograph of a railway bridge, the central section of which has been completely destroyed — the product of 'revenge'? — leaving the tracks dangling into the river. The point of the story is concretised in a visual image: in the prevailing circumstances, no bridging 'Übergang' is possible, between the 'leisure' and work interests of the three men, between private and professional, cooper-ation and specialisation, experience and theory.

An extreme example of this increasing interplay between word

---

10. Cf. Theodor W. Adorno, 'The Essay as Form', *New German Critique* 32 (Spring-Summer 1984), pp. 151–71.

and image in Kluge's writing, is to be found in the 1978 edition of *Schlachtbeschreibung*. '"Die Wünsche [. . .] sind um 1200 etwas sehr Einfaches"' is the most discontinuous text Kluge has so far produced; of its twenty pages, no fewer than ten are taken up with illustrations. These range from medieval pictures, photographs, paintings, illustrations from the Nazi era, to a frame of a modern comic strip. Of the remaining pages, roughly half comprise quotations, including the Grimms' 'Märchen', Michelet, Karl Korsch and a textbook on administrative law. Virtually each passage introduces a new point of view, and there are only residual 'characters'. Wieland's appearance at the outset is, however, crucial, for the text is motivated by the question of how he and thousands of other German soldiers like him came to die at Stalingrad.

The opening section of '"Die Wünsche . . ."' consists simply of two pictures, separated by a brief quotation. The first shows the reality of Germany in the Middle Ages: peasants harvesting, their backs bent with toil. This is followed by the quotation from Karl Korsch from which the title is taken: '"Die Wünsche, die sich in Bewegung setzen, daß einer marschiert, sich töten läßt, sind um 1200 etwas sehr Einfaches . . ."' (SB, p. 300). There follows a painting of a medieval monastery, the embodiment of such wishes. In the next section the narrative proper begins and associates the motifs of marching and wishing with Stalingrad, before moving on to a telescoped account of the history of Wieland's family since the late Middle Ages. Like the 'Lebenslauf' principle in Kluge's first collection, the compression is not merely a shock tactic but a way of making connections that would otherwise be invisible.

Accordingly the rest of '"Die Wünsche . . ."' moves backwards and forwards across hundreds of years. The next passage describes an autopsy performed on a frozen corpse, in which the surgeons are unable to find any trace of 'wishes' or the '"Protest, der nach Stalingrad in Marsch setzt"' (SB, p. 302). With a photograph of a dead German officer as a 'bridge', the perspective switches back to the Middle Ages and the wretched existence of the common people that was the original matrix of such wishes. A Grimm tale about a giant who dared to resist Death himself is followed by a cluster of aphoristic accounts, accompanied by photographs or idealised paintings, of exceptional individual feats during the Second World War. After a densely associative and elliptical theoretical passage on Korsch's theory of 'Blitzkrieg', the perspective reverts yet again to the Middle Ages, with a series of quotations from various sources depicting the expropriation of the peasantry, the betrayal of the epic hero Roland, the peasants' unfounded faith in the Emperor, and the death of Barbarossa after recklessly bathing in the icy waters of a river. 'Barbarossa', the Nazi code-name for the Eastern Campaign, along with blindness to danger and the motif of cold, enable us to associate back to Stalingrad.

One of Kluge's emphases in this text is that we should treat the subjective factor seriously. This includes not only the wishes of individuals but their aggregated form in legends and folk-tales, which are characterised by being ' "mehrdeutig, 'kompakt' [. . .] Einerseits erzählen sie uns über Ereignisse, über Taten und Erlebnisse als Symbole" ' (SB, p. 316, n. 3). These very qualities, compactness, multiple meanings, the symbolic element, characterise Kluge's fictions too.

The final section of ' "Die Wünsche . . ." ' is, typically for Kluge, not an attempt to synthesise and subsume the preceding materials under an 'Oberbegriff' and achieve closure. Instead he tries to push his new interpretation of Stalingrad further. The section opens with a reproduction of Karl Friedrich Schinkel's famous 'Dom über einer Stadt': the apotheosis of the Romantics' idealised image of medieval Germany, painted in the year of liberation from Napoleon, 1813. To it Kluge appends the 'caption': 'Der "Reichs-Gedanke", ein Marsch in Widersprüchen. "Es lebe unser heiliges Deutschland!", ruft Stauffenberg [. . .] als er erschossen wird' (SB, p. 318). In the elliptical and somewhat opaque micro-essay that closes ' "Die Wünsche . . ." ', Kluge argues that, as Stalingrad proved, this 'idea' was a mere formal construct that exploited real human needs and wishes and rested, ultimately, on 'Einbildung' (illusion). Once again the point is delivered most vividly by an association from this, the last word of the text (which contains the idea of 'Bild'), to a visual image. A comic strip shows Hitler and his generals watching through binoculars a successful air attack on an armoured division. Hitler *imagines* this to be the work of the *Luftwaffe* but is corrected by Guderian: 'Nein, mein Führer, das waren unsere Panzer!' (SB, p. 320). However Kluge, having scored with an open goal in front of him, does not leave the matter there. Instead, operating like Ernst Bloch with a dialectical rather than rationalistic concept of ideology, he recognises that people succumb to such 'Einbildung' because it corresponds to real needs within them; and so he appends a qualifying footnote: 'Das "versteht", wer das Reich nicht braucht, weil er nicht in Not ist' (SB, p. 320, n. 3). Otherwise Stauffenberg's last words would, like the peasantry's faith in the Emperor, be incomprehensible.

To produce even such a marginally coherent account of ' "Die Wünsche . . ." ' we have had to abstract from its dense surfaces and antagonistic materials. These include anticipations of future projects. Thus a breathless footnote attributed to 'Korsch' contains a skeletal outline of one of the main arguments underlying *Geschichte und Eigensinn*. Other materials will find their way into *Die Patriotin*: Wieland is the former owner of the film's knee-narrator. The reader ignorant of the rest of Kluge's work may find the components of '"Die Wünsche . . ."' and their juxtapositions intriguing, but would almost certainly be bewildered if he or she tried to make sense of the text as a whole. Although Kluge warns against the latter objective of closure, however much a writer counterpoints verbal and visual discourses and uses fragmenting devices, the reading process is still, necessarily, linear. In that they contain the seeds of future projects, a 'generative' quality is a feature of all Kluge's texts and films. Yet '"Die Wünsche . . ."' goes so far in this direction as to jeopardise its communicative ability, irrespective of whether we try to grasp it as fiction, essay or as mixed-media hybrid of the two. At one level this text is an ultimately private production-process: a laboratory that manufactures motifs and embryonic arguments by confronting found (visual and textual) materials with one another and fusing them with fictional fragments. Yet from another perspective, in the demands it makes on our synthesising capacity and associative phantasy, it is a logical extension of Kluge's 'homeopathic' shock tactics: an assignment for advanced readers. '"Die Wünsche . . ."' also corresponds to the genesis and texture of Kluge's films: by its unfinished and improvisatory quality; its mingling of time-scales in the continuous present of the text ('Jetztzeit'); its use of montage as an organising principle; its confrontation of fictional and documentary materials; its play with text and image and their interactions; and, above all, by its inductive, exploratory momentum. It is to Kluge as film-maker that we must now return.

The persistent early categorisations of Kluge as a film-maker who also occasionally writes fiction have proved inadequate. What is interesting about his more recent fiction is precisely the way in which it has, relatively speaking, begun to emancipate itself from his work in the cinema. The astonishing formal and thematic diversity of *Neue Geschichten* suggests that Kluge has discovered for himself the specificity of literary production. He came to this point not by overcoming his initial scepticism of literature but, typically, by pushing it to its limits (*Schlachtbeschreibung*) and drawing the necessary conclusions in order to revitalise his writing. It was precisely the vast, largely unrealised — and hence 'utopian' — productivity of the cinema glimpsed by Kluge during the early 1960s that simultaneously brought into focus the changed circumstances of literary production and reception. He endorses not only Brecht's contention that people who see films read *and write* (or should write) differently, but also Benjamin's argument that the cinema corresponds to a new stage in the development of human sensibility. Expressed in its most radicalised form: if the latter challenge is met, the substance of a thousand pages or more (Proust) should be contained in a short story of no more than one or two pages. Kluge does not hold this up as a serious criterion but to dramatise how the writer, like the film-maker, must ceaselessly reflect on questions of form. For Kluge, all rules and conventions represent a reduction of human experience and complexity. Accordingly, realism is for him not an imperishable mode, as with Lukács, but a motive and a goal that, as with Brecht, demands constant reassessment.

A recurring motif in Kluge's work is the inability, or refusal, of individuals to 'see', to trust in the concrete evidence of their senses — the 'basis of all knowledge' — and their reliance instead on abstract preconceptions or illusions. This is the common situation of Hitler in '"Die Wünsche . . ."', the Sociologist H. in 'Projekt: Groß-Weißafrika' — who is 'blind, da man das Blicken auf geweißte Kellerwände nicht als "Sehen" bezeichnen kann' (LP, p. 199) — the army command at Stalingrad and the bomber-crews that attacked Halberstadt. That the latter are described as 'eine Justiz im Anflug' (NG, p. 63) reminds us that it was precisely the 'blindness' of the law, its imperviousness to concrete human experience, its hierarchical, deductive and abstract nature, that first stimulated Kluge to turn to the cinema. As this suggests, the cinema is, for Kluge's work, neither merely a repertoire of formal devices nor simply a criterion against which literature's potential is to be determined, but something approximating to both a cognitive ideal and, even, a scale of ethical values. The 'Utopie Film', which Kluge has constantly kept in sight, despite setbacks and disappointments in his own film practice, thus embodies not only a vision of what the cinema could be like but, simultaneously, the belief that the cinema's potential itself signals a utopia in a wider sense: not a concrete vision of a better society, but a model of social and historical understanding that Kluge tries to embody in his own works and methods. This is because film is, by its nature, concrete, cooperative, dynamic and dialectical and has, as the early Soviet film-makers admired by Kluge recognised, the capacity to transcend the boundaries of space and time and assemble vast quantities of disparate material. If this 'constructivist realism' corresponds to Marx's method, the camera-eye is cognate with Benjamin's historical materialist vantage-point,[11] as Kluge makes explicit:

Sehe ich eine Stadt wie z.B. Mainz von dem Beobachterstandpunkt des geschichtlichen Blicks, so rücken keltische Gründung, römische Prägung, mittelalterliches Mainz, Besetzung durch die französischen Revolutionsarmeen, Resurrektion der Revolutions-Umzüge im späteren Mainzer Karneval, preußische Amtsgebäude und Bahnhof, Bombardierung im Zweiten Weltkrieg, Wiederaufbau und industrielle Veränderung zu jener *Bewegung* zusammen, die geschichtlich-wirklich stattfindet. Ich sehe das als *Film*. (GuE, p. 719)

In the light of this it would be reductive and undialectical simply to regard film as the formal parameter of Kluge's work and history as its content. As was already suggested by *Brutalität in Stein*, it is the potential for simultaneity inherent in film that enables the presentation (and perception?) of history as 'Jetztzeit' — the film/history nexus is already present in Benjamin's work — as the aggregate of all past moments in the present, albeit in the form of ruins. Returning now to the phylogenetic perspective with which we began will bring into focus what we have called the ethical dimension of Kluge's film utopia. For Kluge, one of the strongest arguments in favour of film is not that the sensuality of its images is immediate, though, despite the role of the apparatus, film is less abstract than literary language; but, rather, that the images of film have a correlative in the image-making capacity of human memory and imagination. This lends film a 'natural', essential dimension that print, as a symbolic medium, can never have. At the same time, film can not only overcome the artificial compartmentalisation of time into past, present and future, it can also, by means of the associations that its images evoke in the viewer, overcome the no less artificial boundaries between subjective and objective. Kluge's radical displacements of 'normal' chronological sequence (interruption, confusion, acceleration), together with his intensified use of images since the 1970s, are both attempts to appropriate such properties of the cinema for his texts. No less significant, however, is the fact that what film as a medium has the capacity to create, in other words Marx's 'rich totality of many determinations and relations',[12] corresponds to the method and *political-ethical* interest of *Geschichte und Eigensinn*: namely 'Zusammenhang', which can be understood as a

11. According to Benjamin, the historical materialist 'stops telling the sequence of events like the beads of a rosary. Instead, he grasps the constellation which his own era has formed with a definite earlier one. Thus he establishes a conception of the present as the "time of the now" [*Jetztzeit*] which is shot through with chips of Messianic time', 'Theses on the Philosophy of History', in *Illuminations*, London, 1970, p. 265.
12. Karl Marx, *Grundrisse*, London, 1973, p. 100.

sense of totality, meaningful interconnectedness, achieved by human labour. Such totality is not a natural product but requires assembly (montage!) of dispersed and fragmentary materials to overcome the compartmentalisations of capitalist society, although the book's argument also incorporates, as a critical criterion, an essentialist utopia of 'natural' self-regulation. Reconstructing the process whereby Kluge arrived at such a position will also bring into focus how the stages of his thinking correspond to the changing preoccupations of the left in the Federal Republic.

In the early 1960s, like many other intellectuals, Kluge was heavily under the influence of Adorno's pessimistic view of Western society — a pessimism largely motivated by the barbarisms of the Nazi past. Against the background of the Eichmann trial in Jerusalem and the controversy unleashed by the appearance of Fritz Fischer's reinterpretation of German aims in the First World War (both in 1961), an exploration of the explosive question of the relationship between the Third Reich and the Federal Republic was the main impulse underlying Kluge's first collection of fictions, *Lebensläufe*. This question of 'tradition' was then projected further backwards in history in *Schlachtbeschreibung*, to uncover the origins of the catastrophe of Stalingrad: 'Die Ursachen liegen 30 Tage oder 300 Jahre zurück'.[13] A content-oriented view of Kluge as historian makes his first two books seem very much a product of the climate of the time and difficult to relate to his subsequent work. However, we should recall that the other component of Adorno's pessimism, intensified by his experiences in American exile, was motivated by his sense of the liquidation of the individual not just physically, as in Auschwitz, but also culturally and experientially, in the bureaucratic and technocratic organisational forms of work and leisure in modern industrial society. Indeed this question of 'organisation' is just as much a concern of Kluge's as the question of tradition in his first two books, which accounts for the way in which he uses not just compressed narrative (the 'Lebenslauf' model) but also classification to structure his material, employing the latter to bring out the complementary synchronic fragmentation of human experience. In both *Lebensläufe* and even more so in *Schlachtbeschreibung*, individuals were shown to be overwhelmed by the sheer weight of objective forces, the recipe for survival being a cynical pragmatism. In the climate of the CDU-state it is understandable that for signs of hope Kluge had to look to the abstract cultural utopia of the cinema.

The window of history opened by the Student Movement in the

13. Alexander Kluge, *Schlachtbeschreibung*, Olten, 1964, p. 7.

late 1960s was closed again all too swiftly, but not before it had let in a glimpse of concrete utopia and left a dual creative residue of collective experiences of protest on the one hand and of revitalised Marxist theory on the other. After the initial euphoria had evaporated it was clear that the *political* task was to fashion a storehouse of strategy on which the disorientated left could draw. *Öffentlichkeit und Erfahrung* tackled the previously reified question of organisation head on by challenging the hierarchies and divisions of capitalist society in general, and the commodified offerings of the consciousness industry in particular, with a utopian vision of cultural revolution 'from below' energised by a cooperative alliance of subdominant human faculties which had hitherto escaped absorption. The closing sentence of the book outlines the project that would be taken up by the German left throughout the 1970s, though increasingly motivated by melancholy rather than hope: 'Proletarische Öffentlichkeit ist der Name für einen gesellschaftlichen kollektiven Produktionsprozeß, dessen Gegenstand *zusammenhängende* menschliche *Sinnlichkeit* ist' (italics added, ÖuE, p. 486 n. 3). This assertive, confident tone, to be found throughout *Öffentlichkeit und Erfahrung*, was obsolete by the time the book appeared in 1972, the year of the 'Radikalenerlaß'.

With hindsight, the satirical exaggerations of *Lernprozesse* seem more 'realistic'. At one level, most of the stories still depict individuals as victims. If profession was a central category in *Lebensläufe*, this is here narrowed to the work-process itself. Bureaucracy, the law and the Prussian military tradition now take second place to an even more potent instrument of dehumanisation: capitalism itself and the division of labour on which it rests. Whereas the human carriers of deductive, hierarchical and abstract intellectual traditions are, consistent with Kluge's earlier work, still pilloried in *Lernprozesse*, he also concretises themes from *Öffentlichkeit und Erfahrung*. These include the consequences for individuals of the compartmentalisation of time, of the overdevelopment of those human faculties that can be exploited in the work-process, and of the increasing alienation of the worker from his or her product. Kluge's characters react to the latter phenomenon not 'realistically', with resignation, but, clinging to increasingly redundant artisanal notions of perfectionism and satisfaction, with protest. The experience of 'Sinnentzug' provokes a desire for revenge, even though these are — in a phrase from *Öffentlichkeit und Erfahrung* that provides the title of one of the stories — 'Ausbruchsversuche innerhalb der Gefängnismauern'. However the political problem of mobilising the necessary energies remains. The two welders of this story are too drained by the work-process for any initiative: they ram the brick wall the truck they have stolen is facing eight times before making their escape, on foot. Indeed *Lernprozesse* as a whole is a compelling amalgam of Marxist analysis of monopoly capitalism and its human costs on the one hand and Nietzschean nihilism on the other, with the two dimensions fused — with the help of Musil's prophetic sketch of motivation crisis, 'Der deutsche Mensch als Symptom' — in the title story. Even though the dimension of protest is more strongly present than in either of Kluge's two previous fictional works, it still awaits full conceptualisation. It is, significantly, asserted more vigorously in the sensual medium of film, where it is identified with the female protagonists who predominate in Kluge's individual features. The opening words of *Gelegenheitsarbeit einer Sklavin* go further: 'Roswitha fühlt in sich eine ungeheure Kraft, aber sie weiß aus Filmen, daß es diese Kraft auch wirklich gibt' (GeS, p. 143). The 'Utopie Film' is now allied with a perspective, stimulated in part by the rise of the New Women's Movement during the 1970s, that women are the more likely carriers of resistance in our society. This is because, Kluge argues, their specific socialisation and subsequent separation from the production-process through being in the home has enabled them to preserve rudiments of a pre-capitalist mode of production based on human need and use-value. This is manifested most vividly in child-rearing, as *Gelegenheitsarbeit einer Sklavin* depicts; though the fact that Roswitha has to perform abortions to support her family at the same time symbolises the grotesque anomalies of the existing system.

What exactly is being distorted? Not some essential 'human nature' to which we can return but the full development of human potential outlined in the *Paris Manuscripts*: something yet to be discovered rather than something that has been lost. From the 1970s onwards the humanist early Marx is enlisted by Kluge to put the 'Utopie Film' on a materialist footing. This is brought out particularly clearly in his next feature, *In Gefahr und größter Not bringt der Mittelweg den Tod* (1974). The moment of radicalism is already embodied in the title, and underscored by the fact that, whereas Nietzsche provided the grace-notes throughout *Lernprozesse*, here the tone is set by quotations from early Marx — not only 'Sinnlichkeit ist die Basis aller Wissenschaft' but also another precept that crystallises Kluge's project of critical realism in the dynamic and dialectical medium of the cinema: 'Man muß den versteinerten Dingen ihre eigene Melodie vorspielen, um sie zum Tanzen zu bringen'.[14] Indeed in the notes accompanying the script of *In Gefahr und größter Not bringt der Mittelweg den Tod* the goal of film is now defined as the production of 'Sinnlichkeit des Zusammenhangs' (GeS, pp. 212–14),[15] which is what is required to satisfy human 'hunger for meaning' in a world as reified and contradictory as our own.

Kluge's first two fictional works generally depicted the triumph of the objective — organisation, the law, German history — over real human needs. In *Lernprozesse* this analysis of the objective was assimilated to an account of capitalism, whereby the human labour that the latter exploited was shown to contain an element of resistance, however 'unrealistic'. For Kluge such rejection of an inhuman reality principle is the only humanly realistic course of action. His recurrent recourse to childhood, the irrational, the surreal, embodies not just a moment of protest but also, more fundamentally, the conviction that the subjective and imaginary are at least as important as, and inseparable from, the objective and the real: 'Es gibt nichts Objektives ohne die Gefühle, Handlungen, Wünsche, d.h. Augen und Sinne von Menschen, die handeln' (DP, p. 41). In keeping with his intellectual roots in the Frankfurt School, from the mid-1970s Kluge now increasingly enlists Freud as well as Marx. The historical dimension in his fictions was always allied with the life-historical; the intersections between the two dimensions were manifested as 'breaks' in the 'Lebenslauf' of a character. However, in keeping with Kluge's initial pessimism, the objective was shown generally to overwhelm the subjective.

From *Öffentlichkeit und Erfahrung* there was a growing sense of human agency as a factor, but in *Lernprozesse* individuals' energies were still generally misdirected, though the origins and the ultimate goal of such energies were recognised: '"Glück ist die Erfüllung eines Kinderwunsches". Arbeit ist das, was den Zustand des Kinderwunsches wiederherstellt' (LP, p. 163). Even security expert Ferdinand Rieche in *Lernprozesse* is driven by a longing for childhood, to recapture which he would sacrifice everything. But the longing is illusory. Four years later, in a story in *Neue Geschichten*, Kluge gives the quotation from Freud in full: '"Glück ist die Erfüllung eines Kinderwunsches, aber der Satz ist nicht umkehrbar. Die Wünsche sind nicht kinderglück"' (NG, p. 399). The same point is underlined in the powerful and programmatic opening image of *Neue Geschichten*: a double-page photograph of a mother holding her baby at the instant after birth. The caption is a quotation

---

14. Quoted in, Alexander Kluge and Edgar Reitz, 'In Gefahr und größter Not bringt der Mittelweg den Tod', *Kursbuch* 41 (September 1975), p. 45.
15. See also Kluge and Reitz, 'In Gefahr', p. 66.

from Georg Groddeck : '"Da ist eine Mutter, in deren Leib hat man 9 Monate gesessen, sorglos, warm und in allen Freuden"' — to which Kluge has appended the lapidary comment 'ideologisch' (NG, p. 13). Why is this 'ideological'? Because the dream of regression cannot be fulfilled; there is no going back to childhood. In its place Kluge holds up a utopia of constructive labour in the world to create 'Sinnlichkeit des Zusammenhangs': labour motivated by this primal experience of separation, the ultimate source of human wishes and longing. The key concept in Kluge's writing henceforth becomes Marx's ontological notion of 'work' — defined in the widest possible sense — as human self-production. The boundless potentiality and diversity of people and their wishes is symbolised in the opening story of *Neue Geschichten*, where an engineer states that an attempt to reproduce in mechanical terms the faculties of a single human being would cover the entire planet. Thus even 'inhuman' organisational forms, such as the law, the army, the concentration camp, are *products* of human labour as well as destroyers of it. Accordingly, Kluge now focuses less on the human costs of capitalism than on those human faculties and experiences that helped to bring capitalism about. This results in a drastic lengthening of historical perspective. Writing about the development of 'Strategie von oben' in 'Der Luftangriff auf Halberstadt am 8. April 1945' in which Kluge's family home was destroyed, he notes:

Damals waren Gedankengänge das Maß, die auf Trenchard zurückgehen, der wiederum Verdun-Erfahrung hat, selber aus der Kavallerie hervorgegangen, die auf Hannibal zurückgeht, der wieder aufnimmt, was frühe Baumkletterer in der Gattungsgeschichte veranlaßt hat, nahrhafte Amnioten-Eier übergrosser Saurier zu finden, von unten oder von der Seite die Schale aufzubeißen und entweder die Brut dort hineinzuverlegen oder sie für sich selber auszusaugen. (NG, pp. 64–5).

At the same time such a passage, whose compressed chronology is once again not just a literary effect but heuristic, is an extrapolation of the 'Lebenslauf' principle to take in a phylogenetic dimension. Similarly, the historical perspective is lengthened in the new edition of *Schlachtbeschreibung*, where, instead of 300 years, the causes of the disaster are now traced back 800 years in German history: in other words long before the emergence of the Prussian military and philosophical (Kantian) tradition. Kluge now revises his earlier interpretation and rejects the idea that Paulus's Sixth Army was a machine, an instrument of the High Command. What made 300,000 men march to Stalingrad was *their own* 'Arbeitskraft, Hoffnungen,

Vertrauen' (SB, p. 8). This was not, despite appearances, an abstract organisation held together only 'from above': they themselves were the organisation. Kluge's view of Stalingrad has changed precisely because he has followed through the logic of Marx's idea of work as human self-production. For work transforms not only its object, Nature, but also its subject, man. Consequently, if man is what he has made, his past is 'sinnlich' present in the products of his labour: 'Man sieht, wie die Geschichte der *Industrie* und das gewordene *gegenständliche* Dasein der Industrie das *aufgeschlagene* Buch der *menschlichen Bewußtseinskräfte*, die sinnliche vorliegende menschliche *Psychologie* ist . . .' (NG, p. 103). This seminal quotation from the *Paris Manuscripts* is appended, as a 'caption', to a photograph of the ruins of Halberstadt after the bombing-raid: but it applies just as much to Stalingrad, which was equally a product of misdirected labour and 'powers of human consciousness'. 'In solche Not kann nicht *die Natur* bringen' (italics added, SB, p. 9): the question to which Kluge now turns, is what experiences in history could have brought about such a misdirection?

The urgency of this question was intensified by the traumatic events of the 'deutsche Herbst' of 1977, which has been seen as the most serious crisis of legitimacy in the Federal Republic's history. Although Kluge responded almost immediately, in the shape of the collective film *Deutschland im Herbst* (1978), the crisis moved him to throw his energies into a radical interrogation of German history for the second time in his career. This *political* motive now became intermeshed with the phylogenetic perspective on human wishes and faculties that was beginning to developed in *Neue Geschichten*. If Germany's problematic relation to its past is thematised in the film *Die Patriotin* (1979), by means of the 'archaeological' activities of the history teacher Gabi Teichert, the theoretical elaboration of how such a past could have come about, and much else besides, is provided in the epic *Geschichte und Eigensinn*. Kluge's second book with Negt is offered as nothing less than a counterpart of Marx's political economy of capital (the logic of the 'enemy'): a study of the genesis and structure of labour power itself. Negt and Kluge's starting-point is Marx's insight, in the *Grundrisse*, that the historial process is not the result of capital but the latter's precondition. Unlike structural approaches, which in part underlay both *Öffentlichkeit und Erfahrung* and *Lernprozesse*, a historical approach does not simply accept what exists as its object of knowledge but sets out to interrogate the process whereby such a status quo should have come about rather than another. This immediately sets free, in the unrealised potential thereby uncovered, a moment of change.

Against the dispiriting objectivity and weight of German history, Negt and Kluge set 'die einzelnen Eigenschaften, die in diesem Geschichtsprodukt *arbeiten*' (italics added, DP, p. 355). Work is not only a dialectical category, combining subjective and objective, process and product, it also embodies transformation and, therefore, diachrony.

Negt and Kluge draw attention to the utopian energies that have accumulated in German history by identifying which faculties have been underemployed and which dominant: the latter including, notably, the 'Unerbittlichkeit' they detect in the 'deutsche Herbst' on both sides, the state and the Stammheim inmates, as well as in Kant's moral absolutism. This particular faculty is traced back to the experience of 'Trennung', which signifies both division and separation, and on which the argument of *Geschichte und Eigensinn* rests. What is peculiar to German history, Negt and Kluge argue, is that the experience of primary accumulation, whereby peasants were expropriated and thus separated from their (natural) means of production, the land, is not simply a phase but a permanent experience. Aggregated over generations, as in Wieland's family, this has led to an overdevelopment, to an irrational and destructive degree, of the faculty of relentlessness. Means have become elevated to ends for which people are prepared to sacrifice themselves: the supreme symbol of this is, for Kluge, Stalingrad. One consequence has been the phenomenon, intrinsic to capitalism everywhere, of the division of human senses and faculties into those that can be utilised in commodity production and those that cannot and hence remain undeveloped. In particular since modernisation began, the confluence of these two levels of 'Trennung' led to a hypertrophy of those tendencies that have propelled the catastrophes of recent German history. Against this static, bleak and 'abstract' legacy Negt and Kluge set a dynamic, 'cinematic' and sensual utopia of 'Zusammen-hang' that is foreshadowed in the montage forms and encyclopaedic scope of *Geschichte und Eigensinn* itself. Precisely by radicalising their historical perspective beyond the time-span of the German 'tradition' back to the origins of capitalism and beyond, Negt and Kluge can evoke a vision of self-regulation and the full development of all human faculties: 'Nicht nur die menschliche Sinnlichkeit wird geboren durch den anderen Menschen, sondern auch die einzelnen Sinne gewinnen ihre spezifische Eigenschaft als menschliche Sinne durch die Arbeit der *anderen* Sinne. Die Isolierung voneinander macht die Monstren' (GuE, p. 724).

Albeit with vastly greater conceptual range and sophistication, *Geschichte und Eigensinn* is essentially continuing the project that

Kluge first began two decades previously in *Lebensläufe*. This hinges on the axiom that 'neither the life of an individual nor the history of a society can be understood without understanding both'.[16] What is more, the overall shape of *Geschichte und Eigensinn*, as well as its associative texture, corresponds to the underlying concerns of Kluge's work as a whole, in particular his fictions:

> Ein Mensch hat eine Geschichte, d.h. er kollidiert mit der Geschichte. Er wird aus einem persönlichen Lebenskreis hervorgeboren, entwickelt in dieser Form seine Sinne, Wünsche, Organe der Erfahrung; die Anwendung dieser Eigenschaften erfolgt später unter Verhältnissen, die von Versachlichung und Verdinglichung bestimmt sind. Alle diese Formen der Konfrontation von eigentlich zwei Lebensweisen [. . .] bilden den individuellen *Lebenslauf*. Dies ist *die primäre Geschichte, wie sie Menschen erleben*. (GuE, pp. 782–3)

The three sections of *Geschichte und Eigensinn* correspond to this model: the subjective dimension (the genesis of human faculties); the objective dimension (the movement of German history); and their interaction in specific 'Zusammenhänge' or sites (war, human relationships). This mirrors the mechanism of Kluge's fiction, which examines precisely this collision between human energies and reified social and historical realities in the shape of specific exemplary stories — 'Zusammenhänge'. At the same time, to recall the utopian element in the latter category, it is only within such concrete, subjective–objective sites of conflict that the goal of a meaningfully integrated context can ultimately be achieved.

To construct a sense of meaningful interconnectedness out of the fragments we are offered is the challenge we face when reading Kluge's texts. What characterise his writing are the interactions within a text and between texts. As a result one feels that one is repeatedly describing how Kluge's texts work rather than coming to grips with their substance. For Kluge, however, the way a text works *is* the essential part of its substance. To grasp this, we need a more fluid concept than that of dialectic: 'Sobald man vom *Prozeß* und nicht von den bezahlten Resultaten her beobachtet, ergeben sich *Kreisläufe* und vollständige Wechselwirkung' (italics added, GuE, p. 229). This holistic category of 'Kreislauf' is not only fundamental to *Geschichte und Eigensinn*, as the embodiment of an essentialist utopia of self-regulation and dynamism, it also describes the method of the book, which is in a state of perpetual motion. Materials and categories are brought together to yield new thematic and conceptual

16. C. Wright Mills, *The Sociological Imagination*, Harmondsworth, 1970, p. 9.

constellations, in such a way that 'alle Bewegung wieder zu Rohstoff wird' (DP, p. 366). This is, at the same time, an accurate definition of how, at the level of both text and *oeuvre*, Kluge's writing works. If the latter is allowed to interact with our own experience and imagination, as the gaps and breaks enable it to do, the result is a subjective–objective 'Kreislauf'. Despite the common root, this is not easy (for us) to reconcile with the necessarily linear category of a finite human 'Lebenslauf', which Kluge describes in paradoxical fashion as a 'Kreislauf, der sich nicht schließt' (GuE, p. 253). This contradiction can be resolved if in place of the egocentrism of seeing our lives as individual narratives with a beginning and an end, we are prepared to surrender to the flow of generations, the carriers of the flow of history. Our quarrelsome, compartmentalising minds may have striven to deny our interconnectedness, with fatal consequences for ourselves and our planet, but our bodies know.

Author's Note

The following editions and abbreviations are used for Kluge's works: (place of publication is Frankfurt on Main unless otherwise indicated):

DP = *Die Patriotin, Texte/Bilder 1–6*, 1979
GeS = *Gelegenheitsarbeit einer Sklavin. Zur realistischen Methode*, 1975
GuE = *Geschichte und Eigensinn* (with Oskar Negt), 1981
LP = *Lernprozesse mit tödlichem Ausgang*, 1973
NG = *Neue Geschichten. Hefte 1–18: 'Unheimlichkeit der Zeit'*, 1977
ÖuE = *Öffentlichkeit und Erfahrung. Zur Organisationsanalyse von bürgerlicher und proletarischer Öffentlichkeit* (with Oskar Negt), 1972
SB = *Schlachtbeschreibung: Der organisatorische Aufbau eines Unglücks* (augmented edn), Munich, 1978

Also note:

Lebensläufe. Anwesenheitsliste für eine Beerdigung (augmented edn), 1974
Die Macht der Gefühle, 1984
Theodor Fontane, Heinrich von Kleist und Anna Wilde: Zur Grammatik der Zeit, W. Berlin, 1987

Alexander Kluge

Suggested Further Reading

While the majority of the analyses of Kluge's work are contained in literary magazines and periodicals, some of the most useful studies are to be found in two collections of essays, both of which include detailed bibliographies. Especially recommended are the essays by Thomas Böhm-Christl (on *Neue Geschichten*) and the two by Rainer Stollmann (on 'Massensterben in Venedig' and on Kluge and realism) in the first volume, and the pieces by Stollmann (on the Negt/Kluge collaboration) and Anton Kaes (on *Die Patriotin*) in the second:

Thomas Böhm-Christl (ed.), *Alexander Kluge*, Frankfurt on Main, 1983
H.L. Arnold (ed.), *Alexander Kluge*, *Text und Kritik*, Munich, 1985

See also:

Hanno Beth, 'Alexander Kluge', in H.L. Arnold (ed.), *Kritisches Lexikon zur deutschsprachigen Literatur der Gegenwart*, Munich, 1978ff
Theodor Fiedler, 'Alexander Kluge: Mediating History and Consciousness', in Klaus Phillips (ed.), *New German Filmmakers*, New York, 1984, pp. 195–229
Peter Labanyi, '"Eine Felsburg, um welche der Fluß herumströmt": Kriegsmaschinen und Maschinen-Menschen bei Alexander Kluge', in Erhard Schütz (ed.), *Willkommen und Abschied der Maschinen: Literatur und Technik*, Essen, 1988, pp. 162–76
Christian Linder, 'Die Behandlung der Welt. Über Alexander Kluge', *Die Träume der Wunschmaschine*, Reinbek, 1981, pp. 64–111

MORAY McGOWAN

Franz Xaver Kroetz

Franz Xaver Kroetz, who began the 1970s as a complete unknown, had, by 1981 — at the age of thirty-five — had thirty-one plays staged in countless productions and become the most successful German dramatist since Brecht. The decade saw equally marked developments both in Kroetz's work and in his political and aesthetic position, and this chapter aims to review his work in the 1970s in the light of the changes and continuities that have subsequently become apparent.

In the early 1970s, Kroetz's public statements expressed a drastic utilitarianism. Works of art which did not serve the interests of the masses were 'geistige Exkremente' (Kroetz 1976a), writers who did not do so mere 'Musenficker' (WA, p. 592).[1] He damned Max Frisch's *Biografie* (1967) as a 'Privatissimo', and Ionesco and Beckett for their 'Urschleimtaucherei', their 'philosophische Schlamm- und Dreckbauten' (WA, p. 606).

This radical rejection of subjectivity and self-reflection in literature in favour of social criticism, appeared to be confirmed by Kroetz's work. He gained fame initially with plays like *Heimarbeit* (1971)[2] that seemed to be grim records of the material and linguistic poverty of the outsiders and the underprivileged behind the glittering facade of the 'Wirtschaftswunder', part of the fashion for 'Neuer Realismus' exemplified by the plays of Martin Sperr or the films of Fassbinder. Even after the decline of documentary literature, critics and audiences in the early 1970s still expected 'authenticity', a direct relationship with social reality, and believed they saw it in Kroetz's early work, which he claimed was drawn from newspaper reports and from observation: 'Erfindung ist — hoffentlich — wenig dabei'.[3] Kroetz's later work in the 1970s, from *Oberösterreich* (1972) to *Nicht Fisch, nicht Fleisch* (1981), established him as the dramatist of the West German everyman, the 'Kleinbürger' and his/her habits of

---

1. See Author's Note at the end of this essay for key to Kroetz's works. For secondary Literature refer to the Select Bibliography following.
2. Dates are of first production except where stated.
3. *Theater heute*, Jahressonderheft, 1972, p. 65.

thought, speech and consumption. These plays seem at first sight to confirm Rolf-Peter Carl's judgement of Kroetz's work as one, 'das überhaupt nicht zum Ort wird, über sich selbst zu schreiben' (Carl 1978, p. 17).

However, the fundamental change in Kroetz's self-conception as a writer that emerged around 1980 has altered the perspective on his earlier work. In this respect, Kroetz's resignation from the DKP, the German Communist Party, in that year is not only politically significant. Kroetz had joined in 1972, very shortly after his break-through, as what he termed a 'Schutz gegen die Umarmung der Bourgeoisie' (Riewoldt 1985, p. 169). For a time his party commit-ment reflected his bad conscience about his political powerlessness as a writer: 'Ich säße lieber in Bonn im Bundestag', he announced in 1973 (WA, p. 585). He would abandon writing altogether, or write only agitprop plays in future. In fact only *Globales Interesse* (1972) and *Münchner Kindl* (1973) fit this category in any respect. Initially Kroetz echoed, and with the enthusiasm of the convert, often outdid, the party's rhetoric. As the decade progressed, however, and his analytic insight, sharpened by Marxist dialectic, grew, he re-jected both this rhetoric and the party's East European model of socialism. In 1975, he left the Suhrkamp-Verlag rather than see his overwhelmingly positive GDR-report 'Sozialismus auf dem Dorf' (WA, pp. 427–515) go unpublished; in 1985 (having long since returned to Suhrkamp) he rejected the same report as 'grauenhaft verlogen' (Kroetz 1985, p. 78). He became equally disillusioned with the party's dogged adherence to progress in the Marxist sense. Kroetz in 1980 was 'etwas fortschrittsskeptisch' and this pessimism has since increased, though he still rejects that nihilistic gloom which can be used to justify inaction (e.g. FH, pp. 228–9). Since 1980 he has given support to the SPD, the Greens and the DKP, choosing camps according to issues from a position of sceptical independence which he had previously damned as that of an 'elitärer Selbstbestimmer' (Kroetz 1978a).

This move from dogmatism to pluralism is reflected in the trans-formation of Kroetz's aesthetics. In 'Kirchberger Notizen' (1980), a major reexamination of his attitudes to subjectivity, art and politics, he still rejected the search for individual meaning or eternal truths at the expense of social reality and social solidarity, but he also argued that political art, *above all*, should not neglect form: 'Wer im Eifer des Gefechts [. . .] die Form wegwirft, um besser kämpfen zu können, der wirft einen Teil seiner Waffe weg. [. . .] Kunst ohne Zähne, ist keine. Kunst ohne Form, auch nicht' (Riewoldt 1985, p. 172).

He now also accepted the role of subjectivity in literature; indeed he recognised that his own work had always concerned 'meine eigenen, biographie-immanenten, existentiellen Ruinen, die ich versuche, als gesellschaftliche Phänomene zu begreifen und darzustellen' (Kroetz 1980a, p. 18). His work is full of 'Verletzungen, Brüche, Verzweiflungen, Depressionen, Einsamkeiten, Demütigungen, Minderwertigkeitskomplexe, Wunden' (Kroetz 1980c). In this sense it parallels the 'Neue Subjektivität' of the 1970s with which it at first sight seemed so out of step. However, in his plays of the 1970s, Kroetz insists on ordinary working-class characters' right to the identity crisis which from Goethe's *Die Leiden des jungen Werthers* to Botho Strauß's *Die Widmung* (1976) has customarily been reserved for the sensitive bourgeois intellectual. Arguably, this rehabilitation of an archetypal bourgeois theme in socially critical guise aided Kroetz's success with a public whose disillusion with the political demands made on literature in the late 1960s was advanced but still not complete. Despite his increasing emphasis on subjectivity, however, in the 1970s Kroetz held to the optimistic, rationalistic goal of portraying existential crises as social, therefore man-made and changeable, phenomena affecting representative figures whose problems have concrete social and economic origins.

Kroetz's public stance of the early 1970s created a false image of the 'Auto-Didakt [. . .] im proletarischem Milieu aufgewachsen' (Wendt 1974, p. 94). In fact his youth was that of the precocious would-be artist in rebellion against his comfortable lower-middle-class Catholic upbringing and his father's conventional ambitions for him.[4] Kroetz read Kierkegaard, Heidegger, Pascal, Guardini, Thomas Aquinas, Gide, Mauriac, Claudel, Sartre, Hemingway, and Henry Miller as a boy, wrote obsessively from his early teens, and trained as an actor in Munich and Vienna. It is true that between 1966 and 1970 he had numerous irregular and casual jobs and that this experience of proletarian and sub-proletarian life fed many of his early plays. Kroetz always saw himself, however, 'als Künstler im Wartestand' (Kroetz 1980b).

Kroetz acted and directed on the 'Bauerntheater' circuit in the late 1960s, and has described this as his 'künstlerische Geburtsstätte' (see Carl 1978, p. 8). His real artistic home, however, was the Munich avant-garde, particularly the Büchnertheater, where his adaptations of *Julius Cäsar* and of Goncharov's *Oblomov*[5] were per-

4. Principal biographical sources: Blevins 1983, pp. 13–34; Riewoldt 1985, *passim*; Kroetz 1985.
5. With this ironic study of crippling self-awareness, Kroetz, of all authors, and four years before Botho Strauß's *Hypochonder*, was anticipating the new subjectivity of the 1970s.

formed in 1968. This was a period of heady politicisation in West German society when a new upsurge of radicalism seemed to presage the demise of the liberal-democratic consensus. But Kroetz was at this time immersed in a group whose anti-bourgeois rebellion was artistic and not political: 'Wir [. . .] lehnten Politik sogar ausdrücklich ab, fand sie primitiv und unbedeutend.[. . .] Unser Kunstanspruch zuckte wie von der Natter gebissen zurück, wenn er auch nur in die Nähe von Wirklichkeit kam' (Riewoldt 1985, p. 166).

Thus a conflict grew in Kroetz between the art he was trying to practice and the reality he was experiencing — and as an unskilled, casual labourer, this was disproportionately the reality of those who had failed to establish a foothold in the affluent society: 'Alles, was ich beim Arbeiten sah, litt und verstand, konnte ich in "unsere Kunst" nicht einbringen. Mit dem Kopf war ich Künstler und sonst Prolet' (Riewoldt 1985, p. 167). As a result, when Kroetz did achieve his theatrical breakthrough in 1971, his aggressively proletarian, anti-intellectual, utilitarian stance was an expression not just of anger over conditions at the sump of the affluent society, nor just of scorn for the theatrical establishment, but also a revolt against his own immediate past.

Moreover, on the one hand Kroetz's early plays *did* coincide with the realisation, expressed in books like Jürgen Roth's *Armut in der Bundesrepublik* (1974), that in West Germany the 'Randgruppen', the outsiders and the socially disadvantaged, formed a very substantial minority beneath the affluent surface. On the other hand, his early plays are firstly not solely concerned with social outsiders (a misunderstanding indicative of the narrow social experience of many theatre critics): Erwin in *Wildwechsel* (1971) is a lorry-driver; Rustorfer and Ertl in *Hartnäckig* (1971) are publicans; Otto in *Lieber Fritz* (1975) a market gardener; Fräulein Rasch in *Wunschkonzert* (1973) a clerical worker; while *Männersache* (1972) concerns a factory worker and a shopkeeper. Secondly, these plays are in any case more than social reportage. They are also imaginative restatements of Kroetz's personal experience: 'Ich hatte nicht Mitleid, ich hatte gelitten, und das in meinen frühen Stücken dargestellt (Riewoldt 1985, p. 172). The motif of 'Heimarbeit', piecework labour performed in the home, which occurs in the plays *Heimarbeit* (1977), *Geisterbahn* (1975), *Sterntaler* (1977), *Das Nest* (1975), *Heimat* (1980) and *Agnes Bernauen* (1977), is not only a social fact, a metaphor for exploitation and an effective piece of stage-craft, but also articulates the socially isolated and insecure world of Kroetz in the late 1960s, drifting between unskilled casual jobs, rare engagements as an actor, and unsuccessful attempts as a writer.

The same applies to the motif of handicap in *Heimarbeit, Hartnäckig, Stallerhof* (1972) and *Lieber Fritz* (1975): it is both a social reality and a metaphor for the rejection Kroetz experienced before 1971. This motif, however, also recurs obsessively as a metaphor of a humanity tragically denied and denying its own ideal nature, from his earliest texts (e.g. 'Koreanischer Frühling', FP, pp. 7–38, or 'Als Zeus zum letzten Mal kam', FP, pp. 99–130) to his novels *Der Mondscheinknecht* (1981) and *Der Mondscheinknecht. Fortsetzung* (1983), whose central character is the polio victim Anton Kreuzberger, and *Der Nusser* (1986), his adaptation of Ernst Toller's *Hinkemann* (1922). 'Ich glaube, daß wir alle Behinderte sind', remarks Kroetz on the dustjacket of *Der Mondscheinknecht*.

The early plays were seen as epitomising the 'Sprachlosigkeit' of a linguistically, spiritually and materially deprived sub-proletariat, a critical oversimplification for which Kroetz was partly responsible (e.g. his foreword to *Heimarbeit*, quoted in Riewoldt 1985, pp. 63–5). Kroetz's plays were linked with the rediscovered work of Odön von Horváth under the banner of the 'neues Volksstück' (Kroetz himself, in fact, first subtitled a play — *Das Nest* — a 'Volksstück' only in 1974, when most directors and critics were already bored with what was for them a passing fashion): the younger author was seen as continuing the tradition of demonstrating a whole class's linguistic dispossession. So closely did Kroetz's work seem to fit Basil Bernstein's fashionable models of language competence — of a middle-class 'elaborated' code and a working-class 'restricted code' — that one analysis declared: 'Dieser autor geht unverkennbar aus von der gegenwärtigen diskussion um sprachbarrieren und schichtenspezifischen sprachgebrauch' (Burger and von Matt 1974, p. 270). This is unquestionably false; Kroetz's highly crafted dialogues result not from socio-linguistic theory but from empirical observations reshaped according to his acute sense of dramatic effectiveness.

Moreover, just as Bernstein's theories were criticised for unintentionally confirming the hierarchy of class by measuring working-class speech by middle-class norms and neglecting the former's creative and affective potential, so too Kroetz came to reject the label 'Sprachlosigkeit' both for the fatalism it implied and for the way it neglected the elements of humour, struggle and solidarity present even in the bleakest of his plays (e.g. Riewoldt 1985, p. 117).

The early plays are in any case as much theatrical experiments as social documents. In 1985 Kroetz argued that these plays had begun as one direction of formal exploration among many in the late 1960s, before their success determined his concentration in the 1970s on 'realistische Stücke' (Kroetz 1985, p. 76). The plays which appeared in the early 1970s are indeed marked by considerable formal variety, and the starkly reduced dialogue itself represents a radical formal innovation: though it has parallels with the social realism of Edward Bond's *The Pope's Wedding* (1962) and *Saved* (1965), Kroetz's distillation of intensely dramatic interactions out of apparently banal, naturalistic exchanges punctuated by pauses is often closer to the early Harold Pinter (see McGowan 1978). It is certainly artificial: the transcribed interviews with Bavarians in *Chiemgauer Geschichten* (1977), which might have confirmed the much-praised 'Genauigkeit' of his dialogue, share some syntactic features with the plays but are noticeably different (see Betten 1985, p. 253: Hess-Lüttich 1985, pp. 297–302).

Michis Blut (1971), stripped of all the reassuring trivia of naturalist milieu or dialogue, carries 'Sprachlosigkeit' to a formal extreme. Like *Wunschkonzert*, a silent one-person play for which Kroetz demands that 'reale Zeit sei gleich Bühnenzeit' (GS, p. 187), *Dolomitenstadt Lienz* (1972) employs a naturalist 'Sekundenstil'; but it is broken up in Brechtian manner by 'Songs'. The prisoners' dreams of flying, a motif echoed in *Sterntaler* and in *Mensch Meier* (1978) and notably in Kroetz's comments on the staging of *Furcht und Hoffnung der BRD* (1984) — 'ich habe oft das Gefühl, alle Figuren stehen am Fenster und wollen wegfliegen' (FH, p. 8) —, indicate that incarceration is not only a social reality or a restatement of autobiographical experience (Kroetz was once briefly imprisoned in Lienz on a drunk-driving offence) but is also, like handicap, a metaphor for repressed human potential. The bizarre black-comic shootout that ends the original version of *Männersache* anticipates the Kroetz of *Nicht Fisch, nicht Fleisch* (1981) onwards in departing from naturalism to express the essential dynamic of a relationship or psychological state.

Kroetz has always been a man of the theatre — actor and director as well as writer — for whom the documents of despair, such as the knitting-needle abortion scene in *Heimarbeit*, are also powerful stage images. This point is reinforced by the return, in *Bauern sterben* (1985), to the drastic stage imagery of the early plays. Though anchored in the social context of a decaying, economically marginal peasantry, it concentrates human experience into its own metaphorical transcendence. In one scene, while mother and daughter lay out grandmother's corpse, daughter has a miscarriage and lays the stillborn foetus in the worm-eaten stomach of the dead grandmother (BS, p. 9): an image of life as circularity and bleakness (echoing the 'Born astride a grave speech' in Beckett's *Waiting for Godot*) that has nothing more to do with naturalism.

An awareness of the role of subjectivity in Kroetz's work provides another important interpretative approach: his plays explore the relationship between the human being as object of social forces and the human being as conscious subject struggling for self-determination, and in so doing trace a process from object to subject. Kroetz's work is a debate with itself, in which he continually reshapes certain essential dramatic constellations as his own social and aesthetic views and intentions develop.

The characters of very many of his plays are unfree objects, pinballs in a pintable of social forces. Their attempts to fulfil wishes which their social situation simply does not permit only confirm the social processes which have blocked their way out of object existence. The dialogue's sparse Bavarian lower-class 'sociolect' emphasises in its repetitions and unreflected clichés the closed circle of alienation in which the characters live. The aggressions the society generates in them are not turned back on the society, but directed inwards, at members of their family, at the unborn child in the womb, at themselves.

Thus in *Heimarbeit* Willi murders his wife Martha's child by another man (after her own abortion attempt fails), when the real root of his frustration is his own social rejection. Hanni in *Wildwechsel* shoots her father, loses her unwanted child and sinks back into a bovine indifference. 'Wie Tiere projizieren diese Menschen ihre Notsituationen in ihrer Haltung im Stummsein', writes Kroetz in his prologue to *Wunschkonzert*, in which a lonely spinster takes an overdose, tidying herself away as the culmination of the process of alienation which has made her into an object (GS, p. 185).

Only in *Lieber Fritz*, where Fritz and Mitzi temporarily if unsuccessfully reject the norms of their environment, and in *Stallerhof*, do the characters of the early plays take significant steps away from their object existence. Sepp and Beppi attempt, despite their disadvantages and despite the taboos on their relationship, to realise their needs for tenderness. Sepp's abuse of Beppi is a helpless, misdirected step, but at least a step *undertaken*, in contrast to the apathy characteristic of the early plays. The Stallerin's decision not to abort Beppi's child may be cowardice, or it, too, may be an assertion of her natural humanity against the pressure of social norms. However, the surprising optimism of *Stallerhof* is qualified by its sequel *Geisterbahn*. Beppi's spirited attempts to build a new independent life with her child inevitably founder and she kills the baby.

Thus Kroetz's early plays are by no means unremittingly negative. They contain, as in the Beppi plays, celebrations of the human spirit in the worst of circumstances. However, the process of self-

discovery and self-assertion of the subject really begins with
Oberösterreich (1972). Kroetz continued to experiment in the 1970s,
for example with further one-person plays like *Weitere Aussichten*
(1975), with plays on specific political issues such as the morality of
the arms industry in *Die Wahl fürs Leben* or the 'Berufsverbot' debate
in *Verfassungsfeinde* (both written 1973), and with those that attempt
a broader social panorama, such as *Agnes Bernauer* (1977); however,
the mainstream of his work from *Oberösterreich* to *Nicht Fisch, nicht
Fleisch*, those plays, that is, which achieved most critical attention
and popular success, was the depiction of the pressures and contradictions of West German — capitalist — society as manifested in
the nuclear family: the married couple, with or without children.
These people — van-and lorry-drivers (*Oberösterreich*; *Das Nest*),
factory workers (*Mensch Meier*; *Der stramme Max*, 1978), skilled,
highly-paid typesetters (*Nicht Fisch, nicht Fleisch*) — are 'integrated in
the supermarket society of a modern economy' (Innes 1979, p. 232).
From the deprivation of *Heimarbeit* it is a long way to, say, *Der
stramme Max*, where Anna and Max send their daughter Sabine to an
expensive boarding-school to compensate for her working-class origins.

From play to play, the characters become increasingly aware of
and able to articulate the problems they face. Both their language
and their horizons open out. But their economic, social and linguistic growth (compared to the early plays) is accompanied by what
Kroetz calls 'Verkleinbürgerlichung', the largely unquestioning
adoption of petit-bourgeois and middle-class attitudes and aspirations by working-class people (Kroetz 1981, p. 45). Anna and Max's
ambitions for Sabine are symptomatic, as is Otto's refusal to let his
son Ludwig become a worker like himself (*Mensch Meier*). These
attitudes, like the linguistic deprivation of the earlier plays, prevent
the characters from knowing themselves and their true interests,
though the closed circle of plays like *Heimarbeit* is not repeated.
Typically, in the plays of the later 1970s, the male protagonists
experience a socially grounded threat to their petit-bourgeois existence — unemployment, or the economic consequences of a preg-
nancy, for example — which disorientates them sufficiently for
them to recognise their lack of individual identity. This alienation
permeates their whole existence, from the workplace into the marriage bed, as Heinz explicitly remarks in *Oberösterreich* (GS, p. 400).
The motifs of manifest handicap used in the early plays to portray
alienation have gone; but Kroetz now observes more subtle defor-
mations of the thinking and behaviour even of capitalist society's
average members.

Up to this point, Kroetz may seem to share the pessimism of other contemporary authors such as Botho Strauß or Thomas Bernhard, who also portray the human subject as an object of larger determining forces (see Kafitz 1980). However, Kroetz has always remained a humanist, concerned with 'das Zurückfinden zu menschlichen Werten', and to keep 'der Mensch im Mittelpunkt' of his work (Kroetz 1979a, p. 39). And, as he says on the dustcover of *Der Mondscheinknecht*, 'man muß sich wehren, wenn man ein Mensch sein will'. This contrasts markedly with Strauß, for example, whose *Rumor* (1980) challenges the humanist faith in the human being as an active subject, seeing it as long disproved by science and by the universe's indifference. Kroetz's characters, in contrast, initially degraded into objects, struggle to become self-determining subjects and precisely this struggle establishes their identity as human beings (see McGowan 1985).

These plays of the later 1970s can therefore be seen as a sequence of steps towards awareness of self and social reality. Perhaps surprisingly, for a socialist writer, however, Kroetz restricts himself almost exclusively to the depiction of the home life of largely apolitical individual families.

There are three reasons for this: firstly, his strength is portraying small-scale social patterns. His one planned historical drama, *KPD lebt!*, on the Communist Party's period of illegality in the Adenauer era, was abandoned at an early stage (see Riewoldt 1985, pp. 109–15). Agnes Bernauer's image of capitalism as a village of 'Heimarbeiter' threading rosaries works only as a parable not a social panorama.

Secondly, making virtue of necessity perhaps, Kroetz argues against theatrical representations of collective forces: 'das scheitert zwangsläufig, weil das Theater Individuen braucht' (Kroetz 1980a). However, Kroetz portrays not 'great individuals' but the West German everyman; not Peter Siemens but the Siemens workforce. It is the workforce as *individuals* however: despite Kroetz's direct workplace experience, he has almost never attempted to bring the factory onstage; when he does, in *Sterntaler*, it is in a surreal scene in which Karli literally weds his packing machine (WA, pp. 193–4). He argues that 'der Verlust von Arbeit ist spannender als wie die Arbeit tun, ist dramatischer' (Kroetz 1980b). Indeed, what interested Kroetz in this period was the effects of work, unemployment or the threat of the latter on the ordinary West German worker's family life.

Thirdly, despite his own political development, Kroetz in this period sought to create representative characters, and 'typisch ist für unsere Gesellschaft nicht der exemplarische Kommunist, sondern der exemplarische Kleinbürger, der Prolet, der seine Lage noch nicht begreift' (Kroetz 1976b, p. 57): Kroetz portrays the impact of manifestly political phenomena, rationalisation of work processes (*Mensch Meier*; *Nicht Fisch, nicht Fleisch*) or industrial safety (*Der stramme Max*), or indeed unemployment in most of these plays, on fundamentally apolitical individuals. They take at most small, but real, steps away from apolitical consciousness towards a modest awareness, founded on experience and not on theory, of their political and social reality.

This can be observed most clearly in *Das Nest*. The modestly affluent 'Kleinbürger' Kurt and Martha inhabit a deceptive idyll, shattered when Kurt, to meet the consumption targets on the fulfilment of which his breadwinner identity depends, accepts a 'Sonderauftrag' to dump poisonous chemicals and in so doing almost kills his own son. This unleashes an identity crisis in Kurt, deepened by Martha's accusation that he is just a 'dressierter Aff' (WA, p. 241). Kurt realises how much he and Martha have been unthinking objects of social forces. He reports himself to the police and confronts his boss, who scorns him as a 'Würstl' (WA, p. 249). The once self-satisfied Kurt now knows this to be true in capitalist society, but precisely at this point when his boss's affable mask drops to reveal his true opinion, because Kurt has challenged him, Kurt becomes less of a 'Würstl', because he is asserting himself. The human being degraded to object is thus here given the possibility of regaining capacity for action and so of becoming a self-determining subject.

The socio-economic analysis has a Marxist basis: both Kurt, who fails to see the connection between his 63-hour-weeks and his boss's new 60,000 mark car (WA, p. 231), and Martha, who is exploited as a 'Heimarbeiterin', create surplus value for the owners of the means of production. Modern consumer capitalism creates inherently destructive contradictions: even those like Kurt who identify with its values cannot fulfil the expectations it awakes without dehumanising and endangering themselves or their families.

Beside *Das Nest*'s modest plea for social solidarity in its suggestion that with trade-union support Kurt will be stronger in his fight (WA, p. 251), it also reaffirms the role of individual moral fortitude. The characters remain products of social circumstances as in Kroetz's other plays: Kurt and Martha's 'Unmündigkeit', in Kant's terms, is thus not wholly 'selbstverschuldet'. Their 'Ausgang' to enlightenment, however, is very much a matter of individual integrity: now they have recognised how their actions can influence circumstances, it is their responsibility not to be the victims of circumstances. This may seem a surprising verdict from a play-wright who was a communist at the time; here, as elsewhere, Kroetz's critique of capitalism combines with a christian-humanist concern for the individual and his/her moral integrity.

The optimism of *Das Nest* is virtually unique in Kroetz's work; his later plays do not share its exemplary, 'morality play' character. Kroetz's humanism gains dialectic subtlety: he now shows that the step out of object existence not only brings the awakening of con-sciousness and the beginning of self-determination, but also lays bare the painful conflicts between individual and social existence, conflicts which the progress from object to subject may intensify rather than resolve.

In *Mensch Meier*, Otto's dissatisfaction with his identity, or lack of it, as a worker, is expressed in success fantasies (in which the Kroetzean hero's archetypal freedom dream of flying is perverted by Otto's internalisation of hierarchical social values into a dream of running a model-plane factory) and in his refusal to let his son Ludwig take a manual job like himself. Instead, the unemployed Ludwig becomes the target for the aggressions Otto accumulates at work.

This eventually destroys the family. Otto's wife Martha leaves: 'Ich geh weg von dir, Otto, weil ich dich verlaß' (MM, p. 48). These are exactly Martha's words to Willi in *Heimarbeit* (GS, p. 59). But whereas Willi's wife returns, thus restoring, fundamentally un-changed, the fateful order of things, Martha Meier builds her own separate existence. Like Ludwig, who also leaves and becomes a bricklayer, Martha grows by asserting herself. By accepting her identity, she is able to change it, and, within her modest possi-bilities, begin determining her own future.

Otto, in contrast, remains trapped in brooding fantasies, con-vinced his real self is strait-jacketed by his socio-economic status, yet unable to act to free it (MM, p. 58). Life without the prospect of escape from a working-class identity he rejects seems senseless: 'Bevor man anfangt, is alles aus' (MM, p. 45). This, too, is remi-niscent of the 'Born astride a grave' speech in *Waiting for Godot*; but Otto draws this conclusion from the alienation of his specific material existence as an assembly-line worker, the sensation of being little more than a human robot (e.g. MM, pp. 45–6, 53). In the plays of the later 1970s the crises Kroetz's characters experience continue to have social causes.

By the late 1970s Kroetz himself was reaching a crisis. Behind the facade of party loyalty lay increasing frustration with the DKP; behind his status as a world dramatist he agreed with those of his critics who said he was repeating himself: 'Ich lande immer wieder beim Wohnküchen-Gasherd-Realismus' (Kroetz 1979b). After *Der stramme Max* (written 1978), came a two-year gap, followed by Kroetz's resignation from the party, his next play *Nicht Fisch. nicht Fleisch* (1980; premiered 1981) and his first published novel *Der Mondscheinknecht* (1981), which together marked the end of one phase in Kroetz's work and the beginning of a new one.

Nicht Fisch, nicht Fleisch addresses a fundamental question of modern technological society: can technical progress be allowed to take away not only the heavy and dangerous work, but also the satisfying and pleasurable work that gives the human being his or her sense of identity? The social conflicts and contradictions of this issue are, as always in Kroetz's work, registered as they manifest themselves in individuals.

At the time of writing the play, Kroetz was in the process of coming to terms with his own subjectivity (see especially 'Kirchberger Notizen', 1980). In the two male protagonists, the sensitive brooding individualist Edgar and the rational trade-union activist Hermann, two halves of Kroetz's own personality confront one another: the creative artist and the party worker.

Edgar and Hermann are articulate and well-paid typesetters. However, when their firm introduces computer typesetting, the craftsmen have to retrain as machine operators: technical progress robs them of their profession and so of their identity. This awakes in Edgar grim visions of a totally rationalised future in which the individual has no place (e.g. NF, pp. 43–4). Edgar responds with romantic, atavistic dreams of the wilderness, where man daily reasserts his identity in the struggle for existence. And should he die, he says, then let hyenas eat his corpse and carry it 'in ihrem Bauch in allen Himmelsrichtungen' (NF, p. 50). Instead of asserting himself by resisting the material causes of his loss of identity, he dreams of Nirvana, of being dissolved and at the same time preserved in universal nature.

In contrast, Hermann's tenacious optimism is founded on the experience of struggle in the real world against real people. Hermann approves of progress in principle, fighting it only when it manifests itself as rationalisation in the exclusive interests of capital. He scorns Edgar's individualism and declares him a traitor to his colleagues and his class.

Hermann's criticism is countered by the richer imagery of Edgar's speculations and by Helga's accusation that Hermann has set dogma above humanity and abandoned his friend, which echoes the author's verdict on his own previous denial of subjectivity (e.g. FP,

p. 179). At one point Hermann writhes in pain, after his colleagues, tired of his political windbagging, have blown air up his rectum with a bicycle pump. 'Karl Marx persönlich, der durch das Arschloch des Herrn Hermann Zwiebel abfährt', remarks Edgar (NF, p. 76), a drastic metaphor of liberation contemporaneous with Kroetz's departure from the DKP.

Nicht Fisch, nicht Fleisch points to a number of directions Kroetz's work may take. By using two complementary married couples, Kroetz significantly widens his scope while retaining the strengths of the dramatic constellation he has made his trademark. The play is Kroetz's most serious attempt to make drama out of the clash of ideas rather than the subtextual tensions of unarticulated desires and frustrations. The no-man's-land scene (NF, pp. 75–8) gives notice of a move away from 'Wohnküchen-Gasherd-Realismus' without subverting it completely; a move still more pronounced in the variety of form, physical and sociological setting of the fifteen fragmentary scenes of *Furcht und Hoffnung der BRD* (1984), or in the Expressionist 'Stationendrama' form of *Bauern sterben* (1985). In 1985, invited to direct a revival in Stuttgart, Kroetz wanted *Agnes Bernauer* (1977), one of his least 'socially realist' plays of the 1970s (Kroetz 1985, p. 80). Ten years after the proud denial of the role of 'Erfindung' in his writing, Kroetz, in an interview before the 1982 Frankfurt production of *Nicht 'Fisch, nicht Fleisch*, remarked: 'Die Phantasie ist viel wirklicher wie das Leben' (Kroetz 1982, p. 10).

Nicht Fisch, nicht Fleisch points forward in another respect to *Bauern sterben*. Edgar's stance echoes the revolt against technology which contributed in the 1970s to the growth of the land commune movement and the Green Party, and to the popularity of Eastern religions. The conservative tendency that forms one facet of these movements' critique of modern civilisation underlies much of Kroetz's work, as he himself has admitted (Riewoldt 1985, pp. 185–6; see also Töteberg 1985). It emerges in *Bauern sterben* as a daemonisation of urban society: 'Die Stadt ist der Metzger' (BS, p. 23). In the interview cited above, Kroetz revokes *Das Nest*'s support for trade unions, attacking them now for their acceptance of untrammelled technological progress: 'Es ist längst so, daß die Technik und der Fortschritt die Dinge, die mir auf dieser Welt noch Spaß machen, mehr bedrohen als schützen' (Kroetz 1982, p. 4). Later he argues that 'Bruch mit der Tradition führt auch immer zum Lebensverlust', reflected in *Nicht Fisch, nicht Fleisch*'s greater sympathy for the fecund, motherly Helga than the childless careerist Emmi, and in *Bauern sterben*'s requiem for lost 'Heimat': 'Ohne an Bodn stirbtma' (BS, p. 29).

Finally, *Nicht Fisch, nicht Fleisch* points forward, in the unresolved conflict between Edgar's pessimism and Hermann's optimism, to *Der Nusser* (1986). In the same interview, Kroetz indicates his interest as a dramatist in 'das Aufspüren tatsächlicher, nicht mit gutem Willen, Leitartikeln und Tarifverhandlungen auflösbarer Konflikte' (Kroetz 1982, p. 7). Ernst Toller wrote of *Hinkemann* that no social system can eradicate every human pain: 'immer bleibt ein Rest. Aber soziales Leid ist sinnlos, nicht notwendig, ist tilgbar'.[6] Kroetz's Hinkemann-adaptation *Der Nusser* (whose handicap motif brings Kroetz full circle to his very earliest extant work but whose German everyman protagonist has parallels in Kroetz's 'Kleinbürger' plays) focuses on this awareness of the tragic contradictions of life, but linked with the refusal to be blind to the social and therefore changeable causes of human suffering where they do exist: the expectation never to win but the determination to fight.

If Kroetz's demands in the early 1970s for a social realism that championed the underdog were, as he has suggested, primarily motivated by the parallels to his own material reality, if, as he suggested in 1985, 'Mich hat niemals das Volk interessiert' and 'Ich habe mein Leben lang nur von mir geschrieben' (Kroetz 1985, p. 78), then it was inevitable that material success would change his political and aesthetic priorities. Alternatively, one could argue that the thirty-odd plays of the 1970s were a necessary step towards the multi-dimensional and differentiated view of life's contradictions — mutable and immutable — and their literary reflection which his work in the 1980s has begun to demonstrate.

Author's Note

Kroetz's works, as well as essays, statements and interviews published in book form, are referred to by the following abbreviations:

BS = *Bauern sterben, Programmheft der Münchner Kammerspiele*, 1984/85, 8 (subsequently published Frankfurt on Main, 1986)
FH = *Furcht und Hoffnung der BRD*, Frankfurt on Main, 1984
FP = *Frühe Prosa. Frühe Stücke*, Frankfurt on Main, 1983

6. *Eine Jugend in Deutschland*, Reinbek, 1963, p. 161.

GS = *Gesammelte Stücke*, Frankfurt on Main, 1975
MM = *Mensch Meier / Der stramme Max / Wer durchs Laub geht*, Frankfurt on Main, 1979
NF = *Nicht Fisch, nicht Fleisch; Verfassungsfeinde; Jumbo Track*, Frankfurt on Main, 1981
WA = *Weitere Aussichten*, Cologne, 1976

Interviews and statements by Kroetz are identified as follows:

Kroetz 1972 = Hannes Macher, 'Was alles zur Gewalt führt', *Die Zeit*, 23 June 1972, p. 17
Kroetz 1973 = 'Subventionssauerei', *Neues Forum*, 229, February 1973, pp. 58–9
Kroetz 1976a = 'Zur Diskussion: Beiträge vom Bonner Parteitag der DKP: Franz Xaver Kroetz', *kürbiskern* 1976, 3, pp. 163–6
Kroetz 1976b = Ursula Reinhold, 'Interview mit Franz Xaver Kroetz', *Weimarer Beiträge*, 21, 1976, 5, pp. 46–59
Kroetz 1978a = 'Sozialismus aus Liebe zum Vernünftigen', in Fritz J. Raddatz (ed.), *Warum ich Marxist bin*, Munich, 1978, pp. 34–56
Kroetz 1978b = Thomas Thieringer, 'Gut gemeint ist das Gegenteil von Kunst', *Süddeutsche Zeitung*, 23/24.9.1978
Kroetz 1979a = H.L. Arnold, 'Der lebende Mensch ist der Mittelpunkt', in idem (ed.), *Als Schriftsteller leben*, Reinbek, 1979, pp. 35–64
Kroetz 1979b = Carna Zacharias, 'Die Erotik ist zerbrochen', *Abendzeitung*, 22/23.12.1979
Kroetz 1980a = Manfred Beetz, 'Ich schreibe nicht über Dinge, die ich verachte', *Theater heute*, 21, 1980, 7, pp. 18–19
Kroetz 1980b = Interview with Moray McGowan, Kirchberg, 8.9.1980; unpub. recording
Kroetz 1980c = 'Rede an den Wiener Literaturtagen', unpub. ms, 1980
Kroetz 1981 = Donna L. Hoffmeister, 'Ich kann nur schreiben, von dem, was ich sehe', *Modern Language Studies* 11, 1980/81, 1, pp. 38–48
Kroetz 1982 = Ulrike Prokop, 'Ich meine, wenn, dann phantastischer Realismus', *Programmheft des Frankfurter Schauspiels zu Nicht Fisch, nicht Fleisch*, Frankfurt on Main, 1982, pp. 3–22
Kroetz 1985 = 'Ich habe immer nur von mir geschrieben', *Theater 1985*, Velber, 1985, pp. 72–87

Select Bibliography

(* = contains major bibliography)

H.L. Arnold (ed.) (1978), *Franz Xaver Kroetz, Text und Kritik*, 57, 1978

——— and Michael Töteberg (1978 ff.),* 'Franz Xaver Kroetz', in H.L. Arnold (ed.), *Kritisches Lexikon zur deutschsprachigen Gegenwartsliteratur*, Munich, 1978ff.; bibliography by M. Töteberg and U. Voskamp

Anne Betten (1985), *Sprachrealismus im deutschen Drama der siebziger Jahre*, Heidelberg, 1985, pp. 218–90

Richard W. Blevins (1983), *Franz Xaver Kroetz: The Emergence of a Political Playwright*, New York, Berne and Frankfurt on Main, 1983

Elizabeth Boa (1985), 'Kroetz's *Nicht Fisch, nicht Fleisch*: a good red herring?', *German Life and Letters*, 38, 1985, 4, pp. 313–22

Harald Burger and Peter von Matt (1974), 'Dramatischer Dialog und restringiertes Sprechen. Franz Xaver Kroetz in linguistischer und literaturwissenschaftlicher Sicht', *Zeitschrift für germanistische Linguistik*, 2, 1974, pp. 269–98

Denis Calandra (1983), *New German Dramatists*, London, 1983

Rolf Peter Carl (1978), *Franz Xaver Kroetz*, Munich, 1978

Susan L. Cocalis (1981), '"Mitleid" and "Engagement". Compassion and/or political commitment in the dramatic works of Franz Xaver Kroetz', *Colloquia Germanica*, 14, 1981, pp. 203–19

Ernest W.B. Hess-Lüttich (1985), 'Neorealismus und sprachliche Wirklichkeit. Zur Kommunikationskritik bei Franz Xaver Kroetz', in Riewoldt (ed.), *Franz Xaver Kroetz*, pp. 297–318

Donna L. Hoffmeister (1983), *The Theater of Confinement. Language and survival in the milieu plays of Marieluise Fleißer and Franz Xaver Kroetz*, Columbia, S. Carolina, 1983

Christopher D. Innes, (1979), *Modern German Drama*, Cambridge, London, New York and Melbourne, 1979, pp. 222–34

Dieter Kafitz (1980), 'Die Problematisierung des individualistischen Menschenbildes im deutschsprachigen Drama der Gegenwart', *Basis*, 10, 1980, pp. 93–126

Wend Kässens and Michael Töteberg (1976), 'Fortschritt im Realismus? Zur Erneuerung des kritischen Volksstücks', *Basis*, 6, 1976, pp. 30–47

Hajo Kurzenberger (1978), 'Negativ-Dramatik, Positiv-Dramatik', *Text und Kritik*, 57, 1978, pp. 8–19

Moray McGowan (1978), 'Sprache, Gewalt und Gesellschaft. Franz Xaver Kroetz und die sozialrealistischen Dramatiker des englischen Theaters', *Text und Kritik*, 57, 1978, pp. 37–48

——— (1985), 'Botho Strauß and Franz Xaver Kroetz: two contemporary views of the subject', *Strathclyde Modern Language Studies*, 5, 1985, pp. 59–75

Evalouise Panzner (1976), *Franz Xaver Kroetz und seine Rezeption. Die Intentionen eines Stückeschreibers und seine Aufnahme durch die Kritik*, Stuttgart, 1976

Jürgen H. Petersen (1983), 'Franz Xaver Kroetz: Von der Tragödie der Unfreiheit zum Lehrstück für Werktätige', in Gerhard Kluge (ed.), *Studien zur Dramatik in der Bundesrepublik Deutschland*, Amsterdam, 1983, pp. 291–312

Ursula Reinhold (1985), 'Franz Xaver Kroetz — Dramenaufbau und Wirkungsabsicht', in Riewoldt (ed.), *Franz Xaver Kroetz*, pp. 229–51

Otto Riewoldt (ed.) (1985), * *Franz Xaver Kroetz*, Frankfurt on Main, 1985; bibliography by M. Töteberg

Ursula Schregel (1980), *Neue deutsche Stücke im Spielplan: am Beispiel von Franz Xaver Kroetz*, Berlin, 1980

Michael Töteberg (1976), 'Der Kleinbürger auf der Bühne. Die Entwicklung des Dramatikers Franz Xaver Kroetz und das realistische Volksstück', *Akzente*, 1976, 2, pp. 165–73 (also as: 'Franz Xaver Kroetz: the realistic folkplay', *Performing Arts Journal*, 2, Winter 1978, pp. 17–25)

——, 'Ein konservativer Autor', in Riewoldt (ed.), *Franz Xaver Kroetz*, pp. 284–96

[handwritten annotation in top-left margin:] Schneider as exemplum of the political ... the "personal" as oppos... ... of the "gener...*

PETER LABANYI

When Wishing Still Helped
Peter Schneider's Left-Wing Melancholy

For the post-war generation to which Peter Schneider (born 1940) belongs, the 1970s define themselves negatively as the decade that came *after* the revolt of 1967–9. If the watershed of the Student Movement had been preceded, in the cultural sphere, by an endemic crisis of the individual (thematised, in complementary ways, by Adorno and Beckett) its demise unleashed a seemingly no less endemic crisis within the left — which only intensified the personal crisis for Schneider's generation. This explains why, when asked in 1981 about the current goals of the left, Schneider replied in the idiom of liberalism: 'die Ränder zwischen Staat und Individuum immer wieder neu zu ziehen und die Ränder im Sinne des Individuums immer weiter hinauszuschieben'.[1] This can be read as a defensive response, understandable in the light of the traumatic experiences of the left in the Federal Republic since the Student Movement disintegrated. These experiences, epitomised by the dialectic of escalation between terrorism and State repression, are registered, albeit with uneven emphasis, in Schneider's writings. But such a perspective risks reducing a writer to a passive, 'seismographic' role and neglecting the fact that subjectivity is not just a substance of writing but also a motivation. Though this has become increasingly clear in Schneider's work over the years, arguably it has always been the dominant factor, and should warn us against constructing an ideal-type of him as the disappointed student revolutionary who turned in on himself. Such a categorisation sits all too comfortably with liberal and conservative versions of the 'new' 'Zeitgeist' of the 1970s. The media stereotype of a 'turn' from politics to subjectivity has as much to do with fashion, and needs to be relativised by an insistence — exemplified within the Student Movement — that the personal *is* the political. Focusing on this dialectic does justify examining in what ways Schneider can be

1. 'Verweigerung ist nicht genug', interview with Gerhard Bott, in E. Knödler-Bunte (ed.), *Was ist heute noch links?*, Berlin, 1981, p. 46.

regarded as a symptomatic figure of the 1970s. The historicism implicit in the category 'decade' threatens to bring the personal/ political dialectic to rest at the objectivist pole : but only if we forget that the historical is always already mediated through the personal experience of the writer. Schneider's fictions and essays alike are not about the 1970s, the Student Movement, the 'Berufsverbot', etc., but about his experiences of *and during* the decade.

In any case the real movement of history — or of personal life-history — refuses to fit tidily into ten-year blocks. Especially given the overwhelming significance for Schneider of the Student Movement, it would be a distortion to begin an examination of him with *Lenz* (1973) and ignore his writings of the late 1960s. But where are we to stop? Moreover, quite apart from our own role in constructing the object of analysis in the first place, like the characters on the two diverging trains in Wim Wenders' 1974 film, *Falsche Bewegung*, we ourselves as well as our objects are moving. Any starting- and stopping-point is an interpretative intervention, shaped as much by our own historical position as by the interactions of the texts with the real history they mediate and participate in. Since reflection on an historical moment continues (begins in earnest?) once the moment is past, an examination of Schneider and the 1970s would be incomplete without some consideration of *Der Mauerspringer* (1982), which represents a synthesis of and response to the problems thrown up throughout his writing during the decade.

Having decided on a genetic perspective, we should be conscious of the dangers it brings with it: a tendency to chronological determinism and to chalk up easy points with the privileges of hindsight. Both strategies have been criticised by Schneider himself: determinism, because it restricts human freedom; retrospection, because it enables one to present oneself as moving towards a predestined goal and, where necessary, to append the required self-justifications. Compelled under the pressure of the 'Berufsverbot' to review his own political career, Kleff in . . *schon bist du ein Verfassungsfeind* (1975) recognises that, far from being the product of a logical sequence of decisions, a political standpoint is 'nichts weiter als das Ergebnis zahlloser, widersprüchlicher Erfahrungen' (V, p. 18).[2] A genetic approach is validated by its ability to avoid stasis and to bring out not just an historical but a life-historical dynamic too. As Schneider himself would insist, however, it must always be relativised by contingency, a recognition of which is inescapable in an epoch of unprecedented volatility. Yet, as will become apparent, if a belief in

2. See Author's Note at the end of this essay for key.

the role of chance is a guarantor of freedom of action, of individual political choices, it at the same time deprives history of an overall meaning and thus exposes the individual to a melancholy which can rob commitment of its motivating energies: if there is no purpose or pattern, why bother acting? For merely to register contingency does not still what Alexander Kluge calls our 'hunger for meaning'. This tension between necessity and freedom, already articulated two decades ago in a review of Sartre's literary essays (AP, pp. 78–86), is at the heart of Schneider's writing. This must relativise the notion of Schneider as the writer laureate of the New Left who, in the wake of disappointments political and personal increasingly retreats into *belles-lettres* and into himself — a retreat symbolised by his switch from left-wing to mainstream publishers. The expectations raised by the first two fictional works (*Lenz* and *Verfassungsfeind*), which deal respectively with the Student Movement and the 'Berufsverbot', do indeed collapse in the face of the third. Instead of the full-scale treatment in fictionalised form of the problem of terrorism that the historical moment seemed to demand, *Die Wette* (1978) withdrew into apparently timeless emotional quagmires. Whereas the question of terrorism does form the essential backdrop to Schneider's film-script for Reinhard Hauff's *Messer im Kopf* (1979), it resurfaces — the odd essay apart — only after an interval of several years in the mediated guise of the author's correspondence with the convicted member of the Red Army Faction, Peter-Jürgen Boock.

This is a plausible way of reading Schneider's 'disappointing' progress after *Verfassungsfeind* — yet it depends on bringing *expectations* to bear on subsequent texts, on assuming that the political writer's job is to be a kind of chronicler. Such expectations ignore the shifting relationship between the historical process and the dynamic of the writer's own experience. Accompanying and articulating the historical-political momentum within Schneider's writing — an ongoing engagement with the German left and its opponents since the late 1960s — is a ceaseless and intensifying self-scrutiny, which is rooted in generational and biographical particulars. Moreover, while the answers that a writer gives may *formally* appear to be similar, the questions that history is asking are ceaselessly changing.

If we are looking for a constant in Schneider's writing, a clue is provided by a remark in the long *Kursbuch* essay on 'Die Phantasie im Spätkapitalismus und die Kulturrevolution' (1969). Schneider notes how, according to Freud, phantasy becomes the destination of those infantile wishes that are unable to find satisfaction in reality. During the Oedipal phase, the child learns 'die entsprechenden

Lusterwartungen auf die Personen und Gegenstände der Außenwelt zu übertragen. Dabei werden auch die erotischen, nichtkapitalistischen Formen der Aneignung der Objekte, Tasten, Schauen, Riechen usw. [. . .] von der Mutter gelöst und können an anderen Objekten Berfriedigung *suchen*' (AP, pp. 132–3). Thus the child abandons the mother, 'um von nun an *die ganze Welt zur Mutter zu machen*' (italics added, ibid); and the point is illustrated by a quotation from Villon, whose 'love' for 'his' city is invoked in sexual terms.

Such a transference of originally infantile desires on to a world that satisfies few or none of them is bound to lead to an immense accumulation of wishes. The historical remoteness of the allusion to Villon highlights the fact that, in the face of the increasingly reified social world depicted by Schneider in *Ansprachen* and throughout his fiction, the transference will result in a disappointment proportionate to the unreasonableness of the original expectations. The sense of yearning that this provokes is double-edged: it can yield utopian dreams of a 'Heimat', of a reunion with the Other from which we were separated as children; but it can also end in frustration and defensive withdrawal back into the self. Narcissism, 'the final form of individualism', [3] is a diminished sense of the self that engenders a disturbed because dependent relation to the object-world in general and vitiates sexual relationships in particular. The prevalence of narcissism in the post-war Western world has been explained as a strategy of survival in an epoch of endemic economic, cultural and personal insecurity.[4] It stamps Schneider's protagonists, as does the compensatory hunger for sensual experience ('Tasten, Schauen, Riechen') that has, equally, been thematised as characteristic of the 1970s. For infantile narcissism is a phenomenon of the oral phase of development, and it has been argued that in our society — consumer-oriented monopoly capitalism — an oral social character has increasingly replaced the anal impulse that drove entrepreneurial capitalism.[5]

The popular thesis of politicisation followed by a compensatory swing back to subjectivity forgets that the denial of subjectivity was not a feature of 1967–9 but of the Marxist-Leninist cadre-party phase that ensued. Moreover, it tries to harness a global and generational phenomenon — the frantic intensification of subjec-

---

3. Russell Jacoby, *Social Amnesia*, Hassocks, 1977, p. 116.
4. Cf. e.g.: Christopher Lasch, *The Culture of Narcissism*, London, 1980 and *The Minimal Self*, London, 1984; also the German debate on the 'new socialisation type' initiated by Thomas Ziehe, *Pubertät und Narzißmus*, Frankfurt and Cologne, 1975.
5. Cf. Johann August Schülein, 'Von der Studentenrevolte zur Tendenzwende oder der Rückzug ins Private', *Kursbuch* 48 (June 1977), pp. 101–17.

tivity at the moment of its decline — to short-term historical explanation. This is not to deny the importance of factors specific to the Federal Republic, such as the institutionalised political repression of the left by the state from 1972 onwards, which accelerated 'retreat' from political activism (as well as its radicalisation into terrorism). It is simply to emphasise that an adequate analysis of Schneider's preoccupations rests not on any one of the levels of history ('events' during the 1970s), generation (political, cultural and family socialisation during the first two post-war decades) and biography (Schneider's own experiences), but on the interaction between all three. The outcome of this nexus has been so explosive for Germans of Schneider's generation during the late 1960s and 1970s — witness the roll-call of casualties from Rudi Dutschke to Ulrike Meinhof, from Rainer Werner Fassbinder to Bernward Vesper — that it is not surprising that an intense reflection on 'Lebensgeschichte' should be a concern of both Schneider's protagonists and of their creator.

Schneider had been regularly publishing for some ten years before the appearance of *Lenz*, which can be seen to mark the 'beginning' of his literary career only if we ascribe a primacy to fiction over essayism and self-reflection. None the less the main interest of his early reviews is in the signposts they contain towards his subsequent development. Thus for Schneider the core of Weiss's *Marat/Sade* (1964) is the antithesis between political engagement and individualism — which also constitutes the central tension in *Lenz*. Similarly, the discussion of Sartre's essays brings out not only Schneider's sympathy for existentialism as a guarantor of individual freedom but also a shared scepticism about the 'inevitability' of revolution and an affirmation of the principle of non-causality that was to render problematic not only his position during the Marxist-Leninist phase of the Student Movement but his relation to historical materialism in general.[6]

What still marks these early reviews is the lack of a clear political standpoint. The late 1960s did not merely, in the shape of the APO and the campaign against the 'Notstandsgesetze', supply a political focus for students and the new generation of intellectuals. No less importantly, these years provided an opportunity for a collective *exorcism*, via mass demonstrations and other protest actions, of the

---

6. Schneider is strongly attracted by Jacques Monod's existentialist-inspired view of religion, philosophy and sections of scientific knowledge as monuments to humankind's unending effort to deny its own contingency; cf. *Le hasard et la nécessité*, Paris, 1970, p. 63.

frustrations accumulated by this generation during the politically stagnant Adenauer era. This process set free the wishes and desires — and, not least, the anger — that had hitherto been suppressed or found expression only in art (as Schneider detected in the sensuality and vehemence of the *Marat/Sade*) but which now seemed capable of imminent social and political realisation. The speeches and other writings in *Ansprachen* (1970) show the interplay of these factors within the Student Movement. They reveal that, whereas particular campaigns (university reform; Vietnam; the abortive Springer Tribunal, in which Schneider was, along with Dutschke and Enzensberger, closely involved) served as ethical-political crystallisation-points, the real libidinal energies came from elsewhere. One source was the rift between the students and their parents' generation, which was deepened by such reminders of the Nazi past as the Frankfurt Auschwitz trial. Another was a related protest against the reified quality of the everyday life the older generation had established in the Federal Republic, which Schneider captures in *Ansprachen* in a series of vignettes, whose laconic grotesqueness recalls Reinhard Lettau. They focus on how human behaviour is regulated by inhibitions and prohibitions, especially in the area of 'Hausordnungen' and road manners. That minor transgressions result in often violent over-reactions lays bare how individuals' needs have been mistreated in other areas of their lives, how the wishes of the 'Wirtschaftswunder' generation have been attenuated to the desire to cling on to their possessions. By contrast, the protest generation are bursting with needs and wishes they are no longer prepared to suppress.

It is ironic that at the same time as Schneider has found a distinctive voice, he is also driven to question the role of literature. In 'Rede an die deutschen Leser und ihre Schriftsteller', an unashamedly subjective piece, Schneider starts with the concrete — the sterile everyday life of West Berlin as seen from his own window each morning. Once again he draws attention to how capitalism pursues its interests at the expense of human needs : 'Die Leuchtschriften drücken nicht die Wünsche und Leidenschaften der Städtebewohner aus, sondern die von Osram, Siemens und AEG' (AS, p. 32). The conclusions for literature : not only can such a situation provide no inspiration for the writer — though Schneider's acute vignettes as well as *Lenz* belie this — the only adequate response is not to try to describe it but to change it. Traditional art must be combatted because its function has been to protect capitalism from the rebellion of human wishes. Rejecting Adorno's conviction that art's utopian energies depend on its autonomy, Schneider

Peter Schneider

argues that in the new, pre-revolutionary situation, the task of the artist must no longer be to organise wishes in art but to help them find their *political* form. It is not literature as such that is 'dead' but the bourgeois literature that converts the despair of the masses into an object of consumption instead of showing how their oppression can be overcome. Schneider cites Mao's Red Army as the form in which human needs were organised (as against a prayer, a poem, or a novel) during the Long March and observes : '*Natürlich* läßt sich das Modell auf unsere Verhältnisse übertragen' (italics added, AS, p. 38). Such knee-jerk over-confidence is a measure of the 'over-politicisation' of the late 1960s.

The paradox of late capitalism is that its unprecedented unleashing of productive forces has stimulated an unprecedented explosion of human wishes that, owing to the socio-economic inequalities on which it rests, it can only redirect according to its own needs or else frustrate. This qualitatively new form of crisis underlies the widespread recognition during the 1960s that political-economic revolution would be incomplete, would fail to increase human happiness, without an accompanying 'cultural' revolution within everyday life. Accordingly, 'Die Phantasie im Spätkapitalismus und die Kulturrevolution' elaborates ideas (and absorbs passages) from 'Rede an die deutschen Leser und ihre Schriftsteller'. While it reflects in its discourse the Student Movement's re-discovery and subsequent fetishisation of Marxist theory, its conceptual *content* is far removed from the dogmatism of the Marxist-Leninist groups that mushroomed in the wake of the founding of the DKP in 1968. Not only does Schneider enlist, as might be expected, the humanist-utopian Marx of the *Paris Manuscripts* rather than the more economic-systemic *Kapital*; following the example of the Frankfurt School and of Marcuse in particular, he also juxtaposes (though fails to integrate) Marx's affirmation of human needs and sensuality with Freud's theory of wishes, dreams and phantasy.

The 'Phantasie' essay makes clear that the model underlying Schneider's understanding of everyday life in late capitalism is a Freudian one. In our society, human wishes are articulated only in commodified form, as it were already fulfilled, by the mass media; in art and literature these wishes appear, in recognition of the impossibility of their fulfilment, as Kafkaesque nightmares. The coldness, fear and hostility Schneider finds everywhere is explained by the fact that when people's real wishes and needs are frustrated, these express themselves in the form of mass neuroses. In the Federal Republic these neuroses are exacerbated by the trauma of the repressed memory of the Nazi past: but here, as generally elsewhere,

–319–

Schneider's work is short on historical perspective. Apart from its anticipation of the programme of the allegedly 'new' subjectivist tendencies of the 1970s (also foreshadowed at the time in the sexual-revolutionary impulse of 'Kommune I' and the rediscovery of Wilhelm Reich). the 'Phantasie' essay is dated, in both senses, not simply by aggressive over-confidence but — issuing from this — by undigested absorption of Marxist terminology. Yet Schneider does not fully succeed in drowning his personal and political depression in objectivity, as he himself subsequently confessed. The piece is hybrid: comprising not just theoreticist ventriloquism but occasional concrete-experiential elements too. Whereas the essay is ostensibly devoted to strategies for the emancipation of a collective subject, i.e. the working class, the protest and energy impelling it still derive from *individual* experience. Indeed, even in such a largely 'objectivist' essay, Schneider is too candid to conceal an incorrigible individualism that believes that the goal of a cultural revolution is to enable 'die menschliche Ungleichheit' to develop, to invent forms of social life 'in denen man mit gutem Gewissen gewissenlos sein kann, weil kein Mangel an Freundlichkeit herrscht' (AP, pp. 130–1). As the protest movement entered into its 'proletarian' phase, partly inspired by the wave of strikes in September 1969, this mechanism of transference was lost sight of, with fateful consequences for the morale, coherence and sense of direction of the left.

The waning of the strategies of the late 1960s was symbolised by the dissolution of the SDS (Sozialistischer Deutscher Studentenbund) and the emergence of new, contradictory impulses in the shape of Dutschke's 'long march through the institutions' and the foundation of the Red Army Faction. In the years that followed, Schneider began to express his scepticism towards theory in general and towards the Marxist-Leninist turn in the German left in particular, whereby the anti-authoritarian movement increasingly succumbed to authoritarianism within its own structures. During this period he published a number of essays in *Kursbuch* that were based on his experiences: working in an electrical factory; in a Berlin school; and in class struggles in the north of Italy. In each case Schneider pillories the arrogance of a theory that ignores real human wishes and needs and that erects alongside reality a purely intellectual edifice whose criterion is whether it can be instrumentalised in political practice. In each of these pieces Schneider casts himself in the role of a 'participant observer', suggesting that it was through practical work and experiences that the hollow theoreticism of the 'Phantasie' essay was overcome.

There remained, however, what now came to be called the 'subjective factor', and it is this that *Lenz*, Schneider's first extended narrative, set out to explore. He was not the first of the protest generation to venture into this terrain, for his brother Michael Schneider had published a psychological profile of the cadre-party sector of the left, 'Gegen den linken Dogmatismus, eine Alterskrankheit des Kommunismus', in *Kursbuch* as early as 1971, where he anticipated some of *Lenz*'s themes: above all, the relationship between political activism and personality. This immediately raises the question of how *Lenz* should be read. When it appeared, it was received as an intervention in debates about and within the extraparliamentary left, as attacks on Peter Schneider from the Marxist-Leninist wing suggest. At the same time, Schneider has himself warned that it is not to be read autobiographically — notwithstanding its roots in his personal experience – and in 1984 he even suggested that he would be happy for it to be seen as an essentially *unpolitical* work of fiction.[7] This provocative remark is more revealing than might at first seem. What strikes one with hindsight is how *Lenz* now reads as a catalogue of the 'cultural' preoccupations of the non-dogmatic sector of the German left since the early 1970s: not just subjectivity but also its specific components — phantasy, wishes, feelings, utopia, sensuality, the 'rediscovery' of the body, female/male relationships, the crisis of maleness — as well as such more conventional strategic questions as the relationship between intellectuals and the working class or between spontaneity and organisation. In a reference to Lenz's 'hunger for experience', Schneider even anticipates the title of the most imaginative and penetrating analysis of the 1970s, Michael Rutschky's *Erfahrungshunger* (1980).

Rutschky's keyword for the decade is 'disorientation': the situation in which Lenz finds himself. We first encounter him waking from a dream. Dreaming is, as Freud tells us, one means of fulfilling our wishes; what distinguishes the other, phantasy, is that it can be translated into action through its ability to link up with the motor-system, and hence has revolutionary potential. However, for Lenz, as for the Student Movement as a whole, the phase of mass demonstrations is past — and with it the hopes of revolution — giving way to melancholy and introspection. Finding no space in his Maoist group for his personal needs, Lenz's disillusionment with theory and its hypnotic effect on his political colleagues grows. His sense of isolation and loss is intensified by the ending of his relationship with

7. Interview with Helmut Pfeiffer (12 October 1984), *Deutsche Autoren heute* 7, Bonn n.d. [1986], p. 53.

L. Disintegration and stasis are mirrored in the forms of the text. The narrative is episodic, broken up into short, self-contained sections. During the first half, these are introduced by non-specific formulae such as 'An einem anderen Tag . . .' that reflect the lack of development, as one virtually identical day follows another. For Lenz has fallen out of (his) history; he is floating. Yet the moment of waking that opens the book represents a threshold — between unconscious and conscious, wishes and actions, past and present — and so contains the possibility of change.

The first indication of this is Lenz's heightened sensual awareness, recalling that of his namesake in Georg Büchner's novella. He sees the world as if for the first time, with himself at its centre, like the hero of a 'Bildungsroman'. But there is nothing utopian or emancipatory about Lenz's exposure to concrete experience. Nature provokes only fear and disgust. Without the shield of either theoretical concepts or his relationship with L. to filter reality for him, the world is for Lenz a cacophony of sense-impressions. What had attracted him to the working-class L. in the first place was her practical experience of things that existed only in his head, as wishes and ideas. For Lenz is a narcissist in the precise psychoanalytical sense: in the myth, Narcissus is caught between an unrealisable desire for himself and for an absolute Other, Echo. The narcissist thus looks for himself in others, 'finding the self-image in the image of another'.[8] In an individualistic attempt to bridge the gap between classes and fulfil his yearning for the Other, Lenz invested his 'hunger for experience' in this relationship and used it as a springboard 'die Welt mit den Sinnen zu *erobern*' (italics added, L, p. 45).

Lenz's narcissism is the cause of his disturbed relation to the object-world. He can no longer distinguish between the real and the imaginary, outward and inward. He regards other people as resources ('erobern') to satisfy his needs,[9] looking to their otherness to provide him with the sense of identity he lacks. For the narcissist, such a quest is doomed. Thus a casual sexual encounter elicits from the narrator a refusal of description: 'Es war dann sehr schön, es gibt nichts weiteres dazu zu sagen' (L, p. 10). But this is the silence not of tact but of alienation: 'Später, als sie nebeneinander lagen, tat Lenz ihre Zärtlichkeit körperlich weh' (ibid.). Like Schneider's other male protagonists, Lenz simultaneously yearns for and fears

---

8. Juliet Mitchell, *Psychoanalysis and Feminism*, Harmondsworth, 1975, p. 39.
9. Cf. Richard Sennett, 'Destructive Gemeinschaft', in R. Bocock et. al. (eds.), *An Introduction to Sociology*, London, 1980, pp. 91–121; also Sennett, *The Fall of Public Man*, New York, 1977.

involvement with the Other because this brings with it dependence and, thereby, a *loss* of the narcissist's self.[10] Political activism is thus often a kind of occupational therapy to distract from one's personal problems and neuroses. The protagonist's diatribes are fuelled by the same anger and energy that powered Schneider's speeches in *Ansprachen*, but the targets now include the left itself. Lenz harangues his friend B. for the fact that he and his fellow revolutionary intellectuals define their goals and themselves by negation:

> Da ihr die Ziele eures Kampfes immer nur von den Lippen eurer Gegner ablest, tritt nie eine Beruhigung ein, auch nicht wenn der Gegner besiegt ist. [. . .] Ihr wißt nicht, im Namen von was ihr kämpft, oder ihr wißt es, aber ihr habt es nicht drin. Weil ihr nicht für euer eignes Glück kämpft, verteidigt ihr auch nicht das Glück anderer Leute. Ihr seid nicht angreifbar — weil ihr nichts zu verteidigen habt — sondern nur Angreifer. (L, p. 50)

This passage, at the exact centre of the text, argues that the relationship of the left intelligentsia to the working class is — mirroring Lenz's relation to L. — narcissistic: the former look to the latter both to provide a sense of identity and to satisfy their needs by proxy. Before the intelligentsia can be of any use in the class struggle they must, like Lenz, begin to recognise their own needs and 'fight for their own happiness'. If such needs and wishes are repressed, in the interests of party discipline or doctrinal purity, they are likely to assert themselves 'hinter dem Rücken der Gruppe und durch ihre Unterdrückung die Arbeit behindern' (L, p. 28). Lenz's onslaught on B. marks the turning-point: on the following day he decides to leave Berlin for Rome.

At first, it seems as though Lenz's Italian journey will result in self-discovery. He revels in the country's sensuality and sheer otherness, which unlock long-repressed memories of childhood. He is impressed by Pierra's spontaneity, by her principle of fulfilling each wish as soon as it arises, irrespective of the dictates of conscience. The way she relates everything to events in her own past enables her to live more fully in the present — just as people seem to Lenz more alive and imaginative in ruin-filled Rome than in the historyless cities he knew in Germany. Lenz's position, however, is dramatised

10. In 'Die Sache mit der "Männlichkeit". Gibt es eine Emanzipation der Männer?', an early (1974) contribution to the subsequently proliferating discussion by men of the problems of maleness, Schneider maintained that the capacity to separate sex from emotions was typically male (cf. B, p. 229). It is in line with Schneider's mistrust of either/or extremes that he is no less sceptical about 'feministic' men than he is about chauvinists.

as that of the outsider caught between extremes, between neurotics and theoreticians. Rome is merely the antipode of Berlin. If the Marxist-Leninist groups in Germany reduce everything to the contradiction between capital and labour, Pierra's circle are no less infatuated with psychoanalysis: for them the family situation is the determinant of all conflicts, including social ones. Schneider's argument is schematic: if Berlin is the thesis and Rome the antithesis, the synthesis is provided by Trento. *En route*, Lenz realises that he has acquired a healthier relationship to the object-world. He has found the right tempo for his perceptions, no longer wanting immediately to dissolve all phenomena into concepts. Nature has ceased to disgust him, and he can now overcome his latent fears of homosexuality sufficiently to embrace and kiss B. This attempt to incorporate into their friendship an awareness of their bodies now appears no less *politically* significant to Lenz than what they think and say to one another.

As Lenz becomes involved in the community and the local struggles in Trento, where Schneider had himself spent some time, the struggles within himself begin to seem ludicrous. He finds, in a concrete situation, that theory is no longer meaningless. His political work is now motivated by a sense of pleasure, in place of the superego that prevailed within the Marxist-Leninist and Maoist groups. Personal conflicts are not, as in Berlin, repressed but brought out and spontaneously resolved. However, just as Lenz seems to have gained a sense of identity and purpose, he is made to realise that this is, once again, borrowed. So Schneider ends not on a utopian note in Trento but back in Berlin, with Lenz resolving to 'stay'. His journey has not solved his problems. Indeed for a book that affirms the discovery of 'sensuality', there is little trace of this in the text. Schneider denies us visualising description; characters are barely differentiated (projections of the narcissistic protagonist's consciousness?); the discourse is, at the close as well as the beginning, reified, frequently composed of chains of symmetrical sentences and, significantly, placing the subject in first place at the epistemological centre of things: 'Lenz blieb. Er schrieb keine Briefe und telefonierte nicht mehr nach Deutschland. Er sehnte sich nirgends zurück und nirgendwo hin. Er lernte wie ein Kind sprechen, durch Nachahmung und Beobachtung. Es fiel nicht mehr auf, wenn er nach einem Wort fragte, das er nicht verstand. Er ging auf die Versammlungen und redete dort, als gehörte er dazu' (L, p. 83).

How is the outcome of Lenz's learning-process to be interpreted? Is staying in Berlin, where he detects only minor signs of change during his absence, to be grasped as resignation or as recognition that the terrain of political activity in the 1970s is concrete work in the local community? B. by contrast is planning a trip to Latin America. Schneider's ending is cautious, open-ended: Lenz has still not found a goal for his wishes. As a narcissist, could he ever? So perhaps Schneider is right in suggesting that *Lenz* is not to be read as a political book. It is, rather, 'pre-political': an analysis of the predispositions for political involvement, and hence as much about the subjectivity of politics as about the politics of subjectivity. Although Schneider's attack on theoreticism is valid, it is undifferentiated, for both the early Marx he himself uses in the 'Phantasie' essay as well as Ernst Bloch, to give just two examples, ascribe a pivotal role to sensuality and experience. Indeed many of the questions touched on by Schneider in *Lenz* and elsewhere had been *theoretically* elaborated by Oskar Negt and Alexander Kluge in their seminal *Öffentlichkeit und Erfahrung* (1972),[11] which was itself a non-dogmatic by-product — and sublation — of the German left's proletarian turn. Similarly, the exoticism of Lenz's Italian interlude has more to do with the mobilisation of the protagonist's wishes and his quest for an Other than with specific strategic lessons, which Schneider had already provided in a pair of essays in the special Italian number of *Kursbuch* edited by him.[12] All in all Lenz's state of mind derives at least as much from an existential crisis — as the allusions to Büchner imply — as from the demoralisation of the left. To be more precise, the latter entailed that personal crises could no longer be, in the very mechanism Schneider analyses in the book, sublimated through political action.[13]

Historically, the vogue for self-reflection was not merely a response to the dissipation of the Student Movement. It equally corresponded to the new, defensive introspection into which the left was forced by the 'Berufsverbot', which was fully in operation by the time that *Lenz* appeared. If the latter is permeated by melancholy, the mood of Schneider's next fictional narrative, . . . *schon bist du ein Verfassungsfeind* (1975), is paranoia. The pattern of anguished self-scrutiny is sustained, only here the initial stimulus is as much external: a product of the investigative mechanism of the 'Radikalenerlaß' itself. The historical moment is more urgent; the gap

11. See my chapter on Kluge, pp. 270f. above.
12. 'Können wir aus den italienischen Klassenkämpfen lernen?' and 'Die Massen, die Gewerkschaften und die politischen Avantgarden', *Kursbuch* 26 (December 1971), pp. 1–3 and 135–62; Schneider did not reprint the latter in *Die Botschaft des Pferdekopfs*.
13. For further discussion of *Lenz* see also Wilfried van der Will's chapter on 'The Republic of Letters, and the State', pp. 15f.

between narrated time and publication was, unlike *Lenz*, only a matter of months: the book begins in May 1975, shortly before the Baader-Meinhof trial in Stuttgart.

The law has been a key terrain of political debate and conflict throughout the history of the Federal Republic, whose tendency has been to convert intractable political and ideological questions — such as the reconcilability of a Communist Party and the economic 'miracle' — into legal ones. As the countless car-owners and house-holders who take petty private squabbles to court demonstrate, a similar pattern saturates everyday life too: it was here that Schneider began in *Ansprachen*. Such a preoccupation with the law derives from the specific development of the Federal Republic, for which questions of legitimacy and constitutionality have, in the light of the experience of fascism and of the juridical process amid which the West German state was founded, been of central importance. Here, too, the question of historical continuity was crucial: both in the shape of continuity within a largely unreformed judiciary after 1945, as well as in legislation that stirred memories of the Third Reich and its immediate prelude. The campaign against the 'Notstandsgesetze', around which the APO coalesced, was thus challenging the state on the most sensitive ground.

The introduction of the 'Radikalenerlaß' in January 1972 should not be trivialised as the 'revenge' of the fathers' generation against the rebellious sons of 1967–9. It was, rather, an expression of a wider legitimation crisis of the late capitalist state, as it evolved, in the face of diminishing economic prosperity and spreading social disintegration, from liberal towards technocratic-authoritarian forms. In such a situation, as Peter Brückner has argued, education, the process of developing consciousness and transmitting attitudes to the next generation, becomes a seminal political factor,[14] as the late 1960s recognised. This is why it was in particular teachers — the profession of Kleff, the protagonist of *Verfassungsfeind* — who were called upon to demonstrate their loyalty to the state and hence their fitness to participate in the increasingly urgent process of ideological and cultural stabilisation. It was, however, the cost-ineffective disproportion between the vast number of investigations and the handful of actual refusals of career civil servant status ('Verbeamtung') that unmasked the state's strategy as what Oskar Negt has called 'preventive counter-revolution.[15]

14. Cf. Peter Brückner, *Versuch, uns und anderen die Bundesrepublik zu erklären*, W. Berlin, 1978, pp. 163–7
15. Cf. Oskar Negt, 'Die Misere der bürgerlichen Demokratie in Deutschland', *Keine*

As the late 1960s generation left the universities and was absorbed into career patterns, it found itself caught between the (with hindsight, excessive) wishes and hopes mobilised during the Student Movement and the pressures to conform in the new retrenched capitalist world after the Oil Crisis. Lenz's problem may be his rootlessness, but he is thus also without ties, personal or professional. We only surmise that he is a student; he takes a job in a factory out of personal-political rather than financial motives. Above all, he is an *agent*, still apparently capable of shaping his future. Kleff too is, like Lenz, an outsider, also with a radically new perspective on reality — but only because he has been declared a 'Verfassungsfeind'. From the outset, Kleff is, by contrast with Lenz, a *reactor*, whose scope for choice and action is severely curtailed. He represents the next stage in the development of his generation, as it were an institutionalised Lenz.

Although Schneider, who was himself investigated but subsequently cleared after appeal, enlists his personal experience of the 'Berufsverbot', he has emphasised that *Verfassungsfeind* draws on several actual cases. Nevertheless the focus continues to be, as with *Lenz*, on an individual: more explicitly so, in that the text is made up of Kleff's letters to the lawyer he has engaged to help him clear the authorities' 'doubts' concerning his suitability for 'Verbeamtung'. At times these letters read more like journal entries: along with Kleff's horror at being back in a provincial town, an echo of Sartre's *La Nausée*. This Freiburg setting, another autobiographical element, illustrates how the protest generation was in part politicised by frustration with the 'gedämpfte Tonfall, diese verrückte Stille' (V, p. 19) that typified Adenauer's 1950s. Unlike both Lenz and Sartre's Roquentin, however, Kleff can no longer indulge in the cherished existentialist pastime of contemplating his disturbed relations to the object-world, because the threat of 'Berufsverbot' forces him to retrace his political progress. As a result, not only is *Verfassungsfeind* more rooted in a specific historical moment; the narrative itself has a stronger historical component than *Lenz*. This comprises not just the life-history that is pieced together by Kleff but also the 'Radikalenerlaß' itself, which is shown to re-open the question of the German past.

The subjective perspective is now balanced within the text by the interpolation of italicised documentary passages, including actual letters from the authorities to employees under suspicion 'quoted' by

---

Demokratie ohne Sozialismus. Über den Zusammenhang von Politik, Geschichte und Moral, Frankfurt on Main, 1976, pp. 17–46.

Kleff. By confronting extracts from the legislation on the civil service at various periods, Schneider is able to show that the 'Radikalenerlaß' is in line not with the democratic (Weimar) tradition but with the Wilhelmine and Nazi eras — as well as with tendencies in the GDR. The common factor is 'jederzeit': the applicant is bound to uphold the principles of the free-democratic basic order (or of the Third Reich, or the workers' and peasants' state) both during and outside of working hours. The late 1960s axiom that the personal is the political has thus, ironically, been annexed by the state, as it expands itself into the hitherto autonomous domain of the mentalities and opinions of individuals. This is part of a wider process whereby the boundaries of what is objective and subjective, public and private, are being redrawn: the debates on 'Öffentlichkeit' and on the 'subjective factor' within the German left during the 1970s were complementary. It is Kleff's discovery that his assessment by the school authorities will comprise a *'Bewertung der gesamten Persönlichkeit'* (V, p. 8) that impels him to start compiling his own personal file to rival theirs. The problem to which Schneider, like Kleff, addresses himself in *Verfassungsfeind*, is the weight that can still be given to individual experience in an epoch where societalisation ('Vergesellschaftung') is being augmented by increasing 'statification' ('Verstaatlichung').

This is one reason why the utopiá of immediate experience in *Lenz* was merely *asserted*, could not be allowed to infiltrate the book's cool and sceptical discourse, which contrasts with the irresistible but overheated intensity of Bernward Vesper's autobiographical account of a parallel process, *Die Reise* (1977). For the disillusionment described in *Verfassungsfeind* was already visible among the left by the time *Lenz* appeared. This made the writing of *Lenz* an act of attempted re-orientation. To have ignored the need for this, in favour of an unproblematic affirmation of sensuality, would have been an act of bad faith. In *Verfassungsfeind* this utopia of immediate experience is still more remote — located not in Italy but in Africa. Kleff manages to keep in contact with this level of his being through drumming. The latter serves, like dancing in *Lenz*, as a physical exorcism of anger and hatred. Not only did the cult of the body and bodily experience during the late 1960s symbolise rebellion and emancipation, it was, for Schneider at any rate, also a politicising factor: 'Es war ein neues Gefühl für den Körper, eine neue Art, sich zu bewegen, zu sprechen, *und dann erst* ein neues Bewußtsein, das mich anzog' (AP, p. 225, italics added). By contrast, the fetishisation of 'Sinnlichkeit' during the 1970s both signalled a retreat into that part of one's existence that seemed beyond the reach of 'Vergesellschaftung' and 'Verstaatliching' and at the same time, as Rutschky has argued, assumed that physiological answers could be provided to existential questions: in other words, that hunger for meaning could be satisfied by (sensual) experience — a belief that promoted domestic reception of the New German Cinema, significantly the work of Herzog and Wenders above all. Such a shortcircuiting of 'Sinnlichkeit' and 'Sinn', legitimated by a superficial reading of early Marx, is both enticing and regressive: as abreactive protest, this was part of its appeal. Schneider, however, cannot embrace such a body-based Rousseauism, which has latterly taken a less hedonistic and more therapeutic turn, because his affinity with existentialism prevents him from believing that there is any prelapsarian (that is, pre-capitalist) human 'essence' to re-appropriate. At the same time, his allied sense of contingency makes it difficult for him to *envisage* any utopia: a conscious *goal* of striving, not what one discovers when one gets there.

The author's scepticism is in tune with the 'neue Ruhe im Lande' (V, p. 49) registered by Kleff. If this seems a bizarre characterisation of the turmoil that made the 1970s in the Federal Republic a battleground of terrorism and state repression, it is clarified when Kleff adds that what has changed are not the causes for disquiet but the willingness, or the possibility, to articulate it. In the light of this desensitisation, the subtitle to Schneider's collected non-literary journalism from the 1970s — *Essays aus einem **friedlichen** Jahrzent* — is not simply ironic but poignant, marked by a sense of loss. But however widespread and fashionable, this is the perspective of a specific *generational* experience. Although *Verfassungsfeind* contains no affirmative equivalent to the spontaneous class struggles in Trento, other ways of reading the political dynamic of the 1970s are alluded to. There was developing, at the time the book appeared, not just a regrouping of extra-parliamentary forces, as the Brandt–Scheel reform era came to an end, but the sublation of traditional class-based politics by new categories and goals. The abstract and megalomaniac strategy of overthrowing the existing system was replaced by the attempt to establish concrete utopian enclaves in the here and now, in the shape of the 'alternative' Counter Culture. Those questions for which orthodox Marxism had no answer forced their way on to the political agenda. From the mid-1970s, as the Women's Movement was gaining in profile and strength, more subversive and far-reaching analyses of the subjective factor were emerging, while by fixing on identifiable targets, the grass-roots 'Bürgerinitiativen' crystallised protest energies in a non-sectarian manner, above all in the Anti-Nuclear Movement.

Even when utopia is lost sight of, wishes still remain, and thus frustration and melancholy grow. So much so that Kleff, in his confused and imploded state, cannot perceive for himself the new social movements growing up around him, including those nearby at Wyhl, and has to have these pointed out to him by the 'anarchist' Jutta. Their conversation is the crux of *Verfassungsfeind*, because she confronts him with the gap between his former ambitions (Africa correspondent, musician) and the reality of his existence, with his inability to overcome his fear and convert his principles into actions. Kleff is himself aware that, having left Freiburg with so many wishes, he had returned empty-handed. This is, Jutta tells him, because like most people, 'Du nimmst deine *Wünsche* nicht ernst.' (V, p. 95, italics added). Having refused what, he subsequently realises, was a test of his preparedness to go 'underground', Kleff now finds himself boxed in: faced with a 'choice' between retracting his incriminating comment about the right to resist undemocratic laws, and being regarded as a 'traitor' by the left, or alternatively holding out and becoming a 'martyr'. Having opted for the latter, Kleff discovers that he has been outmanoeuvred by the authorities. He is rejected not on account of the comment which led to his investigation but for having passed on details of the investigation. The final paragraph of the text abandons the subjective perspective of Kleff's letters: the authorities are given the last word. We learn that Kleff is not present at his appeal because he has 'disappeared'. As with *Lenz*, the ending is open — has Kleff committed suicide? emigrated to Africa? joined the armed struggle? or has he withdrawn into himself entirely? It is, however, even more difficult to construe this in utopian terms. To the extent that a bibliography of the 'Radikalenerlaß' appears as an appendix — an affirmation if not of hope, at any rate of resistance — Schneider's political commitment is sustained, albeit now even more tinged with melancholy.

Confusion and disorientation were understandable, for the extension of the boundaries of politics to incorporate the personal and aesthetic spheres, proclaimed in the late 1960s as essential to the strategy of cultural revolution, was now being put into practice by the state itself, for the purposes of stabilisation. The chief tool of this process was a 'Verrechtlichung' (juridification) of conflict within the superstructure. If the 'Radikaleneralaß' politicised subjectivity, the new censorship laws, such as Article 88a relating to the 'Befürwortung der Gewalt', represented a 'politicisation of aesthetics'. This was in tune with the media-led witch-hunt against the intelligentsia, which began with the right's perversion of Heinrich

Böll's attack on the methods of *Bild-Zeitung* into 'intellectual bomb-throwing' and advocacy of terrorism. On top of the legacy of disillusion arising out of the fractured hopes of the late 1960s, in such a climate it was to be expected that the self-scrutiny undertaken with *Lenz* and *Verfassungsfeind* should continue. This now took explicitly autobiographical form, in two pieces in Schneider's programmatically titled *Atempause: Versuch, meine Gedanken über Literatur und Kunst zu ordnen* (1977). The first, 'Über den Unterschied zwischen Literatur und Politik' (1976), attempts, amid the prevailing depression and depoliticisation accompanying the Federal Republic's 'Hundertmetersprint in die Vergangenheit' (AP, p. 167), to take some joyless comfort from the thought that, in German history, literary revivals have often accompanied political restoration. This entails a disengagement, a recognition of the lack of synchronisation between literature and politics, which Schneider had coupled together in the late 1960s. For him this is now symbolised by the contradiction between Gorky and Lenin, the architect of the Bolshevik 'Machtergreifung' (AP, p. 172). Such a scandalous borrowing of the standard term for the *Nazi* seizure of power hammers home the fact that Schneider's sympathies lie with Gorky, even though he is well aware that if the Russian workers and soldiers had followed the latter, there never would have been a revolution. By identifying with the self-styled 'heretic' who accepts his contradictions, Schneider is giving voice to his own difficulties in reconciling literature and political commitment. He sees a fundamental conflict between the writer's obligation to integrity — not to suppress opinions, doubts, wishes just because they deviate from the party line — and the self-denial, expediency and discipline so often tactically essential to politics. This was, though presented in somewhat different form, the problem described in *Lenz*. In a sense, however, this is not the real problem. For by 1976 the Marxist-Leninist phase was past its peak and no longer a major issue; the measure of autonomy necessary to art was fully reconcilable with an involvement in spontaneous and non-dogmatic tendencies within the left, as the theoretically saturated films and stories of Alexander Kluge and his ongoing collaboration with the Marxist sociologist Oskar Negt suggested.

The second essay, 'Die Beseitigung der ersten Klarheit', begins by examining Schneider's motives for writing in the light of Orwell's four categories in 'Why I Write': sheer egoism; aesthetic enthusiasm; historical impulse; political purpose. Schneider cannot deny that the first of these, in the form of revenge against his parents, was a major motive. If we extend 'sheer egoism' to include self-understanding, this is probably stronger than any of the others.

Schneider's insistence on the disjunction between literature and politics can, therefore, be understood not simply as marking the differences between the late 1960s and the late 1970s but as an *emancipation*, which would legitimate the apolitical story-collection *Die Wette* (1978). For, of Orwell's categories, 'sheer egoism' and 'political purpose' are the hardest to reconcile. So Schneider takes advantage of his breathing space for personal reflection, to survey his career during the preceding decade and a half, always mindful that 'man kann die Vergangenheit nur mit den Augen der Gegenwart anschauen' (AP, p. 231). He admits that he abandoned his previous literary efforts during the Student Movement not just out of the political conviction that action was more important but, equally, because he was unable to write what he wanted to (namely exorcising drama on the model of Weiss's *Marat/Sade*). But he is most ruthless towards the 'Phantasie im Spätkapitalismus' essay, which was written against the background of Schneider's combined depression at the failure of a relationship and of the Student Movement. With hindsight, he now recognises that the essay's 'trotzige, in Gesetzesform gekleidete Hoffnung' (AP, p. 230) was an intellectual act of will, an attempt to objectify the subjective factor.

However, as *Lenz* makes clear, the repressed always returns, expressing itself in different channels but with a vehemence proportionate to the original repression. The mechanism is the one that Schneider detected throughout the everyday life of the Federal Republic in *Ansprachen*, while in his scrutiny of his early, politically active phase his own vehemence is evident. Thus the title of this afterword to *Atempause* can be read as a 'discarding' of the unperturbed 'clarity' of Schneider's own career in the late 1960s, to which he now has difficulty in relating. He confesses, indeed, that egoism is equally a motive behind the desire for collective emancipation : 'Nicht der Egoismus verfälscht das politische Engagement, sondern der Versuch, ihn zu verheimlichen' (AP, p. 231).

The ground was now cleared for a guilt-free move away from political subject-matter in *Die Wette*. The move was not especially fruitful. Apart from the unflinching dissection of a failed relationship in 'Das Wiedersehen' and the graphic exploration of post-feminist sexual politics in 'Experiment mit mehreren Männern' — both of which seem closest to Schneider's personal experience — the stories lack both conviction and substance: sketches awaiting a richer political and historical canvas to confer purpose on them. Such an attempt at 'pure' subjectivity was merely an undialectical inversion of the 'Phantasie' essay's objectivism. In the light of Schneider's recurrent motif of resisting the pressure to choose between extremes, it is significant that all the stories are concerned with contest and conflict.

The only conceivable echo in *Die Wette* of the events of the 'deutsche Herbst' of 1977 — the kidnapping and murder of Schleyer, the Mogadishu hijacking and raid, the deaths in Stammheim — is in the violence that marks several of the stories. It is curious that Schneider should have returned to central concerns of *Lenz* and *Verfassungsfeind* not in prose narrative but in a film-script for Reinhard Hauff: *Messer im Kopf* (1979). Notwithstanding the specificities of this genre, the latter text is none the less a barometer of Schneider's development towards the end of the decade. It needs to be emphasised, however, that *Messer im Kopf*, as the title suggests, is not a film 'about' terrorism in the sense of the collective *Deutschland im Herbst* (1978) or Margarethe von Trotta's *Die bleierne Zeit* (1981). Terrorism is a backdrop to the drama going on 'inside the head' of the protagonist. Hoffmann's loss of memory and language after being shot in the head, echoing the experience of Rudi Dutschke, can be read as a metaphor for the helpless situation of the intellectual in the late 1970s: lacking a concrete terrain of struggle, intimidated by repressive legislation, vilified by media and politicians, and above all overwhelmed by the 'deutsche Herbst', whose impact on the left was devastating. To underline this: in *Messer im Kopf*, 'Es lebe die Anarchie' is written on the wall of a home for the blind.

Like his predecessors, Lenz and Kleff, Hoffmann is an outsider in a state of crisis; except on this occasion the crisis is entirely personal in origin. It is *chance* that makes him the political football of the police on the one hand, who suspect him of being a 'terrorist' who attacked a policeman with a knife, and of the new actionist and post-theoretical left generation on the other, who stylise him as the 'victim' of police brutality. Similarly, in his only substantial piece engaging with the phenomenon of terrorism, 'Der Sand an Baaders Schuhen' (1978; cf. B), what interests Schneider is how the competing versions of the deaths in Stammheim — suicide versus murder — became polarised and were exploited to extract avowals of loyalty to the state and the left respectively. In this light it is consistent — however disconcerting such 'balance' may be to the extreme left, who recognised in Schneider a former comrade — that the ending in *Messer im Kopf* is, yet again, open: it is for us to decide whether Hoffmann exacts revenge on the policeman who shot him.

Whereas this conflict provides the narrative momentum of *Messer im Kopf*, Schneider's real interest seems to lie elsewhere: in the painful re-learning Hoffmann undergoes after his injury, having to start again from the beginning, like an infant (or Kaspar Hauser). This process is presented as an emancipation, for Hoffmann is granted the utopian dream of a fresh start in life, which enables him to discover an unrepressed sensuality and thereby rebuild his identity: 'Ich sehe jetzt Dinge, die ich früher nicht gesehen habe. Gesehen schon — aber man hat nicht darauf geachtet' (MK, p. 75). His goal is an entirely personal one that recurs throughout Schneider's work: living without fear of his *wishes*. Marx's ideal of making the petrified social relations 'dance' is presented as obsolete in our age of concrete — so one might as well dance anyway, whereby Hoffmann allows all his suppressed feelings to burst forth via his body.

Having stripped away the pressures of first politics and then, by the drastic dramatic device of Hoffmann's shooting, the social itself, Schneider manages to come face to face with the self — himself. Just as the infant begins to sense its own identity by defining itself against its mother, an Other, so too Schneider makes use of a trip to South America for a similar purpose. The lengthy title essay which prefaces his collected political writings of the 1970s, *Die Botschaft des Pferdekopfs* (1980), is no conventional travelogue: its real subject is Schneider and his relation to his own country. Having spent four months away from the Federal Republic in South America and found so much that is uncannily familiar, Schneider returns, sensitised, to discover the alienness of his native land and recognise himself as an outsider. His picture of everyday life in Germany is the same as was presented a decade and a half previously in *Ansprachen*: sterile, muted, reified, and above all with no room for the fulfilment of human *wishes*.

Schneider's reference-point throughout 'Die Botschaft des Pferdekopfs' are the writings of an earlier traveller to South America. What fascinates him is Alexander von Humboldt's 'Ich', which always has the world, the not-I, as its subject, never itself. By contrast the 'Ich' of our own age, like that in Bernward Vesper's *Die Reise*, keeps intruding, is at once both too large and too small. Did it ever really exist, asks Schneider? 'Dieses Ich, dem die äußere Welt nur noch Anlaß für Lust- oder Unlustbezeugungen war, was bewies es außer einem Verlust?' (B, p.12). Schneider is disconcerted to find so much that is familiar in South America because a chief motivation of his journey was that yearning for the Other that will provide a sense of identity. If one does not find this Other, if one is surrounded only by mirror-images of oneself, one cannot escape the fate of confusing oneself with the world: narcissism. Our sense of loss, our hunger for experience, derive from the fact that by dominating and colonising wherever we tread we have remade the world in our image. The reason the narcissist's restless yearning can never be satisfied is because he is ultimately looking for himself. With such an emphasis on subjectivity, hunger for experience, sensuality and narcissism, it is now clear why Schneider placed this essay at the beginning of his collected journalism from the 1970s, for it brings together, by a circuitous route (via the Other!), several of the themes that epitomise the decade.

The close of the 1970s set the seal on the relations between the Great Powers in the shape of the NATO 'dual track' decision of December 1979 to deploy Cruise and Pershing missiles. If the theatre of a subsequent nuclear war was envisaged as Europe, its stage would be the two Germanies, which had obvious implications for their sovereignty and entailed that the 'national question' was dusted off again. This, along with the release obtained through direct confrontation of the 'Ich-Problem' in 'Die Botschaft des Pferdekopfs', motivated Schneider to turn in his fiction once again to an explicitly political theme that was at the same time part of his immediate experience: the 'Siamese City' of Berlin. This forms the subject of an article in *Freubeuter*, 'Aufgegebenes Gelände' (1981), and another scenario for a film with Hauff, *Der Mann auf der Mauer* (1982). *Both* of these texts served as the basis for Schneider's next major prose narrative, *Der Mauerspringer* (1982), a rich amalgam of essay, fiction, and also autobiography. The fact that Schneider has recognised his identity problem does not mean, however, that he has unburdened himself of it. This is the wish of the first-person narrator of *Der Mauerspringer*. The focal point is no longer a single individual. Indeed the narrator is looking for the story of a man, 'der sein Ich verliert und anfängt, niemand zu werden' (MS, p. 23). Mistrustful of the identity offered him by the two German states, such a man would find his place only on the frontier. Schneider expressed this very wish at the close of his autobiographical essay 'Die Beseitigung der ersten Klarheit'. Returning on the 'S-Bahn' from East Berlin to West Berlin, he reflects: 'Da, wo ich lebe, will ich nicht hin. Da, wo ich herkomme, will ich nicht leben. Wer sagt denn, daß entweder der eine oder der andere Bahnhof die Endstation ist?' (AP, p. 234). These words are echoed by Kabe, the 'wall-jumper' of the title, in Hauff's film. They reveal that *Der Mauerspringer* too is a book about identity. Only now the perspective has widened to explore the interrelation between individual and national identity: 'Wo hört ein Staat auf und fängt ein Ich an?' (MS, p. 92). Schneider's protagonists and, as he points out, both German States, seek their identity against an Other. The narrator detects such a motive in his relationship with an East German woman Lena, echoing the 'hunger for experience' unlocked in Lenz by the working-class L.: 'Das Bild, das ich mir anfangs von Lena machte, entsprach einem undeutlichen *Wunsch* nach Vervollständigung, nach einer *Erfahrung*, die ganz außerhalb läge . . .' (MS, p. 94, italics added). Schneider's argument throughout both *Der Mauerspringer* and the article 'Aufgegebenes Gelände' is how what he calls the compulsion to compare — the way in which the two German states define themselves against one another — distorts one's image not only of the other but of one's own state. Against this the book sets the stories of individuals who refuse to succumb to this either/or and insist on achieving a whole (national) identity by moving backwards and forwards between the two Germanies. The article ends on a utopian note, with the image of a 'third way' for Germany, which could be achieved by a refusal to parrot the dogmas of both Washington and Moscow.[16] Schneider, however, does not allow the fictional *Der Mauerspringer* to end with a wish. In the final paragraph, the narrator wakes from a dream, registers the sounds and surveys the objects surrounding him in his room, measuring their longevity against his. But the elegiac makes way for the resigned: the 'walls' of the city outside will still be standing when there is no one left who could go through them.

This closing image brings into focus the relationship between the themes of identity and wishes that we have traced throughout Schneider's work during the 1970s. Separation (division) creates a gap (a barrier), which provokes a sense of loss, along with the wish to overcome this by crossing the barrier and being reunited with what one was separated from. The archetype for this experience is the infant's separation from the mother, the desire to return to whom is the origin of all utopia. This is complicated in the case of male children as the separation is from what is, in terms of gender, an Other. The woman, 'who limits and denies him, is none the less a necessity to him: he attains himself only through that reality which he is not, which is something other than himself', entailing that a man's life is restless 'struggle'.[17] This yearning for an Other underlies the struggle for identity by the male characters in Schneider's fiction. Yet, at the same time, he can criticise the parallel process of defining one's identity against another (opposite extreme) in the political sphere. This paradox is explained by the fact that union with the Other is also felt by the man as a *loss* of self. Hence the fear that Schneider's characters feel when confronted with women's

---

16. Peter Schneider, 'Aufgegebenes Gelände', *Freibeuter* 8 (1981) p. 62.
17. Simone de Beauvoir, *The Second Sex*, Harmondsworth, 1972, p. 171

demands for emotional commitment. They are trapped in an ambivalent state of yearning: desiring the woman when apart from her,
afraid of being swallowed up when with her. But if, as we have
insisted, the personal is the political, it is consistent that Schneider
has, since the Student Movement came to an end, been fascinated
by figures caught between two extremes and unwilling to commit
themselves to either.[18] The attraction of such a position is that, like
the passenger on the 'S-Bahn' as it passes through the no man's land
between East and West Berlin, one is poised in an instant of
freedom, however illusory. For Schneider's insistence on a 'third
way' and defence of the outsider turns out to be none other than a
romantic-existentialist salvage-operation for individualism.

Towards the end of the 1970s, Schneider observed that, for him,
the 'despairing dreams' of terrorism were more realistic than those
of Marcuse about the abolition of capitalism, because at least the
terrorists' starting-point was the 'Tatsache des Scheiterns dieser
Utopie' (BP, p. 209). But, like wishes, utopias do not 'fail'; they can
only fail to be fulfilled, in which case they live on in the shape of
hopes and dreams — embodied in the new collective energies of the
late 1970s and 1980s, such as the Peace and Ecology Movements. It
is notable that Schneider, still playing the individualist, has found it
necessary to distance himself from these movements — from the
Greens by means of pedantic arguments against their 'essentialism'.
Through blindness and the abandonment of hope, it is we who fail
utopia.

To leave matters there would be to fall back on an individualistic
explanation of Schneider's progress as a melancholy though unrepentent individualist. Against this stands the axiom that the 'social
does not "influence" the private; it dwells within it'.[19] Melancholy,
narcissism, a disturbed relation to the object-world, a hunger for
meaning and/or experience, self-definition by negation — these, the
main themes of Schneider's writing, have all been traced, by his
brother Michael Schneider, to the specific family socialisation of the
late 1960s generation. This generation's melancholy expressed
yearning not so much for what one has lost but, owing to the
emotional starvation prevalent in the postwar German family, for
something one had never had.[20] The outcome was, since available

18. It is just such a refusal of impossible 'choices', an ability to sit between two stools
   even at the risk of being labelled 'traitor' by both sides, that Schneider found in
   Peter-Jürgen Boock; cf. Schneider's preface to their correspondence, *Ratte —
   tot . . .*, Darmstadt and Neuwied, 1985, esp. pp. 12–14.
19. Jacoby, *Social Amnesia*, p. 104
20. Cf. Michael Schneider, 'Fathers and Sons Retrospectively: The Damaged Rela-

parental models could not become objects of love, narcissism. This is why, after the momentary existential release of 1967–9, which Michael Schneider interprets as in part motivated by a yearning for compensation for a childhood spent in the shadow of the Third Reich, so many members of the first post-war generation turned inward, not as an escape but to probe their unresolved family conflicts. This argument is underscored by the way in which Peter Schneider has gone back to life-historical bedrock: his most recent fiction depicts just such a father/son relationship, shorthand for the relationship between the Nazi era and the Federal Republic. Given that the pair are Josef and Rolf Mengele, Schneider's title is, intentionally, scandalous: *Vati* (1987). It implies a *wish* that could, even if 'daddy' was no murderer but 'only' a soldier or fellow-traveller, never wholeheartedly be fulfilled for Schneider and his generation. And yet — if we are to live without fear of our wishes, the first step is to acknowledge them.

Author's Note

The following abbreviations are used for Schneider's works:

AP = *Atempause. Versuch, meine Gedanken über Literatur und Kunst zu ordnen*, Reinbek, 1977
AS = *Ansprachen*, Berlin, 1970
B = *Die Botschaft des Pferdekopfs und andere Essays aus einem friedlichen Jahrzent*, Darmstadt and Neuwied, 1981
L = *Lenz*, Berlin, 1973
MK = *Messer im Kopf*, Berlin, 1979
MS = *Der Mauerspringer*, Darmstadt and Neuwied, 1981
V = *. . . schon bist du ein Verfassungsfeind*, Berlin, 1975

Also note:

Die Wette, Berlin, 1978
Totoloquè. Das Geiseldrama von Mexiko-Tenochtitlan, Darmstadt and Neuwied, 1985
Vati, Darmstadt and Neuwied, 1987
Deutsche Ängste: Sieben Essays, Darmstadt and Neuwied, 1987

---

tionship between Two Generations', *New German Critique* 31 (Winter 1984), pp. 3–51.

Peter Schneider

Suggested Further Reading

There is no reliable study of any length in either German or English examining the spread of Schneider's work in the 1970s; articles and essays tend to concentrate on *Lenz*. As general introductions I would recommend:

Michael Buselmeier, 'Nach der Revolte. Die literarische Verarbeitung der Studentenbewegung', in Martin Lüdke (ed.), *Literatur und Studentenbewegung*, Opladen, 1977, pp. 158ff

——, 'Peter Schneider', in H.L. Arnold (ed.), *Kritisches Lexikon zur deutschsprachigen Literatur der Gegenwart* (KLG), Munich, 1978ff
(This article, which has not been revised since 1983, contains details of essays on Schneider and reviews of his work in German periodicals and newspapers.)

Rolf Hosfeld and Helmut Peitsch, 'Weil uns diese Aktionen innerlich verändern, sind sie politisch' (on four novels on the Student Movement, including *Lenz*), *Basis 8*, 1978, pp. 92ff

Helmut Kreuzer, 'Neue Subjektivität. Zur Literatur der siebziger Jahre in der Bundesrepublik Deutschland', in Manfred Durzak (ed.), *Deutsche Gegenwartsliteratur*, Stuttgart, 1981, pp. 82ff

-339-

ANTHONY WAINE

Martin Walser

Much to the surprise of an East German interviewer who was
questioning him about his political and social experiences in the
1970s Martin Walser enthused: 'Also das sind positive Erfahrungen.
In der Literaturszene geht die Entwicklung zwar in Richtung
Verdünnung der Fiktion und Subjektivierung, aber im Rest der
Gesellschaft hat politisches Bewußtsein, Empfindlichkeit und auch
vielleicht Wachheit für Solidarität zugenommen durch alle möglichen Entwicklungen in den siebziger Jahren'.[1] He went on to cite
various events and trends both national and local as grounds for
such optimism. These included the repeal of the 'Berufsverbots-
gesetz' and of Article 88a on censorship, as well as the determined
resistance of the SPD in 1977 to hysterical demands for sweeping
new measures to counter terrorism. In another context Walser
described the SPD's behaviour at this time of national crisis as
having given him 'ein Vertrauen zu dieser Partei [. . .] das mir neu
ist'.[2] He further admitted: 'Ohne die Sozialdemokraten hätte ich
mich den Aufputschern gegenüber ziemlich ohnmächtig gefühlt.
Das muß ich sagen'.[3]
Nevertheless one can still understand Ursula Reinhold's reaction
of surprise on hearing Walser talk in such sanguine terms about the
turbulent decade that had just ended. One must recall how, after the
momentum of his work in the Extra-Parliamentary Opposition of
the late 1960s had driven him to within joining distance of the
Deutsche Kommunistische Partei, Walser had become a favourite
target for the ire and ridicule of many conservative and liberal critics
from 1970 until at least 1976. Paradoxically, as Peter Hamm once
explained, Walser's refusal to blindly serve and obey the party in
these years — he never actually became a member — increased the
intolerance towards him: 'Wäre Walser einfach "ein anderer" gew-

---

1. Ursula Reinhold, *Tendenzen und Autoren. Zur Literatur der siebziger Jahre in der BRD*,
   Berlin, 1982, p. 293.
2. F. Duve, H. Böll and K. Staeck (eds.), *Briefe zur Verteidigung der Republik*, Reinbek,
   1977, p. 156.
3. Ibid., p. 159.

orden, hätte er ins andere Lager übergewechselt (was immer das ist), man hätte tolerant mit ihm sein können [. . .], aber diese übergreifenden Skrupel und Selbstzweifel eines zwischen den Klassen intellektuellen Kleinbürgers, das geht nicht'.[4]

Hamm's reference to Walser's class origins and mentality lays bare a sensitive nerve running throughout the author's biography and one which became painfully entangled in the fissions of the post-'68 era. The upheavals in West German politics in the wake of the 1968 cultural revolution, leaving the left divided and warring, posed many uncomfortable dilemmas for a self-confessed petit-bourgeois socialist like Walser. His struggle to resolve these dilemmas within the DKP foundered tragi-comically in the mid-1970s. In a letter to the present writer (dated 17 August 1986) Walser reflected on his problems with the party: 'ich konnte mich auch mit meinen DKP-Freunden nicht einigen, weil sie so fremdbestimmt waren; für die war ich der unbelehrbare Kleinbürger (gegen den Marx-Engels-Zitate griffbereit vorliegen)'. When Walser finally severed his attachment to the party he had probably reached the point of greatest disillusionment and isolation in his twenty-five-year-long search for an alternative to that of the 'heimatlose Linke'. The title of his next work to appear seems to epitomise Walser's sense of being an outsider: *Jenseits der Liebe* (1976).

Its publication confirmed his continuing banishment by the West German cultural establishment, or so it appeared at the time. The review of the novel in the *FAZ* by Marcel Reich-Ranicki became a *cause célèbre*. It opened with the most deleterious censure imaginable: 'Ein belangloser, ein schlechter, ein miserabler Roman. Es lohnt sich nicht, auch nur ein Kapitel, auch nur eine einzige Seite dieses Buches zu lesen'.[5] This cruel travesty of a review then proceeded to attack the author personally in the kind of rhetoric to which he had been constantly subjected since the time (around 1967) when his *engagement* for causes such as the Anti-Vietnam campaign and the establishment of a Writers' Union had propelled him into the public limelight: 'um 1970 schöpfte Walser, verärgert über Literaturkritiker, Intendanten und Theaterrezensenten, recht plötzlich neue Hoffnungen: Er wandte sich, die Mode vieler bundesdeutscher Intellektueller flink und graziös mitmachend, dem Kommunismus zu. Wenn es mit dem Dichten nicht weitergehen will, ist hierzulande die

4. Peter Hamm, 'Martin Walser und die Reaktion', in W. Brändle (ed.), *Martin Walser. Das Sauspiel. Mit Materialen*, Frankfurt On Main, 1978, p. 434.
5. Marcel Reich-Ranicki, 'Jenseits der Literatur', *Frankfurter Allgemeine Zeitung*, 27 March 1976.

Barrikade des Klassenkampfes ein attraktiver und meist auch gemütlicher Aufenthaltsort, auf jeden Fall aber eine dekorative Kulisse'.[6]

In retrospect, however, the novel *Jenseits der Liebe* marks a clear turning-point in Walser's fortunes, in more senses than one, and, ironically, Reich-Ranicki's calumnies may well have contributed to this. For, as Ursula Bessen has cogently documented,[7] Reich-Ranicki's attacks on Walser almost certainly influenced the majority of critics reviewing *Jenseits der Liebe* to adopt a benevolent stance towards the work out of a sense of solidarity with the defamed author. Hardly any review, irrespective of the writer's opinion of the novel's literary merits, failed to take issue with Reich-Ranicki. Further ammunition from Walser's new found allies was delivered by the twenty-five critics who each month help to compile the book list for the Südwestfunk. They placed *Jenseits der Liebe* in first position for three consecutive months. Walser's rehabilitation continued apace with his next two works, *Ein fliehendes Pferd* (1978), which was even serialised in the *FAZ*, and *Seelenarbeit* (1979). Both books were voted into first place by the same jury and, more tangibly, at least for the author's bank balance, were bought in great numbers by the West German reading public. At the age of fifty-one (i.e. in 1978), Walser was able to 'das eigene Schreiben finanzieren'[8] for the first time in his life. Thus, within the space of one decade, Walser's situation had changed from that of being one of West Germany's *enfants terribles* to one of being feted as a major talent, who was awarded the 'Schiller-Gedächtnis-Preis' in 1980, and in 1981 the most glittering literary prize of all in West Germany, the 'Georg-Büchner-Preis'. Moreover, it should be added as a rather bizarre postscript, he received that same year the Heinrich Heine Medal — presented by none other than Marcel Reich-Ranicki.

Despite such accolades and the overwhelming critical and public success of *Ein fliehendes Pferd* and *Seelenarbeit* one must still view the 1970s as the most prolonged test of Walser's physical, emotional, intellectual and political stamina endured in his thirty-year-long career as a writer. How then did Walser survive this test and emerge with his integrity unsullied and his status enhanced? Part of the answer is to be found in the growing coherence and conviction of a personal philosophy embracing society, politics and culture. At the core of this philosophy stands the writer-intellectual, as the titles of

6. Ibid.
7. K. Siblewski (ed.), *Martin Walser*, Frankfurt on Main, 1981, pp. 214–33.
8. 'Porträt Martin Walser: Ein Gespräch mit Anton Kaes', *The German Quarterly*, 57, 1984, p. 438.

his two volumes of speeches and essays from the 1970s indicate: *Wie und wovon handelt Literatur* (1973) and *Wer ist ein Schriftsteller?* (1979). It is soon apparent that the intellectual in these theoretical writings is not just a possessor and disseminator of knowledge. Nor is he purely the embodiment of a nation's conscience who gives a moral lead to the rest of the population. Moreover his role is most definitely not to be equated with that of the pragmatic expert advising institutions, parties or citizens' action groups. Being an intellectual is not a role or a public duty for Walser but an identity, a sense of selfhood as determining as one's gender, generation or nationality. However, unlike gender or nationality, it is not a fixed identity; it is a dynamic one, changing in response to the pressures of the age and the needs of the individual. It is not only attuned to the present but oriented towards the future. The intellectual projects visions, proffers alternatives, even hints at Utopias. The word 'Veränderung' becomes almost a leitmotif of the speeches and essays of this period, and Walser's view of the self and the world as changing and changeable entities invariably brings to mind the figure of Bertolt Brecht.

Indeed if one wished to chart the development of Walser the intellectual from the slightly cynical, ambivalent 'Hofnarr' figure of the pre-1965 years — satirically transposed into Anselm Kristlein in *Das Einhorn* (1966) — to the politically forthright ideologue of the 1970s, one need look no further than his changed attitude to Brecht. In essay after essay of the 1960s Brecht is portrayed as the idealist *par excellence*, the Marxist with a hankering after old-fashioned heroes and a penchant for exotic settings, whose works are usable only as historical documents. The positive counterweight to Brecht, according to Walser in the 1960s, is Samuel Beckett whom he accords the title 'Kirchenvater der leeren Kirche und des neuen Realismus'[9] in an essay in 1964. Just fifteen years later a quite different evaluation of their respective merits can be heard: 'Beckett und Brecht — durch diese beiden wird das Mögliche vollkommen deutlich. Beckett wird, ob er will oder nicht, zum Verewiger des Zustands, zum Argument gegen die Veränderung, zur Absage an die Geschichte. Brecht ist, auch da, wo er scheinbar folgenlos zelebriert wird, negative Kraft, also aufklärerisch, also verändernd, also ein Mitarbeiter an dem größten Projekt, das Menschen haben können: an der Geschichte'.[10]

Walser's identity as an intellectual is nourished increasingly in the

9. Walser, *Erfahrungen und Leseerfahrungen*, Frankfurt on Main, 1964, p. 91.
10. Idem, *Wer ist ein Schriftsteller?*, Frankfurt on Main, 1979, p. 43.

1970s by his belief in the possibility of progress. He regards himself as he does those intellectuals who have gone before him as vital links in the historical chain: 'Eine lange Zeit hindurch hatten Schriftsteller einen großen Anteil an der Befreiung von der herrschenden Meinung der Religion und der mit der Religion verbündeten Herrschaftsschicht. Schriftsteller haben mitgearbeitet an der Selbstbefreiung des Bürgertums' (WwhL, p. 10).[11] However, literature, and the belief in change and progress do not necessarily always go hand in hand. Whereas intellectuals in the eighteenth and early nineteenth century had served as emancipatory agents in the self-realisation of the bourgeois class, many had since thrown in their lot with it once it had established itself as the ruling class. Nowadays certain writers, whilst clearly not pro-bourgeois, still continue to serve its interests subliminally. They do so, according to Walser, by portraying society as unchangeable, the individual as incorrigible and human existence as predetermined. He singles out the Irishman Beckett, the Englishman Bond and the Austrians Bernhard and Handke as the arch-exponents of this ahistorical 'Weltanschauung'.

In their philosophy suffering appears endemic to the human condition. Walser starts from this premise too, but draws different conclusions. For him the task of critical, realistic literature is to shed light on the root social causes of suffering. Furthermore, it should open up in an exploratory, undogmatic manner possibilities of action which will help to transform the sufferer's situation from one of passivity to one of activity. The verb 'handeln' in the title of the essay collection *Wie und wovon handelt Literatur* does not simply mean, 'to be about' but stresses the dynamic nature of literature (by which Walser understands all forms of writing, not just fiction). Once again he takes his cue from Brecht, when he quotes from his *Thesen für proletarische Literatur* (1940): "Kämpfe, indem du schreibst! Zeige, daß du kämpfst! Kräftiger Realismus!" (WwhL, p. 137).

For whom, or better, for what is Walser writing and fighting in this epoch of retrenchment, of regression ('Rückfall'), his own synonym for the 'Tendenzwende'? Two concepts, which despite their abuse and devaluation in so many quarters, carry more than ever the hopes of the future-oriented Martin Walser, are 'Demokratie' and 'Sozialismus'. Up until the early 1960s many intellectuals, including Walser, had invested their hopes in this direction in the SPD. However, certain developments in this party in the 1960s were perceived as anti-democratic and anti-socialist and so alternatives were sought. Walser's choice, as has already been reported, fell upon

11. See Author's Note at the end of this essay for key.

the DKP but he was to discover that the socialism of this party was outdated, shackled to ideas perfectly appropriate to the mid-nineteenth century but grotesquely inadequate to the needs of a late twentieth-century advanced industrial society in which the 'Klein-bürgertum' was a class whose interests were as valid as those of the industrial proletariat. Not only did the DKP ignore these interests but it also failed to identify itself with the local and national interests, customs, traditions and institutions of the Federal Republic. Orientated to East Berlin and Moscow, the party could never gain an identity which, to use Walser's favourite word in this context, was 'hiesig'.

The concept of 'hiesig' meaning close by, indigenous, natural to one region and culture, is the opposite of 'fremd', signifying that which is foreign, alien, distant. For the patriotic intellectual Walser 'hiesig' becomes one of the leitmotifs of his increasingly secularised gospel of hope and salvation. Not surprisingly we meet the word in the final section, 'Es wird einmal', of *Die Gallistl'sche Krankheit* (1972), which is concerned with the rebirth of Gallistl as an intellectual in search of a new political home. Here Gallistl enunciates some very firm convictions, which can be readily identified as belonging to Walser himself: 'Antisowjetismus käme mir auch blödsinnig vor, trotzdem glaube ich nicht, die Sowjet-Union könne für uns denken. Wenn die Partei etwas Hiesiges wird, schafft sie's. Aber nicht, solange sie mit beiden Beinen im Ausland steht' (DGK, p. 109). And a few lines further on he confesses: 'Ich liebe meine Heimat, übrigens. Und anstatt daß sie in einem Science Fiction unterginge, möchte ich lieber, daß sie mit Mann und Maus in den Himmel käme. Himmel ist ein hiesiges Wort für eine riesige Zukunft' (DGK, p. 111).

It is no coincidence either that the terms 'hiesig' and 'Heimat' are uttered in the same breath. Both signify that sense of belonging, rootedness and harmony which Gallistl/Walser are increasingly searching for as a natural, secular and humane replacement for the religious community he had experienced as a child: 'Ich habe eine Vorstellung von einer besseren Welt: Trockenheit, Wärme, kaum Krach. Menschen, die gerne etwas tun' (DGK, p. 87), and: 'Das erinnert mich an eine Solidarität, die ich als Kind im Christentum empfand, dann nicht mehr' (DGK, p. 101) Throughout the 1970s in essays, speeches, novels and plays Walser searches for this elusive community and becomes one of the first left-wing German intellectuals to free the word 'Heimat' from its trivialised connotations and, of course, from its political-ideological debasement by the National Socialists and their post-war acolytes.[12] In making 'Heimat' one of the central pillars of his philosophy he was thereby paving the way for many other artist-intellectuals of decidedly non-conservative outlook to broach, explore and even celebrate this subject, culminating in Edgar Reisz's film masterpiece bearing that curt yet charged word as its title.[13]

Reitz

The word is certainly highly charged in Walser's usage. In the essay 'Heimatbedingungen' (!) he proclaims: 'Heimat ist ein Zeitwort, ein Prozeßbegriff, denkbar nur als vergangene oder als zukünftige' (WwhL, p. 97). That is, its meaning is not static, but ever evolving and dynamic. It possesses furthermore both historical *and* utopian connotations. In this respect, too, it suits the post-'68 Walser admirably for it can accommodate his growing historical consciousness and at the same time it functions as a channel and reservoir for visions, aspirations and basic needs, not just his own individual ones but those of all his fellow Germans. His task (as an intellectual) is to ensure that it is not a ruling minority who feel at home in the Federal Republic: 'Es wird vor allem an den Intellektuellen liegen, ob dieser Staat Heimat nur für eine Minderheit bleiben soll' (WwhL, p. 96). The concept is therefore quintessentially political, and Walser goes on to spell out precisely how he wishes it to be interpreted: 'Sozialismus und Demokratie sind zwei Wörter für diesen denkbaren Heimatzustand. Heimat könnte man ihn nennen, weil in ihm die Entfremdung, die jetzt die Arbeit beherrscht, zum Verschwinden gebracht werden kann' (WwhL, pp. 98–9).

It hardly needs stressing that Walser's own rootedness in the landscape, culture and history of his native Bodensee region constitutes the tangible reality of 'Heimat' from which the more grandiose and abstract applications of the term derive their substance and their veracity. It forms a remarkably fertile source: in a book of drawings by André Ficus and words by Walser, inevitably entitled *Heimatlob* (1978), the author reminds us of how Celts, Romans and Germanic tribes have each in turn added to the cultural and racial melting-pot so that 'die Luft ist süß von Geschichte' (H, p. 10). He also resurrects for us one monastic writer, often forgotten, who drew inspiration equally from region and religion alike : Heinrich Seuse, he claims, is 'ein Inbegriff dieser Gegend' (H, p. 63).

---

12. In 1968 he had entitled a volume of largely political essays and speeches *Heimatkunde*.
13. For a comprehensive contextualisation of this issue see: Michael E. Geisler, '"Heimat" and the German Left: The Anamnesis of a Trauma', *New German Critique*, 36, 1985, pp. 25–66.

Walser's enthusiastic championing of Seuse along with so many other features of his local homeland is further proof of the author exploring and discovering the identity of a region and in the process finding himself too. Self-discovery and self-realisation are the keynotes of his development as an intellectual in this decade. Consequently the impression gained through studying his theoretical writings is of an integrated and idealistic body of thought. However, one must beware of drawing any facile conclusions from this for his works of fiction, epic or dramatic. These are much more subjective, sombre and ambiguous responses to the world and to his own private needs and shortcomings. In his letter to the present writer Walser drew attention to the relationship between experience and response:

> Anfang der 70er Jahre wurde ich eben von der Atmosphäre gestreift, die sich in den Berufsverboten ausgedrückt hat. Mein Bedürfnis nach realer Demokratie wurde als Überlaufen zum bösen Feind (im Osten) verstanden. Andererseits konnte ich mich auch mit meinen DKP-Freunden nicht einigen, weil sie fremdbestimmt waren. [. . .] Ich habe dann versucht, in Prosa zu reagieren. Schluß mit jeder anderen Reaktionsart. Zuerst wollte ich probieren, ob man genau sein kann, weit gehen kann im Subjektiven, ohne die Gesellschaft aus den Augen, und aus dem Text zu verlieren.

His fiction presents the dilemmas, crises and even tragedies befalling a cross-section of petit-bourgeois characters from the intellectual Gallistl to the grammar-school teacher Halm, from the middle manager Horn to the chauffeur Zürn.

All four figures exemplify how debilitating the struggle to maintain a firm grip on one's existence can be and how necessary therefore it is to know one's true self and one's true interests. One could generalise, with some justification, and say that much of Walser's fiction in the 1970s revolves around the interrelated questions of seeking and maintaining orientation, examining old and new perspectives, and learning to withstand the pressure to assume false or self-damaging standpoints. Walser's earlier figures invariably lacked or ignored this awareness of where they were heading and what they believed in. Hans Beumann is quite explicitly characterised as 'der ziel- und richtungslose, leichthin pendelnde Zuschauer'.[14] His successor, Anselm Kristlein, in the novels *Halbzeit* (1960), *Das Einhorn* (1966) and *Der Sturz* (1973), was largely of the same hue. As his creator was to observe in a comic yet revealing obituary for him some years after the final work of this trilogy was

---

14. Walser, *Ehen in Philippsburg*, Reinbek, 1963 p. 41.

completed: 'Und weil er so wenig standfest war, wurde er in alles hineingezogen, in Erotikintrigen, in Wirtschaftskämpfe, Salonkämpfe, Kulturkämpfe'.[15] Even though *Der Sturz* appeared in 1973, any discussion of the novel necessitates placing it within the trilogy as a whole,[16] an enterprise which would take us too far outside the bounds of what after all is an attempt to identify what is new and different in Walser's work of the 1970s. *Die Gallistl'sche Krankheit* (1972) is a more rational starting-point.

Gallistl is the first of Walser's heroes to break out of the Beumann–Kristlein syndrome. He does so by recognising the symptoms of his disintegrating, deformed personality and writing them down in the form of a medical report. He senses that he has been losing control of his life for many years and is now drifting aimlessly, as one surrealistic sequence makes evident: The key word in his passage is 'treiben', occurring three times, evocative of his possessing no fixed point of reference in his existence: 'Ich verschwand hinter einem Essigbaum. Auf dem Fluß näherte sich ein weißes Motorboot. Es trieb. Ich bemächtigte mich seiner. So entkam ich. Nachts zündete ich Lampions an. Als ich beschossen wurde, löschte ich die Lampions wieder. Seitdem treib ich im Dunkeln. Am Tag treib ich an kleineren Booten vorbei, in denen Leute sitzen, Lesebücher in den Händen' (DGK, p. 60). The image of darkness reinforces Gallistl's sense of having lost control over his existence. His reorientation begins with his decision to distance himself from his old circle of friends and their lifestyle of intellectual egotism and competition: 'Ich gerate in Bewegung. Weg von euch. Weg, weg, weg von euch. Ich will nichts mehr hören' (DGK, pp. 76–7). Reorientation also involves him leaving behind his old self: 'Es handelt sich [. . .] um den Fall einer Trennung von sich selbst' (DGK, p. 86). Gallistl's search for new bearings, for a new standpoint is therefore the search for a new self and a new identity.

Gallistl's search is that of a petit-bourgeois intellectual who rejects his 'natural' class allegiances in order to realign himself within the socialist movement. Although Walser's next novel *Jenseits der Liebe* (1976) is set in the world of business the issue of political alignment is explored further. Between the publication of the two works four years had elapsed, during which time Walser had withdrawn his commitment to the DKP, and the paranoia and hysteria over the

---

15. Idem, 'Nachruf auf einen Verstummten', in *Die Anselm Kristlein Trilogie*, Frankfurt on Main, 1981, p. 364.
16. For more detailed discussion of the trilogy see Heike Doane, *Gesellschaftspolitische Aspekte in Martin Walsers Kristlein-Trilogie*, Bonn, 1978.

question of radicals working within West German institutions, privately owned or state-administered, had grown. These two factors impinge noticeably on the novel's political ambience. Franz Horn, a middle manager with a South German firm manufacturing dentures, is racked with self-doubt. His position within the firm's hierarchy, his still warm relationship with the firm's boss Thiele (despite the latter's promotion of a younger man above Horn) predispose him to show allegiance to the status quo. However, his politics have become more left-wing and he is courted by the Communist member of the works council for his support (in the form of his signature to appear in a newspaper advertisement on behalf of the DKP). Horn agrees but fears privately that his support, once known publicly, could have repercussions on his standing in the firm. Furthermore, Horn, whilst warming to Heinz Murg (the communist in question), has personal reservations about the DKP's lack of a West German profile. Parallels to Gallistl's soul-searching in 'Es wird einmal' are clearly visible.

However, in contrast to Gallistl who has freed himself from his former circle of bourgeois friends, Horn has less room for manoeuvre. Especially in view of his age — he is in his late forties — he is dependent on his boss's confidence, just as he is on that of his colleague-cum-rival Liszt. Aware of his dependency and resentful of it, enjoying their personal friendship yet unsure of its genuineness Horn had abreacted his anger and frustration at home, beaten his wife and children and fled in fear and guilt. The interconnections between all these facets of his past and present behaviour have never been consciously explored or articulated until this point, as Horn prepares for a business trip to Coventry. Instead they have been concealed, repressed and misinterpreted. The trip to England becomes a crisis as the truth of the situation crystallises: 'Zum ersten Mal gelang es ihm, sich wirklich durch und durch als der Scheißkerl zu fühlen, der er war' (JdL, p. 121). This awareness of his real though acutely negative self unleashes a concatenation of further insights, and accompanying destructive and self-destructive urges, ending with his attempted suicide. He fails, and, as we know from the sequel *Brief an Lord Liszt* (1982), he returns to his job and, more importantly, to his family.

His journey to England therefore proves to be a decisive turning-point, for it provides him with the all-important distance from familiar reality, which had become deceptive and disorientating. *Jenseits der Liebe* shows how the individual gradually learns to interpret his situation more realistically (i.e. less self-deceptively), but it does make clear also how complex this process of interpretation is in a modern society purporting to be humane, democratic and open but which is in reality the reverse: 'Und das Groteske: er hatte jahrelang dieses Gerüst aus Höflichkeit und Rücksicht nicht bemerkt' (JdL, p. 119). The gaining of a more objective perspective on his confusing circumstances is a crucial task for the 'Kleinbürger' in particular, whose (negative) identity was once defined thus by Walser: 'Ein Kleinbürger ist jemand, der sich selbst ausbeutet, und auch dazu bereit ist und darin seinen Stolz sieht und seine Seligkeit und seine Misere. Das wird dann in Seelenarbeit bewältigt.'[17]

The reference in the last sentence to the actual title of his novel *Seelenarbeit* (1979) points to one possible, critical interpretation of the story of Franz Horn's cousin from the hamlet of Wigratsweiler. The novel takes us into the heart and soul and even bowels of the 'little man', Franz Xaver Zürn, who is the proud and loyal chauffeur of his firm's boss, Gleitze, and has been so for the past fifteen years. This period of his life, however, has been very similar to that of his cousin Franz Horn. He has been leading a double existence. His real self and the self he is obliged to present daily (and often nightly too) to his mild-mannered, cultured boss are moving further and further apart. His spiritual labours to keep the two selves in some kind of harmony are proving more and more stressful. His body (especially his intestines) is subconsciously reacting against it and his mind is too (he collects knives clandestinely). Like the other repressed and unstable figures of Walser's 1970s symphony[18] he experiences frequent sensations and outbursts of anger, but it is impotent rage which merely effects more inner turmoil. His surname Zürn is painfully apposite.

Three experiences, however, help Xaver Zürn to decode his oppressive reality more truthfully and to rechannel his emotions, especially anger, more appropriately, by resisting the oppression rather than internalising it. His life-long habit — the result of his mother's influence — of reading the legends of martyrs is gradually superseded by a passionate interest in the historical analysis of the Peasant Wars. Secondly, he discovers by accident a diary by another chauffeur called John Frey in which Frey learns to see through his National Socialist employers. Finally, and quite crucially, Xaver is admitted to a Tübingen hospital at the behest of his boss who, under the guise of benevolence, is exercising his despotism merely to ensure that his servant Xaver is physically reliable to continue as his

17. Reinhold, *Tendenzen und Autoren*, p. 290.
18. In his letter to the present writer Walser saw in the figures of Horn, Halm and Zürn the potential for a 'Gegenwarts-Symphonie'.

chauffeur.[19] On leaving the clinic after five days of painful, humili-
ating and ultimately negative examinations Xaver's new perspective
begins to be translated into self-knowledge, self-respect and self-
protection:

> Er hatte so oft, so lange der Meinung der Umwelt über sich selber
> zugestimmt, daß ihm sein wahres Selbstgefühl nur noch wie etwas
> Vergangenes einfiel. Es war ihm fast schon fremd. Aber unvermindert
> übriggeblieben war, wie wichtig ihm sein Selbstgefühl war, gegenüber
> allem, was sonst jemand über ihn sagen konnte. So schwach es war,
> nichts würde er zäher verteidigen, als dieses Schwache, kaum mehr
> wahrnehmbare Selbstgefühl. (S, p. 170)

Making a stand and resisting alienating, threatening forces, even if
such action remains an abstraction because of the 'Kleinbürger''s
powerless and isolated socio-economic position, are the emergent,
positive developments in Walser's work of the 1970s, and contrast
sharply with the willing adaptability and naïve opportunism of his
earlier conformist figures.

How exposed and vulnerable Xaver Zürn remains, despite his
positive insights, is reinforced when Xaver is relieved of his duties as
chauffeur and demoted to the post of fork-lift truck operator in
Gleitze's works. The news is as shattering and disorientating to
Xaver as his medical 'overhaul' was in the Tübingen clinic. He does
find himself again, however, and arrives at further valuable interpretations of his experiences. The importance of knowing one's
mind, literally and figuratively, of establishing where one stands,
especially in relation to others, i.e. having a standpoint, are perceived now as the true safeguards against the danger, especially
acute for the 'Kleinbürger', of losing one's sense of self, of becoming
alienated from one's own body and soul. Soul work ('Seelenarbeit')
therefore need not only be the negative celebration of one's powerlessness and suffering, which Walser one-sidedly and provocatively
described it as being in the interview with Ursula Reinhold. It can
trigger a productive and indeed liberating process of recognition and
reorientation, which leaves the individual at a higher level of self-
awareness: 'und Agnes hat gesagt, Gleitzes seien nicht gut. Du
könntest so etwas nie sagen. Aber Agnes kann das sagen. Der
Kollege Frey hatte einen Standpunkt. Wenn man nicht Agnes'
Leute-Empfindungsfähigkeit hat, braucht man einen wertvollen

19. For a more detailed interpretation of this episode see: Anthony Waine, 'Pro-
    ductive Paradoxes and Parallels in Martin Walser's *Seelenarbeit*', *German Life and
    Letters*, 34, 1981, 3, pp. 297–305.

Standpunkt. Besonders gegen solche von vornherein bewährten Menschen. Gleitze ist ein Bischof. Aber ja. Und du hast das nicht bemerkt' (S, p. 284).

In this self-appraisal (mirroring Horn's new perspective on his boss Thiele) it is indicative that he identifies himself with the symbolically named John Frey. Both Frey and Zürn, professionally qualified to steer machines and their passengers throughout the land, are shown learning to map-read the network of human relationships more efficiently and plot their own course through life more rationally. The above quotation also significantly includes his wife Agnes and confirms how she too serves as a positive model for forging an existence in which the individual is in harmony with both himself and his environment (the true meaning of 'Heimat'!). In no previous work has the wife been portrayed so affectionately and her role in relation to her husband's identity rendered so pivotal as in *Seelenarbeit*: 'Durch Agnes war er möglicher als ohne sie. Ohne sie käme er sich schädlicher vor. Sie macht etwas wieder gut' (S, p. 294). In such an unstable and opaque world, marriage, fragile as it may sometimes appear itself, is presented by Walser as one of the fixed points of human existence; any threats or challenges to it, whether they emanate from within the male partner or from the environment, need to be resisted at all costs.

Such a situation, dramatically heightened, obtains in a work wedged in between *Jenseits der Liebe* and *Seelenarbeit*. *Ein fliehendes Pferd* (1978) is of a quite different complexion from these two novels in that the social, economic and political undercurrents of the 1970s are here much more tenuous. This has not prevented one critic from claiming that part of the novella's success derived from having captured the prevailing mood:

Auch ohne empirische Überprüfung wird doch kaum jemand in Zweifel ziehen können, daß im Jahre 1978 die wichtigsten *Motive* der Novelle auf ausgesprochenen fruchtbaren Boden fallen mußten. [. . .] Eine ausgebreitete Diskussion über "midlife crisis" beschäftigte damals alle Medien (und etwa nicht auch Menschen?) "Beziehungsprobleme" standen auf der Tagesordnung, und nicht nur in der APO-Generation. Der Soziologie-Boom war längst durch einen Psychologie-Boom abgelöst; Identität/ Subjektivität/Spontaneität/Kommunikation/Interaktion stand auf den neu umlaufenden Münzen; nicht mehr so gern in Zahlung genommen wurden Gesamtgesellschaft/objektive Entwicklungstendenz/ Organisation/ Agitation/Klassenkampf.[20]

20. Volker Bohn, 'Ein genau geschlagener Zirkel. Über *Ein fliehendes Pferd*', in Siblewski (ed.), *Martin Walser*, pp. 155–6.

It may well be true that the publication of the novella happened against an especially propitious backdrop, but the work's real strength (and fascination for readers of both sexes) lies in the timelessness and universality of its subject-matter, in its unearthing of psycho-physiological layers of the male's conscious and subconscious make-up which are eternal; his sexual anxiety (Helmut), his sexual prowess (Klaus); his repressed libido (Helmut), his flaunted lasciviousness (Klaus); his sense of phallic inadequacy (Helmut), his masculinity fetischism (Klaus). Helmut subconsciously relates Eros to death, Klaus relates it to life. Helmut feels guilt towards his wife over his sexual abstinence, Klaus feels instinctively compelled to give his wife sexual satisfaction regularly. Both deify the youthful, voluptuous female; for Helmut it is a fantasy, for Klaus a reality. The latter has ditched his first wife and married Helene, twenty years his junior.

Helmut fears Klaus as a rival; Klaus savours the rivalry with Helmut. Helmut's preferred route in life is flight; Klaus's is fight. Helmut seeks peace in nature (the forests exert a womb-like fascination on him); Klaus seeks to defy and conquer it (surviving the raging storm). Klaus is fending off the encroachment of middle age; Helmut has accepted this inevitability with melancholic resignation and is conditioning himself to post-middle age. Klaus is proud of his body; Helmut experiences a sense of self-repugnance. Helmut's endeavours to cling on to his perspectives and steer himself through the crisis (symbolised by the 'Pinne' on the boat) is put to the sternest test in his confrontation with Klaus. In pitching these conflicting moods, fantasies and philosophies into an escalating dramatic struggle (waged over five days during a holiday on Lake Constance) Walser creates that erotic and psychological tension and narrative momentum which are the virtues of so many great novellas, not just those found in German literature. This is a second major reason for the book's success.

A further explanation of the novella's effectiveness lies in the fact that Walser, in presenting us with two opposed personality-types and lifestyles, compels us to identify and evaluate their contrasting perspectives — as the quotation from Kierkegaard's *Entweder/Oder* preceding the text indirectly encourages us to — with a view to determining our own priorities and positions more exactly. No other book of Walser's has made the reader so conscious of the necessity for orientating oneself realistically and of the dangers (to ourselves and others) where we fail to do so. In fact the image of the runaway horse suggests a violent breaking free from fixed positions without regard for oneself or others and with no awareness of direction or goal. Similarly the raging storm on the lake, especially as seen through Helmut's eyes, symbolises loss of direction, loss of control, loss of self: 'Helmut wußte nicht, wie er in diesem Toben und Knallen und Knattern mit diesem lächerlichen Stück Holz etwas ausrichten sollte. Er hatte das Gefühl, es sei Mitternacht' (EfP, p. 119).

The novella is of course not simply about Helmut's dilemma of orientation but about Klaus Buch's too. Much of the work's ironic impact results in fact from the reader's gradual awakening to the fact that he too is undergoing the same kind of crisis. How profound this is emerges with his wife's chilling monologue when her husband is believed drowned. The images she chooses echo the storm on the lake and alert the reader once more to the danger of disorientation and dislocation, and the suffering which ensues for the individual and his/her relationships: 'Es kam mir immer mehr so vor, als müsse ich einen Ertrinkenden über Wasser halten' (EfP, p. 140), and 'Er war auf dem falschen Dampfer. Und mich hat er auch auf diesen falschen Dampfer gezwungen. Darum weiß ich, wie das ist, auf dem falschen Dampfer zu sein. Das ist die Hölle' (EfP, p. 138). Klaus's failure to choose the right direction has resulted in his young dependent wife suffering the same fate. Helmut's desperate attempts to deceive the world about his real self, his inability and refusal to let even his wife see his true self, have harmed their relationship too. This self has now been exposed to him with the gravity and clarity experienced by Franz Horn during his business trip to Coventry and by Xaver Zürn whilst in the Tübingen clinic. Correct orientation is dependent on being in harmony with one's real self, no matter how uncomfortable and shocking the discovery of that repressed identity may at first be. The alternative is living a false existence, that is, one of self-contradiction and self-alienation.

The creation of Helmut Halm (1978), Xaver Zürn (1979), Franz Horn (1976) and initially Josef Gallistl (1972) not only helped Walser to fill the vacuum in his epic repertoire, left by the defunct representative of post-war Germany, Anselm Kristlein, but gave him a flexibility in the exploration of his country's post-1968 experiences which one individual medium such as Kristlein could never have realistically provided. The autobiographical authenticity and appropriateness of these four petit-bourgeois heroes — for this is what they are — in their quest for self-understanding and self-realisation provide a further explanation for Walser's own success in riding the storms of the 1970s. The continuity and diversity of his epic programme seem to complement the coherence and maturity of his theoretical work examined earlier. Only in one sphere of his artistic and intellectual production did Walser appear to make little progress, namely the theatre. There is a certain irony here in that at the end of the 1960s Walser was more firmly established in the public eye as a dramatist than as a prose writer. It should be remembered that he had written 'only' one novel during that decade, namely *Das Einhorn* (1966), whilst his six stage plays and three major essays on the theatre had contributed to the renaissance of the West German theatre and helped to sever its umbilical cord from Brecht, Frisch and Dürrenmatt.

Before concluding this chapter with a brief analysis of Walser's two stage plays of the 1970s, *Ein Kinderspiel* (1971) and *Das Sauspiel* (1975), it is worth speculating about the reasons for the theatre's coolness not to say antagonism towards Walser's dramatic works. In the 1960s the West German theatre had developed an identity as a moral and political institution thanks to plays such as Walser's own, notably *Eiche und Angora* (1962) and *Der Schwarze Schwan* (1964), along with those of Rolf Hochhuth, Peter Weiss, Heinar Kipphardt and latterly Tankred Dorst. In a certain sense the theatre had helped to raise the consciousness of West Germans concerning their recent history and its repercussions on the present and thereby paved the way for the protest movement of the late 1960s. The action thereupon literally moved from the stage to the streets, where the young left-wing radicals were soon denouncing the theatre as bourgeois and divorced from reality. Walser experienced their scorn first-hand at the beginning of the rehearsals for *Ein Kinderspiel* (1971): 'Dem Berliner Schauspieler Michael König, für die Rolle des Asti zunächst nach Stuttgart engagiert, war Walsers Politik nicht progressiv genug. Nach zehn Probetagen verließ er protestierend die Bühne. Walsers Stück, so König im APO-Jargon, reproduziere nur die bürgerlichen Kreisläufe, statt die Möglichkeiten ihrer Überwindung zu zeigen'.[21]

For many theatre directors and theatre critics, on the other hand, the West German theatre had become far too progressive, and a reaction against the politicisation of the theatre in the preceding decade as well as against the extremism of cultural groupings on the left (with whom they most certainly identified Walser) spread in the course of that decade. Handke, Bernhard, Strauß and Beckett were now favoured authors, painting as they did highly sensitive portraits of tortured individuals, whose suffering, however, was rooted as much in the existential situation of man as in any specific social or historical conflicts. The semi-documentary historical plays of the

---

21. 'Zwang zur Politik', *Der Spiegel*, 26 April 1971, p. 184.

1960s with their uncomfortable messages for present-day audiences (especially Germans) were no longer desirable. With reference to *Das Sauspiel* Walser explained how he had 'mein dramatisches Heil beim historischen Stoff gesucht (und nicht gefunden). Das heißt: die Theater wollen keine solchen Stücke, die im historischen Gewand auf die Gegenwart verweisen' (letter to present writer). Nevertheless it was possible for some committed authors like Franz Xaver Kroetz to establish themselves, but his case is a special one. By concentrating in the early plays on Germany's outsiders Kroetz did not compel his bourgeois audiences, as Walser's plays have always done, to identify themselves with the characters on the stage. Instead they were allowed to experience a mixture of titillation and pity at watching tales of extraordinary country folk. When Kroetz did begin to delineate more socially integrated figures in the period around *Das Nest* (1974) the likes of Kurt and Martha were still sufficiently quaint and folksy not to make the audience feel too threatened by the underlying social critique. Furthermore, Kroetz's neo-naturalism made no excessive demands on an audience's intellect or imagination.

Ein Kinderspiel, on the other hand, comprising stream-of-consciousness monologues, the switching between time levels as flashbacks are inserted, the deliberate role-playing of the two younger characters and their stylised language, is far removed from Kroetz's 'Volksstück' realism. The avant-garde techniques are combined with a subject which had become potentially explosive for middle-class families since 1968, when the first act takes place. The subject treated is the changed relationship between the younger generation and their parents, which manifests itself in communication difficulties between the two sides, in acts of verbal and even physical aggressions, especially on the part of the repressed, emotionally manipulated children (who in the play are a brother and sister in their early twenties), but also in conflicts between the young people themselves about what course of action to pursue (subjective, anarchistic or critical), both within the domestic sphere and in society at large.

Their ability to act effectively, i.e. rationally and maturely, is retarded by their emotional hang-ups, which are attributed partly to their family upbringing and partly to social conditioning. Through acting out stages in their childhood and youth they perceive the causes of their deformed identities. This appears to work better with the girl, Bille, than with Asti, who despite the self-detachment afforded by the therapeutic role-playing, is still essentially infantile, egocentric and irrational at the end of the first act, which culminates in his attempted seduction of his wealthy father's much younger second wife before his father's very eyes — hardly a revolutionary action destined to destroy capitalist society! Nevertheless this first version of 1971 did give some cause for believing that a new generation of young Germans was at least searching for possibilities of reorientation during the watershed of 1968.

Not so the second act, written and set in 1975 and first performed in Regensburg in 1978. Viewing events mainly from the perspective of the father, now sixty-five and his wife Irene, thirty-four, we learn how son and daughter have each responded to the changes in the political climate since the halcyon days of 1968. Asti and Bille went in opposite directions. The sister became a terrorist before dropping out of this scene, disillusioned, and now works in a bank, whilst the brother has become a wealthy businessman, designing and manu-facturing children's construction kits. He is now as cynical as he was in 1968: 'Ganz ohne Terror, Schwester, möchten wir nicht mehr sein. Solange da noch so rumgeballert wird, sind wir EINE Nation. Das schweißt uns doch ganz schön zusammen. Arbeiter, Unterneh-mer. Solidarität der Demokraten, verstehst du' (EK, p. 366). Ter-rorism serves the purpose of consolidating the status quo! It is tempting to read into such statements evidence of Walser's pessi-mism regarding the dashed hopes of the late 1960s. But this would be to overlook the message of the first act in which self-emancipation and self-understanding were being initiated by the children and the potential both for personal and political change was being released from beneath the strata of conformist conditioning.

The same confrontation, only from a different historical perspec-tive, between rebellious, idealistic young people, eager for change, and an establishment actively resisting change and persecuting those seeking it, is also at the heart of Walser's first historical drama and most political play to date, *Das Sauspiel*. Although it was originally written for a theatre in Nuremberg, the city in which the drama is set, the changing political climate of the first half of the 1970s led to conflicts between the author and the theatre manage-ment, so that it was transferred to Hamburg and premiered there at the end of 1975. A dozen more theatres had planned to perform it but the combination of several savage reviews in the vein of Reich-Ranicki's infamous invective (*Das Sauspiel* gave Walser a foretaste of what was to come three months later with the publication of *Jenseits der Liebe*) and the election year of 1976 scuppered all hopes of the play being seen elsewhere. In making the 'Tendenzwende' im-plicitly the subject of his play, Walser became a victim of the very syndrome he exposes via the analysis of a previous 'Tendenzwende'

in 1526, following the post-Reformation upheavals and the subjugation of the peasants. It was not the conservatives whose behaviour
angered him most, as the wind of change swept through the Federal
Republic, but that of the liberals and of the formerly left-wing
intellectuals who had so nimbly changed their allegiances after 1970
and realigned themselves with the Establishment. Of course many of
these same intellectuals were the reviewers for the leading national
newspapers and magazines who were sitting in judgement on a man
who was daring to impugn their integrity!

In scenes such as 'Politik in der Badstube' and 'Die Intellektuellen liefern ab' Walser examines the parallels between 1526 Germany
and the Federal Republic of the 1970s. Then and now intellectuals
whose progressive views had helped to unsettle and even destroy
outdated traditions, beliefs and structures were now retreating from
their earlier standpoints. Confronting them was a minority of ideal-
ists, in the play the Anabaptists, embracing a kind of Christian
communism, who wished to take the reforms achieved a stage
further beyond that of bourgeois emancipation. Many of these
strictly non-violent revolutionaries who believed in genuine frater-
nity and equality had been outlawed, their leaders imprisoned or
even arbitrarily sentenced to death. Parallels to the radical factions
of contemporary Germany and their treatment are quite intentionally provoked, but with the crucial distinction that in Walser's
portrayal these radical Christians totally oppose violence. Thus
there can be no identification between the Anabaptists and the
German terrorists, a fact overlooked by most of the play's commentators who were too preoccupied with Walser's critical portrayal of
intellectuals to pay any serious attention to the positive role of the
Anabaptists.

The established intellectuals, represented by Albrecht Dürer,
Faust, Melanchton, Hans Sachs and others, fear for their own
security, status and wealth, should further radical changes take
place. When the city's political rulers approach them to lend their
intellectual authority to the planned use of force against the radical
peasants and evangelists, the intellectual elite of Nuremberg is faced
with a dilemma: do they as critical thinkers question and challenge
the actions of the ruling class (and risk some form of punishment
themselves) or do they provide the ideological rationale needed to
legitimise these actions (and save their own skin)? In portraying the
dilemma of prominent and less prominent intellectuals such as the
folk-singer Jörg Graf, who comes to grief through his failure to
adhere to one fixed position and code, Walser is proffering a self-
critical document of his own experiences in the 1970s and those of

his fellow workers in the 'Bewußtseins-Industrie' (Enzensberger).

The very fact that he should devote two years (1973–5) to producing such a detailed historical and social analysis, at the centre of which stands a true cross-section of artist-intellectuals, is further proof of the claim made early on in this chapter that for Walser's progress through the 1970s his self-conception as an intellectual was decisive. Few contemporary German writers gave so much thought to, placed so much emphasis on and wrestled so stubbornly with the nature of the intellectual's consciousness and his conscience. Even if his reflections and judgements were given short shrift at the time we can now, from our vantage-point, appreciate them as the positive achievements of one particular individual who refused to abrogate his social and historical responsibilities by shying away from the dilemmas and demands of a democracy in a critical period of development. Walser was only too well aware of how German intellectuals of both left and right have ceased to publicly question their own ideology and identity at times of national crisis or when under severe personal pressure (as Walser certainly found himself during most of this decade) and opted for the apparently more secure alternative of an 'inner emigration', only to discover that such a perspective was suicidal, for themselves and for their fellow human beings. Walser's legacy from the 1970s was to demonstrate how the intellectual and the petit-bourgeois could and indeed should realise himself as the subject of German history provided that he knew who he really was, where he stood and towards which ends he was working.

Author's Note

The following editions and abbreviations are used for Walser's works (place of publication is Frankfurt on Main unless otherwise stated):

DGK = *Die Gallistl'sche Krankheit*, 1972
EfP = *Ein fliehendes Pferd*, 1978
EK = *Ein Kinderspiel*, 1970
H = *Heimatlob*, Friedrichshafen, 1978
JdL = *Jenseits der Liebe*, 1976
S = *Seelenarbeit*, 1979
WwhL = *Wie und wovon handelt Literatur*, 1973

Also note the following works cited above (place of publication is Frankfurt on Main unless otherwise stated; * indicates part of *Die Anselm Kristlein Trilogie*, published as a collected edition, Frankfurt on Main, 1981):

Halbzeit, 1960*
Ehen in Philippsburg, Reinbek, 1963
Erfahrungen und Leseerfahrungen, 1964
Das Einhorn, 1966*
Der Sturz, 1973*
Das Sauspiel, 1975
Wer ist ein Schrifsteller?, 1979
Brief an Lord Liszt, 1982 (sequel to *Jenseits der Liebe*)

Suggested Further Reading

Werner Brändle, *Die dramatischen Stücke Martin Walsers. Variationen über das Elend des bürgerlichen Subjekts*, Stuttgart, 1978

Keith Bullivant, *Realism Today*, Leamington Spa and New York, 1987, esp. pp. 213–20

Ulrike Hick, *Martin Walsers Prosa. Möglichkeiten des zeitgenössischen Romans unter Berücksichtigung des Realismusanspruchs*, Stuttgart, 1983

Anton Kaes, 'Porträt Martin Walser' (Interview), *German Quarterly*, 1984, vol. 3, pp. 432–49

Klaus Siblewski (ed.), *Martin Walser*, Frankfurt on Main, 1981

Anthony Waine, *Martin Walser*, Munich, 1980

On Walser's role as a key West German intellectual see:

Keith Stuart Parkes, 'Martin Walser — The View from the Lake', *Writers and Politics in West Germany*, London, 1986, pp. 205–25

MARTIN KANE

Culture, Political Power and the Aesthetics of Resistance
Peter Weiss's
Die Ästhetik des Widerstands

In delivering his *laudatio* to mark the posthumous award of the 'Büchner-Preis' to Peter Weiss in 1982, Walter Jens remarked: 'Nicht dreimal, fünf- und sechsmal muß einer dieses große, dem *Ulysses* ranggleiche Buch lesen [. . .]'.[1] Whether *Die Ästhetik des Widerstands* will indeed take its place alongside Joyce's novel or be able to sustain comparison with Proust's *A la Recherche du Temps Perdu* or Musil's *Mann ohne Eigenschaften* — works whose artistic and intellectual density continues to tease response from fresh generations of scholars and general readers — only time will tell. What is certain, however, is that like those earlier gargantuan masterpieces, *Die Ästhetik des Widerstands* — with the almost a thousand sides which make up its three volumes — raises considerable problems of approach and interpretation. Genia Schulz's recent speculations about the controlling core of the novel revived memories of all the hesitancies with which the book's initial reviewers attempted to categorise it: 'Ist eine ästhetische Theorie oder eine Theorie des Widerstands das organisierende Zentrum, der Geschichtsbegriff oder das Modell der Autobiographie, der Bildungsroman oder eine proletarische Variante davon?'[2] Peter Weiss himself — if we follow the copious comments and jottings in his notebooks from the years 1971 to 1980 which provide an indispensable commentary on the genesis of the novel — was, particularly in the early stages of its conception, uncertain about the precise nature of what he had embarked upon. Direction, purpose and above all the scope of the work seem to have expanded organically with the writing of it. In an

1. Walter Jens, 'Fremdlinge sind wir im eigenen Haus . . . Laudatio auf Peter Weiss', *Jahrbuch der Deutschen Akademie für Sprache und Dichtung*, Darmstadt, 1982, vol. 2, p. 85.
2. Genia Schulz, *"Die Ästhetik des Widerstands"* — *Versionen des Indirekten in Peter Weiss' Roman*, Stuttgart, 1986, p. 7.

interview with Burckhardt Lindner in May 1981 Weiss described how he had conceived the book initially in much more modest terms as a novel about the resistance to fascism: 'Ursprünglich sollte der Roman nur *Der Widerstand* heißen; ich hatte anfangs geplant, ein Buch über den antifaschistischen Widerstand zu schreiben und mir auch nur *ein* Buch vorgestellt'.[3] In this same interview he also distances himself from his own interpretation of the novel given after the first volume had appeared. In subsequently much-quoted remarks made to Rolf Michaelis he had, in 1975, described the project as 'eine Wunschautobiographie. Eine Selbstbiographie, die in sehr vielem meiner eigenen Entwicklung folgt, die aber gleichzeitig das Experiment macht: wie wäre ich geworden, wie hätte ich mich entwickelt, wenn ich nicht aus bürgerlich-kleinbürgerlichem Milieu käme, sondern aus proletarischem'.[4] Now, in the Lindner interview, he seems to be distancing himself from the 'Wunschautobiographie' conception as well as from the notion that the novel is about proletarian resistance alone. He notes: 'Das Wort Wunschautobiographie kam in einem Interview flüchtig auf und wurde danach wie eine Rubrik gesetzt' and goes on to comment on the way that class differences had melted away as exiles from different social background were united by the struggle against fascism.

What gradually emerges when confronted with these various debates about the nature of *Die Ästhetik des Widerstands* is that Weiss has written not so much a novel as an elaborate cultural and political thesis. In seeking a linking feature amidst its complexity of themes and narrative strands one might be tempted to settle for the proposition that ignorance is the most effective of political shackles. Weiss, in his attempt to gather together the manifestations of class conflict as they have been mirrored in art throughout the ages, argues that ruling elites from time immemorial have maintained their ascendancy not merely by force, but — and generally to greater effect — by denying knowledge (and specifically cultural knowledge) to a subjugated majority. In the notebooks we read that what is at stake here is 'den Widerstand gegen Unterdrückungsmechanismen, wie sie in ihrer brutalsten faschistischen Form zum Ausdruck kommen, und [. . .] den Versuch zur Überwindung einer klassenbeding-

3. 'Zwischen Pergamon und Plötzensee oder Die andere Darstellung der Verläufe. Peter Weiss im Gespräch mit Burkhardt Lindner', in Karl-Heinz Götze and Klaus R. Scherpe (eds.), *"Die Ästhetik des Widerstands" lesen. Über Peter Weiss*, *Argument — Sonderband AS 75*, W. Berlin, 1981, p. 150.
4. 'Es ist eine Wunschautobiographie. Peter Weiss im Gespräch mit Rolf Michaelis über seinen politischen Gleichnisroman', *Die Zeit*, 10 October, 1975.

Peter Weiss

ten Aussperrung von den ästhetischen Gütern —';[5] while at an early point in the first volume of the novel itself the first-person narrator — who may be closely identified with Weiss ('Wer ist dieses Ich? Ich selbst bin es. Das Buch eine Suche nach *mir selbst*')[6] — comments:

> Untrennbar von der ökonomischen Begünstigung war die Überlegenheit des Wissens. Zum Besitz gehörte der Geiz, und die Bevorteilten versuchten, den Unbemittelten den Weg zur Bildung so lange wie möglich zu verwehren. Ehe wir uns Einblick in die Verhältnisse verschafft und grundlegende Kenntnisse gewonnen hatten, konnten die Privilegien der Herrschenden nicht aufgehoben werden. Immer wieder wurden wir zurückgeworfen, weil unser Vermögen des Denkens, des Kombinierens und Folgerns noch nicht genügend entwickelt war. Der Beginn einer Veränderung dieses Zustands lag in der Einsicht, daß sich die Hauptkraft der oberen Klassen gegen unsern Wissensdrang richtete. Seitdem war es das Wichtigste, uns eine Schulung zu erobern, eine Fertigkeit auf jedem Gebiet des Forschens, unter der Verwendung aller Mittel, der Verschlagenheit und der Selbstüberwindung. Unser Studieren war von Anfang an Auflehnung. Wir sammelten Material zu unserer Verteidigung und zur Vorbereitung einer Eroberung. (ÄdW, 1, p. 53)[7]

The general conclusion to be drawn about these observations — that education and access to a heritage of culture are potentially the great social and political emancipators — is that they are not particularly new. Where the originality of Weiss's trilogy lies is in its attempt to grasp them on such a grand scale and in the form of lightly fictionalised political and cultural history. It is clear that 'Auflehnung' as it is expressed here, and 'resistance'as it emerges throughout the novel, are both aesthetic and political concepts and that crucial to their definition is the notion of what Weiss elsewhere calls a 'Kämpfende Ästhetik'.[8] In the dramatisation and exploration of this notion lies the fascination which the novel exerts over the reader. Throughout its three volumes, and against the backdrop of a discussion about the relation, across the ages, between the act of artistic creativity and power, the same question is posed repeatedly and in varying form: what function did art have, what role did it play in the dark years preceding and during the era of fascist dominance? In his *Zeit* interview with Rolf Michaelis, Weiss points

---

5. Peter Weiss, *Notizbücher 1971–1980*, vol. 1, Frankfurt on Main, 1981, p. 419.
6. Ibid., vol. 2, p. 539.
7. References to Weiss's *Die Ästhetik des Widerstands* (ÄdW) are used throughout this essay for the following editions: vol. 1 (Frankfurt on Main, 1975); vol. 2 (Frankfurt on Main, 1978); vol. 3 (Frankfurt on Main, 1981).
8. Idem, *Notizbücher 1971–80*, vol. 1, p. 420.

us in the direction of an answer when he notes: 'Die Ästhetik des Widerstands soll andeuten, daß es darum geht, sich kulturelle Werte zu erobern und gleichzeitig gegen den Faschismus zu kämpfen'. But what, we inevitably ask, is the connection between the acquisition of 'cultural values' and the concept of political struggle? What is the nature of a literary endeavour which seeks to interweave an account of the doomed struggle of a valiant few to resist the tyrannies of fascism with extensive interpretative comment on a bewildering sweep of examples from the plastic and literary arts ranging from the Pergamon Altar to Picasso's *Guernica*, from Géricault's *The Raft of Medusa* to Franz Kafka's novels? The notebooks offer some preliminary guidance here, as for instance when Weiss talks of an 'Ästhetik, die nicht nur künstlerische Kategorien umfassen will, sondern versucht, die geistigen Erkenntnisprozesse mit sozialen und politischen Einsichten zu verbinden — '.[9] What is expressed here as tentative theory becomes the central concern of the novel, anchored and illustrated in discussion of specific works of literature and, above all, of the visual arts. It is sometimes forgotten that for almost twenty years Peter Weiss considered himself as 'Immer in erster Linie Maler',[10] which explains why the most detailed and intensive aesthetic discussions are about paintings.

The first volume of the novel opens in Berlin in September 1937 and moves with the narrator — as has been noted, an autobiographical figure, but one who has been moulded into a proletarian and politically conscious version of the author's own earlier self — to Spain and the Civil War. In a climate of increasing political precariousness, members of the shattered Communist Party meet to sustain and develop their political and aesthetic ideals. The avid autodidacticism of the narrator and Coppi — young, educationally deprived factory workers, the product of evening education classes which serve as 'Sammelpunkt für Proleten und abtrünnige Bürger' (ÄdW, 1, p. 15) — is fed by the student Heilmann. Knowledgeable beyond his years and coming from a privileged bourgeois background, Heilmann initiates a discussion which, beginning with the Pergamon marbles and the Heracles legend, wanders somewhat sporadically through to Bosch and Piero della Francesca and eventually the art and literature of the twentieth century. Aided and abetted by the spirit of Arnold Hauser and Ernst Fischer (Weiss acknowledges in the *Notizbücher* Hauser's *Sozialgeschichte der Kunst und Literatur* and Fischer's *Erinnerungen und Reflexionen* published in 1969 as important

9. Ibid., p. 420.
10. Ibid., p. 119.

source material for his novel),[11] we are witness to an unmistakably
Marxist approach to the understanding of art and to a process of
enlightenment with an emphatic political purpose. To repeat and
expand a remark of the narrator: 'Unser Studieren war von Anfang
an Auflehnung. Wir sammelten Material zu unsrer Verteidigung
und zur Vorbereitung einer Eroberung [. . .]. Unser Weg heraus
aus der geistigen Unterdrückung war ein politischer. Alles, was auf
Gedichte, Romane, Gemälde, Skulpturen, Musikstücke, Filme oder
Dramen Bezug nahm, mußte erst politisch durchdacht werden'
(ÄdW, 1, pp. 53 and 56). It is a compelling tale, although the
judgements which the companions arrive at in their attempt not
merely to acquire bourgeois notions of culture, but to grasp and
interpret art in the light of their own struggle towards political
awareness vary considerably; sometimes they have immediate conviction; at others, what at first sight appears merely eccentric will,
with perseverance, yield new and revealing perspectives. It is perhaps the attempt to forage literature for images reflecting the
oppressed proletarian experience which produces the least expected
booty. A lengthy analysis of *Das Schloß*, for instance, in which the
world of the castle and the village is brought into intimate comparison with the lives and daily work experience of the three companions
and where the crumbling shabby edifice run by feeble and embittered officials is equated with the 'Gebäude des Kapitalismus',
leads to the conclusion that 'Was Kafka geschrieben hatte, war ein
Proletarierroman' (ÄdW, 1, p. 179). The purist may regard as a
diminishment of K's high aspirations the condemnation of him as
one who wishes merely to be acknowledged by the Castle authorities
in his professional capacity, and who does not recognise, let alone
rebel against, the fundamental iniquities of a system to which he is
implicitly subservient. The more generous reader, on the other
hand, will see this interpretation as a tribute to the multivalency of
Kafka's metaphor.

Any reservations, however, which might arise about the sure-
footedness of the judgements in literary matters do not apply when
Weiss's narrator is discussing painters and paintings. One immediately recognises, for instance, in the rough-hewn gestures of Cour-
bet's workmen in *The Stonebreakers* the revolutionary spirit of the 1848
barricades as well as the encouragement for future struggles which
the artist has incorporated into their defiant attitudes. Similarly, we
are quickly persuaded of the false consciousness which marks the
humble diligence of the idealised factory workers in the Prussian

11. Ibid., p. 168.

court painter Adolf Menzel's *Das Eisenwalzwerk* of 1875:

> die Wachsamkeit des bärtigen Vorarbeiters am Hebel, beim Entgegen-nehmen des Walzstücks, das Abschrubben der verrußten Körper, . . . wies auf ein einziges Thema hin, auf die Arbeit, auf das Prinzip der Arbeit [. . .]. Es handelte sich nicht um die Arbeit, [. . .] als Vorgang der Selbstverwirklichung, sondern um Arbeit geleistet zu niedrigstem Preis und zu höchstem Profit des Arbeitkäufers [. . .]. Die Lobpreisung der Arbeit war eine Lobpreisung der Unterordnung. (ÄdW, 1, p. 354).

The German workman as Menzel had portrayed him here was the creation — part figment, part reality — of an artist who could conceive of the industrial labourer only in terms of the politically illiterate wage-slave, as 'den deutschen Arbeitsmann aus Bismarcks und Wilhelms Reich unangefochten vom kommunistischen Mani-fest, in seiner einzigen Befugnis, wacker zu sein' (ÄdW, 1, p. 355). Comments such as these form part of a lengthy comparison of Menzel's painting with the picture *Streik* of 1886 by the relatively little-known German-American artist Robert Koehler. *Das Eisen-walzwerk* is seen as a work of art in which every detail is designed to bolster and glorify the existing order of things. The melodramatic lighting of the picture and the romantic presentation of its subject-matter, pose — for the imagined admiring nineteenth-century audi-ence — no disturbing questions about the true nature of the econ-omic and social relations between capital and labour. It is left to the contemporary reader, mobilised by the narrator's critical Marxist perspective, and viewing the picture through his eyes, to see it for what it is: a hymn of praise to nineteenth-century industrial capital-ism in all its arrogant swagger.

Robert Koehler's painting *Streik* which was displayed at the World Exhibition in Paris in 1899 provides the narrator — in its dramatisation of class solidarity and intimations of proletarian revolt — with welcome compensation for Menzel's smug vision of the world of work. He describes how Koehler, who was born in 1850 in Hamburg and died in 1917 in poverty in Minneapolis composes his 'unverstelltes Zeugnis vom Antagonismus zwischen den Klassen' in starkly theatrical fashion. Against a grim industrial background a factory owner has just emerged from his elegant mansion to confront the leader of an angry group of striking workers and their wives and children whose whole demeanour stands in jagged contrast to that of Menzel's complaisant labourers:

> Er stand auf der obersten Stufe der Treppe, hinterm ornamentierten gußeisernen Geländer, vornehm gekleidet, mit Stehkragen, Manschetten,

Zylinder, weißhaarig, blaß und verbissen, die Finger der Rechten ange-
hoben, als hielten sie eine Zigarre, die Hand aber war leer, ihre Geste
drückte Überraschung, kraftlose Abwehr aus. Überragte er auch die vor
ihm Stehenden und war seine Haltung auch noch geprägt von der
Selbstsicherheit einer Klasse, die sich das Aufgeben ihrer Vorrechte nicht
denken konnte, so war doch ersichtlich, daß ihm gegenüber eine Stärke
anwuchs, die ihm ohne geringste Mühe seine Vergänglichkeit beibringen
könnte. Rückwärts gedeckt von den Steinquadern seines Hauses, vom
erschrocknen Diener jedoch schon halb verlassen, stand er in käsiger
Würde vor den Arbeitern, die sich erregt zusammenscharten, und sein
ganzer Mut bestand darin, daß es ihm unvorstellbar war, sie könnten den
Schritt zu ihm hinauf tun und ihn von seinem Podest reißen. (ÄdW, 1,
p. 358)

Whereas in Menzel's picture the factory owner could contemplate
his possessions — men and machines — in a mood of serene
self-satisfaction, with the painter sharing in and supporting his
proprietorial attitudes, here in Koehler's painting the artist is at one
with the viewpoint of the workers; it is they who dominate the
picture, whose power is in the ascendant, threatening the existing,
unjust order of things.

Analysis and observation of the kind we are witness to in the
comparison of Menzel and Koehler constitute some of the most
illuminating and exciting passages in the whole novel. We are also
willing participators in the affirmative response to the savage political caricatures of George Grosz and Otto Dix and the innovative
photomontages of John Heartfield: it is not difficult to recognise the
special role played by the work of these three artists in the political
development of the narrator and his companions and in reinforcing
their 'Haß gegen Habgier und Eigennutz, gegen Ausbeutung, Untersuchung und Folter' (ÄdW, 1, p. 169). On the other hand some
reservations are likely to arise when invited to consider the views of
these three young communists on the subject of modernism:

So verlief unser Bildungsgang nicht nur konträr zu den Hindernissen der
Klassengesellschaft, sondern auch im Widerstreit zum Grundsatz einer
sozialistischen Kultursicht, nachdem die Meister der Vergangenheit
sanktioniert und die Pioniere des zwanzigsten Jahrhunderts exkommuni-
ziert wurden. Wir bestanden darauf daß Joyce und Kafka, Schönberg
und Strawinski, Klee und Picasso der gleichen Reihe angehörten, in der
sich auch Dante befand, mit dessen Inferno wir uns seit einiger Zeit
beschäftigten. (ÄdW, 1, p. 79)

In relation to the debates in the 1930s among Marxist intellectuals about the nature of a socialist art, views such as these have a
very heretical feel to them. What is at work here in this complete

rejection of the line being proposed by the Comintern cultural critics of the time? Hardly an authentic or credible stance on the part of these proletarian devotees of culture. It is surely the elegant critical intelligence of Weiss which — in rejecting the contemporary party view which regarded the narrative innovations of Joyce, Kafka, Gide et al. as the product of bourgeois decadence — proposes instead that the challenge these innovations made to prevailing aesthetic norms were, in turn, a threat to the social structures which those norms underpinned.

It is with reluctance that one criticises a novel which — in terms of its ability to provoke and stimulate — has few rivals in postwar German literature; and yet it is on just this point — the question of authorial voice — that one is confronted with its least satisfactory aspect.

Possible misgivings about the authenticity of Weiss's narrator — the sense maybe that he remains, in this first volume at least, little more than a shadow, a curiously bloodless creature who serves as a channel for ideas, a filter for the vestiges of setting and rudimentarily outlined experience in which the novel's vast stretches of cultural and historical discussion are embedded — may be attributed to Weiss's desire to make him a proletarian, politicised version of his own younger self. This idealised, would-be autobiographical figure was born on 8 November, the same day as Weiss, but one year later in 1917, almost to the moment when Lenin was ordering the arrest of Kerensky's Provisional Government. The use of the narrator to trace the tortuous strands of the development of German socialism in the interwar years — partly through the disillusioned account of his father, partly through his association with the KPD in Berlin and the International Brigade in Spain — tend to reduce him to a mere device; to make him a thing of symbol rather than of flesh and blood. This weakness is extended beyond the figure of the narrator to other areas of the novel and Weiss's inability to fully integrate character and ideas. It is aggravated by the gap between the sophistication of those ideas and the figures in the novel who advance them. Heilmann and the narrator's father, for instance, are little more than ventriloquist's dummies whose sole purpose is to articulate Weiss's own highly intelligent grasp of complex subject-matter. The long conversation between the narrator and his father on the consequences of the short-lived German revolution of 1918–19 is an illustration of this. The account of the failure of the left to capitalise on the situation and of the counter-revolutionary treachery of the SPD which led to the collapse of the Soldiers' and Workers' Councils, seems to be — apart from the acknowledged political bias of the narrator — a straightforward presentation of historical evidence leavened with eye-witness accounts. In other words Weiss the novelist who has set up the fictional father–son relationship is, in his eagerness to set the record straight in the light of his particular beliefs, rapidly left behind by Weiss the Marxist historian. As in the case of the reinterpretation of the Heracles legend where we are similarly reminded at intervals of the source of the tale, the periodic interpolation of 'sagte mein Vater' does not adequately counter the impression that it is Weiss himself and not his creations who are engaged in fashioning this elaborate account.

What emerges from all of this is something of a discrepancy in the novel. On the one hand Weiss wishes to present us with a narrator who, by virtue of his proletarian origins, is culturally and education-ally deprived; on the other he cannot avoid crediting him and his similarly handicapped companions with the weight of his own voluminous knowledge and scholarship. In every thought, in every observation of his narrator can be detected a learning and an experience of culture which could only have been acquired and digested in long years of concentrated effort. We marvel at what the narrator, at the tender age of nineteen, already has under his belt: not only Cooper, Defoe, Dickens, Marryat, Melville, Swift, Poe, Conrad, Jack London, Zola, Gorky, Barbusse, Andersen, but also Nexö, Kläber, Gotsche, Holz, Bredel, Marchwitza, Rolland, Trakl, Hauptmann, Wedekind, Gide, Hamsun, Weinert, Becher, Benn, Plievier, Döblin, Seghers, Kisch, Weiskopf, Wolf, Brecht and Canetti, along with van Gogh's letters, Gauguin's diaries, the writ-ings of Lunacharsky, Tretyakov, Trotsky and utterances on cultural questions by Marx, Engels and Lenin. It may well be, as Jurek Becker has recently argued, that: 'Es ist eine seit zweitausend Jahren stillschweigende Vereinbarung zwischen Schriftstellern und Lesern, daß die fiktiven Erzähler von Rollenprosa gelegentlich zu Erkenntnissen gelangen und auf Formulierungen kommen dürfen, zu denen sie nach aller Erfahrung im sogenannten wirklichen Leben nur außerordentlich selten in der Lage wären'.[12] Nevertheless this by no means comprehensive survey of the narrator's impressive reading does stretch somewhat the bounds of credibility. It suggests that he could quite reasonably have contemplated exchanging his humble labouring job at Alfa Laval for an occupation more suited to his intellec-tual talents; a chair in Comparative Literary Studies perhaps?

12. See Volker Hage, 'Wie ich ein Deutscher wurde. Eine Begegnung mit Jurek Becker in Berlin und Anmerkungen zu seinem Roman *Bronsteins Kinder*', *Die Zeit*, 3, October 1986.

Implausibilities of this kind are the main weakness, particularly of the first volume of the novel. Coppi, Heilmann and the narrator remain rather anaemic figures whose function is to articulate the admittedly fascinating essayistic excursions on art and politics. A similar verdict could be delivered on the narrator's father to whom is allocated the task not only of being Herbert Wehner's collocutor, but is also responsible for conveying the history of the bitter infighting between Social Democrats and Communists during the Weimar Republic which was to leave the way free for the rise of Nazism.

It should, however, be interpolated here that not all critics have shared this negative view of Weiss's narrative technique and his reduction of character to mere mouthpiece. Genia Schulz, in a long and elaborate argument about the use of 'indirekte Rede' in the novel points us to a quite different way of looking at this problem. In *Die Ästhetik des Widerstands*, she maintains, it is not a matter of Marxist historiography in novel form: we are not being presented with a body of cultural, political history from a particular ideological perspective but are being invited to decipher — in a spirit of critical appraisal — various modes of 'imitated discourse'. The use of 'indirekte Rede' with the 'Konjunktivistische Vorbehalt' embedded in it means that at all points what is being narrated is also simultaneously being subjected to scrutiny and question. What we are presented with is not reality, or a particular view of it, but 'das Nach-schreiben des Redens über sie, der Meinungen und Gedanken, die den Ereignissen folgen oder sie begleiten'.[13] This interpretation puts in a somewhat different light the long passages of what Schulz calls 'quasi-wissenschaftliche marxistisch-leninistische Politiksprache' (she gives here as an example an extract from a discussion in vol. 2, pp. 100f., on the dwindling possibility of a popular anti-fascist front). Passages such as this, she argues, are not to be taken at face value: the use of subjunctive and indirect speech induces a distancing element and leads her to conclude that 'die Sprache der *Ästhetik des Widerstands* "erinnert" nur an das abstrakte Polit-Vokabular und seine Syntax, ist nicht identisch damit'.[14]

Genia Schulz also has an answer to the supposed implausibility — explored above — of the narrator figure. To find sympathy for Weiss's creation, however, — as well as for Schulz's account of him — one has to virtually abandon any traditional notion of what a narrator who is also part of the action might be. She understands him to be not so much a person as an 'Allegorie der revolutionären

13. Schulz, *"Die Ästhetik des Widerstands"*, p. 11.
14. Ibid., p. 12.

Arbeit', an 'Ich' who is 'bloße Inkarnation des "Ich spreche" des Textes, Ausdruck des "Ich höre" — und damit auch der Ort einer weitgespannten Ausdrucksfähigkeit, insofern es die verschiedenen rezipierten Diskurse "beherrscht" '. This 'Ich' is a passive witness to the events of the novel, is one who can 'als kollektives Bewußtsein auftreten' and in whom 'alle möglichen Meinungen und Behauptungen enthalten sind'.[15] This is an ingenious argument. Whether it can satisfactorily annul misgivings about the nature of the narrator, or enable the average reader to bear with Weiss through certain extensive passages which read like digests of official GDR history, is another question.

The second volume of Peter Weiss's *Die Ästhetik des Widerstands* picks up at the point where the first left off. It finds the narrator amidst the remnants of the International Brigade in Paris in September 1938, and plunges immediately into the continuation of the two main concerns of Weiss's mammothly ambitious enterprise — namely the creation of a dramatised topography of Germany's anti-fascist intellectuals on the eve of the Second World War, and the search for politically sustaining values among milestones in the literary and plastic arts stretching back to the Pergamon marbles and forward to Bertolt Brecht.

In this second volume, the narrator takes on a much more palpable contour. This is due in part to the fact that his autodidactic quest and his political blooding in Spain have given him a firmer sense of identity, but also one suspects because the experience of finding his feet in Sweden (after the brief sojourn in Paris) overlaps with the author's own. It is at this point that the personal aspect of Weiss's involvement in this project becomes much more clear cut. He is himself well-familiar with the lot of the *emigré* and refugee but, as we see from his earlier autobiographical novels, *Fluchtpunkt* (1969) and *Abschied von den Eltern* (1961), the political and aesthetic concerns of the German Marxist intellectuals depicted in *Die Ästhetik des Widerstands*, and of the working-class narrator through whose consciousness their experience is filtered, were not those of the younger, politically undeveloped Peter Weiss. His formative, radicalising experience was Vietnam, not fascism; his commitment, as well as his Marxism, stems from the 1960s, not the 1930s. Characteristic of Weiss's earlier attitudes is the following passage from *Fluchtpunkt*. The speaker here is Hoderer, the refugee doctor from Berlin who will later crop up in *Die Ästhetik des Widerstands* under his real name Max Hodann:

15. Ibid., p. 44.

Der Sinn deines Überlebens könnte sein, daß du erkennst, wo das Übel liegt und wie es zu bekämpfen ist. Du trägst noch am Ballast deiner bürgerlichen Herkunft. Du weißt, da ist alles verfault und zum Untergang bestimmt, aber du wagst nicht, dich mit einem Schnitt davon zu trennen. Deine Arbeitsversuche bleiben fruchtlos, solange sie nicht dem Kampf um die Veränderung der Gesellschaft dienen. Du bist verloren, wenn du dich nicht einordnen kannst in eine Solidarität. Doch ich mißtraute allen Bindungen, allem Aufgehen in gemeinsamen Ideen, ich konnte noch nicht nach weiten Perspektiven suchen und nach einer politischen Zugehörigkeit, ich mußte mich an die kleinen fragmentarischen Bilder halten, die meine eigenen Erfahrungen spiegelten. Nur in diesen Bildern konnte ich erkennen, auf welche Weise ich in die Zeit gehörte, alles andere mußte Konstruktion bleiben.[16]

One is tempted to speculate that there is an element of bad conscience involved here, that *Die Ästhetik des Widerstands* is, on one level, an exercise in the alleviation of feelings of guilt. In the light of this, the attempt to place himself — through his fictional narrator — in the elite company of Germany's left-wing intellectuals in Nazi Germany and in exile may be viewed as the attempt to recapture lost ground and opportunities — to rework and make his own, in the light of later wisdom, an experience which, due to intellectual callowness, had earlier eluded him.

The elaborate description and analysis of the Pergamon Altar at the beginning of the first volume established the terms of the aesthetic debate in the novel in which art was to be seen as the mirror held up to class antagonism throughout the ages. It reflected, as Peter Weiss indicated in his interview with *Die Zeit*: 'Oben und Unten, Herrscher und Beherrschte, der ewige Kampf zwischen den Klassen. Dieses Thema geht durch und wird noch stärker werden im zweiten Teil'. The extended contemplation, at the beginning of the second volume, of Géricault's *The Raft of the Medusa* narrows this broad perspective down to the narrator's own circumstances. Géricault, the French Romantic, is seen as a 'Sohn des Vierzehnten Juli' (ÄdW, 2, p. 22) who was doomed to fret out his days in a post-revolutionary age. In his portrayal of the survivors of the *Medusa*, French colonial officials and their families wrecked off the island of Arguin *en route* for Senegal, the narrator sees mirrored the sudden plunging into disorder of his own life and the scramble for survival following the defeat of the Republican Army in the Spanish Civil War. And yet Géricault offers Weiss more than an image of disaster. In the gestures of certain of the figures aboard the raft is found an

16. Peter Weiss, *Fluchtpunkt*, 4th edn, Frankfurt on Main, 1969, pp. 59–60.

element of hope and optimism. From this work of a painter of revolutionary aspiration who was able in his art to compensate for a life frustrated by a system of suppression and destruction, the narrator derives fresh strength:

> Er, der eingreifen wollte in das System der Unterdrückung und Destruktivität, sah sich zugrundegehn als Geschlagner. Und doch war es mir noch nie so deutlich geworden, wie in der Kunst Werte geschaffen werden konnten, die ein Versperrtsein, eine Verlorenheit überwanden, wie mit der Gestaltung von Visionen versucht wurde, der Melancholie Abhilfe zu leisten. Vielleicht verstand er nicht, welche Kräfte es waren, die ihn niederhielten, vielleicht war seine Gebrochenheit so groß, daß er sich den Schlüssel zur Deutung der freigelegten Zeichen versagte, im Handwerklichen aber ging er bewußt genug vor, um zu erkennen, daß er mit seiner malerischen Sprache andern den Weg bereitete. Wie er selbst Linien weitergeführt hatte, die von Michelangelo, Tintoretto, Caravaggio ausgegangen waren, so wiesen Daumier, Courbet, Degas, in seiner Art auch van Gogh, mit dem Strich ihrer Pinsel auf Géricault hin. Plötzlich interessierte es mich nicht mehr, die Rätsel seines Lebens zu lösen. Alles, was ich wissen wollte, war mir bekannt. Mit seinem Geben und Nehmen stand er in den universellen Beziehungen und Verbindungen, die den Grund der künstlerischen Tätigkeit ausmachten. (ÄdW, 2, p. 33)

This response to Géricault and his art anticipates a central preoccupation of the novel which is explored more fully in relation to Brecht during the period from Easter 1939 to April 1940 which he spent in Sweden. Having also made his way to Stockholm, Weiss's narrator, now a factory worker, finds himself, through his affiliations with the Communist Party and an eagerness to make up for the educational deprivations of his proletarian origins, in the role of Brecht's part-time, unpaid researcher. With the spectre of National Socialism rolling ever closer, the dramatist, his trunk full of unpublished manuscripts, is shown as pressing relentlessly on with new plans and projects. Not in a spirit of head-in-the-sand aestheticism, of art as refuge, but in the unshakeable belief that art could fix and frame, in these times of cultural nadir, invaluable lessons and encouragement for the struggle against fascism. We observe Brecht in two roles — as an individual passionately concerned with the passage of daily political realities, and as a dramatist constantly in search of theatrical forms and metaphors which would allocate the transient and ephemeral their appropriate place in the historical process. It should be noted *en passant*, however, that there is also a preoccupation here with Brecht the human being which adds a fascinating psychological dimension to the novel, fleshing out the aesthetic and political debate at this point. The legend is

demythologised somewhat as Brecht is shown as being totally ruthless in exploiting the energies of his helpers and devotees to further
his own work.

The discussion of Brecht — and particularly the duality of political observer and dramatist in him — is skilfully exploited by Weiss
to locate both his discussion of the Spanish Civil War — and
particularly the failure of the left to overcome its rifts and dissensions — alongside his concern to find adequate images for the actual
physical horror of the war. This ambience enables Weiss to pass
quite naturally from discussion of the ideological factors, the political manoeuverings and errors which led not only to the disarray and
collapse of the Republican forces in Spain, but also to the dashing of
hopes of an anti-fascist popular front throughout the whole of
Europe, to his reflections — those of the artistic consciousness —
about how to convey the appalling realities of the Civil War. The
one finds its expression in the discussions of the *emigré* intellectuals
who gather clandestinely, in constant fear of the virulently anti-
communist Swedish authorities, around Brecht at his temporary
refuge on the island of Lindingö — the other in the paintings of
Brueghel with which Brecht is seen to be preoccupied. The apocalyptical landscapes of *The Triumph of Death* or *Dulle Griet* furnish
the narrator with images commensurate with his experience of the
Spanish atrocities, while for Brecht they grimly anticipate the cataclysm which will engulf Europe as the inevitable consequence of the
crumbling of democracy in the face of fascism.

> War die Schwelle zum Irrealen einmal überschritten, so nahmen die
> Erscheinungen, wie Brueghel sie wiedergegeben hatte, eine unmittelbare
> Faßbarkeit an. Die Materialisation des großen beschuppten Gesichts, mit
> dem einen leeren, dem andern dunkel glänzenden Auge, den gleich
> Fensterläden aufgeklappten Lidern, dem scheußlichen Rattenschwanz,
> der sich aus einem der Nasenlöcher ringelte, der steinernen, zu einem
> Warttum auswachsenden Stirn, dem klaffenden Rachen, aus dem sich
> eine wimmelnde Kloake ergoß, es war der Tyrann, wie er sich aufgebaut
> hatte in allen Ländern, in denen der Kampf ausgetragen, erstickt, wieder
> angefacht wurde. (ÄdW, 2, p. 150)

It is not only the art of Brueghel, however, which can provide
grim visions entirely appropriate to current realities. In his preliminary work on Engelbrekt, the fourteenth-century Swedish popular hero, Brecht is shown — in characteristic fashion — as foraging
the past for ways of understanding the present. The dramatist builds
the failure of Engelbrekt's revolutionary endeavour to shatter the
grip of feudalism into an embryonic comment (the play was never

completed) on the European left of his own day. Engelbrekt's fatal slowness in grasping the ruthlessness of the power structures with which he was confronted becomes an image of present derelictions and a significant pointer for Brecht's democratic, anti-fascist contemporaries. The political lesson was, of course, learned too late and the failure of the Engelbrekt project to ever come to fruition seems symptomatic of the failure of art in this period.

These somewhat depressing deliberations on the relation between art and politics in dark times foreshadow the arguments of the third and concluding part of Peter Weiss's trilogy in which there seems to be a substantial revision of the very sanguine earlier view of the role which art might play. This third volume — the result of Weiss's inability to accommodate his material in initially one, and subsequently two volumes — was conceived as both 'Epilogband' and as 'eine Hadeswanderung'.[17] It is, in its coverage of the war years, the depiction of a two-fold journey through hell. On the one hand we are witness, after the highpoint of solidarity in Spain — 'den Höhepunkt unsrer Zuversicht' (ÄdW, 3, p. 43) — to the process of inexorable disintegration of the left and the collapse of all hopes for a popular front. On the other we see — and for this the party itself, with its repressive, authoritarian policies, is largely responsible — the gradual whittling away of all aspirations for the supportive role of culture in the political struggle: 'Dies war des Furchtbare, daß die Partei, deren Aufgabe es gewesen wäre, für die Befreiung der Kultur zu wirken, ihre schöpferischen Denker vernichtete und nur die Schablonen noch gelten ließ' (ÄdW, 3, p. 151). As the resistance organisations in Sweden and Nazi Germany during the war are gradually and brutally eliminated, a depressing account is drawn up of the failure of progressive art forms in the years leading up to the fascist take-over to exert any real influence on political and social developments. It is left to Funk, KPD functionary and Chairman of the proletarian 'Kulturverband' to document the achievements of socialist art in the 1920s, and the unique possibilities for political activity they embodied and the failure to make them bear political fruit:

Schon war manches politische Vorhaben unmerklich zu einer kulturellen Aktion geworden. Durch Aufklärung und Bildung war die Möglichkeit einzugreifen größer geworden, es ging der Partei darum, die Erkenntnisse aus dem verangnen Jahrzehnt zu vertiefen, sie durch Einsichten zu ergänzen, die bereits von einer revolutionären Veränderung der Anschauungen sprachen. Unsre Literatur, Kunst und Musik, unser Theater,

17. Idem, *Notizbücher 1971–1980*, vol. 2, p. 661.

unsre Debatten erreichten ihren Höhepunkt, alles, was in diesem Jahrhundert begonnen worden war, kam zu einer einzigartigen Erfaltung. Wir können uns heute, nach dem alles, was Ausdruckskraft besitzt, auseinandergerissen wurde, kaum mehr vorstellen, was wir damals an Forschungsresultaten, an künstlerischen Manifestationen besaßen. Es waren nicht nur die Werke eines Piscator, Brecht, Weill und Eisler, eines Grosz, Dix, Schlemmer, Nolde, Beckmann und Klee, eines Döblin, Musil, Broch, Jahnn oder Benjamin, es war die gesamte Atmosphäre aus Vitalität, aus unbegrenzter Phantasie, aus Lust am Experimentieren, die das kulturelle Leben ausmachte, jeden Tag gab es neue Entdeckungen, wir waren gewiß, daß nun eine Umwälzung einsetzen werde, um den ganzen Menschen zu ergreifen, und die um so denkwürdiger wäre, als dieses Land zum ersten Mal überhaupt eine nationale Identität erhalten hatte. Wie aber konnte geschehn, fragt er, daß zugleich mit diesem kulturellen Aufstieg das Niedrigste, das es im Wesen der Menschen gab, zu einer Ausbreitung kam, die sich innerhalb weniger Jahre stärker erwies, als alle Klarsicht. Wie konnten sich diese Meilensteine auf dem Weg zu einem bessern und gerechtern Leben so einfach von der Verdummung umstürzen lassen, wie konnte sich dieser kritische und poetische Geist vom Pöbel vertreiben lassen. (ÄdW, 3, pp. 84–5)

The sober answer to his despairing question as to how this cultural and political debacle could come about is given him by his fellow party member Fritz Bischoff: 'Vielleicht entglitt uns die Kultur, weil uns die Politik mißglückte. Was wir für fertig hielten, waren Visionen and Utopien' (ÄdW, 3, p. 85). The narrator, too, reflects with some bitterness along similar lines as he recalls the hopes which had been ignited in him and his companions in their contemplation of the Pergamon frieze and how utterly those hopes had been dashed:

Als Erobrer hatten sie sich damals gesehn, die Güter der Kultur hatten sie für sich in Anspruch genommen, hatten geglaubt, daß sie, die über so viel Wissen, so viele geistige Leistungen verfügten, nie unterworfen werden könnten von denen, die menschlichen Schöpfungen verhöhnten, und dennoch waren diese ihnen wieder überlegen, von ihnen würden sie sich packen und in den Dreck treten lassen müssen. (ÄdW, 3, p. 187)

But is this chilling taking of stock in fact the last word which Peter Weiss has to offer? Not quite. In the very last lines of the novel the narrator stands once more — this time in his imagination — in front of the frieze and seems, in his grasp of the symbolism inherent in the rampant lion's paw and the interpretation of it in terms of his own political vision, to be offering a slender ray of hope. In imitation of the power of the lion's gesture the narrator and his companions' müßten selber mächtig werden dieses einzigen Griffs, dieser weit ausholenden und schwingenden Bewegung, mit der sie den furcht-

baren Druck, der auf ihnen lastete, endlich hinwegfegen könnten'
(ÄdW, 3, p. 268).

Suggested Further Reading

Heinz Ludwig Arnold (ed.), *Peter Weiss*, Munich, 1982

——, *Peter Weiss*, *Text und Kritik*, No. 37, 2nd edn, Munich, 1982

Karl Heinz Götze and Klaus Scherpe (eds.), *Die Ästhetik des Widerstands lesen. Über Peter Weiss*, Berlin, 1981 (Sonderband of *Das Argument*, No. 75)

Alexander Stephan (ed.), *Die Ästhetik des Widerstands*, Frankfurt on Main, 1981

Jochen Vogt, *Peter Weiss*, Reinbek, 1987

Heinrich Vormweg, *Peter Weiss*, Munich, 1981 (Autorenbücher 21)

PART III

Conclusion

KEITH BULLIVANT

From the 1970s into the 1980s

Classification of literature according to period is always a somewhat
risky enterprise and, even where relatively successful, brings with it
the inevitable and unavoidable danger of schematisation that has to
exclude even important work that does not 'fit in'. The other main
problem is of over-hasty categorisation, as was made in the early
1970s with the so-called 'Tendenzwende'. While it was true in the
case of a number of writers such as Born, Handke and Strauß that
their 'Neue Innerlichkeit' was accompanied by a turning away from
such interest in political life as they had, there is ample evidence in
this volume and elsewhere that much literature was still highly
politicised, with the intellectual life of the period concerned with
major political issues of the day — the 'Berufsverbot', the terrorist
threat and its concomitant aspects, such as public attacks on writers
seen as 'sympathisers' and the increased and, at times, hostile
surveillance network of the state being the main, but by no means
the only, ones. In addition, the 'Reportagen' of Günter Wallraff, the
publications of the 'Werkkreis Literatur der Arbeitswelt' and of
socially engaged writers such as Max von der Grün, Michael Scharang and Franz-Josef Degenhardt, represented various forms of
so-called operative writing, designed to influence political opinion.
While there was, inevitably, some overlap from the 1970s into the
1980s, it is now clear that a change has taken place: apart from the
spectacular publishing success of Wallraff's *Ganz unten* (1985), operative writing has faded from the scene, with the Werkkreis publications in the Fischer Bücherei being discontinued, while a change in
the social climate has, by and large, meant that the dominant
political issues of the previous decade are no longer pressing. There
has also been, it would appear, a questioning of the sort of political
writing that was so prominent in the 1970s, even by avowedly
left-wing writers: thus Gerd Fuchs has spoken out against the 'krude
Inhaltsästhetik' of the Werkkreis, which for him amounted to 'die
DGB-offizielle Kunstideologie' which was mistakenly trying 'die
Kunst für politische Zwecke zu instrumentalisieren'.[1] Michael

1. 'Gerd Fuchs im Gespräch', in Matthias Altenburg (ed.), *Fremde Mütter, fremde*

Schneider too has rejected the 'platte Politisierung der Literatur' which, in the process, reduces the latter 'zur Dienstmagd der Tagespolitik'. He proceeds to emphasise that, while he is conservative in matters of literary form, he remains a political radical, and the implied distinction made by Schneider and Fuchs between political activity and their aims as writers of imaginative literature — a distinction made back in the early 1960s by Walter Jens and one which writers such as Grass and Siegfried Lenz have always represented — would seem to be shared by many major writers in the 1980s. This reclaiming by writers of a special voice in the area of politics on the basis of their standing as authors is demonstrated most clearly in the early years of the 1980s by their involvement in the 'Friedensbewegung'. In 1981 and in 1983 two 'Begegnungen zur Friedensförderung' took place in Berlin, in which well-known authors from both German states participated, amidst great publicity, with these discussions being complemented by the 'Krefelder Appell' of 1981, supported by a wide range of artists, by the meeting of writers from a number of countries in The Hague and the 'Internationale Literaturtage' in Cologne (both 1982) and by the publication by a number of West German writers of the 'Heilbronner Erklärung' of 1983. In addition there has been public support of the Peace Movement through appearances at public rallies, most notably Böll's address to the largest such occasion (in Bonn) in November 1983.

Time has moved on, however, and it has now become clear that the Peace Movement failed to achieve its short-term objective of preventing the stationing of a new generation of missiles on West German soil; such encouraging signs as there have been in the matter of arms reduction have taken place on the stage of world politics. This lack of success led a young writer such as Hanns-Josef Ortheil to call into question the 'impact' claimed for the engaged literary figure: 'Plötzlich waren auch die Schriftsteller enttarnt. Sie standen da als die sorgenvollen, kummerbeladenen Bürger, zu denen sie in diesen Zeiten [. . .] geworden sind'.[2] At much the same time Martin Lüdke and Delf Schmidt were claiming that the generation represented by Böll, Enzensberger, Walser and their contemporaries, which had in the past 'ein Stück Demokratie verwirklicht',[3] had gone into premature retirement, while statements made by

---

Väter, fremdes Land, Hamburg, 1985–6, p. 26. Cf. also in this section the interview with Michael Schneider in this volume, p. 72.
2. H.J. Ortheil, 'Das Kalkutta-Programm', *Literaturmagazin 19*, Reinbek, 1987, p. 91.
3. 'Editorische Notiz', *Literaturmagazin 19*, p. 8.

younger writers had revealed no burning commitment to the role which their elders had previously occupied. By this time Böll was dead, but the eerie absence of Günter Grass from the election campaign of January 1987 could indeed be interpreted as a lessening of political energies. Walser's own assessment of his position reveals another factor: while the ageing Böll took the line that the Greens represented the appropriate forum for the political activities of his latter years — 'wir haben inzwischen eine Partei im Parlament', he proclaimed at the Bonn Peace Demonstration — Walser felt that the rise of 'die Grünen' at last freed him from a political involvement that had been forced upon him in the 1960s and 1970s, but which was essentially alien to the creative writer: 'am Mikrophon in einer größeren Versammlung sprechend, habe ich mich nicht wohlgefühlt, es war nicht mein Element, sondern ich habe es für notwendig gehalten./ Ich bin in der Hinsicht eigentlich sehr froh, daß die Grünen entstanden sind, daß also unser Herumempfinden einen politischen Ausdruck oder eine politische Form gefunden hat. Mich entlastet das'.[4] Hans Magnus Enzensberger, so often a useful indicator of underlying trends, has also clearly left his political commitment of the late 1960s behind. The death of Böll meant for him the end of an era, in which certain authors were allocated the 'alte Präzeptorenrolle', functioning as necessary counter-weights to the authority of Konrad Adenauer, but they had now become redundant: 'Ich glaube, es ist eine Vergesellschaftung solcher Rollen eingetreten. Wir haben Böll verloren. Aber dafür haben wir Amnesty und Greenpeace'.[5] Michael Buselmeier has also taken the line that the time of writers as 'Berufsaufklärer' has come to an end: these 'Relikte der Adenauer-Ära' can now only manifest a 'linke Unschuld', which 'angesichts dessen, was wir über Machtpolitik wissen (können), traurig komisch wirkt'.[6]

Walser's statement indicates a retreat of literature from the centre-stage of politics into its own domain. The sense of a return to basics, the rescuing of literature from its short-term role as the handmaiden of politics, which is echoed by Gerd Fuchs, Michael Schneider, Hermann Peter Piwitt and others, is reflected in the mid-1980s by a large number of works of narrative fiction: there has been a remarkable revival in the 'Novelle', beginning in 1978 with the astonishing success of Walser's *Ein fliehendes Pferd* and followed by Dieter Wellershoff's *Die Sirene* (1980), since when the trend has

---

4. Walser interviewed by U.E. Ziegler, *die tageszeitung*, 30.9. 1985.
5. Enzensberger, 'Die Gesellschaft ist keine Hammelherde', *Der Spiegel*, 4, 19.1. 1987.
6. *Literaturmagazin 19*, p. 35.

continued unabated. In 1987 Walser again turned to this classical form with his 'Novelle' of the Two Germanies, *Dorle und Wolf*, while Patrick Süskind, (*Das Parfum*, 1985, and *Die Taube*, 1987), Uwe Timm (*Der Mann auf dem Hochrad*, 1984, and *Der Schlangenbaum*, 1986) and Carl Amery (*Die Wallfahrer*, 1986), have, in their different ways, signalled a return to skilfully crafted, linguistically rich prose-writing. Moreover, Dieter Wellershoff (*Der Sieger nimmt alles*, 1983) and Dieter Lattmann (*Die Brüder*, 1985) have attempted — albeit unsuccessfully — to revive the social novel of the nineteenth century. Other writers have turned to memory as the source of inspiration and legitimation for writing, examples here being Klaus Stiller's *Weihnachten* (1980) and *Das heilige Jahr* (1986), Peter Härtling's *Felix Guttmann* (1985), Walter Kempowski's last volume of his 'Deutsche Chronik', *Herzlich willkommen* (1984), Elisabeth Freundlich's recon-struction of the life of her grandfather, *Der Seelenvogel* (1986) and Ludwig Harig's rich 'Roman meines Vaters', *Ordnung ist das ganze Leben* (1986). Highly personal experience forms the basis of the writing of Brigitte Kronauer (*Rita Münster*, 1983, and *Berittener Bogenschütze*, 1986), Gernot Wolfgruber (especially *Die Nähe der Sonne*, 1985), Lothar Baier's *Jahresfrist* (1985), Dieter Wellershoff's volume of stories *Der Körper und die Traüme* (1986) and the novels of Martin Walser. The regeneration of subjective prose has been paralleled by a similar pattern in the field of lyric poetry, which has left behind the activist and 'Parlando' styles of the 1970s and returned to personal experience as the source of poetic inspiration (in, for example, the work of Peter Maiwald, Ulla Hahn and Michael Krüger). Here too there has been a renewed concern with classical forms and styles — Jürgen Theobaldy, for example, one of the leading exponents of the 'pop' style of the 1970s, returned in *Die Sommertour* (1983) to rhyming verse and the form of the sonnet. Perhaps the most extreme example in this area of the interest in conventional forms is given by the great success of Rose Ausländer.

This lively literary scene in the areas of prose and poetry in the 1980s is particularly astonishing if we go back to the earlier years of the decade. The theme of mankind facing an imminent demise had first been (re-)introduced in somewhat jocular fashion by Hans Magnus Enzensberger in his *Der Untergang der Titanic* (1978). With greater seriousness, Sarah Kirsch and Günter Kunert, who viewed the catastrophes facing the human race from various directions with little hope that man's reason could avert them, felt that they had to register the impact of this in literature. The drift of Kunert's argument ought, logically, to have led him to cease writing, instead his pessimistic view of the world has formed the corner-stone of three volumes of poetry — *Abtötungsverfahren* (1980), *Stilleben* (1983) and *Berlin beizeiten* (1987). Wolfgang Hildesheimer, on the other hand, one of the other major voices raised in the catastrophe debate, has been more consistent. In the mid-1970s he had already been predicting the 'End of Fiction', on the grounds that 'unser Leben außer Kontrolle gerät', when the *a priori* of writing was 'daß die Bedingungen menschlichen Lebens auf dieser Welt von der Vernunft geschaffen werden, die in letzter Stunde Abhilfe schafft'.[7] Hildesheimer's short-term solution as a writer, as he has described it, was to escape back into the nineteenth century through the writing of *Marbot* (1981), but by 1984 the catastrophe facing man, unlike former threats, was irreversible and, as a result, he felt 'absolut gelähmt' as a writer.

The conclusion — namely, to stop writing — that Hildesheimer draws from his analysis of the world situation differs from that of Günter Grass, who otherwise shares his reading of the crisis facing mankind and his essentially modernist view of the nature of literature. Instead of abandoning writing, however, Grass feels that the 'Abschied von den beschädigten Dingen [. . .] müßte mitgeschrieben werden', so that, at the very least, we can 'einander die Angst nehmen'.[8] To some extent Grass had already done this in his 'erzählender Essay' *Kopfgeburten oder Die Deutschen sterben aus* (1980), in which the existential problems caused by awareness of the predicament of mankind are fused with autobiographical and documentary material, much in the manner of his earlier *Aus dem Tagebuch einer Schnecke* (1972). In *Die Rättin* (1986), however, in which the destruction of the human race stands centre-stage, he resumes the style of *Der Butt* (1977). A female rat which the narrator is given for Christmas induces a series of dreams which add up to a vast canvas of the dangers posed for mankind by atomic weapons, 'Waldsterben', acid rain and new techniques in genetic engineering, which will also bring with them the death of our literary heritage (including the works of Grass himself). We are confronted with a nightmarish vision of a known world, the human population of which has been destroyed; it is now inhabited only by rats. The novel lacks, however, the tragi-comic intensity brought by the economy of style in Kurt Vonnegut's *Galapagos* (1985) (which *does* do precisely what Grass demands of contemporary writing) escalating instead into lengthy and self-indulgent stories of the elderly Oskar Matzerath

---

7. Hildesheimer, 'The End of Fiction', *Merkur*, 30, 1976, p. 68. Cf. further in this connection 'Der Mensch wird die Erde verlassen', interview with Hildesheimer, *Stern*, 12.4. 1984, pp. 58–60.
8. Grass, 'Die Vernichtung der Menschheit hat begonnen', *Die Zeit*, 3.12. 1982.

Conclusion

and the Koljaiczek clan from *Die Blechtrommel* and a series of clumsy references back to *Der Butt* through the portrayal of a count of the increase in the jelly-fish population, carried out by a group of women in the polluted waters of the western Baltic.

Leaving aside the response of literary critics to *Die Rättin*, which demonstrated yet again the extreme volatility of the 'Literaturbetrieb' in the Federal Republic, it was quite clear from the reaction of younger writers to the situation of writing and the writer in the mid 1980s that it was very different from the modernist position of an older generation. The 'apokalyptisches Krisengerede, das niemand mehr zu irgend etwas verpflichtet',[9] ignored the fact that 'das Leben mit der Bombe, das Leben in der Katastrophe [längst] in den Alltag gerutscht [ist]'.[10] Gerhard Köpf considered it impossible for literature to come to grips with this situation through conventional literary means; instead, the writer had to 'sein Ich, seine Welt und die Zeiten verwandeln, [. . .] sie kraft poetischer Vorstellung und Phantasie überhaupt neu [. . .] schaffen'.[11] This essentially postmodernist position, rejecting the role of literature as a means of illuminating the world and stressing instead the capacity of literature, as produced by the gifted 'Dichter', to transcend the limits of rationality and open up new plains of consciousness — the 'resublimation' of literature, of which Moray McGowan writes in his essay on 'Neue Subjektivität' (p. 67) and which was anticipated in the 1970s in Nicolas Born's *Die Welt der Maschine* (1977) — , is one that during the 1980s has moved to the forefront of attention, with the work of Botho Strauß and Peter Handke receiving particular interest.

Strauß, who in his first attempt to free literature 'aus den Niederungen der totalen Entmythologisierung des Schreibens', *Der junge Mann* (1984), had expressed the contemporary need in writing for 'die lebendige Eintracht von Tag und Traum, von adlergleichem Sachverstand und geringfügigem Schlafwandel',[12] addressed himself specifically to the position adopted by Grass and Hildesheimer in his *Niemand anderes* (1987). The narrative voice in this collection of prose pieces claims that 'die enthemmte Nüchternheit' of the 'fantastischen Angstszenarien [. . .] die emsig und achtlos das Unheil ausmalt, dieses eher herbeizieht als abwendet' (p. 132)[13] The world is, he continues, not empty, literature is not coming to an end, but it is

---

9. Hans Christoph Buch, *Literaturmagazin 19*, p. 32.
10. Gerhard Köpf, ibid., p. 66.
11. Ibid., p. 69.
12. Strauß, *Der junge Mann*, Munich, 1984, p. 11.
13. Munich, 1987; references in the text are to this edition.

the end for the writer as 'Kulturkritiker'. A different writer, the 'Esoteriker', the 'Eingeweihte des verborgenen Wissens — und des geschonten Lebens', addresses himself to the search for 'die Verbindung zu Ordnungen jenseits des sozio-zentrischen Lebens überhaupt' (p. 147). In some respects that is reminiscent of the 'George-Kreis' and of aspects of Hofmannsthal's cultural criticism: those few 'Dichter', 'die der Allgemeinheit Kraft spenden, müssen Durchdrungene sein, nicht Durchschauer' (p. 150), the world needs the 'mystisches Geleit' of these 'Romantiker des Wissens', the latter-day Novalis' and Schlegels, to reach the 'Technosophie' that is true wisdom.

Strauß's notion of an authentic existence transcending the confines of social organisations had, as Michael Linstead shows elsewhere in this volume, been anticipated since the early 1970s in the work of Peter Handke. In his aphoristic *Phantasien der Wiederholung* (1983) Handke stresses that the role of 'Dichtung' — a term which he presumably chooses carefully to distinguish it from lesser forms of writing — should be the rediscovery of 'das Mythisch-Monumentale', with the job of the 'Dichter' as a priest-like figure being 'den Mythos ein*bürgen*'.[14] In the subsequent and stylistically similar *Nachmittag eines Schriftstellers*(1987) he addresses himself to the other aspect of the writer, the suffering induced by his social isolation and — with a very strong allusion to Goethe's Tasso — his fear of 'Verstummen', his ability to articulate the 'Urtext' within him in a way that recognises that 'das Gefüge' of his work is of paramount importance. In addition, although Handke had elsewhere stated that whoever 'das Gerede über die Endzeit mitmacht, ist kein Künstler',[15] the writer is faced with the difficulty, 'einfach die lieben Dinge des Planeten walten lassen, in Gestalt einer Strophe oder eines Absatzes auf einen Baum', when confronted with the possibility of the destruction of the world.[16]

The quasi-theoretical position implied in these aphoristic works achieves its first full expression in Handke's novel *Die Wiederholung* (1986), which can be regarded, to some extent, as a return to the 'Bildungsroman'. The childhood of the narrator is akin to that of Hesse's Peter Camenzind, in that his gifts isolated him from his fellows and cut off his childhood, taking him away from his native village into the nearby town. He now attempts to reconstruct his childhood by going to the area of Yugoslavia from which his family

---

14. Handke, *Phantasien der Wiederholung*, Frankfurt on Main, 1983, pp. 68, 88.
15. Quoted by Hildesheimer, *Stern*, 12.4. 1984.
16. Handke, *Nachmittag eines Schriftstellers*, Salzburg and Vienna, 1987, p. 72.

originally came, unleashing in the process memories which carry along the narration, revealing the 'Erzähler in mir, eben noch wahrgenommen als der heimliche König'.[17] His journey, 'nicht in ein früheres Leben, sondern in ein geahntes' (p. 151), reveals to him, as he passes through the countryside, that he is blessed with being an 'Entzifferer', whose reception and interpretation of the signs in the world of nature work as an antidote 'zu der Dinglast [. . .], so als werde die Erdenschwere, durch die Entzifferung, aufgehoben in eine Luftschrift, oder in ein frei dahinfliegendes einziges Wort aus lauter Selbstlauten' (p. 115). His journey confronts him with the magic of the poet's material, language — especially, in a manner reminiscent of Gerd Gaiser's *Gib acht in Domokosch* (1959) and *Am Paß Nascondo* (1960), the rich mysteries of older languages — and, ultimately, his authentic self as poet, who should never forget 'daß ich die Welt werden kann und mir selber wie dieser das auch schuldig bin' (p. 258). Like a pilgrim to the oracle he comes eventually to the true centre of the earth, a simple hut, 'wo in der bildstockkleinen Höhlung seit jeher der Erzähler sitzt und erzählt' (p. 289), a place that will, he feels, survive even a nuclear holocaust. Even should that not be so, his enshrining in 'Erzählung' of the unspoiled landscape is the best way of securing it in perpetuity, for 'die Sonne der Erzählung' which honours the poet will continue to shine for ever, even after the destruction of the world.

The disturbing proximity of Handke's novel to the regressive mysticism of Hesse and Gaiser has gone largely unnoticed, it — like Strauß's *Der junge Mann* (1984) and *Niemand anderes* (1987) it was ecstatically received by a number of major West German critics. Joachim Kaiser praised the 'hohen Ton', with which 'alles Groß-städtische, Zivilisatorische, Verbindliche' was banished; instead the work was rich in 'Handkes originelle, reiche Kraft, nicht Literatur über Literatur zu machen oder distanziert ironisch Zeitkritik am schlecht Bestehenden zu üben, die ja mittlerweile auch jeder Esel von sich geben kann'. Instead, the novel demonstrated Handke's capacity 'etwas zu sehen, was so noch niemand sah, Daseins-Funken poetisch in Sternbilder zu verwandeln'.[18] His comparison, in a highly positive sense, was with Hesse and George. It is, as always with contemporary literature, difficult to know how long this post-modernist tendency will last, but it clearly marks a major break

17. Handke, *Die Wiederholung*, Frankfurt on Main, 1986, p. 109. Subsequent references in the text are to this edition.
18. Joachim Kaiser, 'Peter Handkes hohe Heimatkunst', *Süddeutsche Zeitung*, 1.10.1986.

with the socio-critical nature of writing that has dominated since the 1960s. One sentence from *Die Wiederholung*, more than any other sums up that decisive shift and the nature of Handke's view of 'Dichtung': 'Der Schein, er lebe, und sei mein Stoff!' (p.190)

Bibliographical Note

Specialised bibliographical information, as considered appropriate by the contributors, has been added at the end of the chapters. Further detailed bibliographies on the individual authors are contained in *Kritisches Lexikon zur deutschsprachigen Gegenwartsliteratur* (KLG), edited by Heinz Ludwig Arnold (Munich, 1978ff.). Below is listed recommended secondary literature on the period of the 1970s available in autumn 1988; to keep abreast of relevant publications appearing after this date, readers are advised to consult the appropriate sections of *Germanistik* and the bibliographical information provided by the various Modern Language associations in English-speaking countries.

K. Briegleb and S. Weigel (eds.), *Hansers Sozialgeschichte der deutschen Literatur*, vol. 12, *Die Literatur der Gegenwart ab 1968*, Munich, 1989

K. Bullivant and H. J. Althof (eds.), *Subjektivität — Innerlichkeit — Abkehr vom Politischen? Tendenzen der deutschsprachigen Literatur der 70er Jahre*, Bonn, 1986 (DAAD)

K. Bullivant, *Realism Today. Aspects of the Contemporary West German Novel*, Leamington Spa and New York, 1987

P. Demetz, *After The Fires. Writing in the Germanies, Austria and Switzerland*, New York, 1986

M. Durzak (ed.), *Deutsche Gegenwartsliteratur*, Stuttgart, 1981

P.U. Hohendahl and P. Herminghouse (eds.), *Literatur der DDR in den siebziger Jahren*, Frankfurt on Main, 1983

Th. Koebner (ed.), *Tendenzen der deutschen Gegenwartsliteratur*, 2nd edn, Stuttgart, 1984

H. Kreuzer and K.W. Bonig (eds.), *Entwicklungen der 70er Jahre*, Gerabronn, 1978

Literaturmagazin 1–, Reinbek, 1972–

J. Lodemann, 'Die Literatur der 70er: Von radikaler Zeitkritik zu neuer Innerlichkeit?', in *Bund und Bibliothek*, 32, 1980, pp. 383ff.

P.M. Lützeler and E. Schwarz (eds.), *Deutsche Literatur in der Bundesrepublik seit 1965*, Königstein, 1980

G. Mattenklott and G. Pickerodt, *Literatur der siebziger Jahre*, Berlin, 1985 (Sonderband 108 of *Das Argument*)

F.J. Raddatz, *Die Nachgeborenen. Leseerfahrungen mit zeitgenößischer Literatur*, Frankfurt on Main, 1982

Bibliographical Note

M. Reich-Ranicki, *Entgegnung. Zur deutschen Literatur der siebziger Jahre*, Stuttgart, 1981

D. Roberts (ed.), *Tendenzwenden. Zum Kulturwandel der siebziger Jahre*, Berne, 1984

R. Schnell (ed.), *Die Literatur der Bundesrepublik. Autoren, Geschichte, Literaturbetrieb*, Stuttgart, 1986

S. Weigel, *Die Stimme der Medusa. Schreibweisen in der Gegenwartsliteratur von Frauen*, Dülmen/Westf., 1987

About the Contributors

Keith Bullivant: Professor of German, University of Florida. Publications on German literature and thought in the nineteenth and twentieth centuries including *Literature in Upheaval*, 1974 (with R.H. Thomas); *Realism Today*, Berg Publishers, 1987; and (as editor) *The Modern German Novel*, Berg Publishers, 1987.

Helen Chambers: Lecturer in German Language and Literature at Leeds University. Publications include 'Thomas Bernhard Checklist', *Theatrefacts*, 12, 1976; *Supernatural and Irrational Elements in the Work of Theodor Fontane*, 1980; and 'Mond und Sterne in Fontanes Werken', *Fontane-Blätter*, 37, 1984.

Donna L. Hoffmeister: Professor of German Literature, University of Colorado. Publications on twentieth-century German literature including *The Theatre of Confinement: Language and Survival in the Milieu Plays of Marieluise Fleißer and Franz Xaver Kroetz*, 1983.

Martin Kane: Senior Lecturer in German and European Studies, University of Kent. Publications include *Weimar Germany and the Limits of Political Art: A Study of the Work of George Grosz and Ernst Toller*, 1987, as well as various articles on East and West German literature.

Peter Labanyi: Lecturer in German, National Institute for Higher Education, Limerick. Publications include 'The Ironies of Ernst Ottwalt', in T. Bourke (ed.), *Neglected German Progressive Writers*, vol. 1, 1984; '"Die Gefahr des Körpers": A Reading of Otton Weinger's *Geschlecht und Charakter'*, in G.J. Carr and Eda Sagarra (eds.), *Fin de Siècle Vienna*, 1985; 'Images of Fascism: Visualization and Aestheticization in the Third Reich', in Michael Laffan (ed.), *The Burden of German History 1919–1945*, 1988.

Michael Linstead: Sometime Lecturer in German at University College Dublin and Lancaster University. Publications on Peter Handke including 'Peter Handke' in Keith Bullivant (ed.), *The Modern German Novel*, Berg Publishers, 1987; also work on contemporary British literature.

Moray McGowan: Professor of German, University of Sheffield. Publications include 'Botho Strauß', in Keith Bullivant (ed.), *The Modern German Novel*, Berg Publishers, 1987; *Marieluise Fleißer*, 1987 ('Autorenbücher'); and numerous articles on German literature of the twentieth century.

About the Contributors

J.H. Reid: Reader in German, University of Nottingham. Publications include *Heinrich Böll: Withdrawal and Re-emergence*, Oswald Wolff, 1973; 'Heinrich Böll: From Modernism to Post-Modernism', in Keith Bullivant (ed.), *The Modern German Novel*, Berg Publishers, 1987; *Heinrich Böll: A German for his Time*, Berg Publishers, 1987; *The New East German Literature: Writing without Taboos*, Berg Publishers, 1989; and numerous articles on post-war East and West German literature.

David Roberts: Reader in German, Monash University. Publications include *Artistic Consciousness and Political Consciousness: The Novels of Heinrich Mann 1900–1938*, 1971; *Tendenzwenden*, 1984; 'Recent Developments in the German Novel', in Keith Bullivant (ed.), *Modern German Novel*, Berg Publishers, 1987; and numerous articles on modern German literature.

John Sandford: Reader in German, University of Reading. Editor of *German Life and Letters*. Publications include *The Mass Media of the German-Speaking Countries*, 1976; *The New German Cinema*, 1980; *Landscape and Landscape Imagery in R.M. Rilke*, 1980; *The Sword and the Ploughshare: Autonomous Peace Initiatives in East Germany*, 1983; as well as numerous articles on German literature, politics, cinema, press and broadcasting.

Julian Sierra-Ballester: Graduate of the University of Adelaide where he is now researching for his doctorate.

Anthony Stephens: Professor of German, University of Adelaide. Publications include *Rainer Maria Rilke's 'Gedichte an die Nacht'*, 1972; *Rilke's 'Malte Laurids Brigge'*, 1974; *Nacht, Mensch und Engel: Rilke's Gedichte an die Nacht*, 1978; 'Christa Wolf' (with Judith Wilson), in Keith Bullivant (ed.), *The Modern German Novel*, Berg Publishers, 1987; and numerous articles on German literature of the nineteenth and twentieth centuries.

Dennis Tate: Lecturer in Modern Languages, University of Bath. Publications include *The East German Novel: Identity, Community, Continuity*, 1984; 'The Novel in the German Democratic Republic', in Keith Bullivant (ed.), *The Modern German Novel*, Berg Publishers, 1987; (as co-editor), *European Socialist Realism*, Berg Publishers, 1988; and various articles on GDR literature.

Wilfried van der Will: Reader in German, University of Birmingham. Publications include *Pikaro heute*, 1967; *The German Novel and the Affluent Society*, 1968 (with R.H. Thomas); *Arbeiterkulturbewegung in der Weimarer Republik*, 1982 (with R.A. Burns); 'Approaches to Reality through Narrative Perspectives in Johnson's Prose', in Keith Bullivant (ed.), *The Modern German Novel*, Berg Publishers, 1987; and numerous articles on German culture since the eighteenth century.

Anthony Waine: Lecturer in German Studies, Lancaster University. Publications include *Martin Walser: The Development as Dramatist*, 1978; *Martin Walser*, 1980 ('Autorenbücher'); and 'Martin Walser', in Keith Bullivant (ed.), *The Modern German Novel*, Berg Publishers, 1987.

Juliet Wigmore: Lecturer in Modern Languages, University of Salford. Publications include 'Ingeborg Bachmann' in Keith Bullivant (ed.), *The Modern German Novel*, Berg Publishers, 1987.

Index